Freaking Romance

Snailords

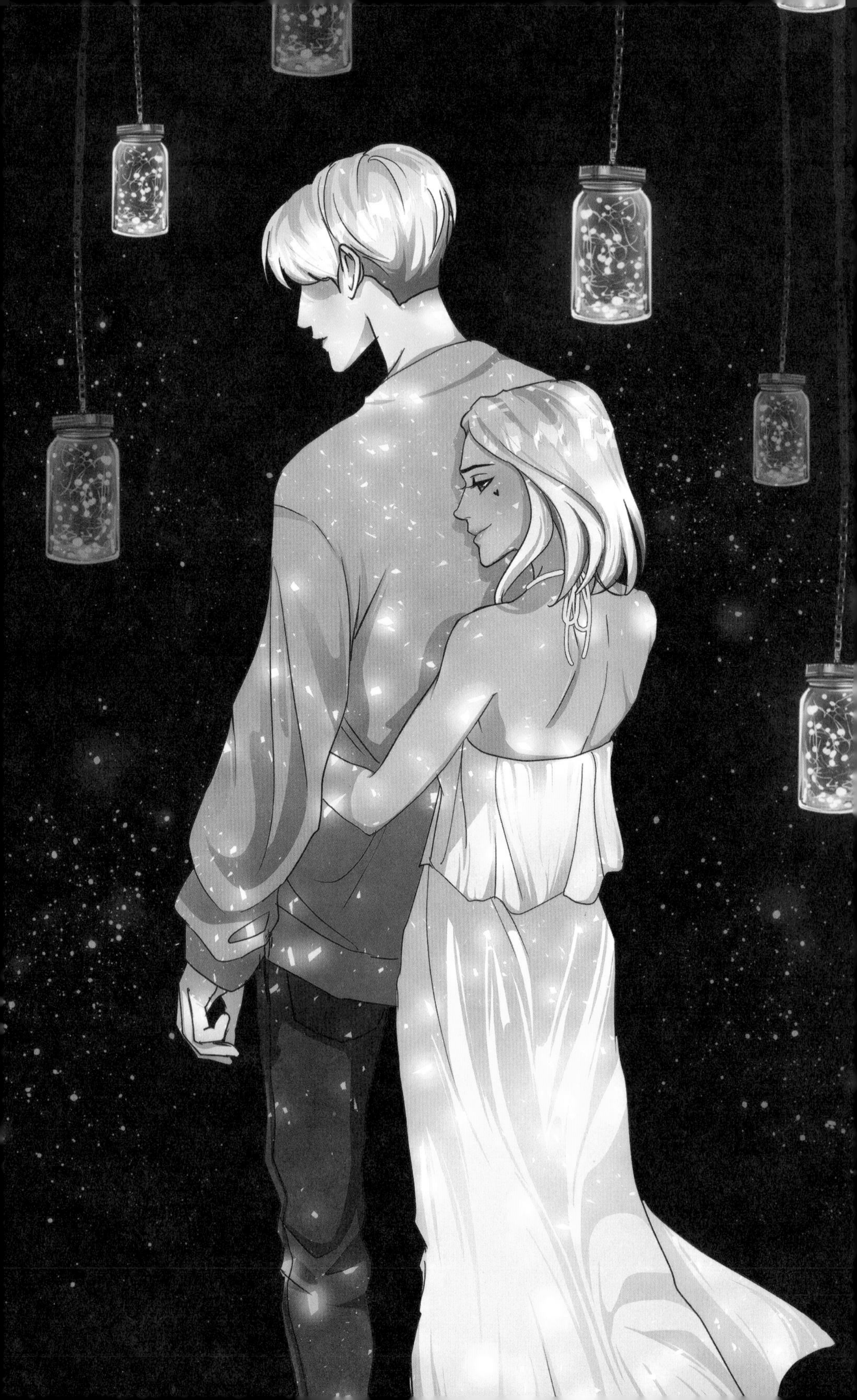

Freaking Romance

Snailords

VOLUME 2

BOBBIE CHASE, EMMA HAMBLY *Editors*
NIKO DALCIN *Sequential Story Designer*
RHYS EUSEBIO & MARIA WEHDEKING *Publication Designers*
PATRICK McCORMICK *Senior Manager, Production*
DELANEY ANDERSON *Production Editor*

WEBTOON
UNSCROLLED™

FREAKING ROMANCE • VOLUME 2

Published in Canada by WEBTOON Unscrolled, a division of Wattpad WEBTOON Studios, Inc.
36 Wellington Street E., Suite 200, Toronto, ON M5E 1C7

The digital version of *Freaking Romance* was originally published on WEBTOON.com in 2018.

www.WEBTOONUnscrolled.com

First WEBTOON Unscrolled edition: June 2024

ISBN: 978-1-99025-992-0

Library and Archives Canada Cataloging in Publication information is available upon request.

CONTENT WARNING: Depictions of emotional abuse and threats of violence toward animals.

Printed and bound in Canada

1 3 5 7 9 10 8 6 4 2

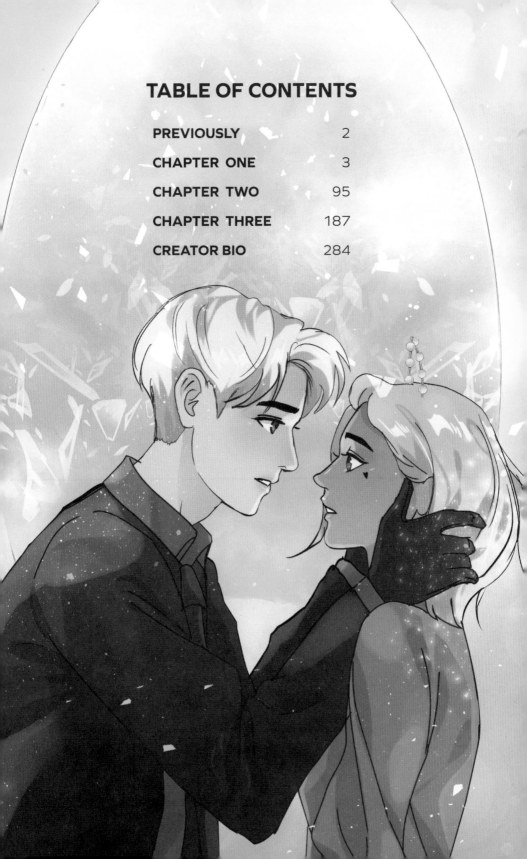

TABLE OF CONTENTS

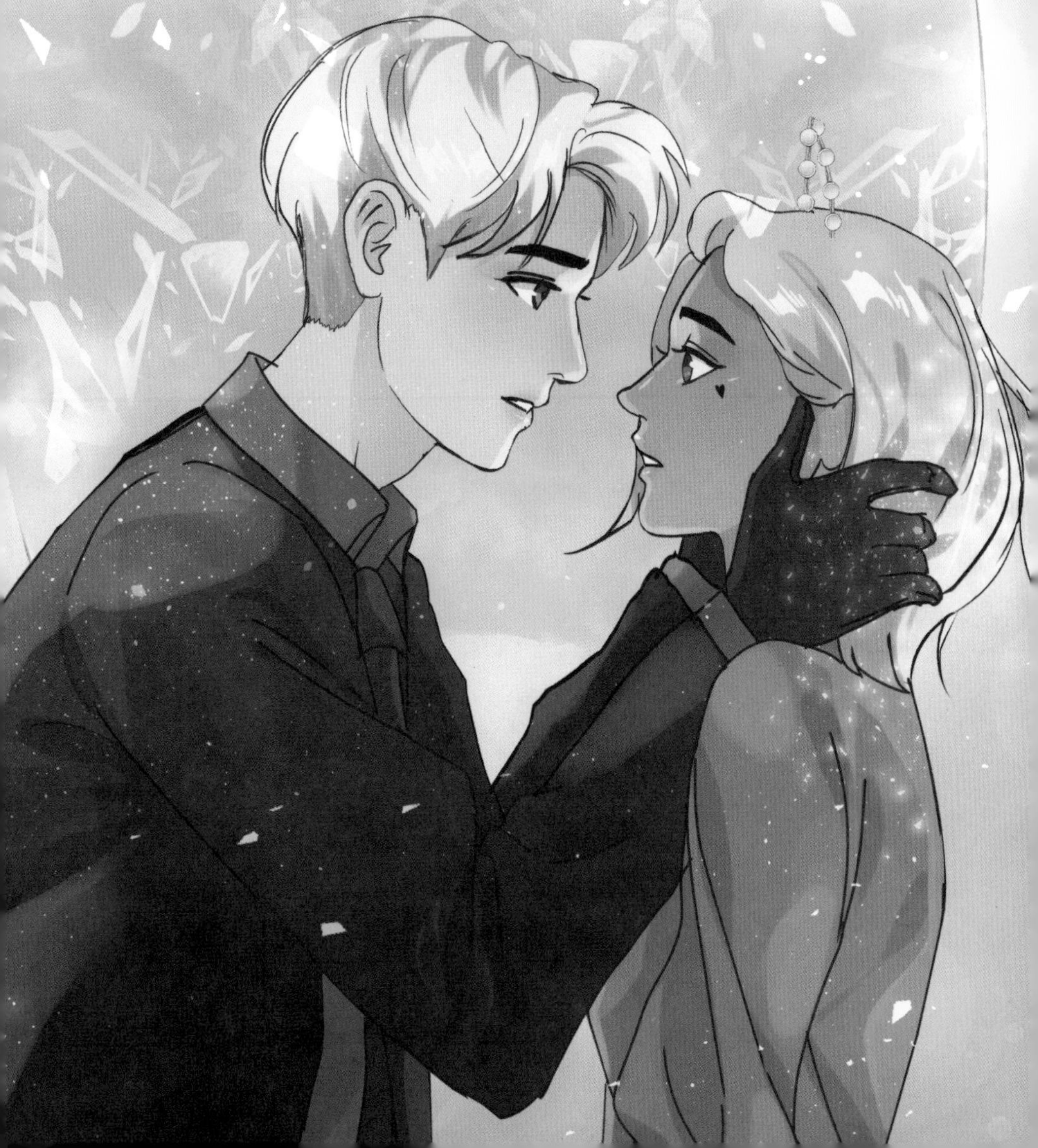

Previously...

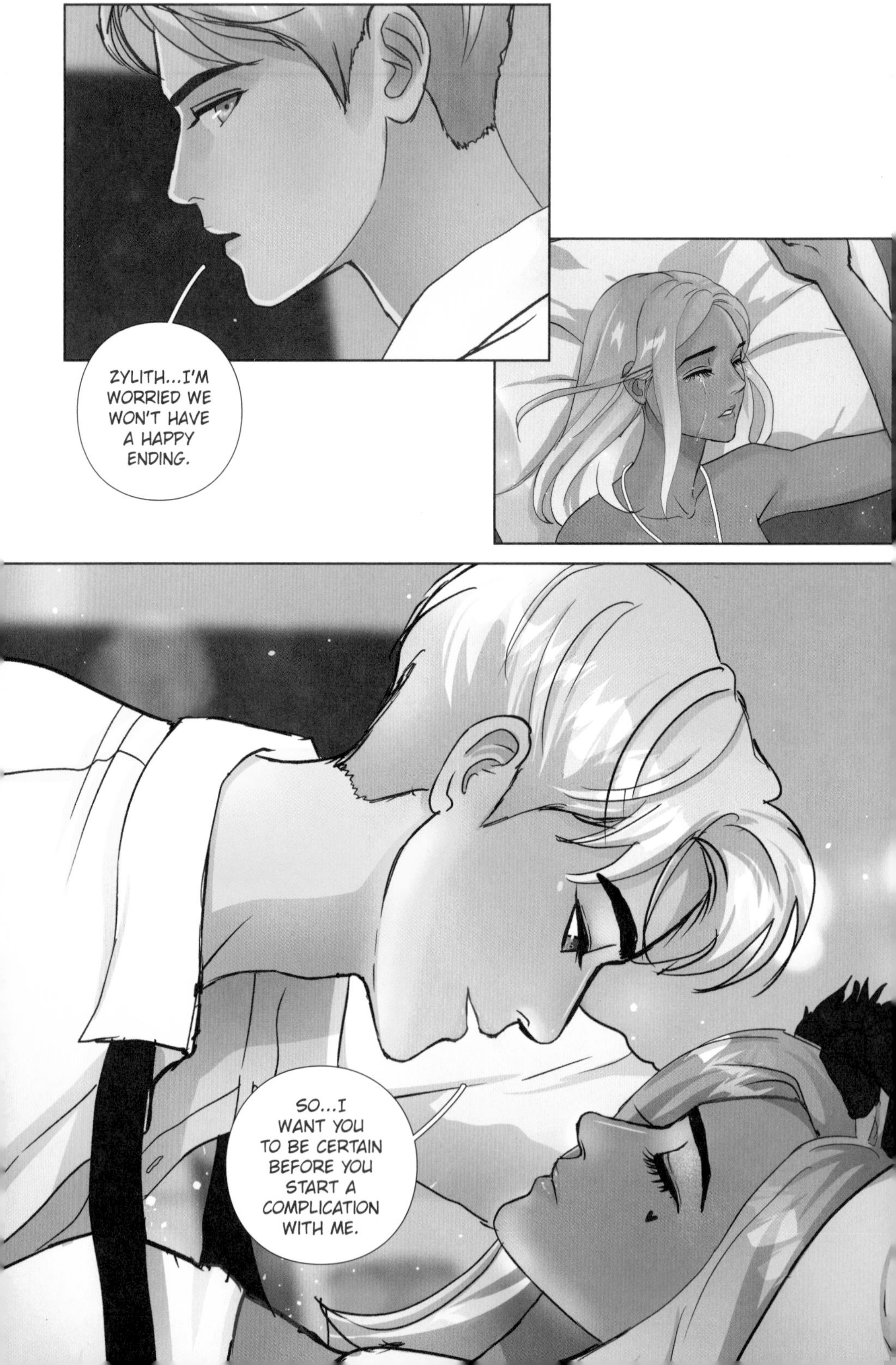
ZYLITH...I'M WORRIED WE WON'T HAVE A HAPPY ENDING.
SO...I WANT YOU TO BE CERTAIN BEFORE YOU START A COMPLICATION WITH ME.

CHAPTER ONE

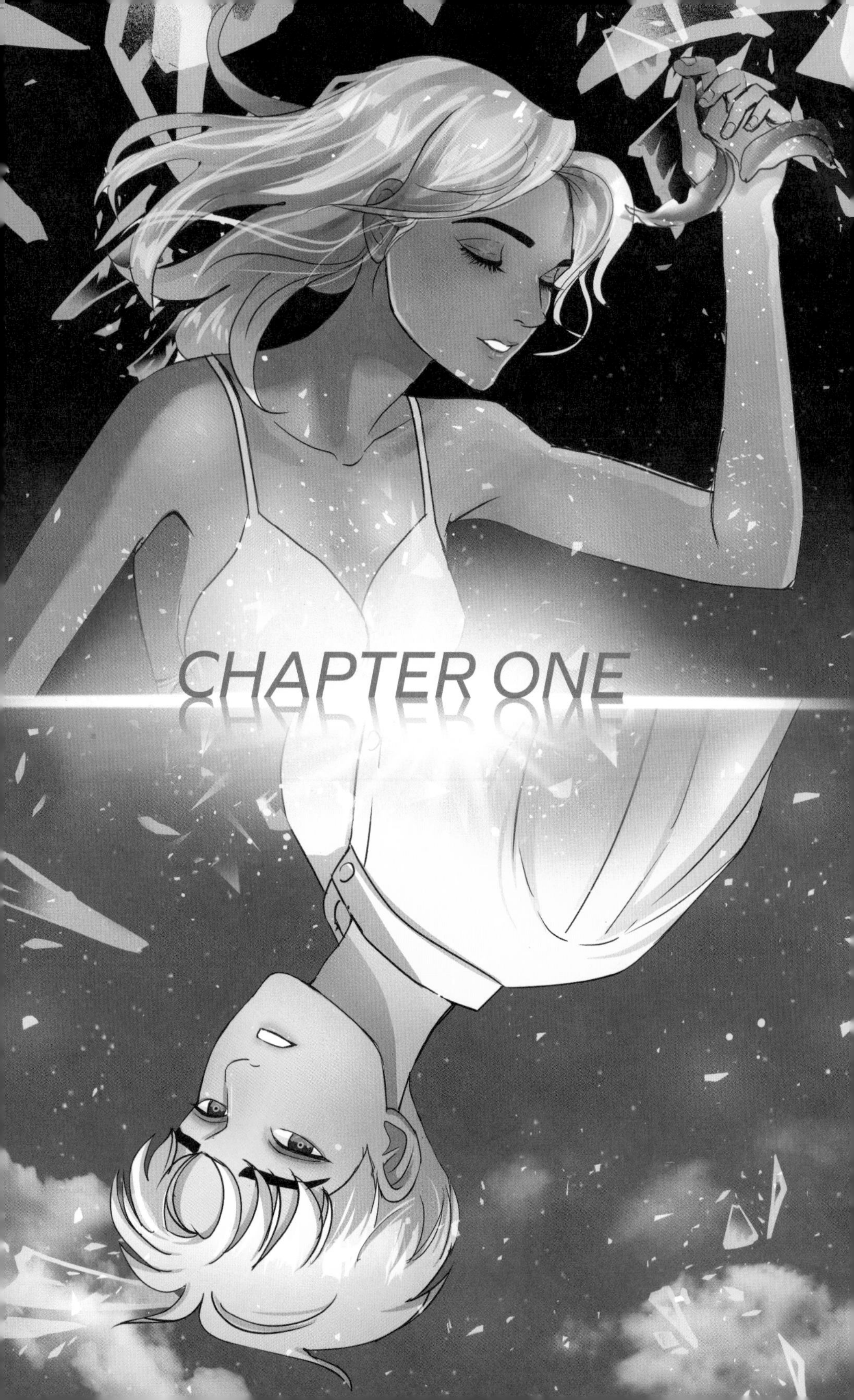

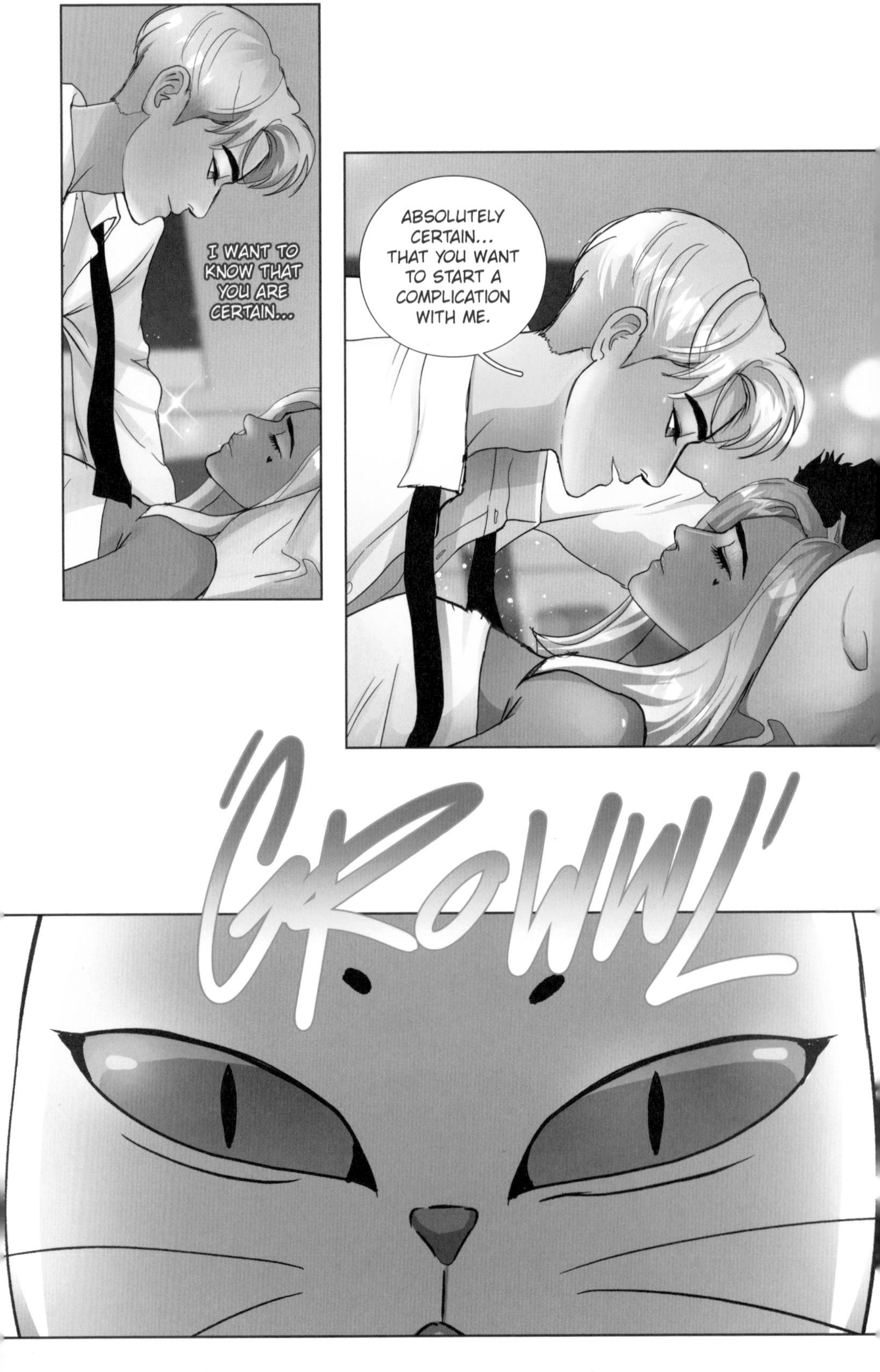
I WANT TO KNOW THAT YOU ARE CERTAIN...
ABSOLUTELY CERTAIN... THAT YOU WANT TO START A COMPLICATION WITH ME.
'GROWL'

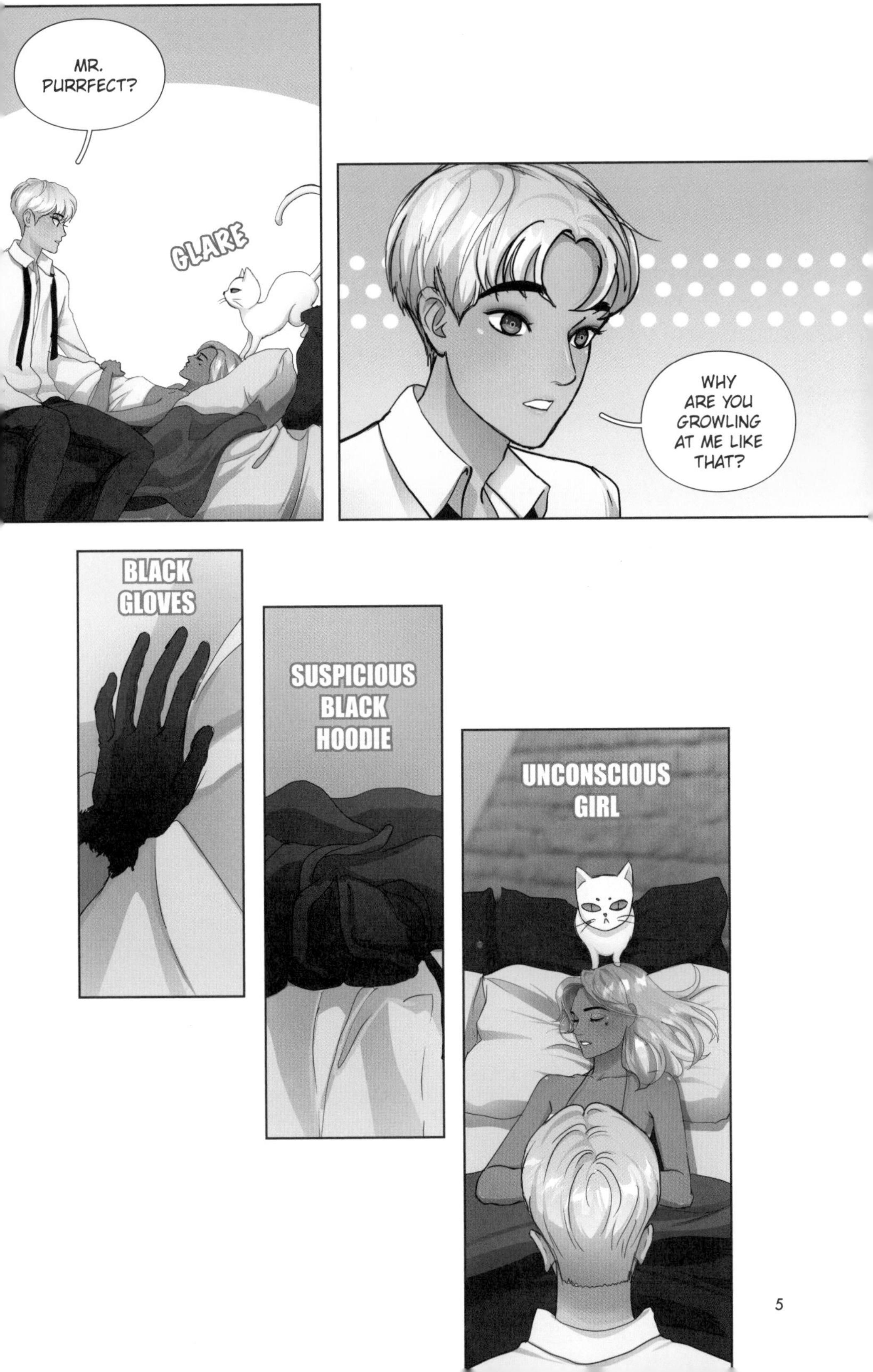
MR. PURRFECT?
GLARE
WHY ARE YOU GROWLING AT ME LIKE THAT?
BLACK GLOVES
SUSPICIOUS BLACK HOODIE
UNCONSCIOUS GIRL

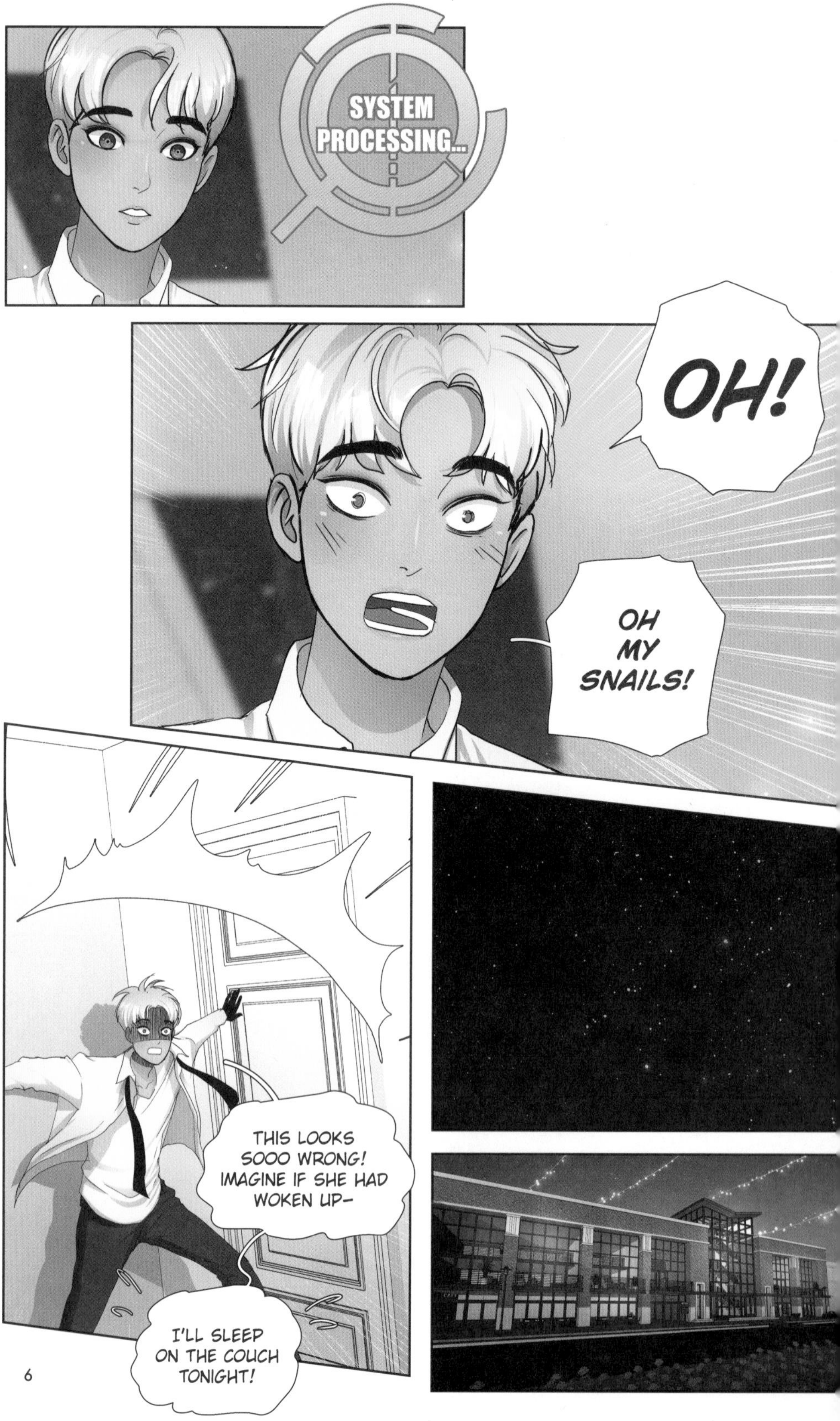
SYSTEM PROCESSING...
OH!
OH MY SNAILS!
THIS LOOKS SOOO WRONG! IMAGINE IF SHE HAD WOKEN UP-
I'LL SLEEP ON THE COUCH TONIGHT!

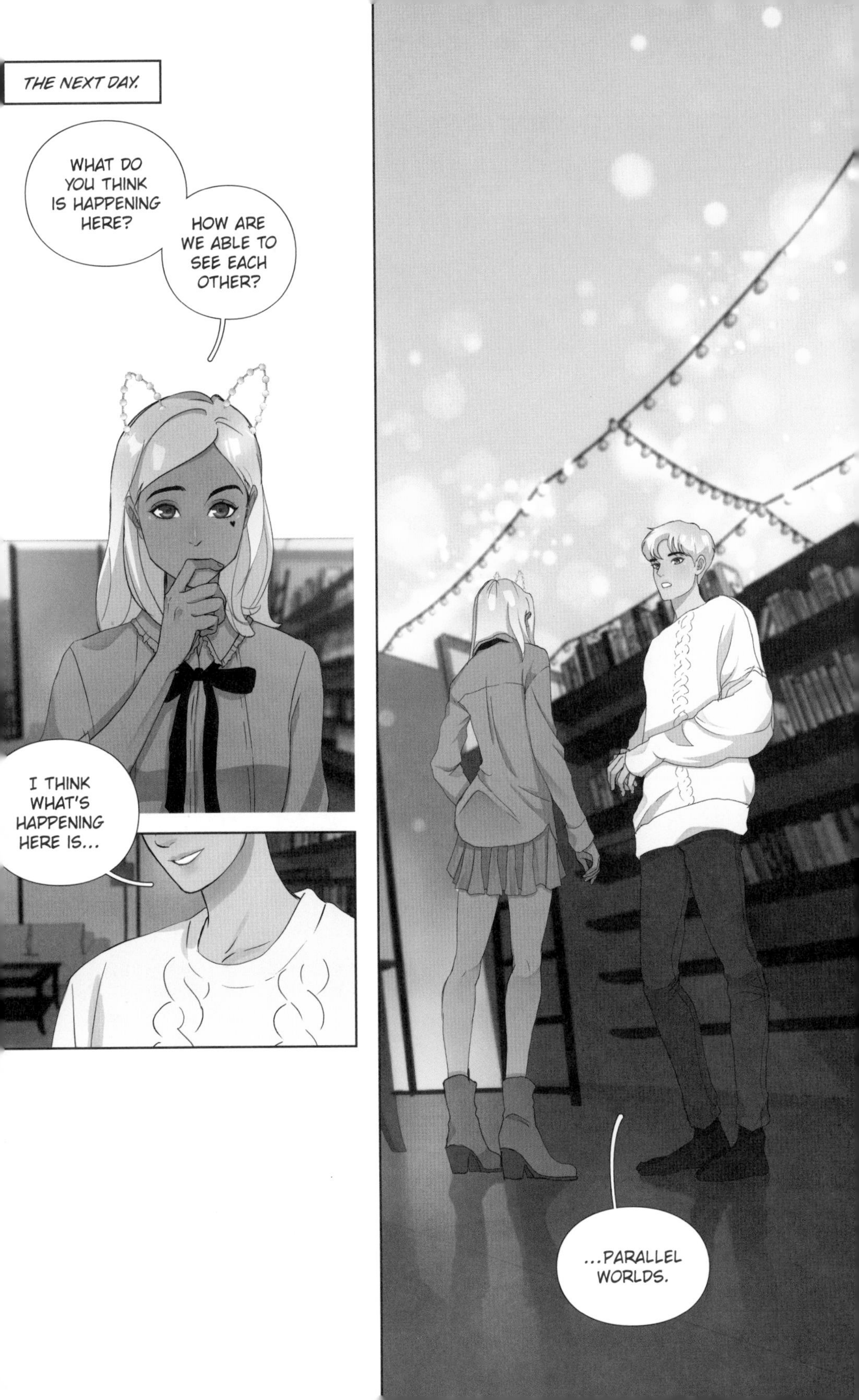
THE NEXT DAY.
WHAT DO YOU THINK IS HAPPENING HERE?
HOW ARE WE ABLE TO SEE EACH OTHER?
I THINK WHAT'S HAPPENING HERE IS...
...PARALLEL WORLDS.

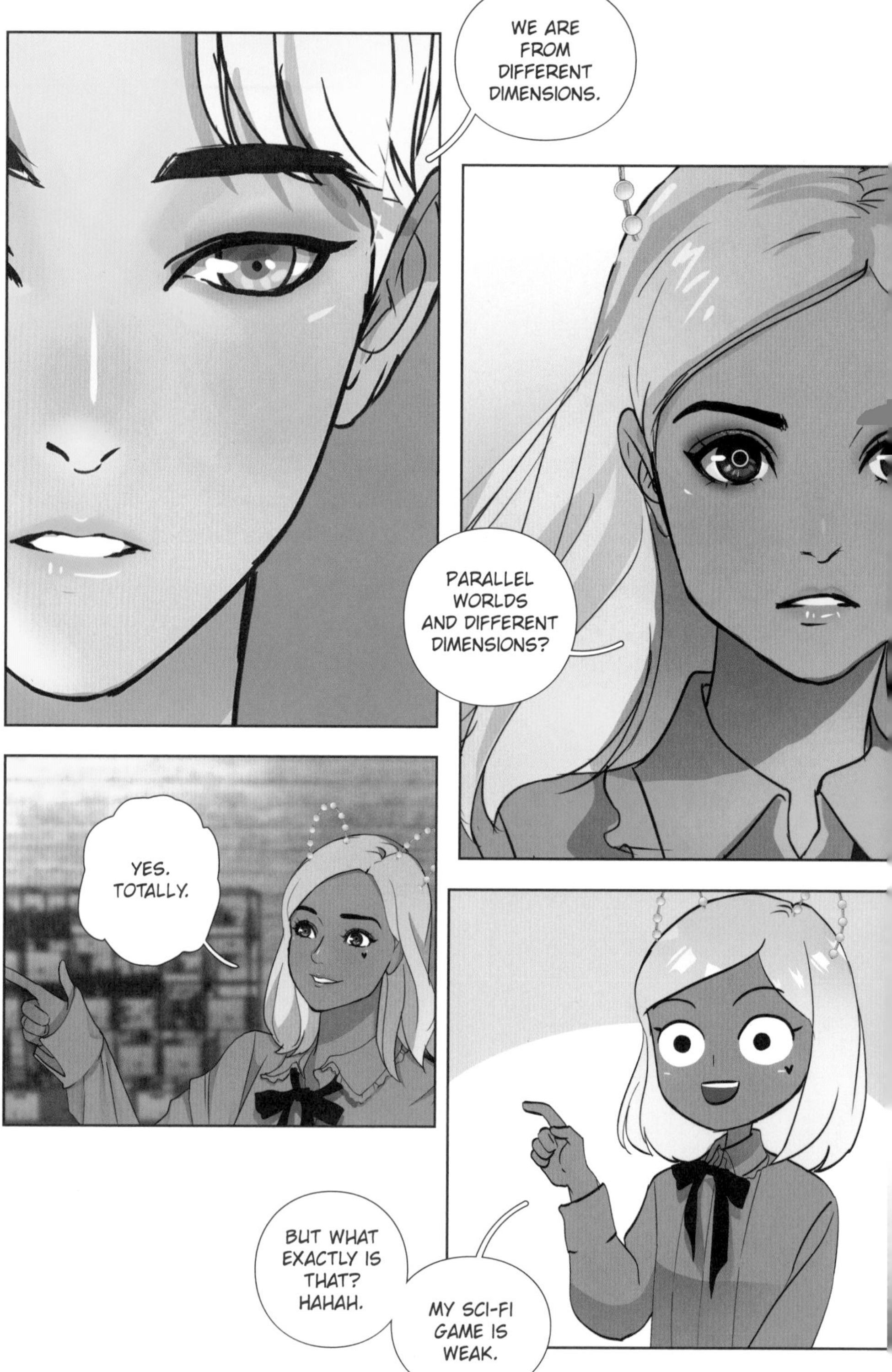
WE ARE FROM DIFFERENT DIMENSIONS.
PARALLEL WORLDS AND DIFFERENT DIMENSIONS?
YES. TOTALLY.
BUT WHAT EXACTLY IS THAT? HAHAH.
MY SCI-FI GAME IS WEAK.

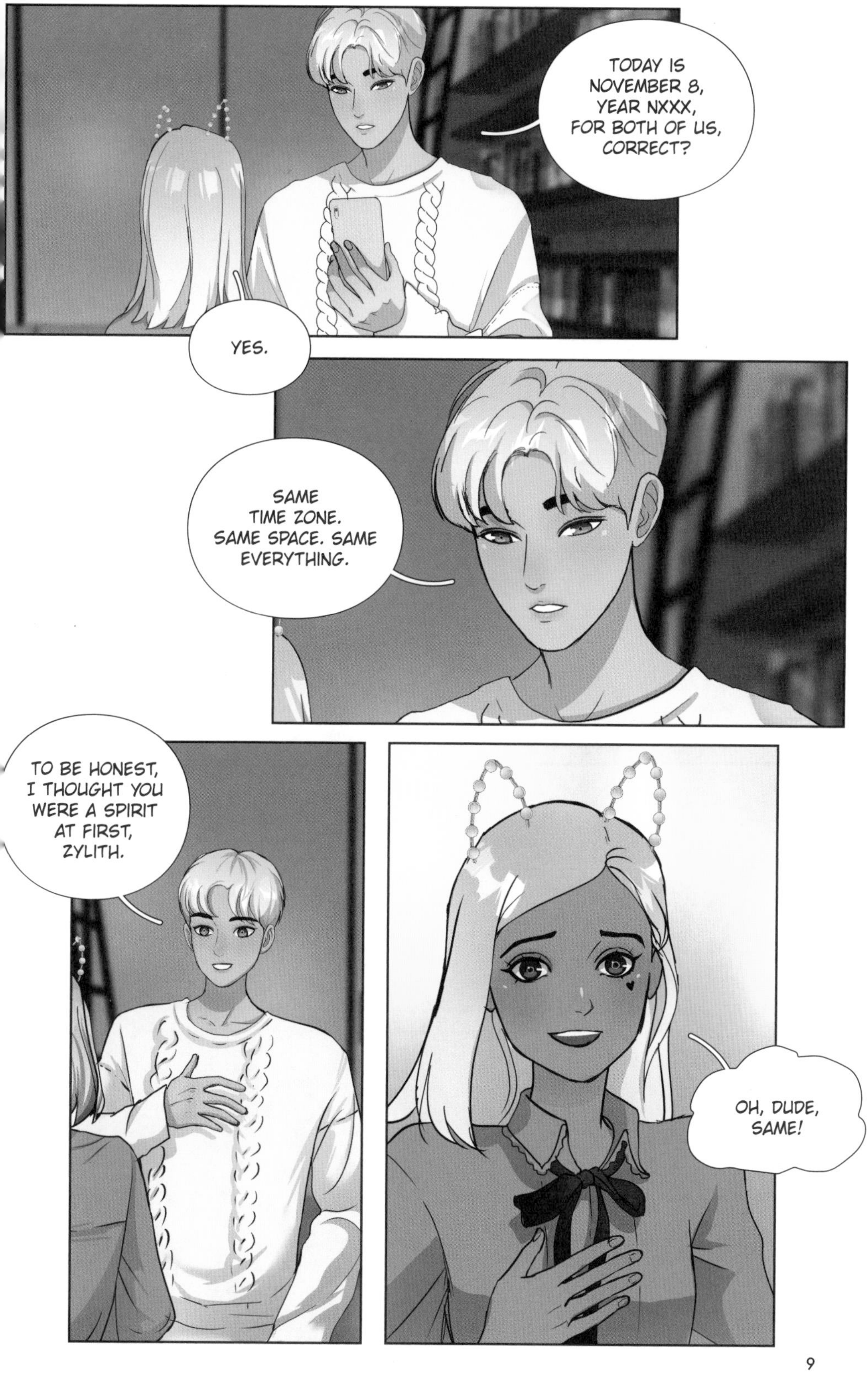
TODAY IS NOVEMBER 8, YEAR NXXX, FOR BOTH OF US, CORRECT?
YES.
SAME TIME ZONE. SAME SPACE. SAME EVERYTHING.
TO BE HONEST, I THOUGHT YOU WERE A SPIRIT AT FIRST, ZYLITH.
OH, DUDE, SAME!

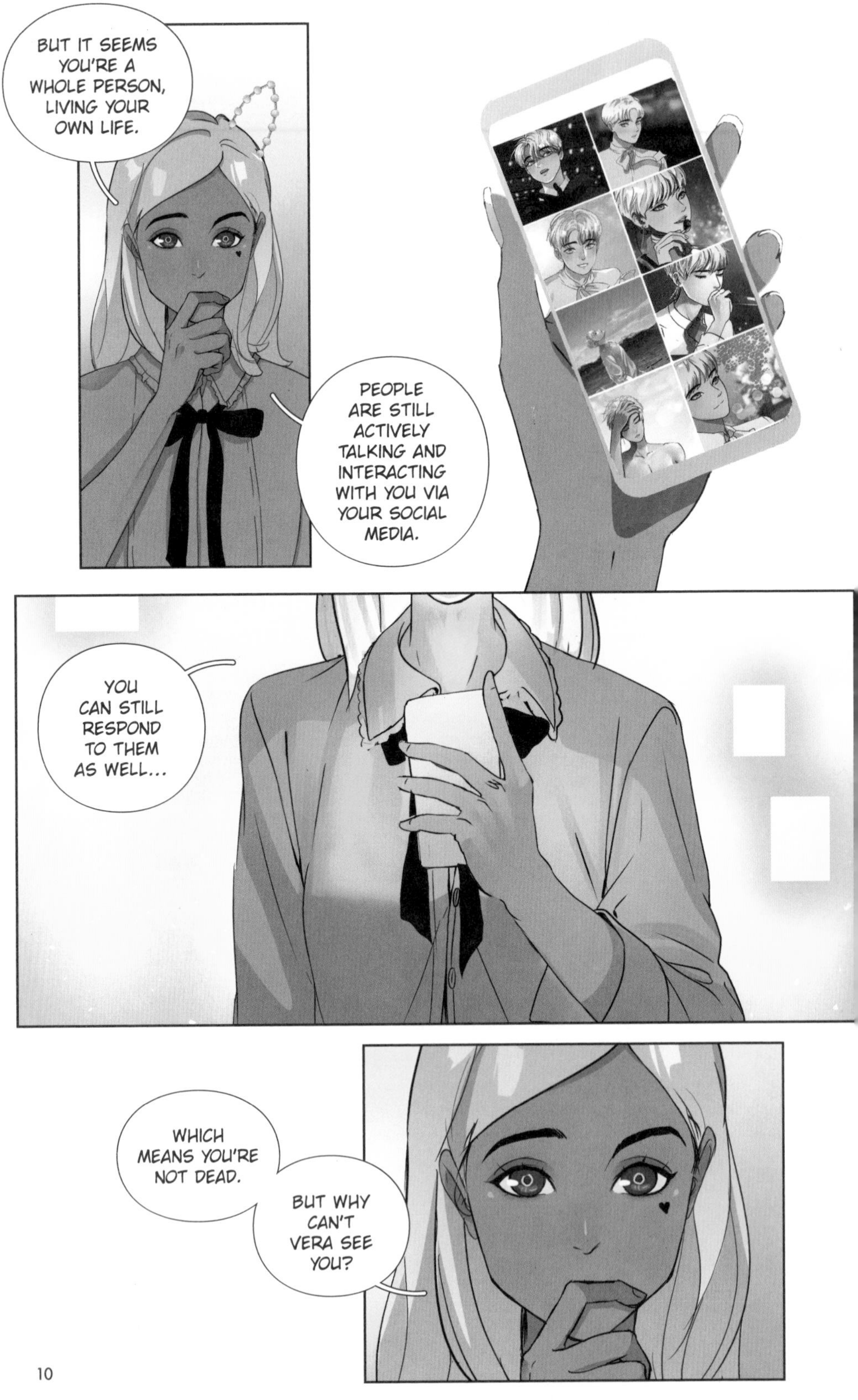
BUT IT SEEMS YOU'RE A WHOLE PERSON, LIVING YOUR OWN LIFE.
PEOPLE ARE STILL ACTIVELY TALKING AND INTERACTING WITH YOU VIA YOUR SOCIAL MEDIA.
YOU CAN STILL RESPOND TO THEM AS WELL...
WHICH MEANS YOU'RE NOT DEAD.
BUT WHY CAN'T VERA SEE YOU?

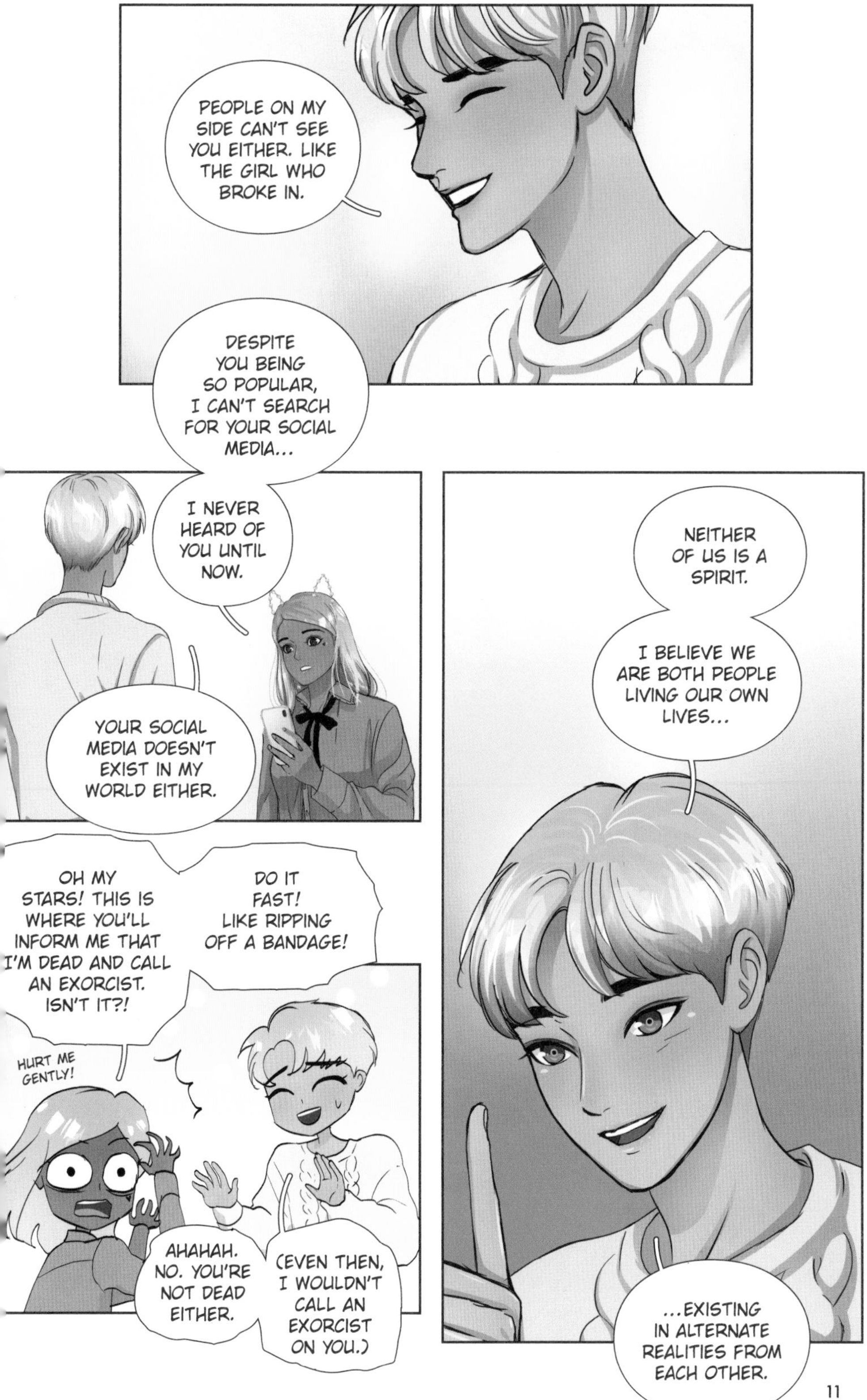
PEOPLE ON MY SIDE CAN'T SEE YOU EITHER. LIKE THE GIRL WHO BROKE IN.
DESPITE YOU BEING SO POPULAR, I CAN'T SEARCH FOR YOUR SOCIAL MEDIA...
I NEVER HEARD OF YOU UNTIL NOW.
YOUR SOCIAL MEDIA DOESN'T EXIST IN MY WORLD EITHER.
OH MY STARS! THIS IS WHERE YOU'LL INFORM ME THAT I'M DEAD AND CALL AN EXORCIST. ISN'T IT?!
DO IT FAST! LIKE RIPPING OFF A BANDAGE!
HURT ME GENTLY!
AHAHAH. NO. YOU'RE NOT DEAD EITHER.
(EVEN THEN, I WOULDN'T CALL AN EXORCIST ON YOU.)
NEITHER OF US IS A SPIRIT.
I BELIEVE WE ARE BOTH PEOPLE LIVING OUR OWN LIVES...
...EXISTING IN ALTERNATE REALITIES FROM EACH OTHER.

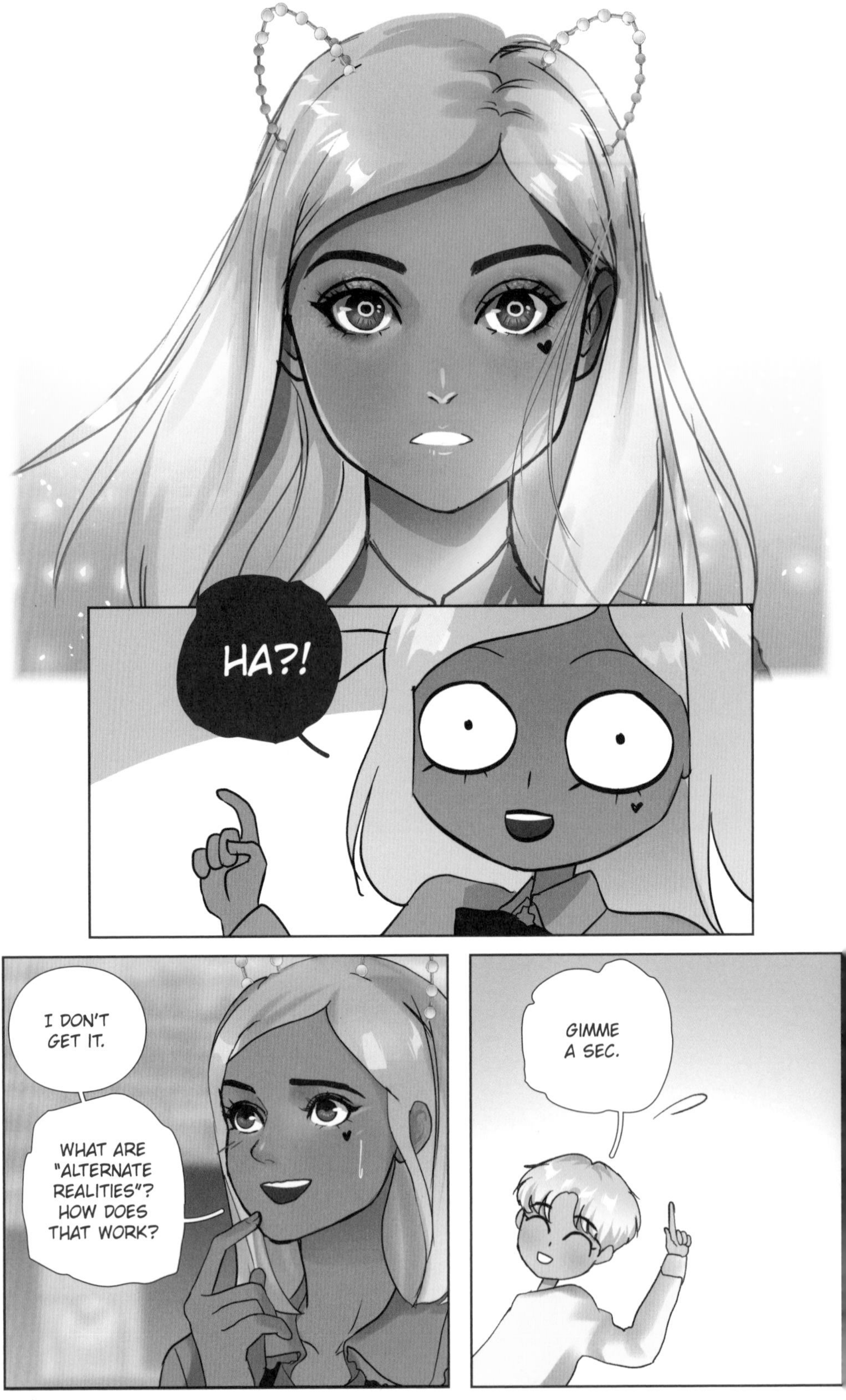
HA?!
I DON'T GET IT.
WHAT ARE "ALTERNATE REALITIES"? HOW DOES THAT WORK?
GIMME A SEC.

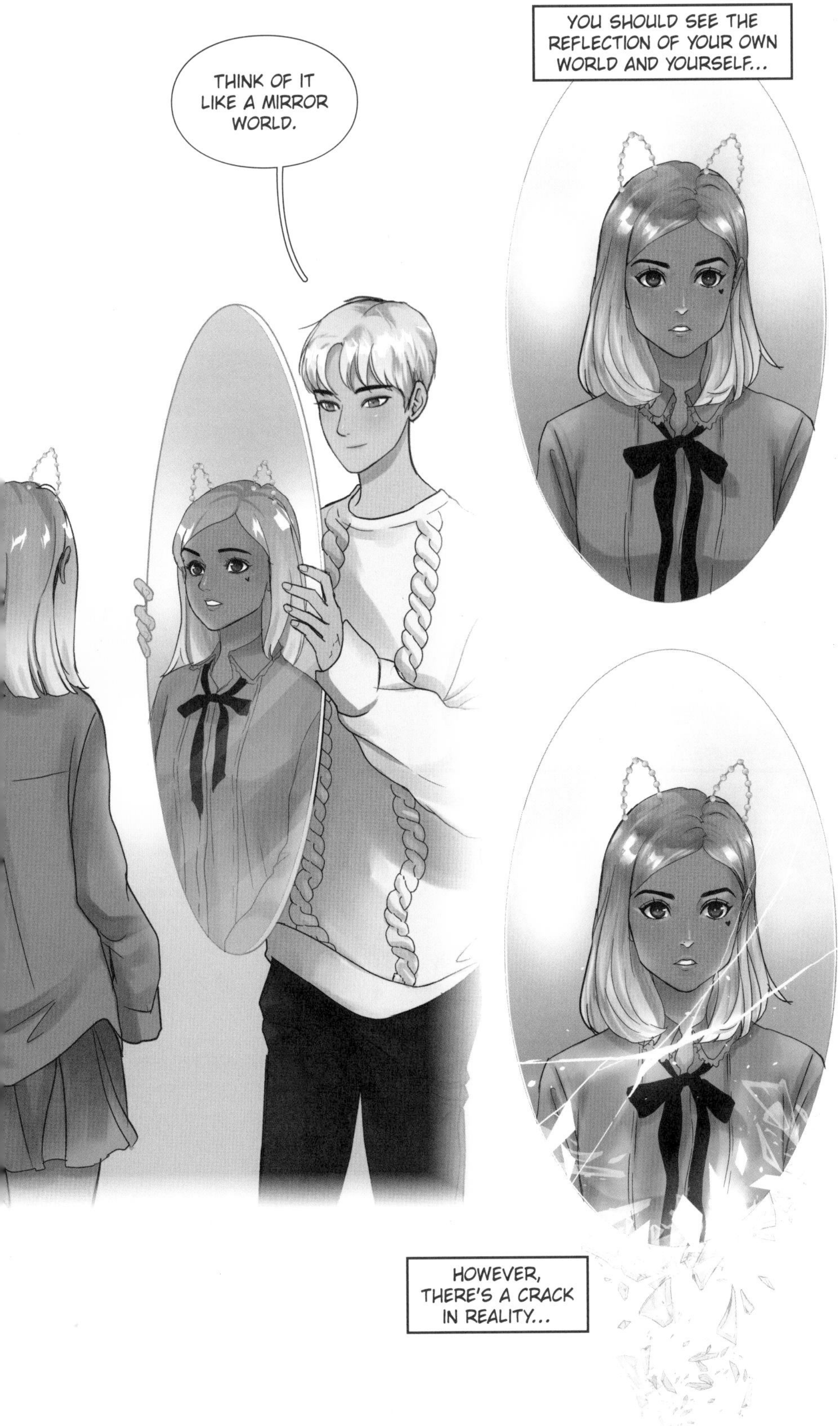
THINK OF IT LIKE A MIRROR WORLD.
YOU SHOULD SEE THE REFLECTION OF YOUR OWN WORLD AND YOURSELF...
HOWEVER, THERE'S A CRACK IN REALITY...

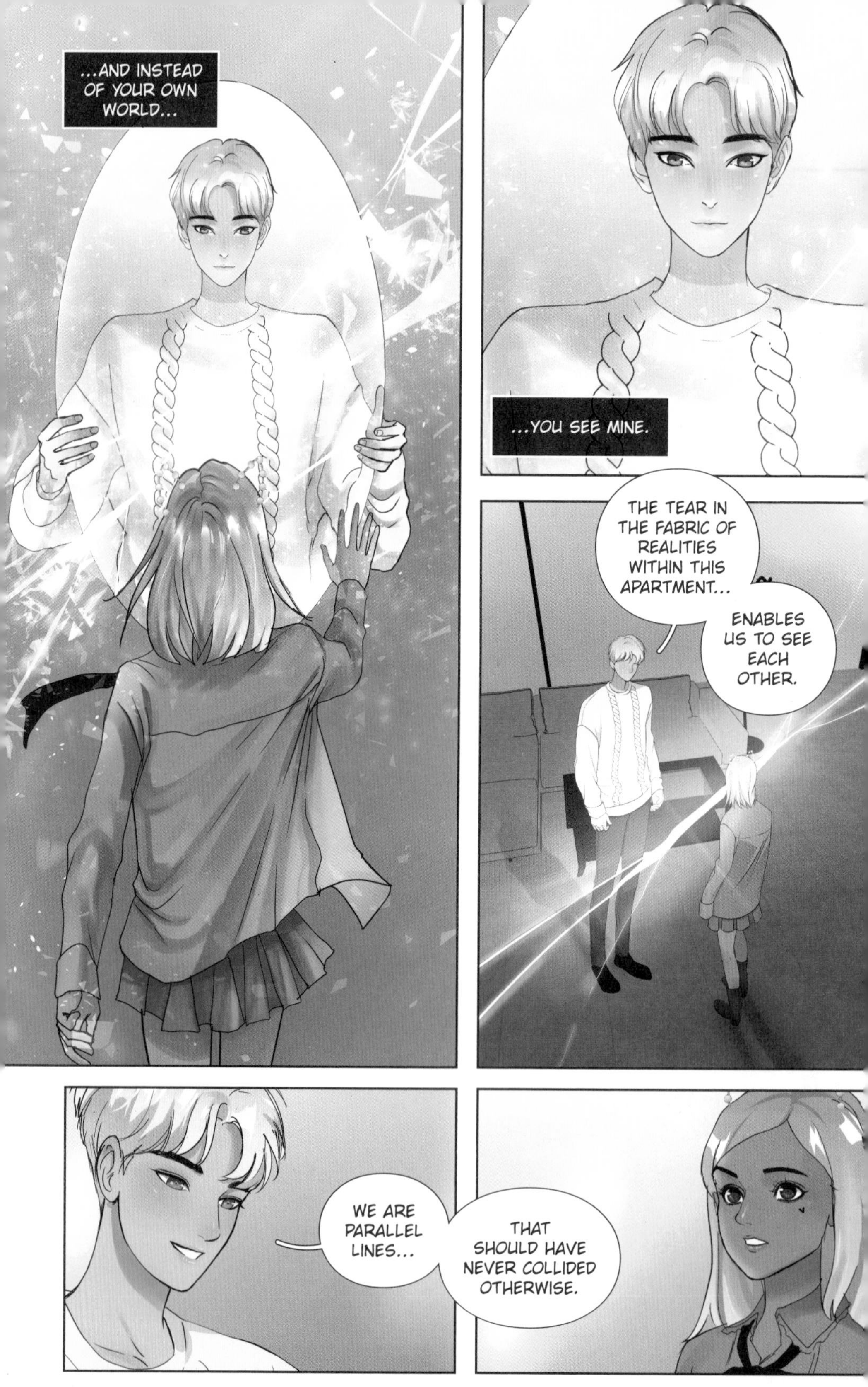
...AND INSTEAD OF YOUR OWN WORLD...
...YOU SEE MINE.
THE TEAR IN THE FABRIC OF REALITIES WITHIN THIS APARTMENT...
ENABLES US TO SEE EACH OTHER.
WE ARE PARALLEL LINES...
THAT SHOULD HAVE NEVER COLLIDED OTHERWISE.

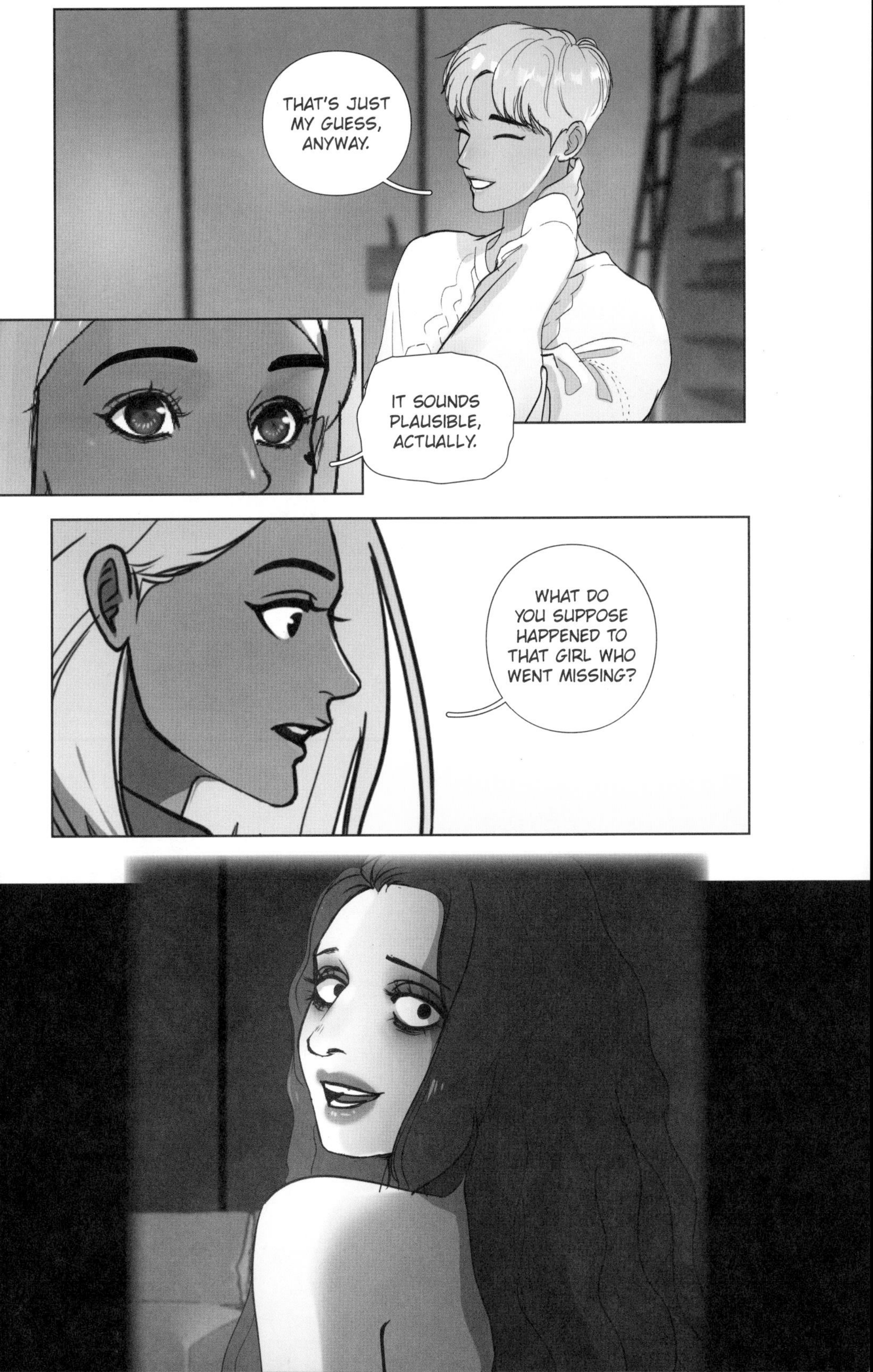
THAT'S JUST MY GUESS, ANYWAY.
IT SOUNDS PLAUSIBLE, ACTUALLY.
WHAT DO YOU SUPPOSE HAPPENED TO THAT GIRL WHO WENT MISSING?

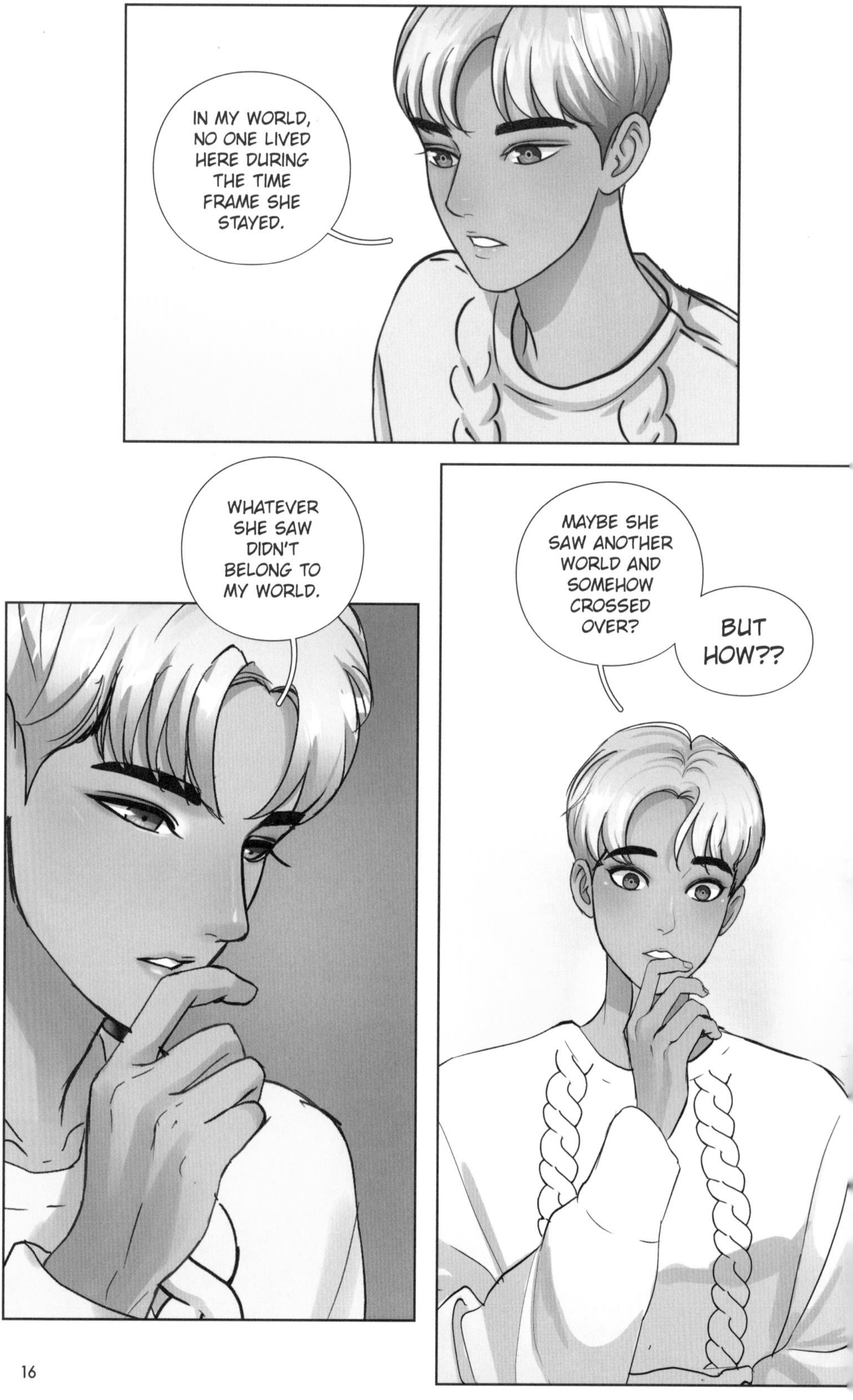
IN MY WORLD, NO ONE LIVED HERE DURING THE TIME FRAME SHE STAYED.
WHATEVER SHE SAW DIDN'T BELONG TO MY WORLD.
MAYBE SHE SAW ANOTHER WORLD AND SOMEHOW CROSSED OVER?
BUT HOW??

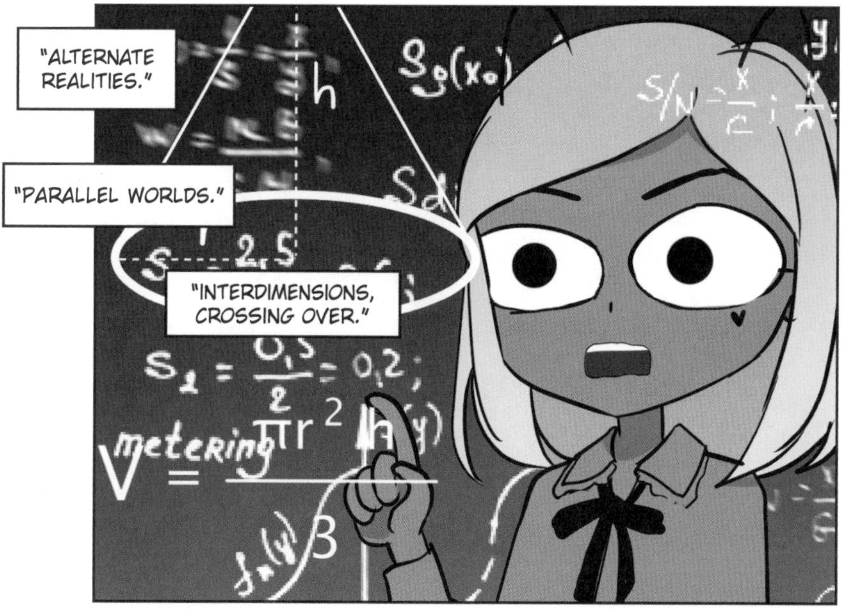
"ALTERNATE REALITIES."
"PARALLEL WORLDS."
"INTERDIMENSIONS, CROSSING OVER."
metering

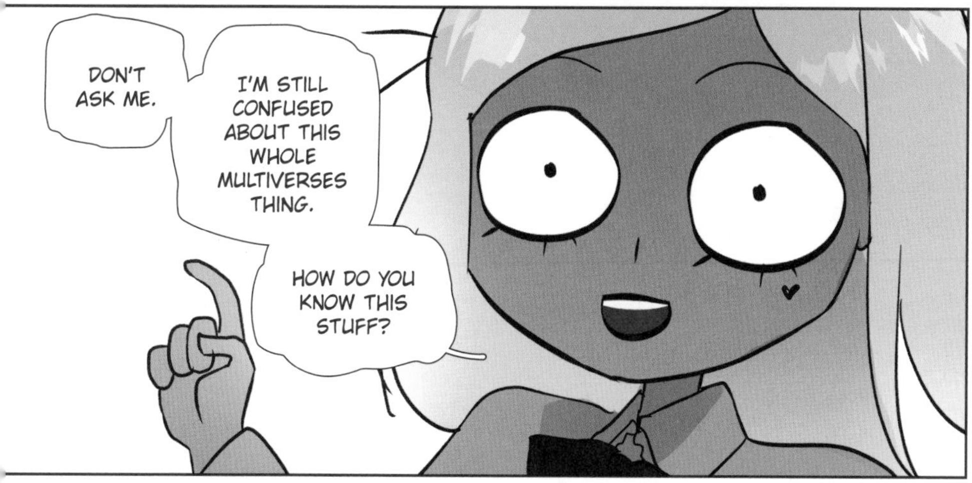
DON'T ASK ME.
I'M STILL CONFUSED ABOUT THIS WHOLE MULTIVERSES THING.
HOW DO YOU KNOW THIS STUFF?

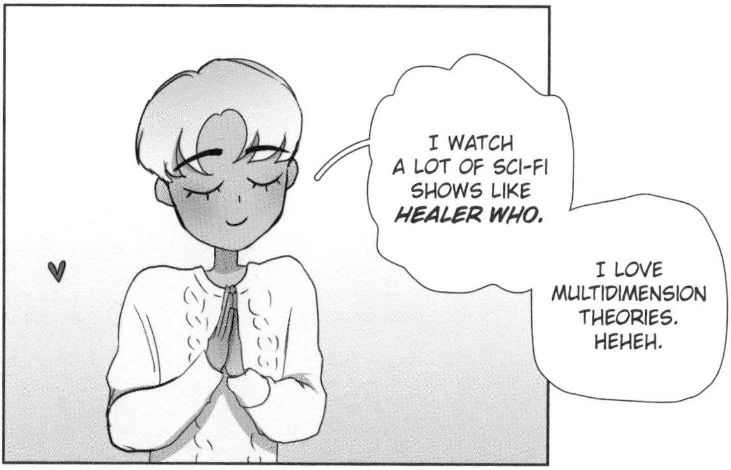
I WATCH A LOT OF SCI-FI SHOWS LIKE ***HEALER WHO.***
I LOVE MULTIDIMENSION THEORIES. HEHEH.

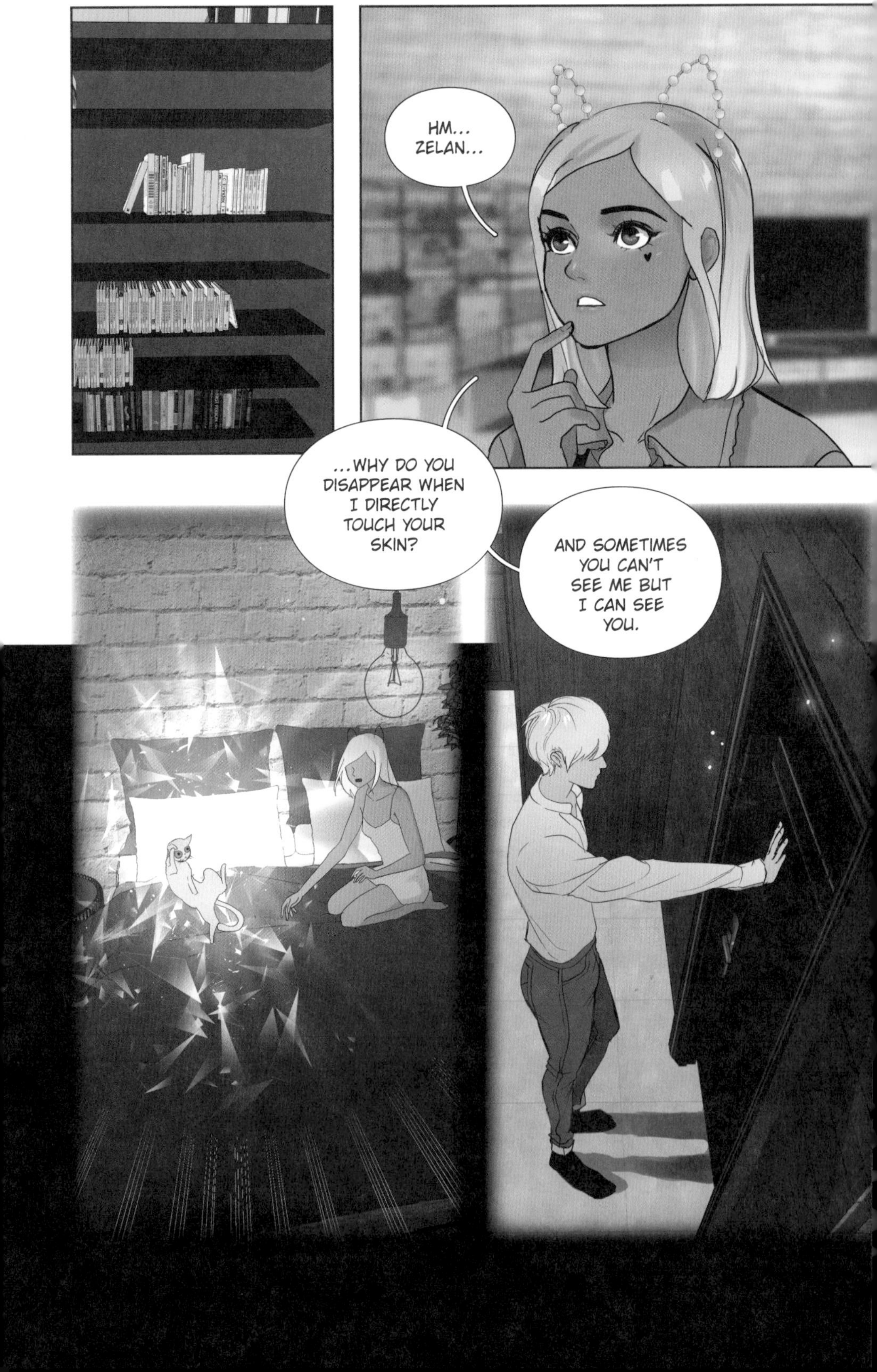
HM... ZELAN...
...WHY DO YOU DISAPPEAR WHEN I DIRECTLY TOUCH YOUR SKIN?
AND SOMETIMES YOU CAN'T SEE ME BUT I CAN SEE YOU.

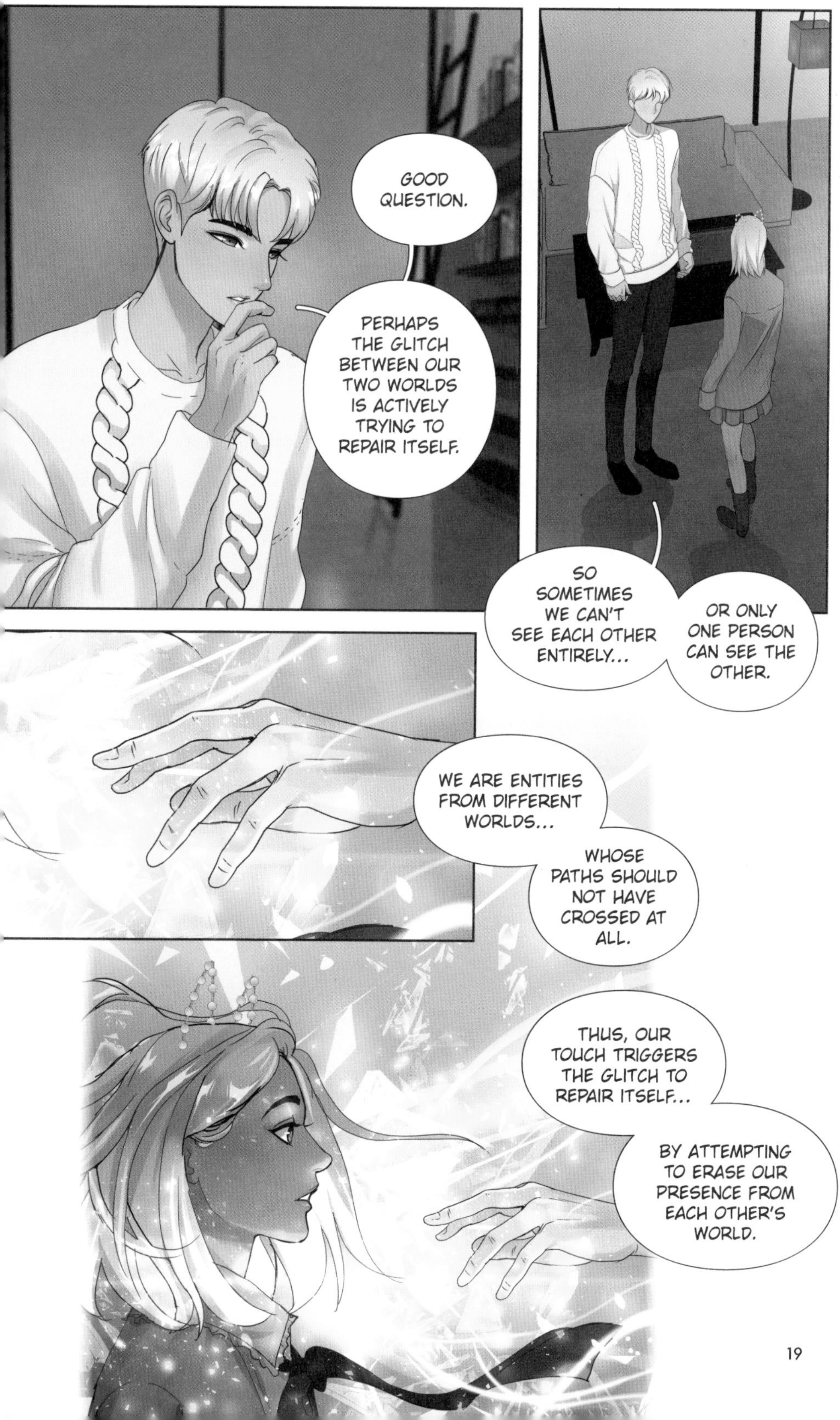
GOOD QUESTION.
PERHAPS THE GLITCH BETWEEN OUR TWO WORLDS IS ACTIVELY TRYING TO REPAIR ITSELF.
SO SOMETIMES WE CAN'T SEE EACH OTHER ENTIRELY...
OR ONLY ONE PERSON CAN SEE THE OTHER.
WE ARE ENTITIES FROM DIFFERENT WORLDS...
WHOSE PATHS SHOULD NOT HAVE CROSSED AT ALL.
THUS, OUR TOUCH TRIGGERS THE GLITCH TO REPAIR ITSELF...
BY ATTEMPTING TO ERASE OUR PRESENCE FROM EACH OTHER'S WORLD.

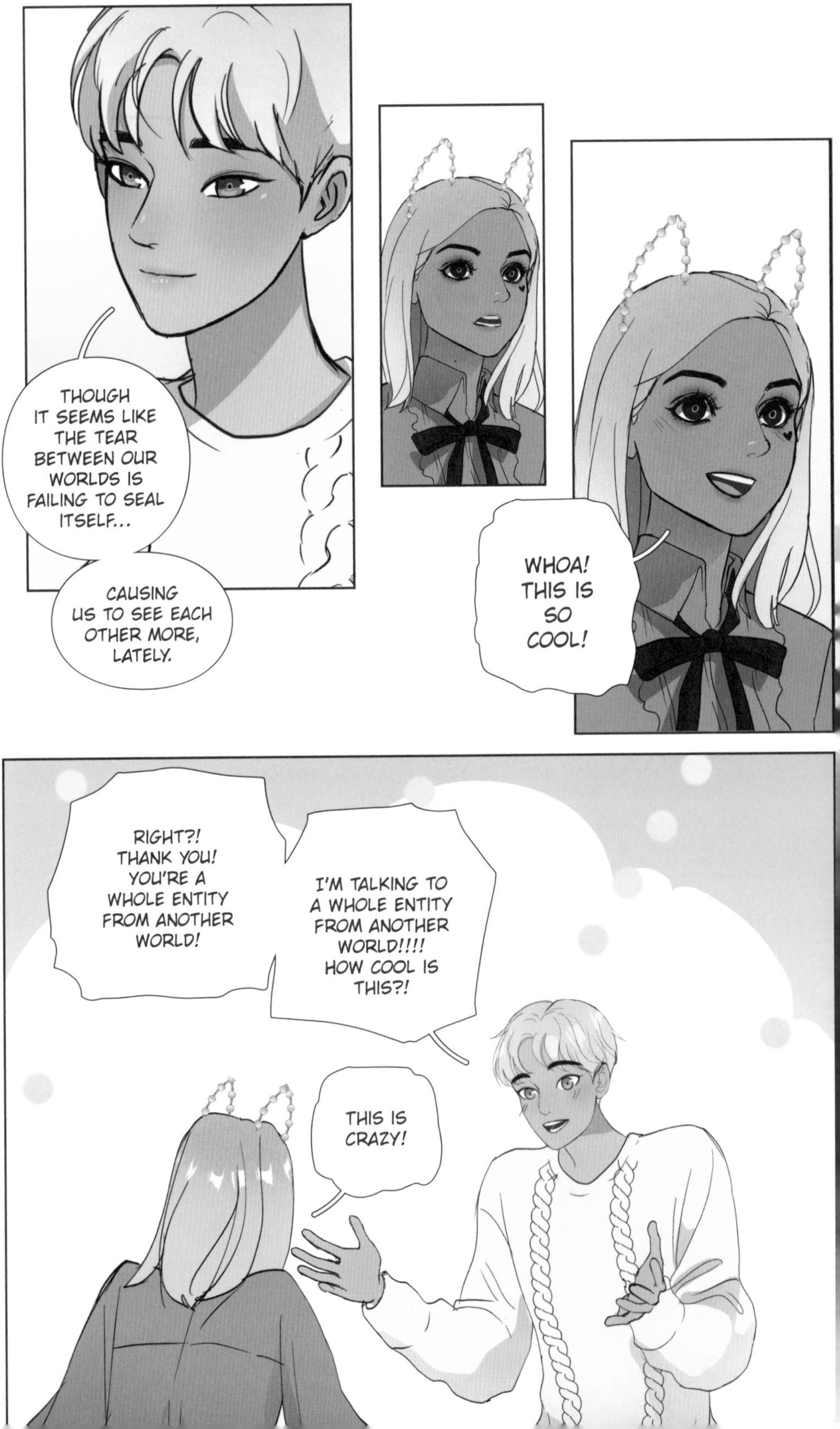
THOUGH IT SEEMS LIKE THE TEAR BETWEEN OUR WORLDS IS FAILING TO SEAL ITSELF...
CAUSING US TO SEE EACH OTHER MORE, LATELY.
WHOA! THIS IS SO COOL!
RIGHT?! THANK YOU! YOU'RE A WHOLE ENTITY FROM ANOTHER WORLD!
I'M TALKING TO A WHOLE ENTITY FROM ANOTHER WORLD!!!! HOW COOL IS THIS?!
THIS IS CRAZY!

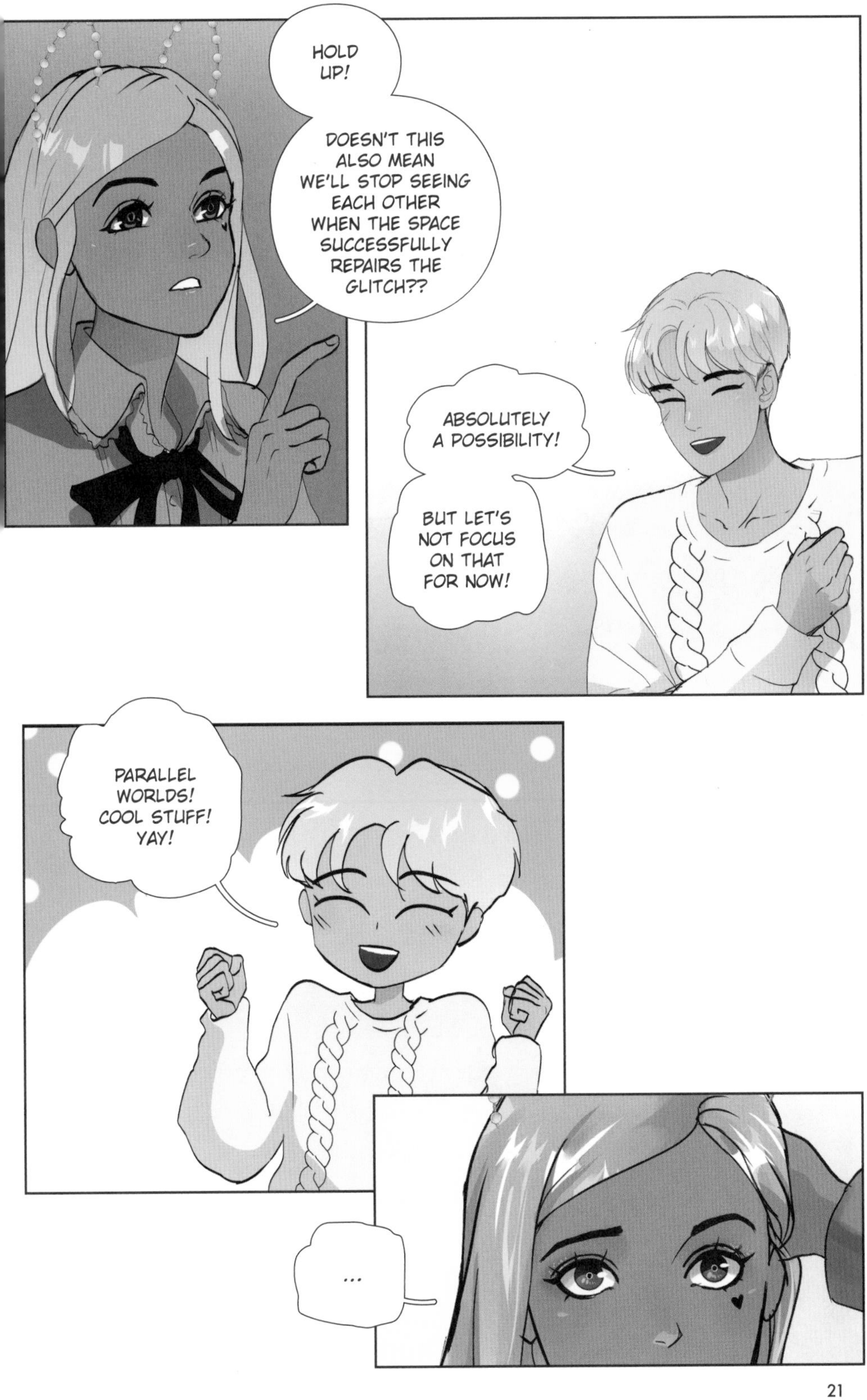
HOLD UP!
DOESN'T THIS ALSO MEAN WE'LL STOP SEEING EACH OTHER WHEN THE SPACE SUCCESSFULLY REPAIRS THE GLITCH??
ABSOLUTELY A POSSIBILITY!
BUT LET'S NOT FOCUS ON THAT FOR NOW!
PARALLEL WORLDS! COOL STUFF! YAY!
...

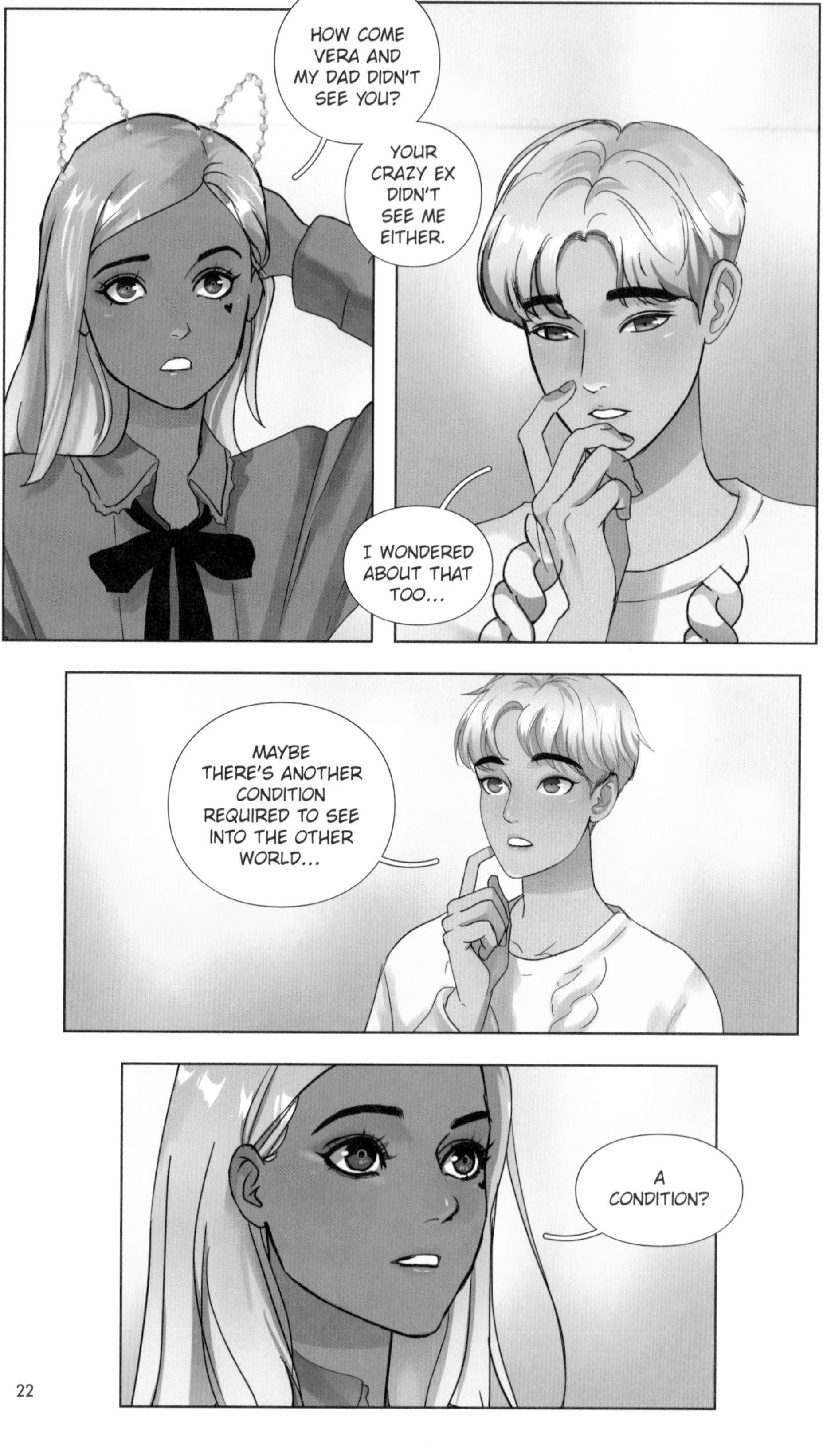
HOW COME VERA AND MY DAD DIDN'T SEE YOU?
YOUR CRAZY EX DIDN'T SEE ME EITHER.
I WONDERED ABOUT THAT TOO...
MAYBE THERE'S ANOTHER CONDITION REQUIRED TO SEE INTO THE OTHER WORLD...
A CONDITION?

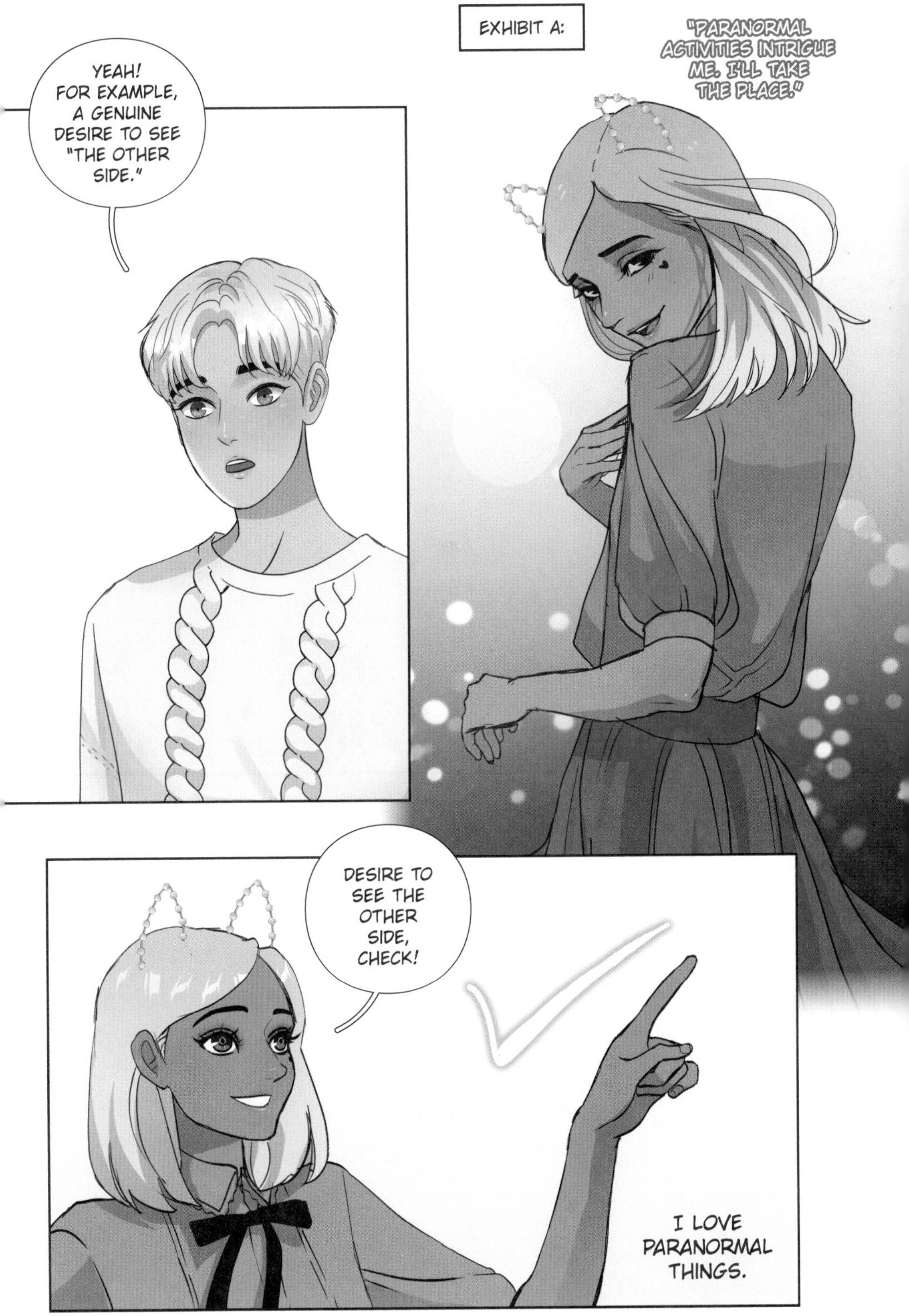
YEAH! FOR EXAMPLE, A GENUINE DESIRE TO SEE "THE OTHER SIDE."
EXHIBIT A:
"PARANORMAL ACTIVITIES INTRIGUE ME. I'LL TAKE THE PLACE."
DESIRE TO SEE THE OTHER SIDE, CHECK!
I LOVE PARANORMAL THINGS.

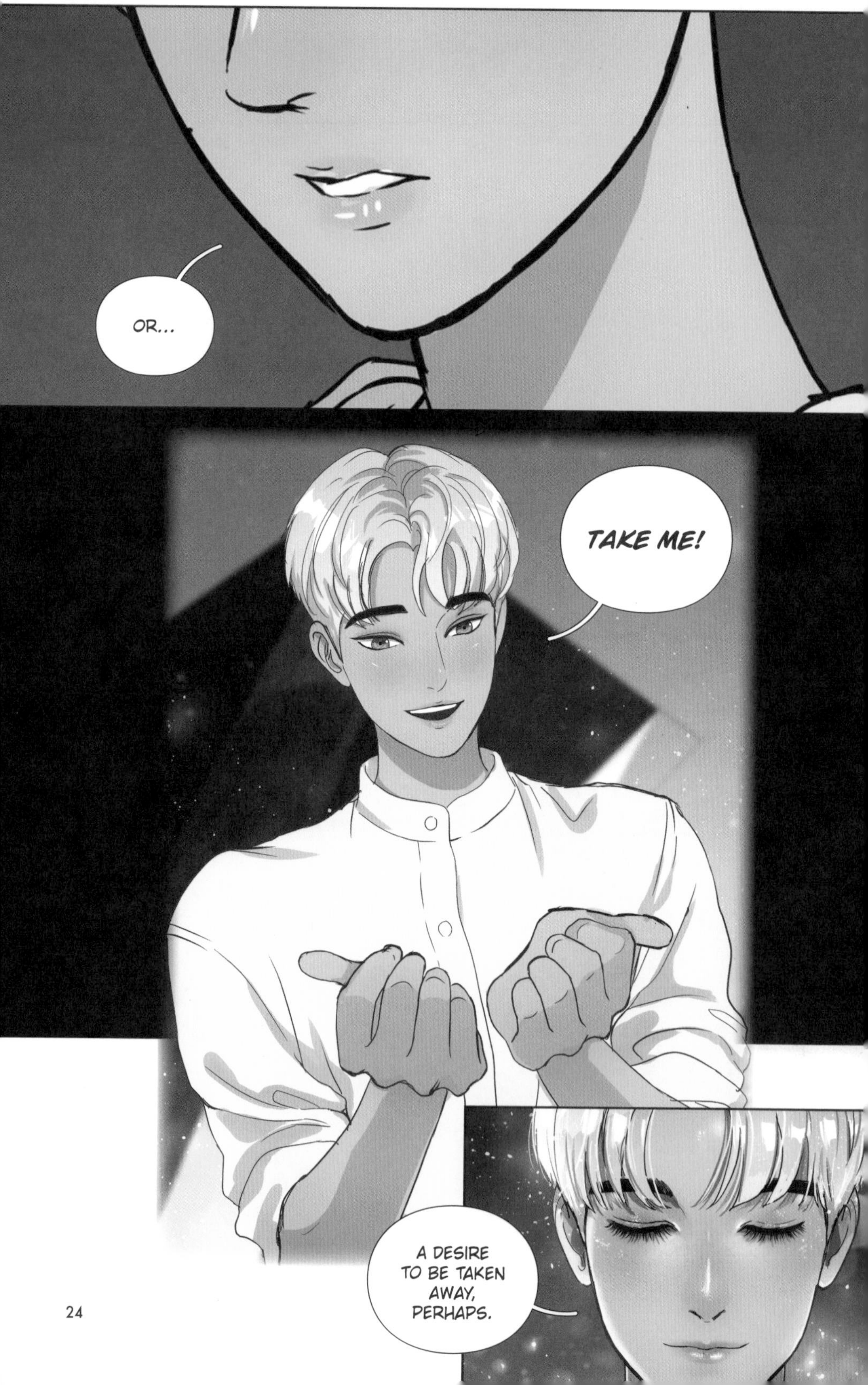

OR...
TAKE ME!
A DESIRE TO BE TAKEN AWAY, PERHAPS.

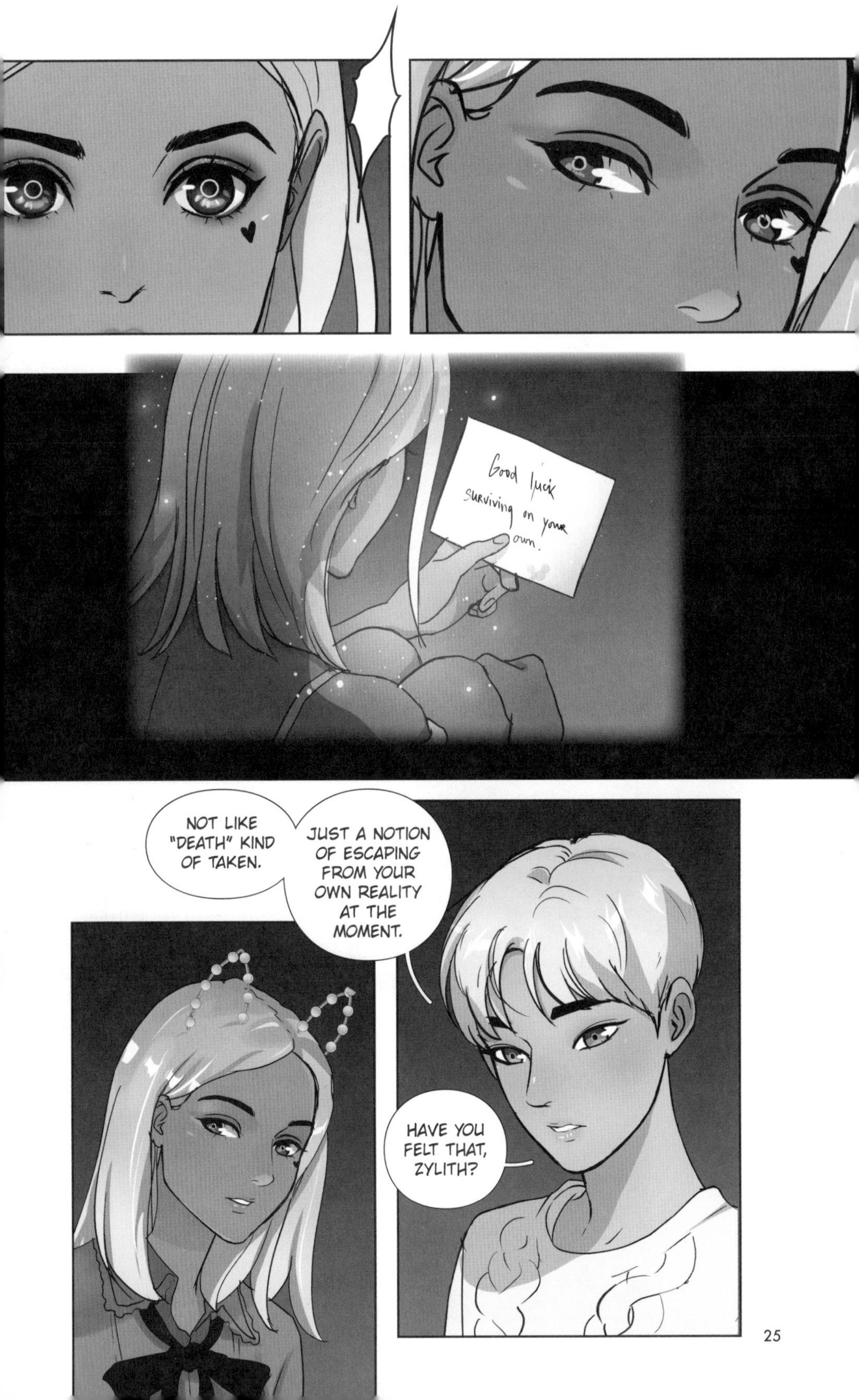
Good luck surviving on your own.
NOT LIKE "DEATH" KIND OF TAKEN.
JUST A NOTION OF ESCAPING FROM YOUR OWN REALITY AT THE MOMENT.
HAVE YOU FELT THAT, ZYLITH?

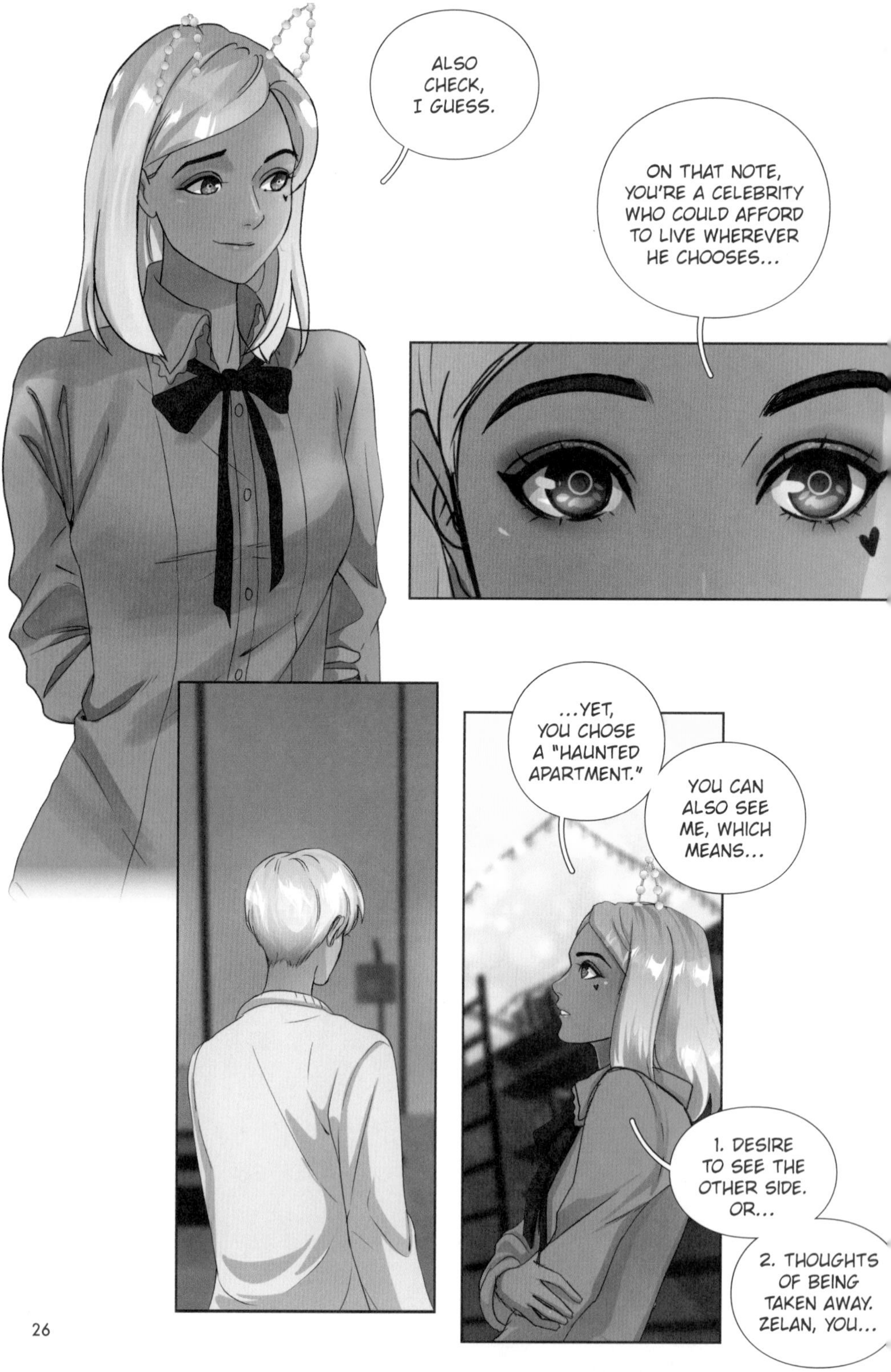
ALSO CHECK, I GUESS.
ON THAT NOTE, YOU'RE A CELEBRITY WHO COULD AFFORD TO LIVE WHEREVER HE CHOOSES...
...YET, YOU CHOSE A "HAUNTED APARTMENT."
YOU CAN ALSO SEE ME, WHICH MEANS...
1. DESIRE TO SEE THE OTHER SIDE. OR...
2. THOUGHTS OF BEING TAKEN AWAY. ZELAN, YOU...

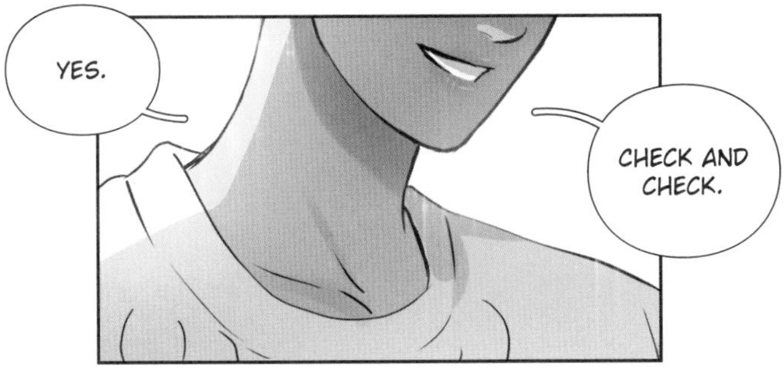
YES.
CHECK AND CHECK.

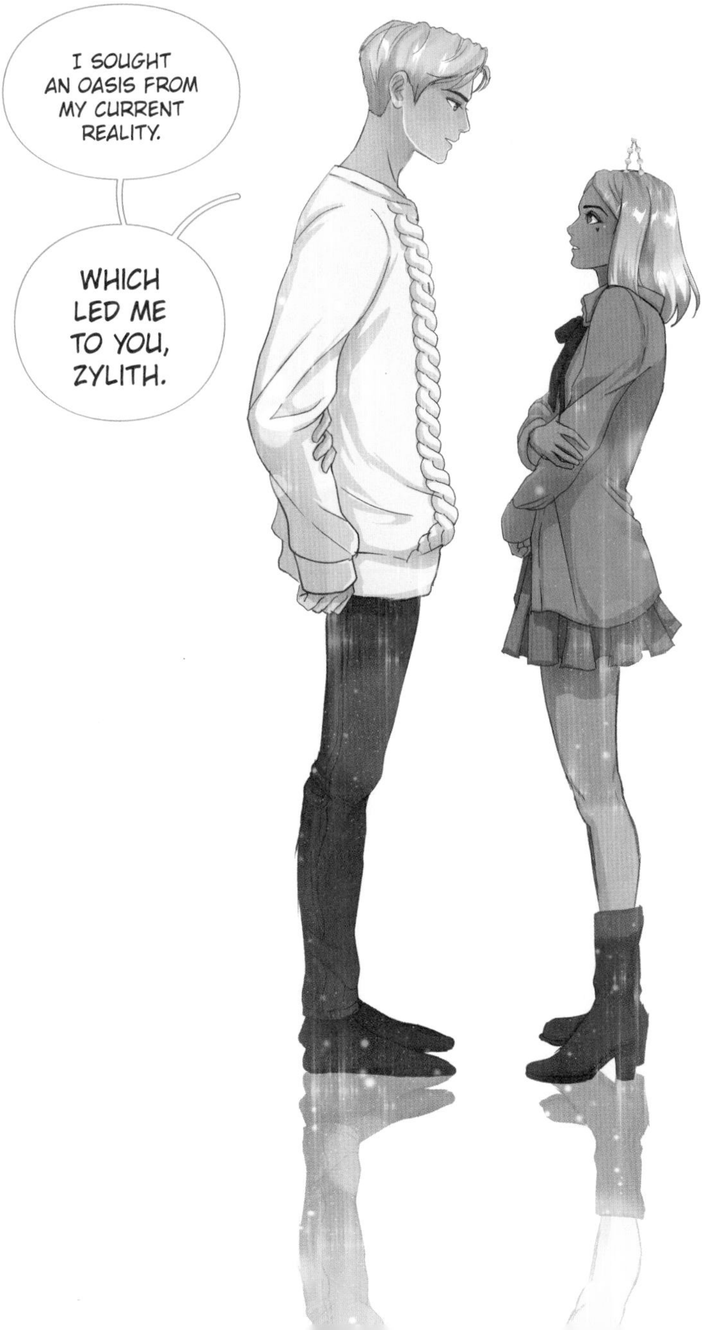
I SOUGHT AN OASIS FROM MY CURRENT REALITY.
WHICH LED ME TO YOU, ZYLITH.

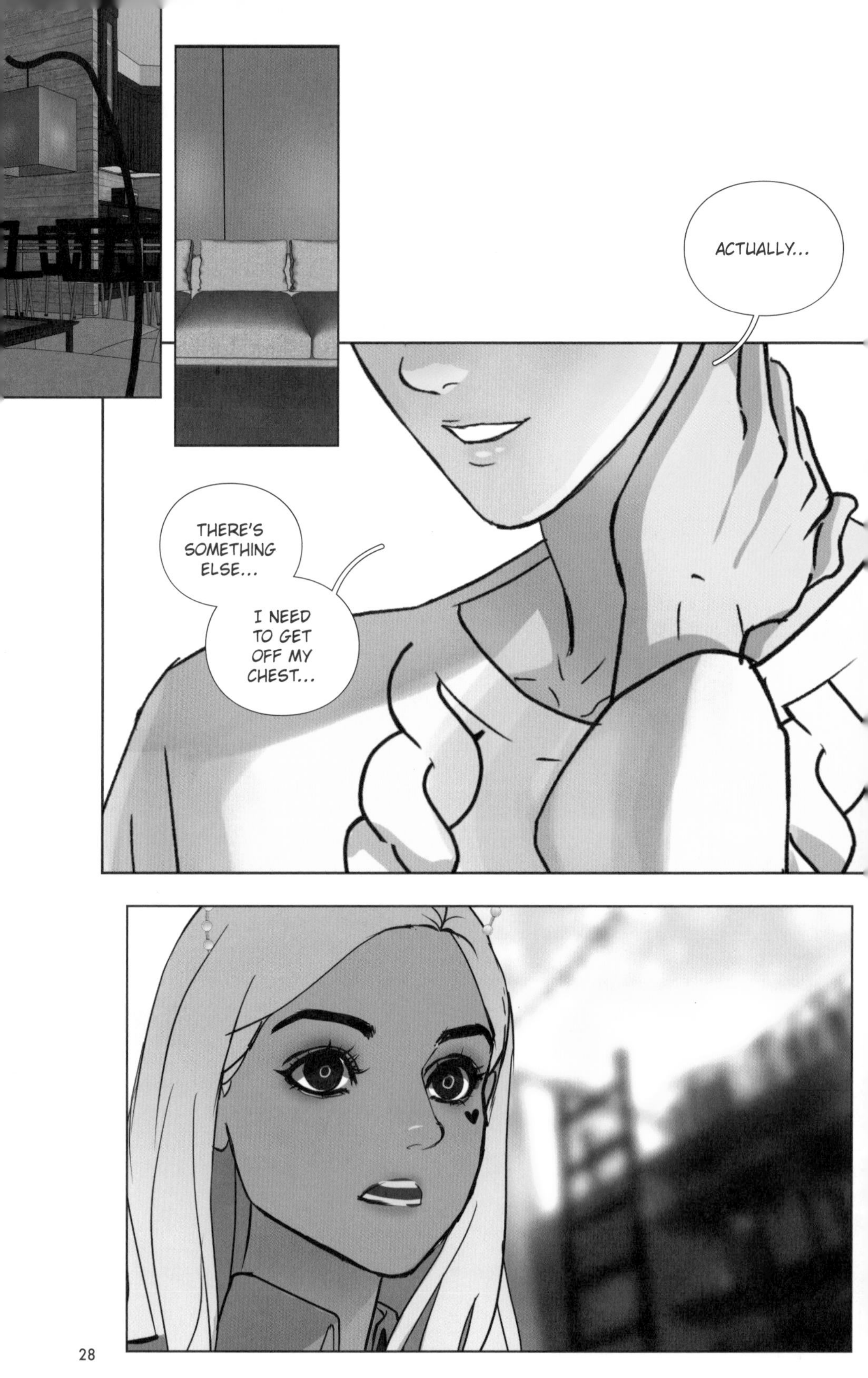
ACTUALLY...
THERE'S SOMETHING ELSE...
I NEED TO GET OFF MY CHEST...

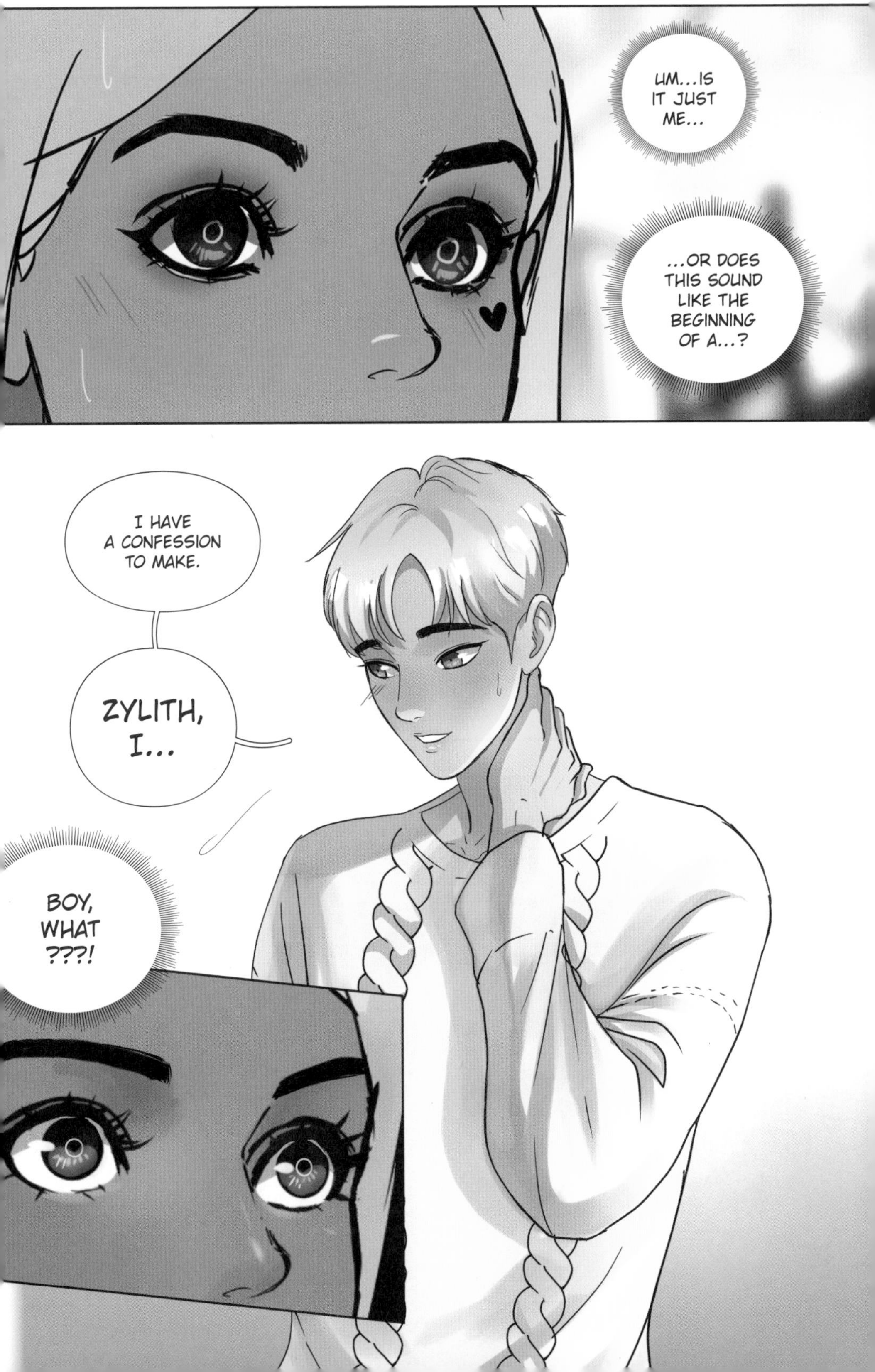
UM...IS IT JUST ME...
...OR DOES THIS SOUND LIKE THE BEGINNING OF A...?
I HAVE A CONFESSION TO MAKE.
ZYLITH, I...
BOY, WHAT ???!

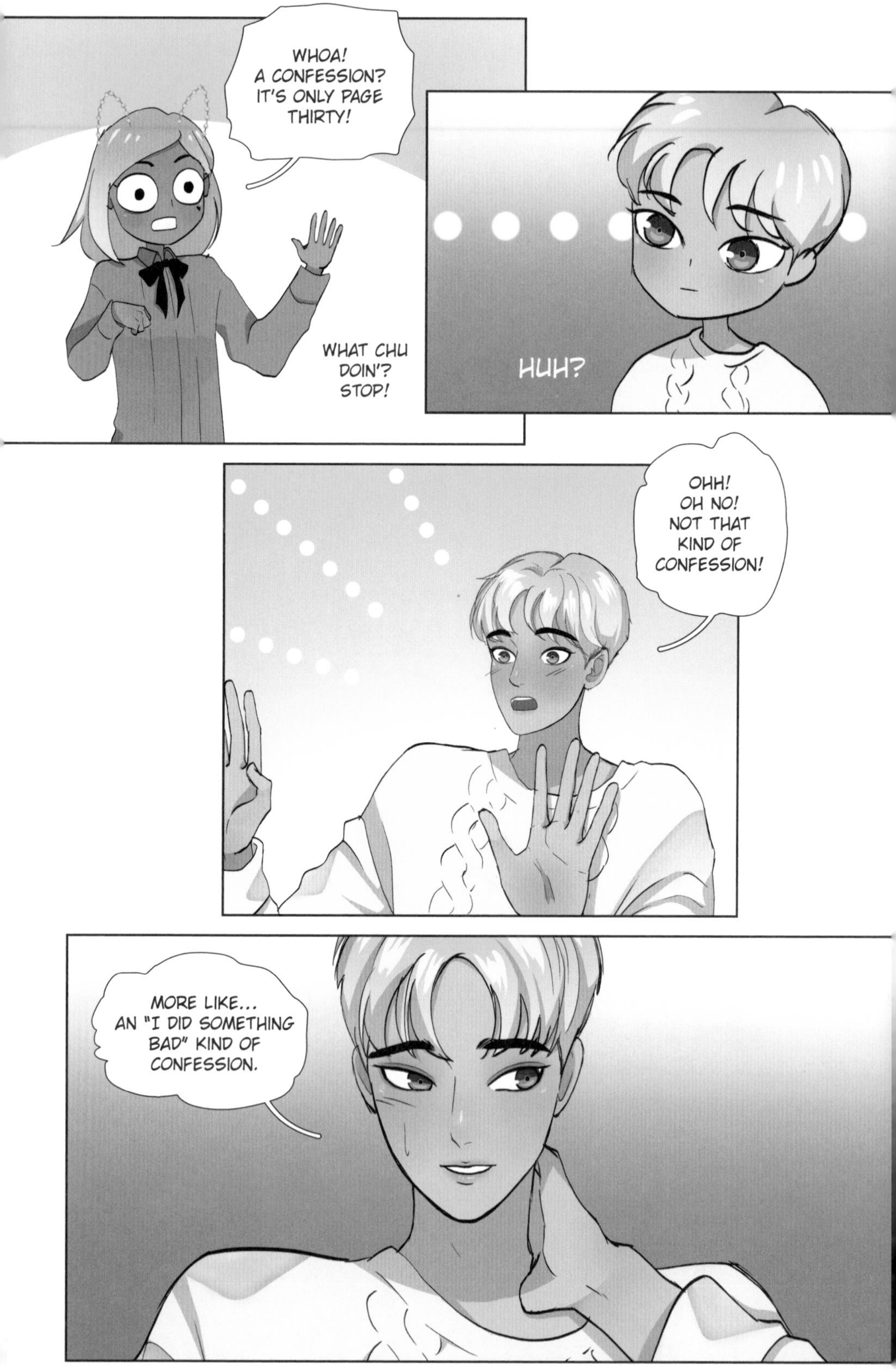
WHOA! A CONFESSION? IT'S ONLY PAGE THIRTY!
WHAT CHU DOIN'? STOP!
HUH?
OHH! OH NO! NOT THAT KIND OF CONFESSION!
MORE LIKE... AN "I DID SOMETHING BAD" KIND OF CONFESSION.

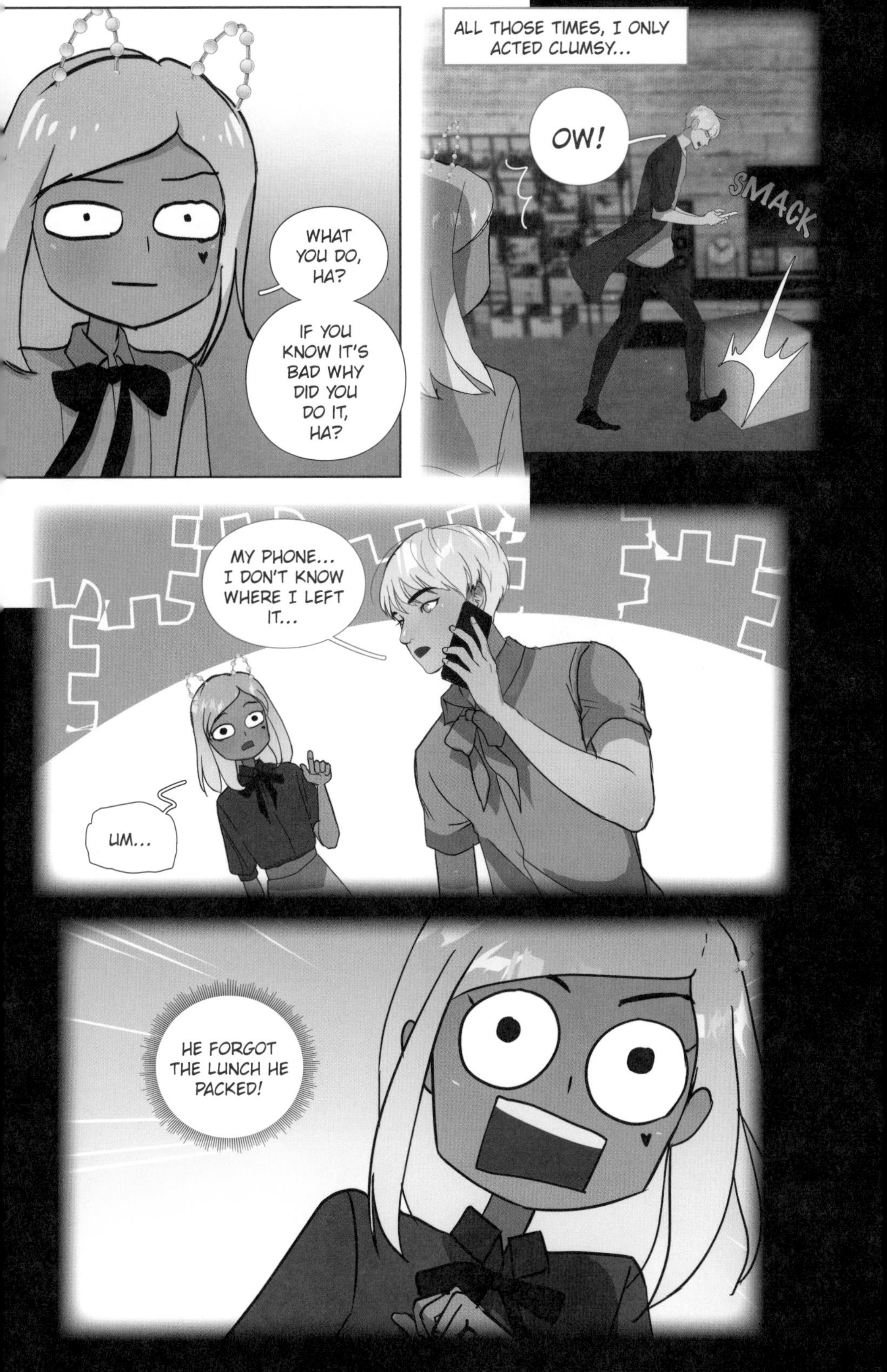
WHAT YOU DO, HA?
IF YOU KNOW IT'S BAD WHY DID YOU DO IT, HA?
ALL THOSE TIMES, I ONLY ACTED CLUMSY...
OW!
SMACK
MY PHONE... I DON'T KNOW WHERE I LEFT IT...
UM...
HE FORGOT THE LUNCH HE PACKED!

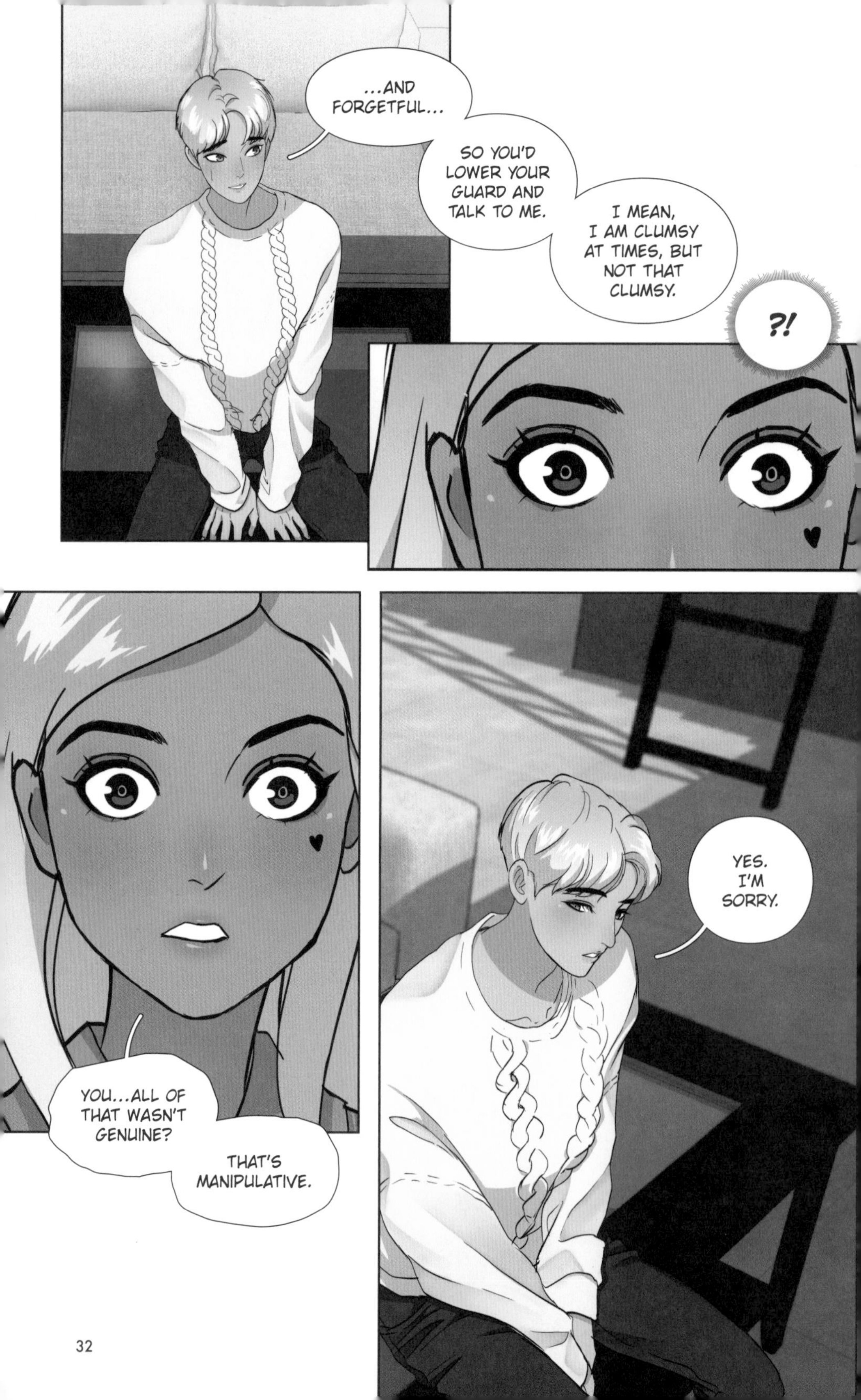
...AND FORGETFUL...
SO YOU'D LOWER YOUR GUARD AND TALK TO ME.
I MEAN, I AM CLUMSY AT TIMES, BUT NOT THAT CLUMSY.
?!
YOU...ALL OF THAT WASN'T GENUINE?
THAT'S MANIPULATIVE.
YES. I'M SORRY.

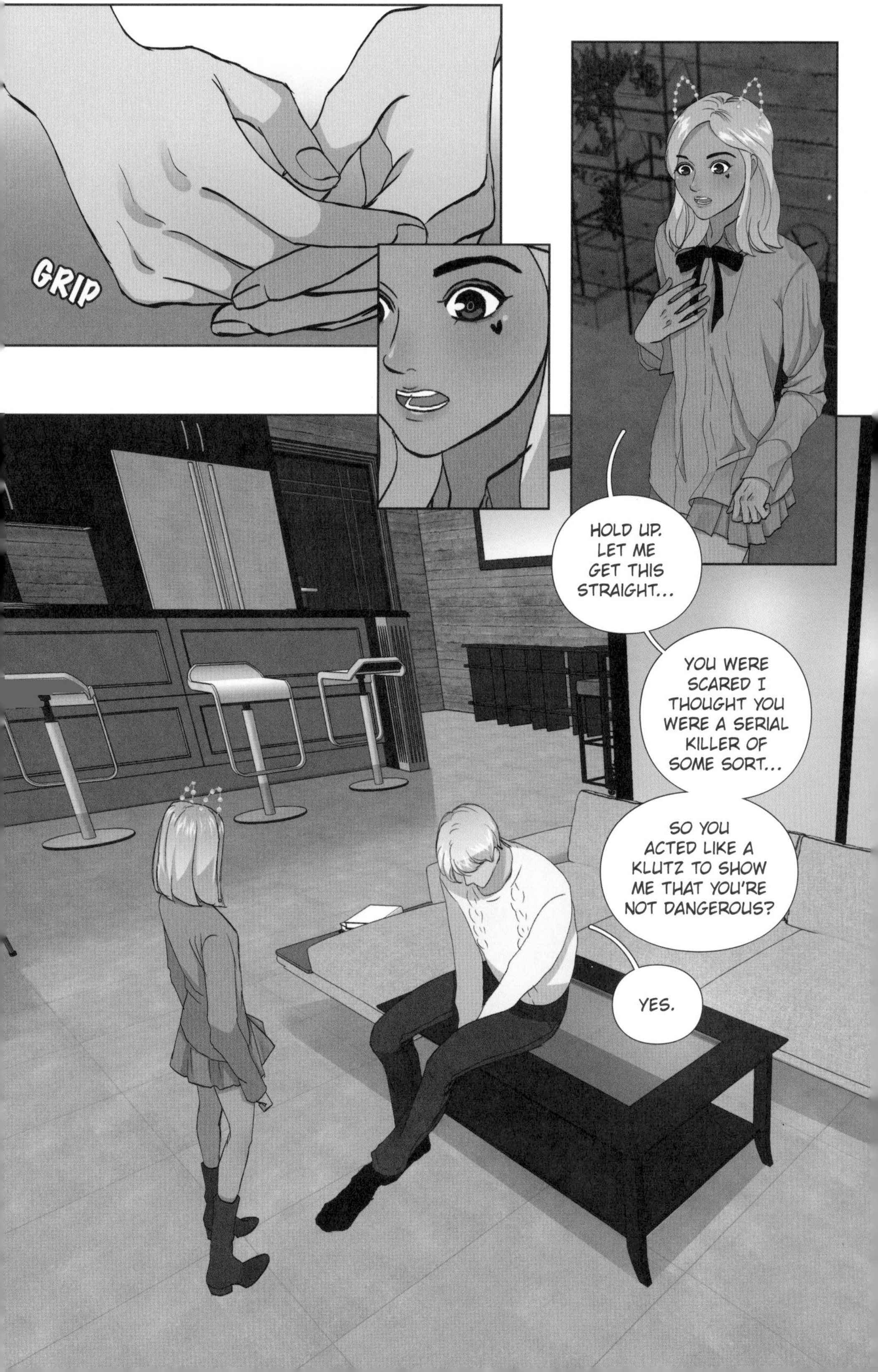
GRIP
HOLD UP. LET ME GET THIS STRAIGHT...
YOU WERE SCARED I THOUGHT YOU WERE A SERIAL KILLER OF SOME SORT...
SO YOU ACTED LIKE A KLUTZ TO SHOW ME THAT YOU'RE NOT DANGEROUS?
YES.

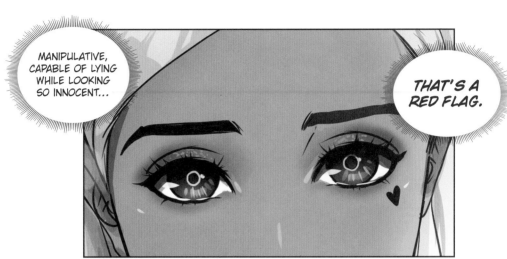

MANIPULATIVE, CAPABLE OF LYING WHILE LOOKING SO INNOCENT...

THAT'S A RED FLAG.

ANYTHING ELSE I SHOULD KNOW ABOUT?

NO, THAT'S ALL.

UM, OKAY. BUT LIKE WHY DIDN'T YOU JUST WALK UP TO ME...

...AND EXPLAIN YOURSELF LIKE A NORMAL PERSON?

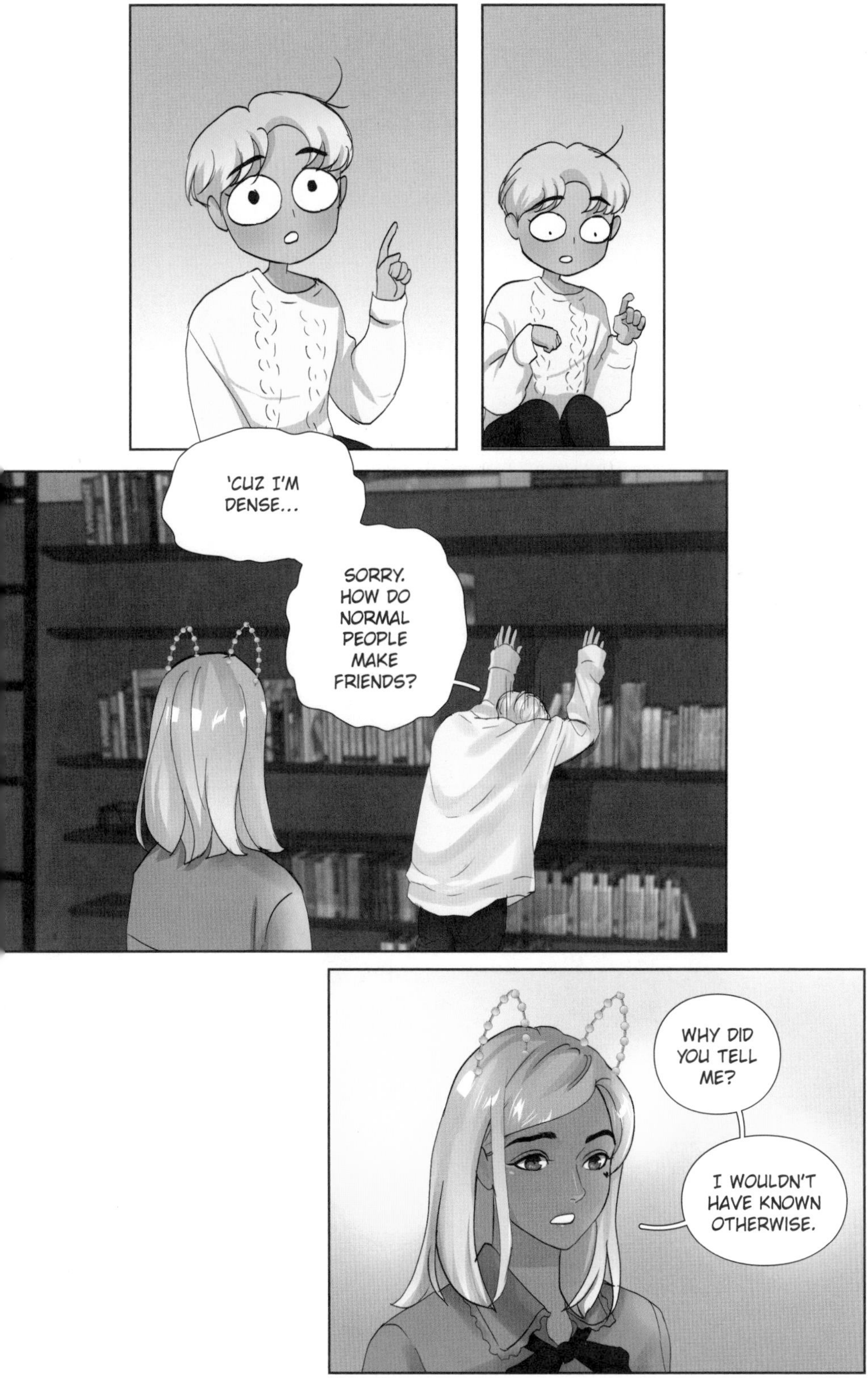

'CUZ I'M DENSE...
SORRY. HOW DO NORMAL PEOPLE MAKE FRIENDS?
WHY DID YOU TELL ME?
I WOULDN'T HAVE KNOWN OTHERWISE.

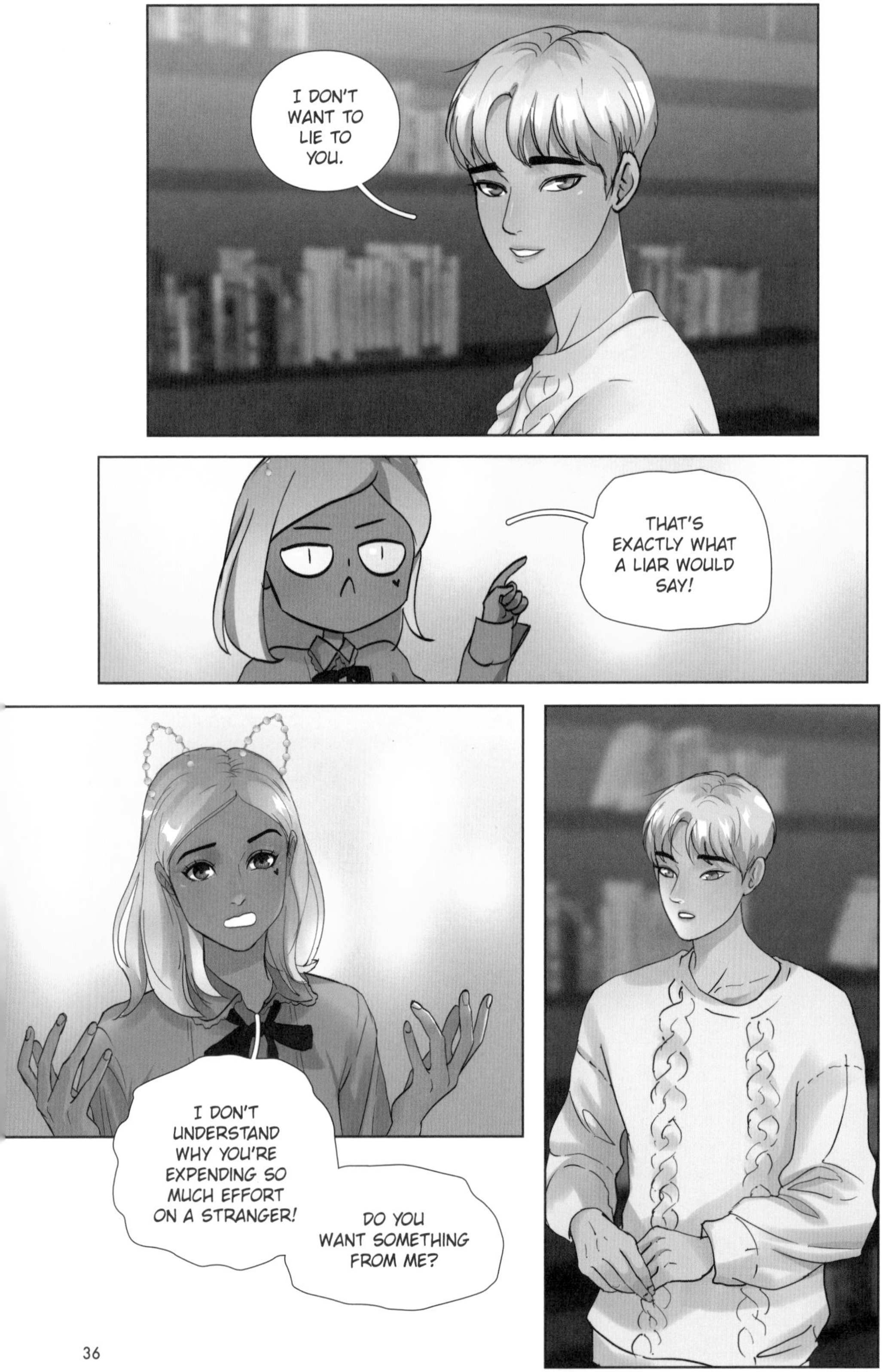
I DON'T WANT TO LIE TO YOU.
THAT'S EXACTLY WHAT A LIAR WOULD SAY!
I DON'T UNDERSTAND WHY YOU'RE EXPENDING SO MUCH EFFORT ON A STRANGER!
DO YOU WANT SOMETHING FROM ME?

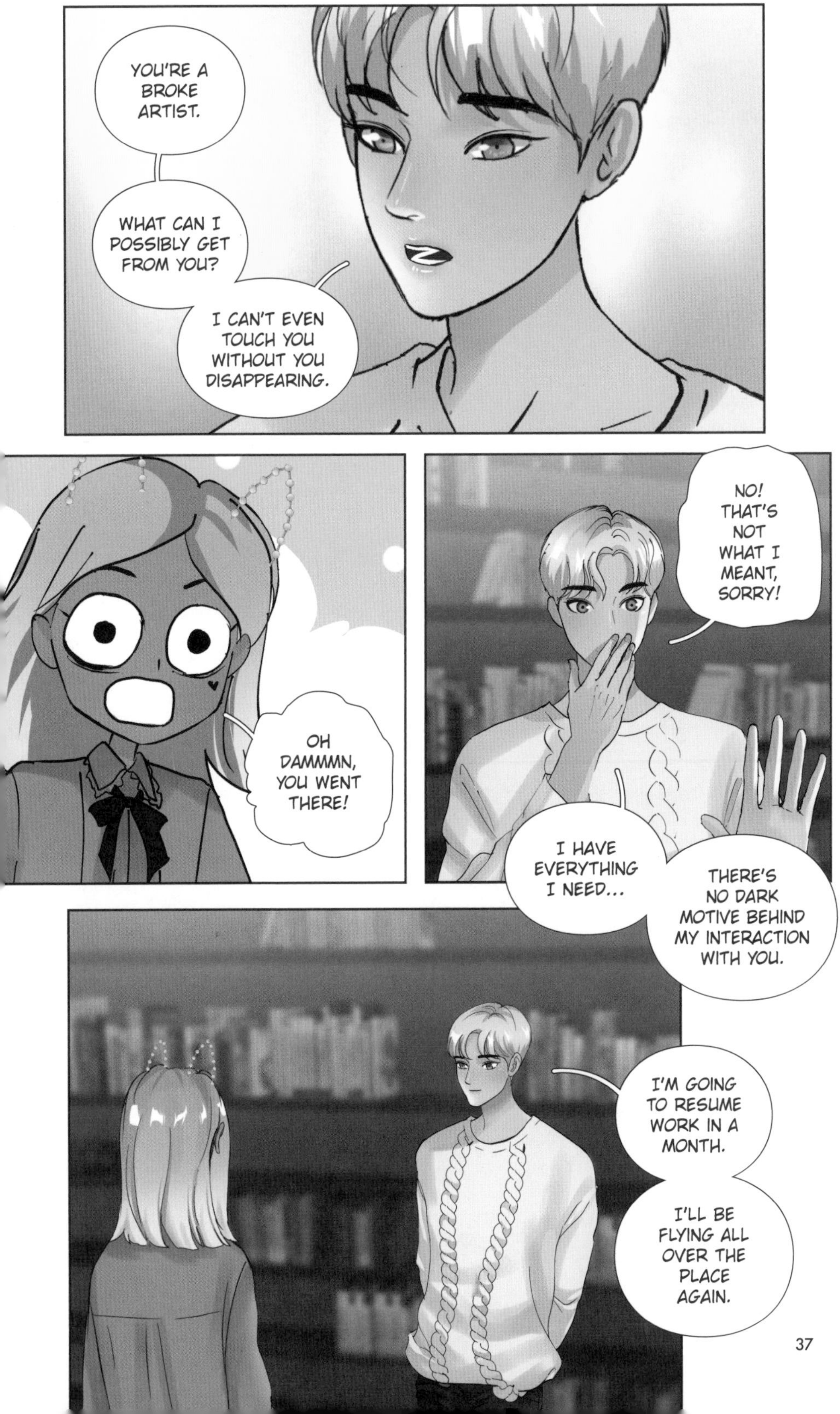
YOU'RE A BROKE ARTIST.
WHAT CAN I POSSIBLY GET FROM YOU?
I CAN'T EVEN TOUCH YOU WITHOUT YOU DISAPPEARING.
OH DAMMMN, YOU WENT THERE!
NO! THAT'S NOT WHAT I MEANT, SORRY!
I HAVE EVERYTHING I NEED...
THERE'S NO DARK MOTIVE BEHIND MY INTERACTION WITH YOU.
I'M GOING TO RESUME WORK IN A MONTH.
I'LL BE FLYING ALL OVER THE PLACE AGAIN.

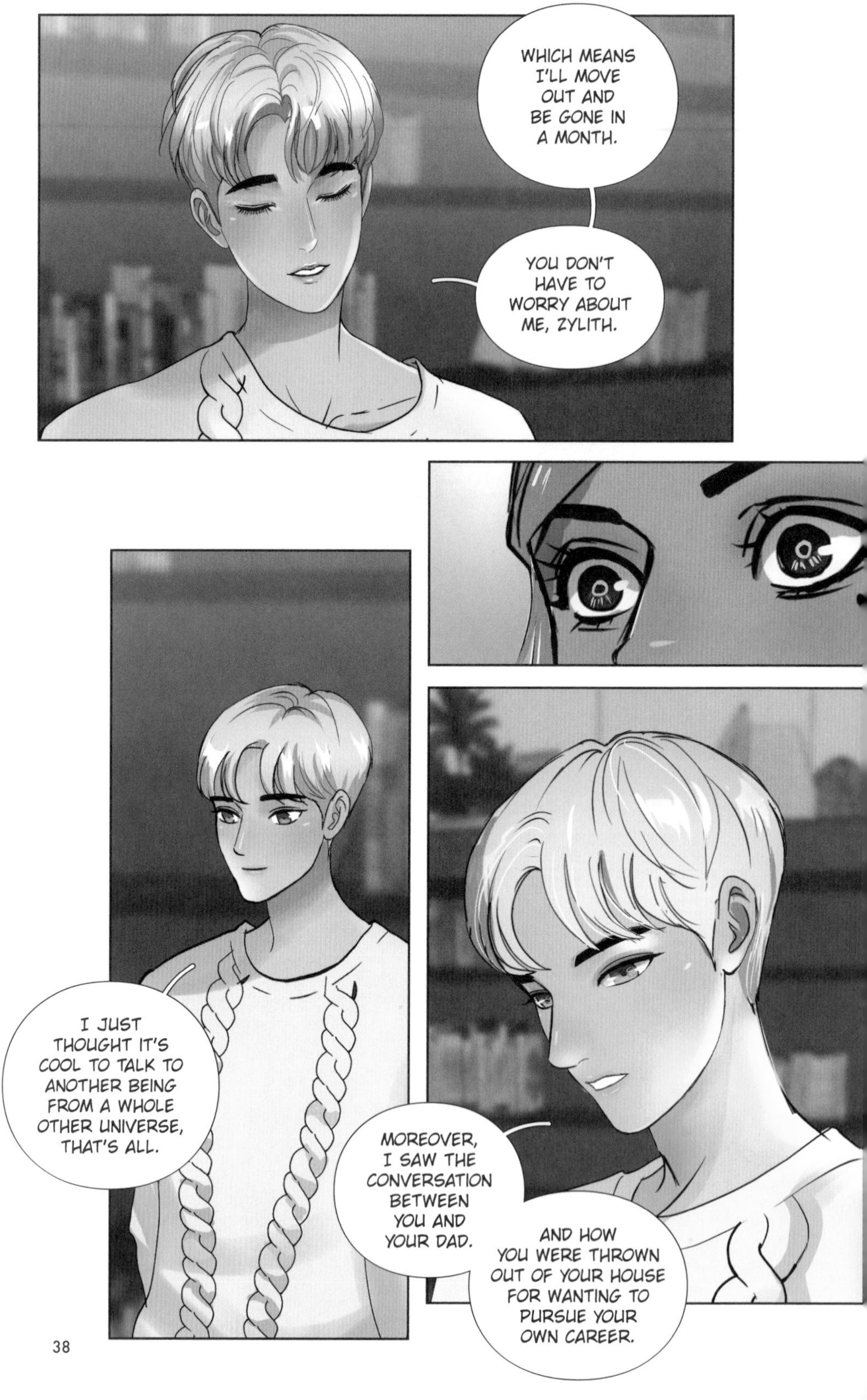
WHICH MEANS I'LL MOVE OUT AND BE GONE IN A MONTH.
YOU DON'T HAVE TO WORRY ABOUT ME, ZYLITH.
I JUST THOUGHT IT'S COOL TO TALK TO ANOTHER BEING FROM A WHOLE OTHER UNIVERSE, THAT'S ALL.
MOREOVER, I SAW THE CONVERSATION BETWEEN YOU AND YOUR DAD.
AND HOW YOU WERE THROWN OUT OF YOUR HOUSE FOR WANTING TO PURSUE YOUR OWN CAREER.

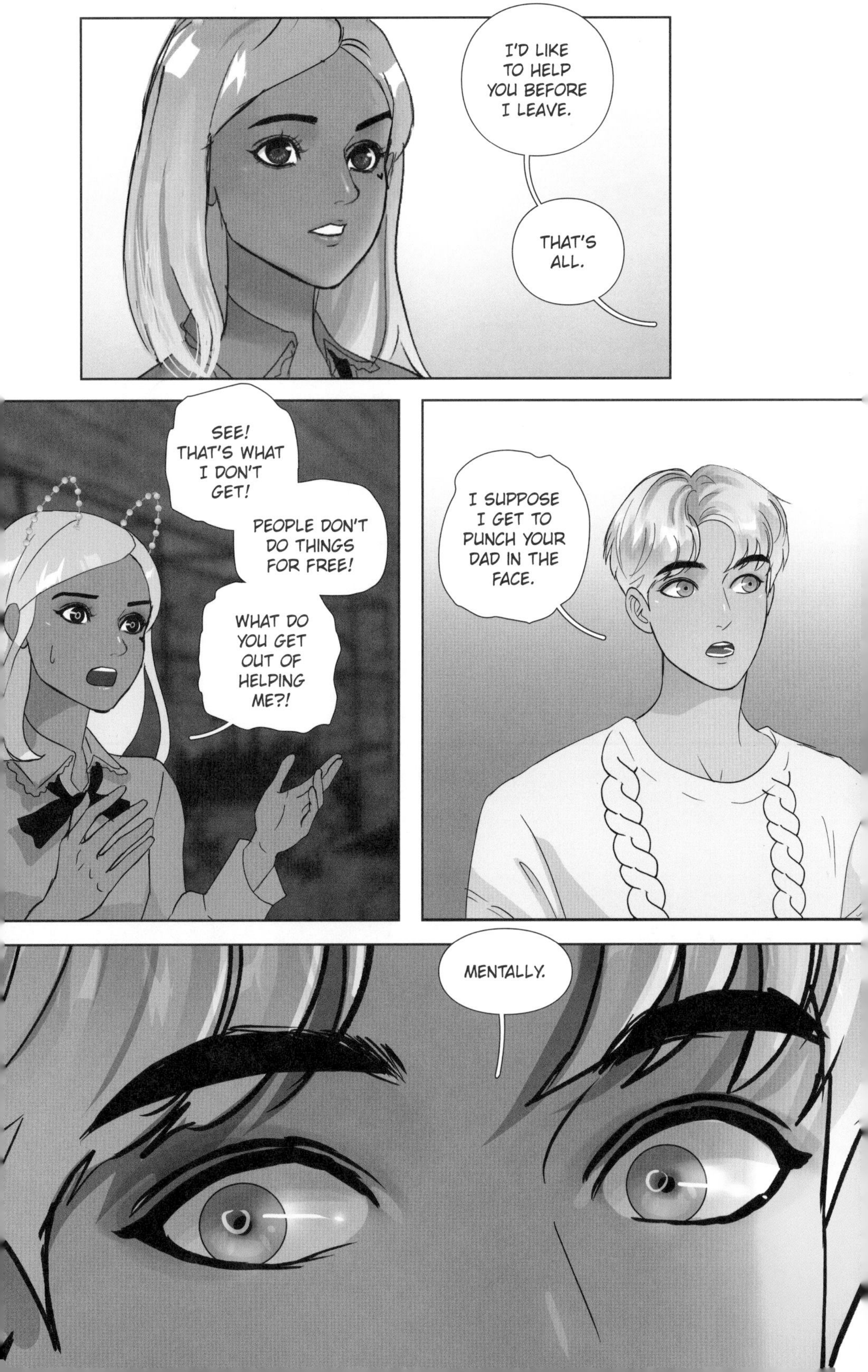
I'D LIKE TO HELP YOU BEFORE I LEAVE.
THAT'S ALL.
SEE! THAT'S WHAT I DON'T GET!
PEOPLE DON'T DO THINGS FOR FREE!
WHAT DO YOU GET OUT OF HELPING ME?!
I SUPPOSE I GET TO PUNCH YOUR DAD IN THE FACE.
MENTALLY.

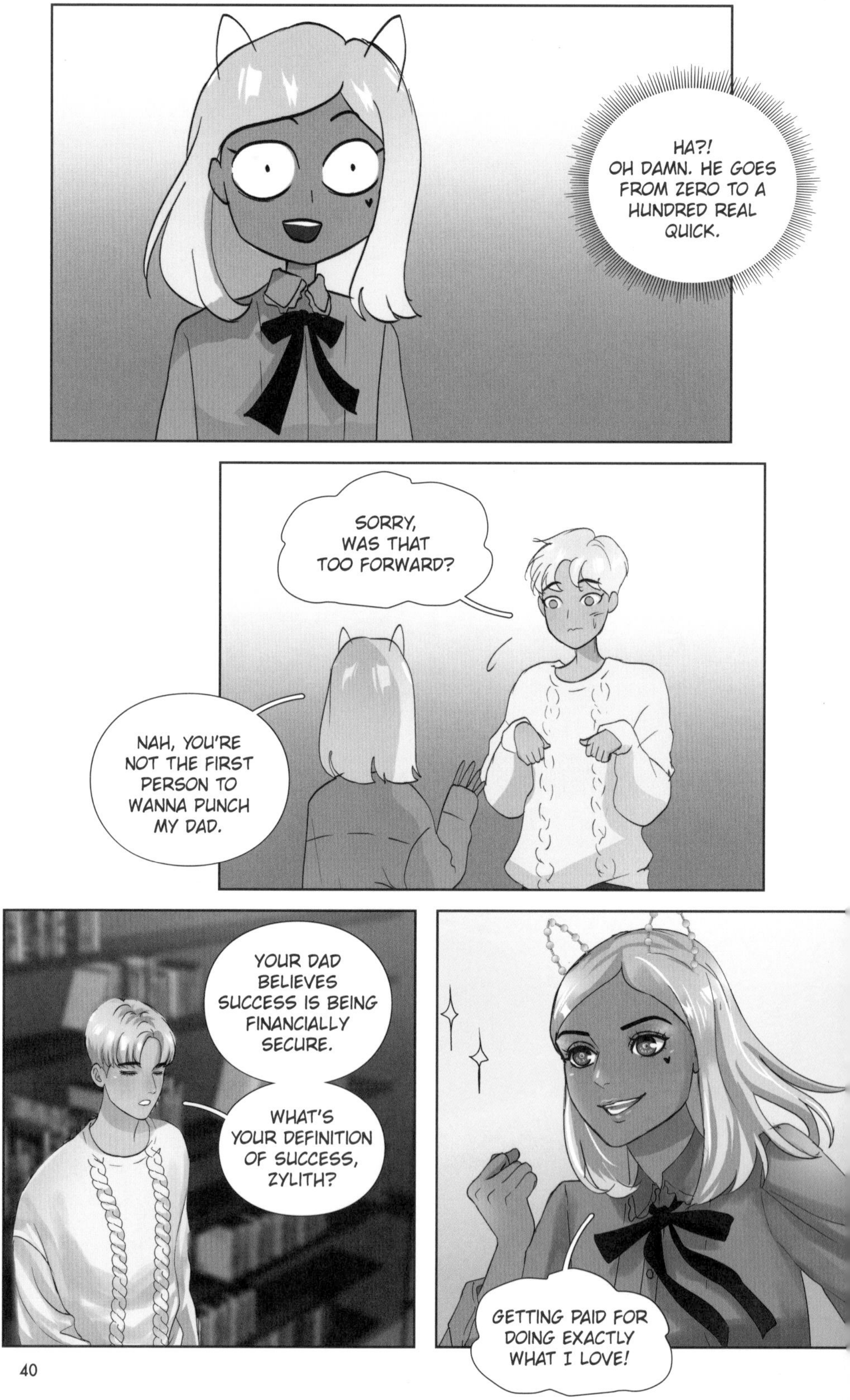
HA?!
OH DAMN. HE GOES FROM ZERO TO A HUNDRED REAL QUICK.
SORRY, WAS THAT TOO FORWARD?
NAH, YOU'RE NOT THE FIRST PERSON TO WANNA PUNCH MY DAD.
YOUR DAD BELIEVES SUCCESS IS BEING FINANCIALLY SECURE.
WHAT'S YOUR DEFINITION OF SUCCESS, ZYLITH?
GETTING PAID FOR DOING EXACTLY WHAT I LOVE!

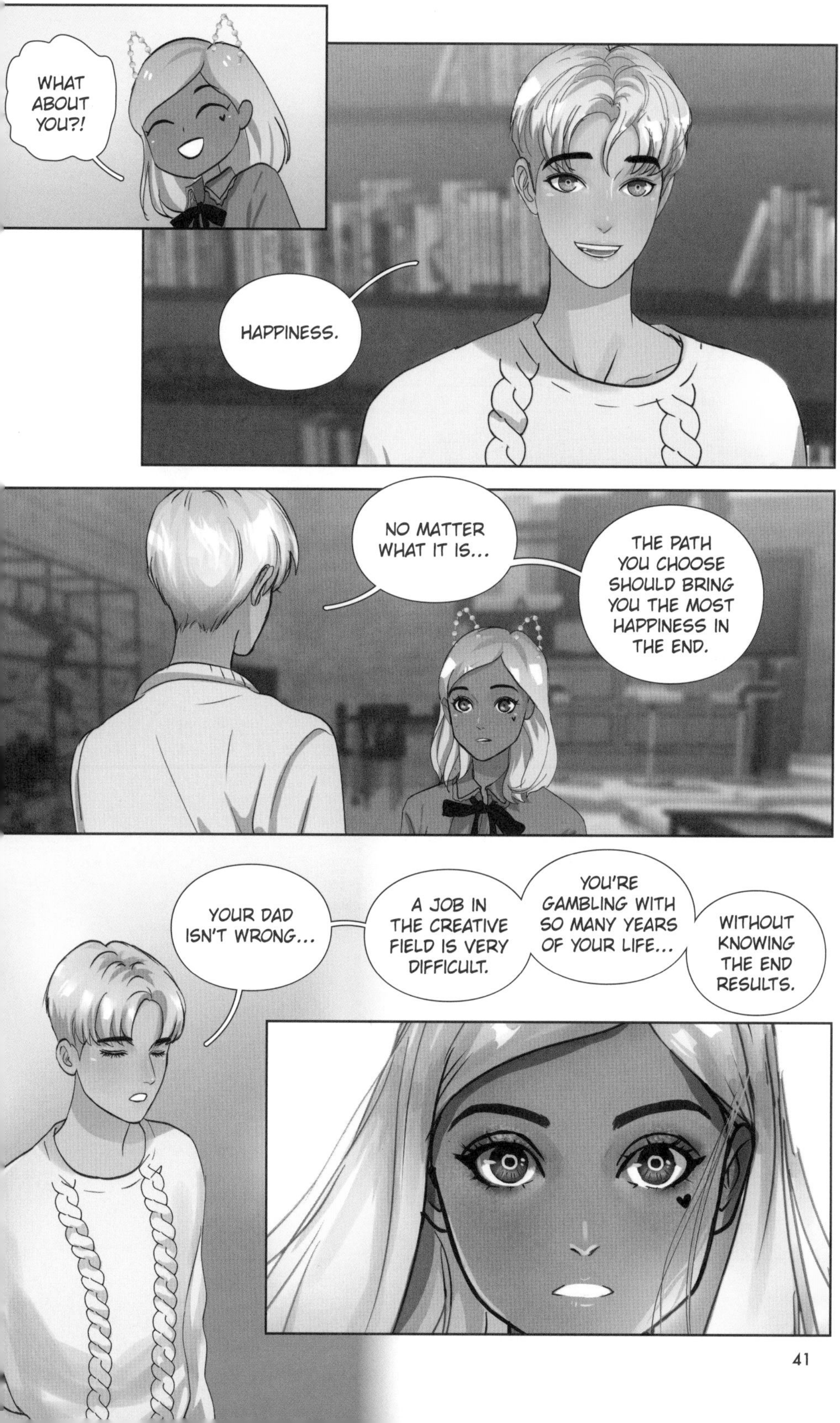
WHAT ABOUT YOU?!
HAPPINESS.
NO MATTER WHAT IT IS...
THE PATH YOU CHOOSE SHOULD BRING YOU THE MOST HAPPINESS IN THE END.
YOUR DAD ISN'T WRONG...
A JOB IN THE CREATIVE FIELD IS VERY DIFFICULT.
YOU'RE GAMBLING WITH SO MANY YEARS OF YOUR LIFE...
WITHOUT KNOWING THE END RESULTS.

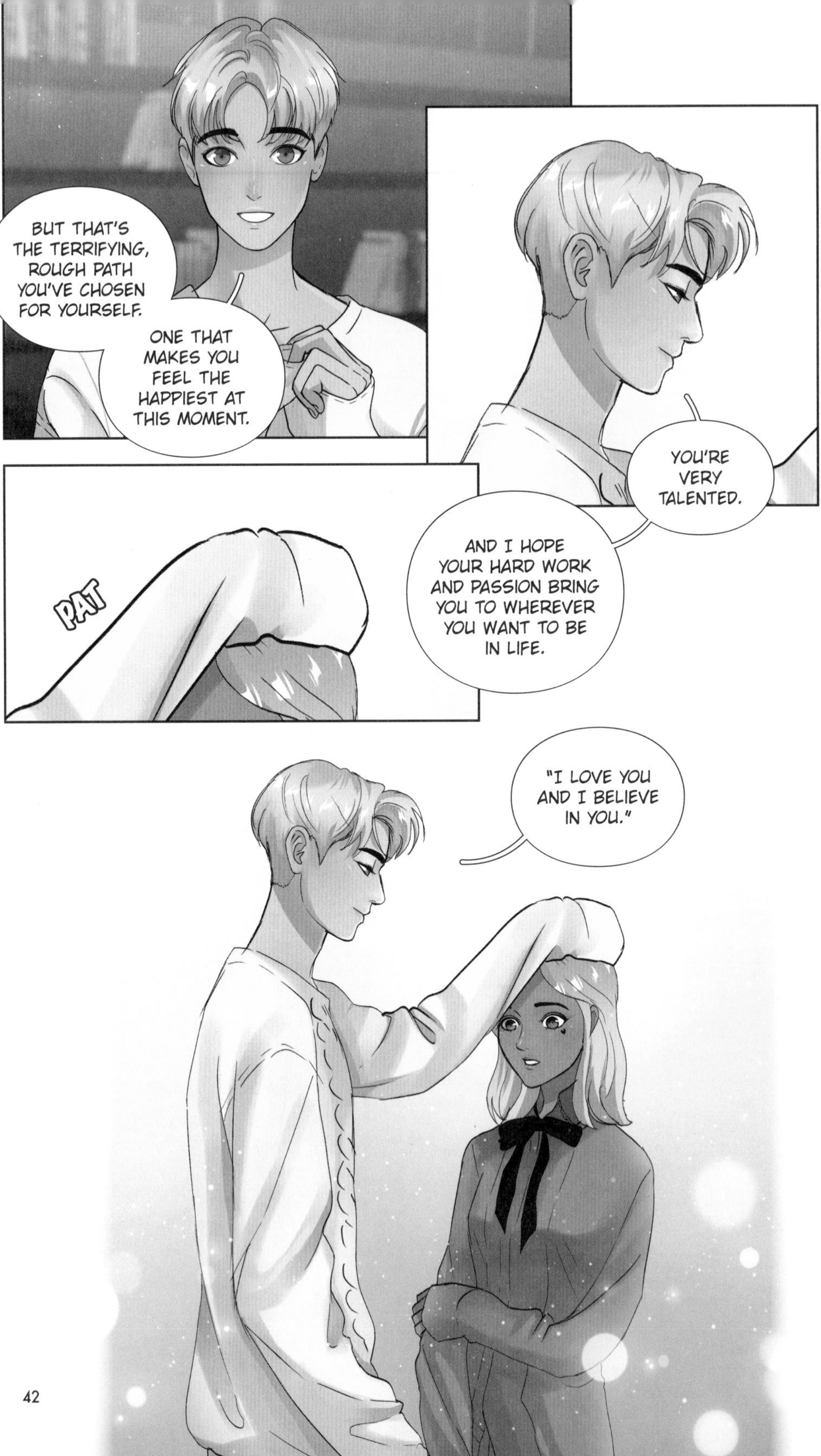
BUT THAT'S THE TERRIFYING, ROUGH PATH YOU'VE CHOSEN FOR YOURSELF.
ONE THAT MAKES YOU FEEL THE HAPPIEST AT THIS MOMENT.
YOU'RE VERY TALENTED.
PAT
AND I HOPE YOUR HARD WORK AND PASSION BRING YOU TO WHEREVER YOU WANT TO BE IN LIFE.
"I LOVE YOU AND I BELIEVE IN YOU."

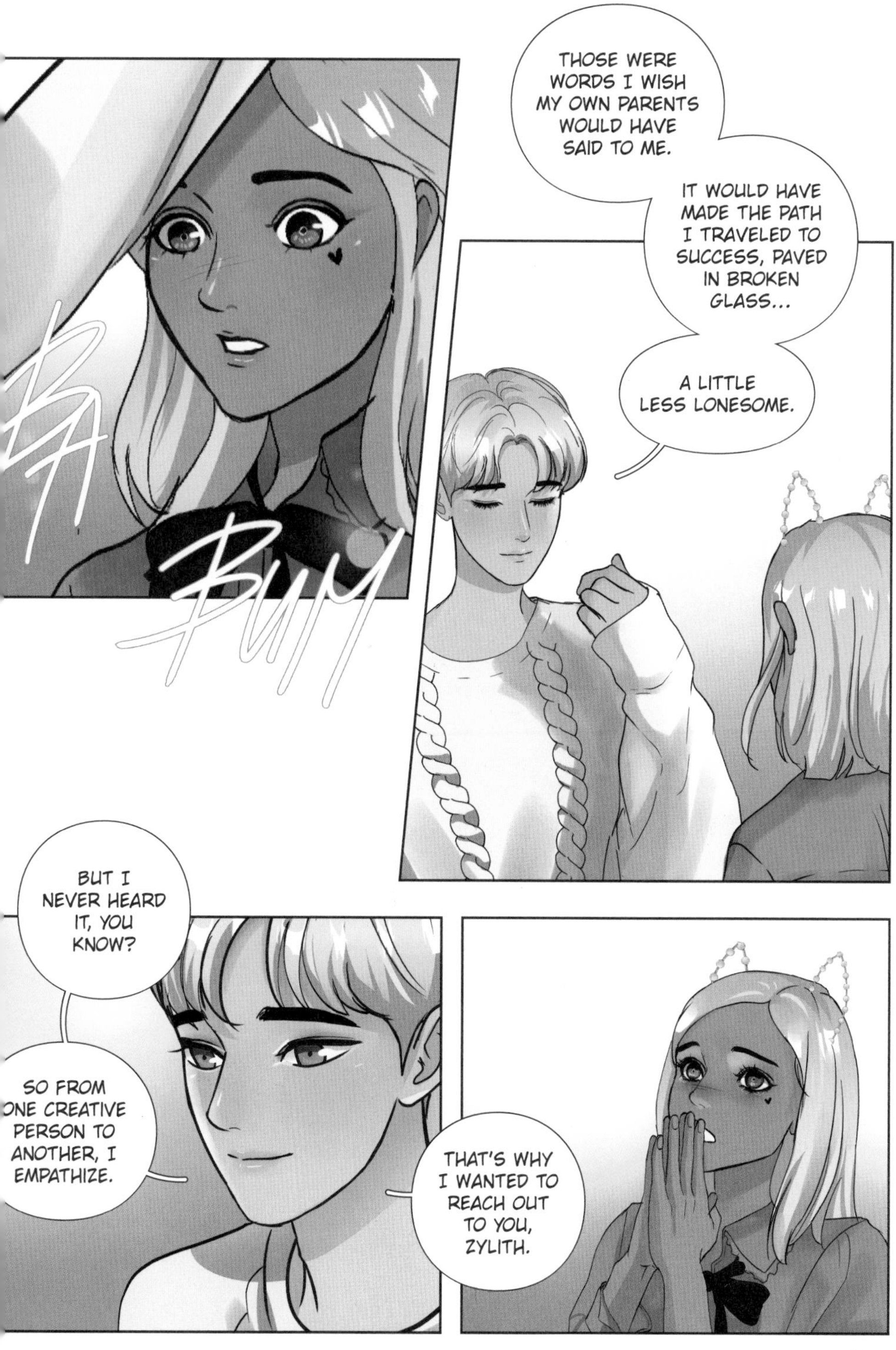
BA
BUM
THOSE WERE WORDS I WISH MY OWN PARENTS WOULD HAVE SAID TO ME.
IT WOULD HAVE MADE THE PATH I TRAVELED TO SUCCESS, PAVED IN BROKEN GLASS...
A LITTLE LESS LONESOME.
BUT I NEVER HEARD IT, YOU KNOW?
SO FROM ONE CREATIVE PERSON TO ANOTHER, I EMPATHIZE.
THAT'S WHY I WANTED TO REACH OUT TO YOU, ZYLITH.

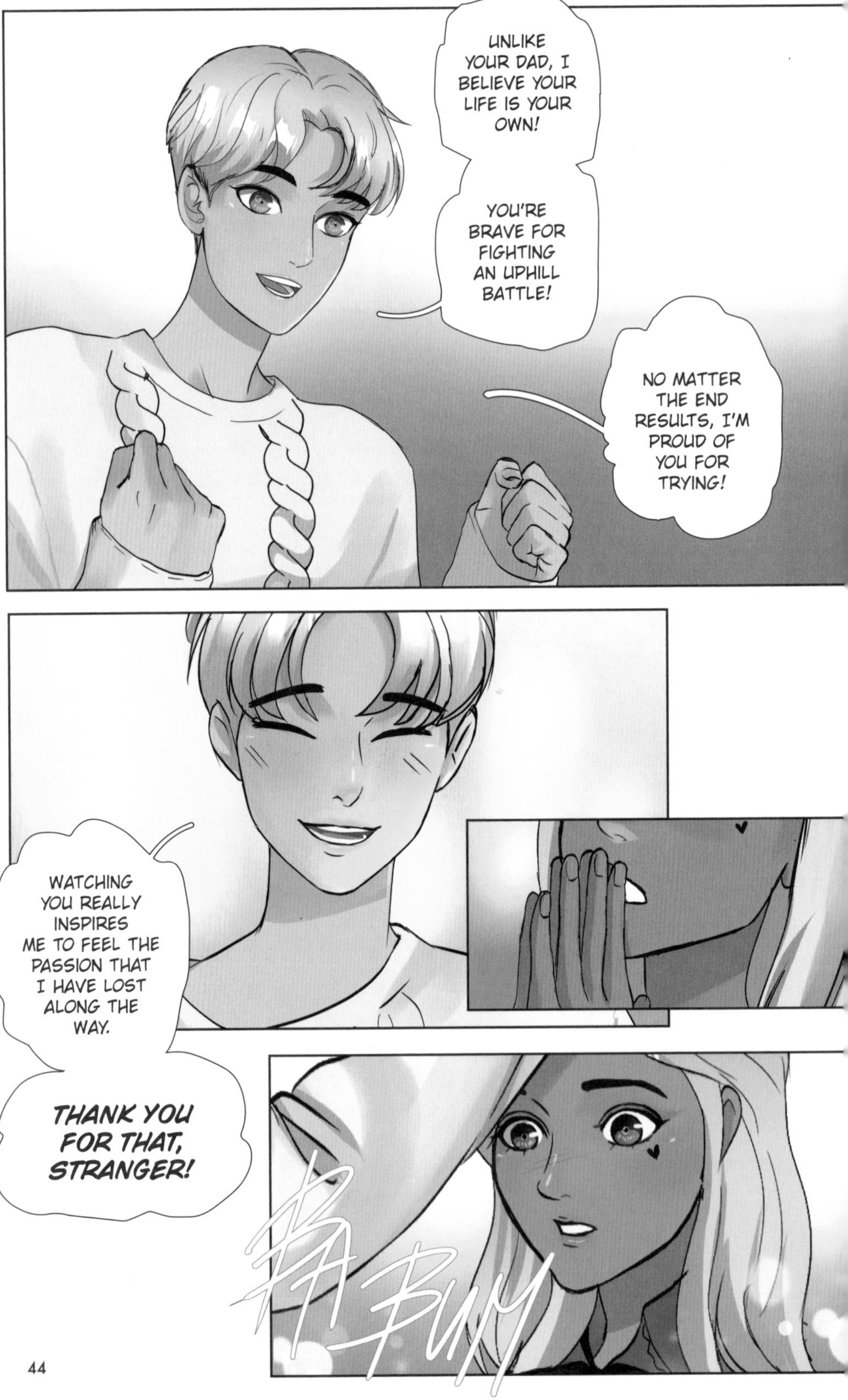
UNLIKE YOUR DAD, I BELIEVE YOUR LIFE IS YOUR OWN!
YOU'RE BRAVE FOR FIGHTING AN UPHILL BATTLE!
NO MATTER THE END RESULTS, I'M PROUD OF YOU FOR TRYING!
WATCHING YOU REALLY INSPIRES ME TO FEEL THE PASSION THAT I HAVE LOST ALONG THE WAY.
THANK YOU FOR THAT, STRANGER!
BA-BUM

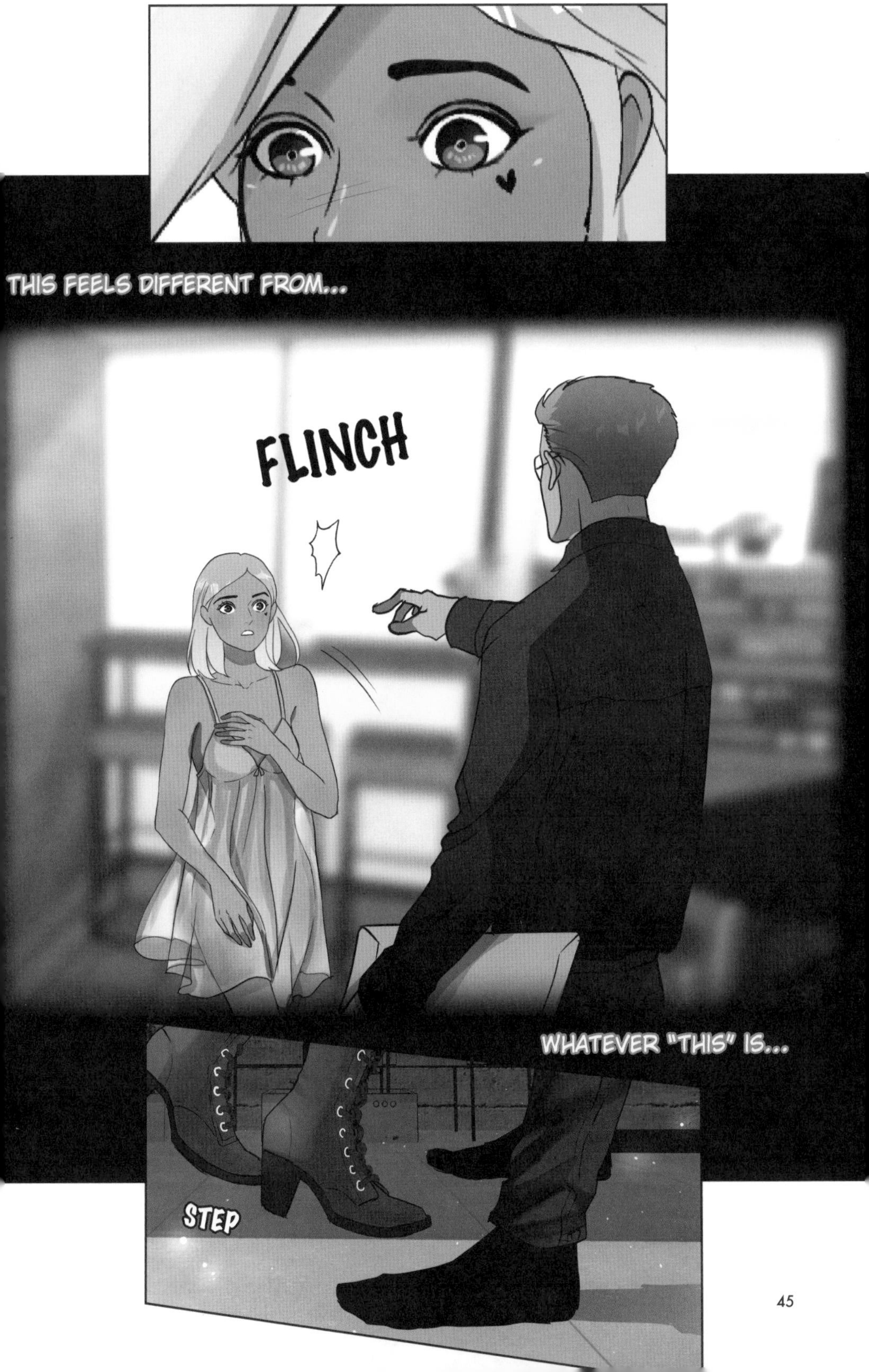
THIS FEELS DIFFERENT FROM...
FLINCH
WHATEVER "THIS" IS...
STEP

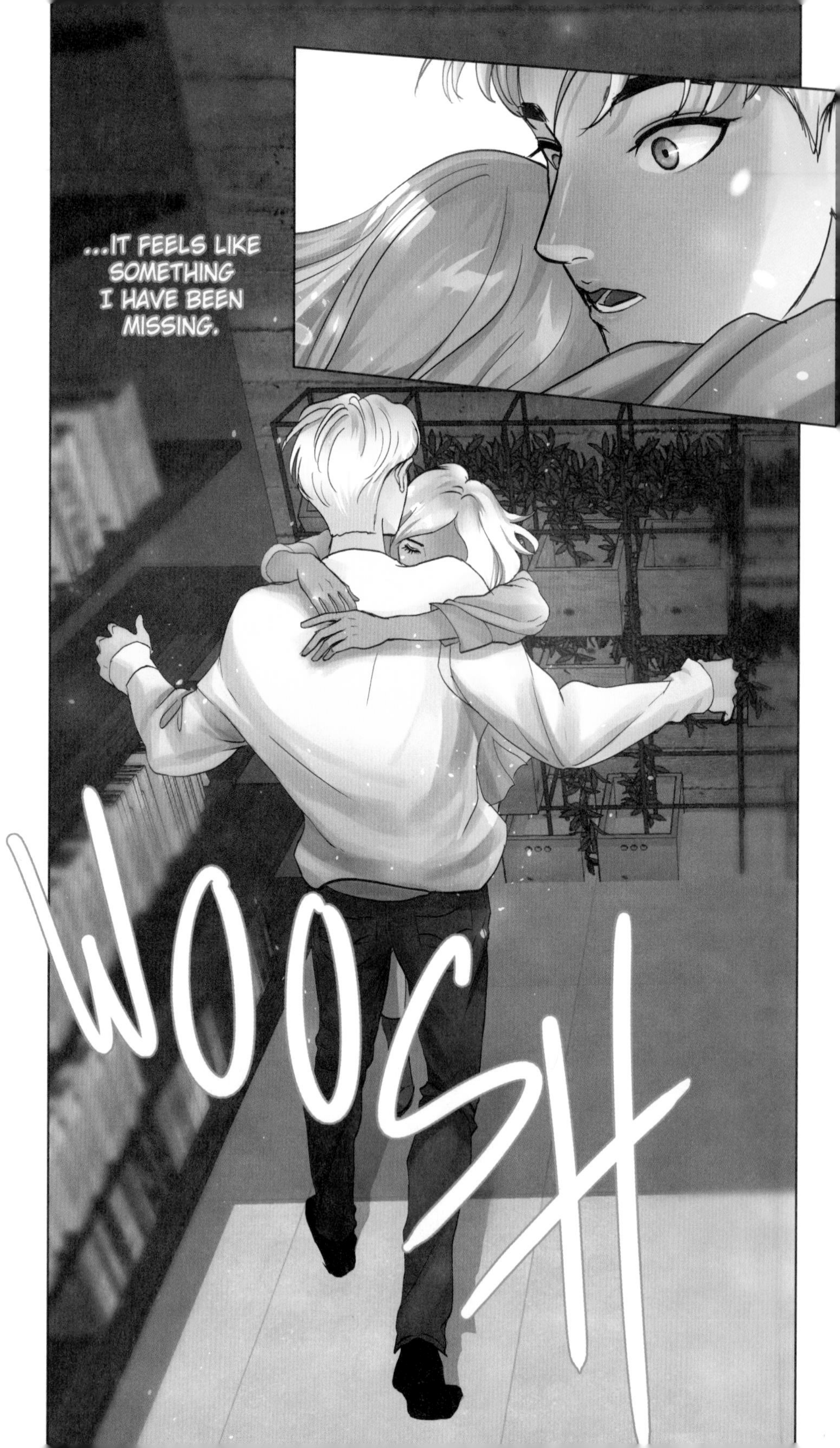
...IT FEELS LIKE SOMETHING I HAVE BEEN MISSING.
WOOSH

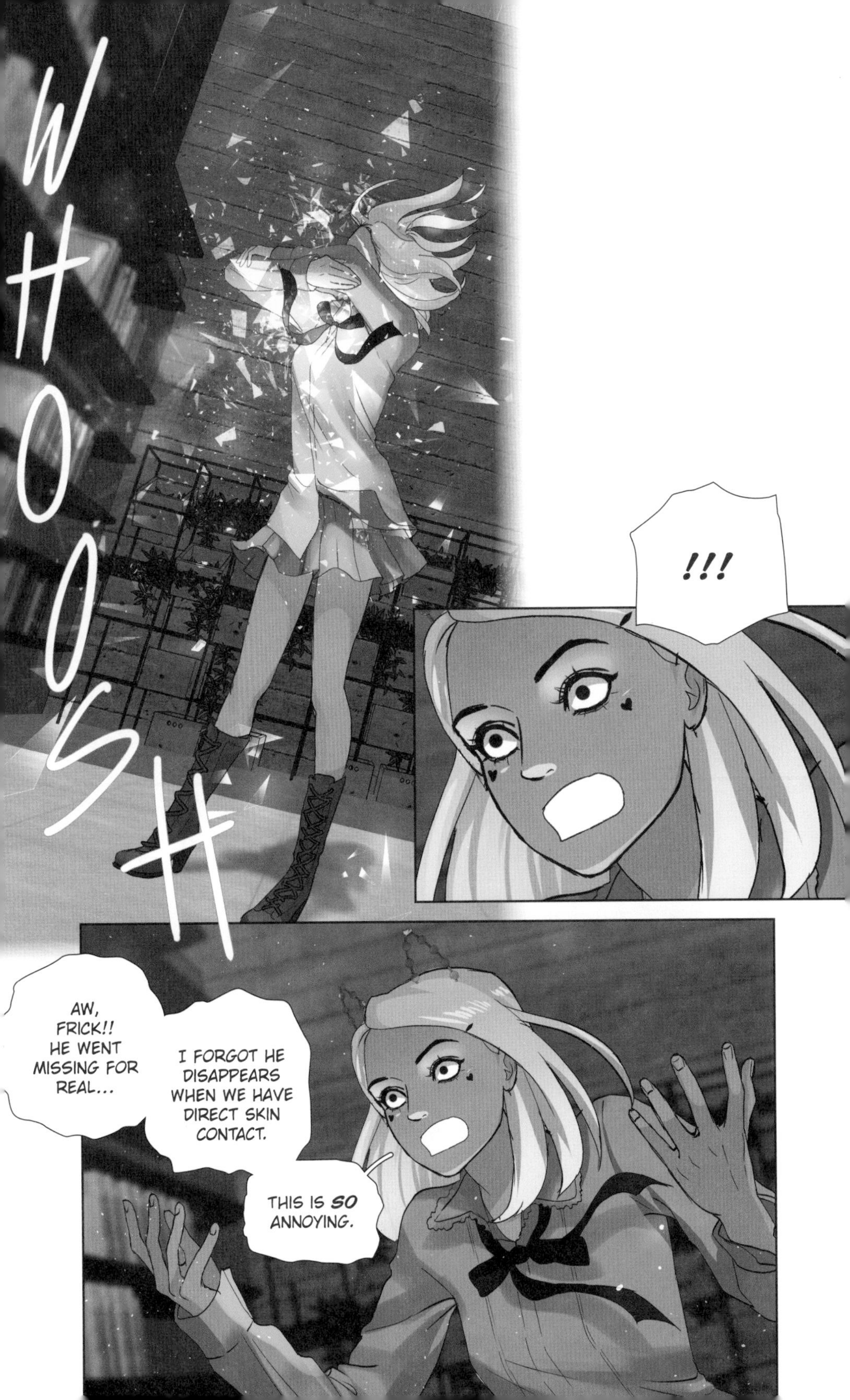
WHOOSH
!!!
AW, FRICK!! HE WENT MISSING FOR REAL...
I FORGOT HE DISAPPEARS WHEN WE HAVE DIRECT SKIN CONTACT.
THIS IS *SO* ANNOYING.

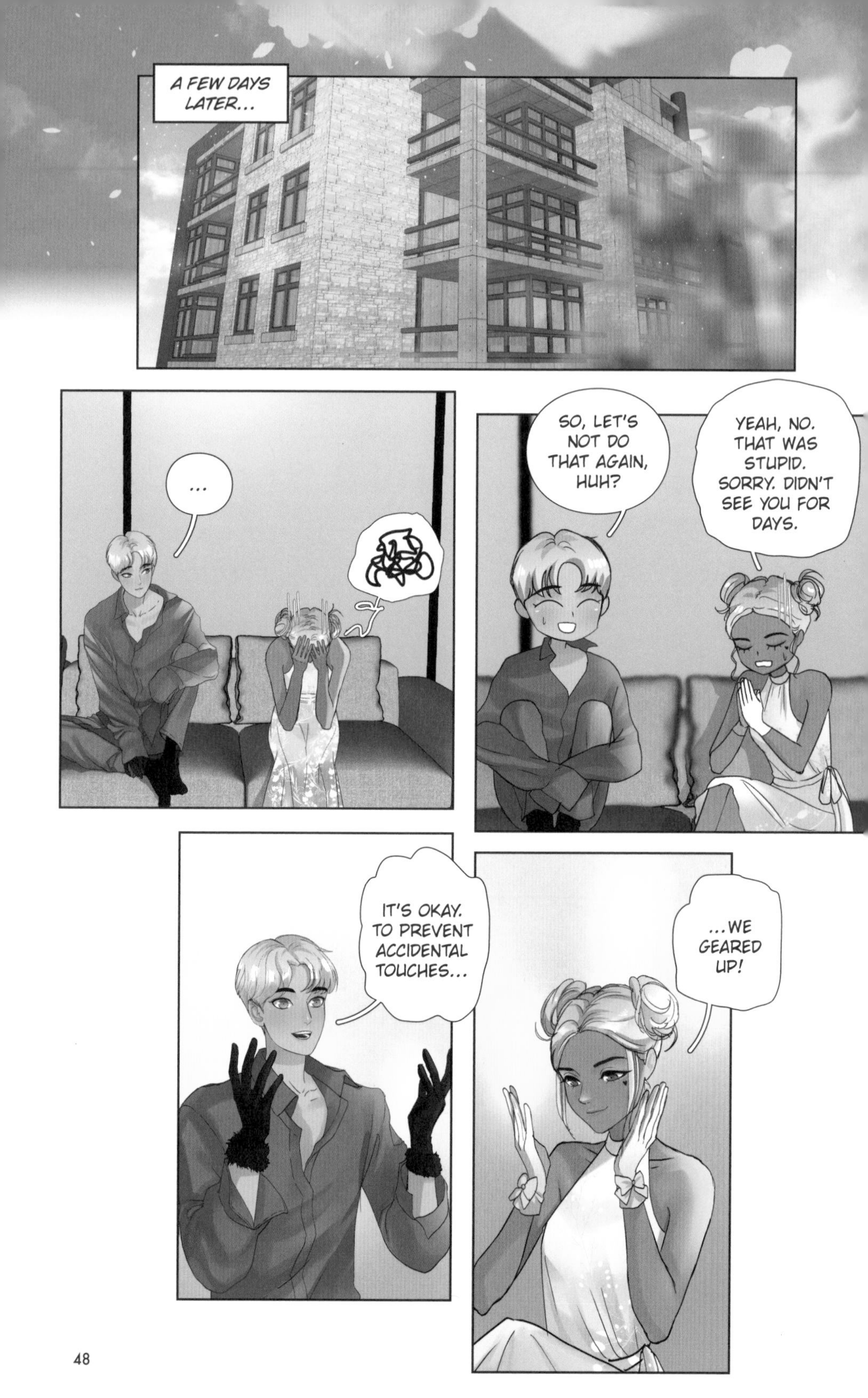
A FEW DAYS LATER...
...
SO, LET'S NOT DO THAT AGAIN, HUH?
YEAH, NO. THAT WAS STUPID. SORRY. DIDN'T SEE YOU FOR DAYS.
IT'S OKAY. TO PREVENT ACCIDENTAL TOUCHES...
...WE GEARED UP!

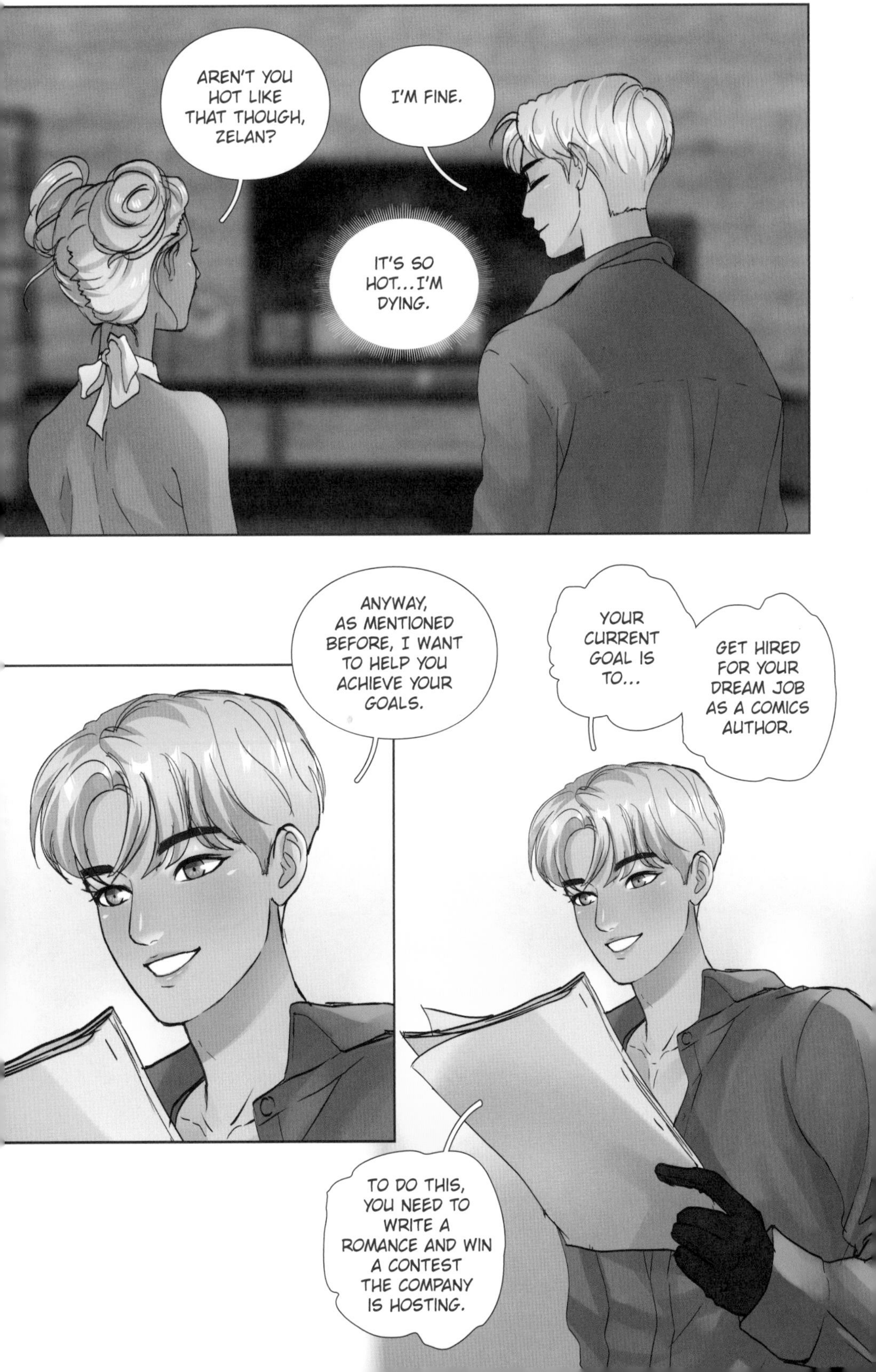
AREN'T YOU HOT LIKE THAT THOUGH, ZELAN?
I'M FINE.
IT'S SO HOT...I'M DYING.
ANYWAY, AS MENTIONED BEFORE, I WANT TO HELP YOU ACHIEVE YOUR GOALS.
YOUR CURRENT GOAL IS TO...
GET HIRED FOR YOUR DREAM JOB AS A COMICS AUTHOR.
TO DO THIS, YOU NEED TO WRITE A ROMANCE AND WIN A CONTEST THE COMPANY IS HOSTING.

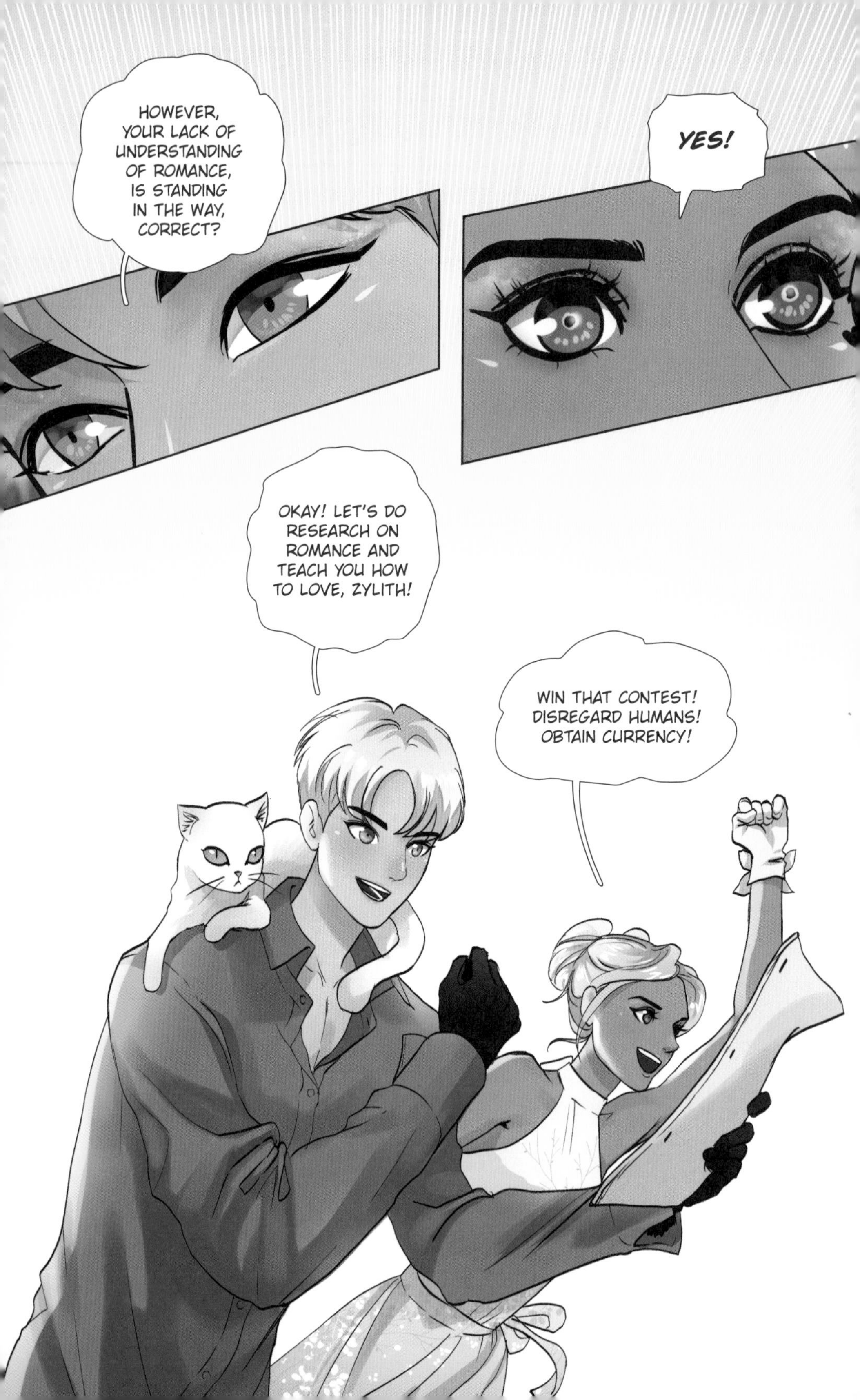
HOWEVER, YOUR LACK OF UNDERSTANDING OF ROMANCE, IS STANDING IN THE WAY, CORRECT?
YES!
OKAY! LET'S DO RESEARCH ON ROMANCE AND TEACH YOU HOW TO LOVE, ZYLITH!
WIN THAT CONTEST! DISREGARD HUMANS! OBTAIN CURRENCY!

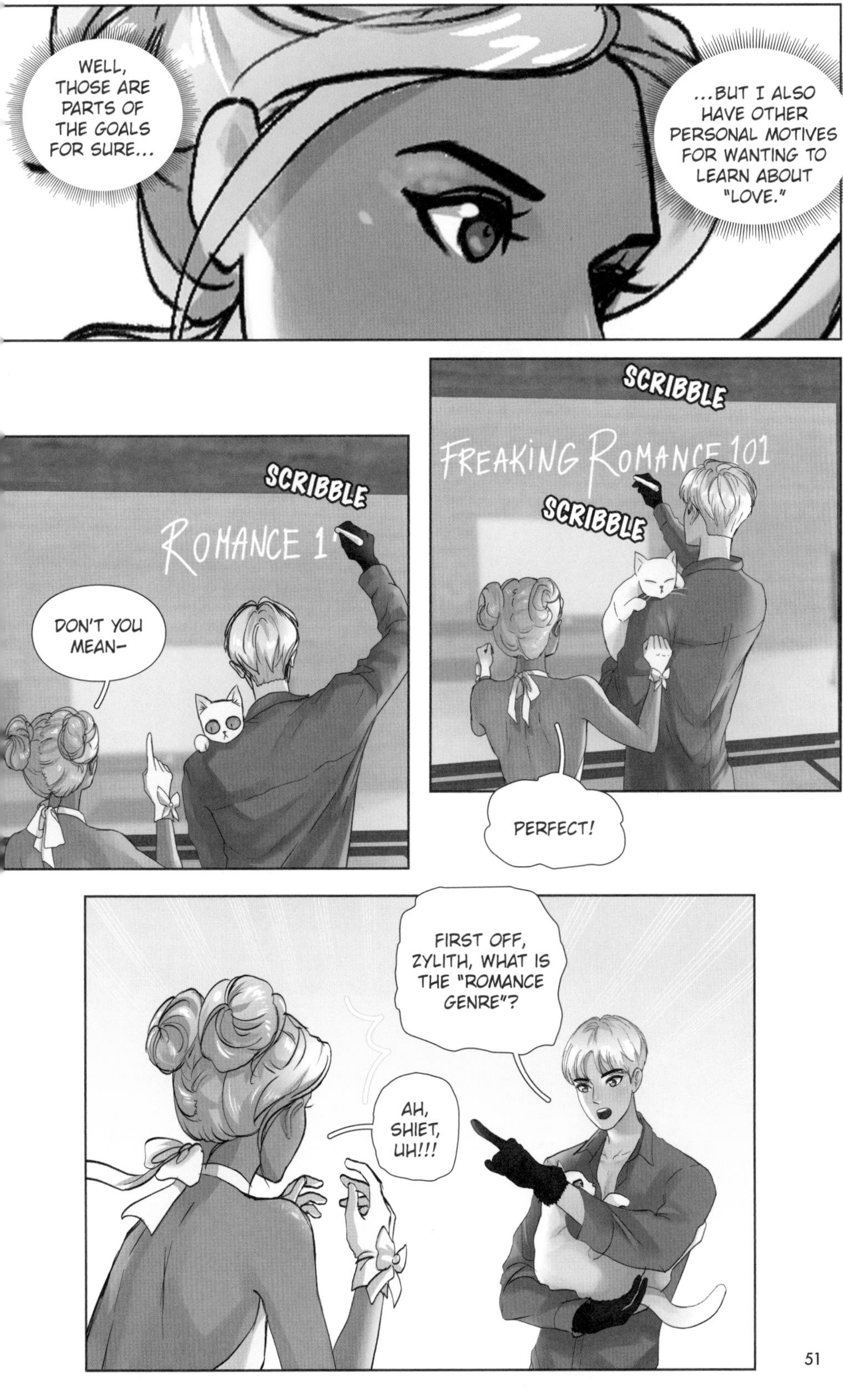

WELL, THOSE ARE PARTS OF THE GOALS FOR SURE...
...BUT I ALSO HAVE OTHER PERSONAL MOTIVES FOR WANTING TO LEARN ABOUT "LOVE."
SCRIBBLE
ROMANCE 1
DON'T YOU MEAN-
SCRIBBLE
FREAKING ROMANCE 101
SCRIBBLE
PERFECT!
FIRST OFF, ZYLITH, WHAT IS THE "ROMANCE GENRE"?
AH, SHIET, UH!!!

STORIES WHERE A POPULAR BOY FALLS FOR A NOT POPULAR GIRL...

AND THEN HIS EX COMES AROUND AND RUINS EVERYTHING!

"A" FOR EFFORT! BUT NOT REALLY!

A ROMANCE IS A LOVE STORY ANSWERING THE QUESTION...

FREAKING ROMANCE

WHAT IS THE ROMAN

"WILL THIS CO MAKE T

..."WILL THIS COUPLE SURVIVE THROUGH TRIALS AND HARDSHIPS, AND REMAIN A COUPLE UNTIL THE END?"

SCRIBBLE SCRIBBLE

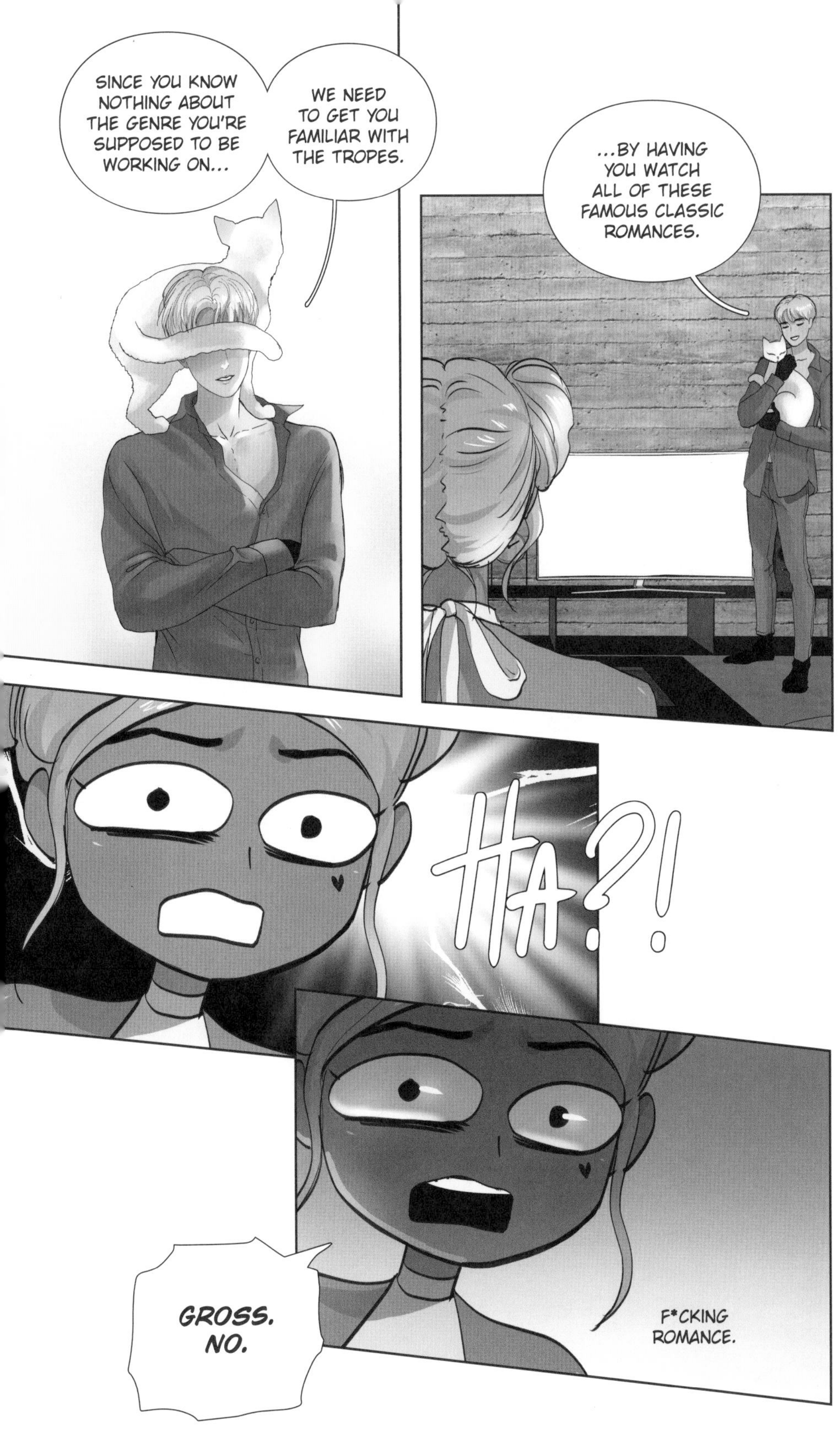
SINCE YOU KNOW NOTHING ABOUT THE GENRE YOU'RE SUPPOSED TO BE WORKING ON...
WE NEED TO GET YOU FAMILIAR WITH THE TROPES.
...BY HAVING YOU WATCH ALL OF THESE FAMOUS CLASSIC ROMANCES.
HA?!
GROSS. NO.
F*CKING ROMANCE.

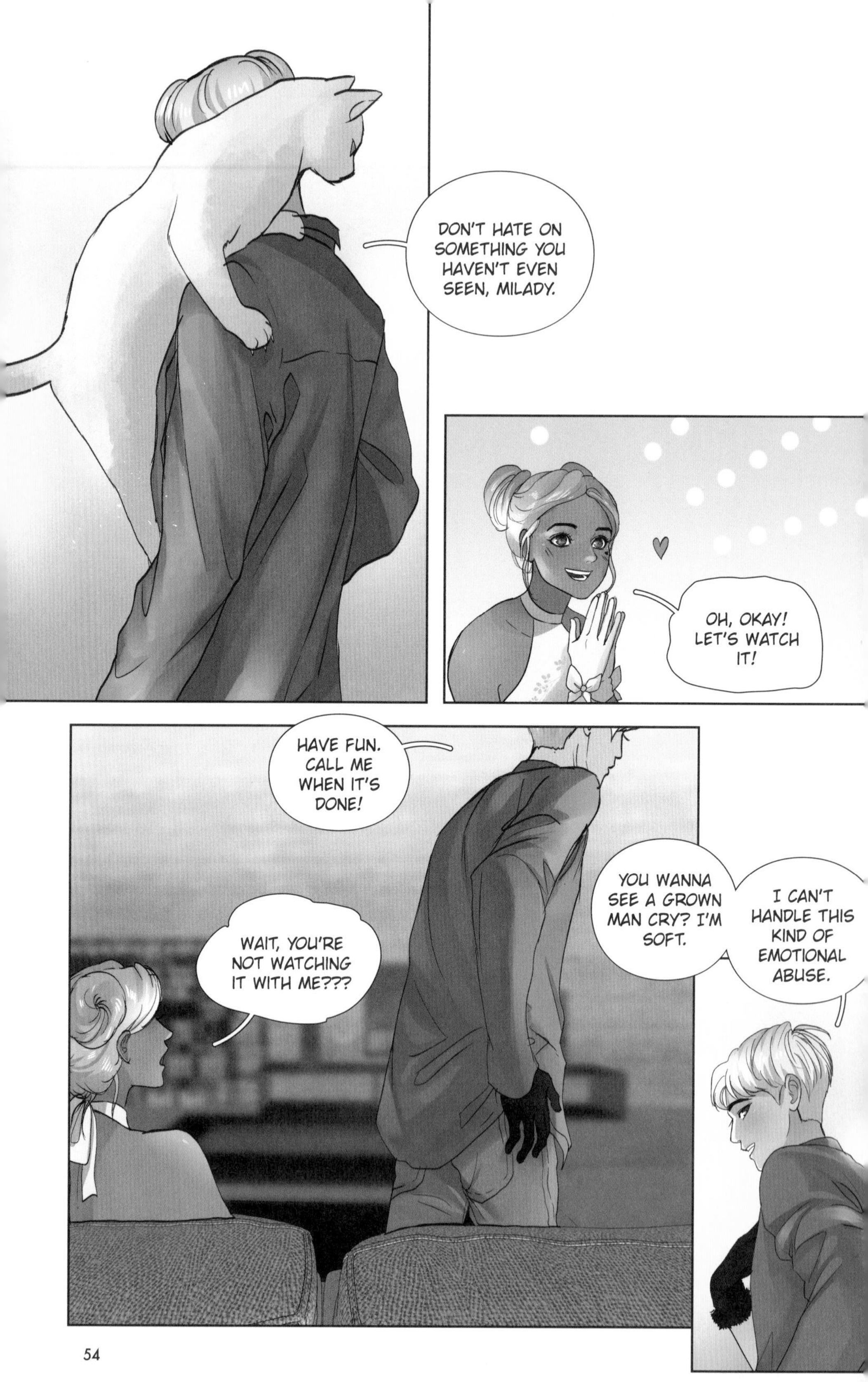
DON'T HATE ON SOMETHING YOU HAVEN'T EVEN SEEN, MILADY.
OH, OKAY! LET'S WATCH IT!
HAVE FUN. CALL ME WHEN IT'S DONE!
WAIT, YOU'RE NOT WATCHING IT WITH ME???
YOU WANNA SEE A GROWN MAN CRY? I'M SOFT.
I CAN'T HANDLE THIS KIND OF EMOTIONAL ABUSE.

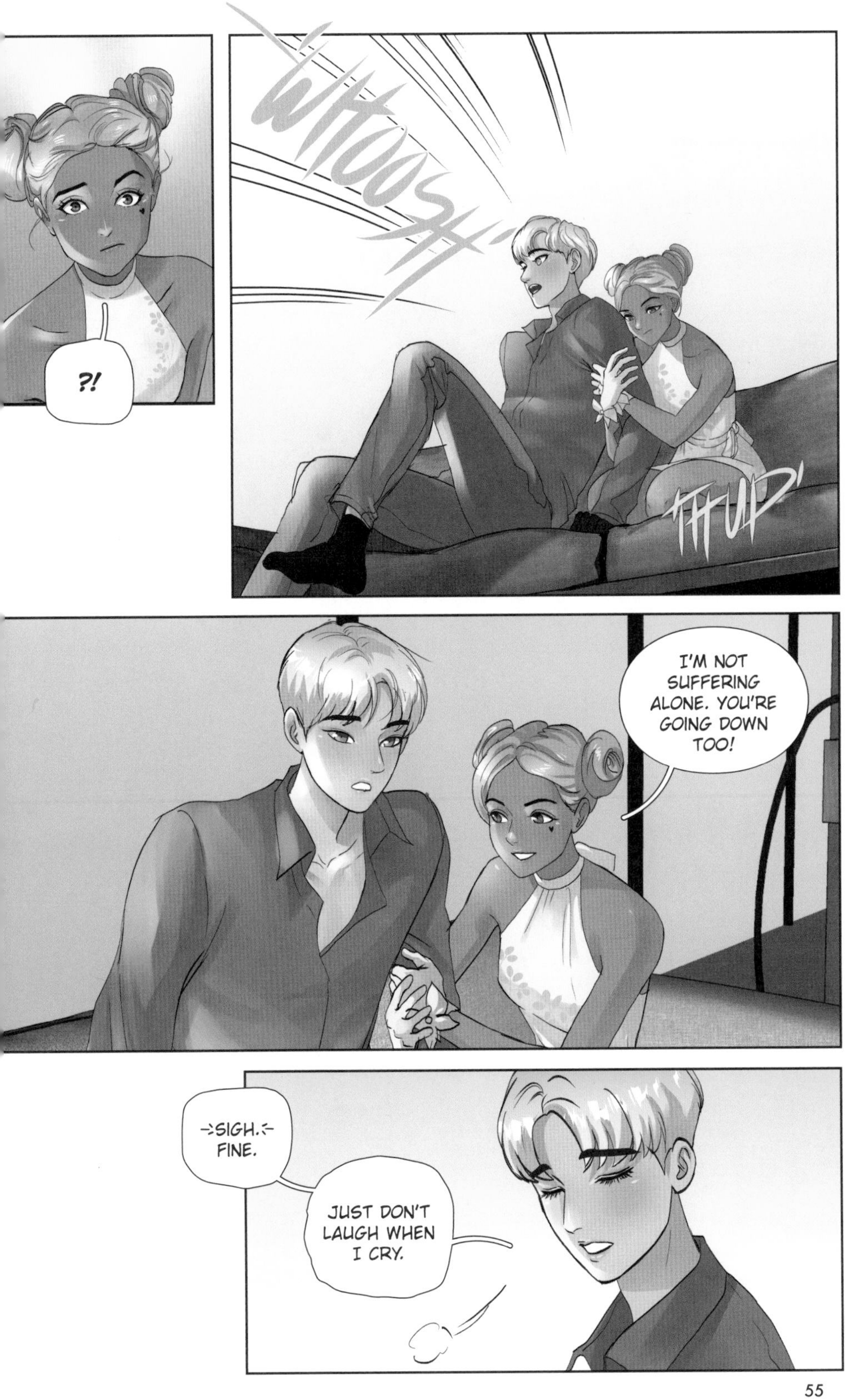
?!
WHOOSH
THUD
I'M NOT SUFFERING ALONE. YOU'RE GOING DOWN TOO!
~SIGH.~ FINE.
JUST DON'T LAUGH WHEN I CRY.

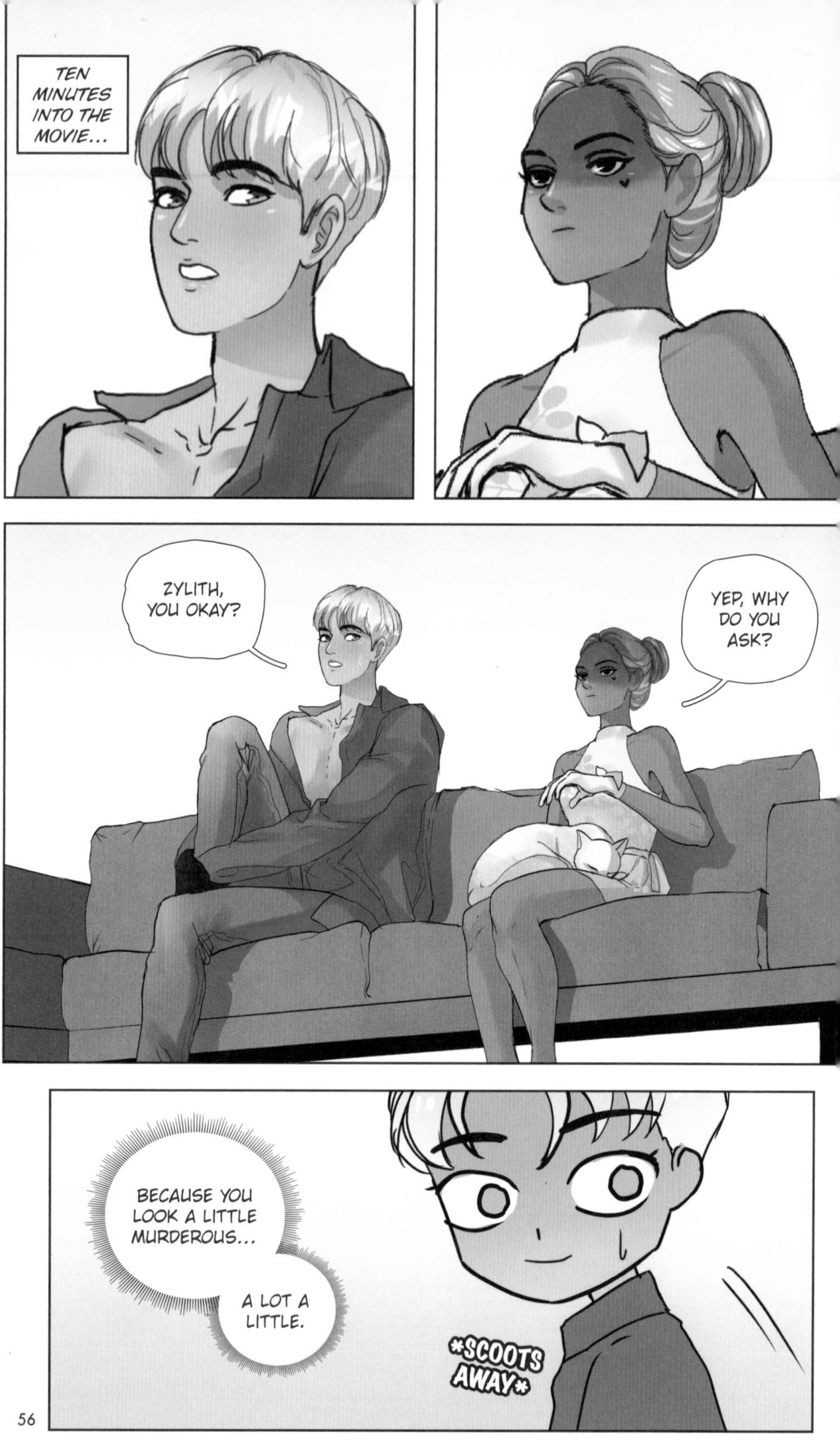
TEN MINUTES INTO THE MOVIE...
ZYLITH, YOU OKAY?
YEP, WHY DO YOU ASK?
BECAUSE YOU LOOK A LITTLE MURDEROUS...
A LOT A LITTLE.
SCOOTS AWAY

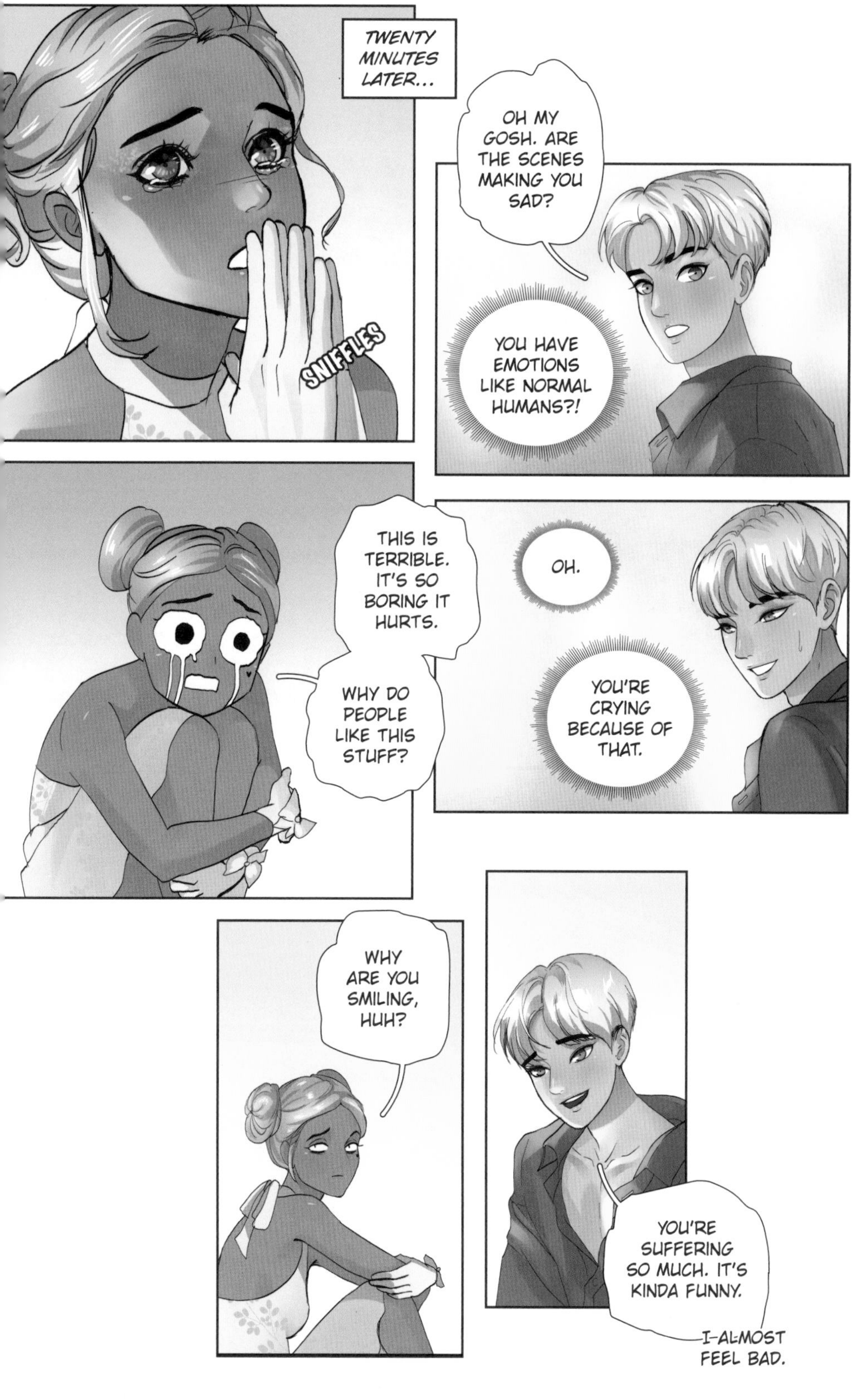
TWENTY MINUTES LATER...
SNIFFLES
OH MY GOSH. ARE THE SCENES MAKING YOU SAD?
YOU HAVE EMOTIONS LIKE NORMAL HUMANS?!
THIS IS TERRIBLE. IT'S SO BORING IT HURTS.
WHY DO PEOPLE LIKE THIS STUFF?
OH.
YOU'RE CRYING BECAUSE OF THAT.
WHY ARE YOU SMILING, HUH?
YOU'RE SUFFERING SO MUCH. IT'S KINDA FUNNY.
I-ALMOST FEEL BAD.

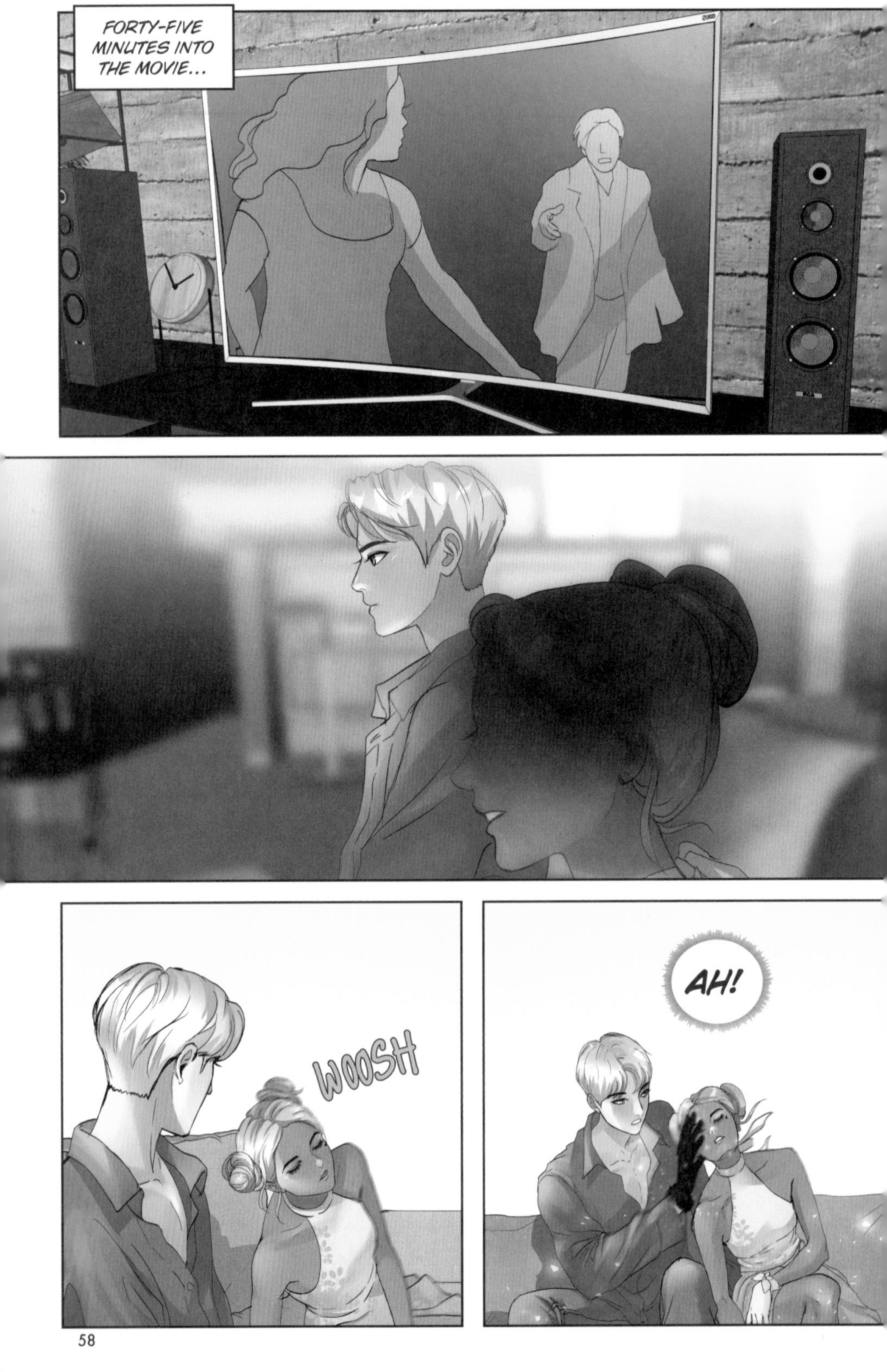
FORTY-FIVE MINUTES INTO THE MOVIE...
WOOSH
AH!

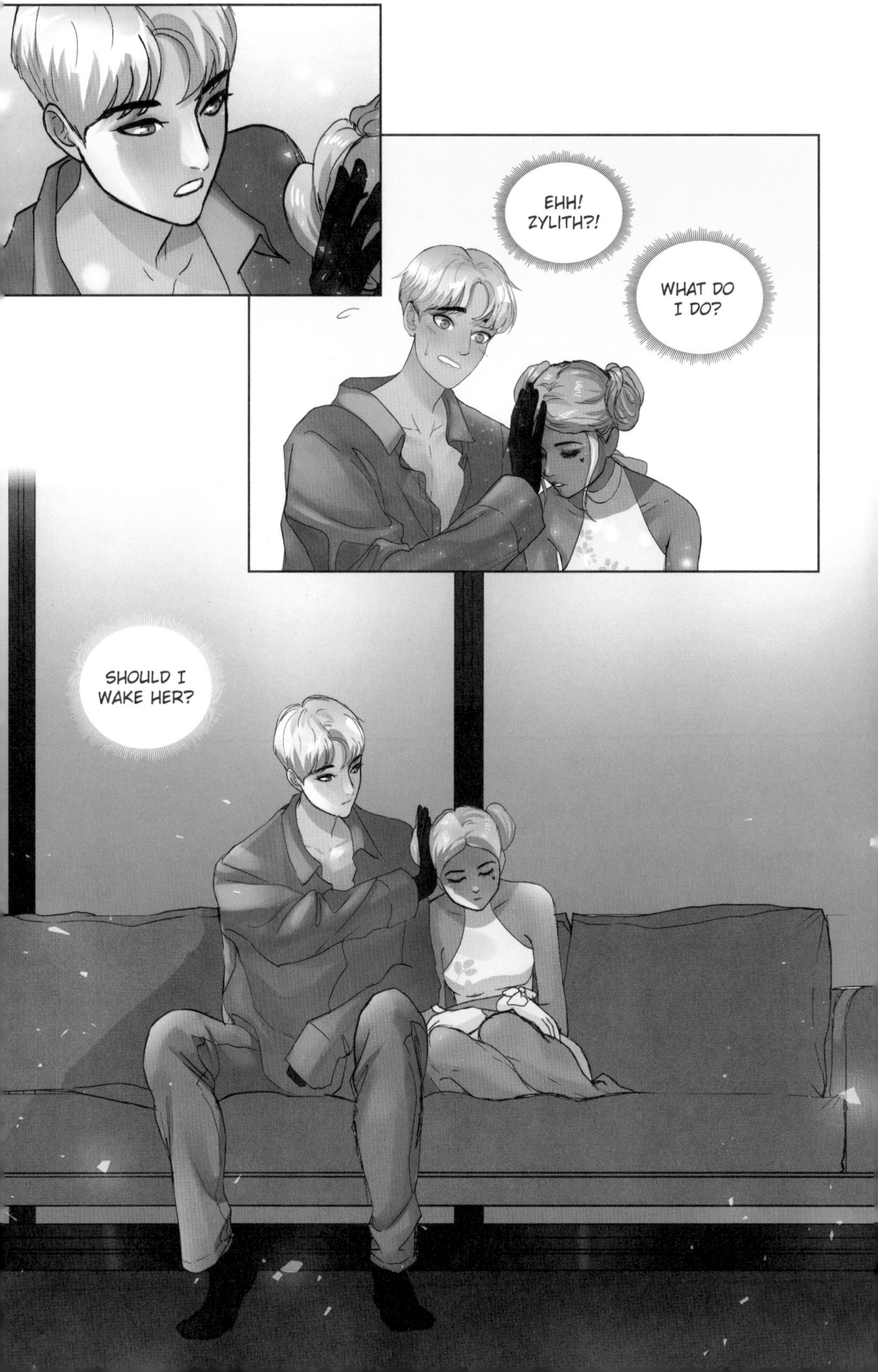
EHH! ZYLITH?!
WHAT DO I DO?
SHOULD I WAKE HER?

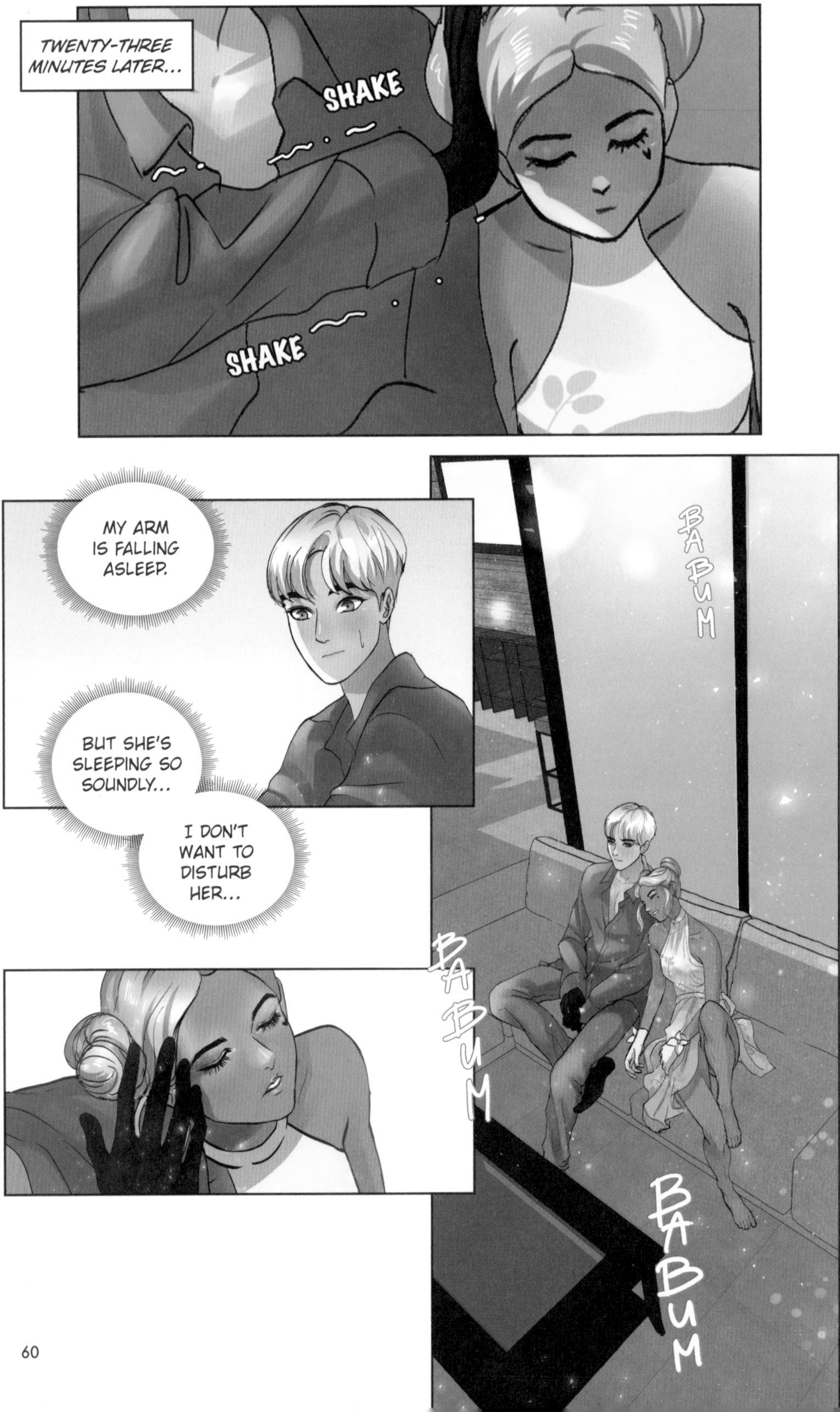
TWENTY-THREE MINUTES LATER...
SHAKE
SHAKE
MY ARM IS FALLING ASLEEP.
BUT SHE'S SLEEPING SO SOUNDLY...
I DON'T WANT TO DISTURB HER...
BABUM
BABUM
BABUM

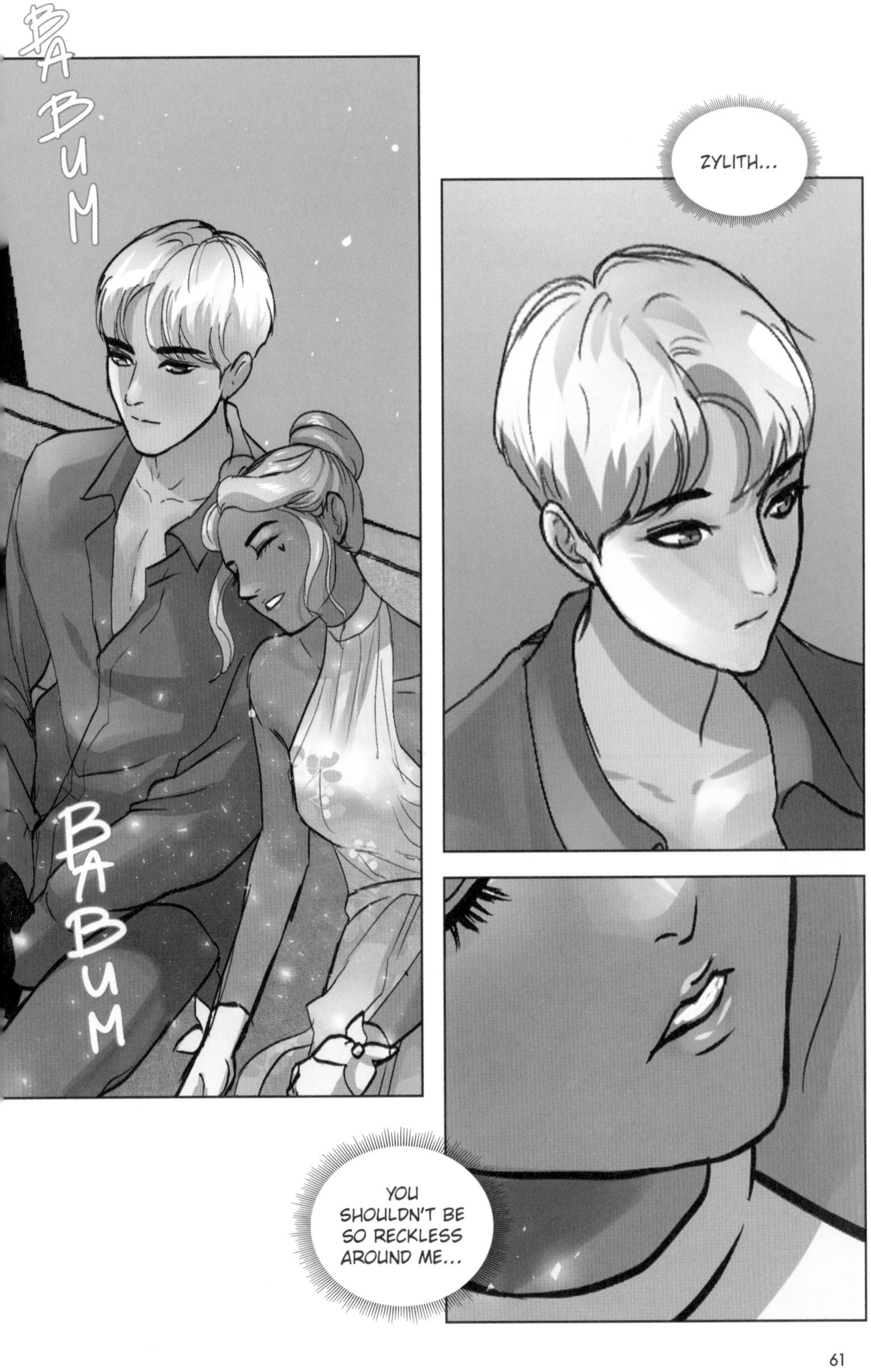
BA BUM
BA BUM
ZYLITH...
YOU SHOULDN'T BE SO RECKLESS AROUND ME...

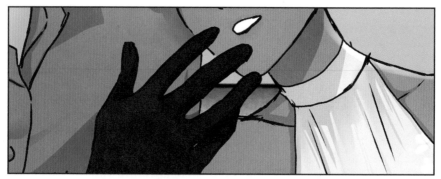

SQUISH

YOU'RE BORED TO DEATH. THIS IS NOT WORKING.

AHHHH! SORRY!!! PUT IT BACK ON AGAIN. I'LL STAY AWAKE!

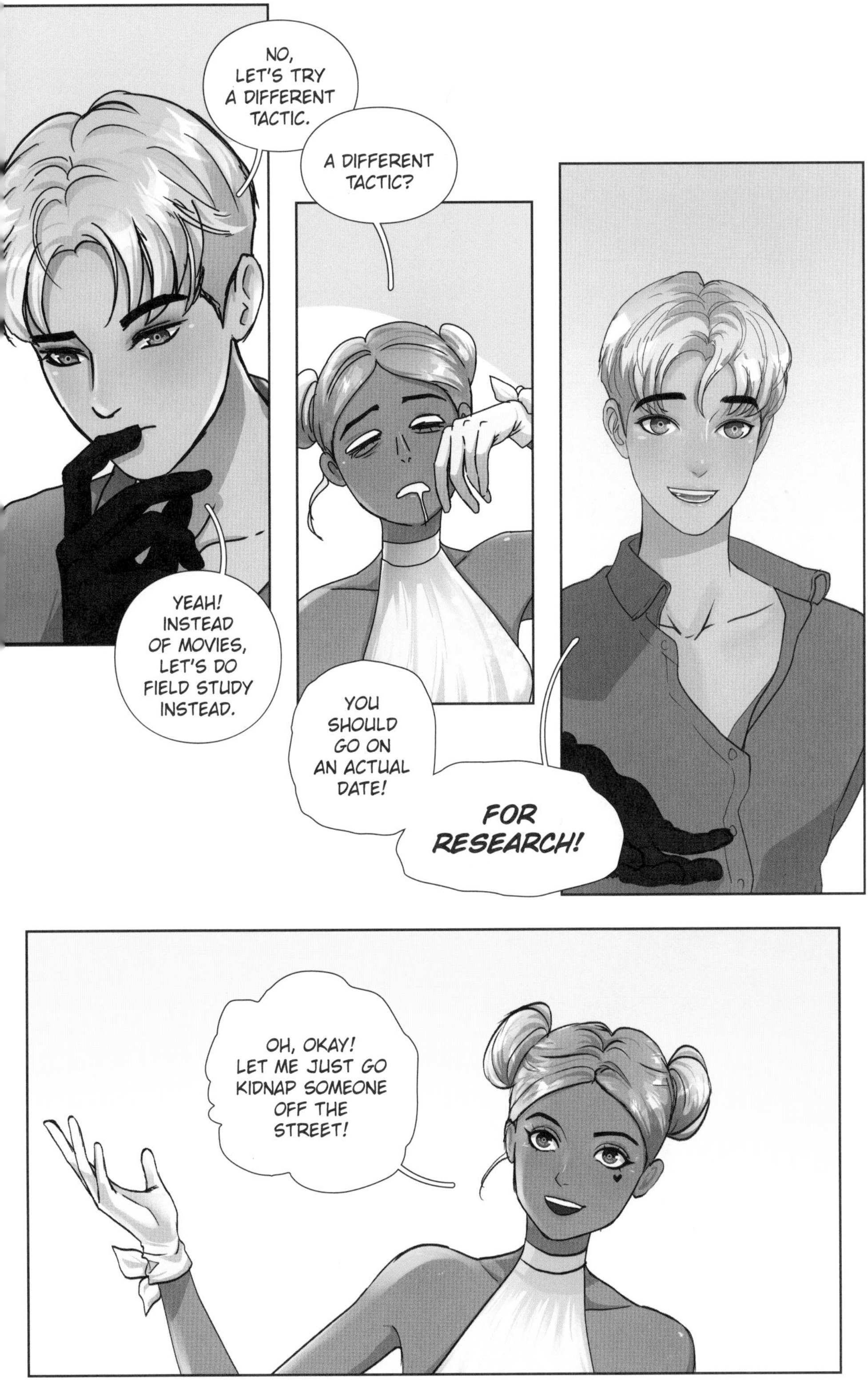
NO, LET'S TRY A DIFFERENT TACTIC.
A DIFFERENT TACTIC?
YEAH! INSTEAD OF MOVIES, LET'S DO FIELD STUDY INSTEAD.
YOU SHOULD GO ON AN ACTUAL DATE!
FOR RESEARCH!
OH, OKAY! LET ME JUST GO KIDNAP SOMEONE OFF THE STREET!

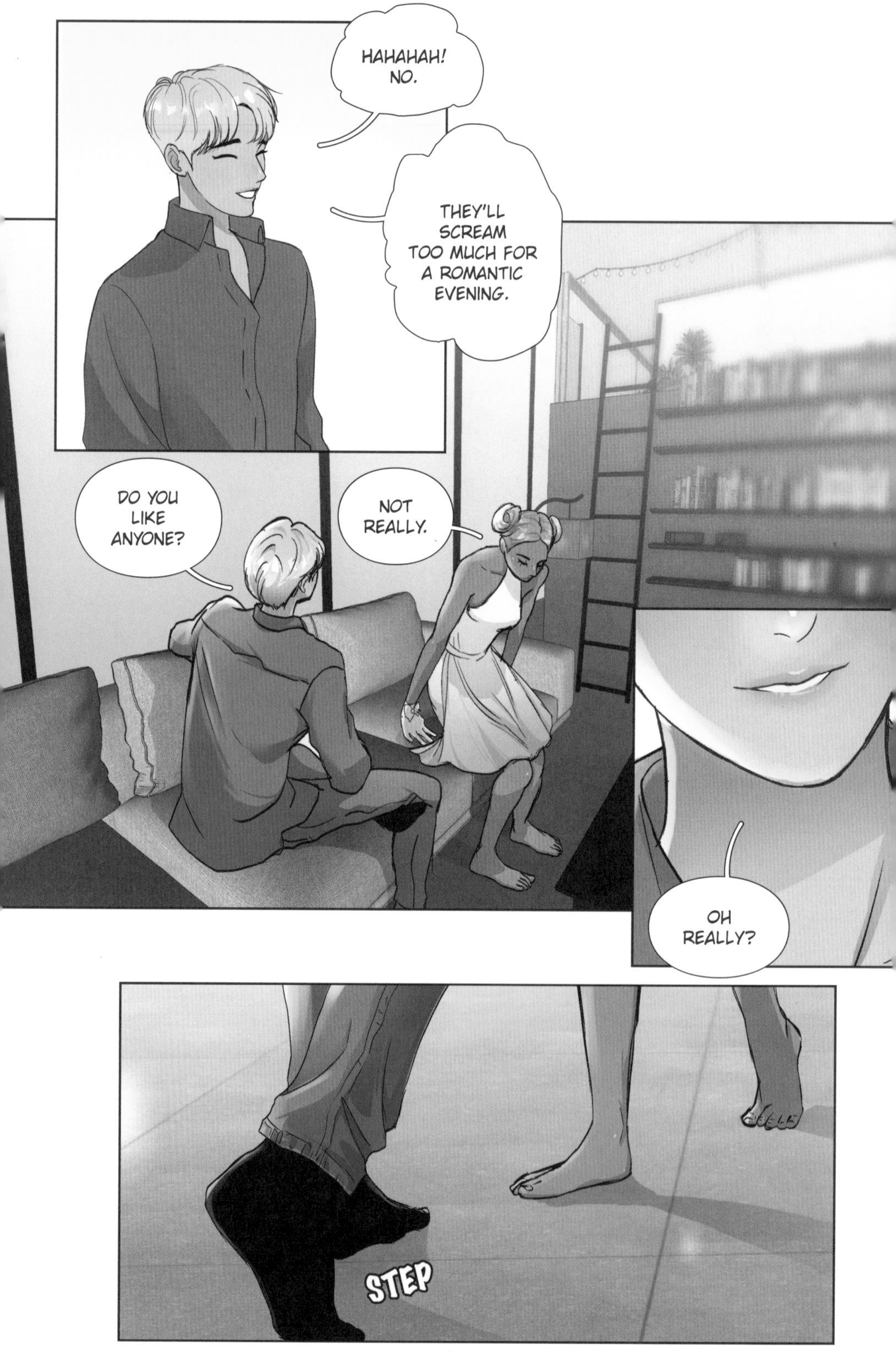
HAHAHAH! NO.
THEY'LL SCREAM TOO MUCH FOR A ROMANTIC EVENING.
DO YOU LIKE ANYONE?
NOT REALLY.
OH REALLY?
STEP

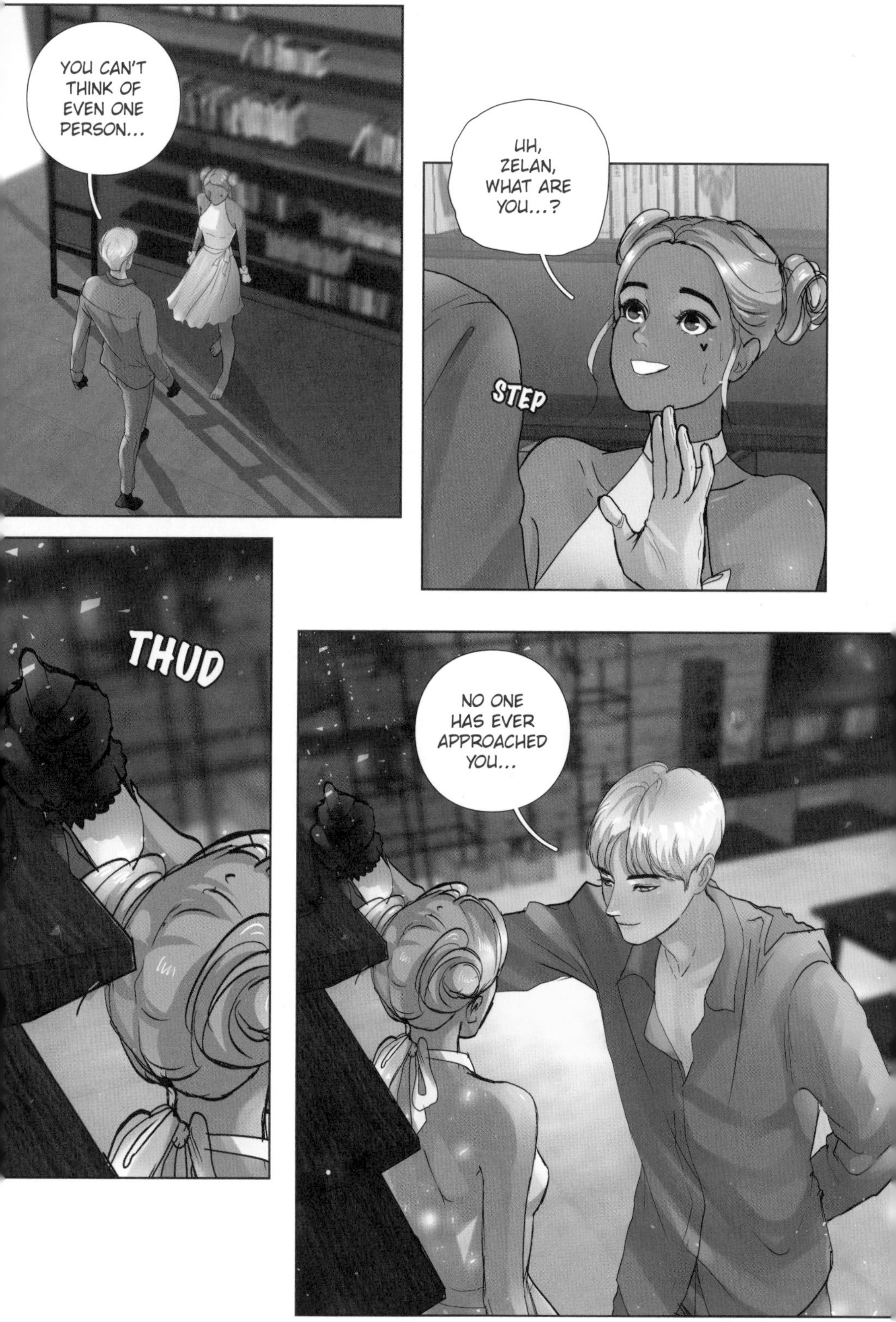
YOU CAN'T THINK OF EVEN ONE PERSON...
UH, ZELAN, WHAT ARE YOU...?
STEP
THUD
NO ONE HAS EVER APPROACHED YOU...

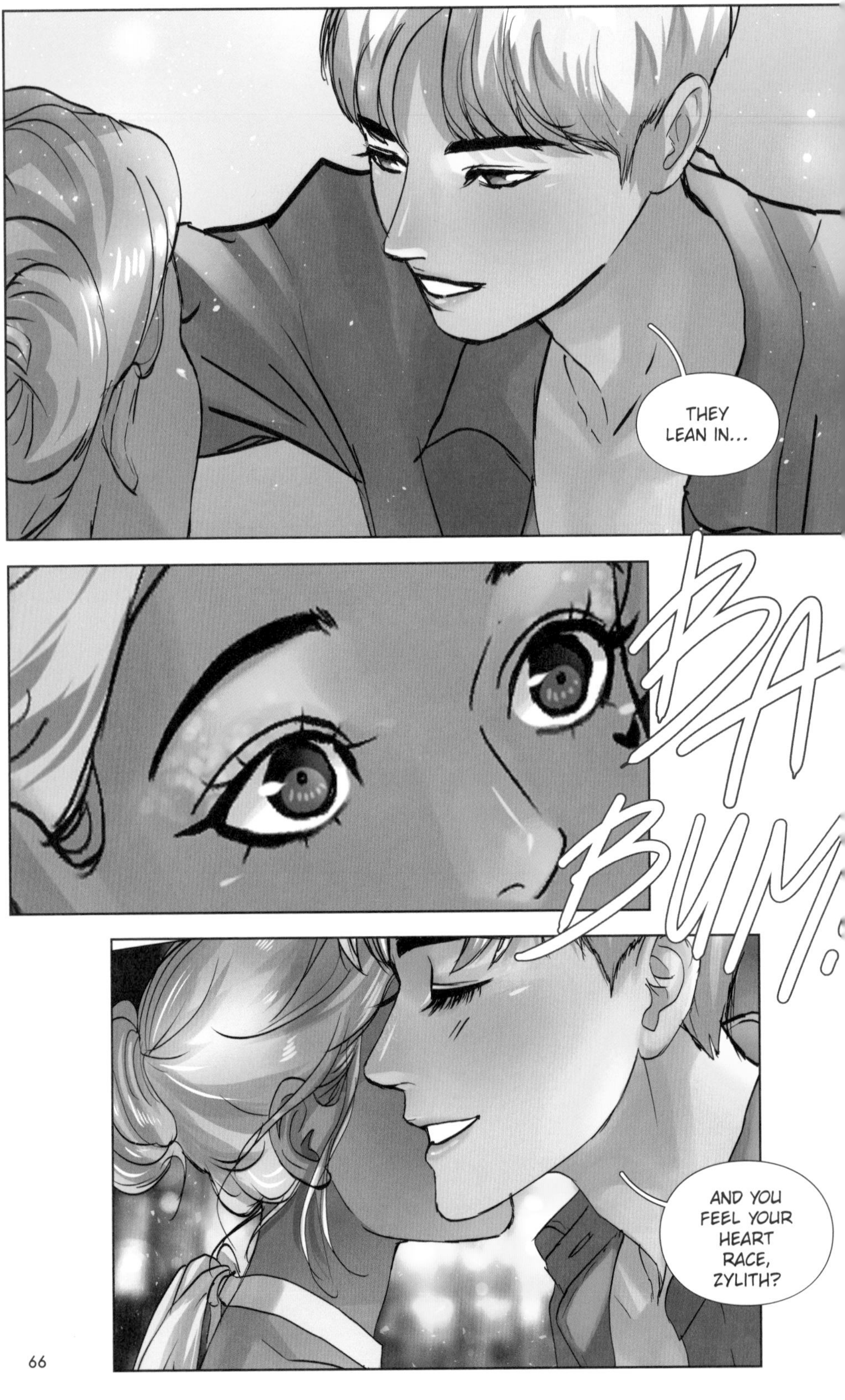
THEY LEAN IN...
BA BUM!
AND YOU FEEL YOUR HEART RACE, ZYLITH?

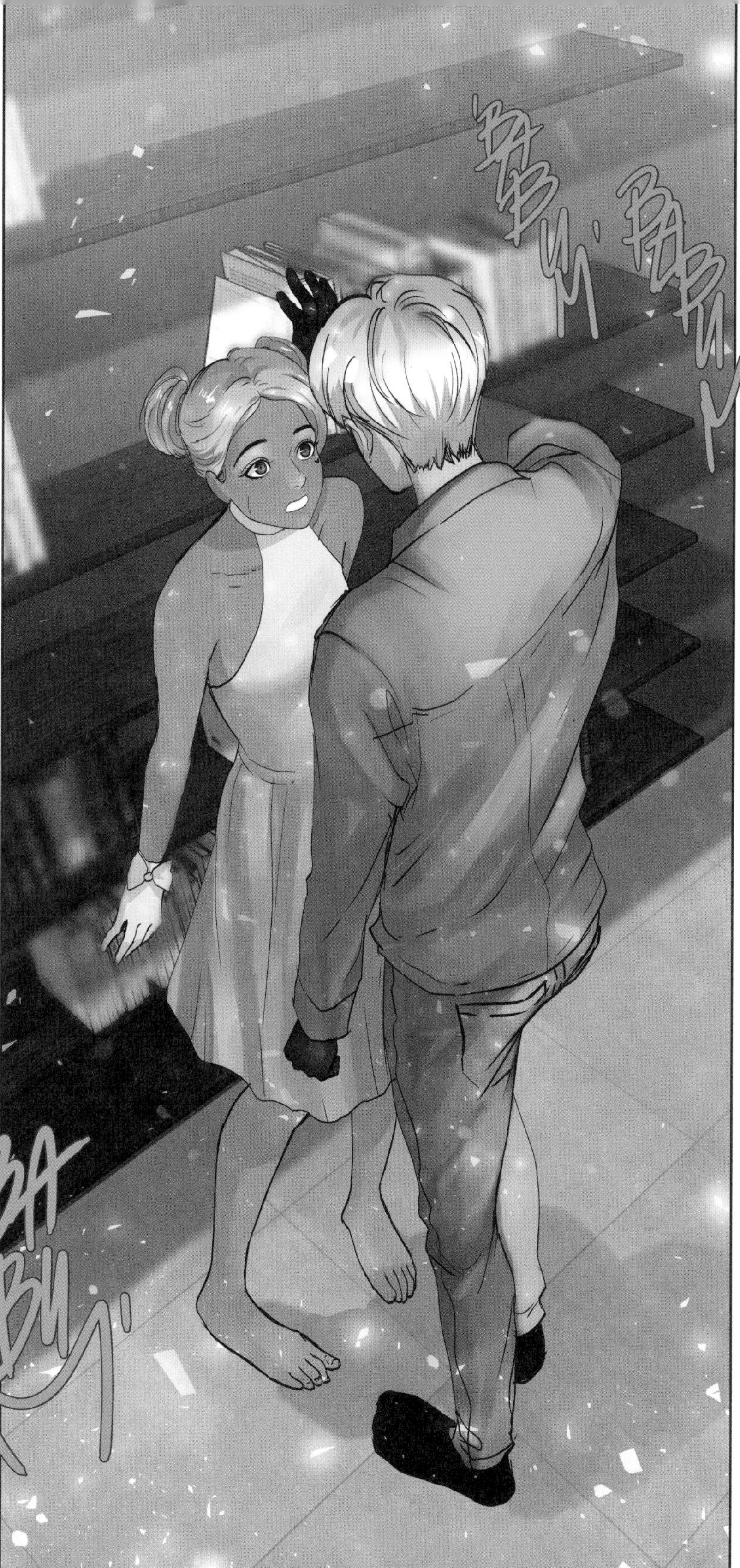

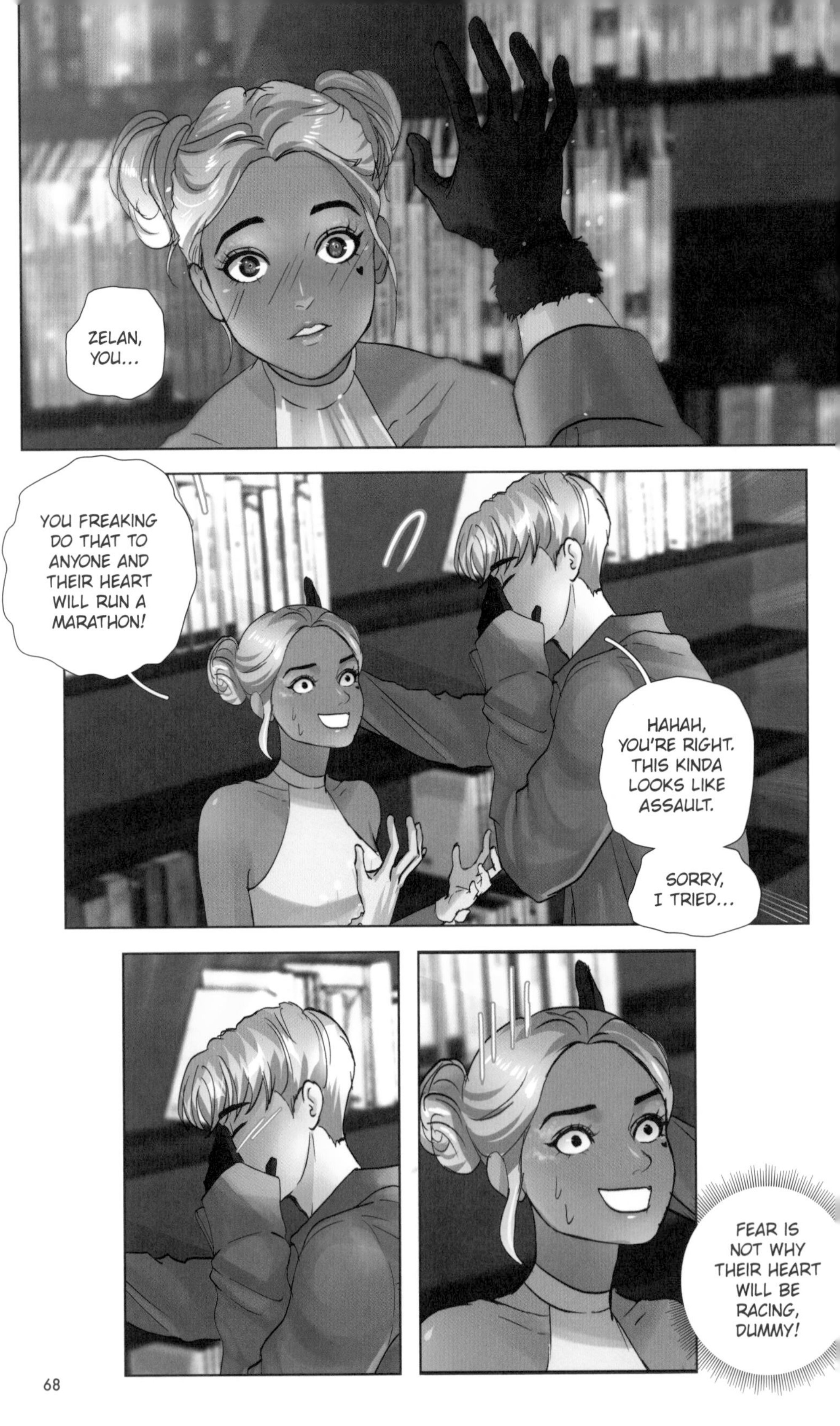
ZELAN, YOU...
YOU FREAKING DO THAT TO ANYONE AND THEIR HEART WILL RUN A MARATHON!
HAHAH, YOU'RE RIGHT. THIS KINDA LOOKS LIKE ASSAULT.
SORRY, I TRIED...
FEAR IS NOT WHY THEIR HEART WILL BE RACING, DUMMY!

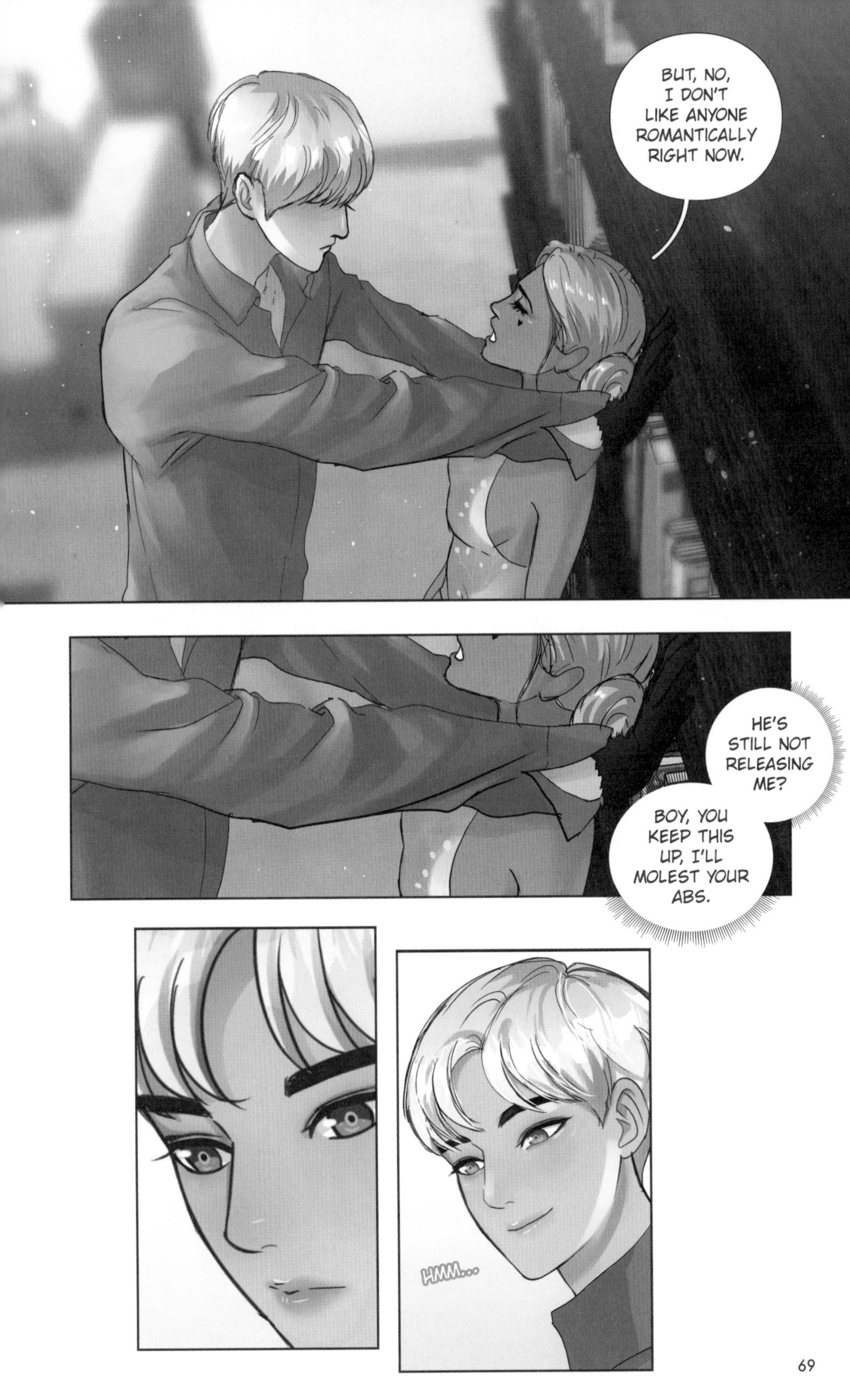
BUT, NO, I DON'T LIKE ANYONE ROMANTICALLY RIGHT NOW.
HE'S STILL NOT RELEASING ME?
BOY, YOU KEEP THIS UP, I'LL MOLEST YOUR ABS.
HMM...

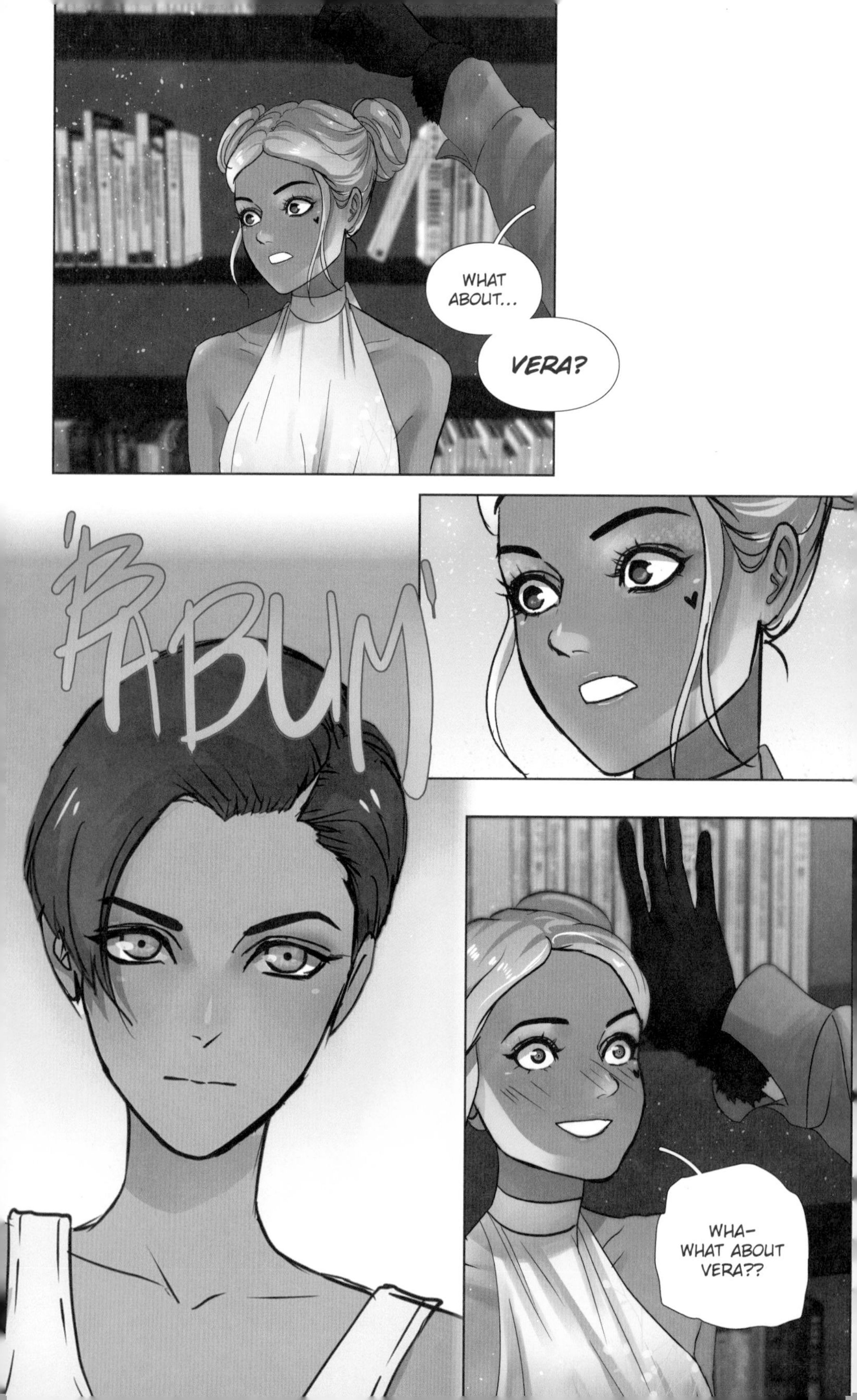
WHAT ABOUT...
VERA?
'BABUM'
WHA- WHAT ABOUT VERA??

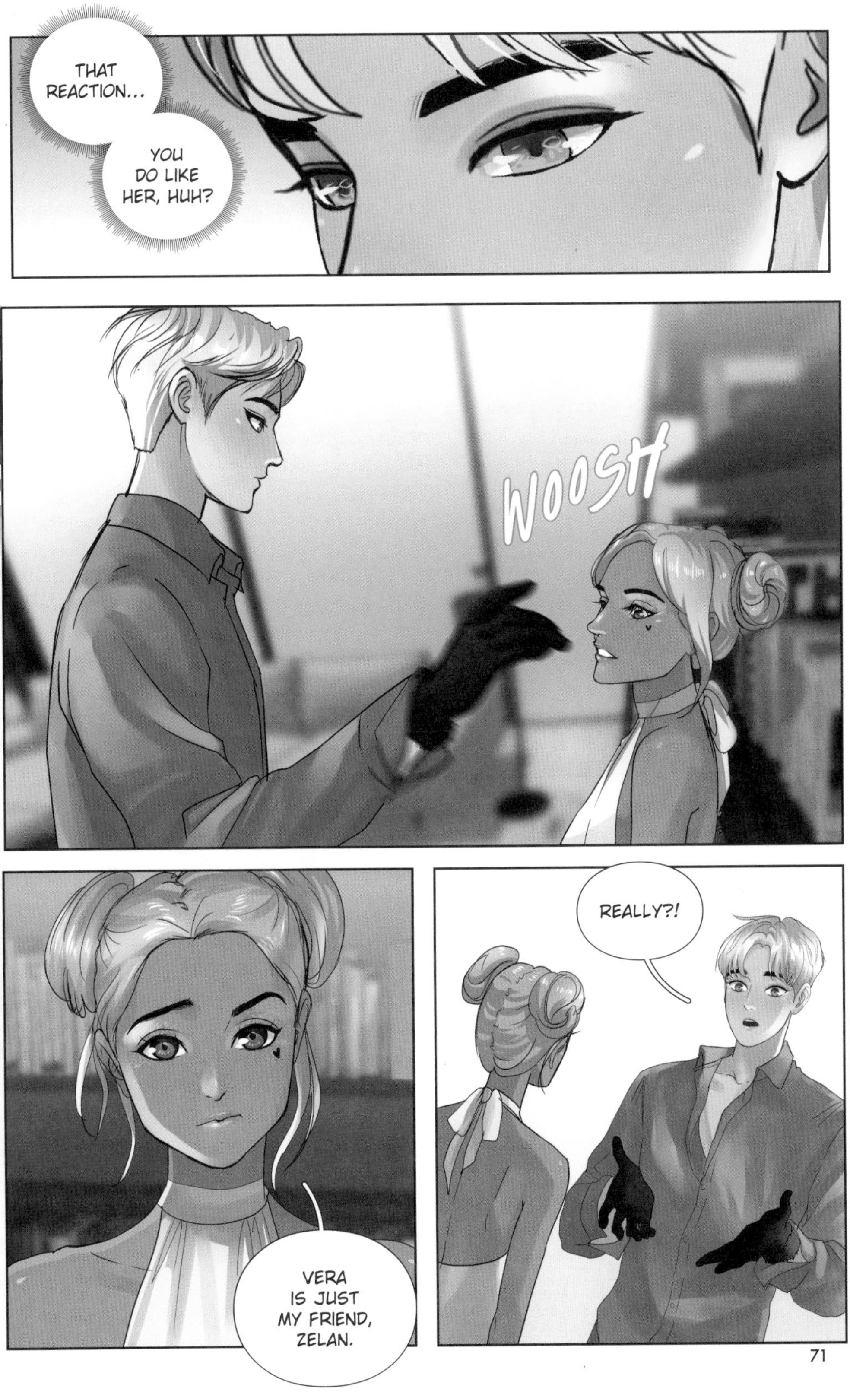
THAT REACTION...
YOU DO LIKE HER, HUH?
WOOSH
VERA IS JUST MY FRIEND, ZELAN.
REALLY?!

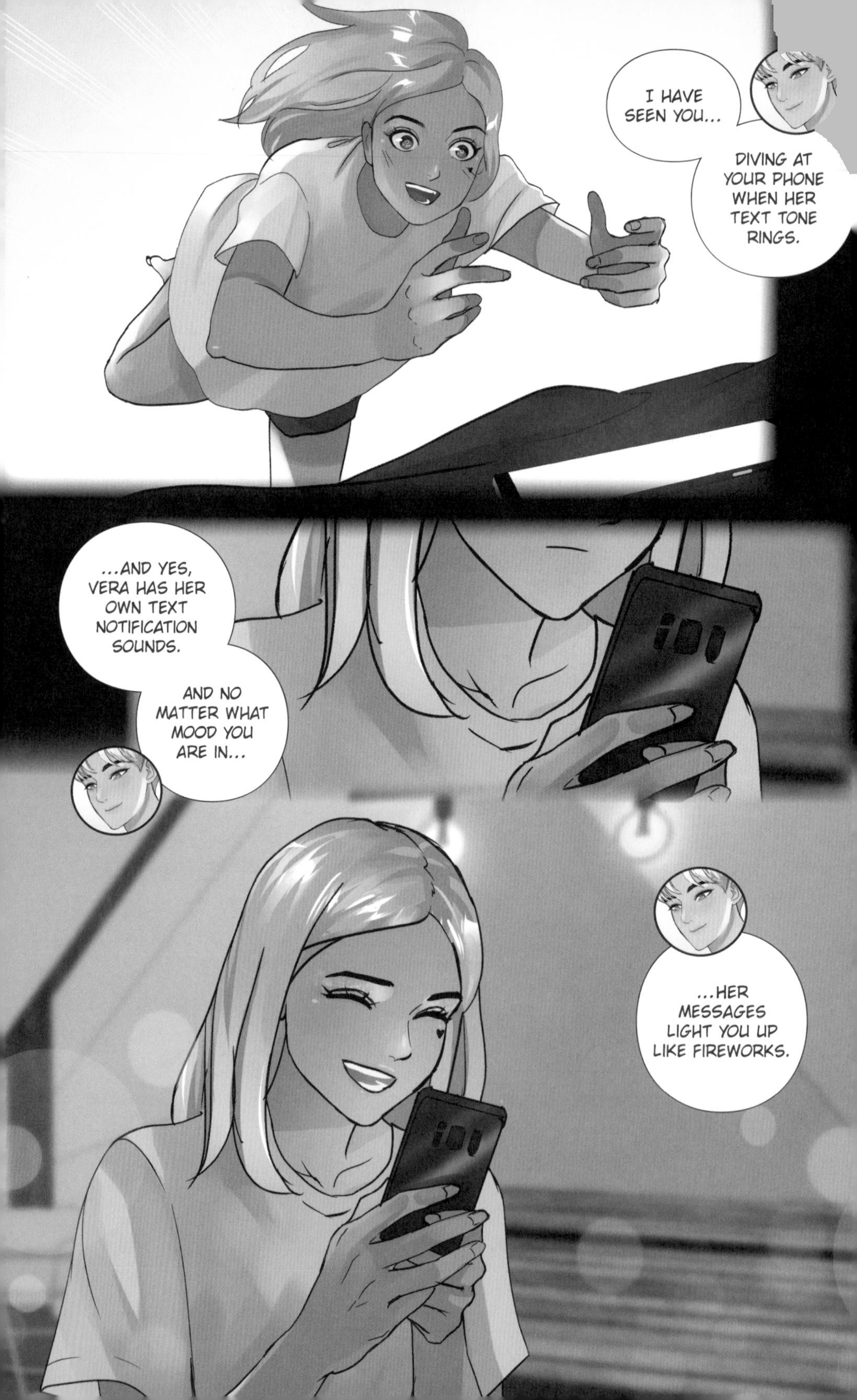
I HAVE SEEN YOU...
DIVING AT YOUR PHONE WHEN HER TEXT TONE RINGS.
...AND YES, VERA HAS HER OWN TEXT NOTIFICATION SOUNDS.
AND NO MATTER WHAT MOOD YOU ARE IN...
...HER MESSAGES LIGHT YOU UP LIKE FIREWORKS.

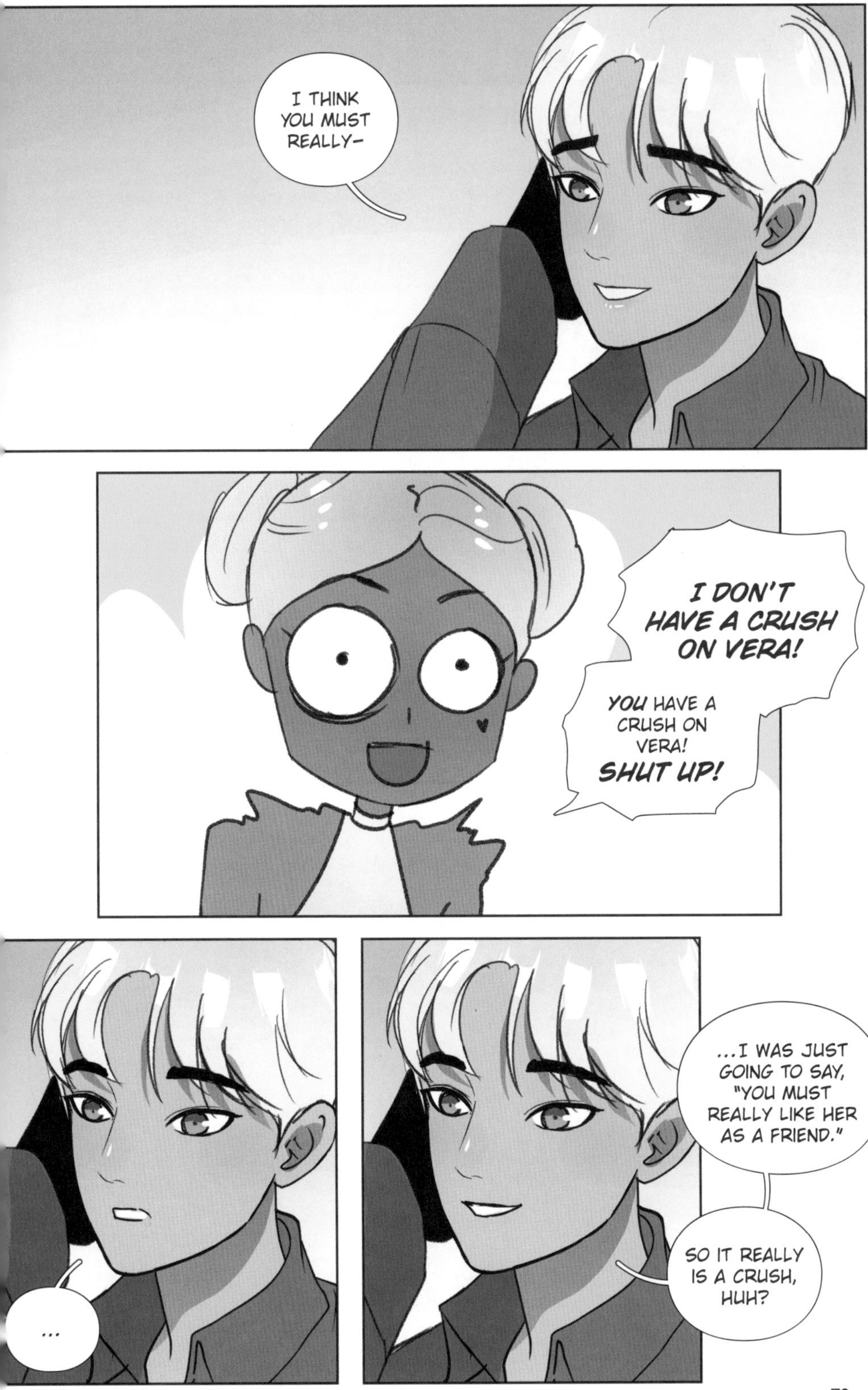
I THINK YOU MUST REALLY-
I DON'T HAVE A CRUSH ON VERA!
YOU HAVE A CRUSH ON VERA! SHUT UP!
...
...I WAS JUST GOING TO SAY, "YOU MUST REALLY LIKE HER AS A FRIEND."
SO IT REALLY IS A CRUSH, HUH?

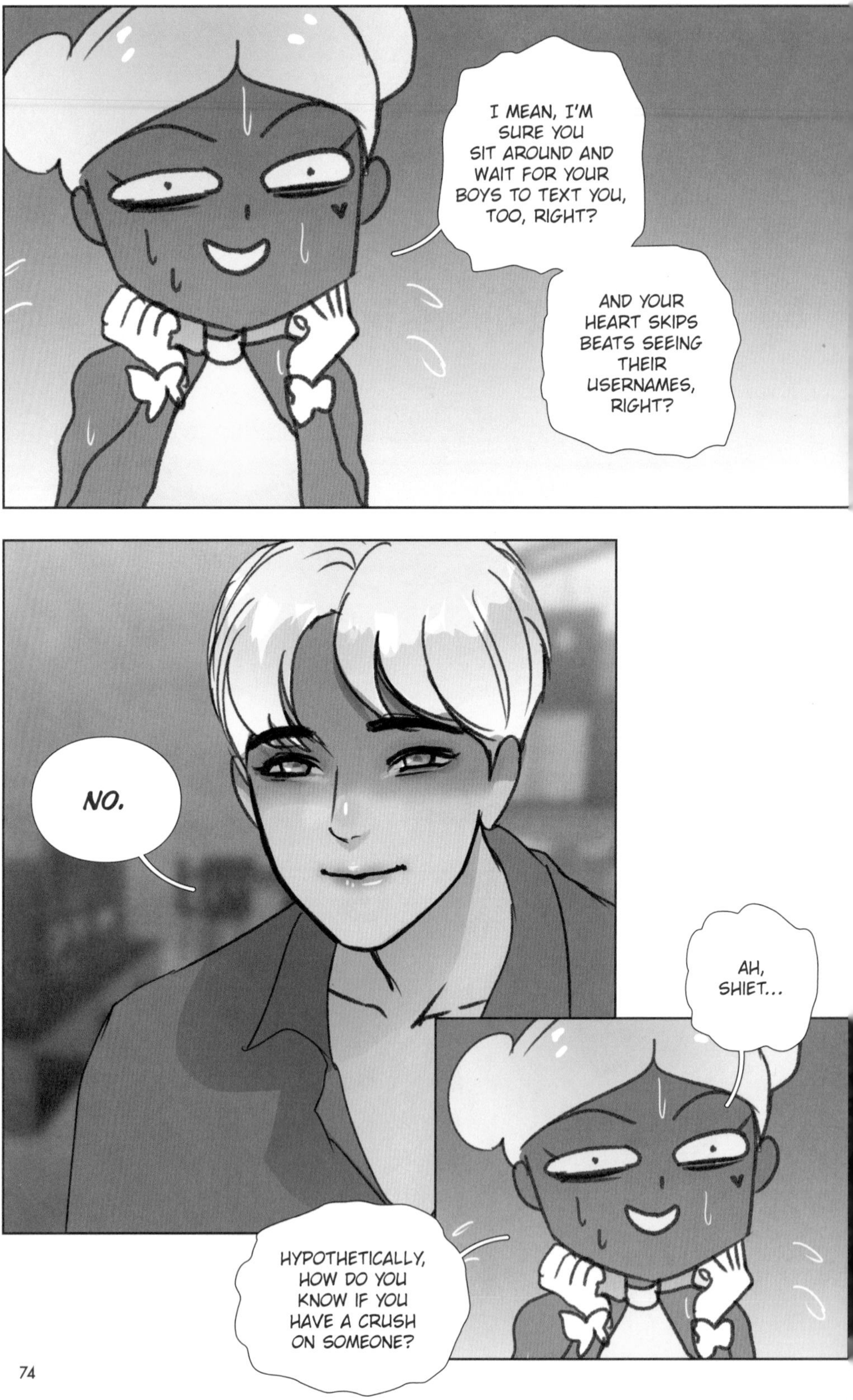
I MEAN, I'M SURE YOU SIT AROUND AND WAIT FOR YOUR BOYS TO TEXT YOU, TOO, RIGHT?
AND YOUR HEART SKIPS BEATS SEEING THEIR USERNAMES, RIGHT?
NO.
AH, SHIET...
HYPOTHETICALLY, HOW DO YOU KNOW IF YOU HAVE A CRUSH ON SOMEONE?

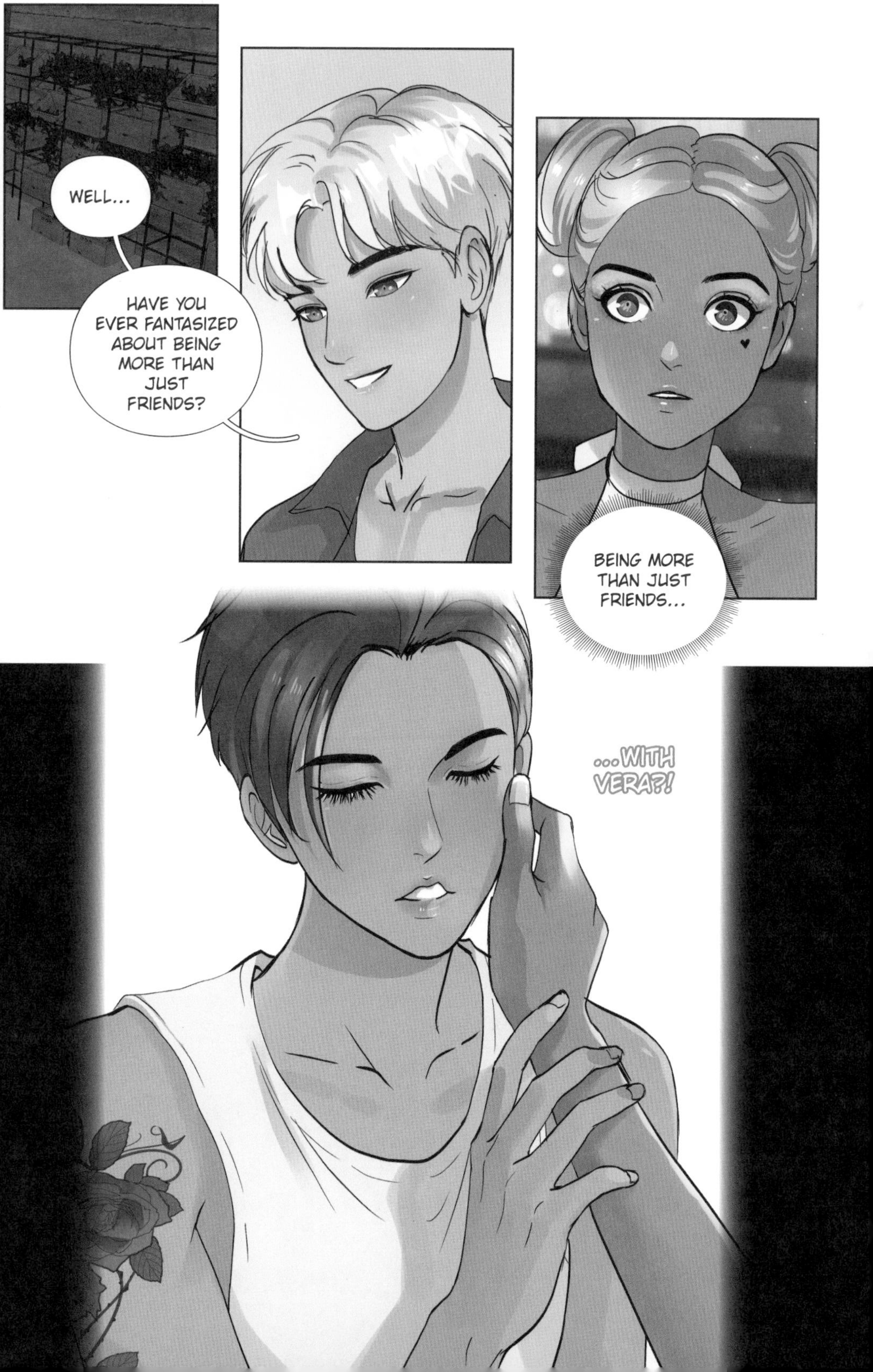
WELL...
HAVE YOU EVER FANTASIZED ABOUT BEING MORE THAN JUST FRIENDS?
BEING MORE THAN JUST FRIENDS...
...WITH VERA?!

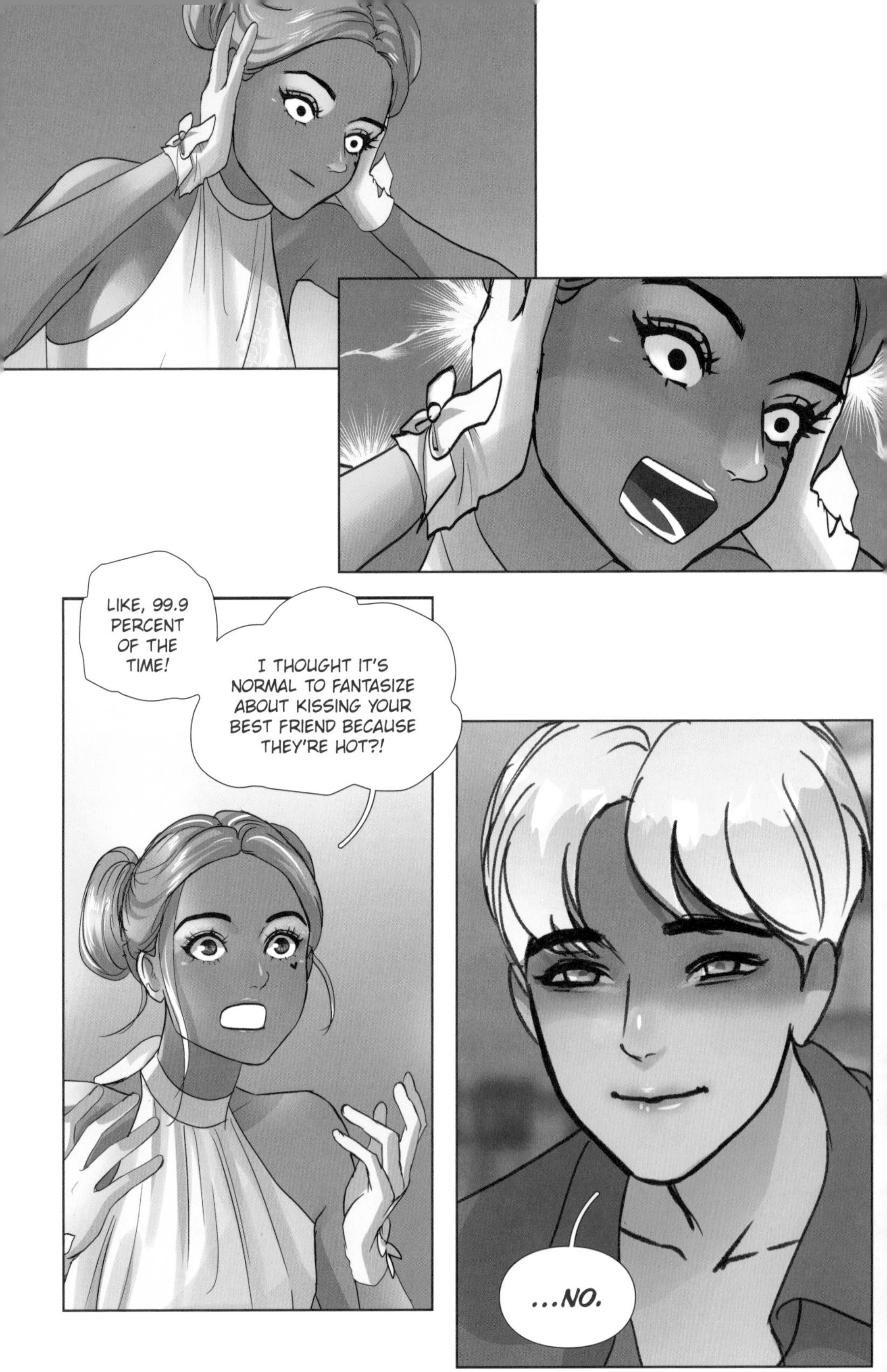
LIKE, 99.9 PERCENT OF THE TIME!
I THOUGHT IT'S NORMAL TO FANTASIZE ABOUT KISSING YOUR BEST FRIEND BECAUSE THEY'RE HOT?!
...NO.

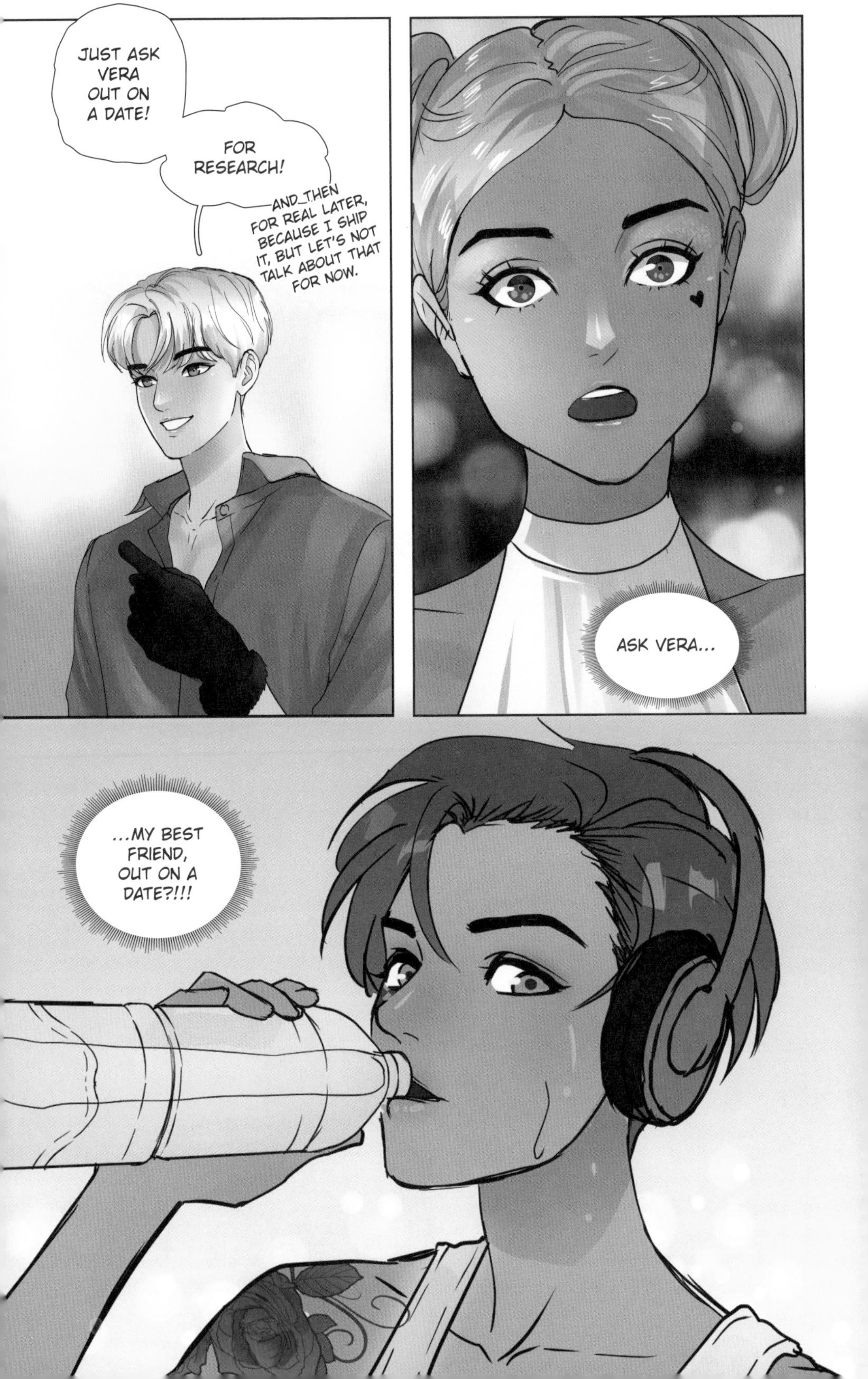
JUST ASK VERA OUT ON A DATE!
FOR RESEARCH!
AND THEN FOR REAL LATER, BECAUSE I SHIP IT, BUT LET'S NOT TALK ABOUT THAT FOR NOW.
ASK VERA...
...MY BEST FRIEND, OUT ON A DATE?!!!

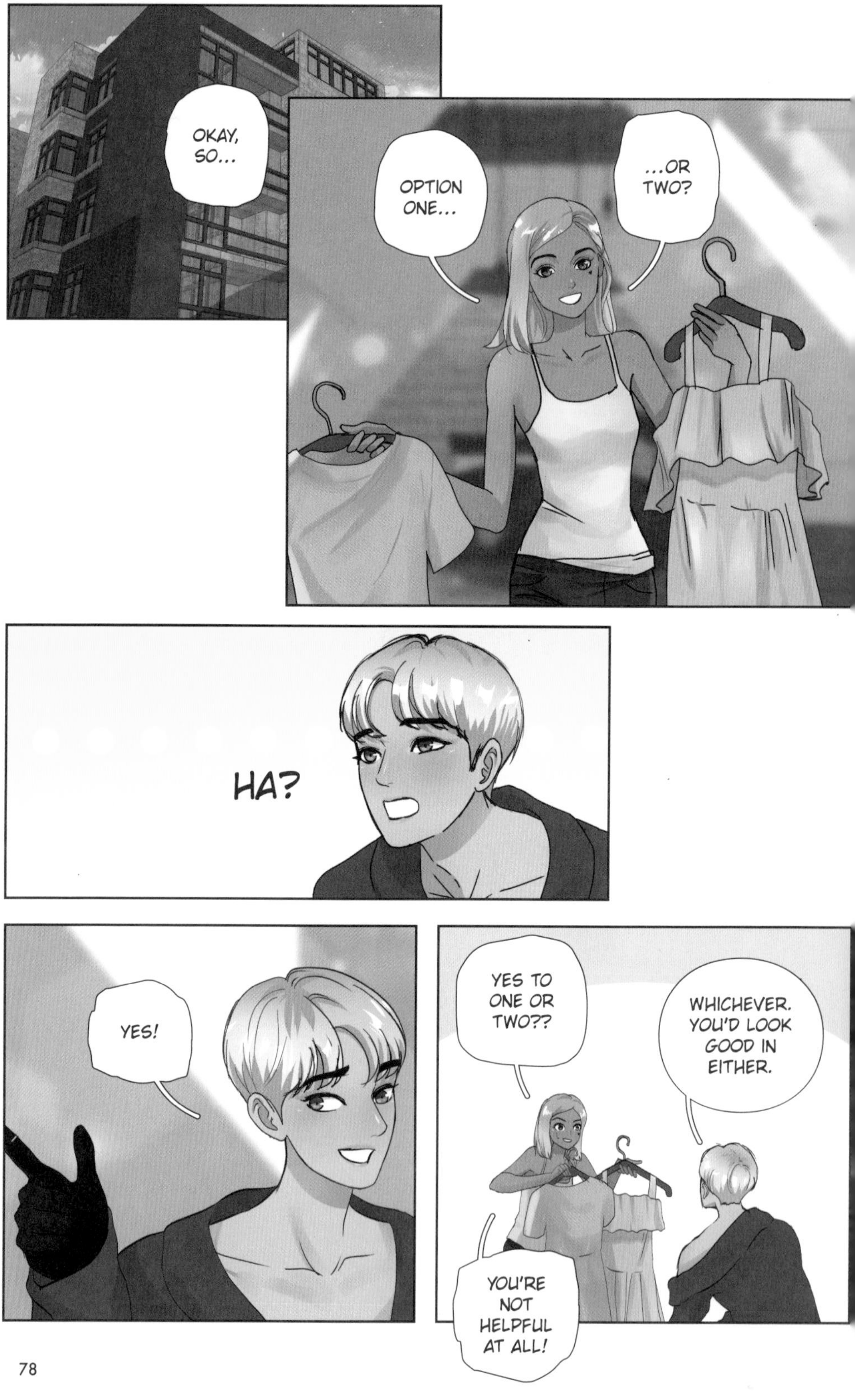
OKAY, SO...
OPTION ONE...
...OR TWO?
HA?
YES!
YES TO ONE OR TWO??
WHICHEVER. YOU'D LOOK GOOD IN EITHER.
YOU'RE NOT HELPFUL AT ALL!

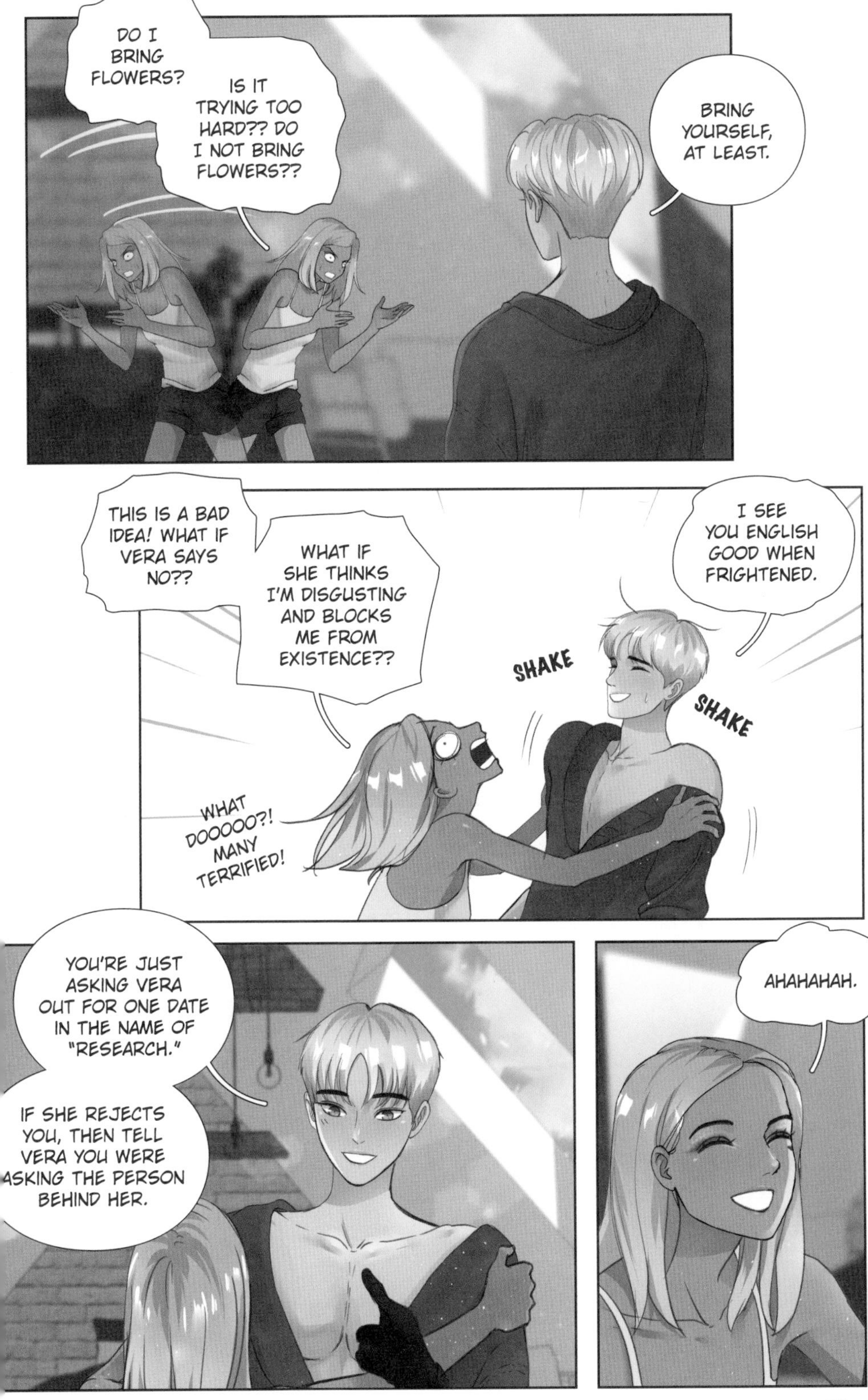
DO I BRING FLOWERS?
IS IT TRYING TOO HARD?? DO I NOT BRING FLOWERS??
BRING YOURSELF, AT LEAST.
THIS IS A BAD IDEA! WHAT IF VERA SAYS NO??
WHAT IF SHE THINKS I'M DISGUSTING AND BLOCKS ME FROM EXISTENCE??
I SEE YOU ENGLISH GOOD WHEN FRIGHTENED.
SHAKE
SHAKE
WHAT DOOOOO?! MANY TERRIFIED!
YOU'RE JUST ASKING VERA OUT FOR ONE DATE IN THE NAME OF "RESEARCH."
IF SHE REJECTS YOU, THEN TELL VERA YOU WERE ASKING THE PERSON BEHIND HER.
AHAHAHAH.

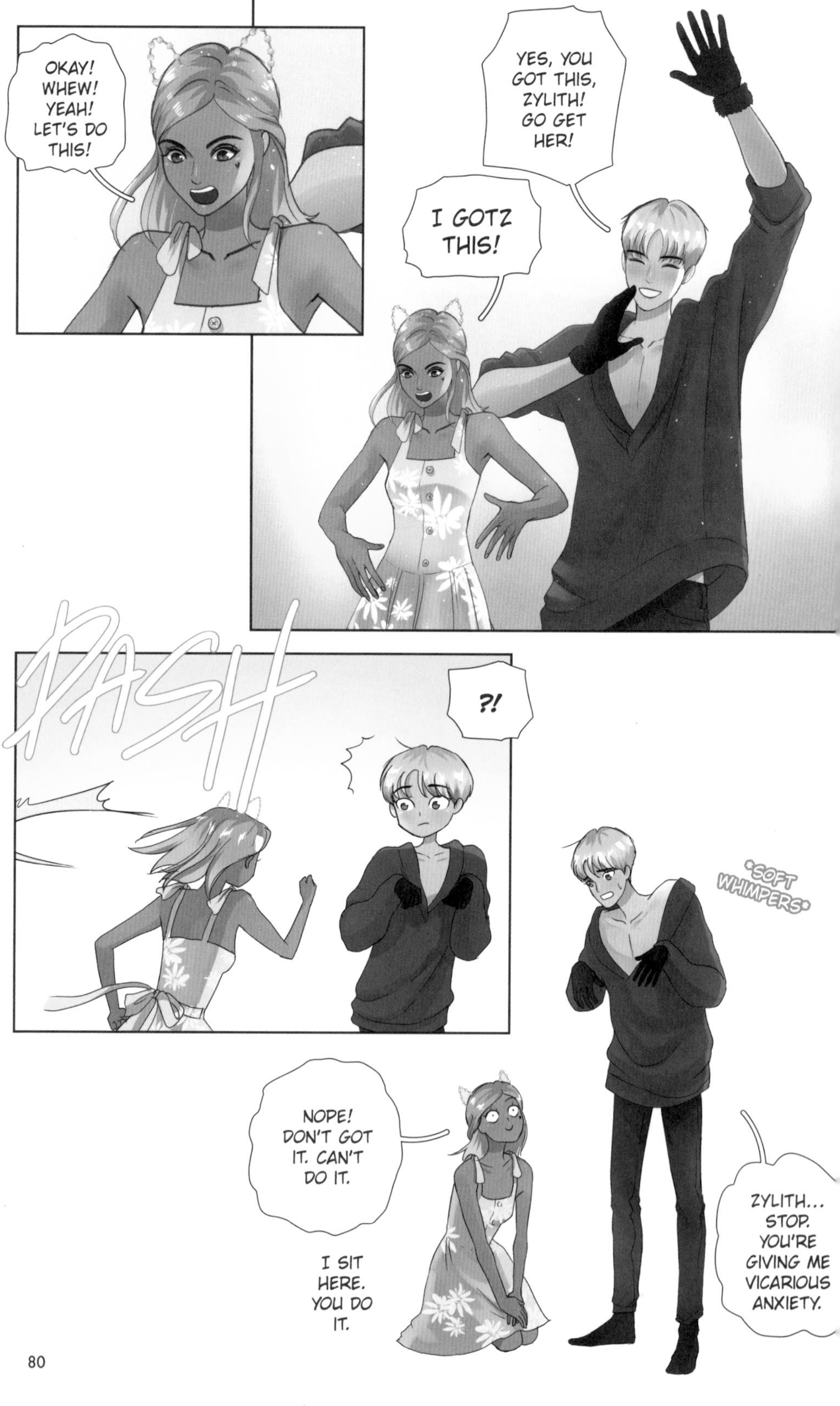
OKAY! WHEW! YEAH! LET'S DO THIS!
YES, YOU GOT THIS, ZYLITH! GO GET HER!
I GOTZ THIS!
DASH
?!
SOFT WHIMPERS
NOPE! DON'T GOT IT. CAN'T DO IT.
I SIT HERE. YOU DO IT.
ZYLITH... STOP. YOU'RE GIVING ME VICARIOUS ANXIETY.

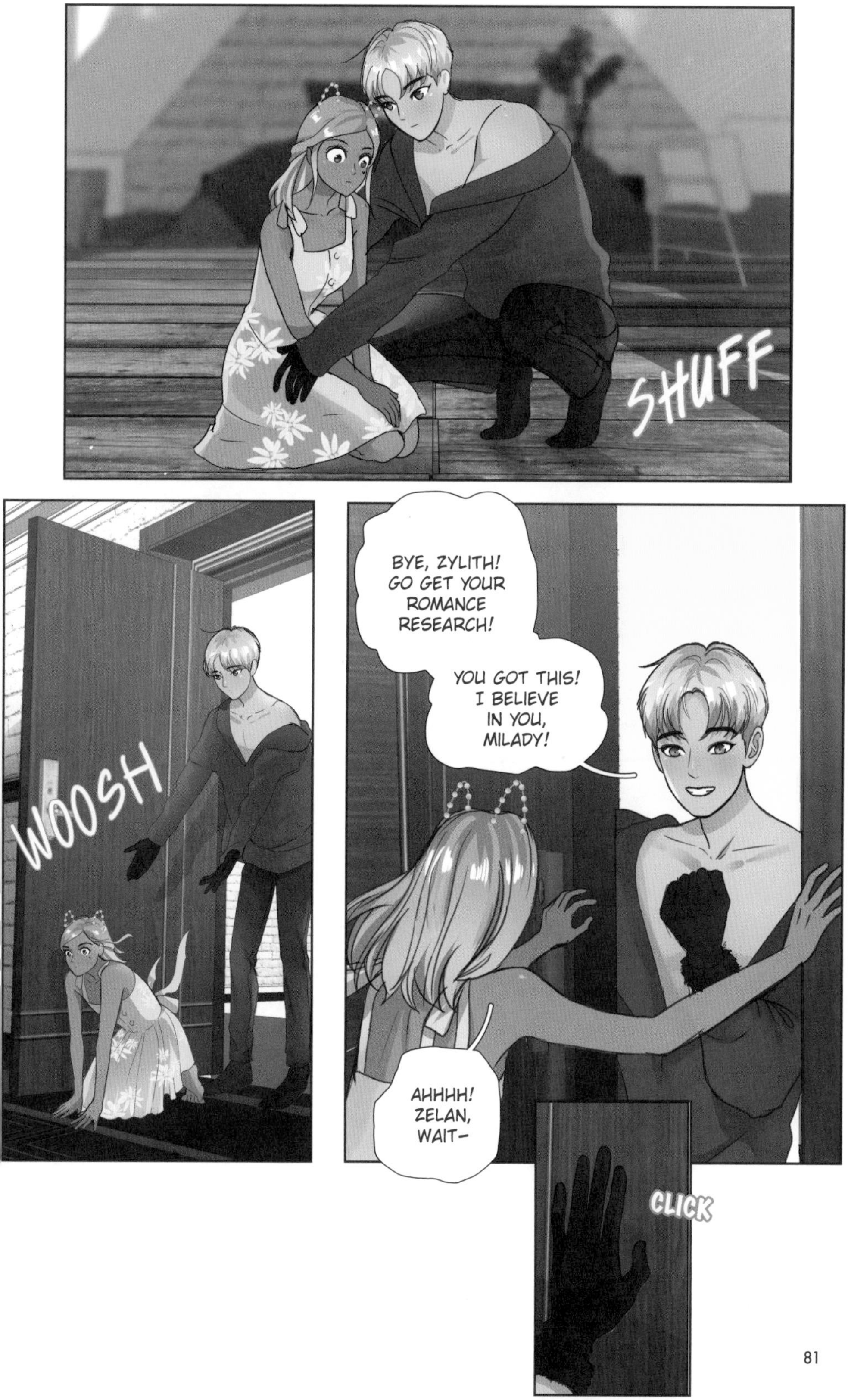
SHUFF
WOOSH
BYE, ZYLITH! GO GET YOUR ROMANCE RESEARCH!
YOU GOT THIS! I BELIEVE IN YOU, MILADY!
AHHHH! ZELAN, WAIT-
CLICK

SIGH...

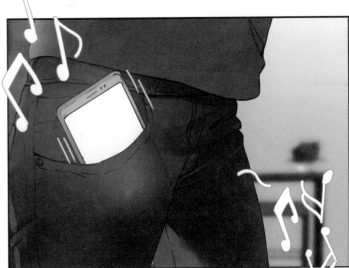

MY LITTLE BROTHER IS CALLING?

AUSHI

🔋 12:48 PM

...e to answer

ZELAN!

MOM IS—

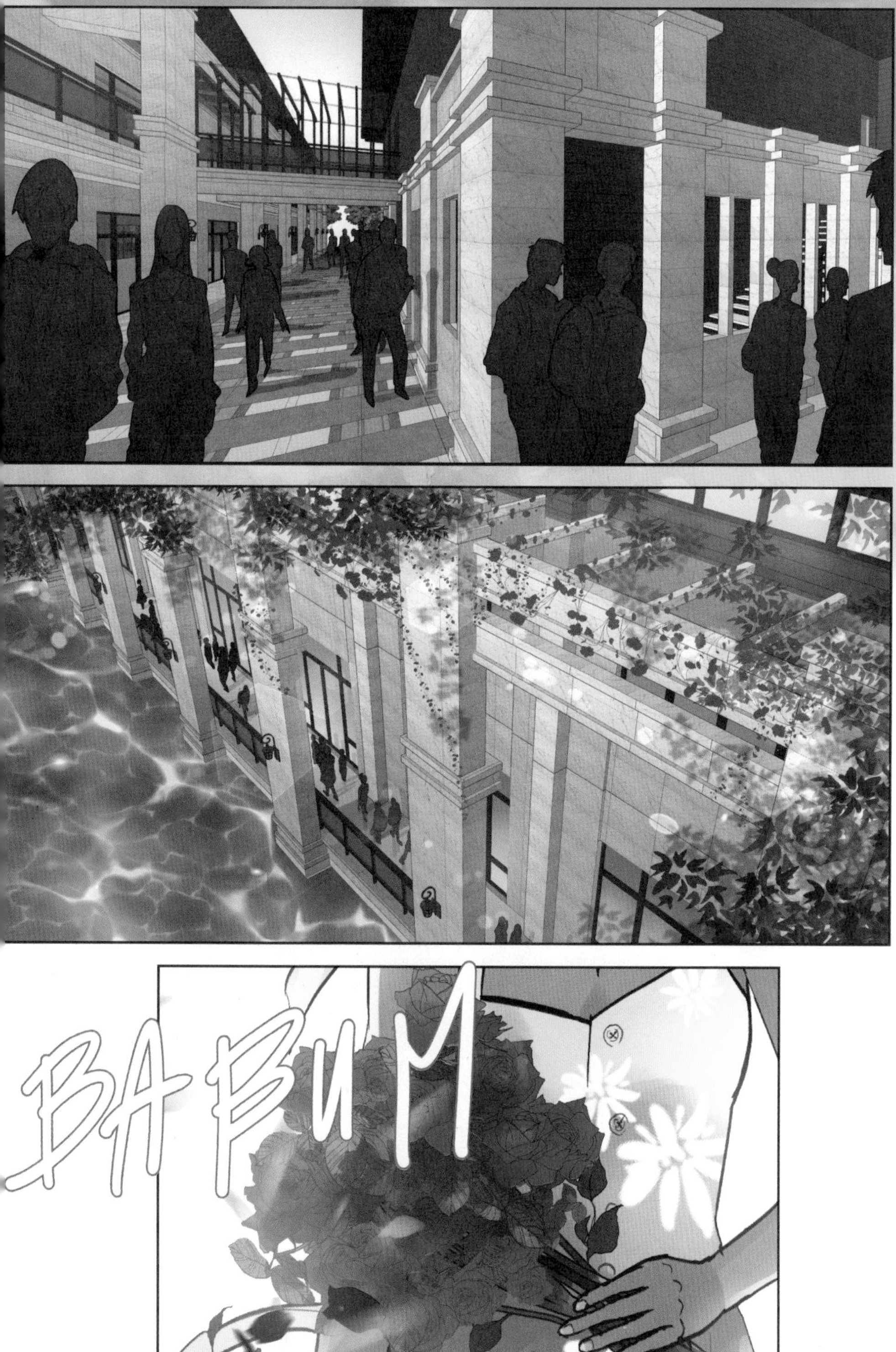
ВАБИМ

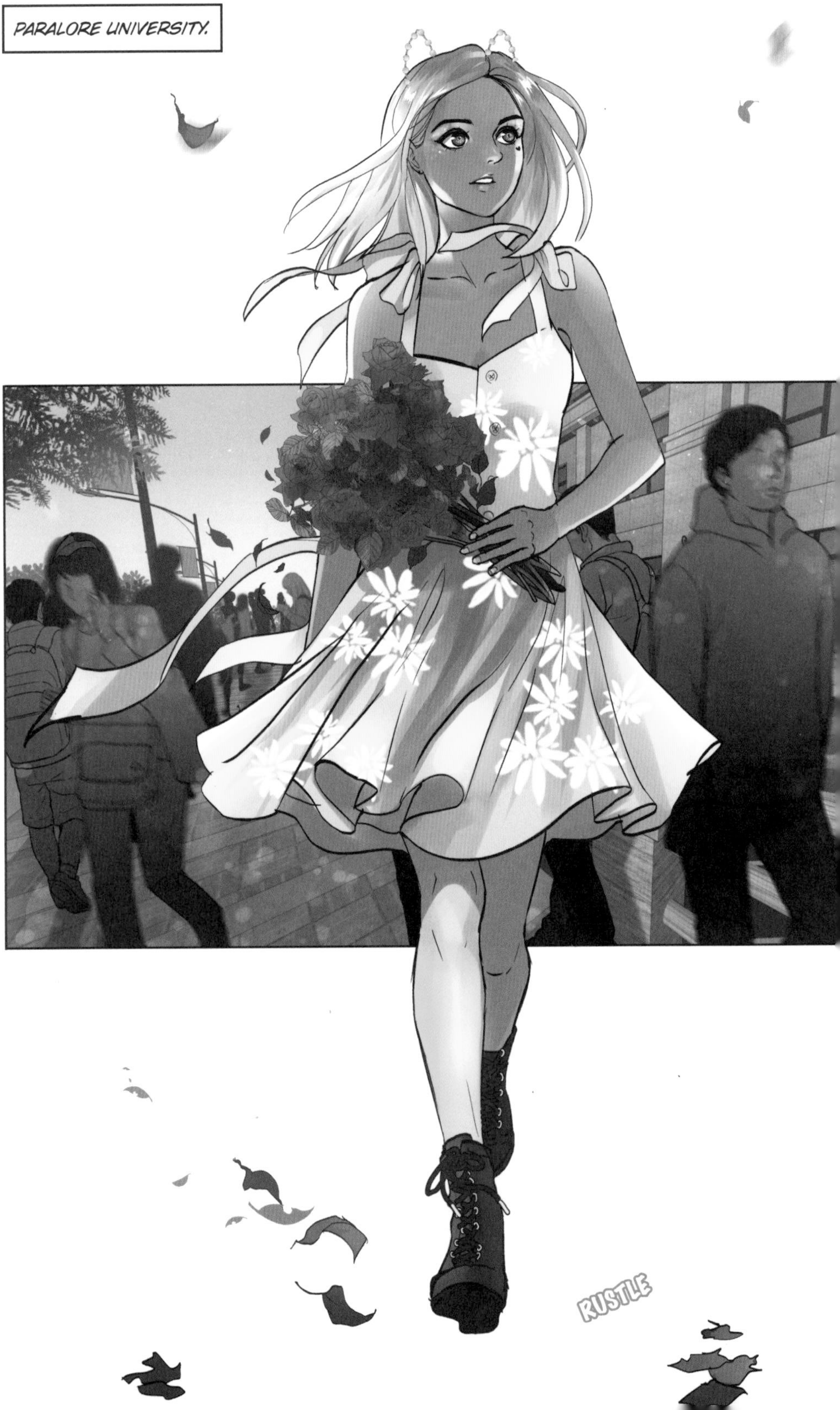
PARALORE UNIVERSITY.
RUSTLE

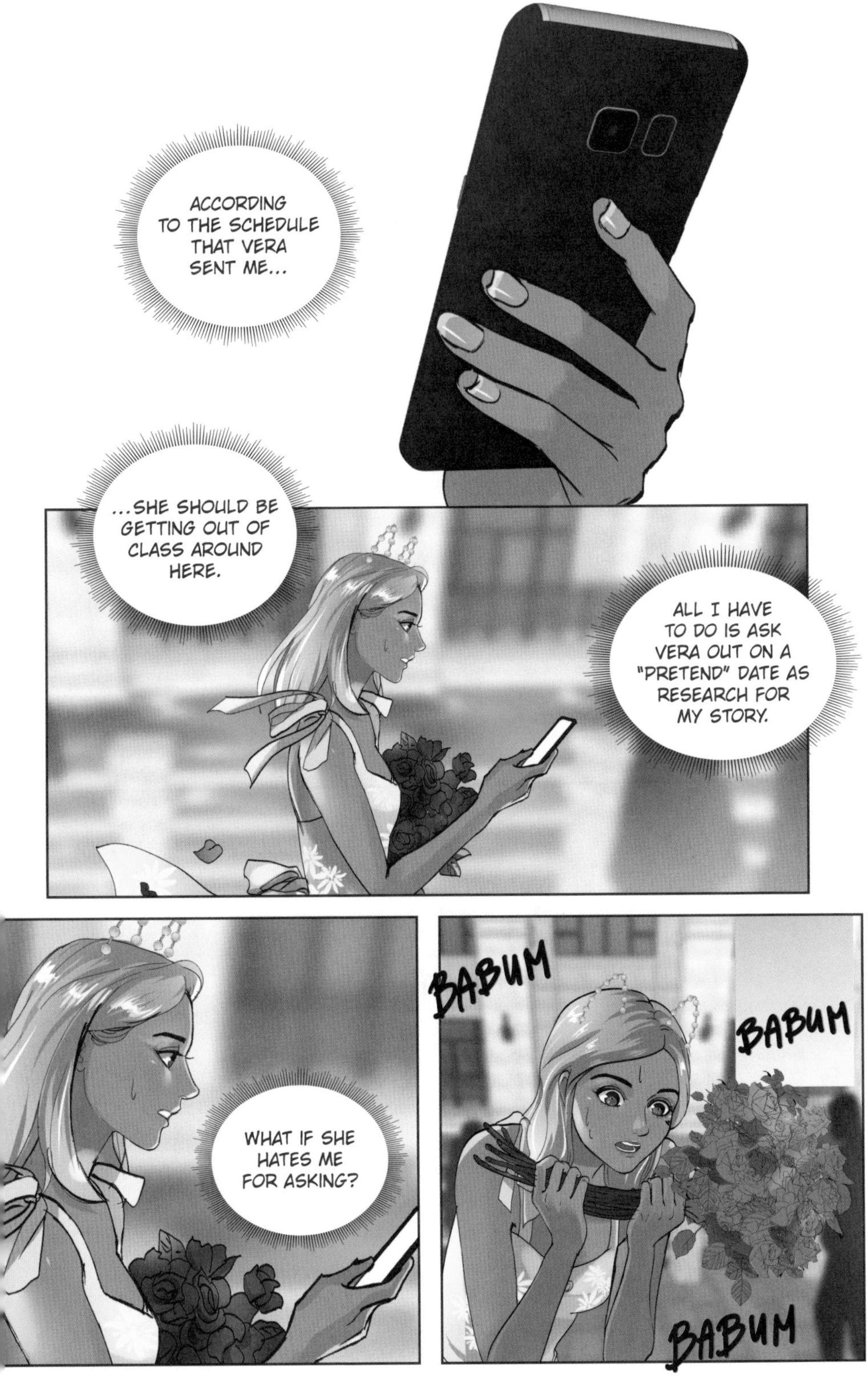
ACCORDING TO THE SCHEDULE THAT VERA SENT ME...
...SHE SHOULD BE GETTING OUT OF CLASS AROUND HERE.
ALL I HAVE TO DO IS ASK VERA OUT ON A "PRETEND" DATE AS RESEARCH FOR MY STORY.
WHAT IF SHE HATES ME FOR ASKING?
BABUM
BABUM
BABUM

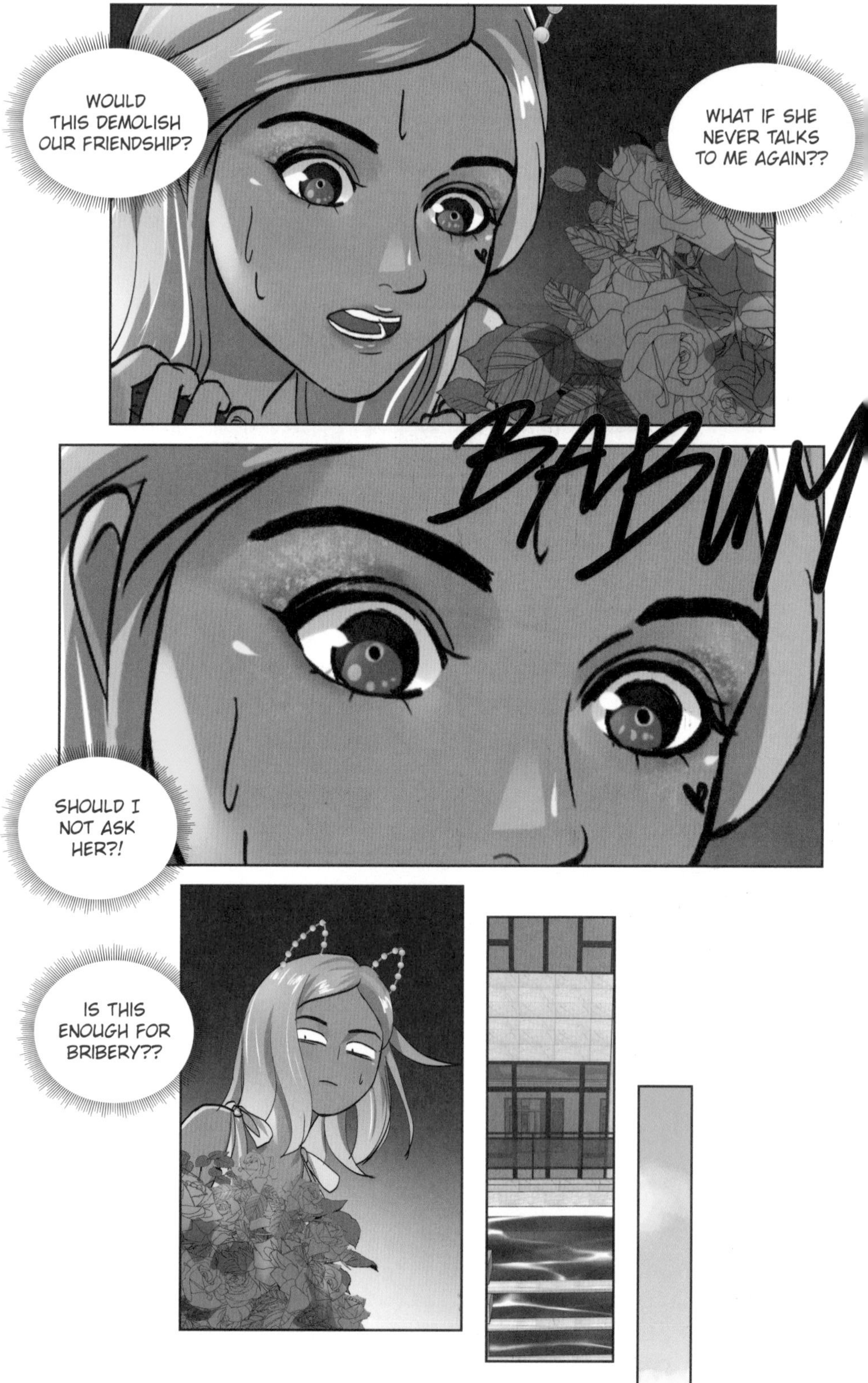
WOULD THIS DEMOLISH OUR FRIENDSHIP?
WHAT IF SHE NEVER TALKS TO ME AGAIN??
BABUM
SHOULD I NOT ASK HER?!
IS THIS ENOUGH FOR BRIBERY??

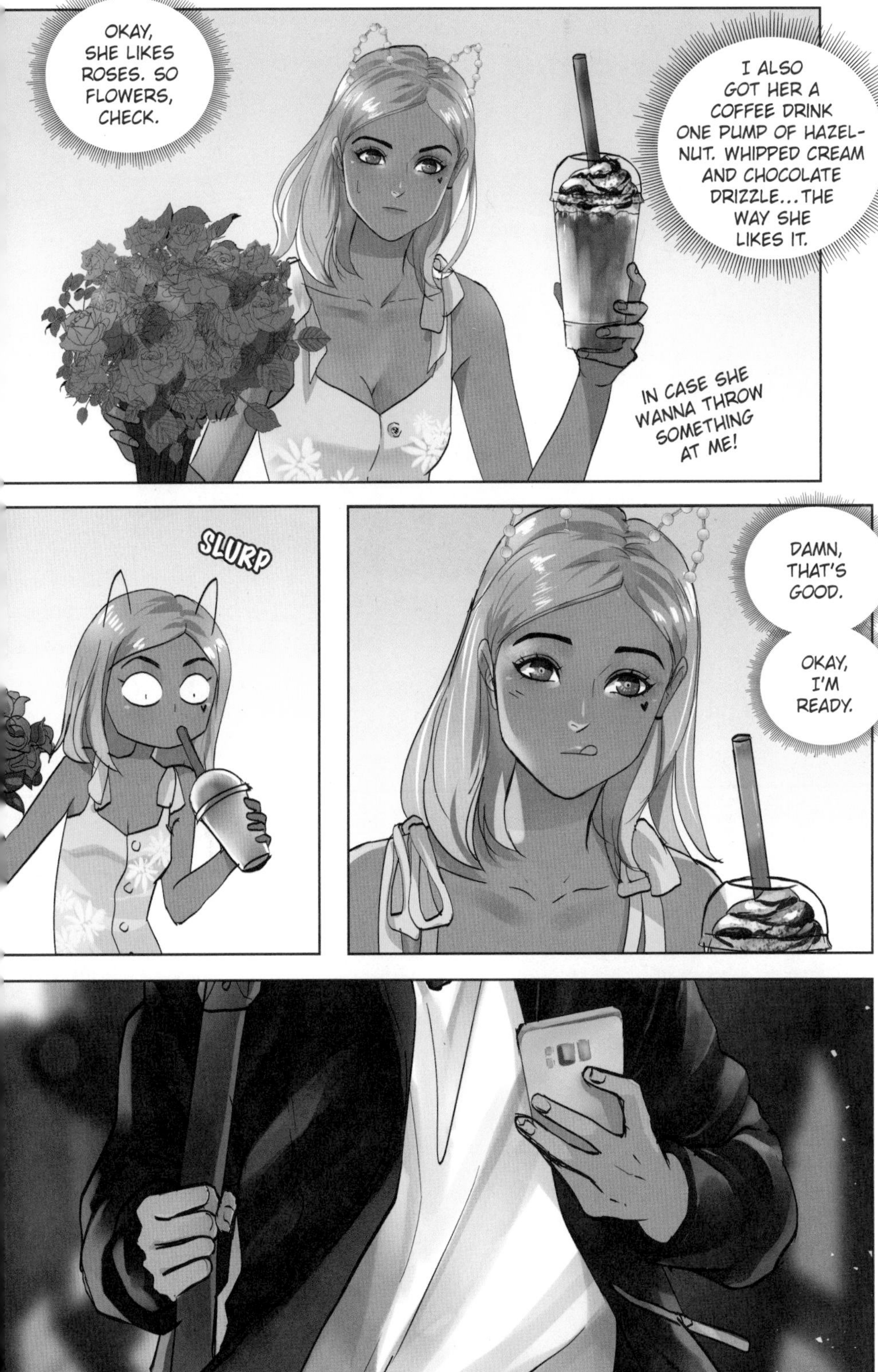
OKAY, SHE LIKES ROSES. SO FLOWERS, CHECK.
I ALSO GOT HER A COFFEE DRINK ONE PUMP OF HAZEL-NUT. WHIPPED CREAM AND CHOCOLATE DRIZZLE...THE WAY SHE LIKES IT.
IN CASE SHE WANNA THROW SOMETHING AT ME!
SLURP
DAMN, THAT'S GOOD.
OKAY, I'M READY.

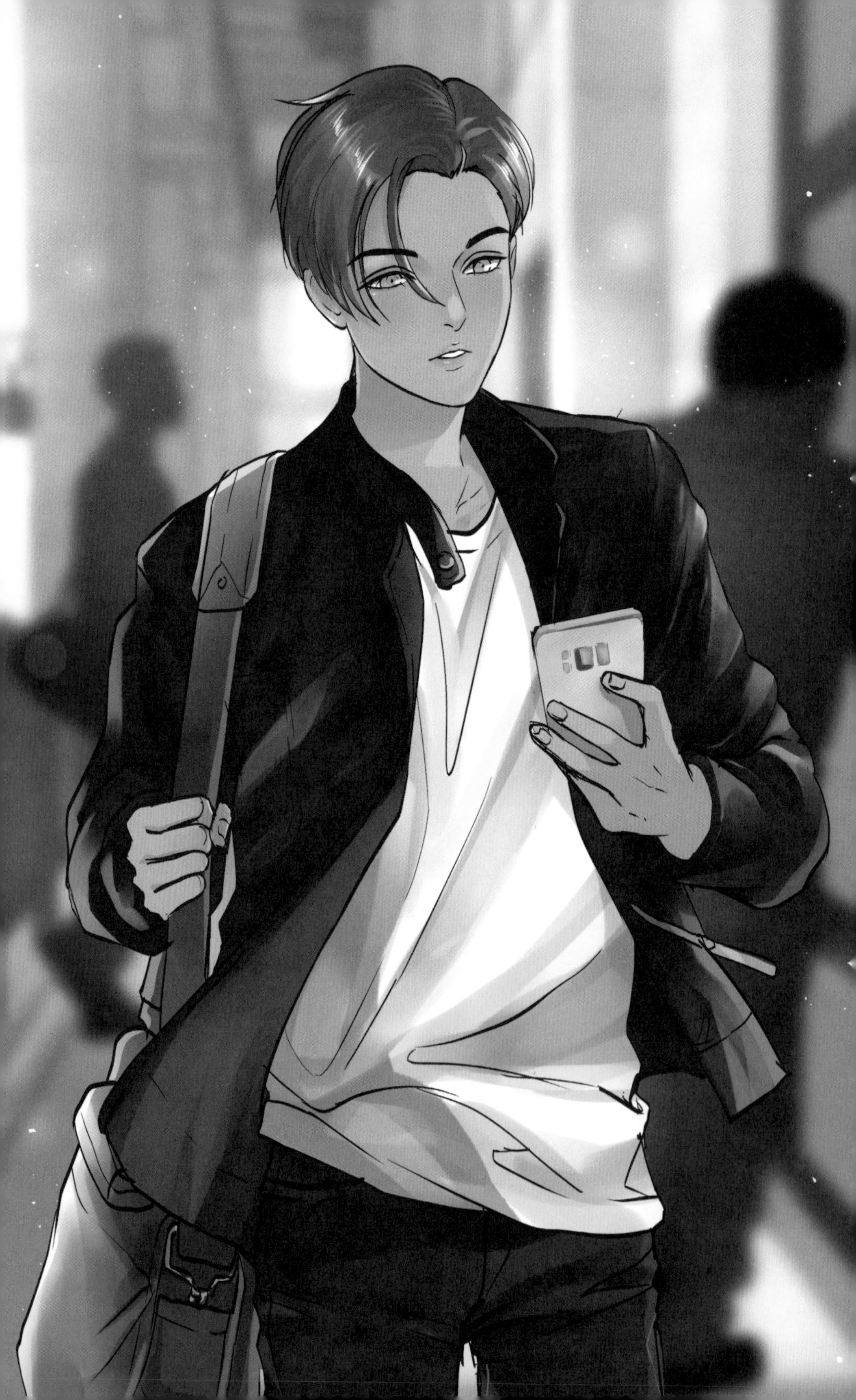

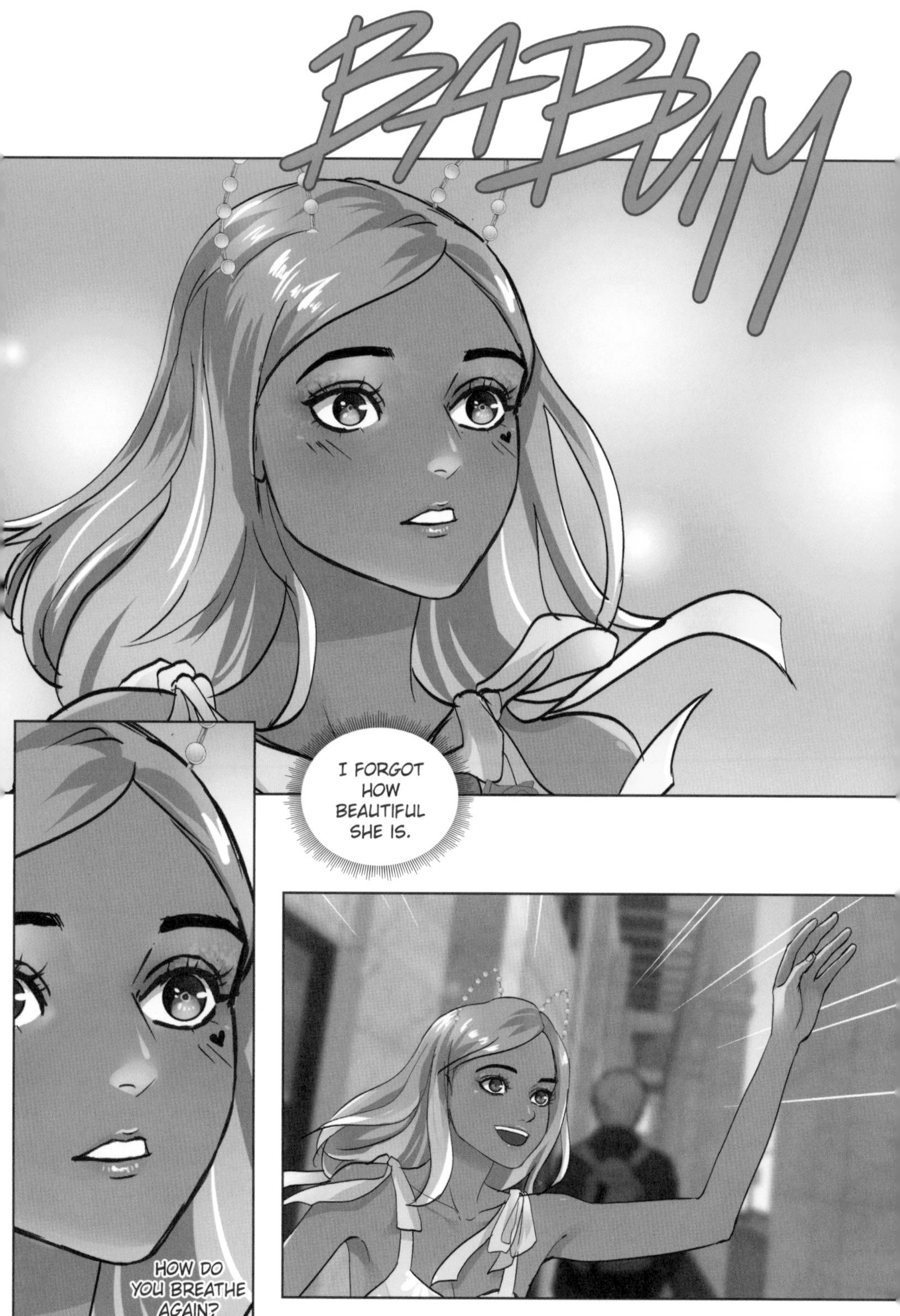
BA-BUM
I FORGOT HOW BEAUTIFUL SHE IS.
HOW DO YOU BREATHE AGAIN?

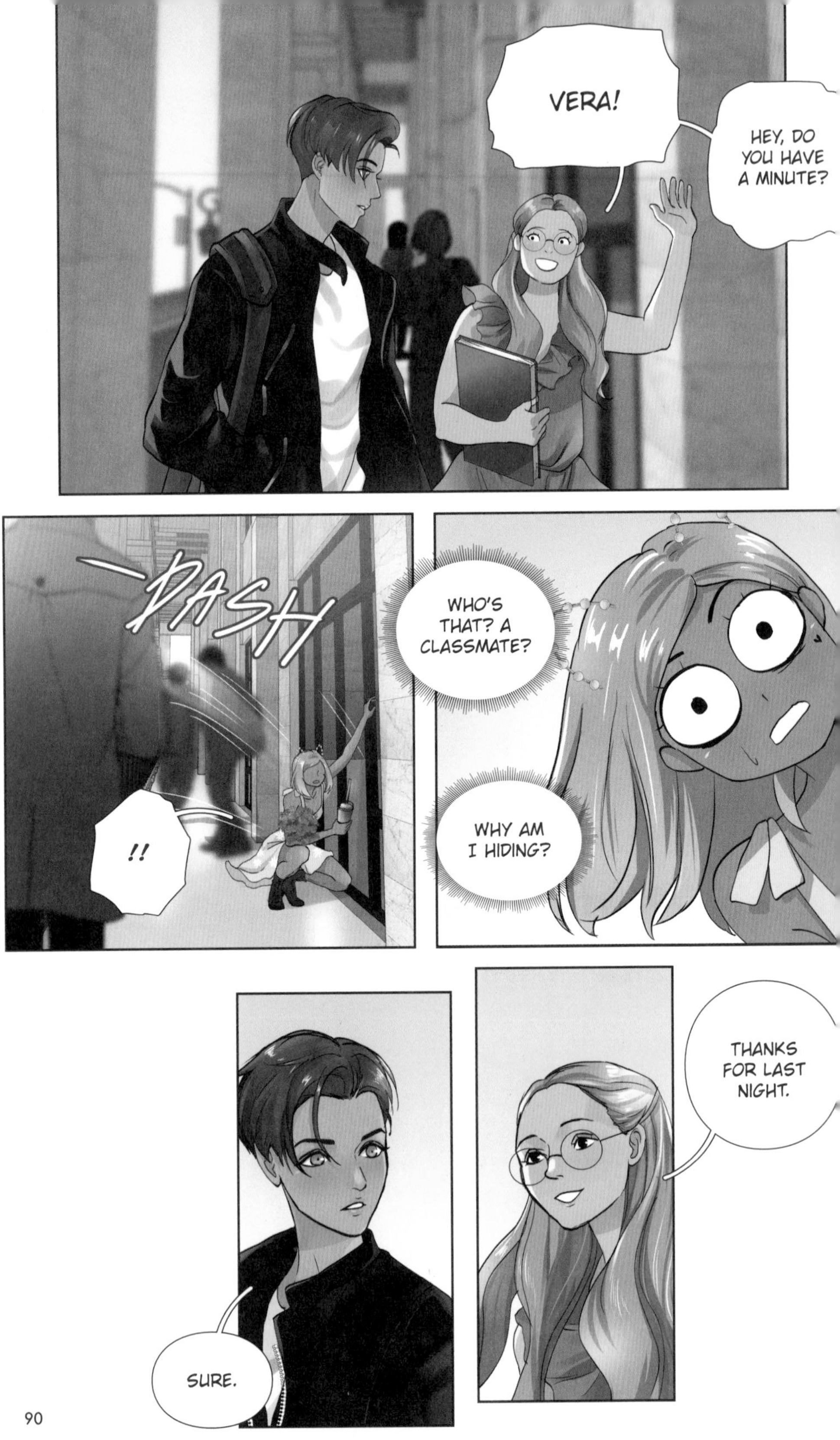
VERA!
HEY, DO YOU HAVE A MINUTE?
DASH
!!
WHO'S THAT? A CLASSMATE?
WHY AM I HIDING?
SURE.
THANKS FOR LAST NIGHT.

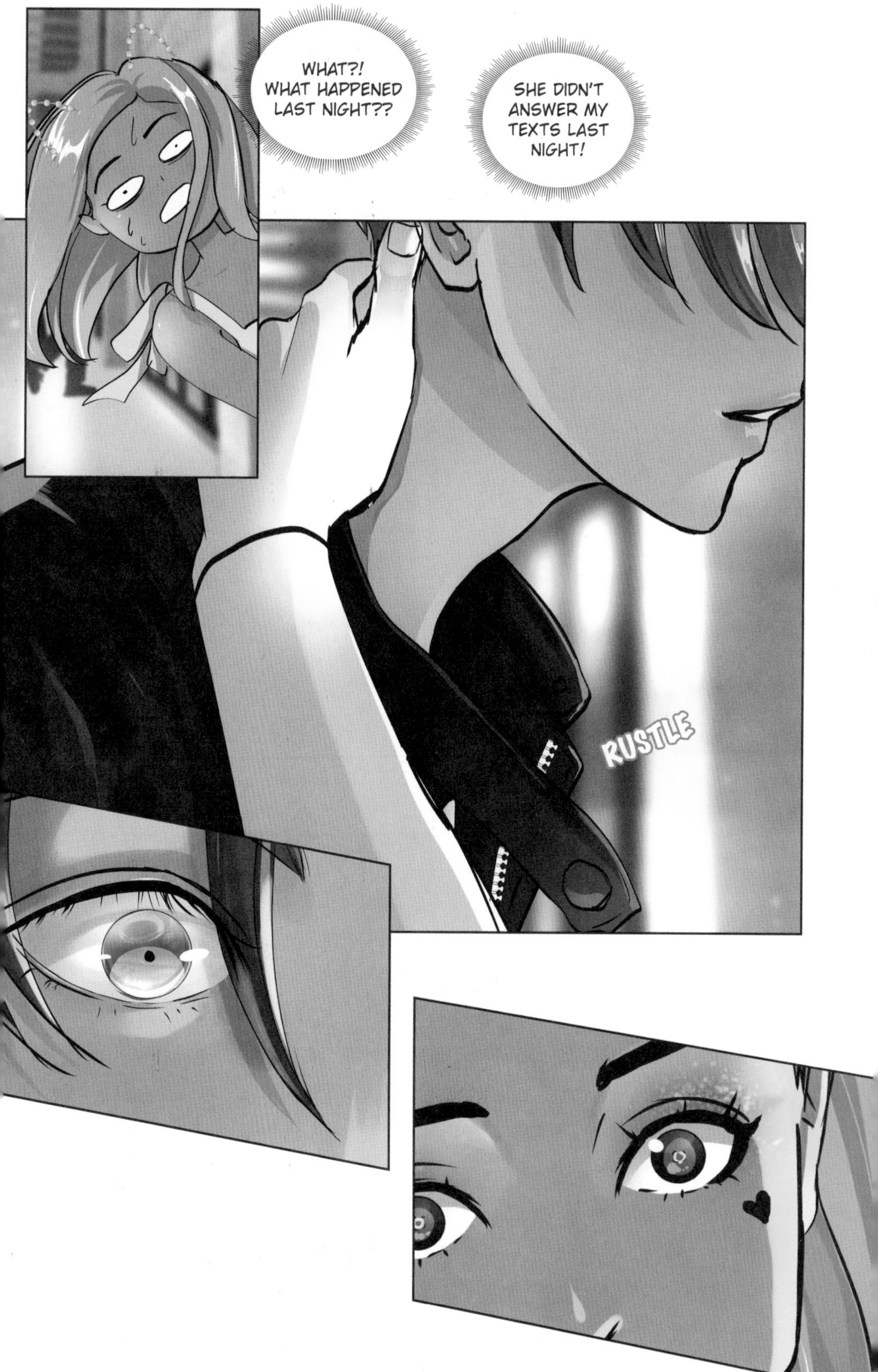
WHAT?! WHAT HAPPENED LAST NIGHT??
SHE DIDN'T ANSWER MY TEXTS LAST NIGHT!
RUSTLE

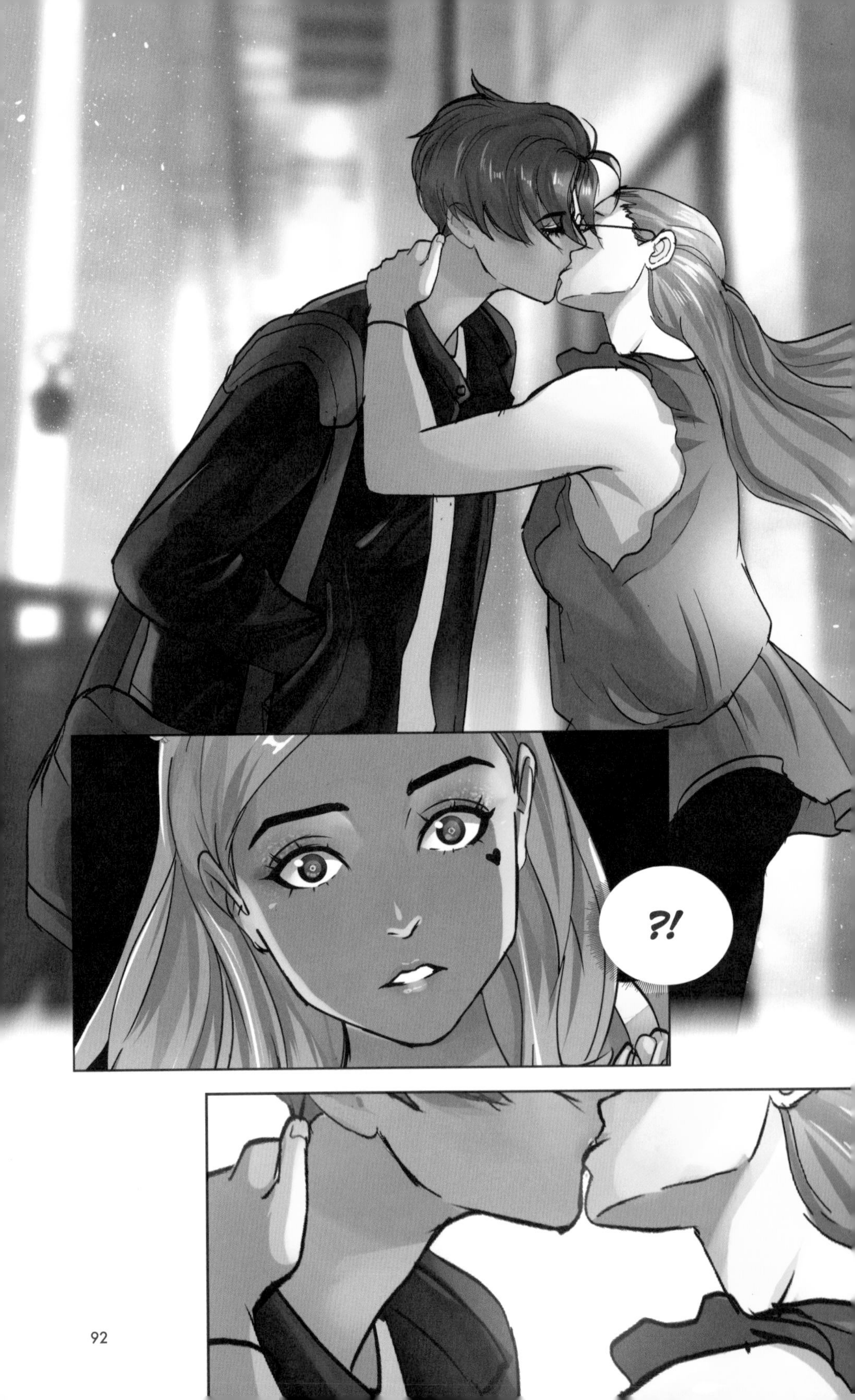
?!

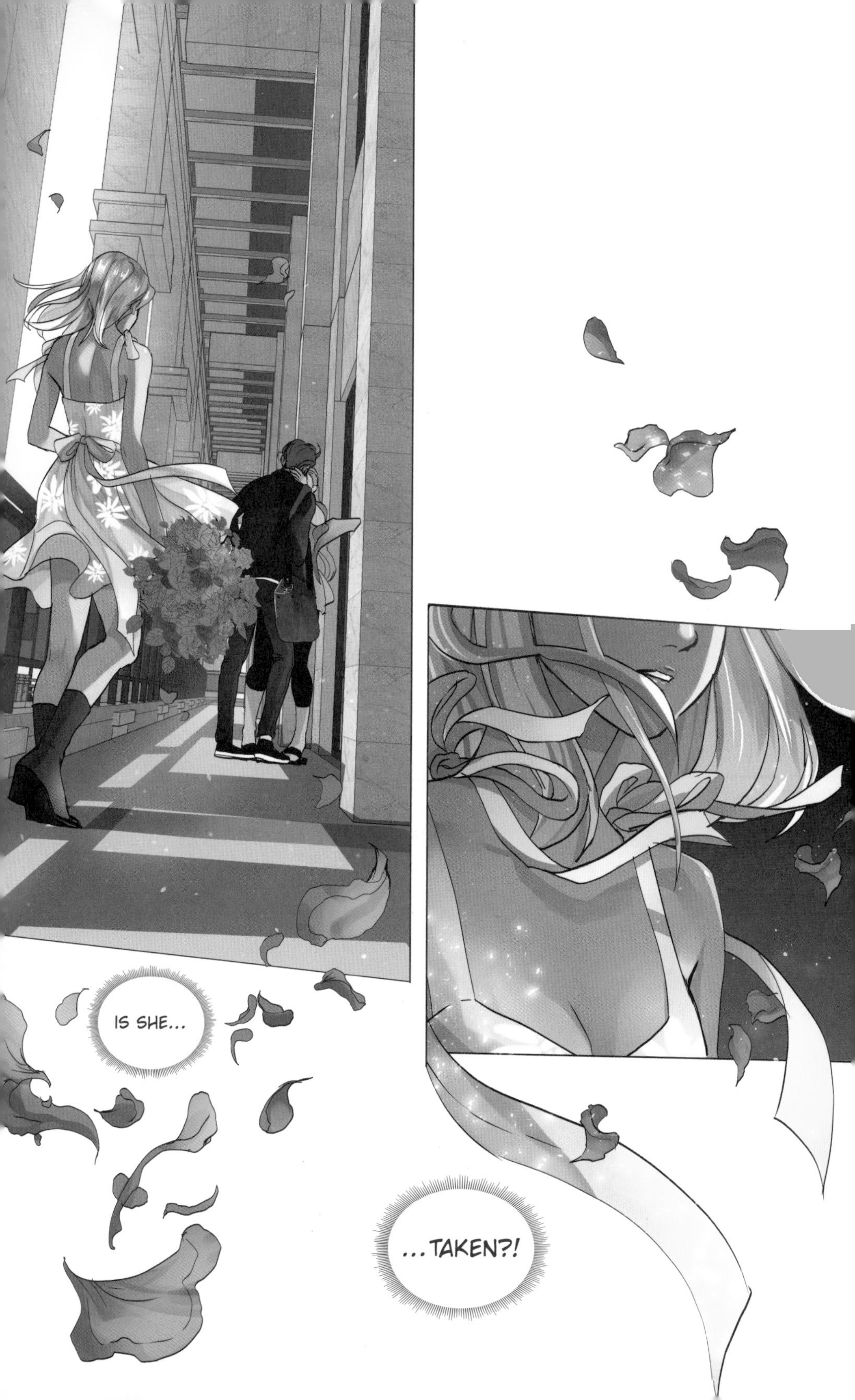
IS SHE...
...TAKEN?!

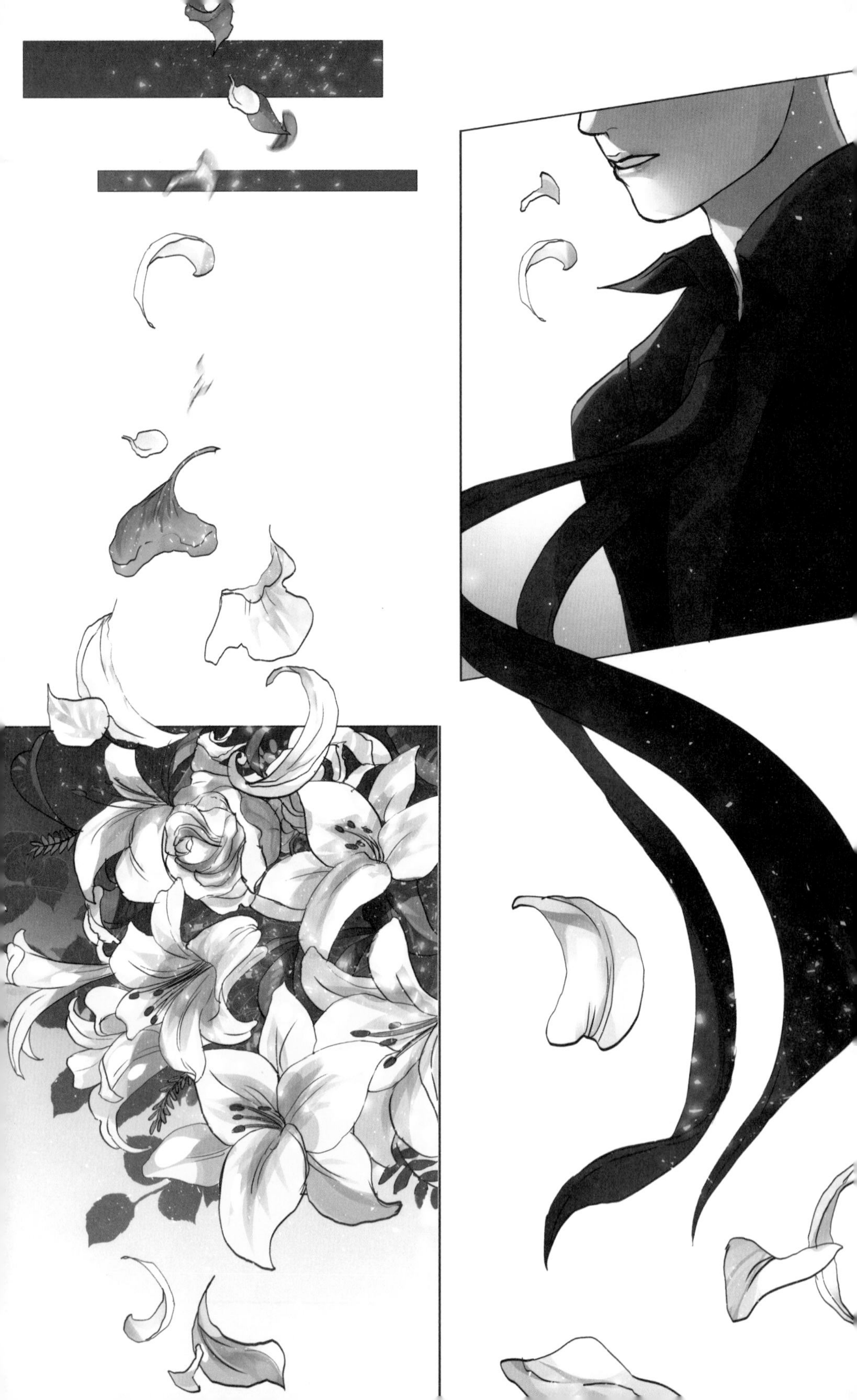

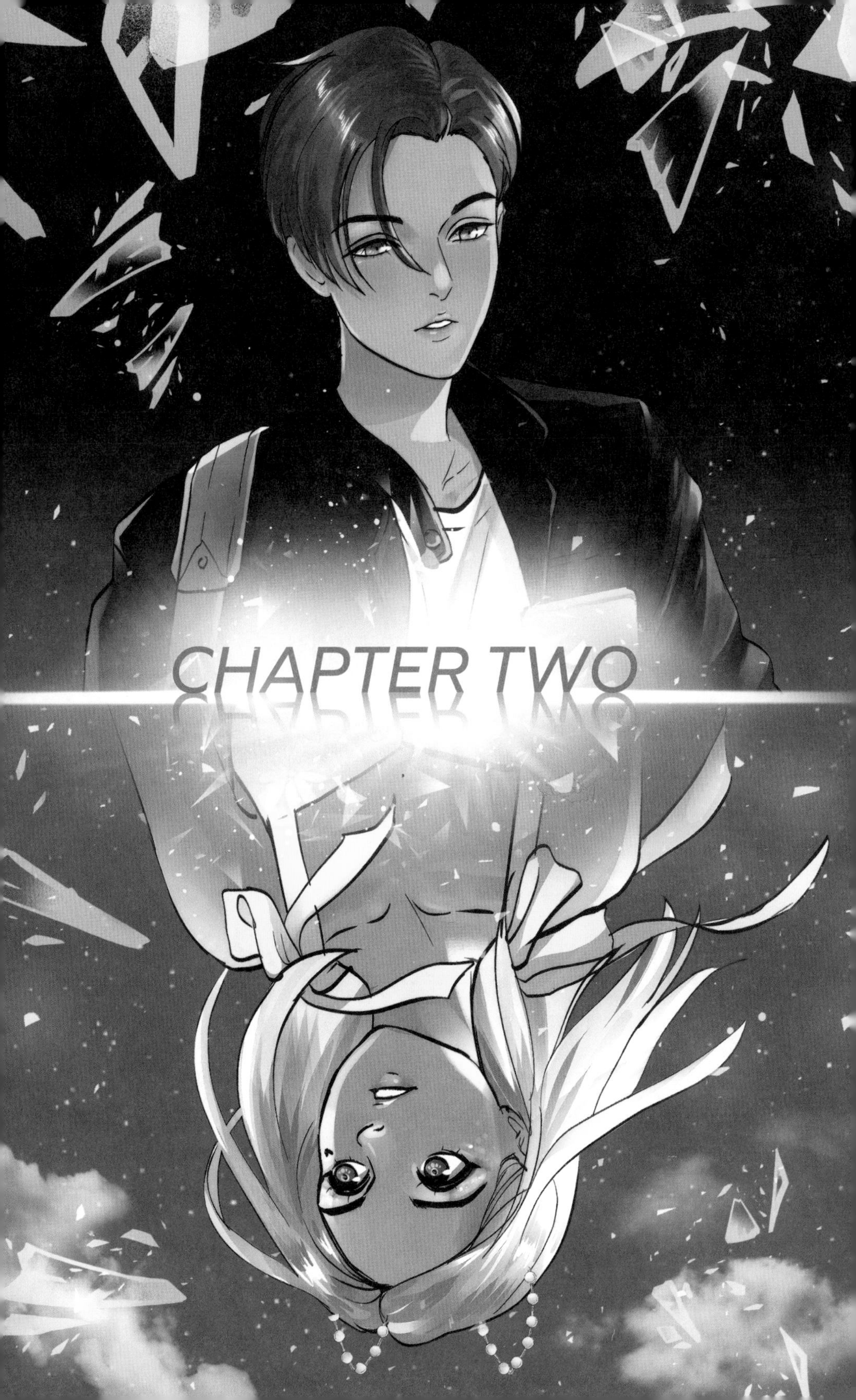
CHAPTER TWO

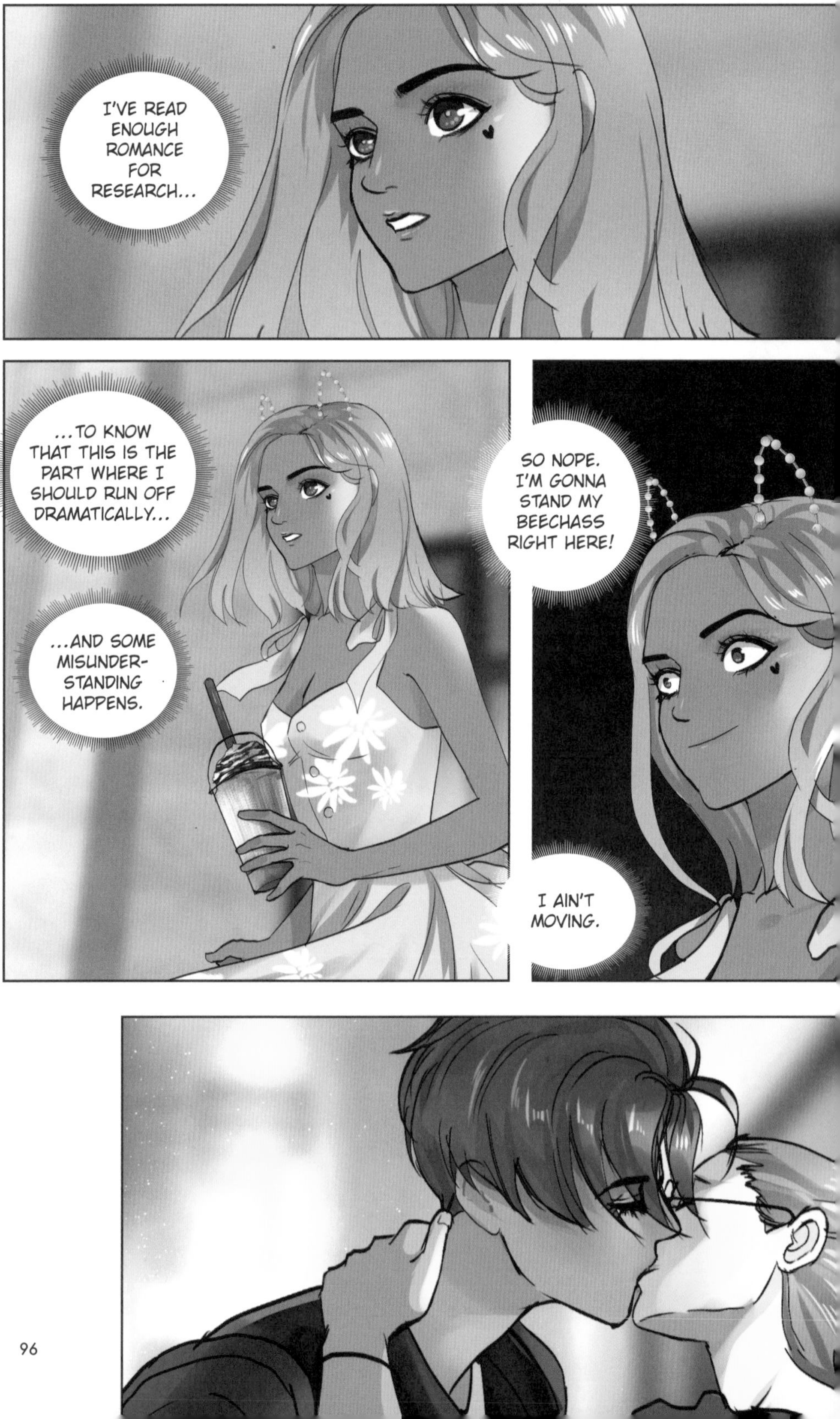
I'VE READ ENOUGH ROMANCE FOR RESEARCH...
...TO KNOW THAT THIS IS THE PART WHERE I SHOULD RUN OFF DRAMATICALLY...
...AND SOME MISUNDER-STANDING HAPPENS.
SO NOPE. I'M GONNA STAND MY BEECHASS RIGHT HERE!
I AIN'T MOVING.

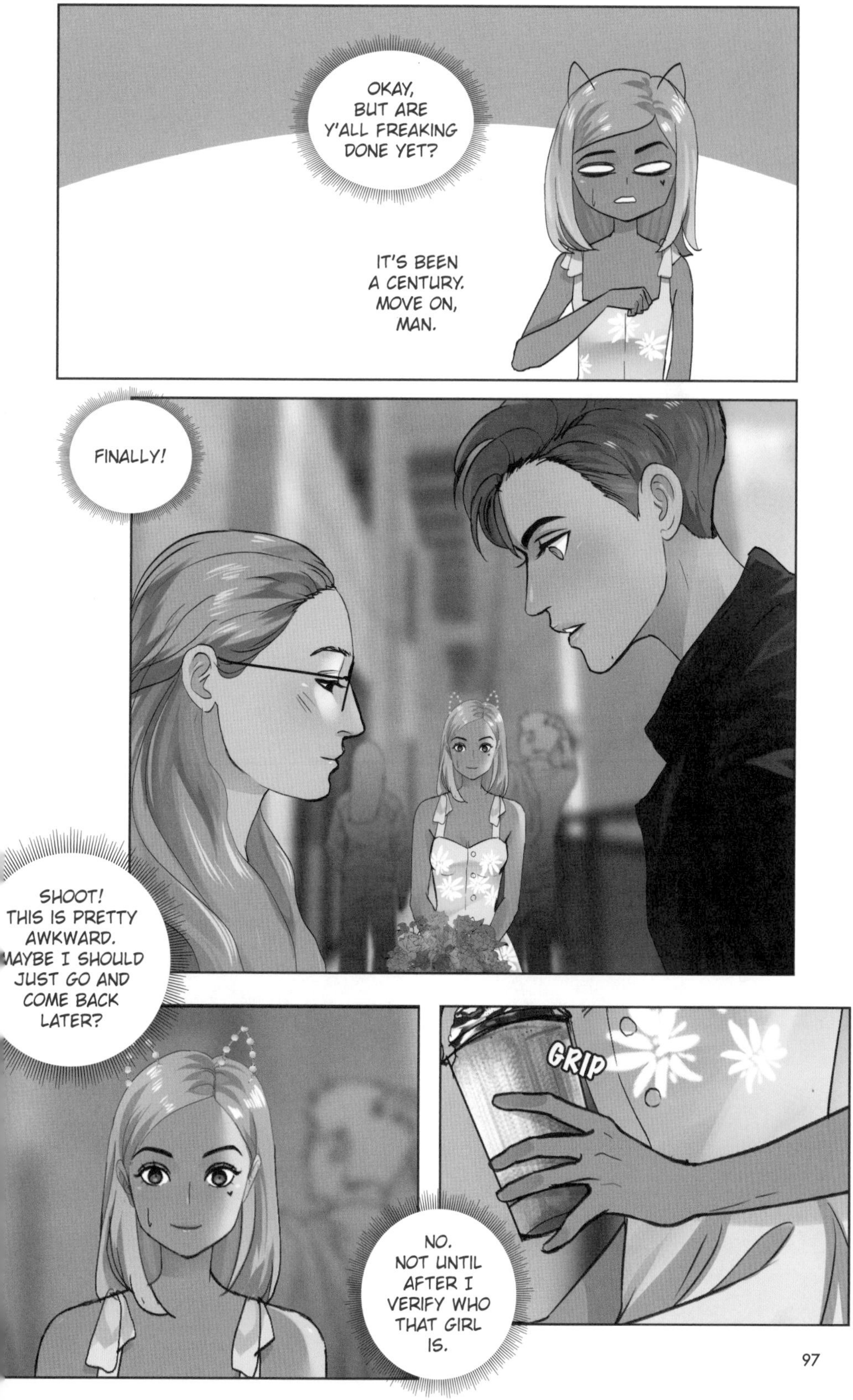
OKAY, BUT ARE Y'ALL FREAKING DONE YET?
IT'S BEEN A CENTURY. MOVE ON, MAN.
FINALLY!
SHOOT! THIS IS PRETTY AWKWARD. MAYBE I SHOULD JUST GO AND COME BACK LATER?
GRIP
NO. NOT UNTIL AFTER I VERIFY WHO THAT GIRL IS.

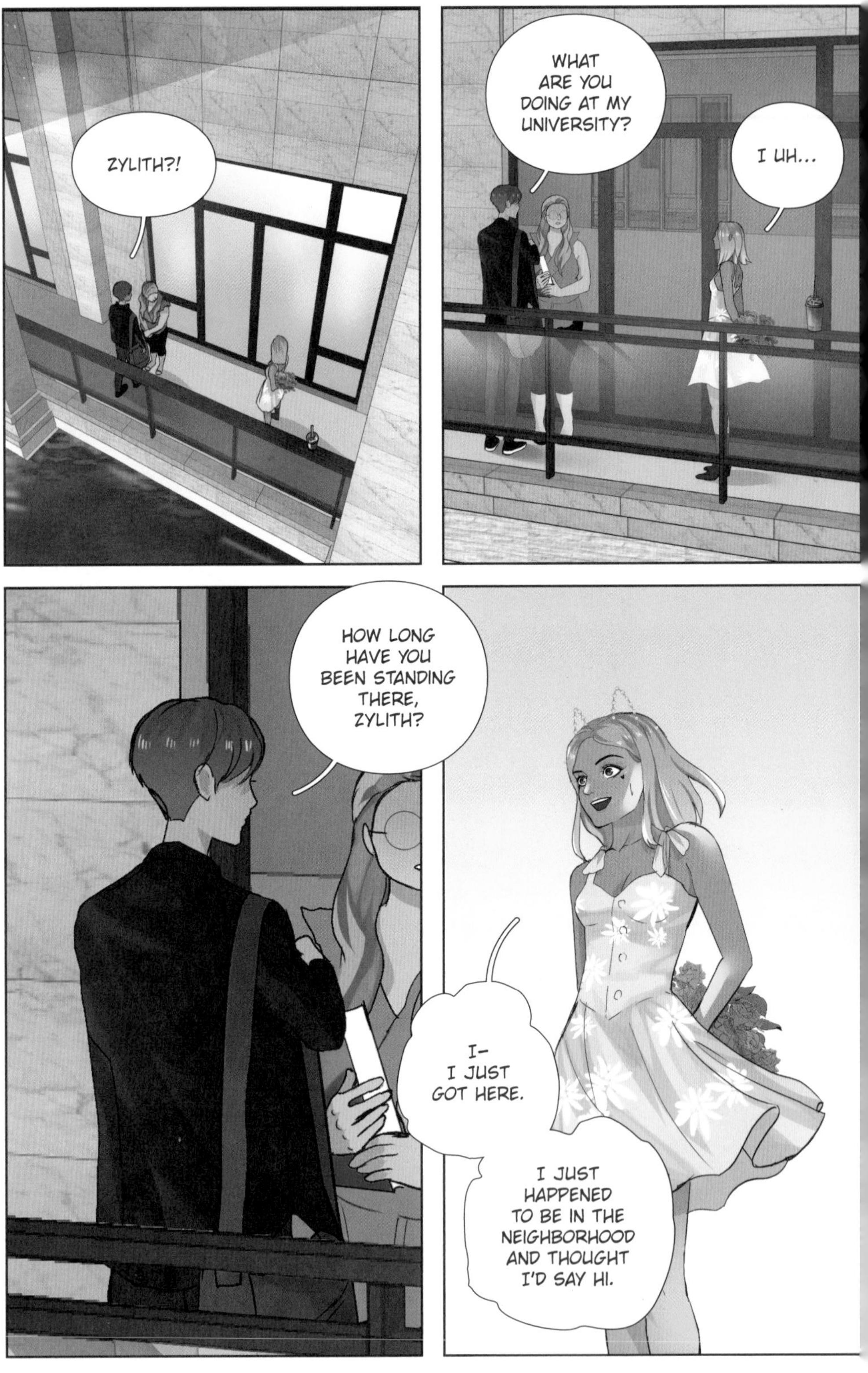
ZYLITH?!
WHAT ARE YOU DOING AT MY UNIVERSITY?
I UH...
HOW LONG HAVE YOU BEEN STANDING THERE, ZYLITH?
I– I JUST GOT HERE.
I JUST HAPPENED TO BE IN THE NEIGHBORHOOD AND THOUGHT I'D SAY HI.

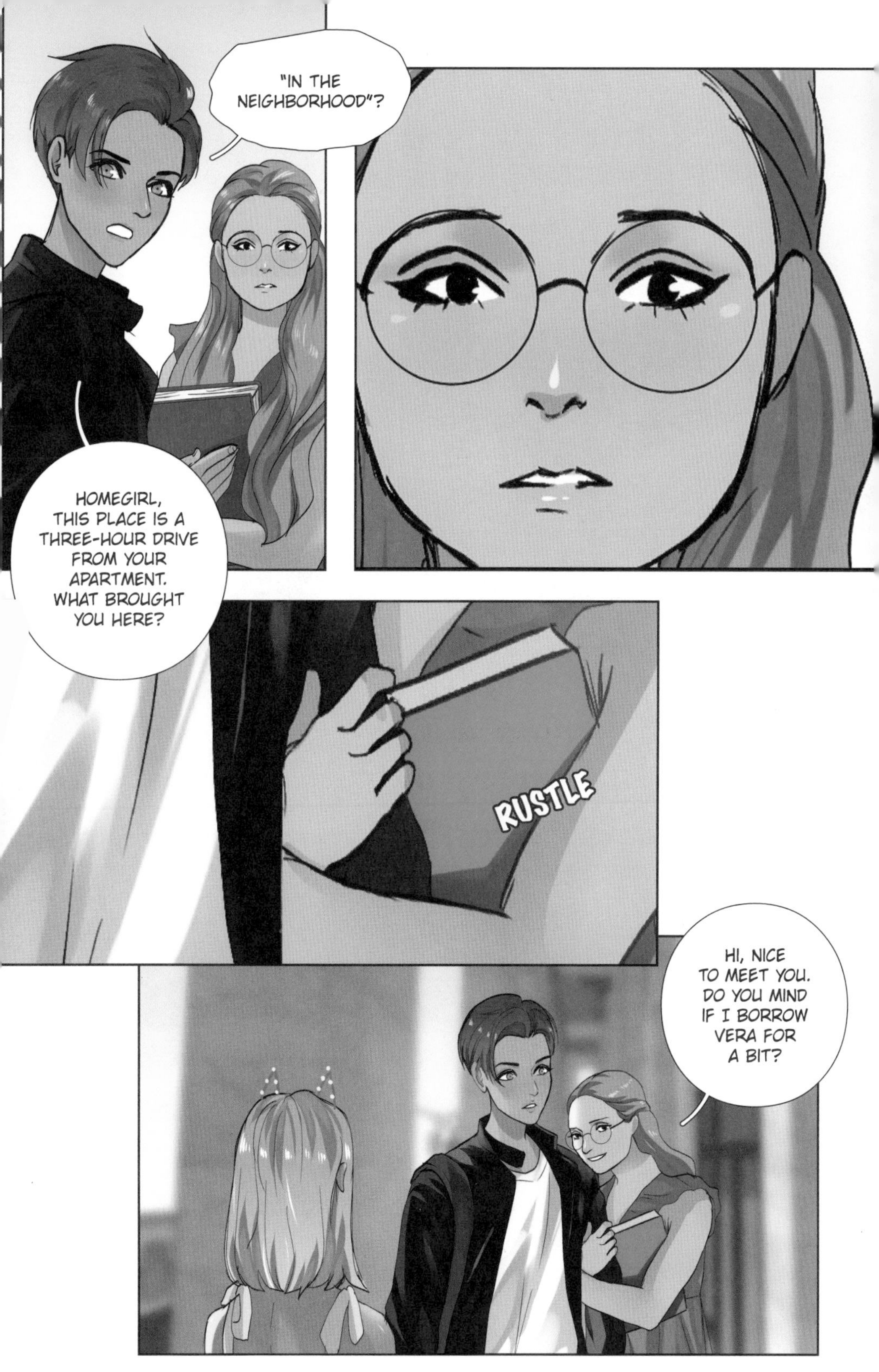
"IN THE NEIGHBORHOOD"?
HOMEGIRL, THIS PLACE IS A THREE-HOUR DRIVE FROM YOUR APARTMENT. WHAT BROUGHT YOU HERE?
RUSTLE
HI, NICE TO MEET YOU. DO YOU MIND IF I BORROW VERA FOR A BIT?

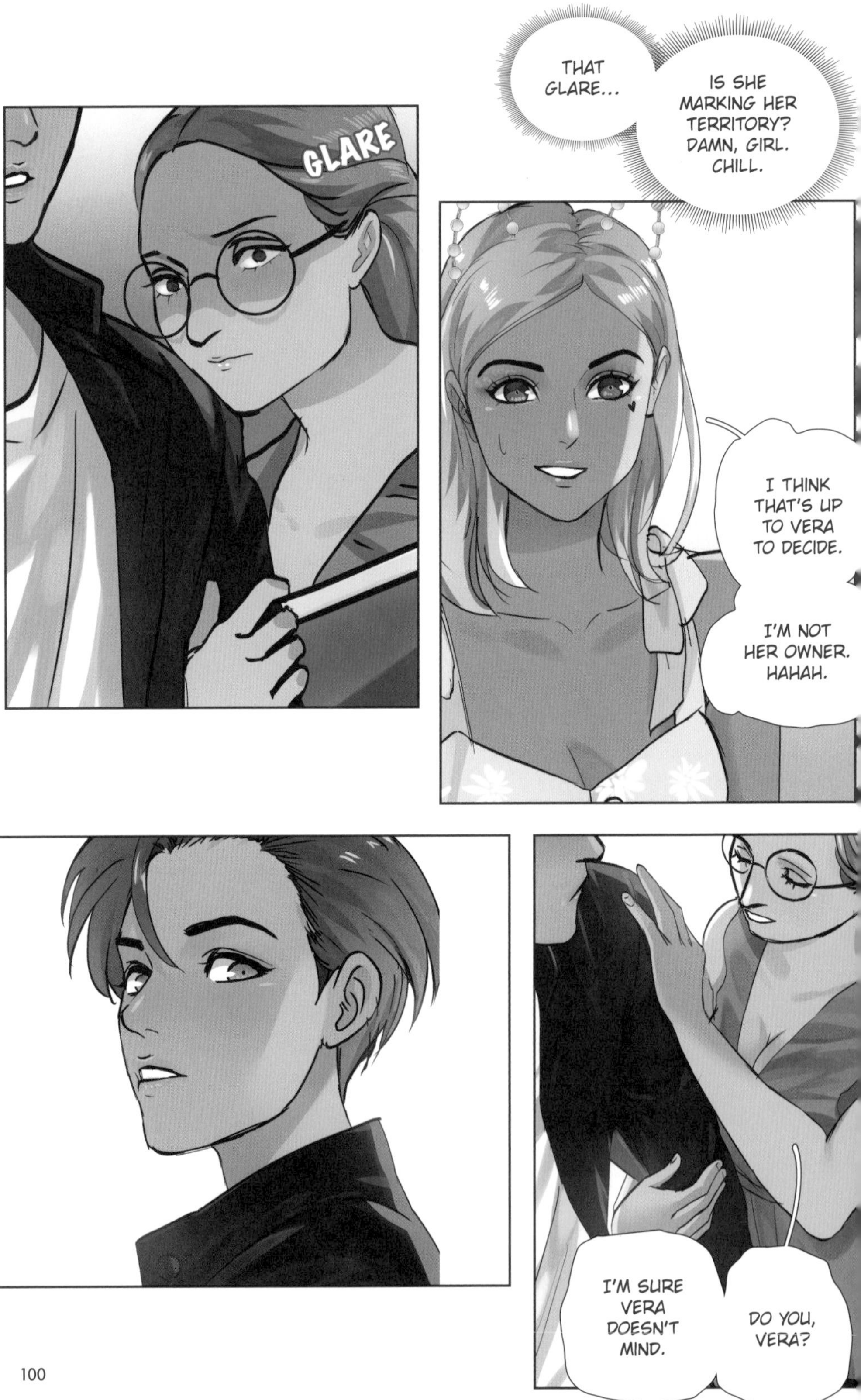
GLARE
THAT GLARE...
IS SHE MARKING HER TERRITORY? DAMN, GIRL. CHILL.
I THINK THAT'S UP TO VERA TO DECIDE.
I'M NOT HER OWNER. HAHAH.
I'M SURE VERA DOESN'T MIND.
DO YOU, VERA?

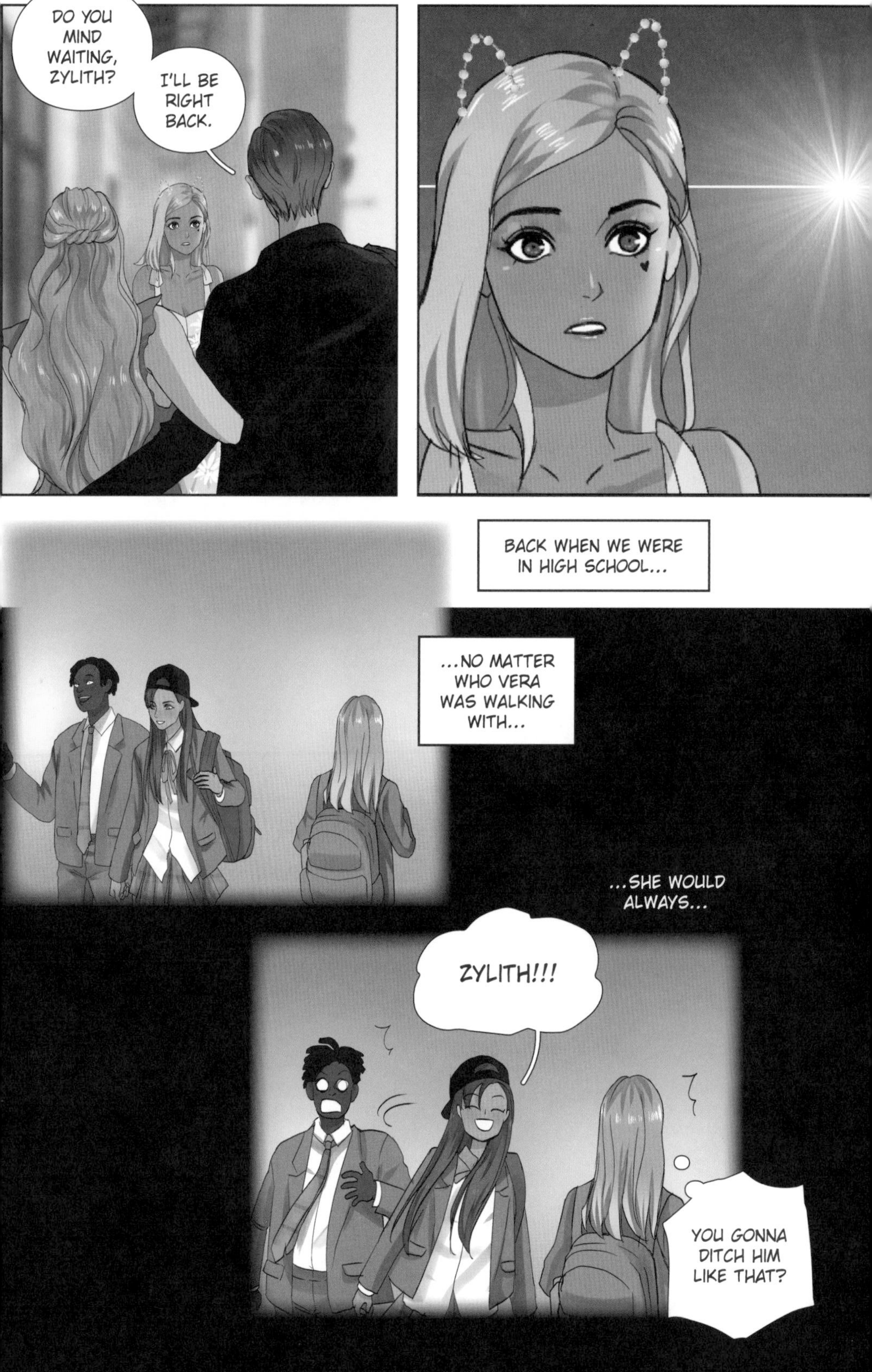
DO YOU MIND WAITING, ZYLITH?
I'LL BE RIGHT BACK.
BACK WHEN WE WERE IN HIGH SCHOOL...
...NO MATTER WHO VERA WAS WALKING WITH...
...SHE WOULD ALWAYS...
ZYLITH!!!
YOU GONNA DITCH HIM LIKE THAT?

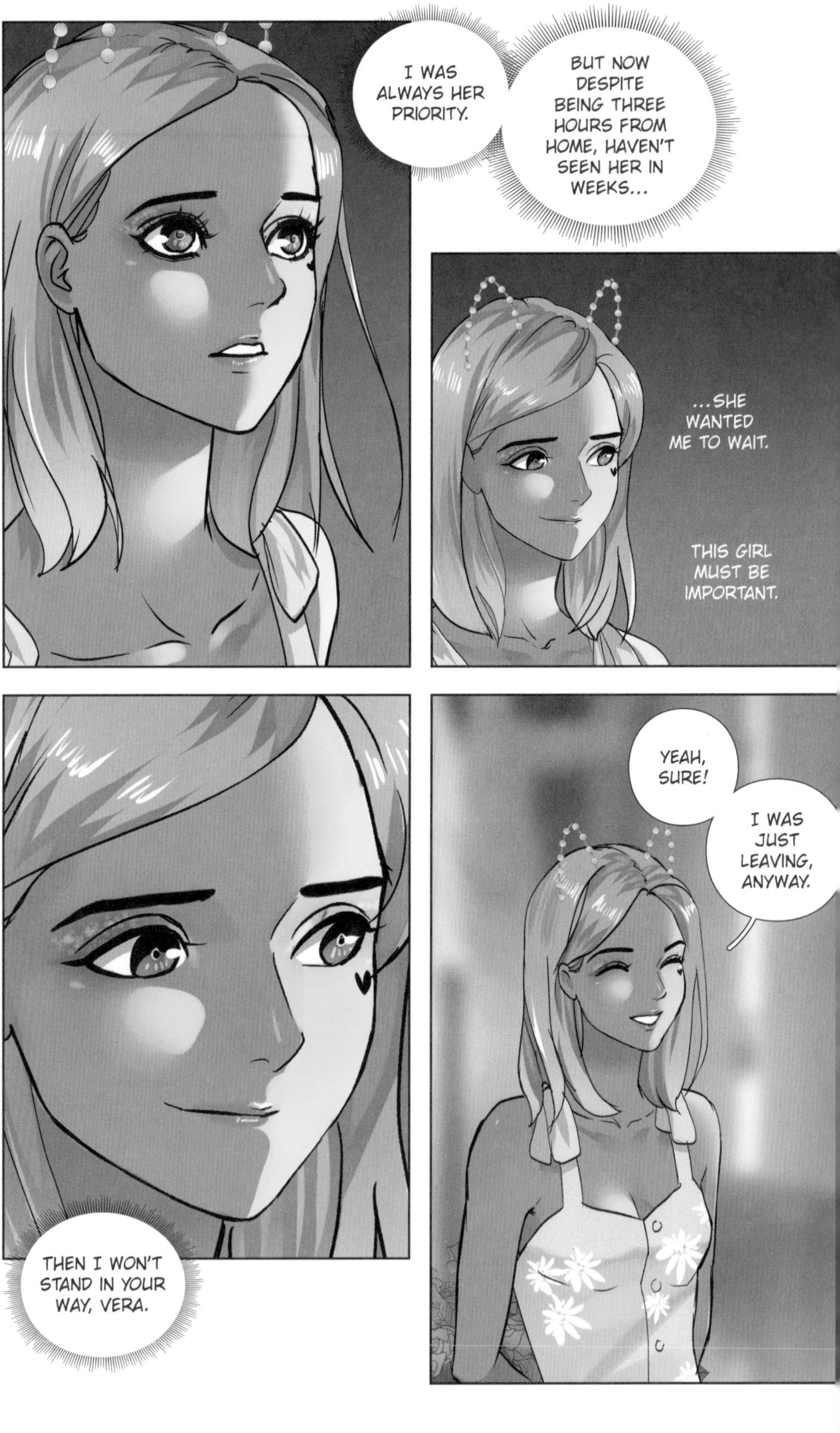
I WAS ALWAYS HER PRIORITY.
BUT NOW DESPITE BEING THREE HOURS FROM HOME, HAVEN'T SEEN HER IN WEEKS...
...SHE WANTED ME TO WAIT.
THIS GIRL MUST BE IMPORTANT.
THEN I WON'T STAND IN YOUR WAY, VERA.
YEAH, SURE!
I WAS JUST LEAVING, ANYWAY.

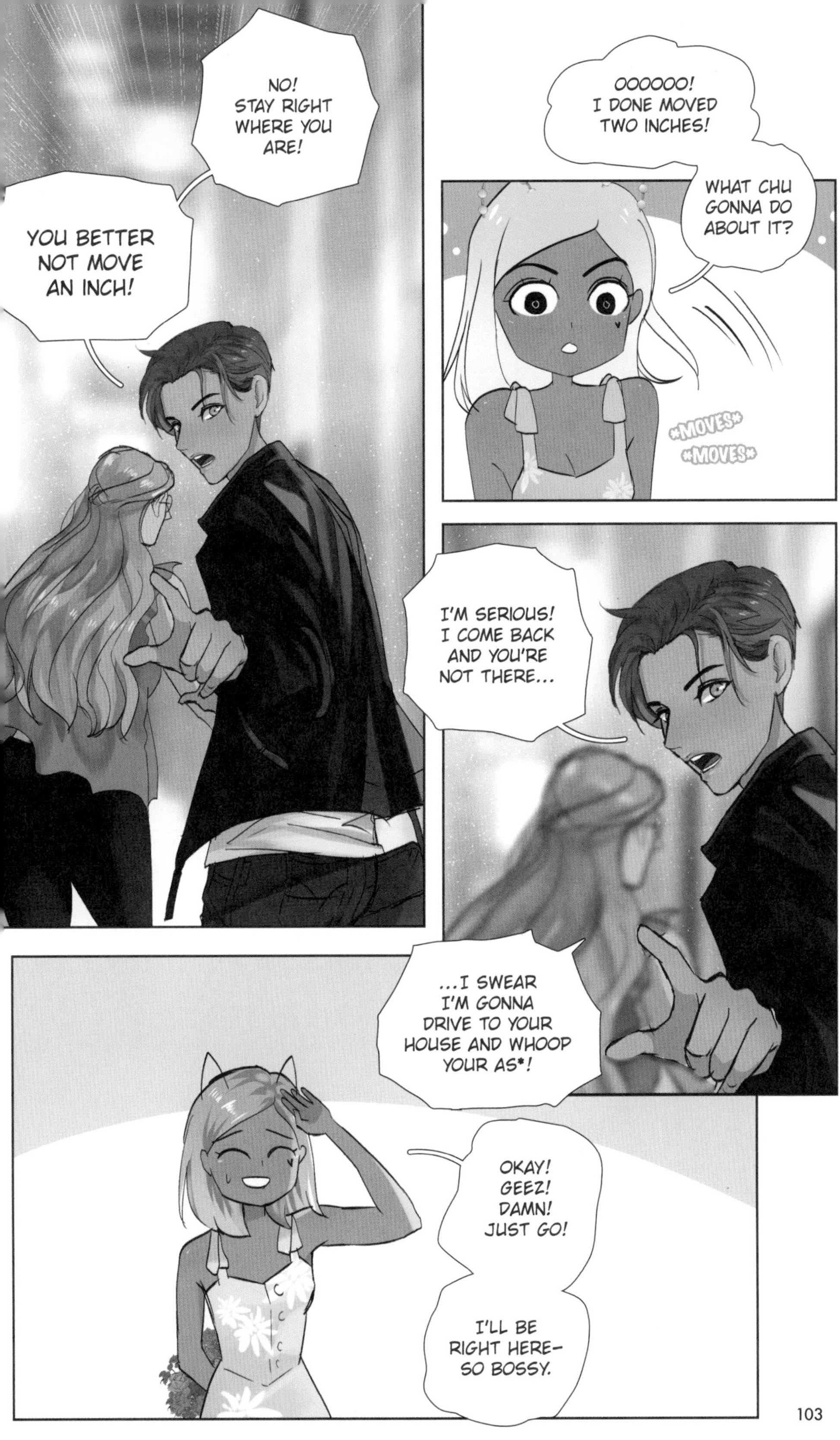
NO! STAY RIGHT WHERE YOU ARE!
YOU BETTER NOT MOVE AN INCH!
OOOOOO! I DONE MOVED TWO INCHES!
WHAT CHU GONNA DO ABOUT IT?
MOVES
MOVES
I'M SERIOUS! I COME BACK AND YOU'RE NOT THERE...
...I SWEAR I'M GONNA DRIVE TO YOUR HOUSE AND WHOOP YOUR AS*!
OKAY! GEEZ! DAMN! JUST GO!
I'LL BE RIGHT HERE- SO BOSSY.

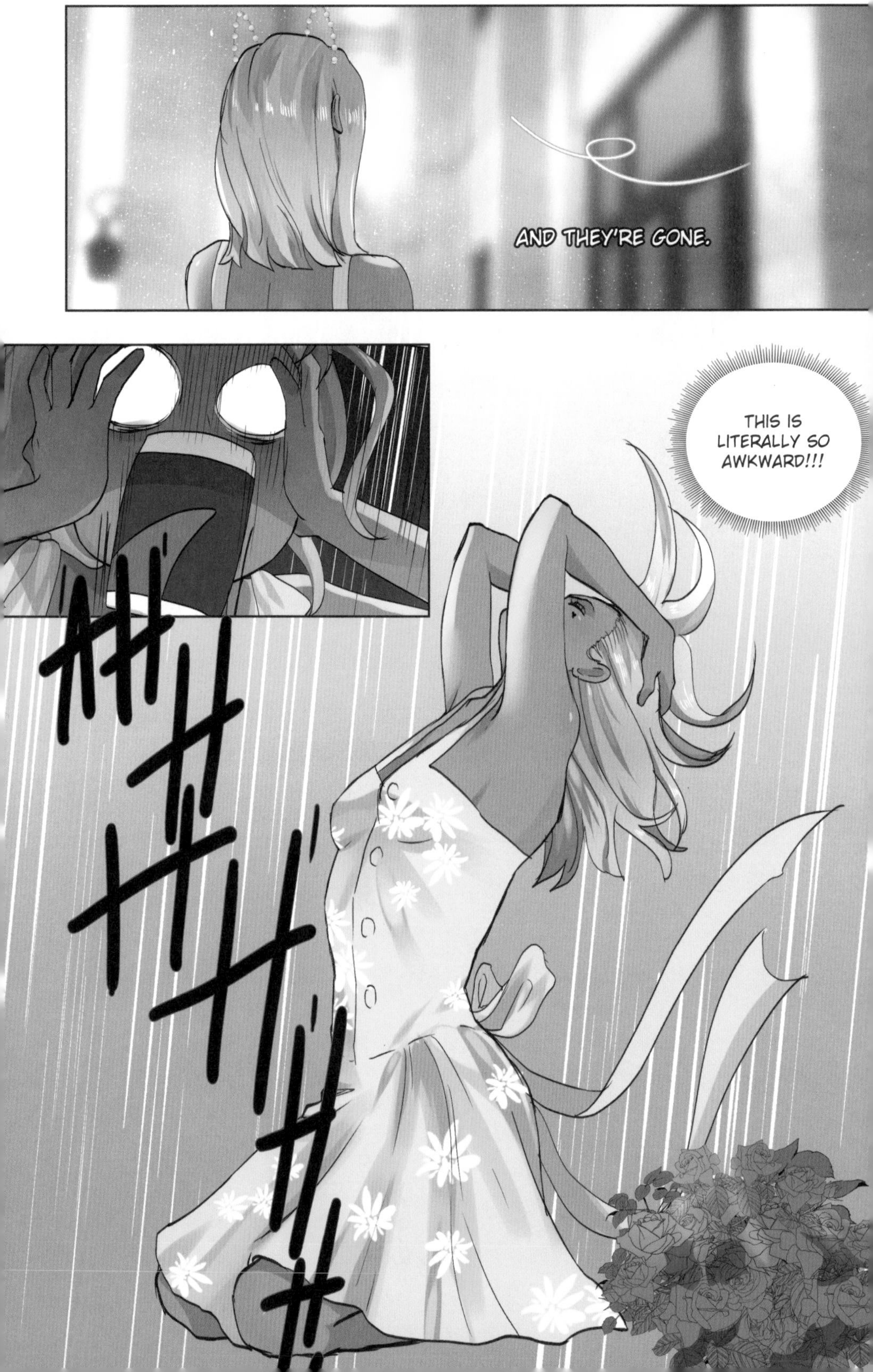
AND THEY'RE GONE.
THIS IS LITERALLY SO AWKWARD!!!

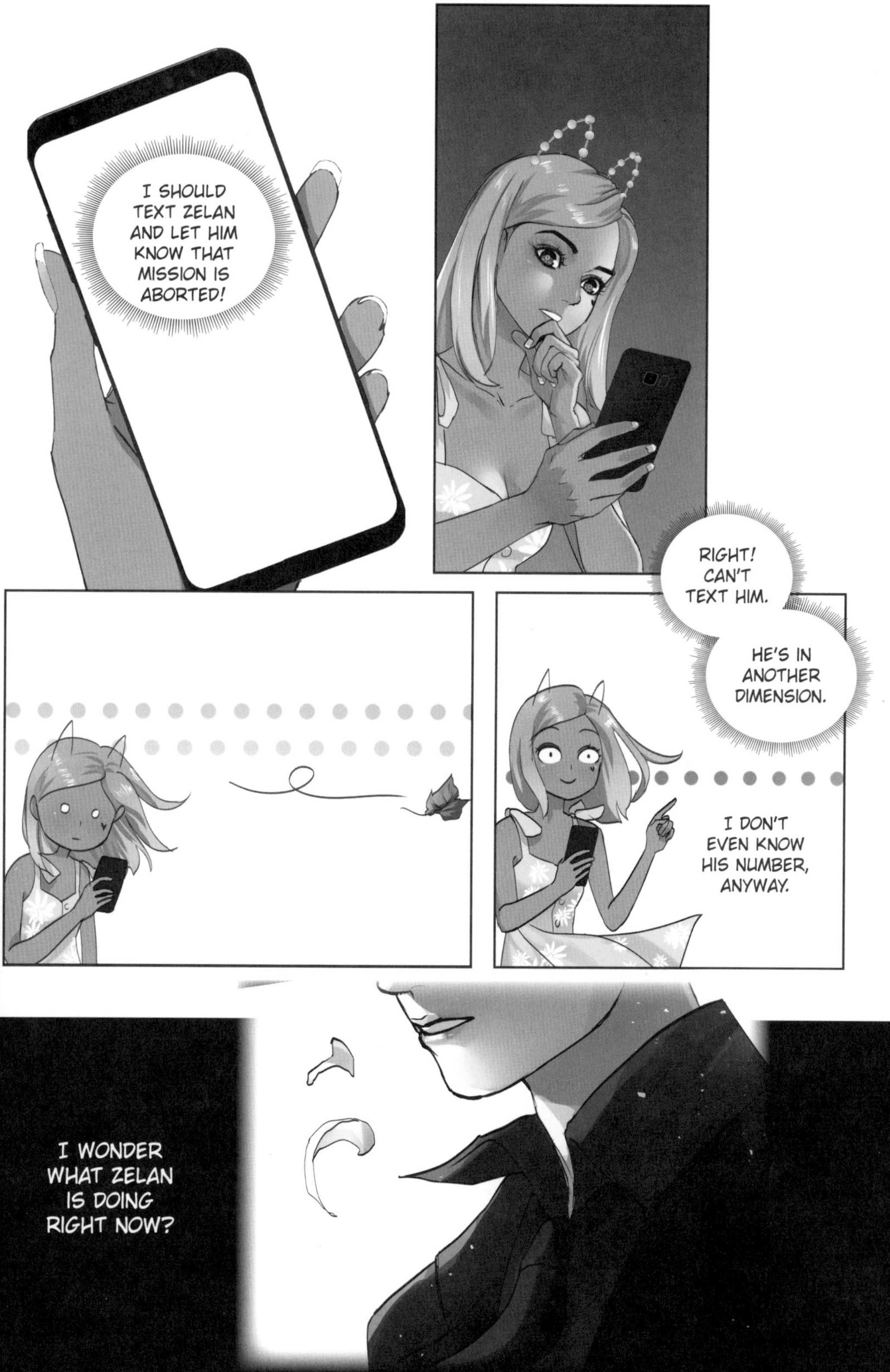
I SHOULD TEXT ZELAN AND LET HIM KNOW THAT MISSION IS ABORTED!
RIGHT! CAN'T TEXT HIM.
HE'S IN ANOTHER DIMENSION.
I DON'T EVEN KNOW HIS NUMBER, ANYWAY.
I WONDER WHAT ZELAN IS DOING RIGHT NOW?

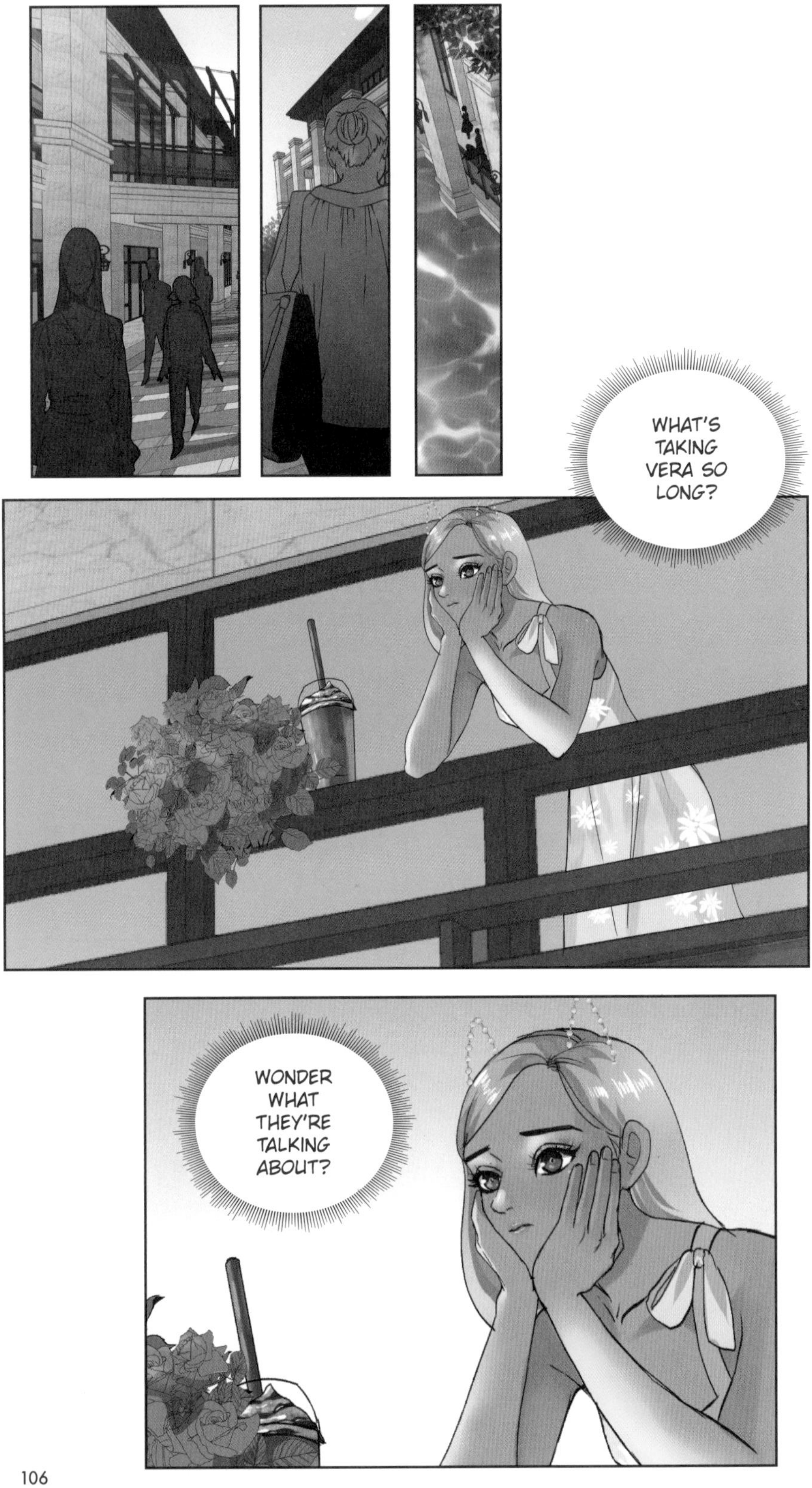
WHAT'S TAKING VERA SO LONG?
WONDER WHAT THEY'RE TALKING ABOUT?

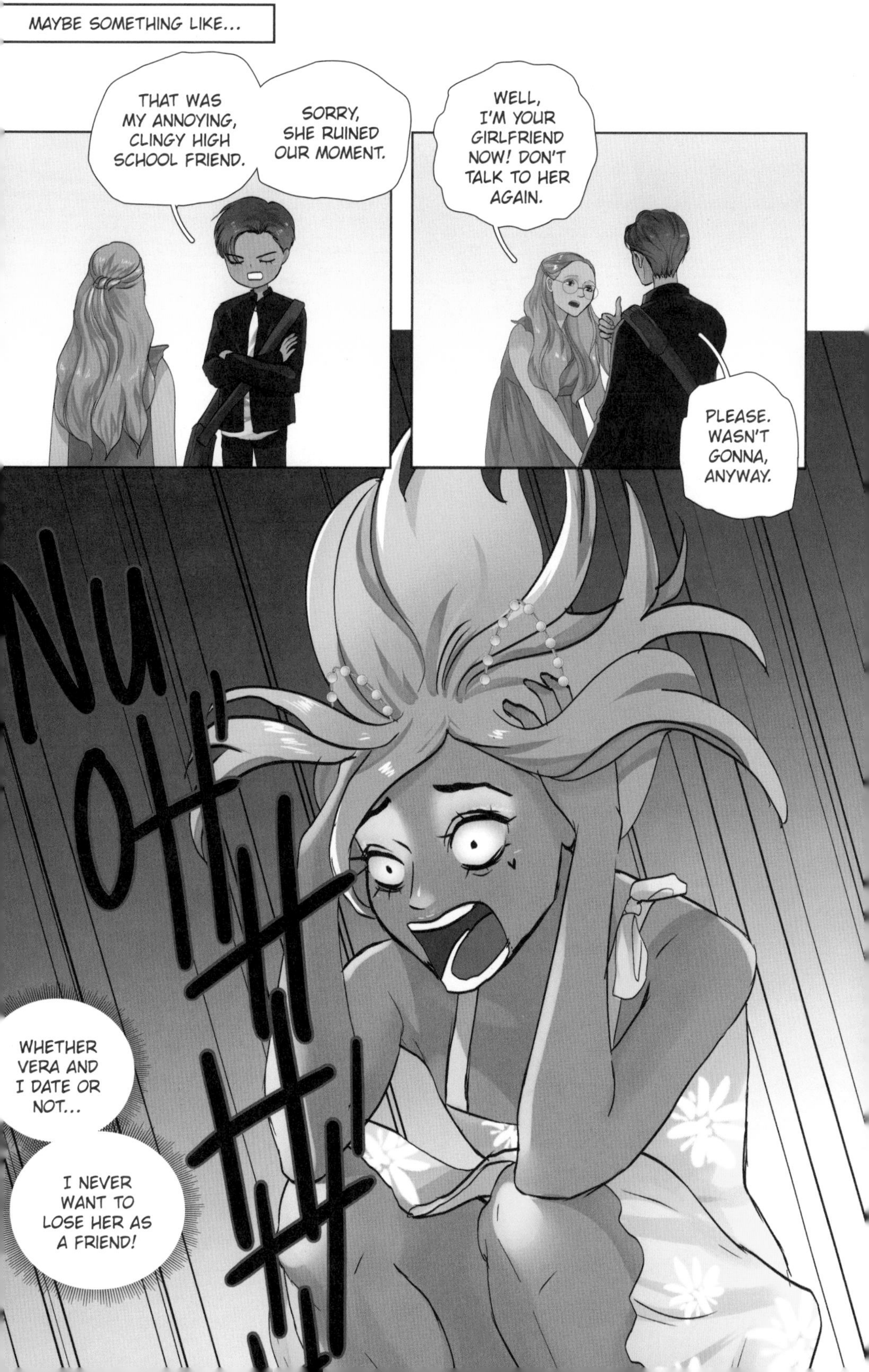
MAYBE SOMETHING LIKE...
THAT WAS MY ANNOYING, CLINGY HIGH SCHOOL FRIEND.
SORRY, SHE RUINED OUR MOMENT.
WELL, I'M YOUR GIRLFRIEND NOW! DON'T TALK TO HER AGAIN.
PLEASE. WASN'T GONNA, ANYWAY.
NUOHHHH!!
WHETHER VERA AND I DATE OR NOT...
I NEVER WANT TO LOSE HER AS A FRIEND!

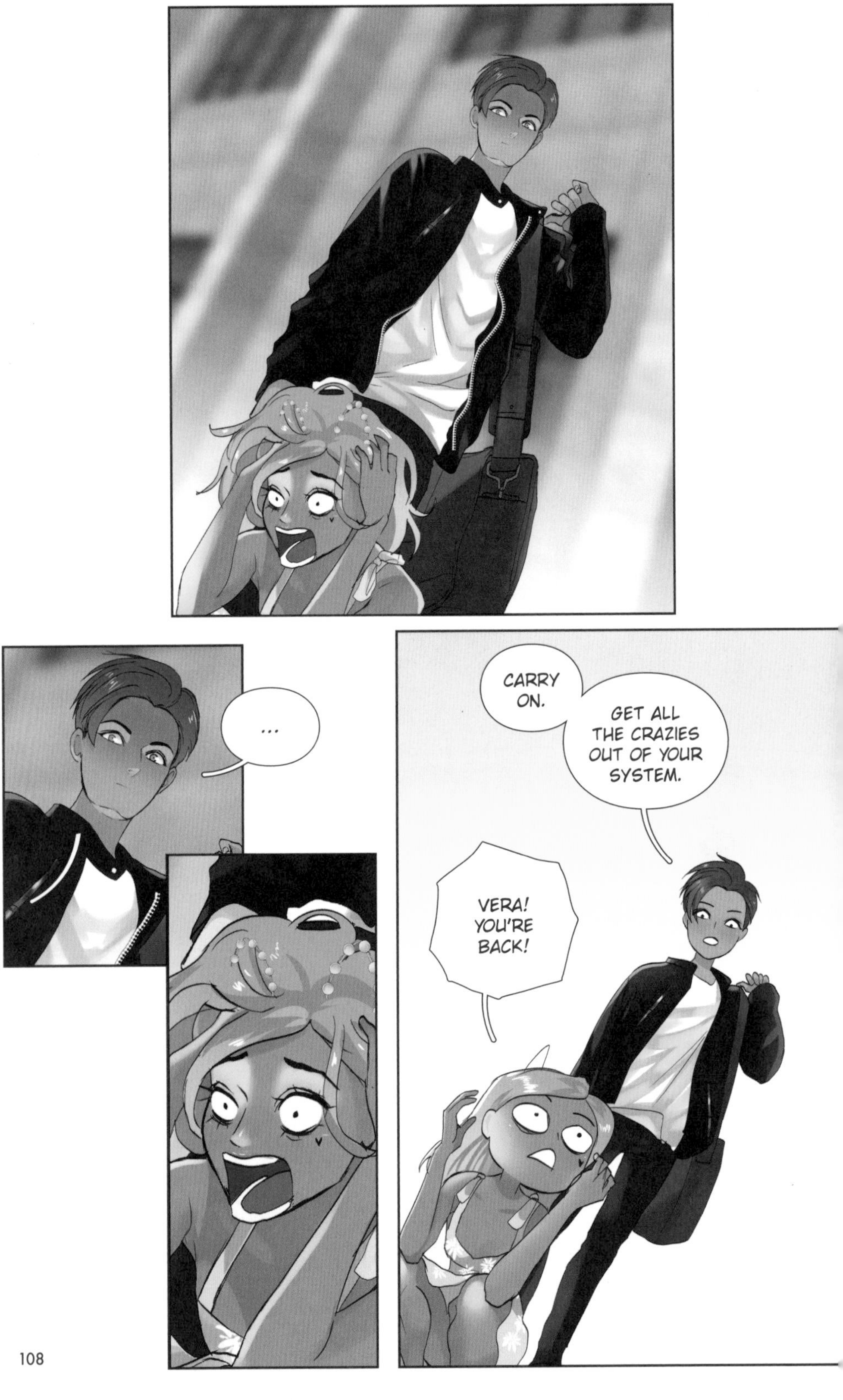
...
CARRY ON.
GET ALL THE CRAZIES OUT OF YOUR SYSTEM.
VERA! YOU'RE BACK!

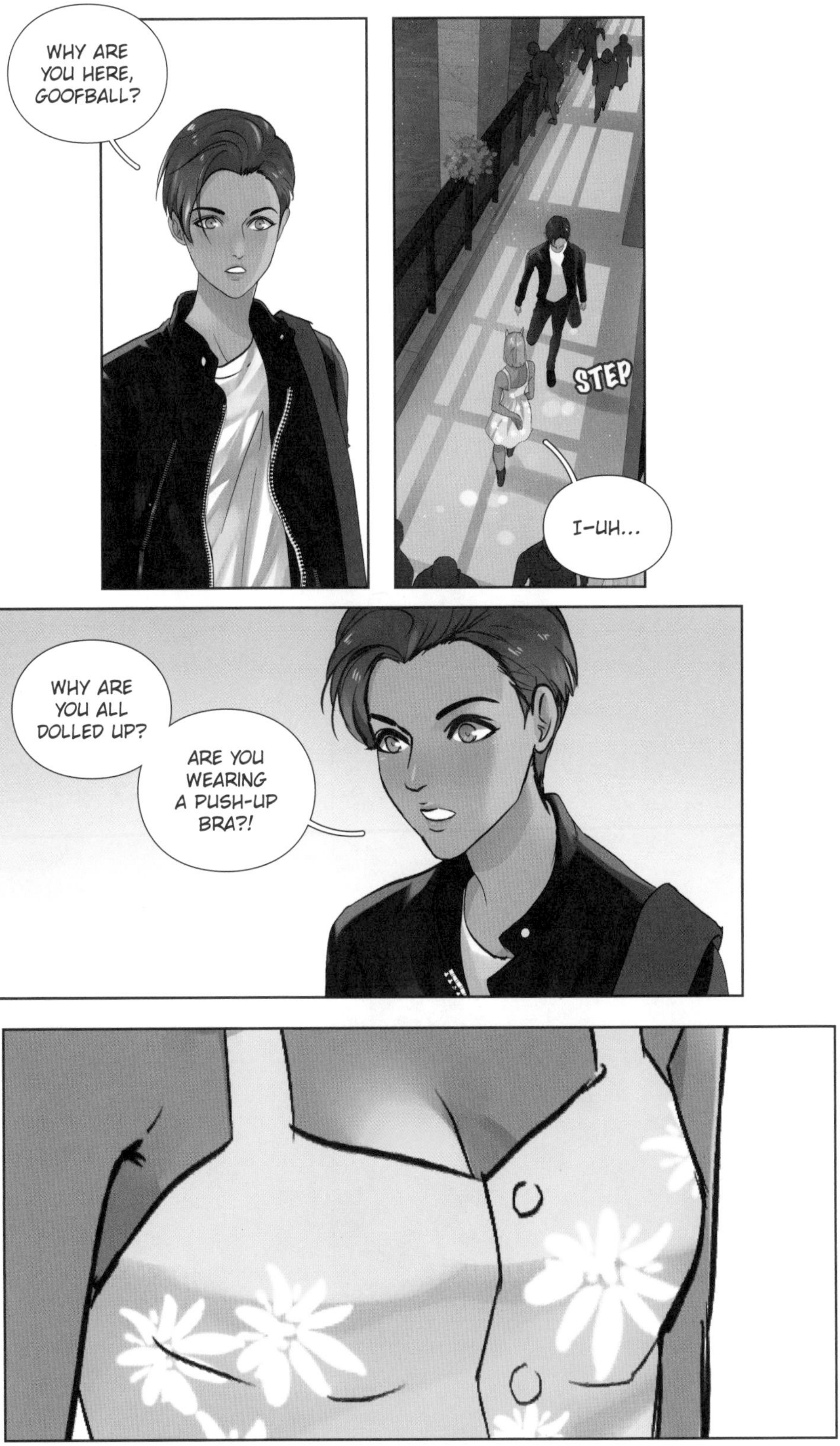
WHY ARE YOU HERE, GOOFBALL?
STEP
I-UH...
WHY ARE YOU ALL DOLLED UP?
ARE YOU WEARING A PUSH-UP BRA?!

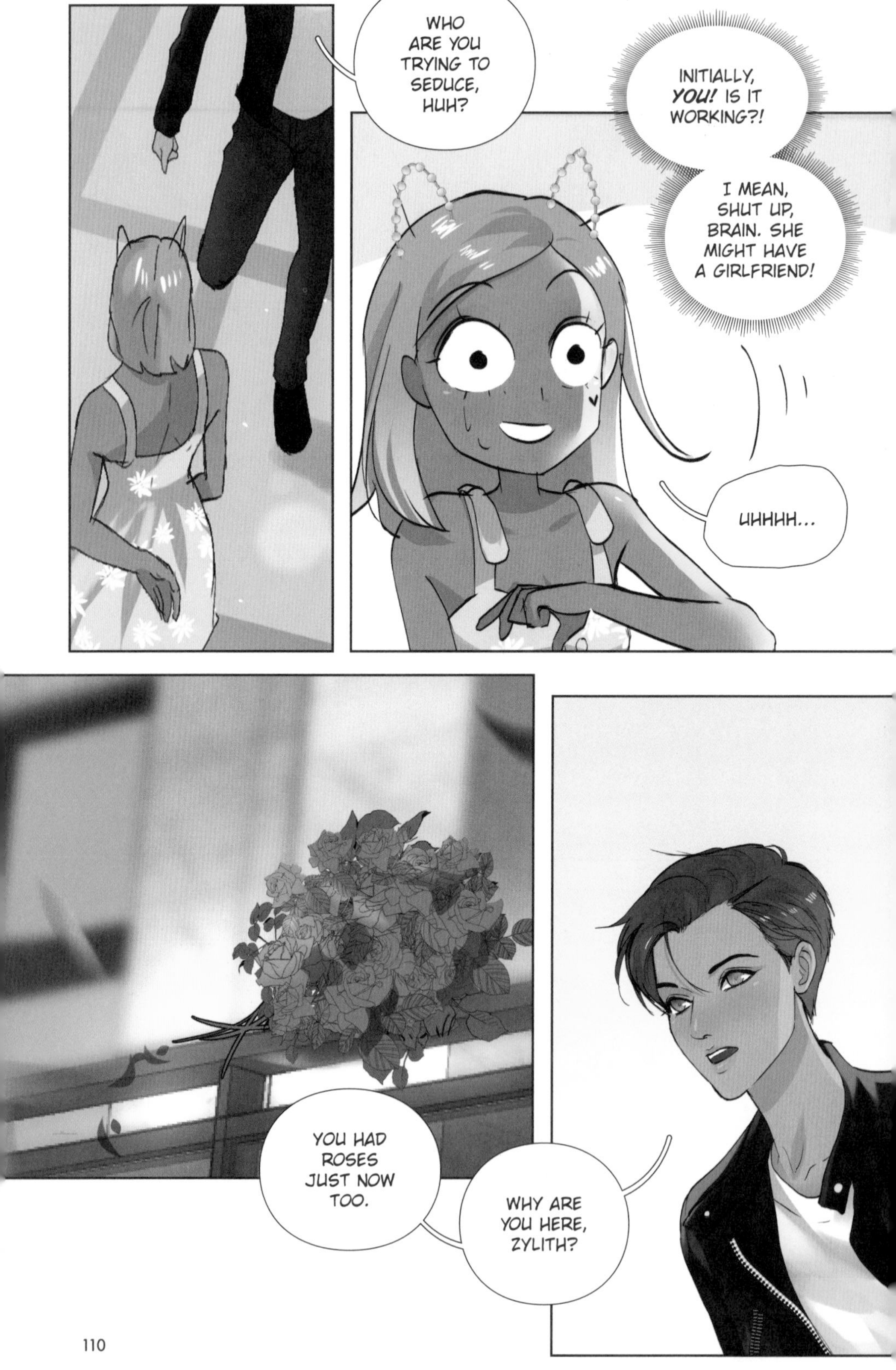
WHO ARE YOU TRYING TO SEDUCE, HUH?
INITIALLY, ***YOU!*** IS IT WORKING?!
I MEAN, SHUT UP, BRAIN. SHE MIGHT HAVE A GIRLFRIEND!
UHHHH...
YOU HAD ROSES JUST NOW TOO.
WHY ARE YOU HERE, ZYLITH?

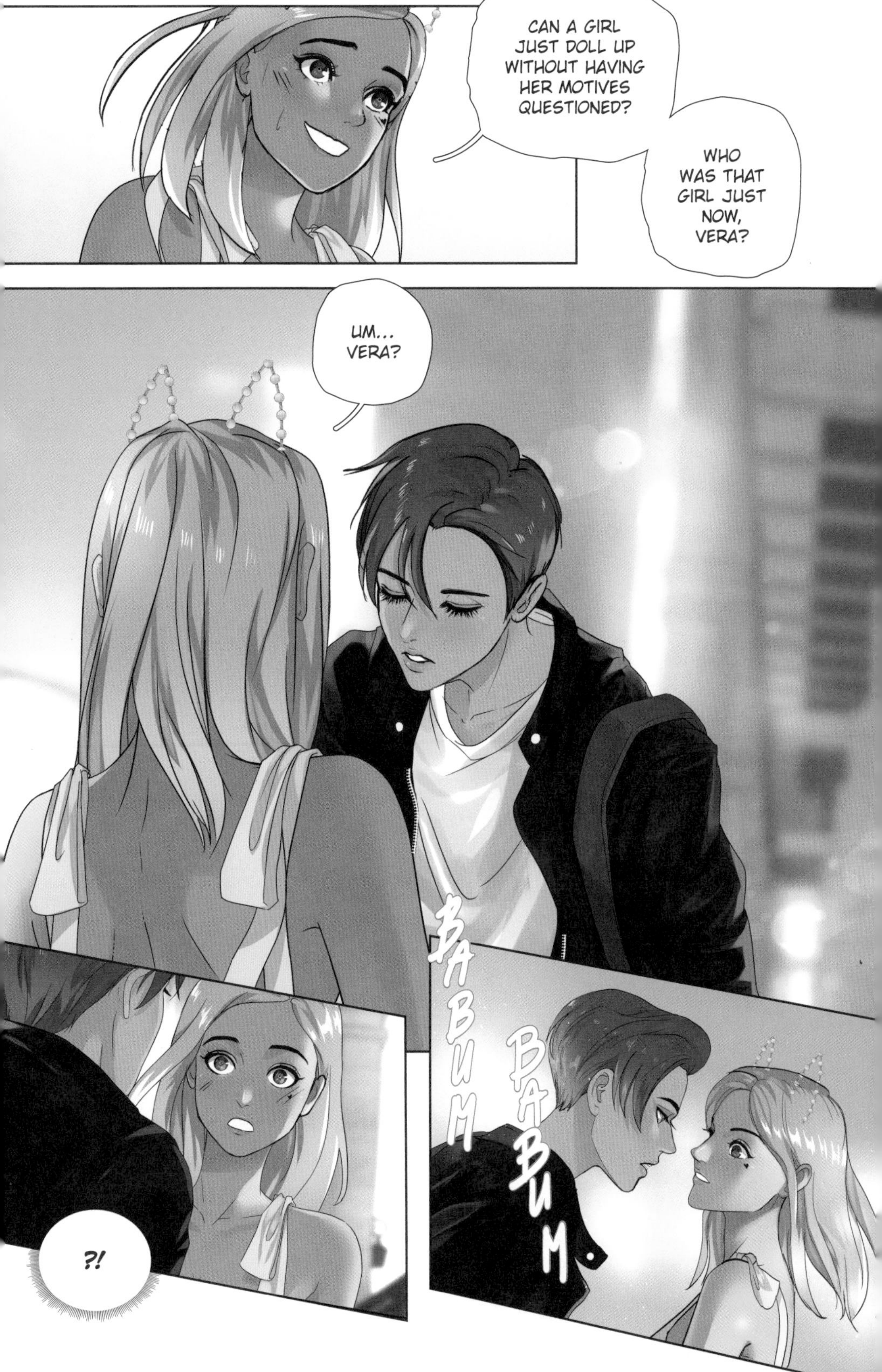
CAN A GIRL JUST DOLL UP WITHOUT HAVING HER MOTIVES QUESTIONED?
WHO WAS THAT GIRL JUST NOW, VERA?
UM... VERA?
?!
BABUM
BABUM.

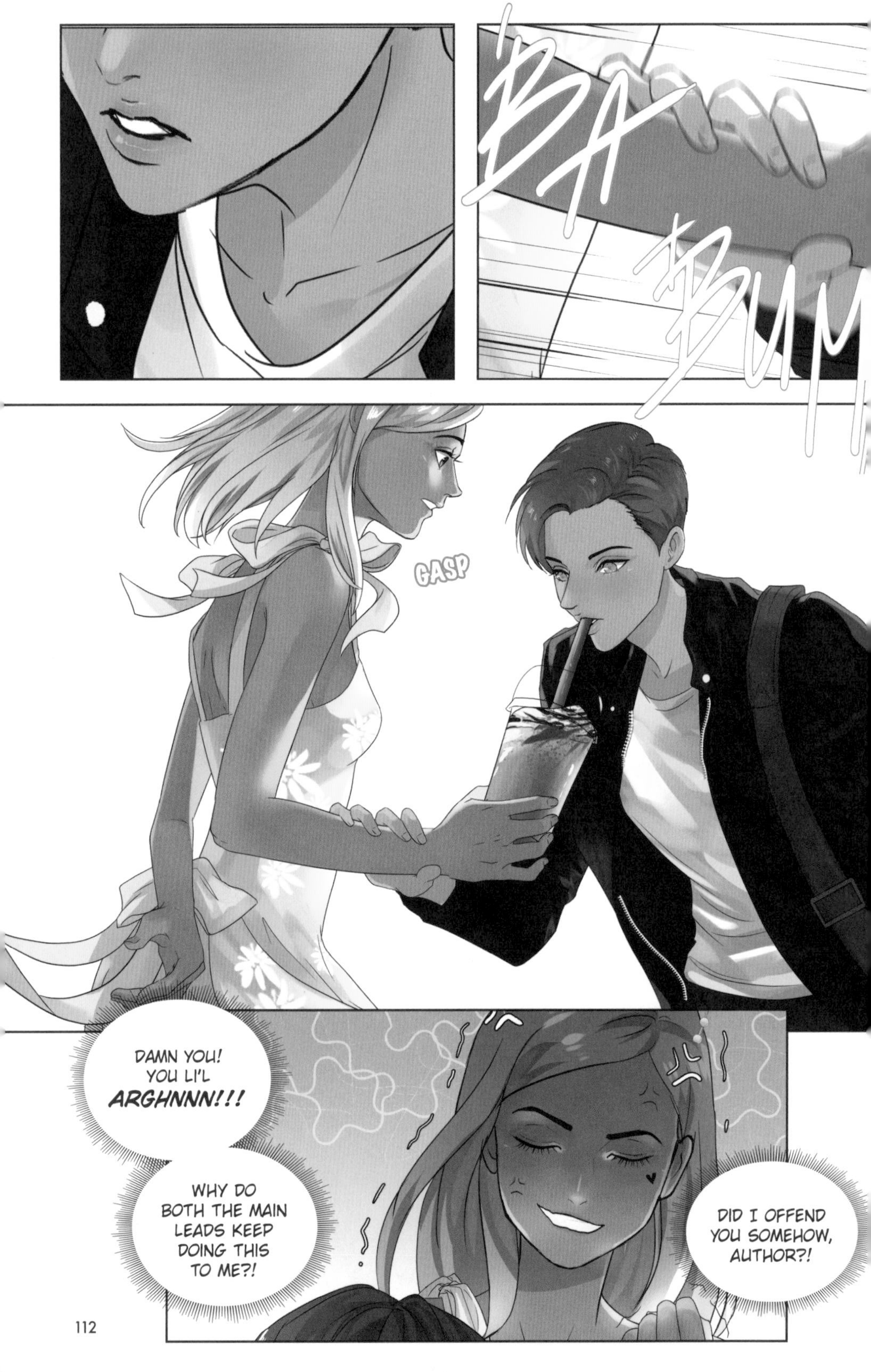
BA BUM
GASP
DAMN YOU! YOU LI'L ARGHNNN!!!
WHY DO BOTH THE MAIN LEADS KEEP DOING THIS TO ME?!
DID I OFFEND YOU SOMEHOW, AUTHOR?!

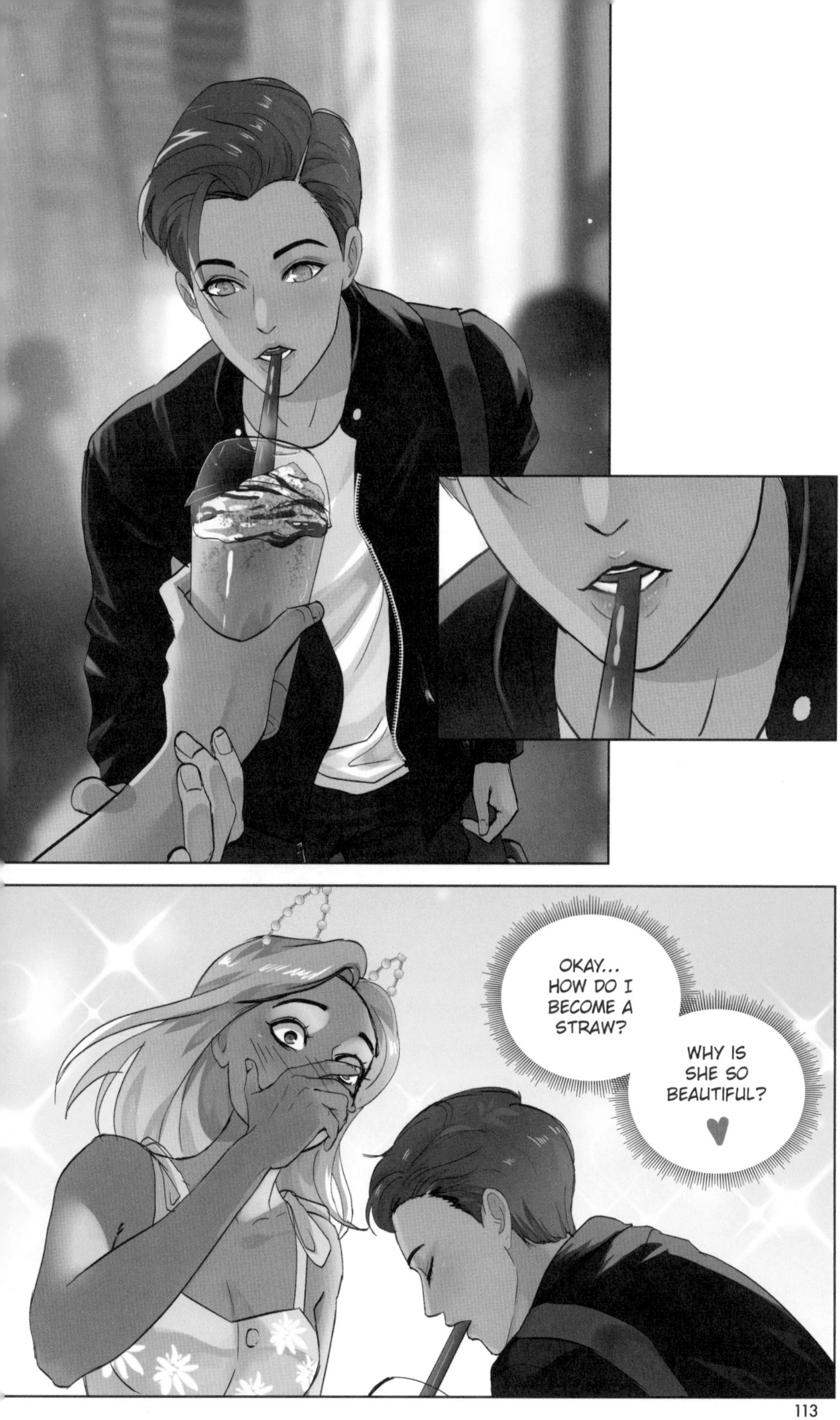
OKAY... HOW DO I BECOME A STRAW?
WHY IS SHE SO BEAUTIFUL? ♥

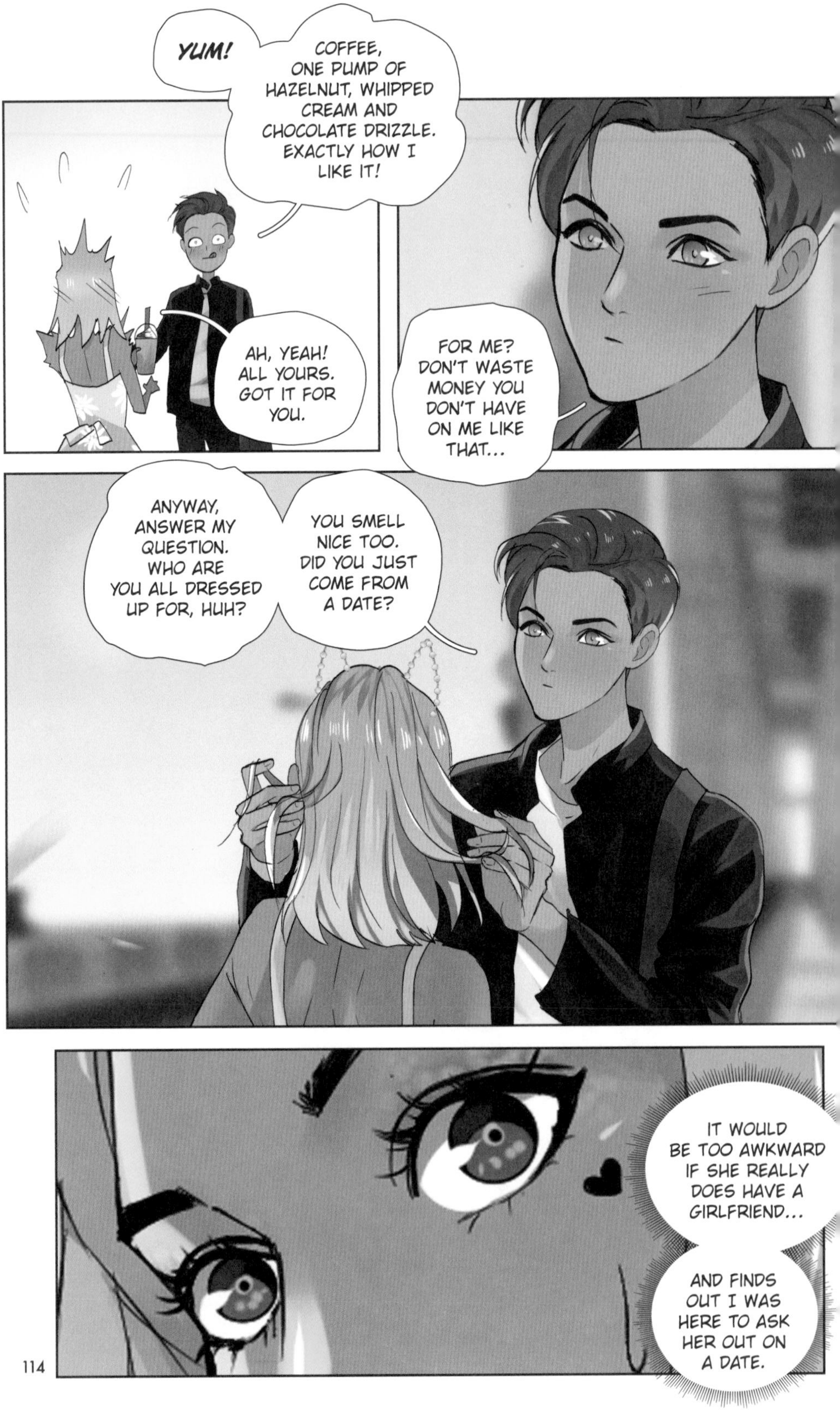
YUM!
COFFEE, ONE PUMP OF HAZELNUT, WHIPPED CREAM AND CHOCOLATE DRIZZLE. EXACTLY HOW I LIKE IT!
AH, YEAH! ALL YOURS. GOT IT FOR YOU.
FOR ME? DON'T WASTE MONEY YOU DON'T HAVE ON ME LIKE THAT...
ANYWAY, ANSWER MY QUESTION. WHO ARE YOU ALL DRESSED UP FOR, HUH?
YOU SMELL NICE TOO. DID YOU JUST COME FROM A DATE?
IT WOULD BE TOO AWKWARD IF SHE REALLY DOES HAVE A GIRLFRIEND...
AND FINDS OUT I WAS HERE TO ASK HER OUT ON A DATE.

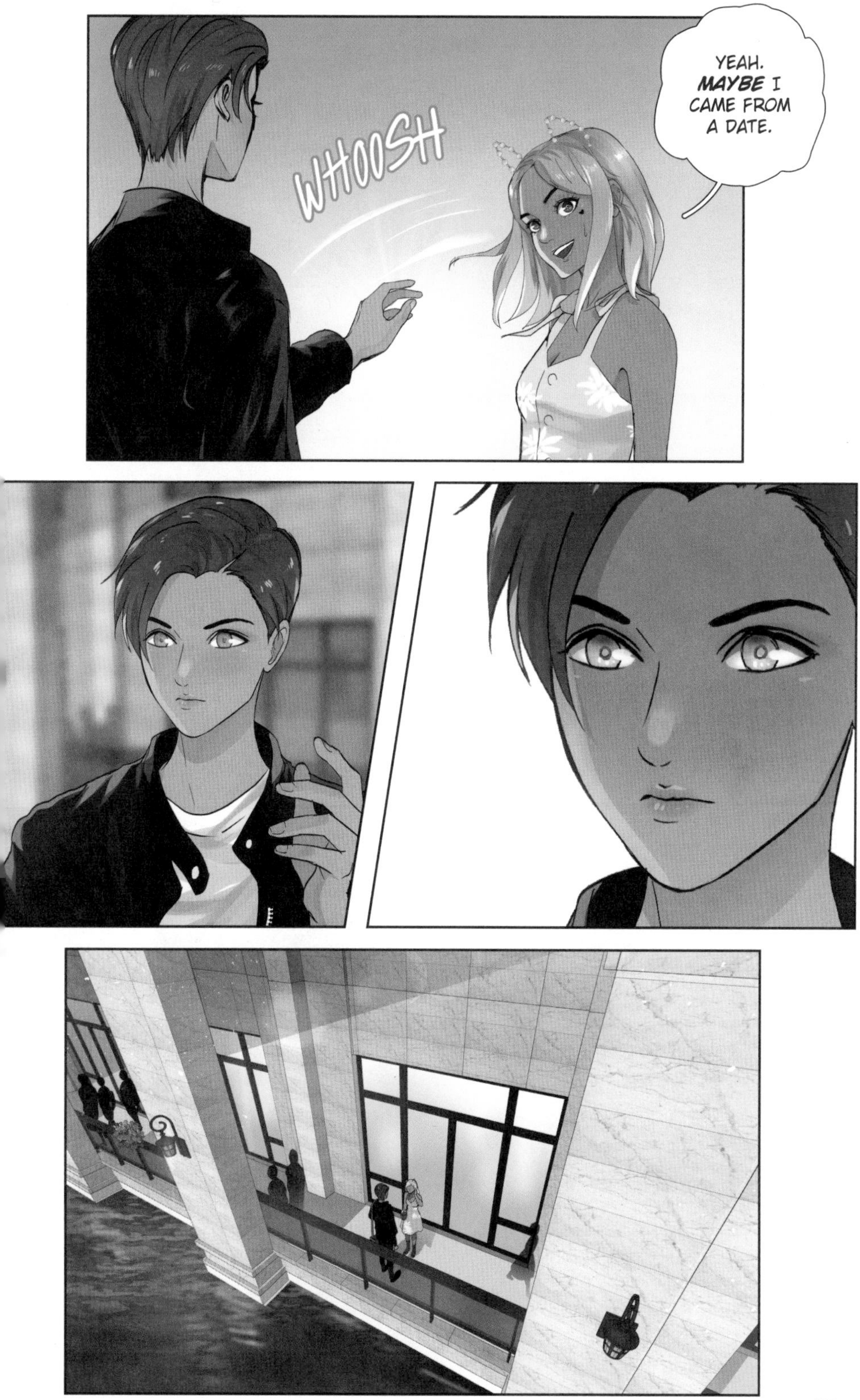
WHOOSH
YEAH. **MAYBE** I CAME FROM A DATE.

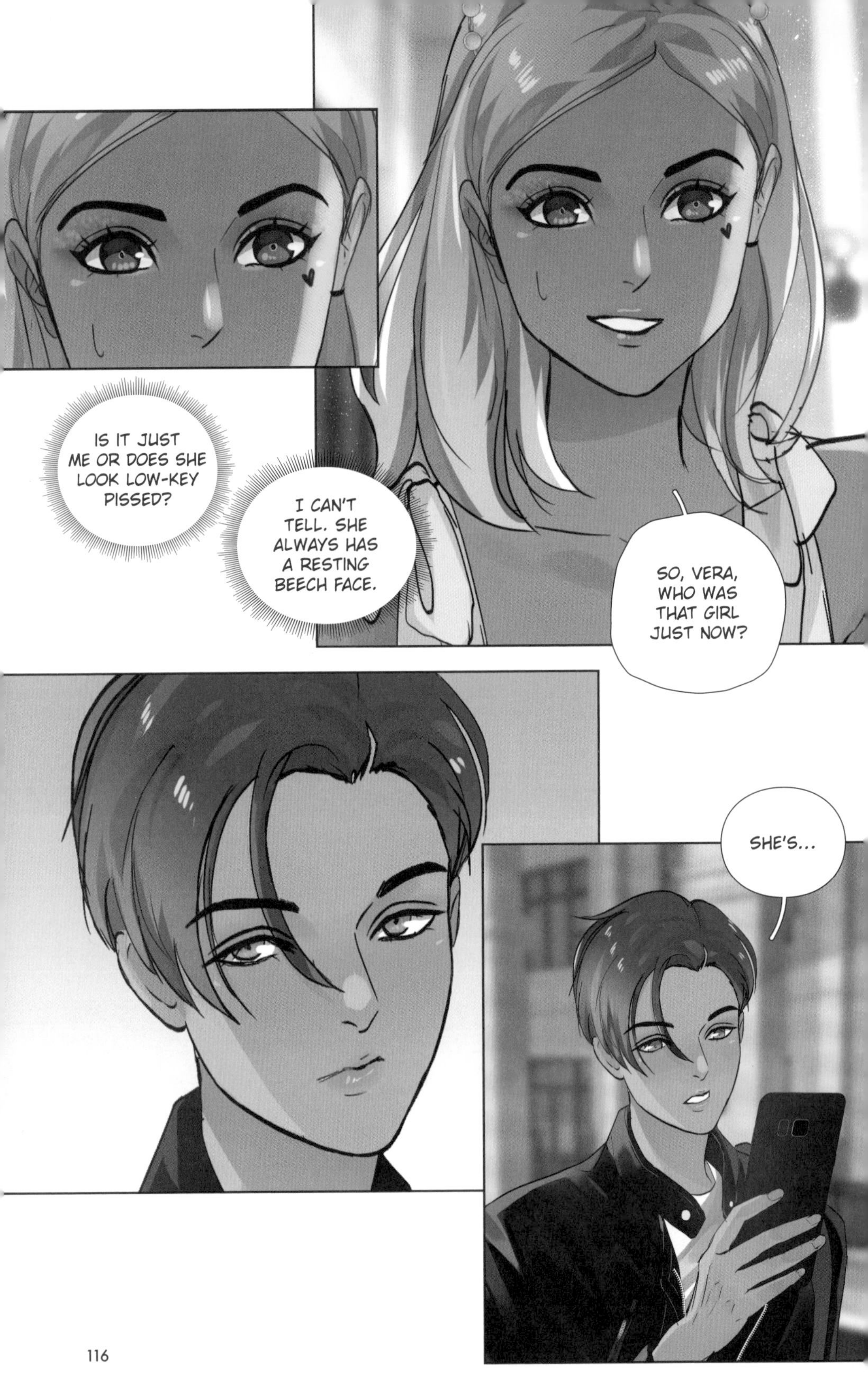
IS IT JUST ME OR DOES SHE LOOK LOW-KEY PISSED?
I CAN'T TELL. SHE ALWAYS HAS A RESTING BEECH FACE.
SO, VERA, WHO WAS THAT GIRL JUST NOW?
SHE'S...

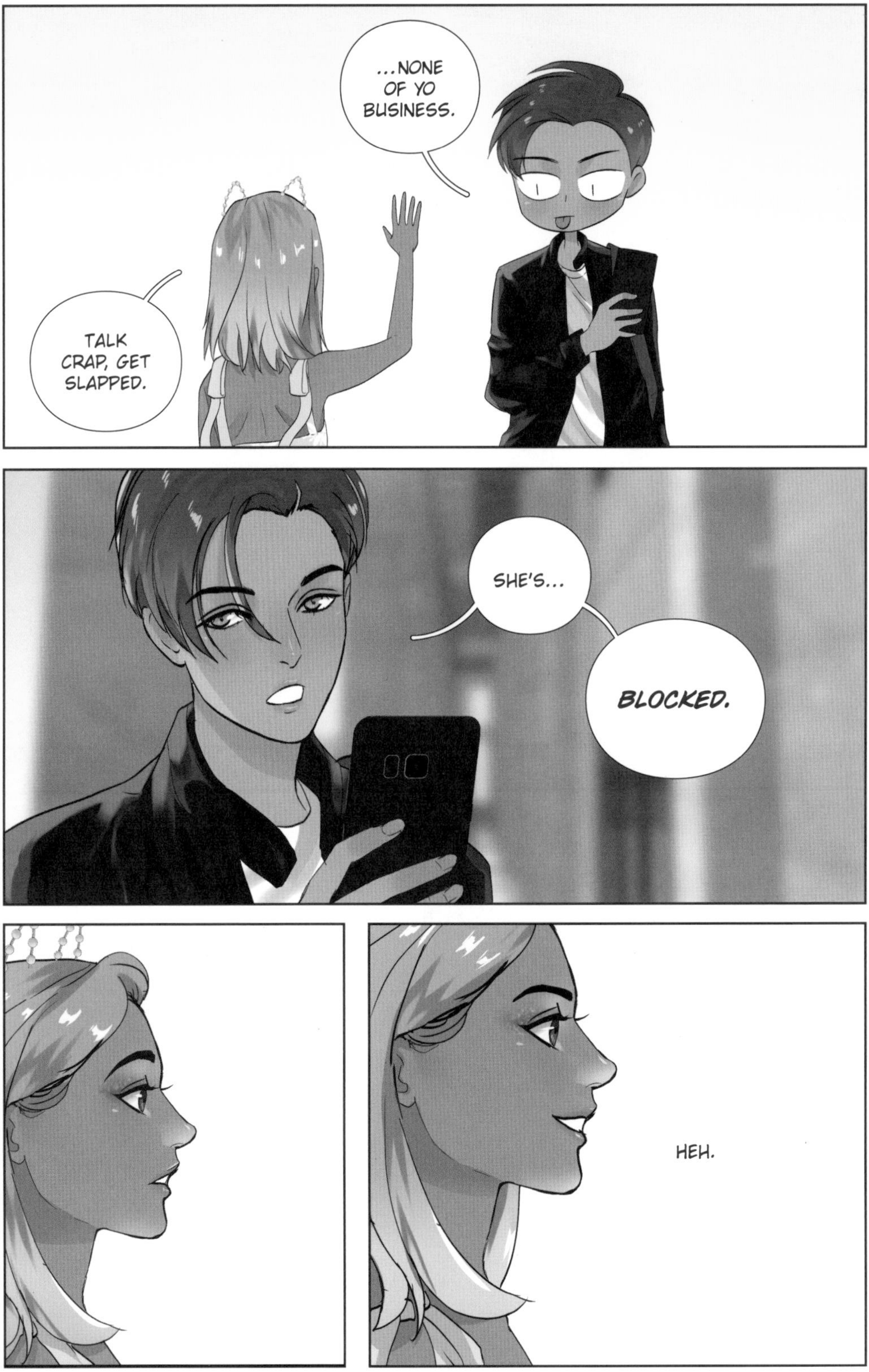
...NONE OF YO BUSINESS.
TALK CRAP, GET SLAPPED.
SHE'S...
BLOCKED.
HEH.

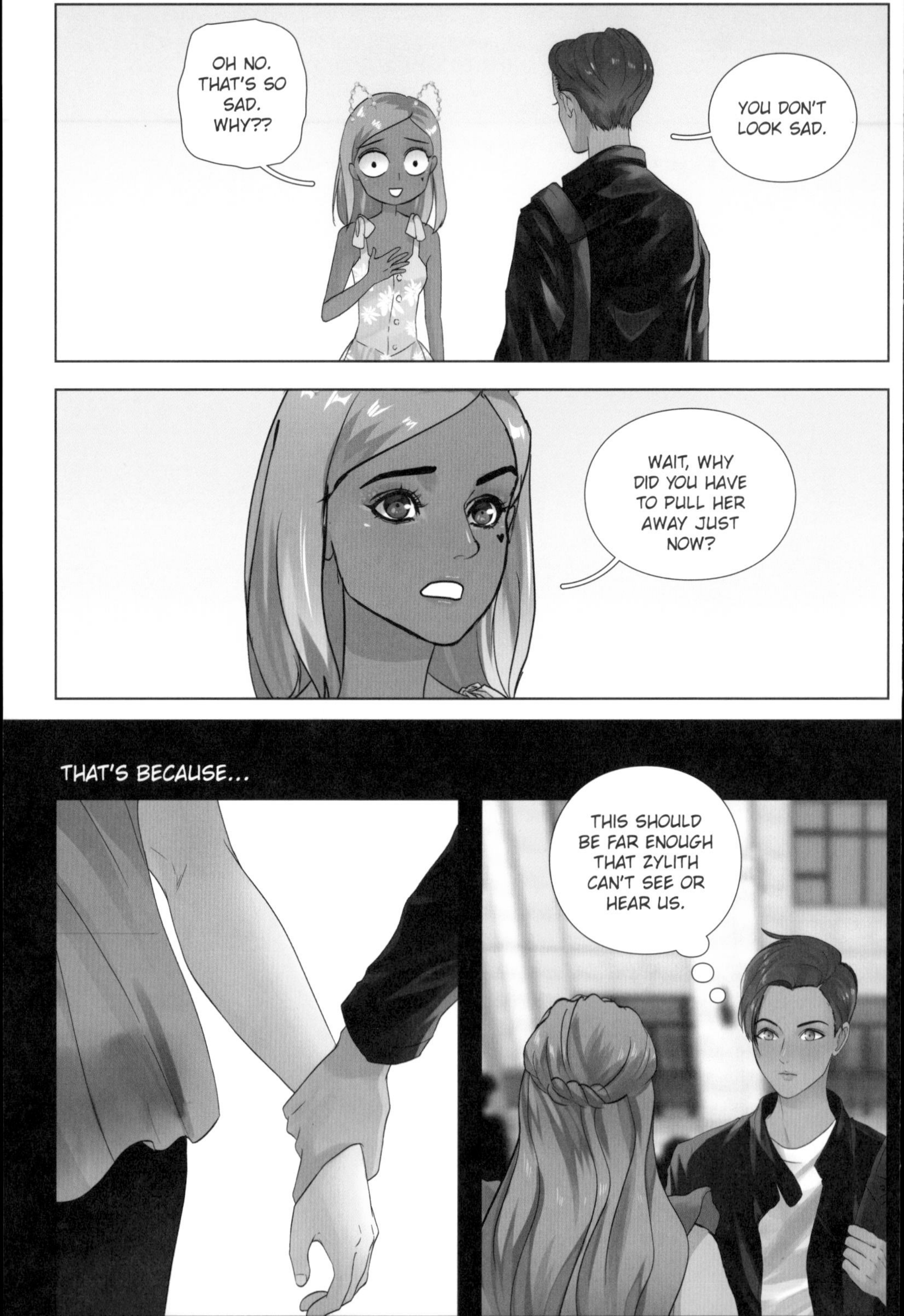
OH NO. THAT'S SO SAD. WHY??
YOU DON'T LOOK SAD.
WAIT, WHY DID YOU HAVE TO PULL HER AWAY JUST NOW?
THAT'S BECAUSE...
THIS SHOULD BE FAR ENOUGH THAT ZYLITH CAN'T SEE OR HEAR US.

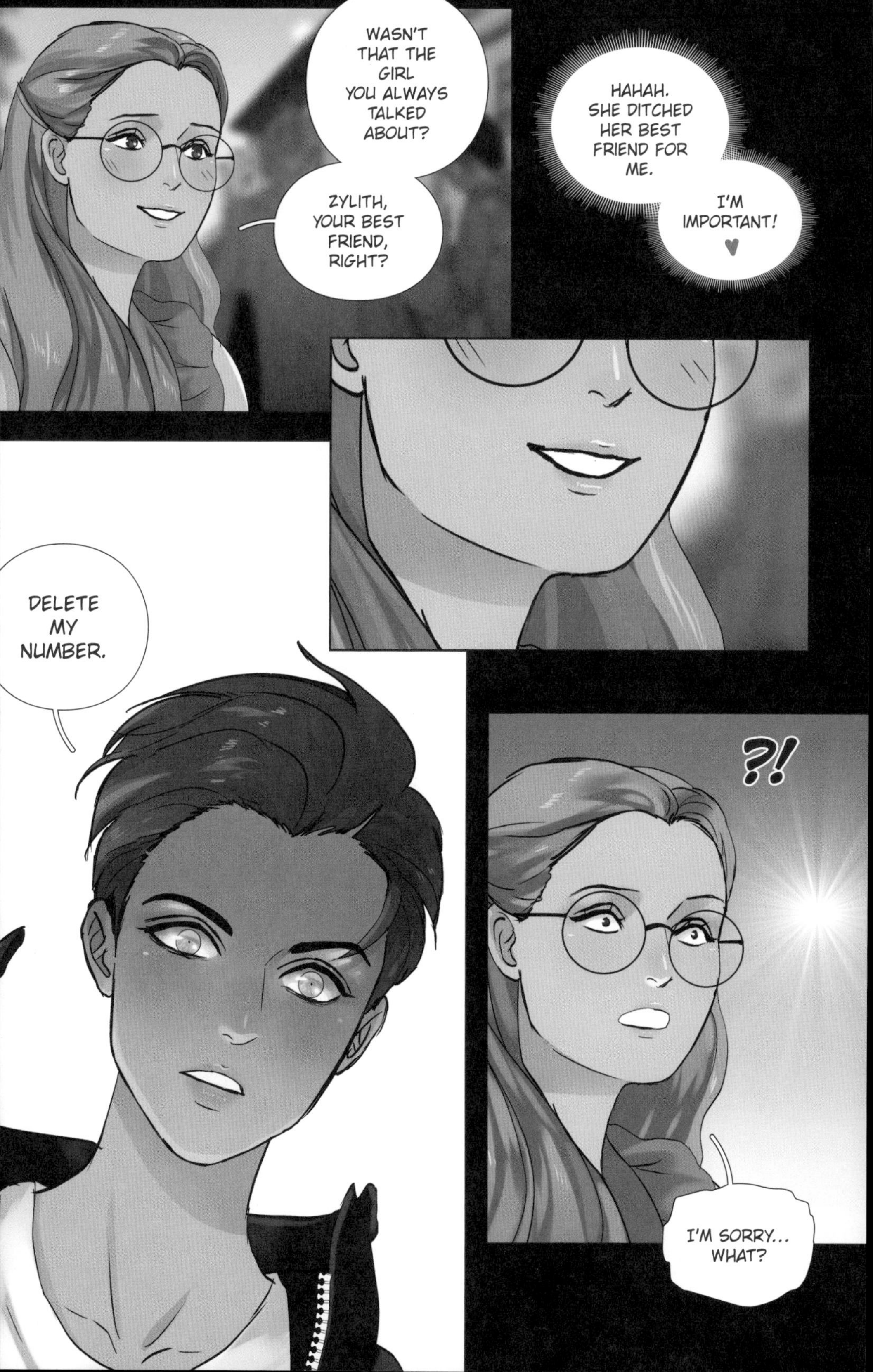
WASN'T THAT THE GIRL YOU ALWAYS TALKED ABOUT?
ZYLITH, YOUR BEST FRIEND, RIGHT?
HAHAH. SHE DITCHED HER BEST FRIEND FOR ME.
I'M IMPORTANT! ♥
DELETE MY NUMBER.
?!
I'M SORRY... WHAT?

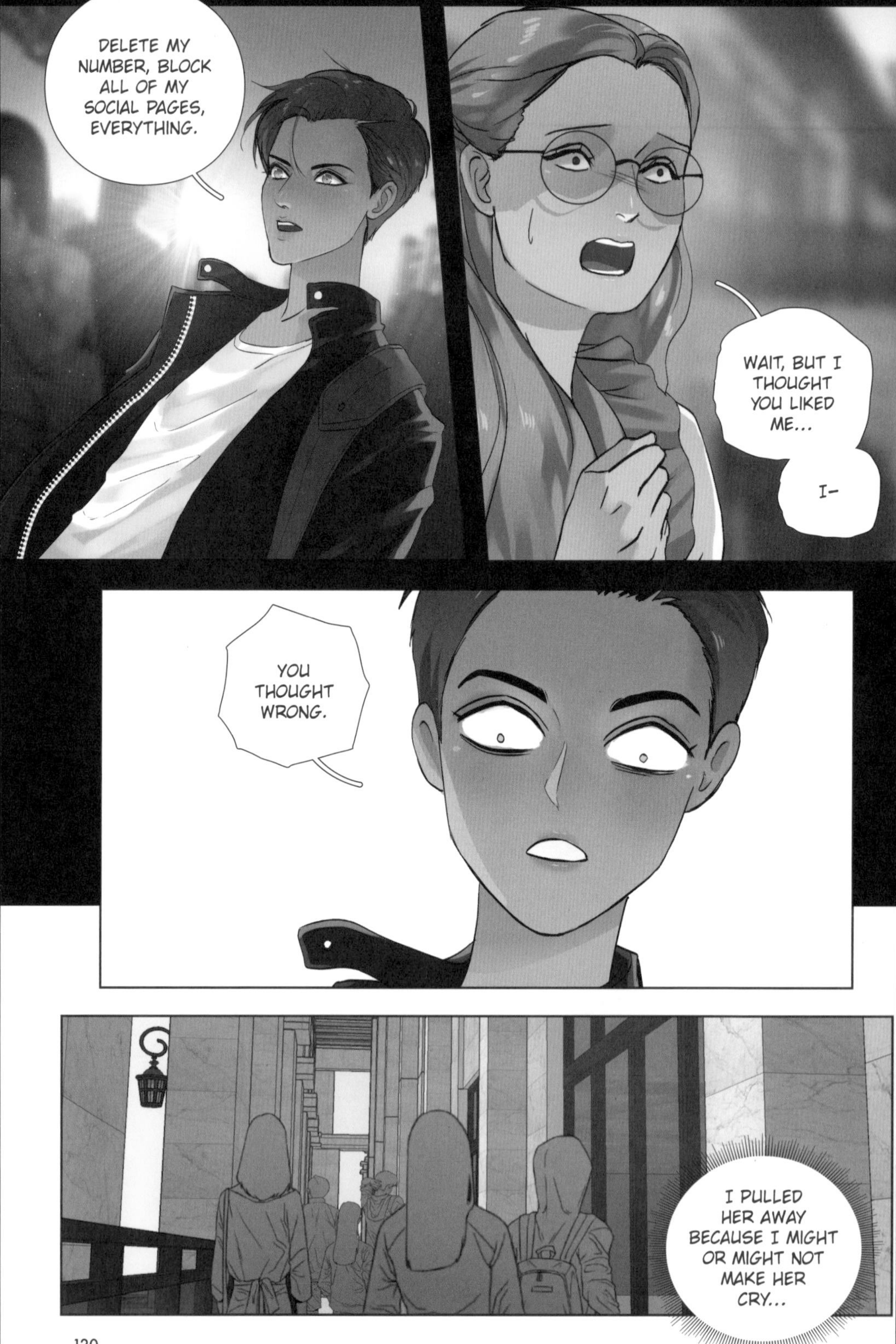
DELETE MY NUMBER, BLOCK ALL OF MY SOCIAL PAGES, EVERYTHING.
WAIT, BUT I THOUGHT YOU LIKED ME...
I-
YOU THOUGHT WRONG.
I PULLED HER AWAY BECAUSE I MIGHT OR MIGHT NOT MAKE HER CRY...

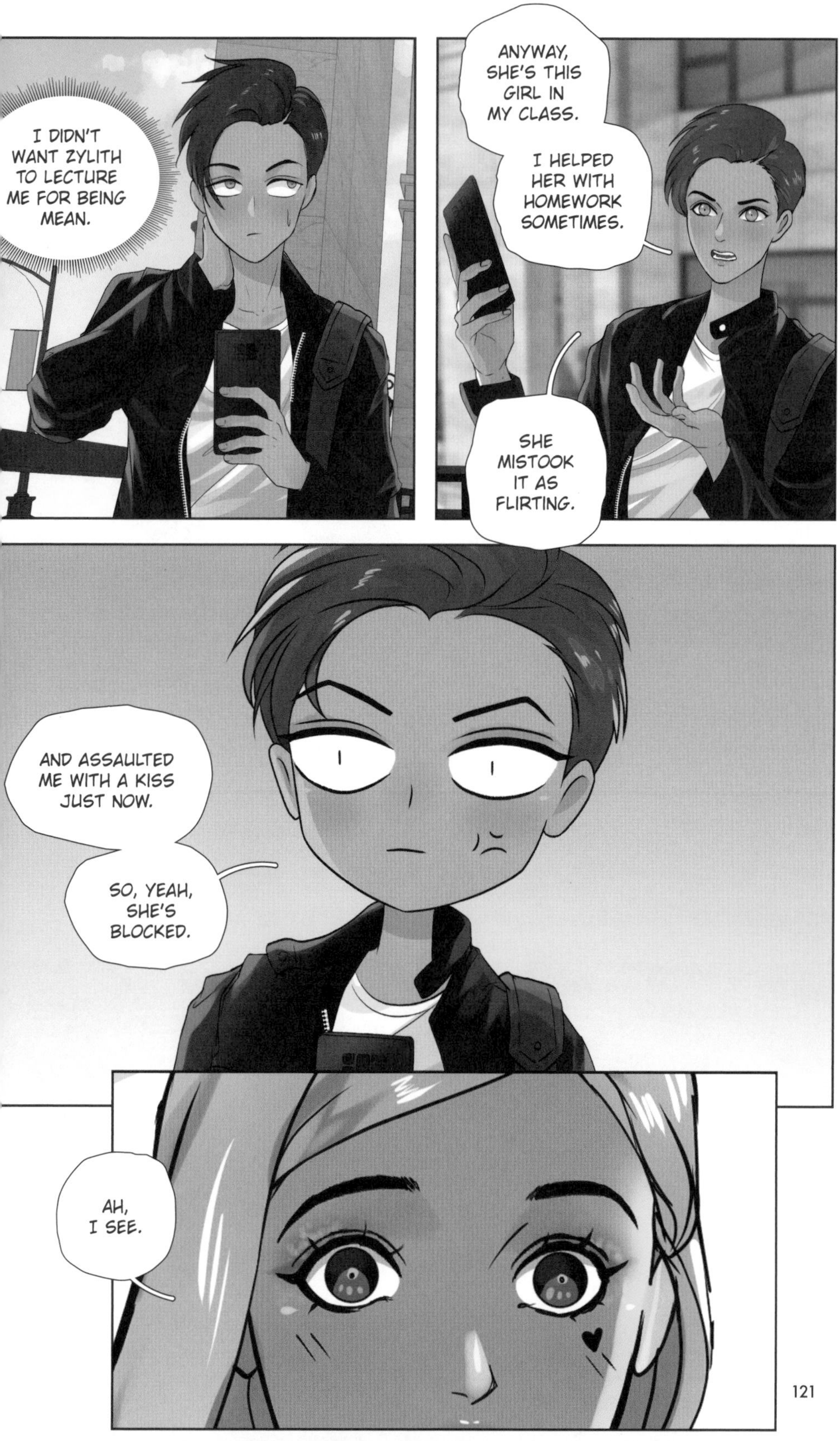
I DIDN'T WANT ZYLITH TO LECTURE ME FOR BEING MEAN.
ANYWAY, SHE'S THIS GIRL IN MY CLASS.
I HELPED HER WITH HOMEWORK SOMETIMES.
SHE MISTOOK IT AS FLIRTING.
AND ASSAULTED ME WITH A KISS JUST NOW.
SO, YEAH, SHE'S BLOCKED.
AH, I SEE.

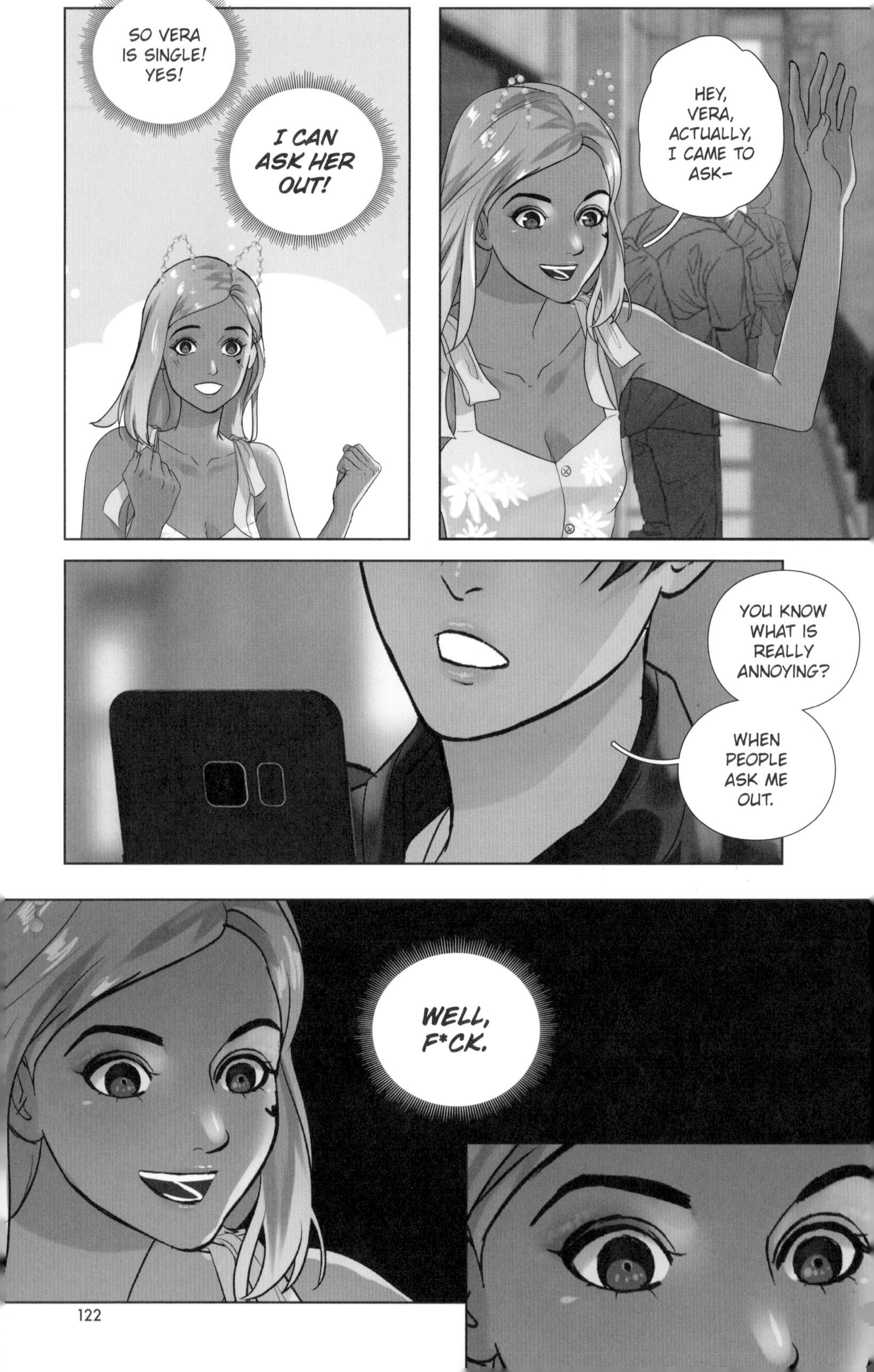
SO VERA IS SINGLE! YES!
I CAN ASK HER OUT!
HEY, VERA, ACTUALLY, I CAME TO ASK-
YOU KNOW WHAT IS REALLY ANNOYING?
WHEN PEOPLE ASK ME OUT.
WELL, F*CK.

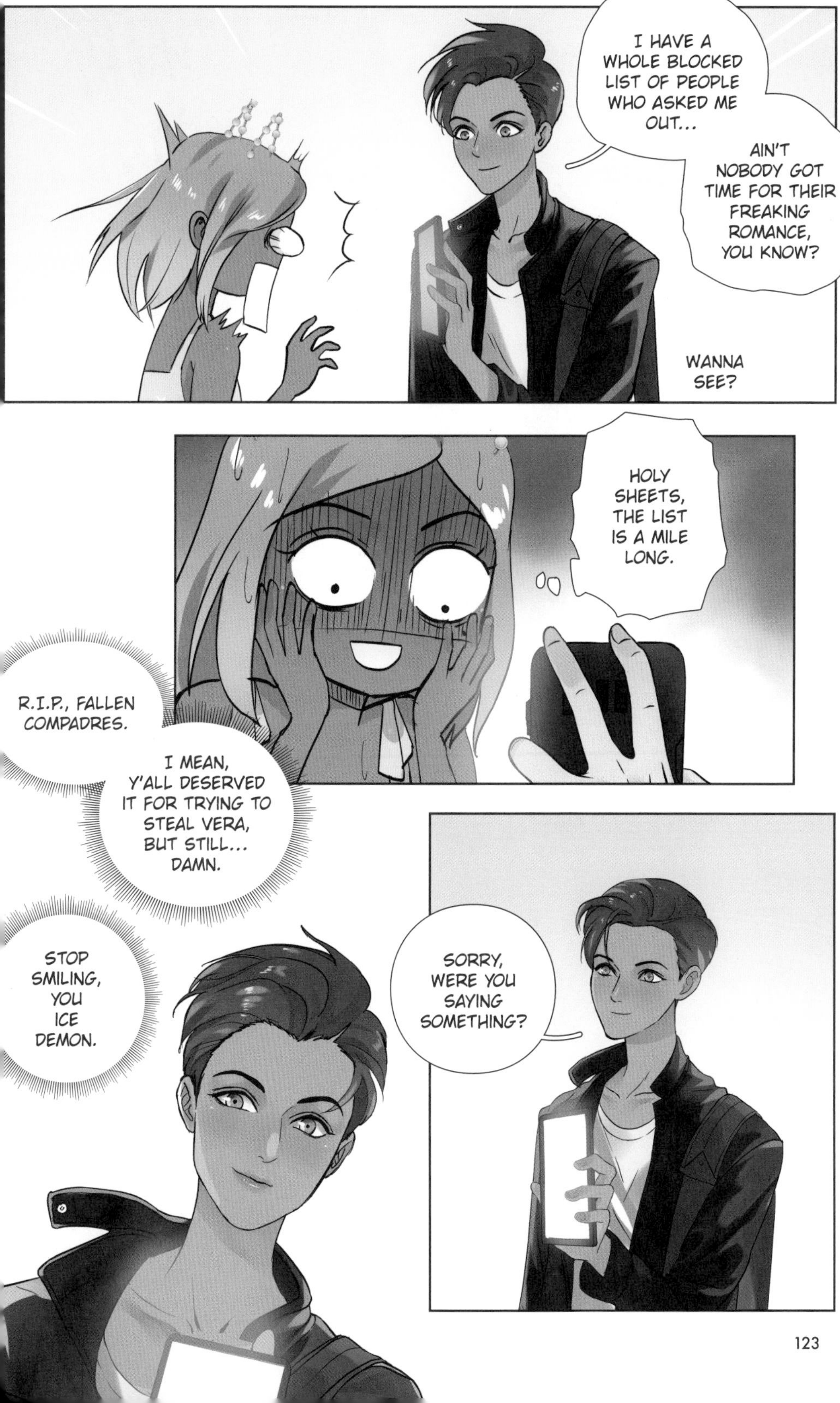
I HAVE A WHOLE BLOCKED LIST OF PEOPLE WHO ASKED ME OUT...
AIN'T NOBODY GOT TIME FOR THEIR FREAKING ROMANCE, YOU KNOW?
WANNA SEE?
HOLY SHEETS, THE LIST IS A MILE LONG.
R.I.P., FALLEN COMPADRES.
I MEAN, Y'ALL DESERVED IT FOR TRYING TO STEAL VERA, BUT STILL... DAMN.
STOP SMILING, YOU ICE DEMON.
SORRY, WERE YOU SAYING SOMETHING?

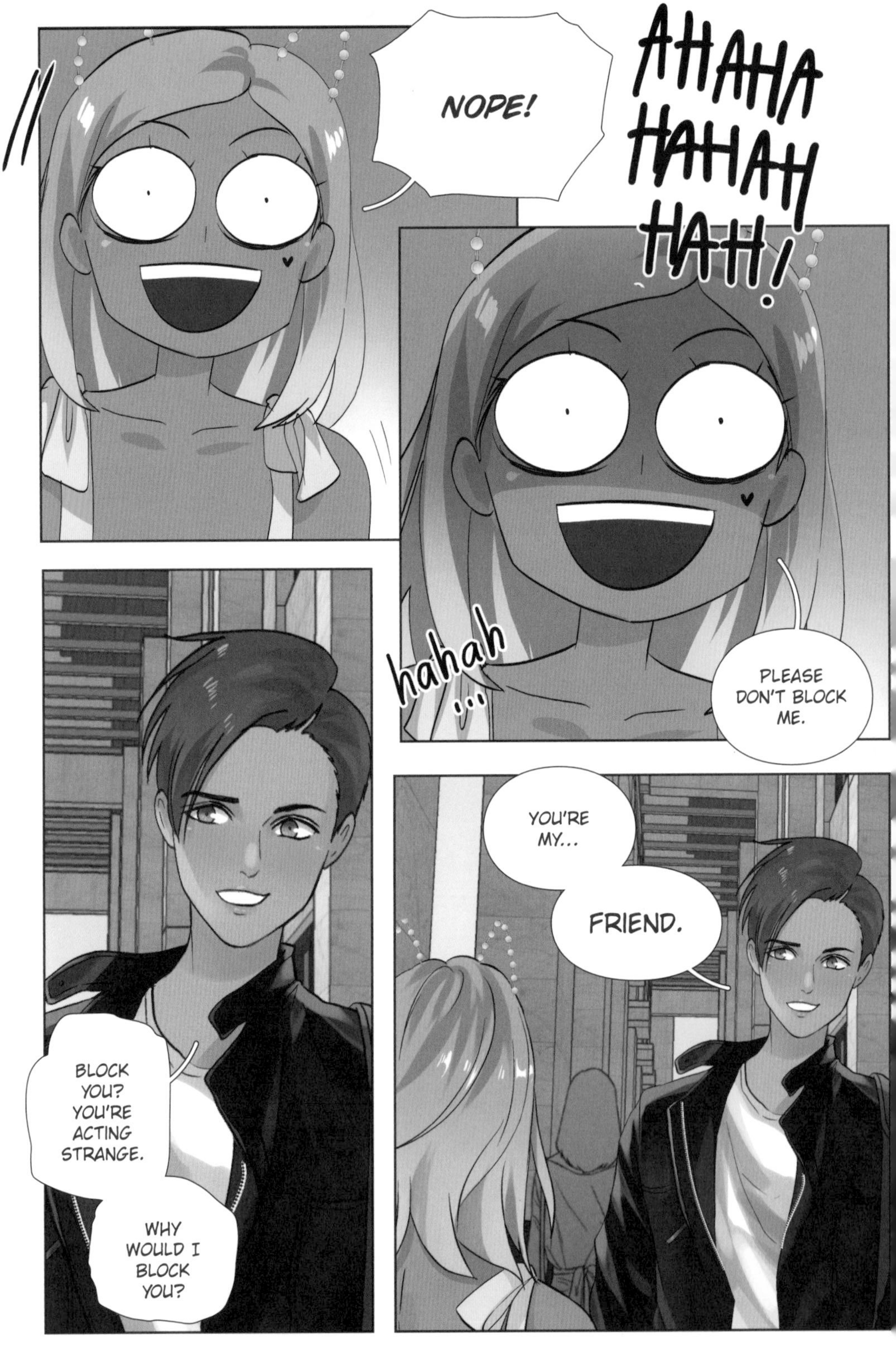
NOPE!
AHAHA HAHAH HAH!
hahah...
PLEASE DON'T BLOCK ME.
BLOCK YOU? YOU'RE ACTING STRANGE.
WHY WOULD I BLOCK YOU?
YOU'RE MY...
FRIEND.

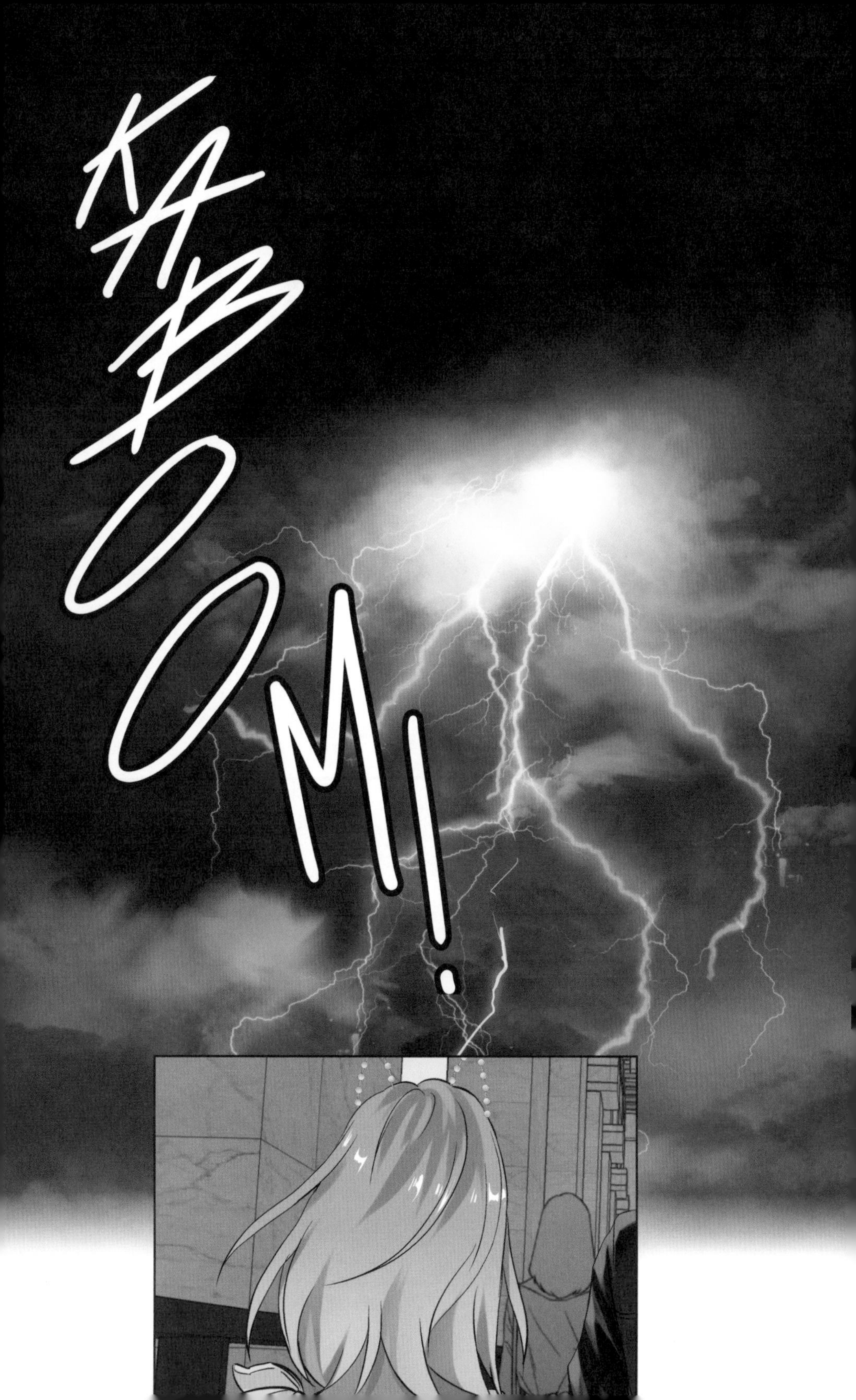
KABOOM!

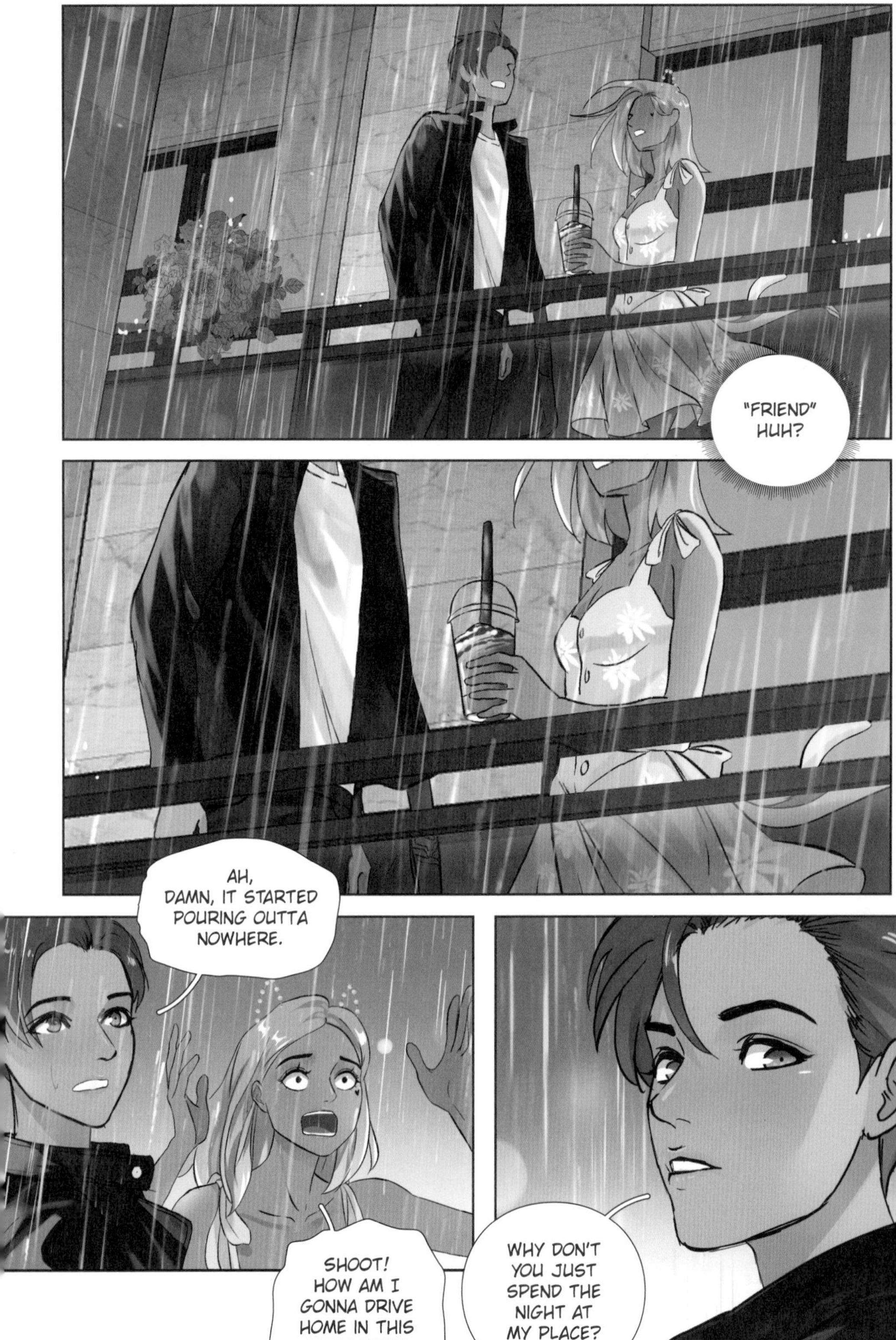
"FRIEND" HUH?
AH, DAMN, IT STARTED POURING OUTTA NOWHERE.
SHOOT! HOW AM I GONNA DRIVE HOME IN THIS WEATHER??
WHY DON'T YOU JUST SPEND THE NIGHT AT MY PLACE?

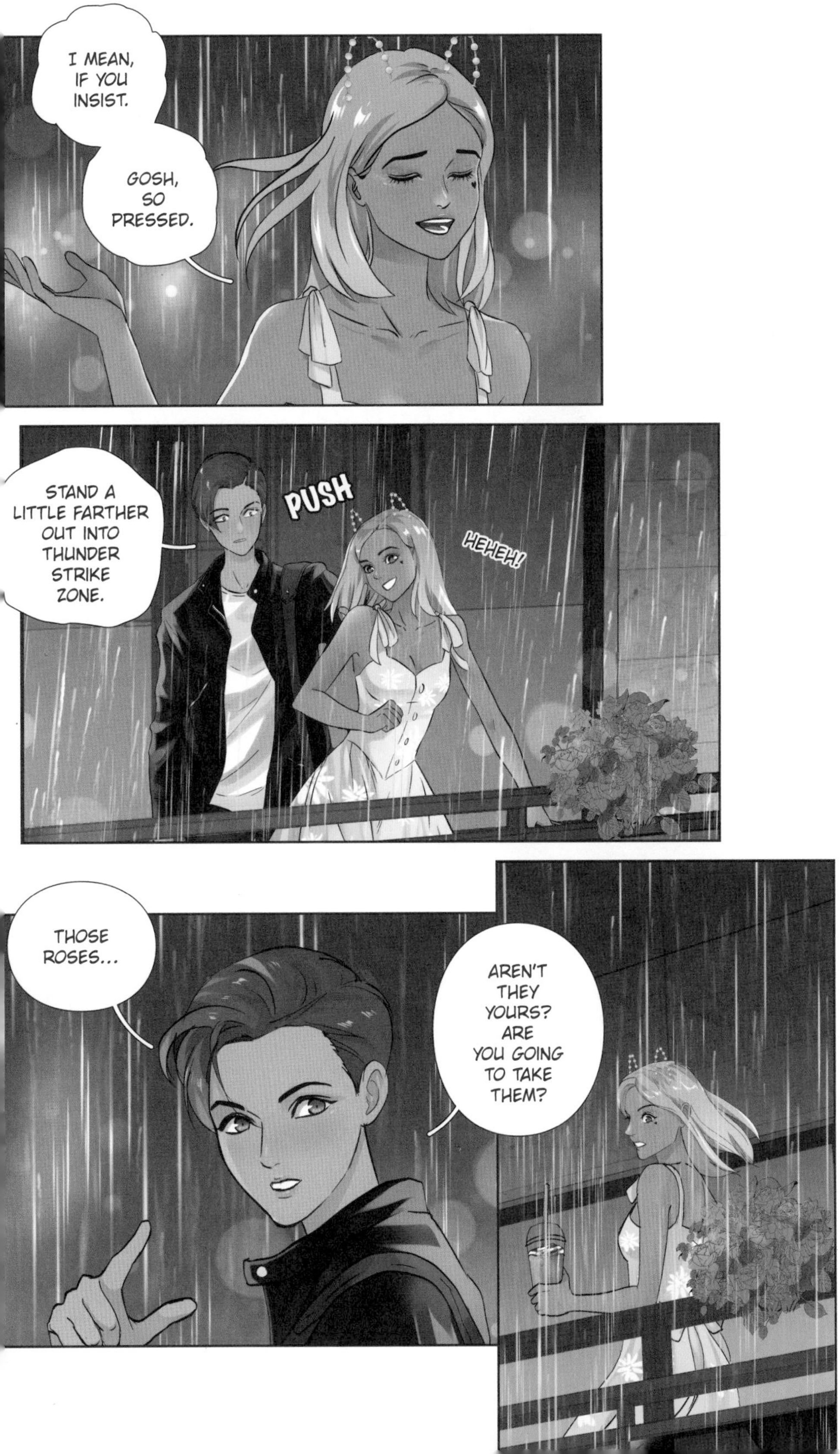
I MEAN, IF YOU INSIST.
GOSH, SO PRESSED.
STAND A LITTLE FARTHER OUT INTO THUNDER STRIKE ZONE.
PUSH
HEHEH!
THOSE ROSES...
AREN'T THEY YOURS? ARE YOU GOING TO TAKE THEM?

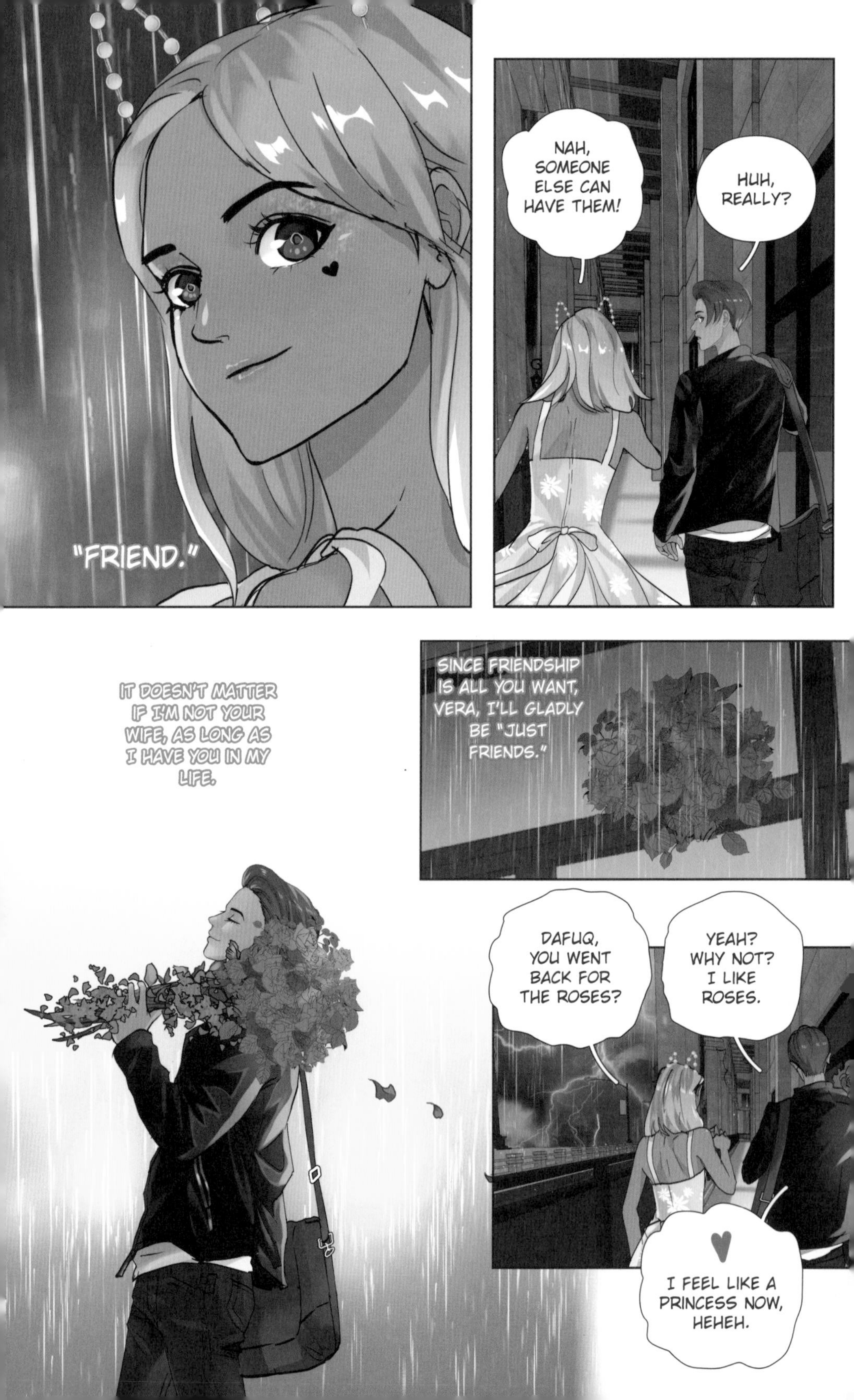
"FRIEND."
NAH, SOMEONE ELSE CAN HAVE THEM!
HUH, REALLY?
IT DOESN'T MATTER IF I'M NOT YOUR WIFE, AS LONG AS I HAVE YOU IN MY LIFE.
SINCE FRIENDSHIP IS ALL YOU WANT, VERA, I'LL GLADLY BE "JUST FRIENDS."
DAFUQ, YOU WENT BACK FOR THE ROSES?
YEAH? WHY NOT? I LIKE ROSES.
I FEEL LIKE A PRINCESS NOW, HEHEH.

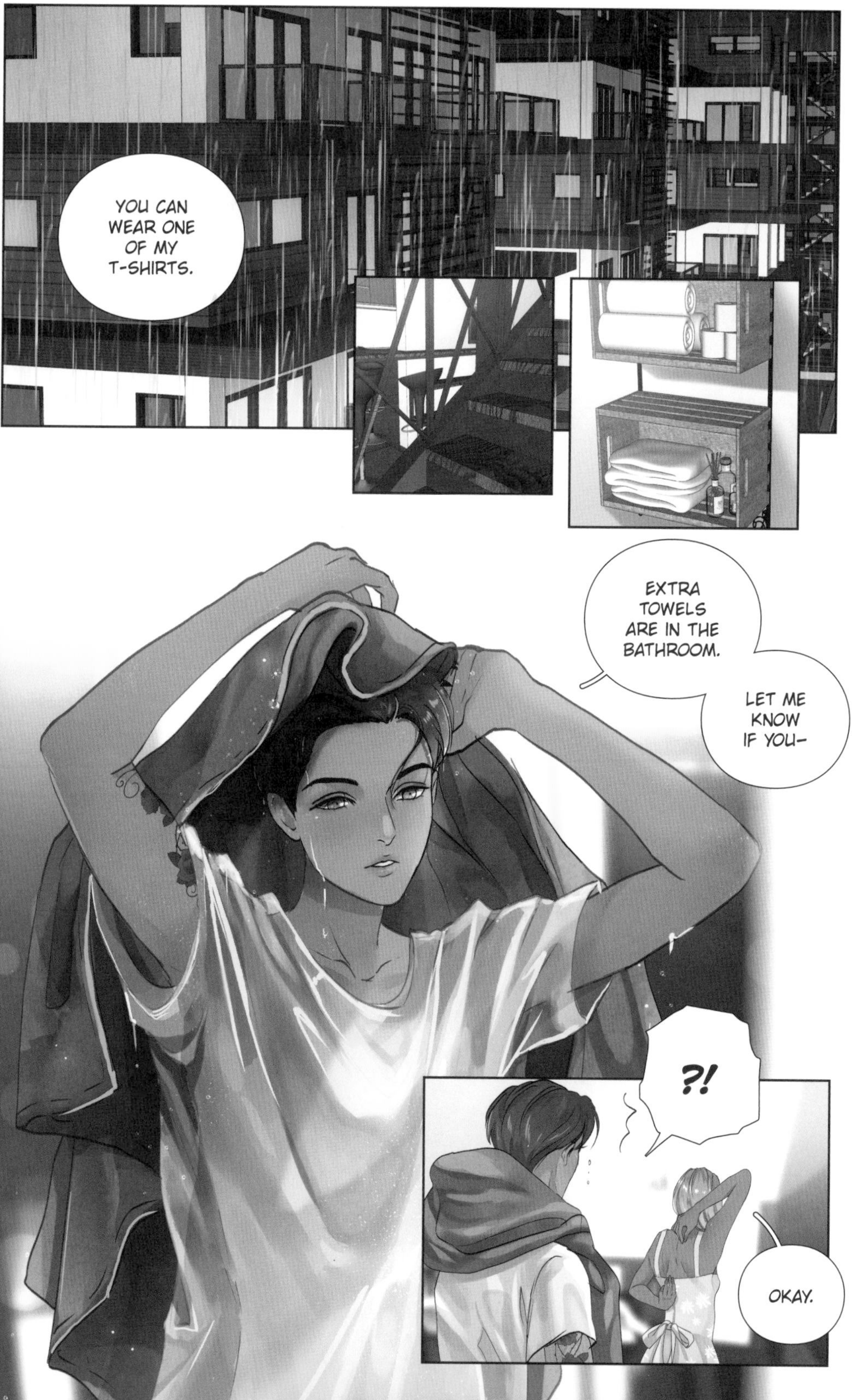
YOU CAN WEAR ONE OF MY T-SHIRTS.
EXTRA TOWELS ARE IN THE BATHROOM.
LET ME KNOW IF YOU-
?!
OKAY.

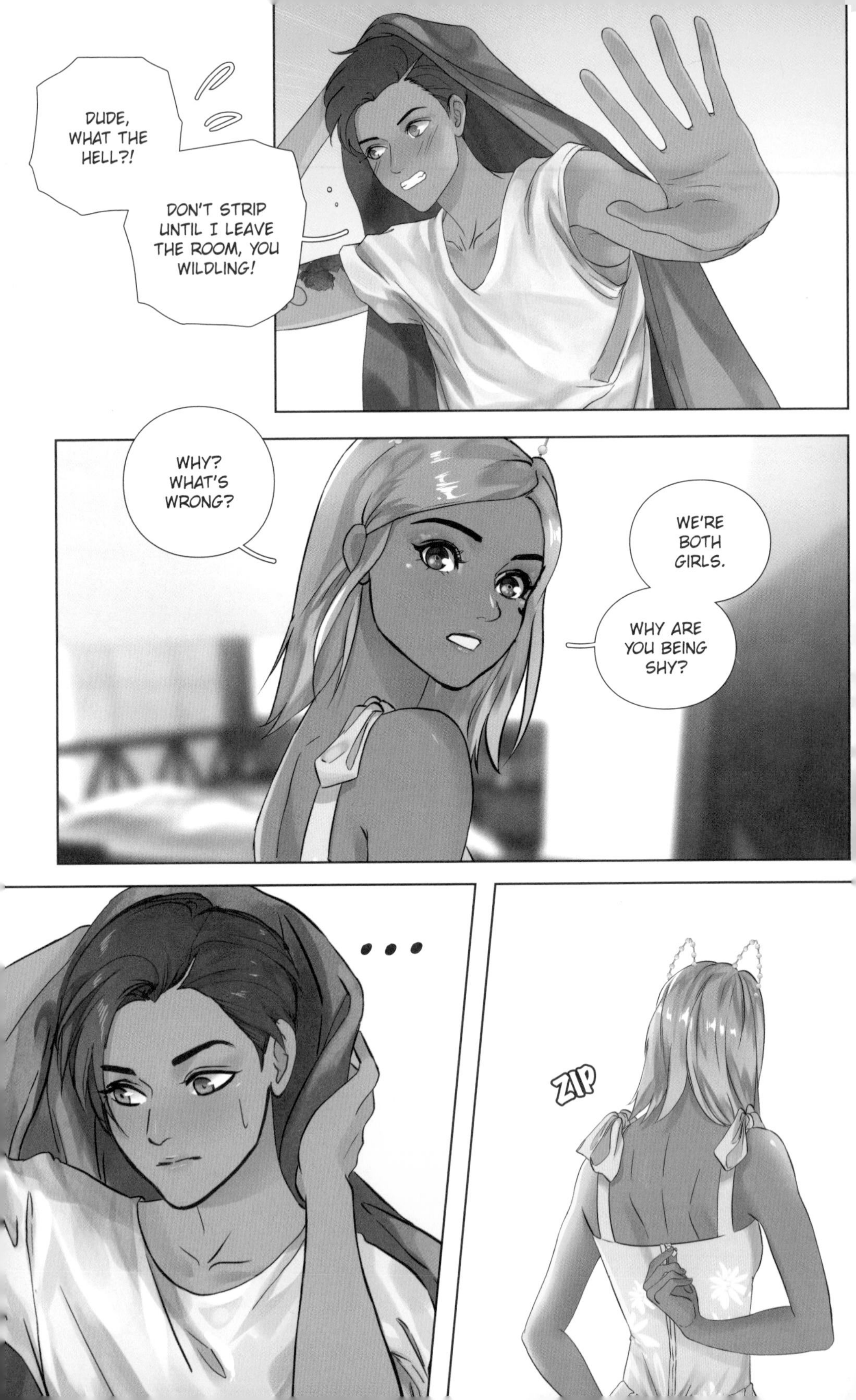

DUDE, WHAT THE HELL?!
DON'T STRIP UNTIL I LEAVE THE ROOM, YOU WILDLING!
WHY? WHAT'S WRONG?
WE'RE BOTH GIRLS.
WHY ARE YOU BEING SHY?
...
ZIP

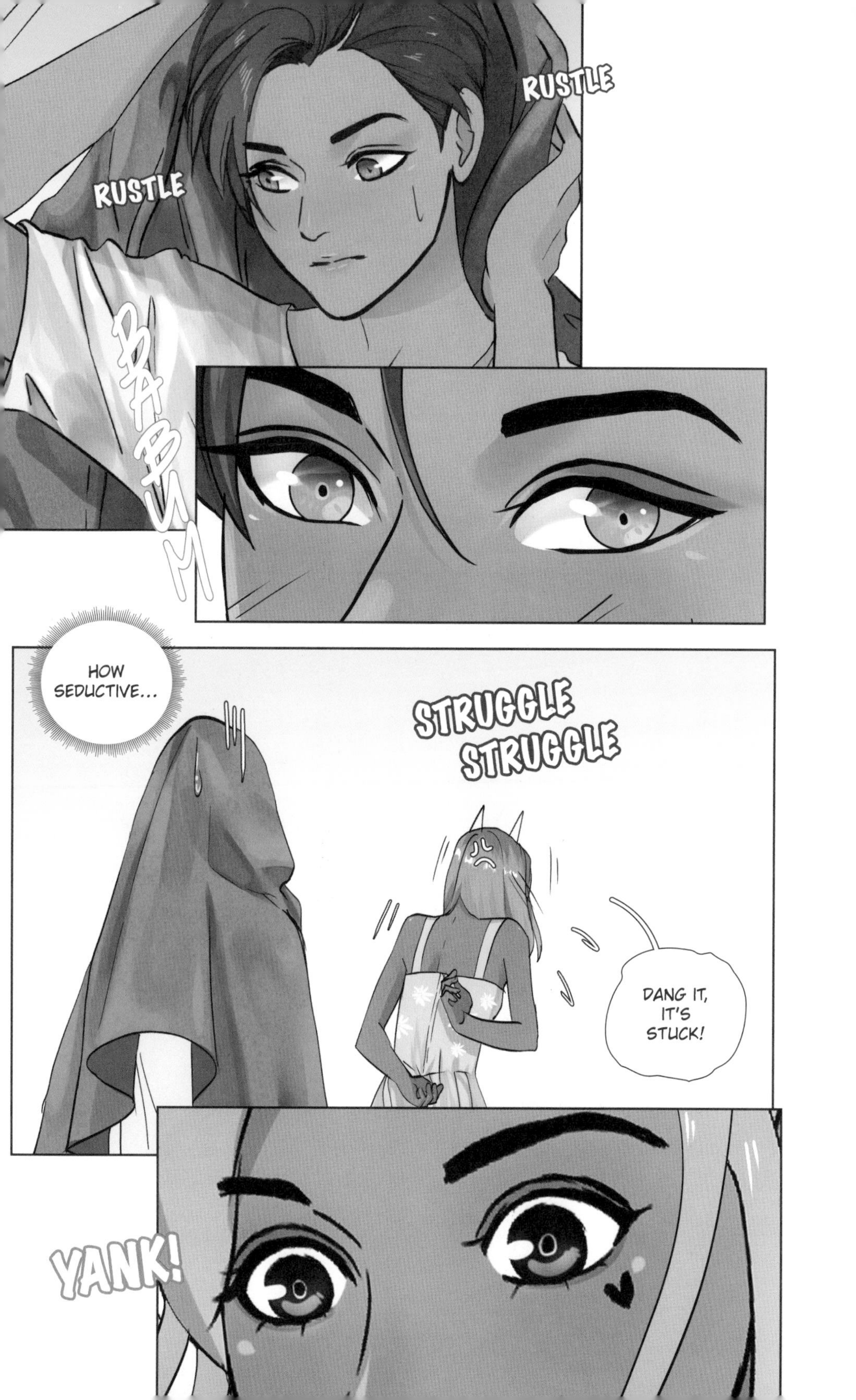
RUSTLE
RUSTLE
BABUM
HOW SEDUCTIVE...
STRUGGLE STRUGGLE
DANG IT, IT'S STUCK!
YANK!

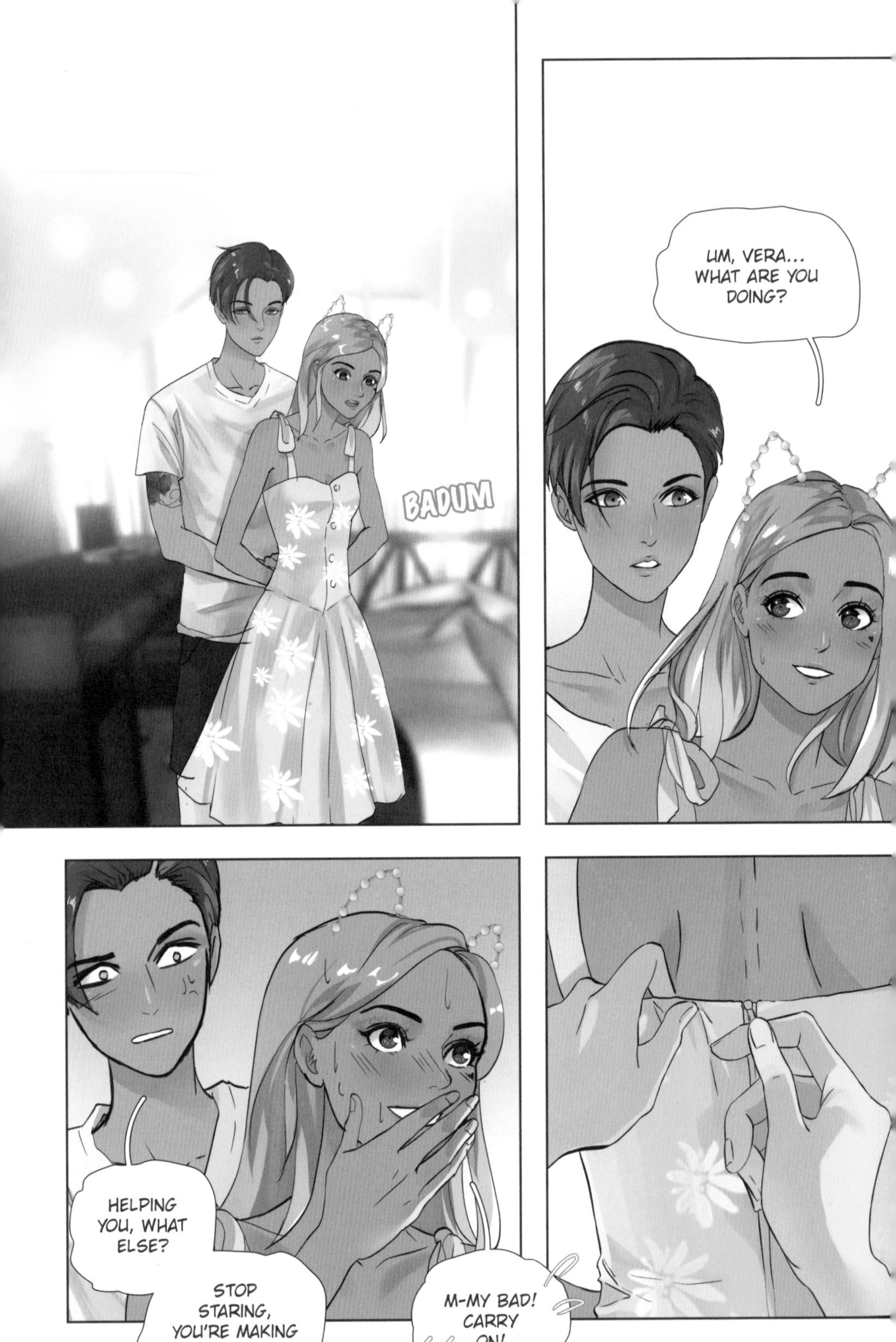
BADUM
UM, VERA... WHAT ARE YOU DOING?
HELPING YOU, WHAT ELSE?
STOP STARING, YOU'RE MAKING THIS AWKWARD.
M-MY BAD! CARRY ON!

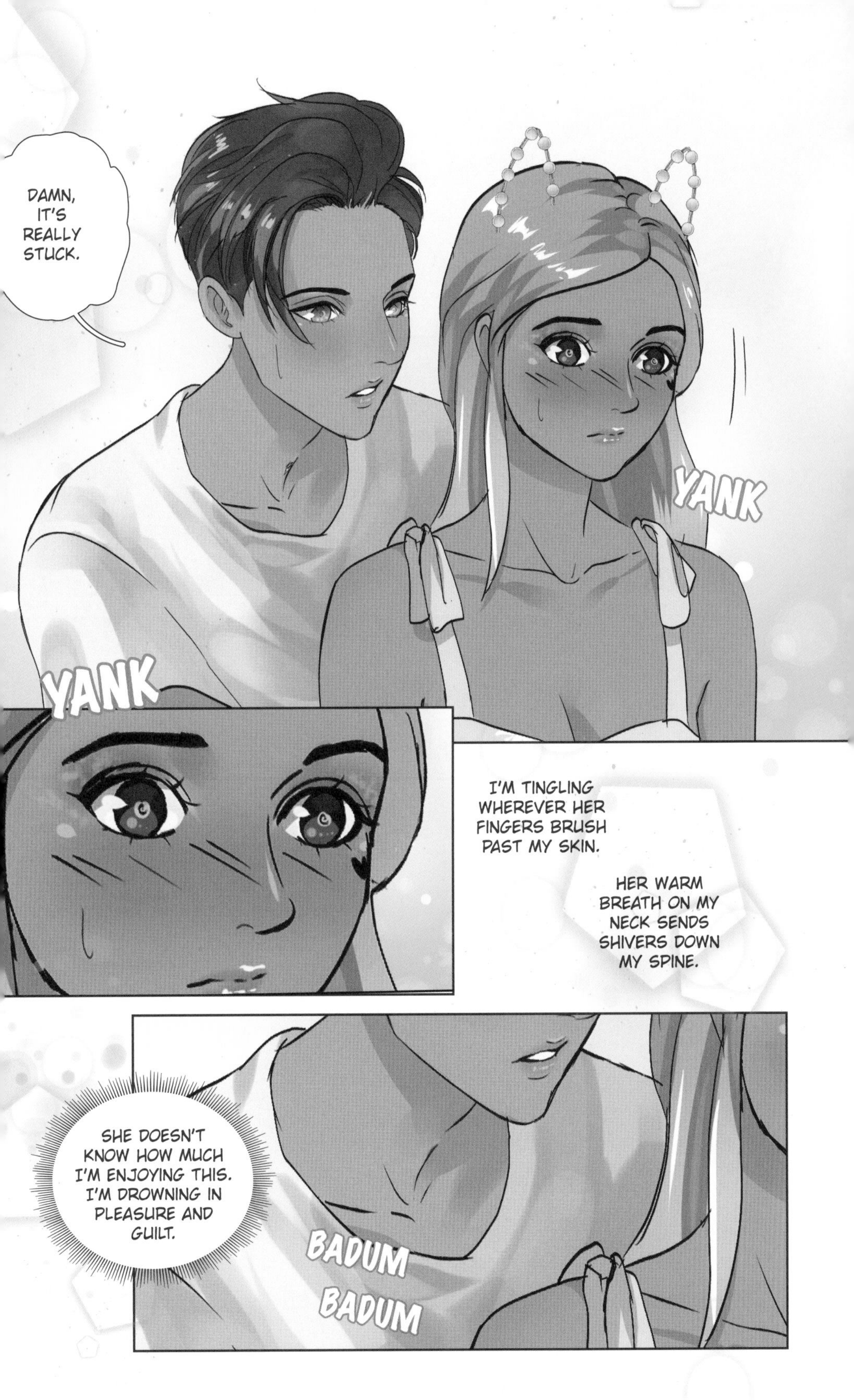
DAMN, IT'S REALLY STUCK.
YANK
YANK
I'M TINGLING WHEREVER HER FINGERS BRUSH PAST MY SKIN.
HER WARM BREATH ON MY NECK SENDS SHIVERS DOWN MY SPINE.
SHE DOESN'T KNOW HOW MUCH I'M ENJOYING THIS. I'M DROWNING IN PLEASURE AND GUILT.
BADUM
BADUM

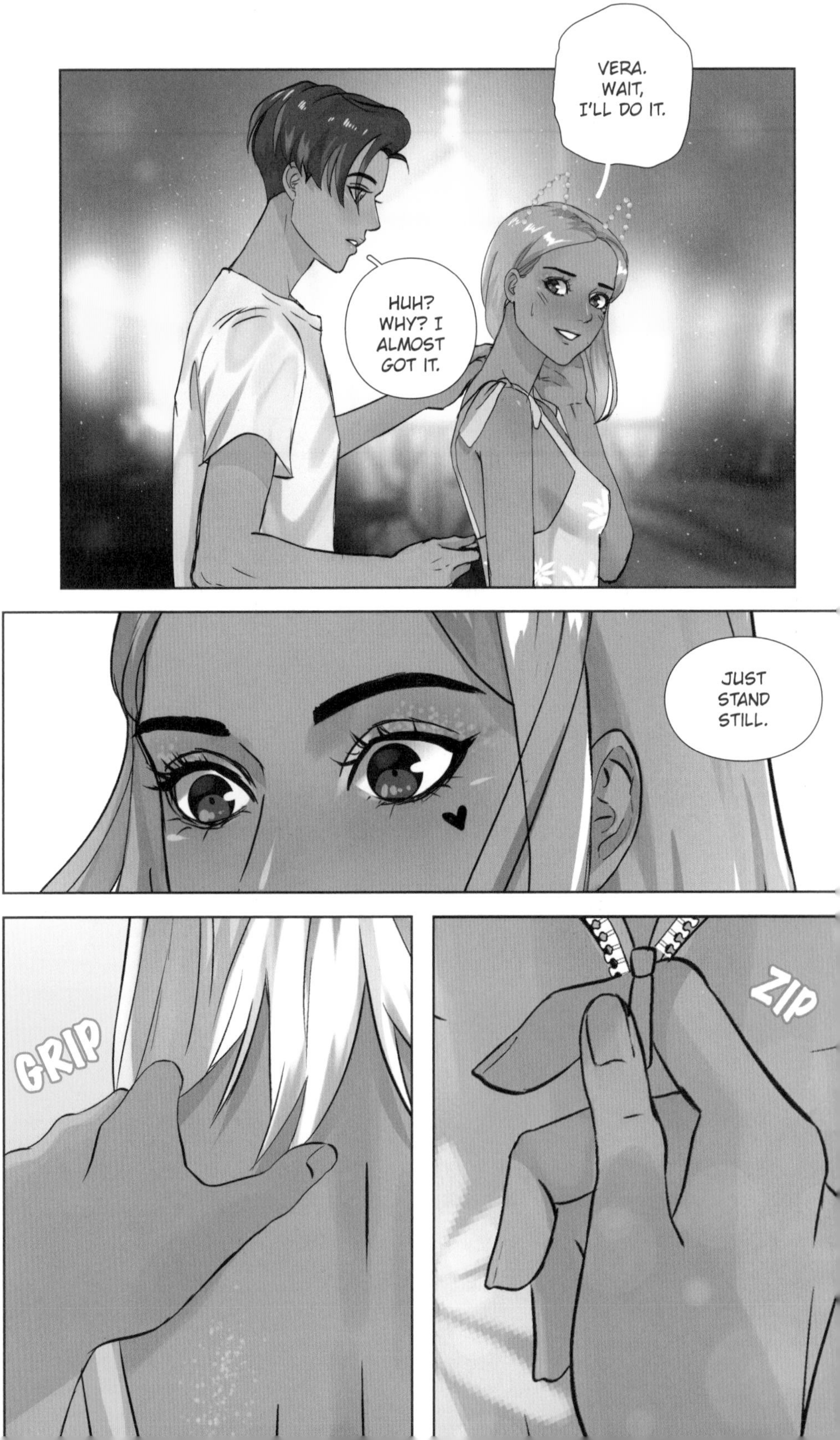
VERA. WAIT, I'LL DO IT.
HUH? WHY? I ALMOST GOT IT.
JUST STAND STILL.
GRIP
ZIP

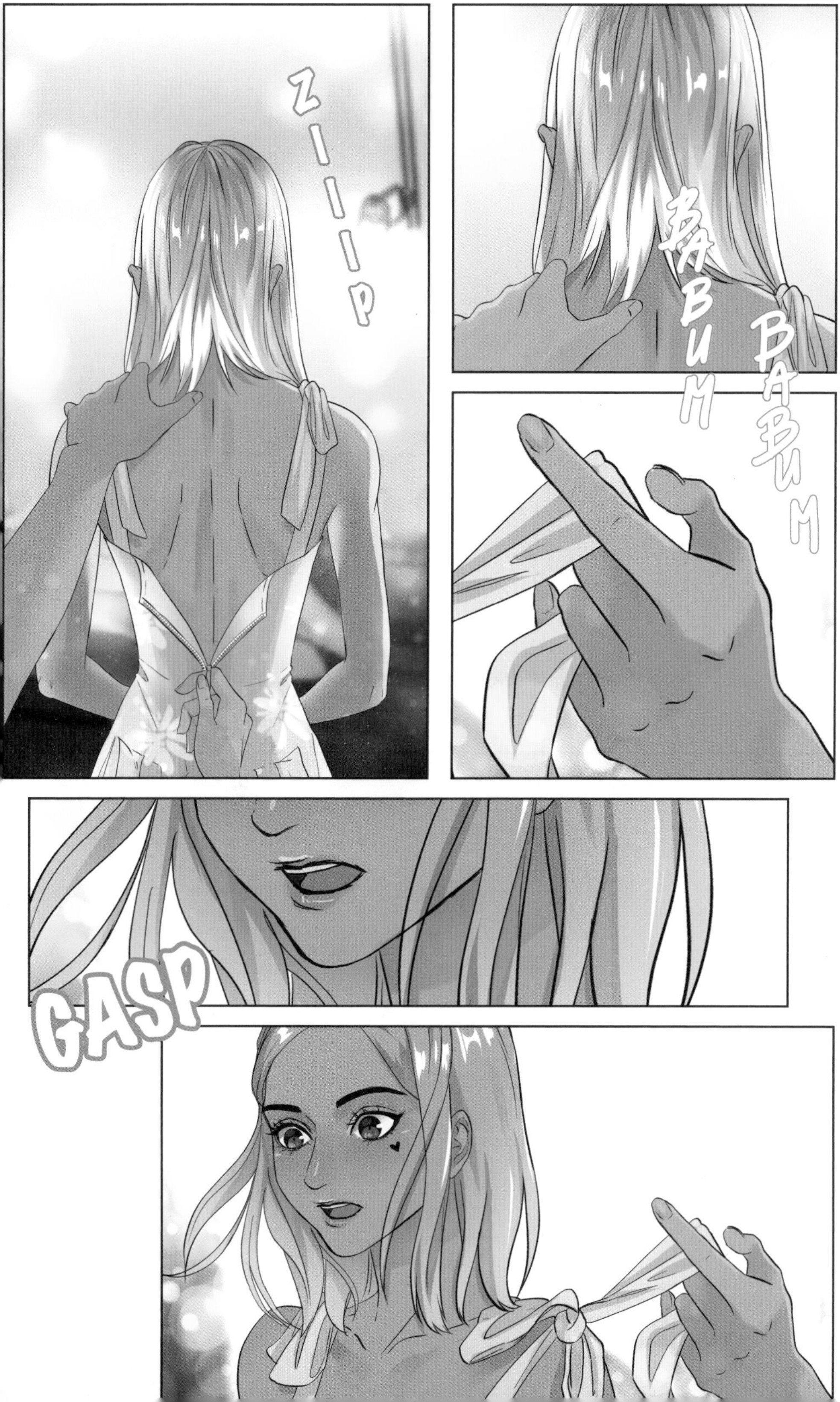
ZIIIP
BABUM
BABUM
GASP

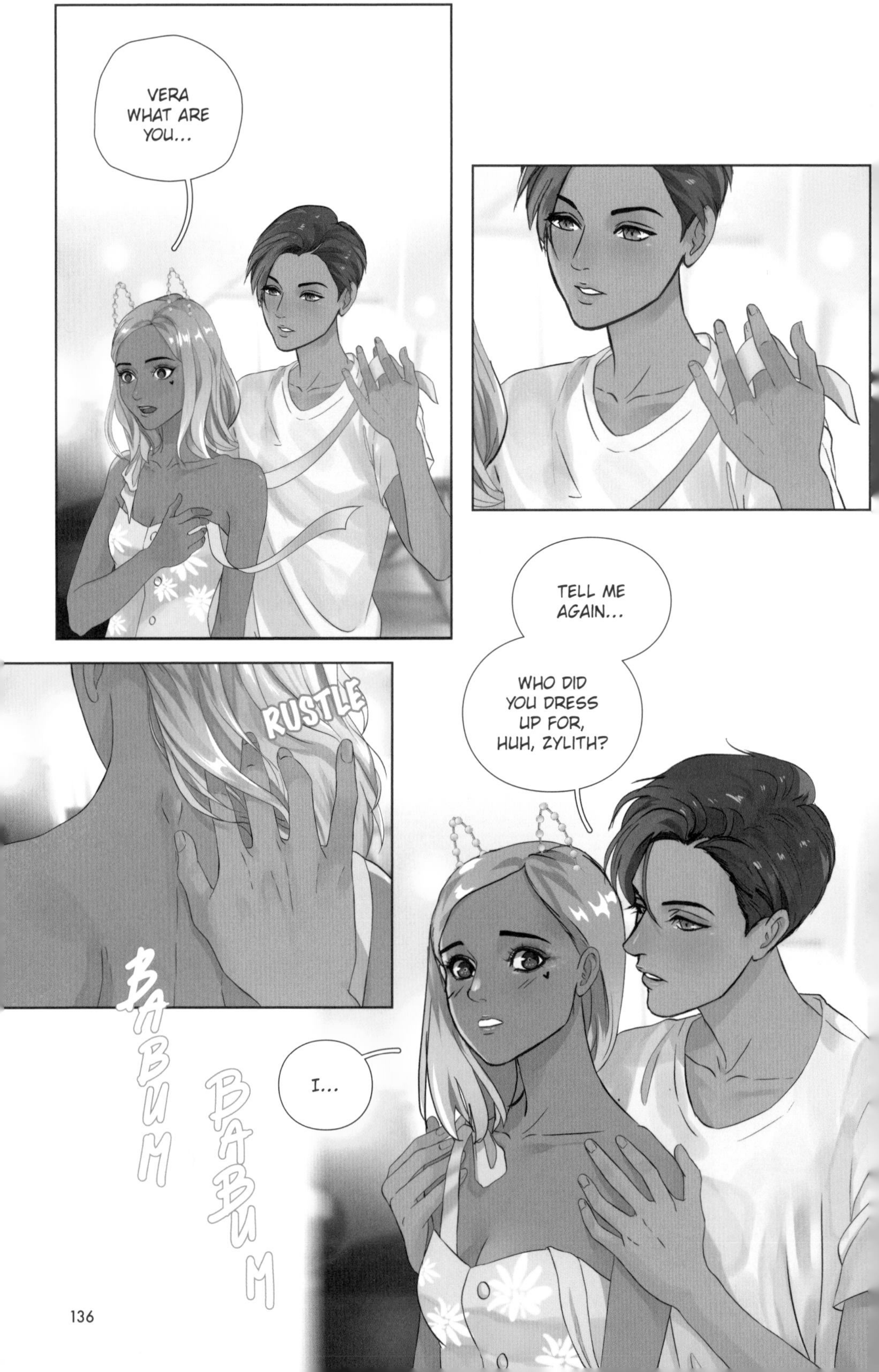
VERA WHAT ARE YOU...
RUSTLE
BA BUM
BA BUM
TELL ME AGAIN...
WHO DID YOU DRESS UP FOR, HUH, ZYLITH?
I...

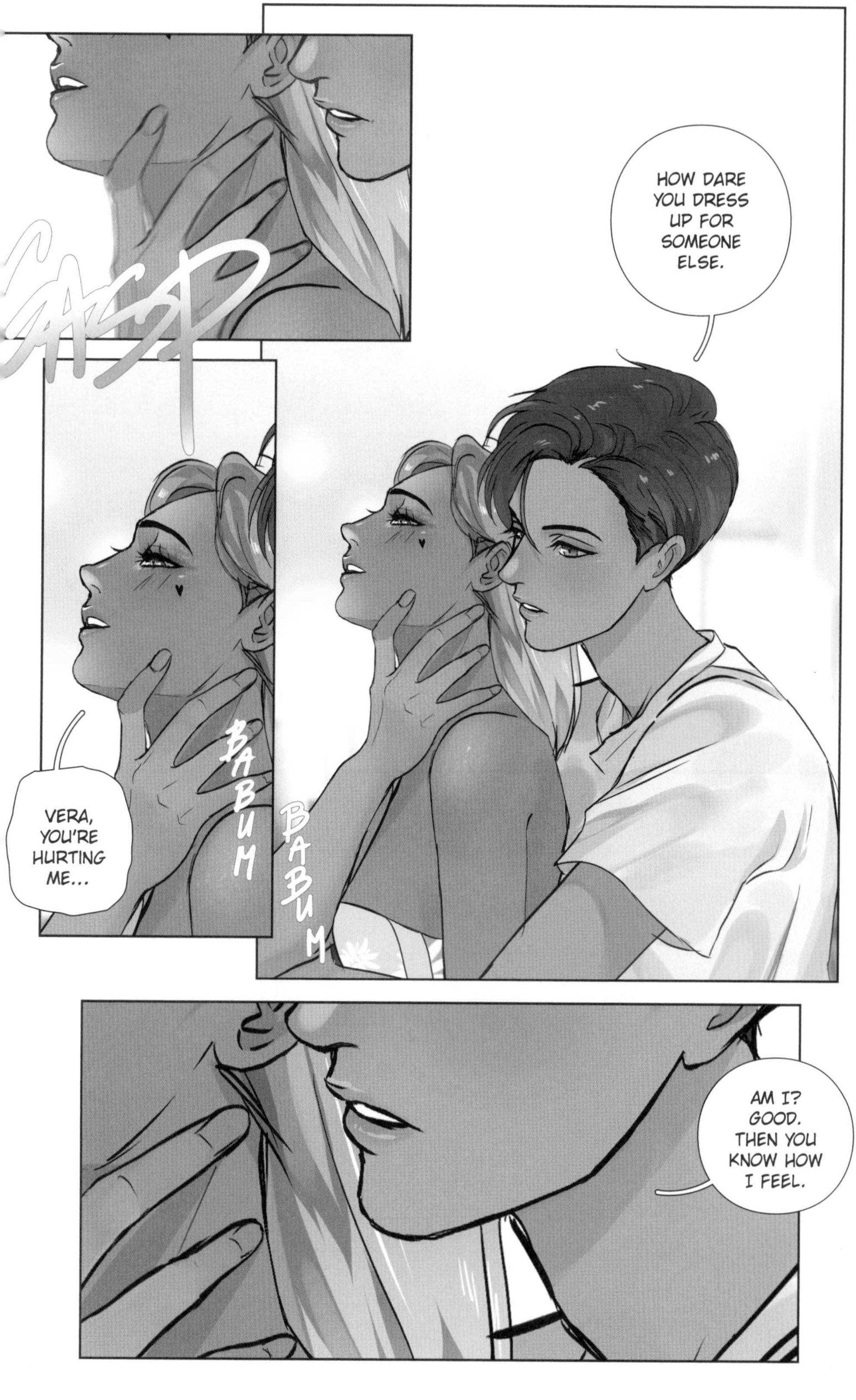
GASP
VERA, YOU'RE HURTING ME...
BABUM
HOW DARE YOU DRESS UP FOR SOMEONE ELSE.
BABUM
AM I? GOOD. THEN YOU KNOW HOW I FEEL.

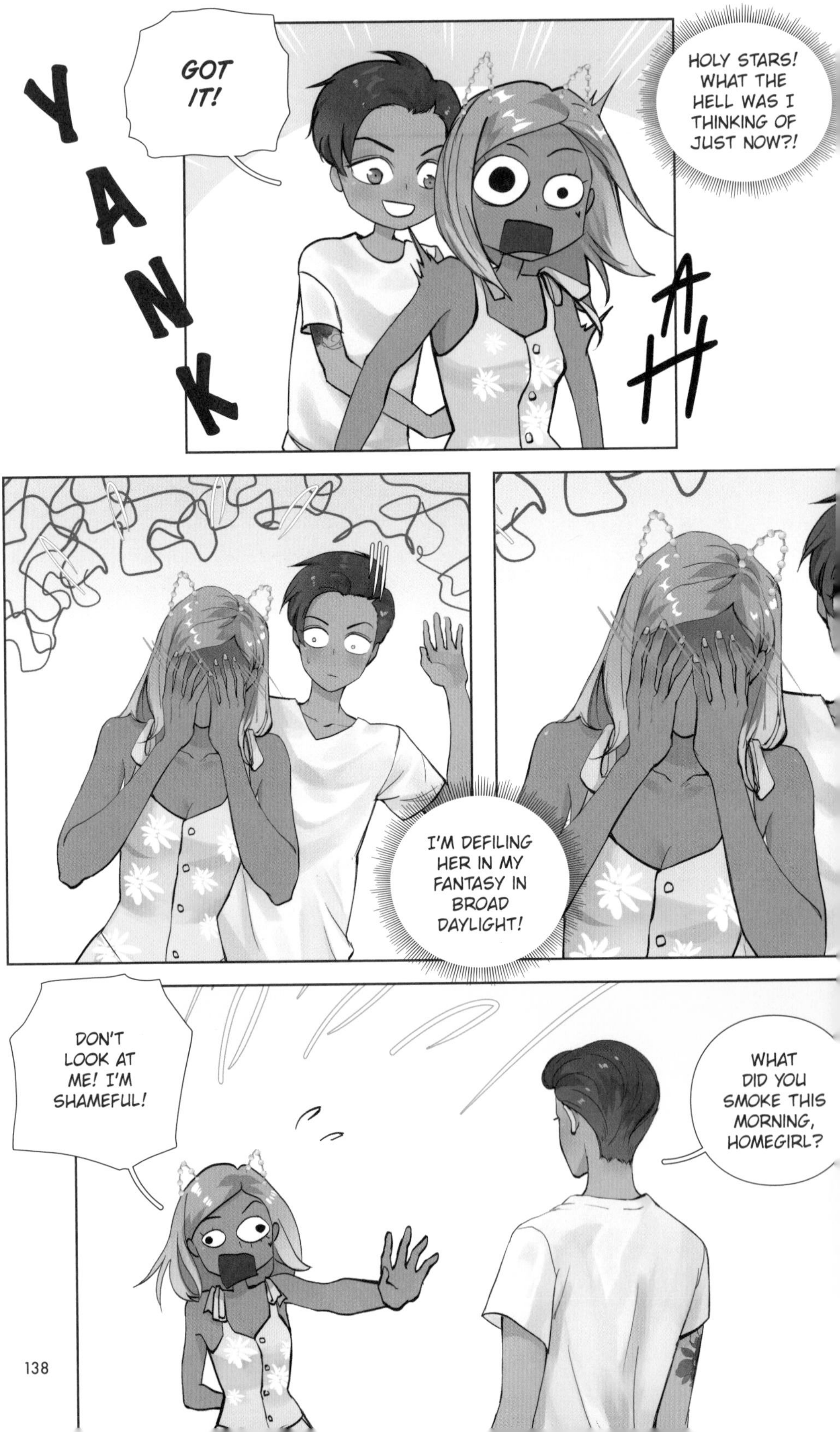
YANK
GOT IT!
HOLY STARS! WHAT THE HELL WAS I THINKING OF JUST NOW?!
AH
I'M DEFILING HER IN MY FANTASY IN BROAD DAYLIGHT!
DON'T LOOK AT ME! I'M SHAMEFUL!
WHAT DID YOU SMOKE THIS MORNING, HOMEGIRL?

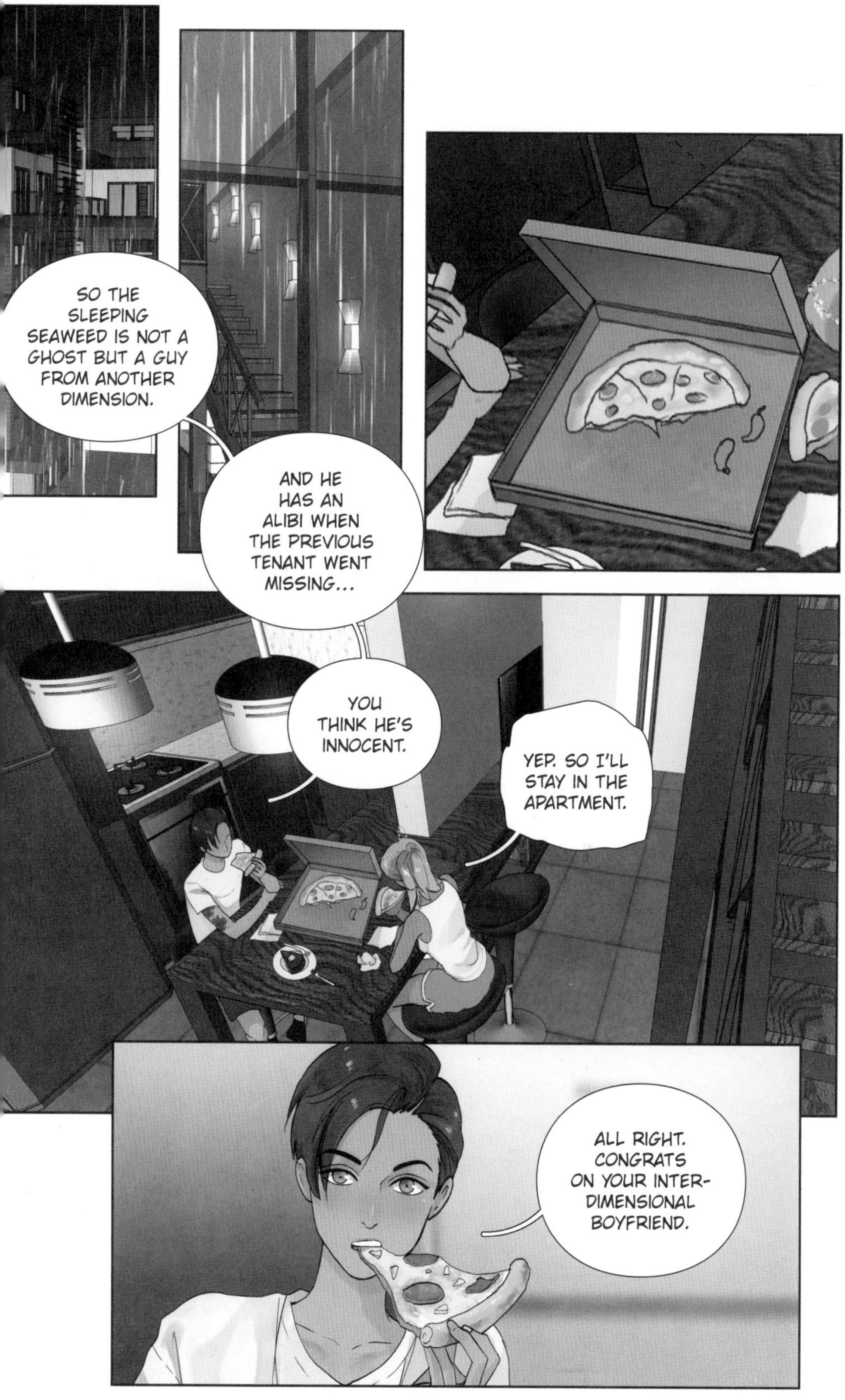
SO THE SLEEPING SEAWEED IS NOT A GHOST BUT A GUY FROM ANOTHER DIMENSION.
AND HE HAS AN ALIBI WHEN THE PREVIOUS TENANT WENT MISSING...
YOU THINK HE'S INNOCENT.
YEP. SO I'LL STAY IN THE APARTMENT.
ALL RIGHT. CONGRATS ON YOUR INTER-DIMENSIONAL BOYFRIEND.

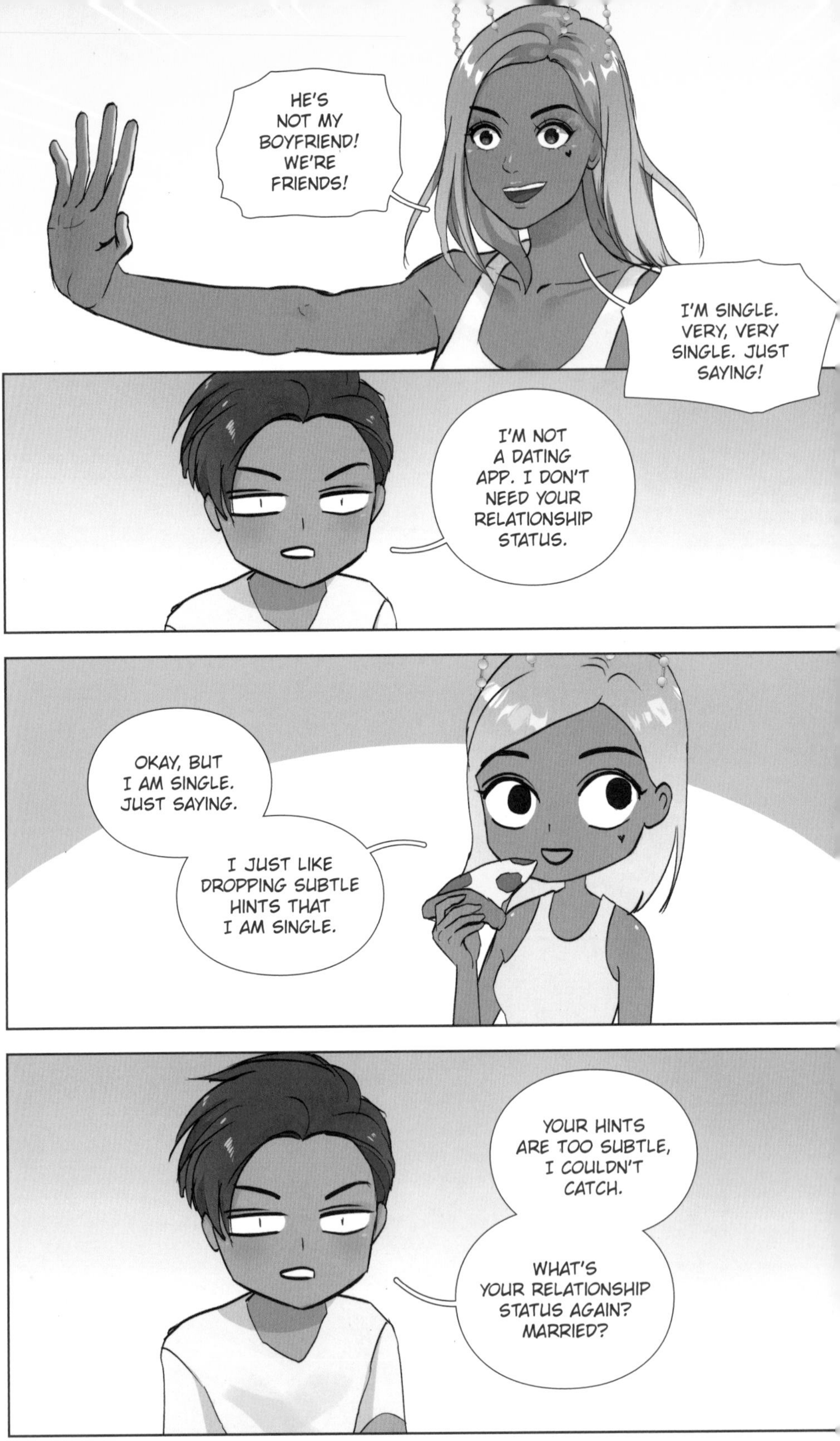
HE'S NOT MY BOYFRIEND! WE'RE FRIENDS!
I'M SINGLE. VERY, VERY SINGLE. JUST SAYING!
I'M NOT A DATING APP. I DON'T NEED YOUR RELATIONSHIP STATUS.
OKAY, BUT I AM SINGLE. JUST SAYING.
I JUST LIKE DROPPING SUBTLE HINTS THAT I AM SINGLE.
YOUR HINTS ARE TOO SUBTLE, I COULDN'T CATCH.
WHAT'S YOUR RELATIONSHIP STATUS AGAIN? MARRIED?

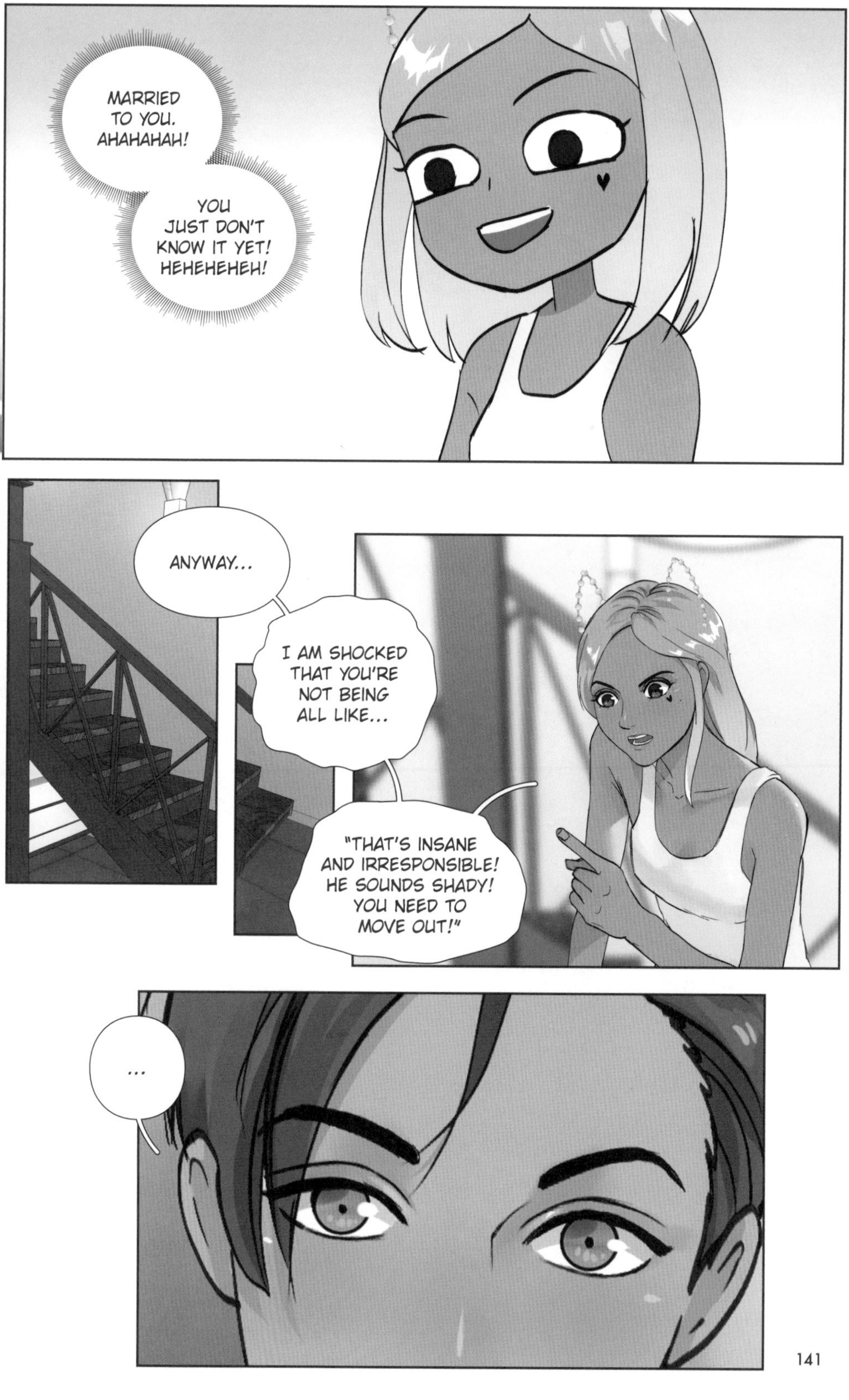
MARRIED TO YOU. AHAHAHAH!
YOU JUST DON'T KNOW IT YET! HEHEHEHEH!
ANYWAY...
I AM SHOCKED THAT YOU'RE NOT BEING ALL LIKE...
"THAT'S INSANE AND IRRESPONSIBLE! HE SOUNDS SHADY! YOU NEED TO MOVE OUT!"
...

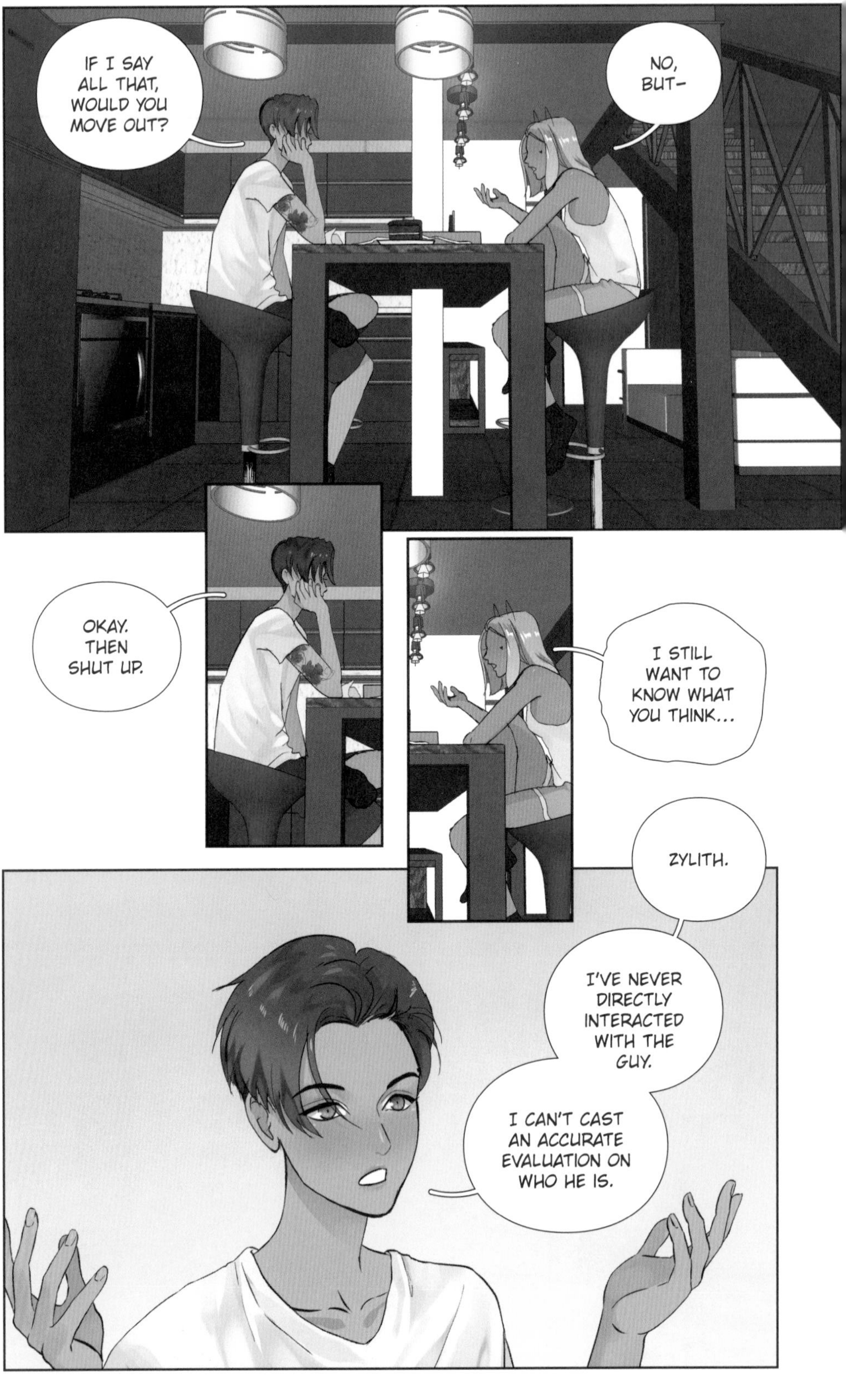
IF I SAY ALL THAT, WOULD YOU MOVE OUT?
NO, BUT-
OKAY. THEN SHUT UP.
I STILL WANT TO KNOW WHAT YOU THINK...
ZYLITH.
I'VE NEVER DIRECTLY INTERACTED WITH THE GUY.
I CAN'T CAST AN ACCURATE EVALUATION ON WHO HE IS.

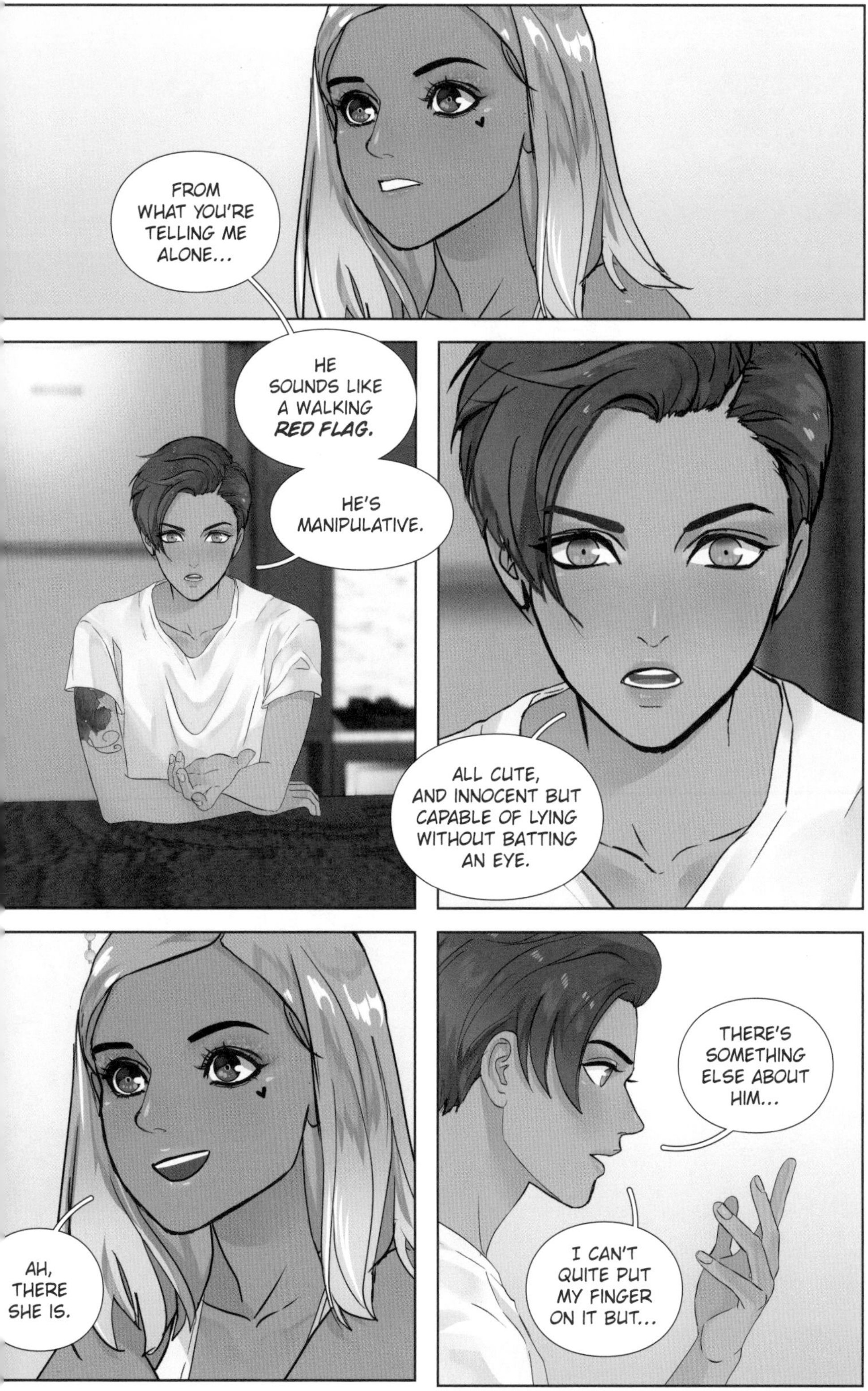
FROM WHAT YOU'RE TELLING ME ALONE...
HE SOUNDS LIKE A WALKING RED FLAG.
HE'S MANIPULATIVE.
ALL CUTE, AND INNOCENT BUT CAPABLE OF LYING WITHOUT BATTING AN EYE.
AH, THERE SHE IS.
THERE'S SOMETHING ELSE ABOUT HIM...
I CAN'T QUITE PUT MY FINGER ON IT BUT...

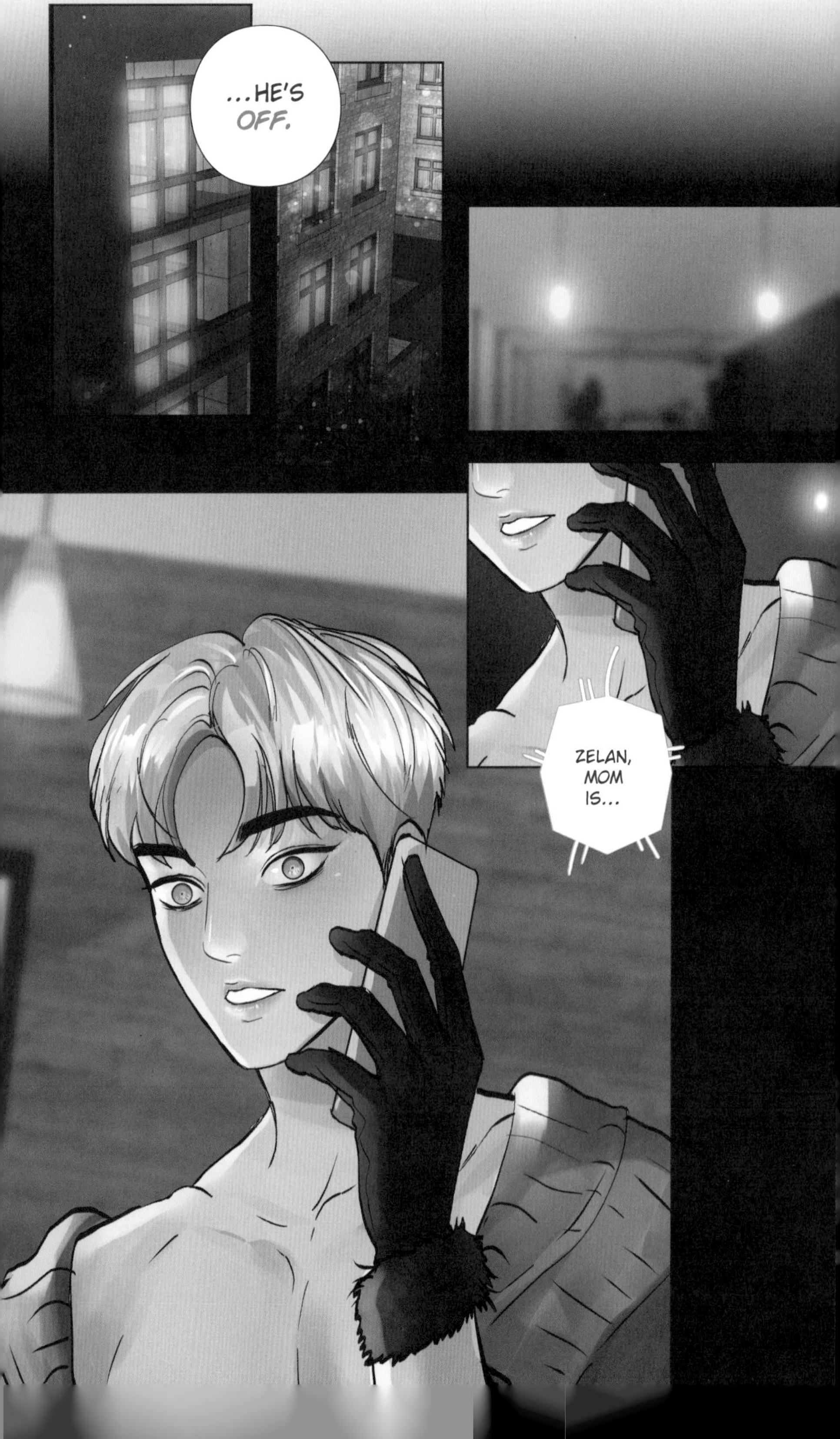
...HE'S OFF.
ZELAN, MOM IS...

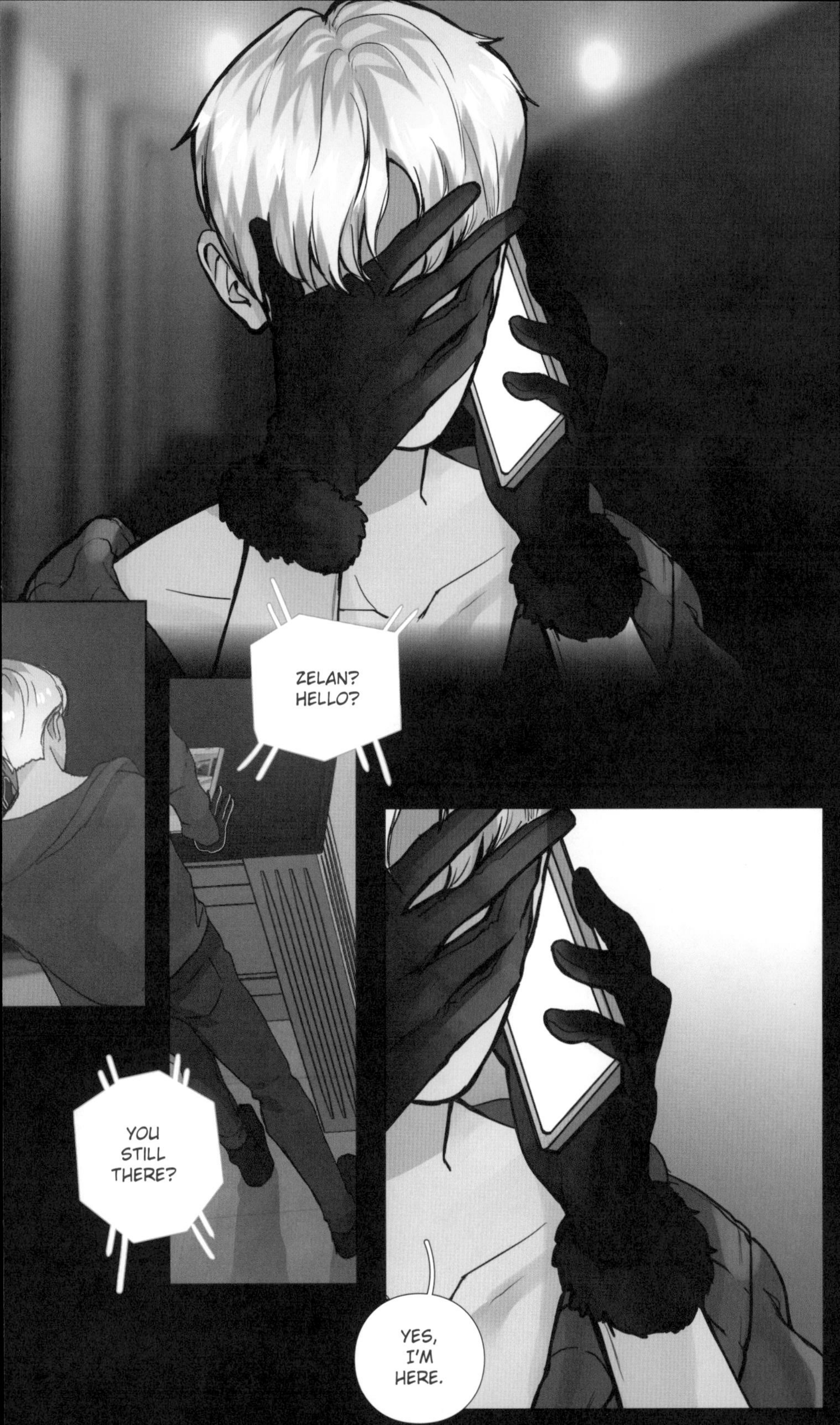
ZELAN? HELLO?
YOU STILL THERE?
YES, I'M HERE.

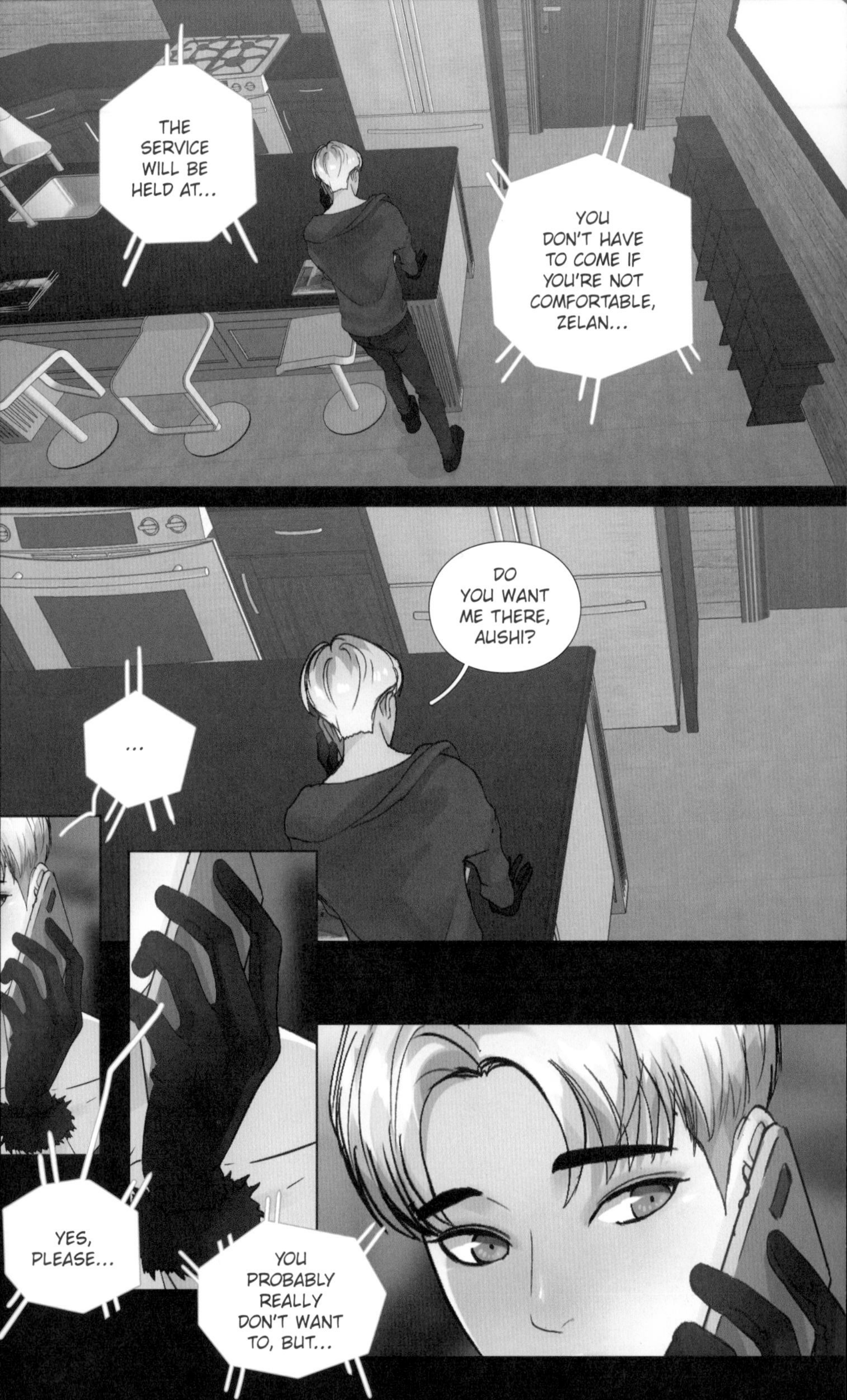
THE SERVICE WILL BE HELD AT...
YOU DON'T HAVE TO COME IF YOU'RE NOT COMFORTABLE, ZELAN...
DO YOU WANT ME THERE, AUSHI?
...
YES, PLEASE...
YOU PROBABLY REALLY DON'T WANT TO, BUT...

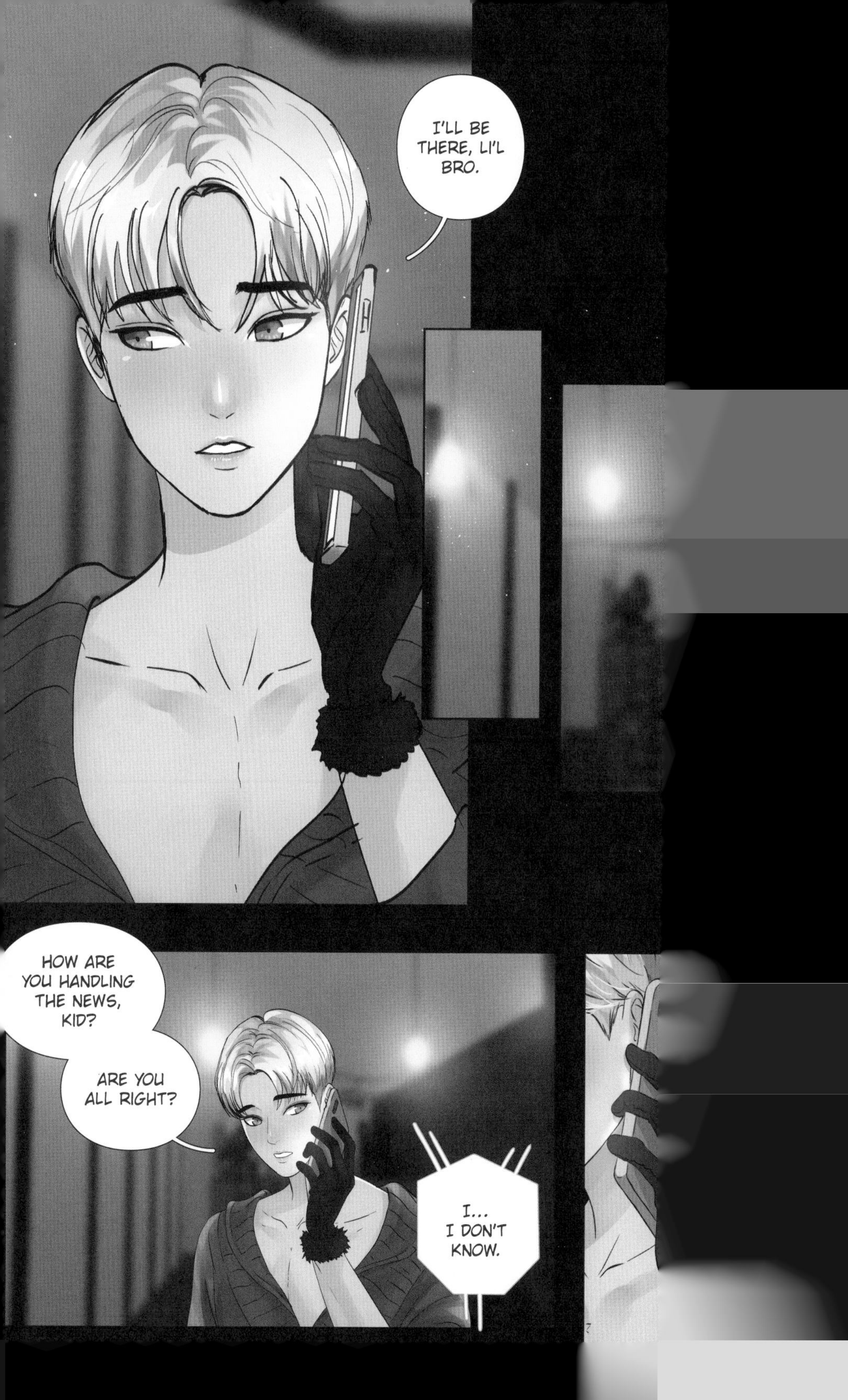
I'LL BE THERE, LI'L BRO.
HOW ARE YOU HANDLING THE NEWS, KID?
ARE YOU ALL RIGHT?
I... I DON'T KNOW.

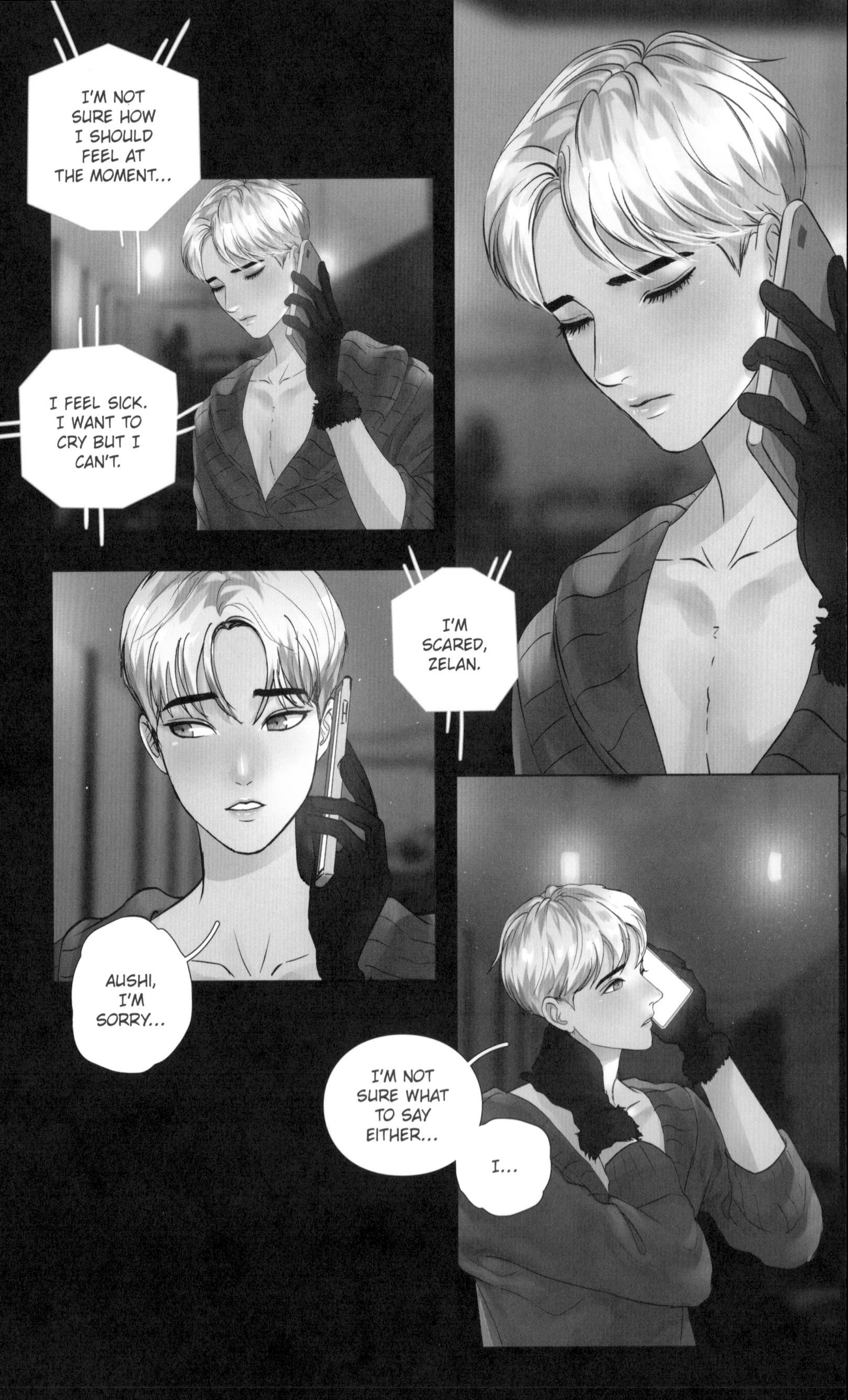
I'M NOT SURE HOW I SHOULD FEEL AT THE MOMENT...
I FEEL SICK. I WANT TO CRY BUT I CAN'T.
I'M SCARED, ZELAN.
AUSHI, I'M SORRY...
I'M NOT SURE WHAT TO SAY EITHER...
I...

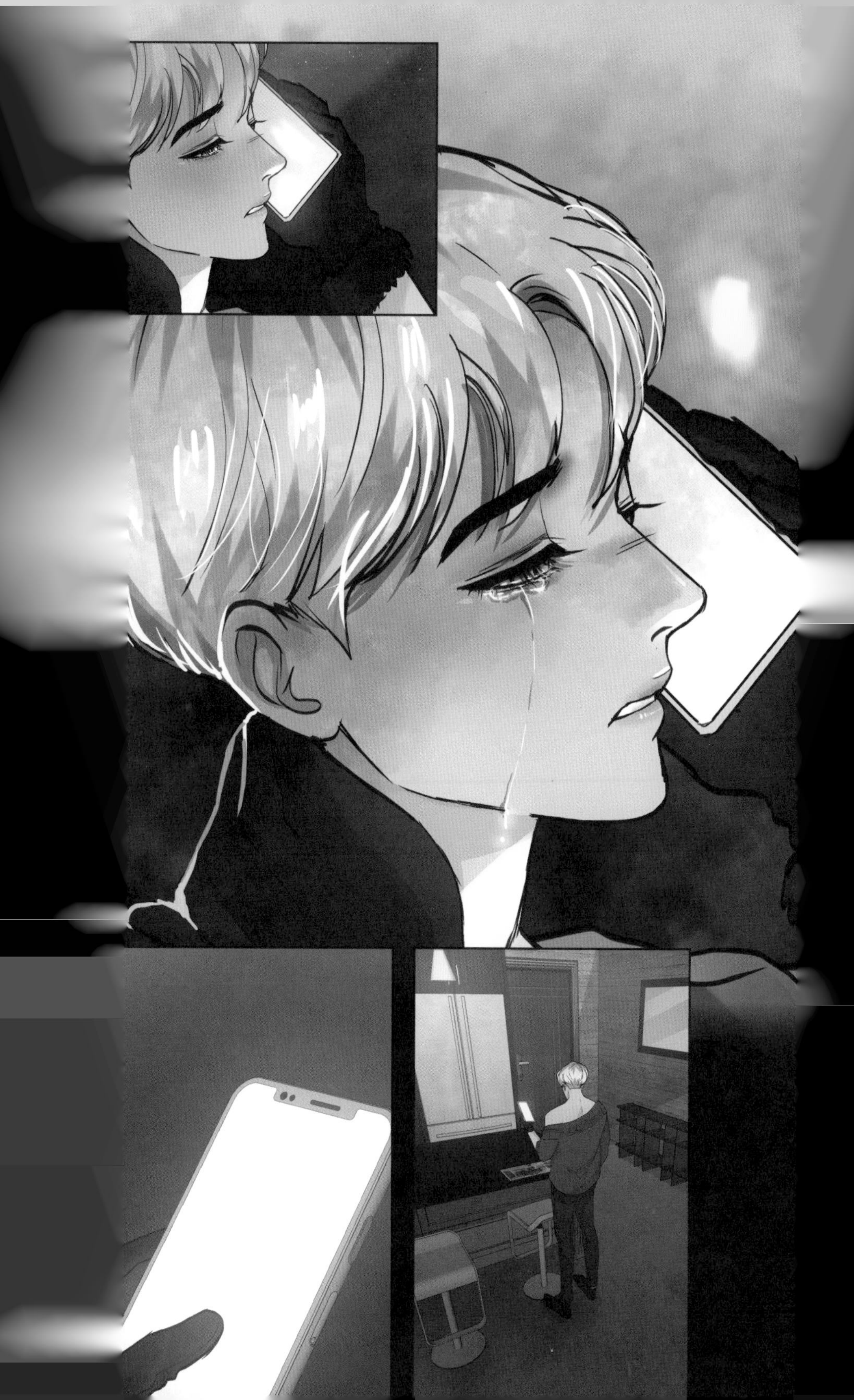

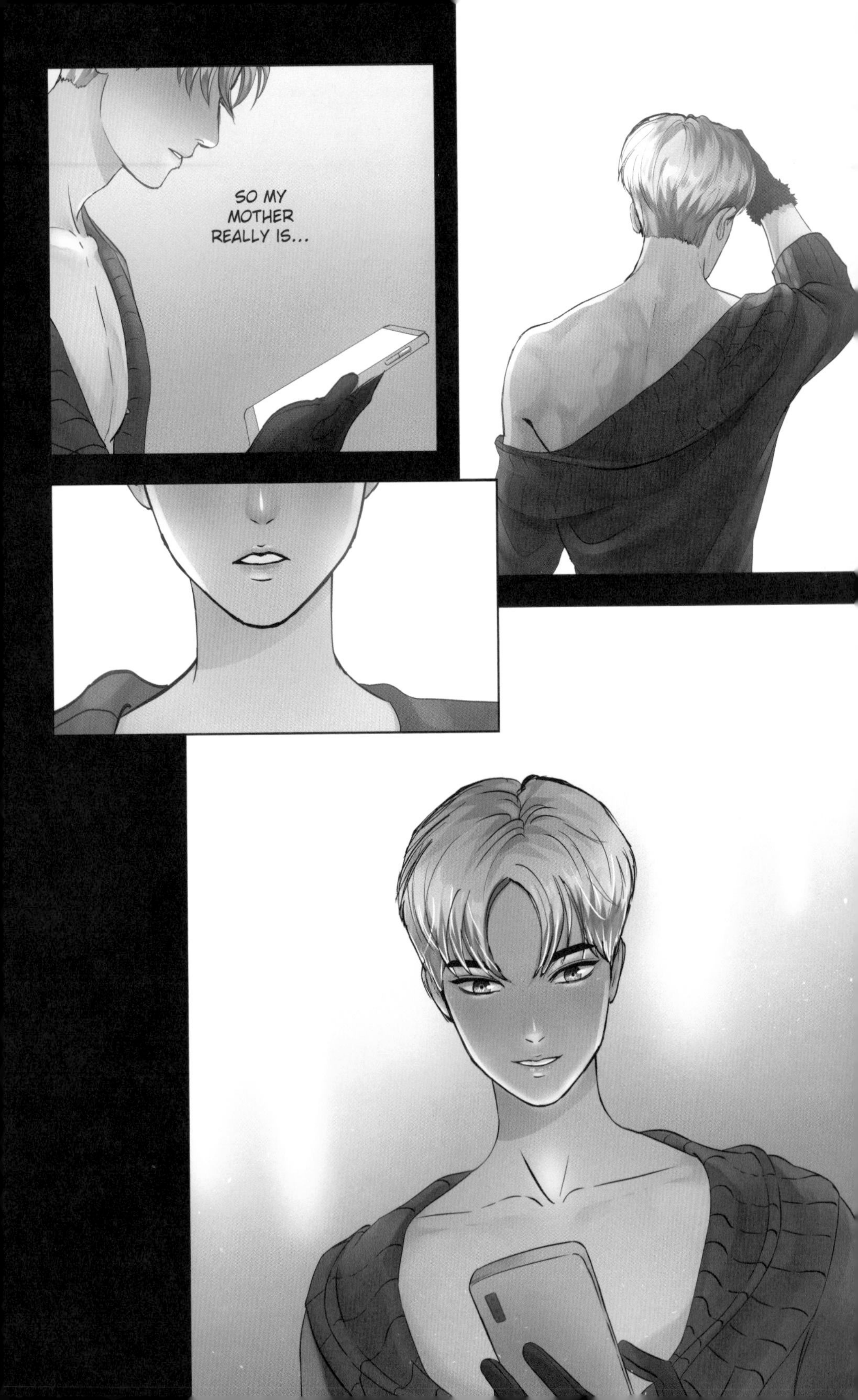
SO MY
MOTHER
REALLY IS...

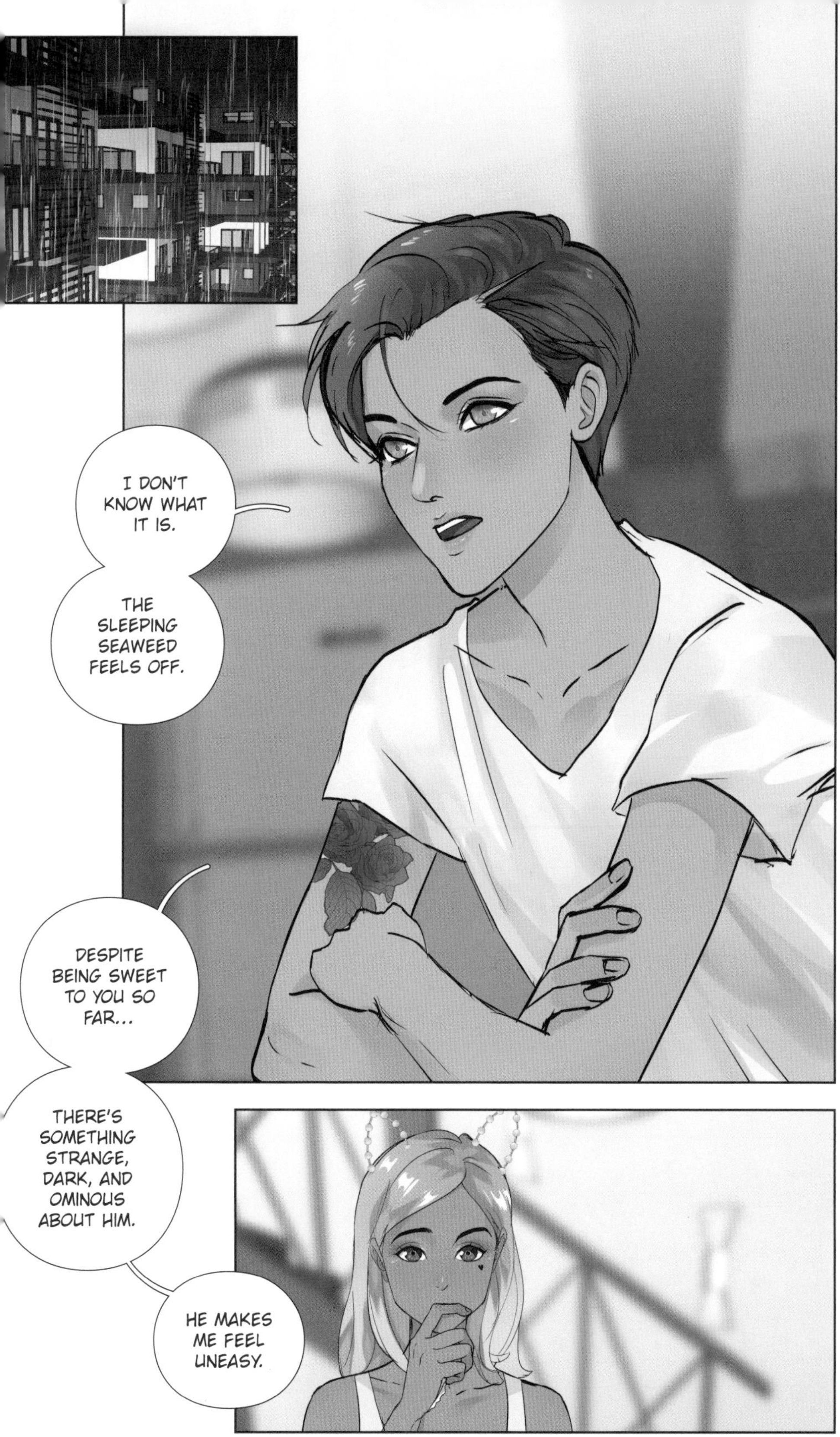
I DON'T KNOW WHAT IT IS.
THE SLEEPING SEAWEED FEELS OFF.
DESPITE BEING SWEET TO YOU SO FAR...
THERE'S SOMETHING STRANGE, DARK, AND OMINOUS ABOUT HIM.
HE MAKES ME FEEL UNEASY.

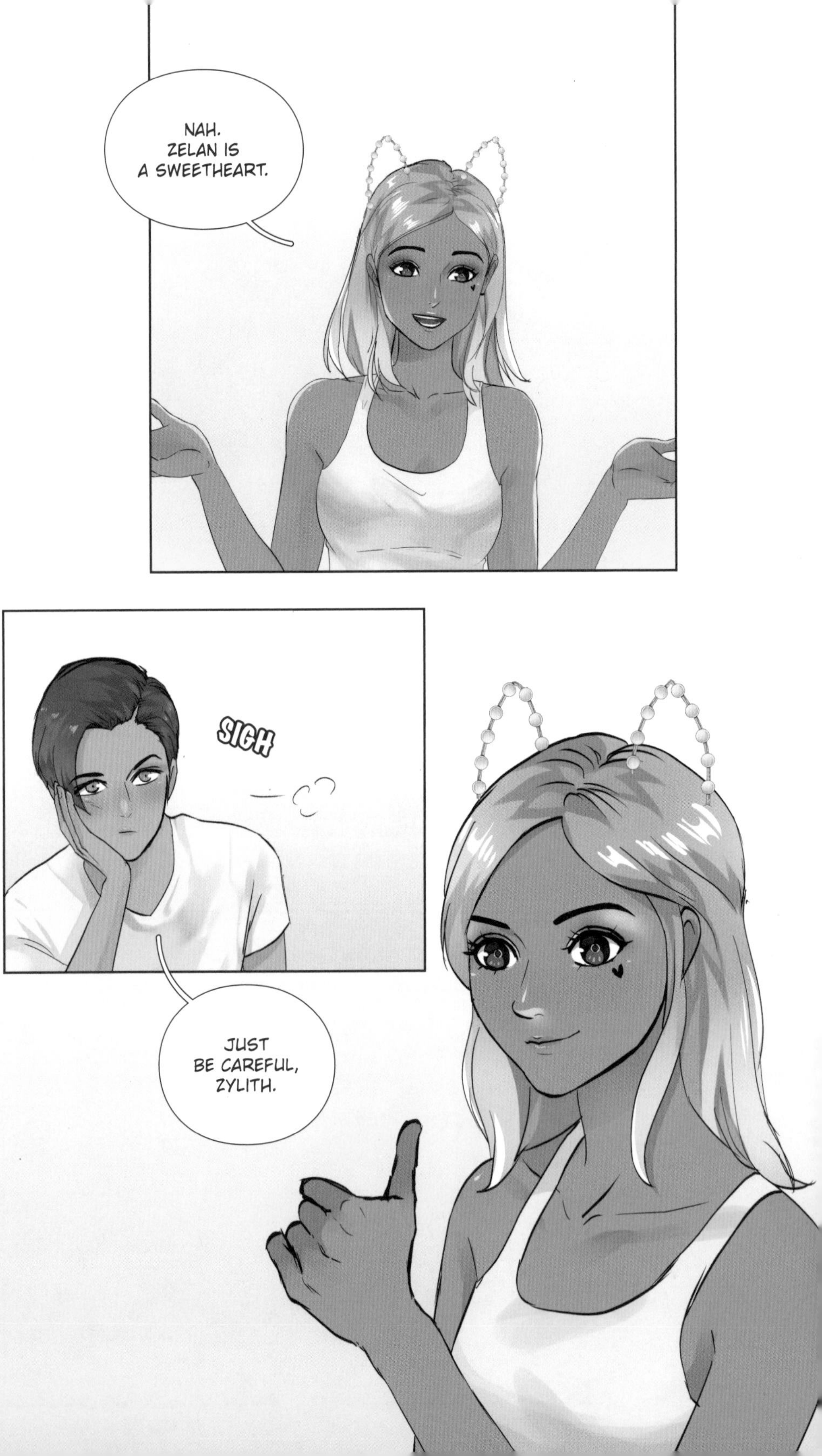
NAH.
ZELAN IS
A SWEETHEART.
SIGH
JUST
BE CAREFUL,
ZYLITH.

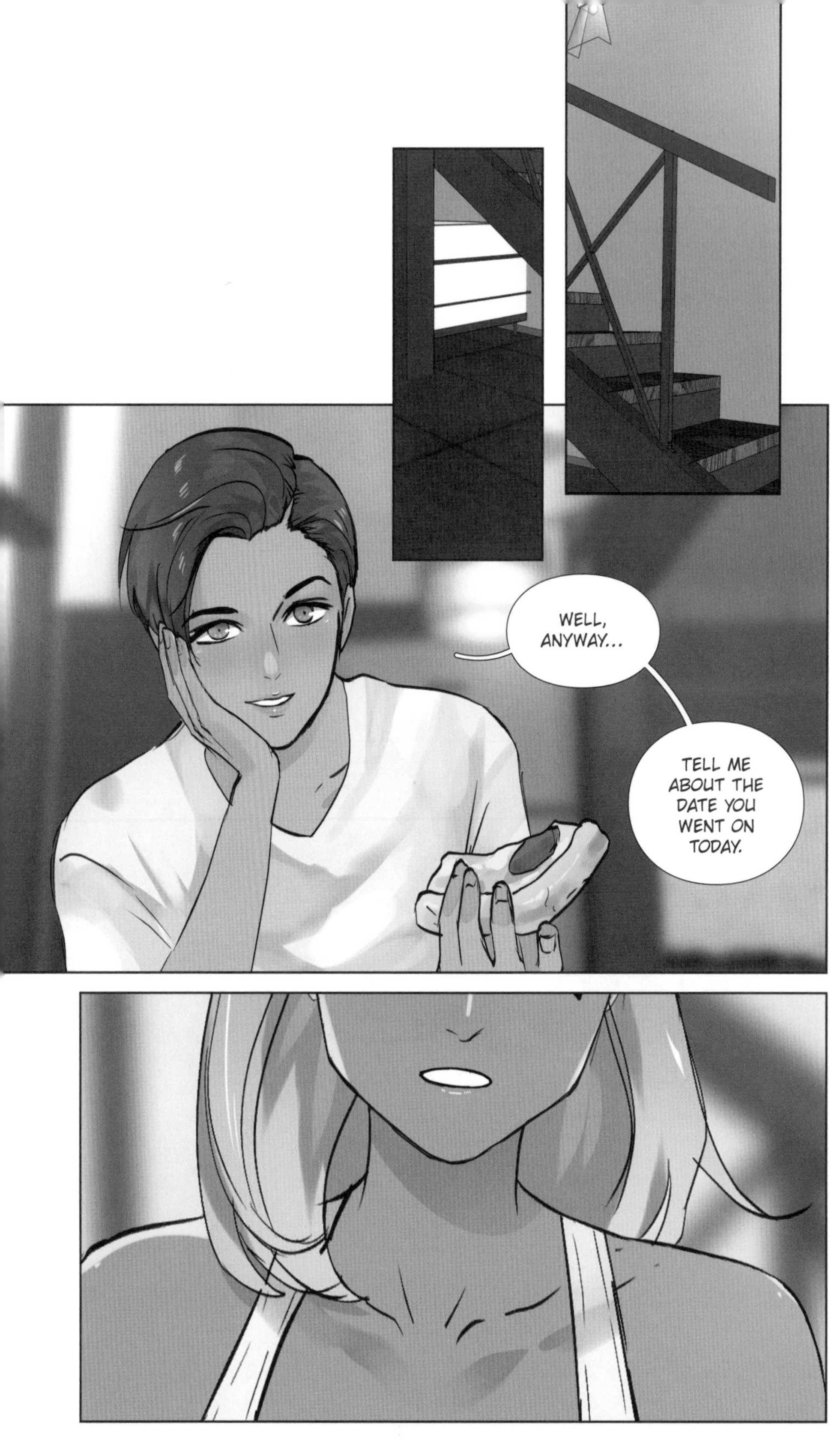
WELL, ANYWAY...
TELL ME ABOUT THE DATE YOU WENT ON TODAY.

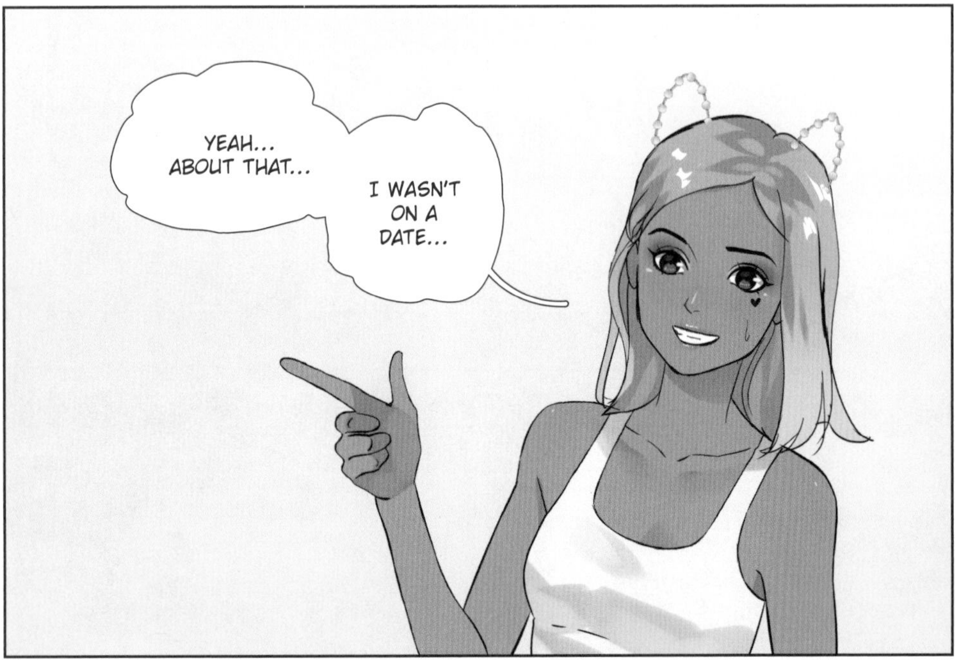
YEAH... ABOUT THAT...
I WASN'T ON A DATE...
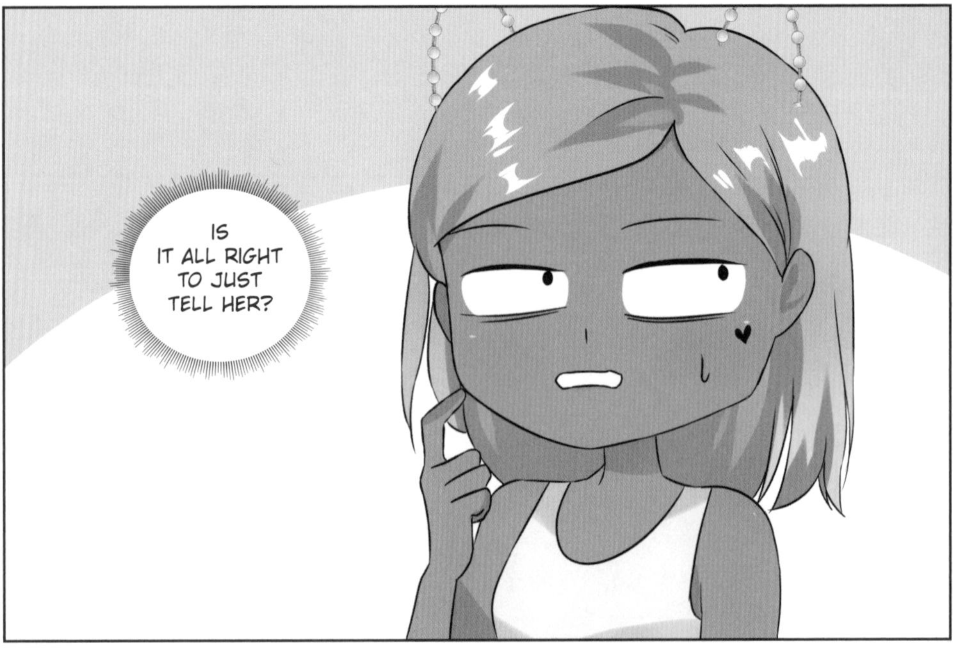
IS IT ALL RIGHT TO JUST TELL HER?

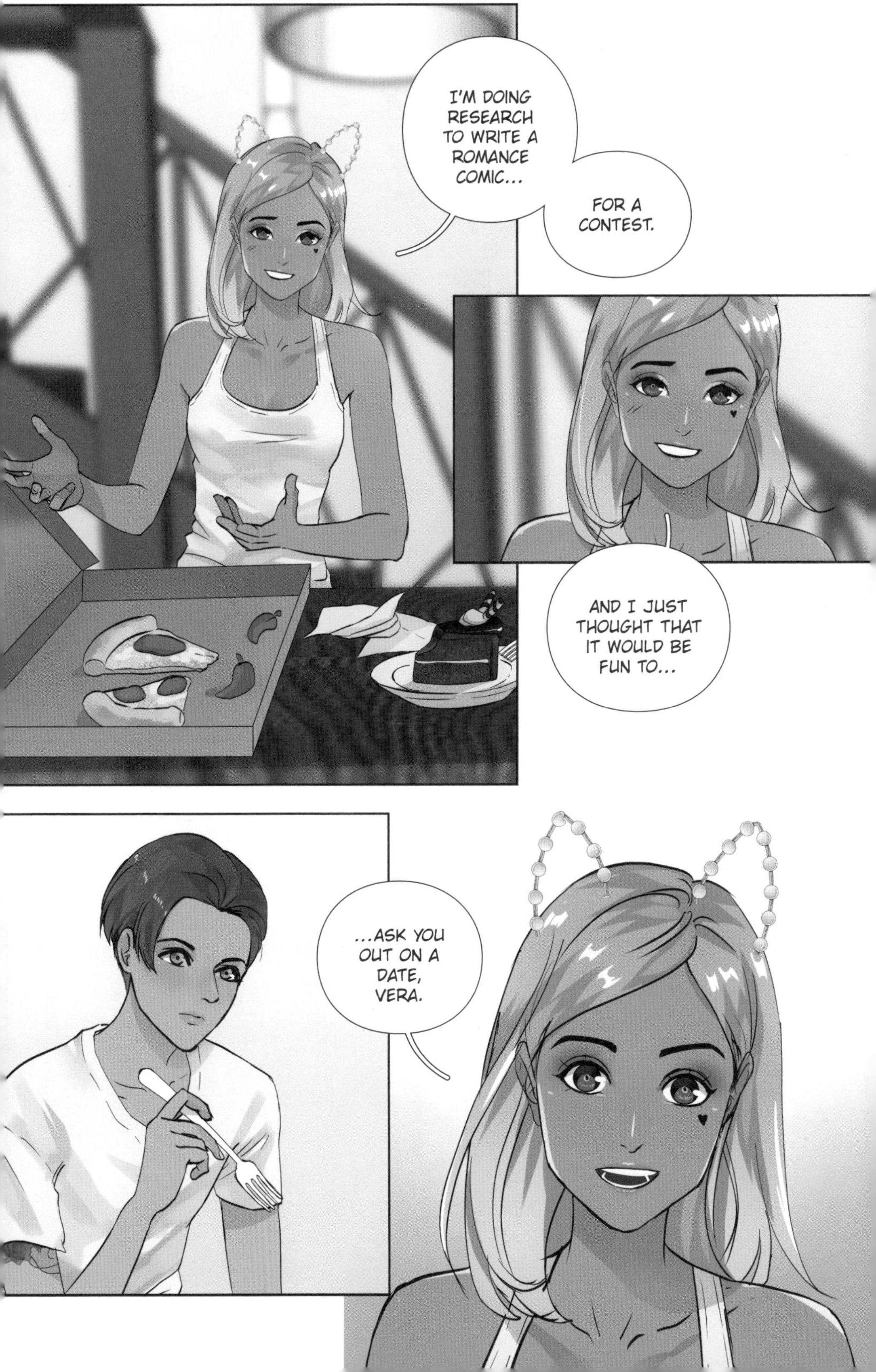
I'M DOING RESEARCH TO WRITE A ROMANCE COMIC...
FOR A CONTEST.
AND I JUST THOUGHT THAT IT WOULD BE FUN TO...
...ASK YOU OUT ON A DATE, VERA.

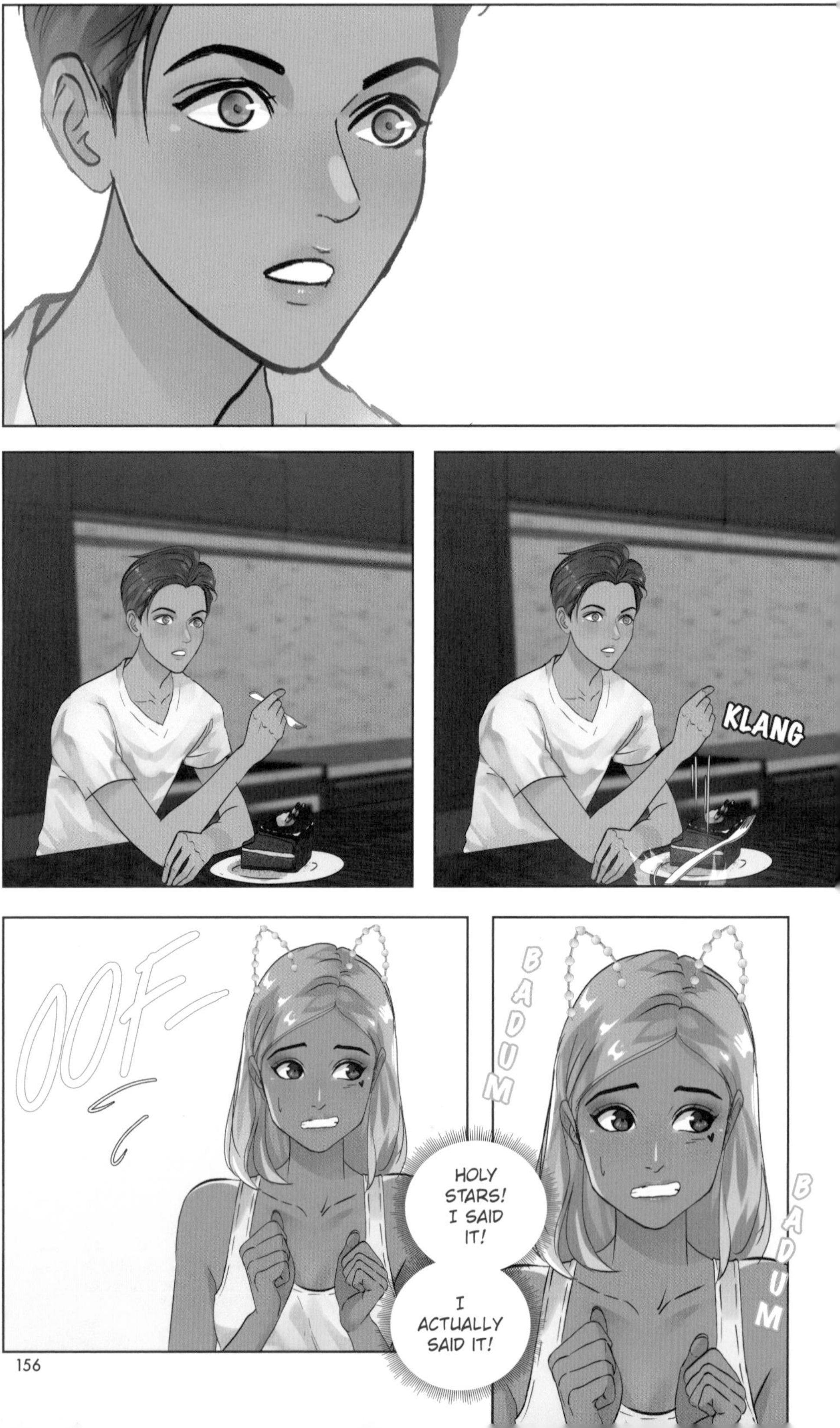
KLANG
OOF—
BADUM
HOLY STARS! I SAID IT!
I ACTUALLY SAID IT!
BADUM

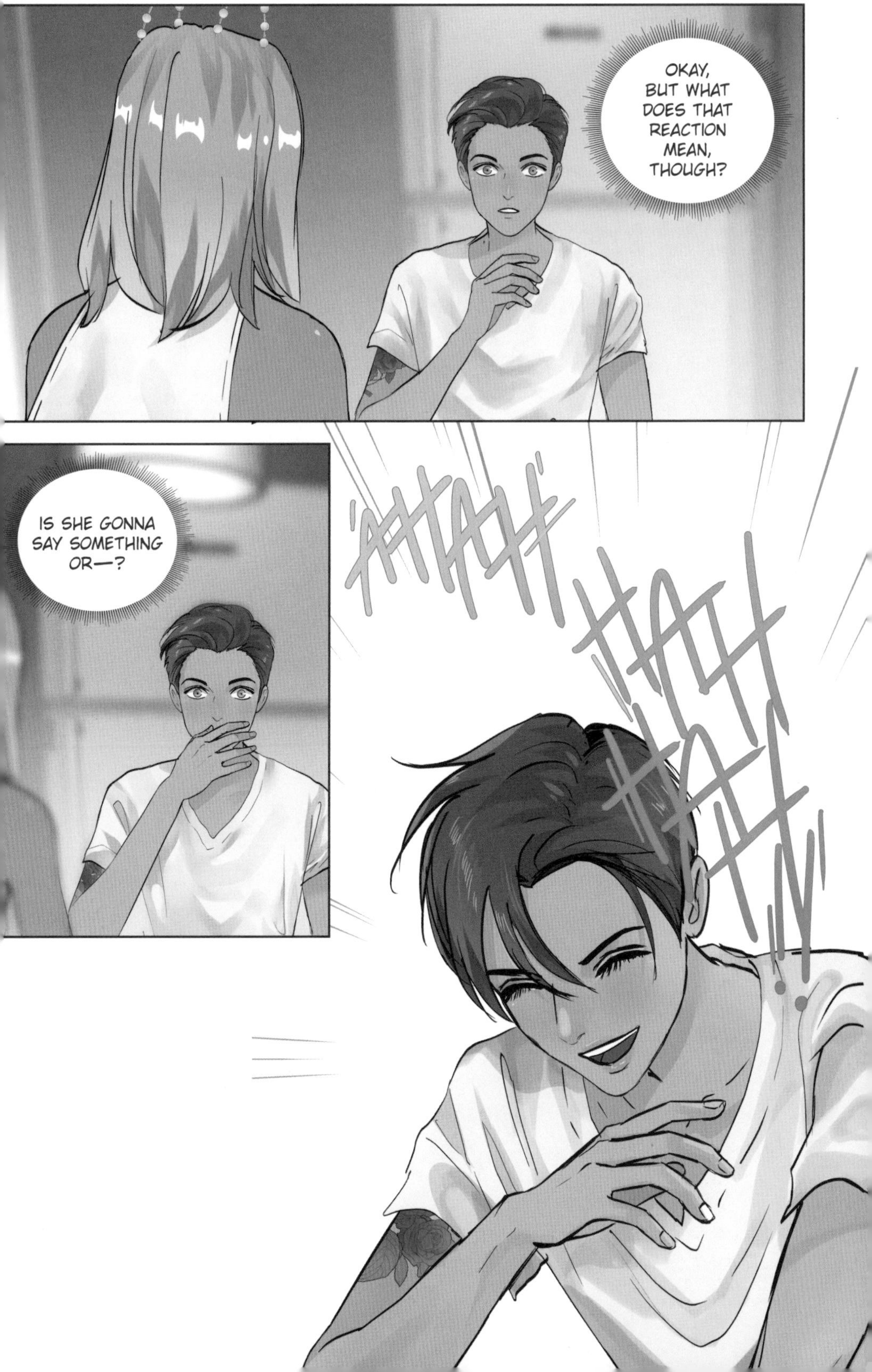
OKAY, BUT WHAT DOES THAT REACTION MEAN, THOUGH?
IS SHE GONNA SAY SOMETHING OR—?
AHAH HAH HAH HAH!!

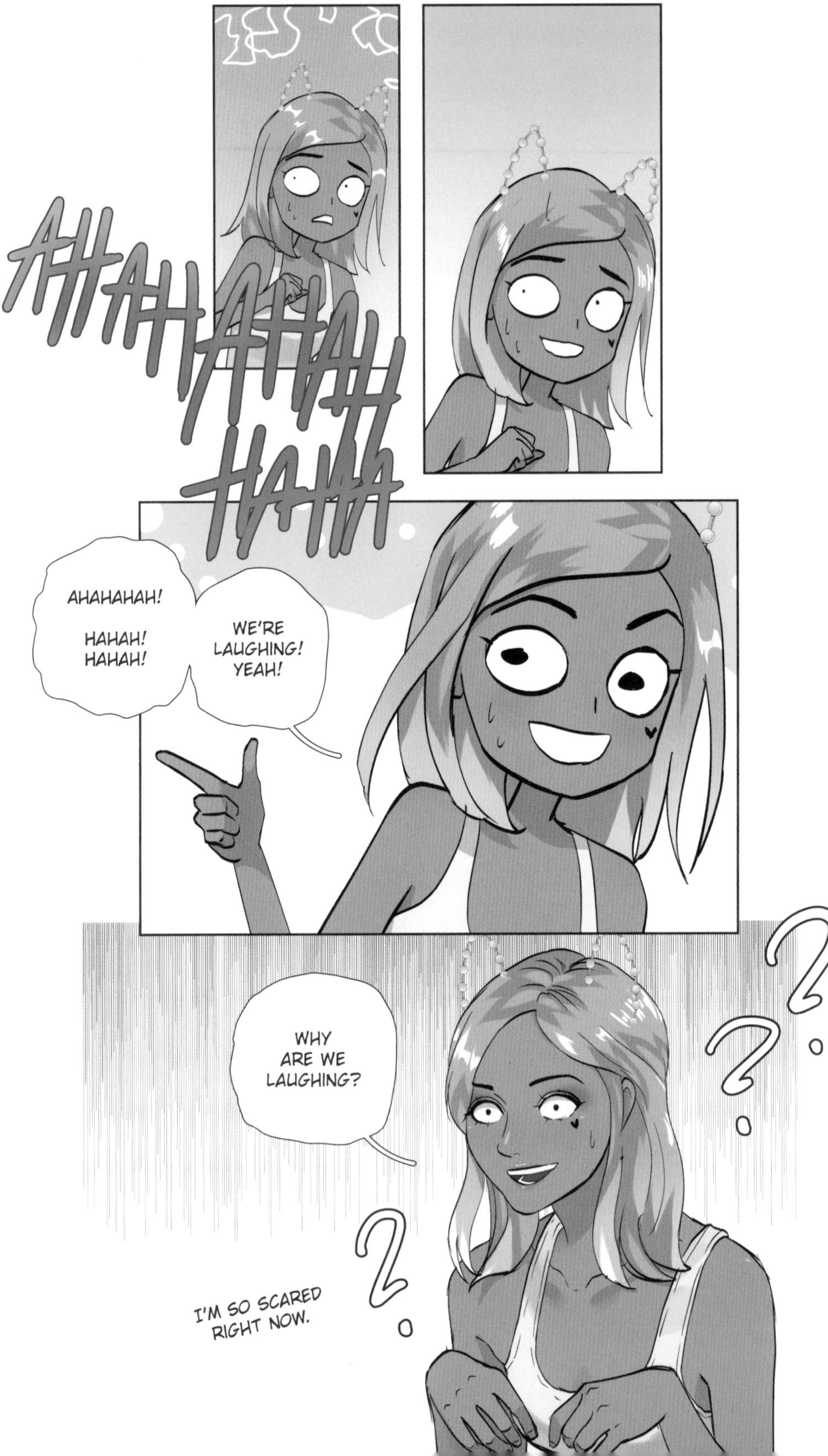
AHAHAHAHAH HAHA
AHAHAHAH! HAHAH! HAHAH!
WE'RE LAUGHING! YEAH!
WHY ARE WE LAUGHING?
I'M SO SCARED RIGHT NOW.

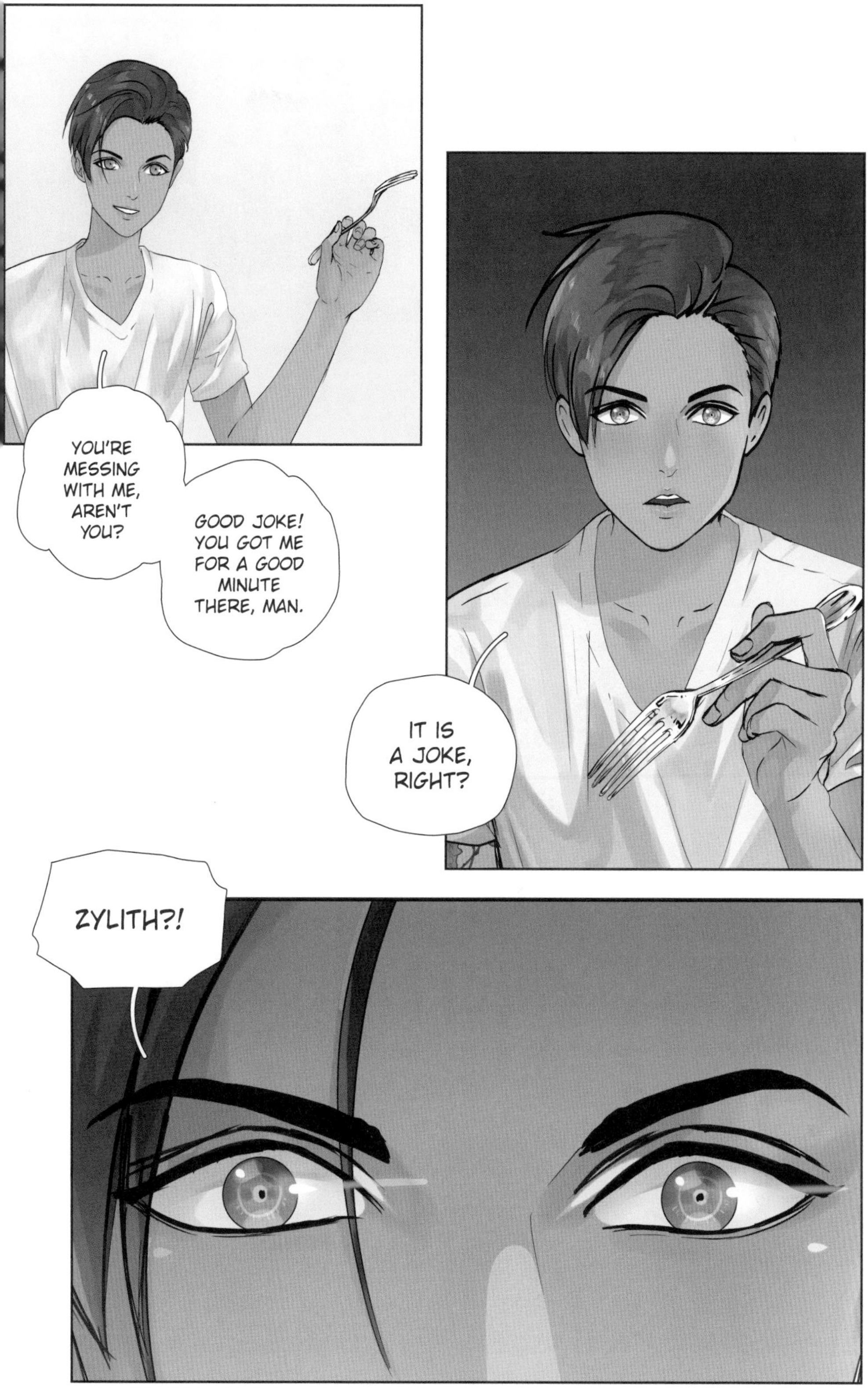
YOU'RE MESSING WITH ME, AREN'T YOU?
GOOD JOKE! YOU GOT ME FOR A GOOD MINUTE THERE, MAN.
IT IS A JOKE, RIGHT?
ZYLITH?!

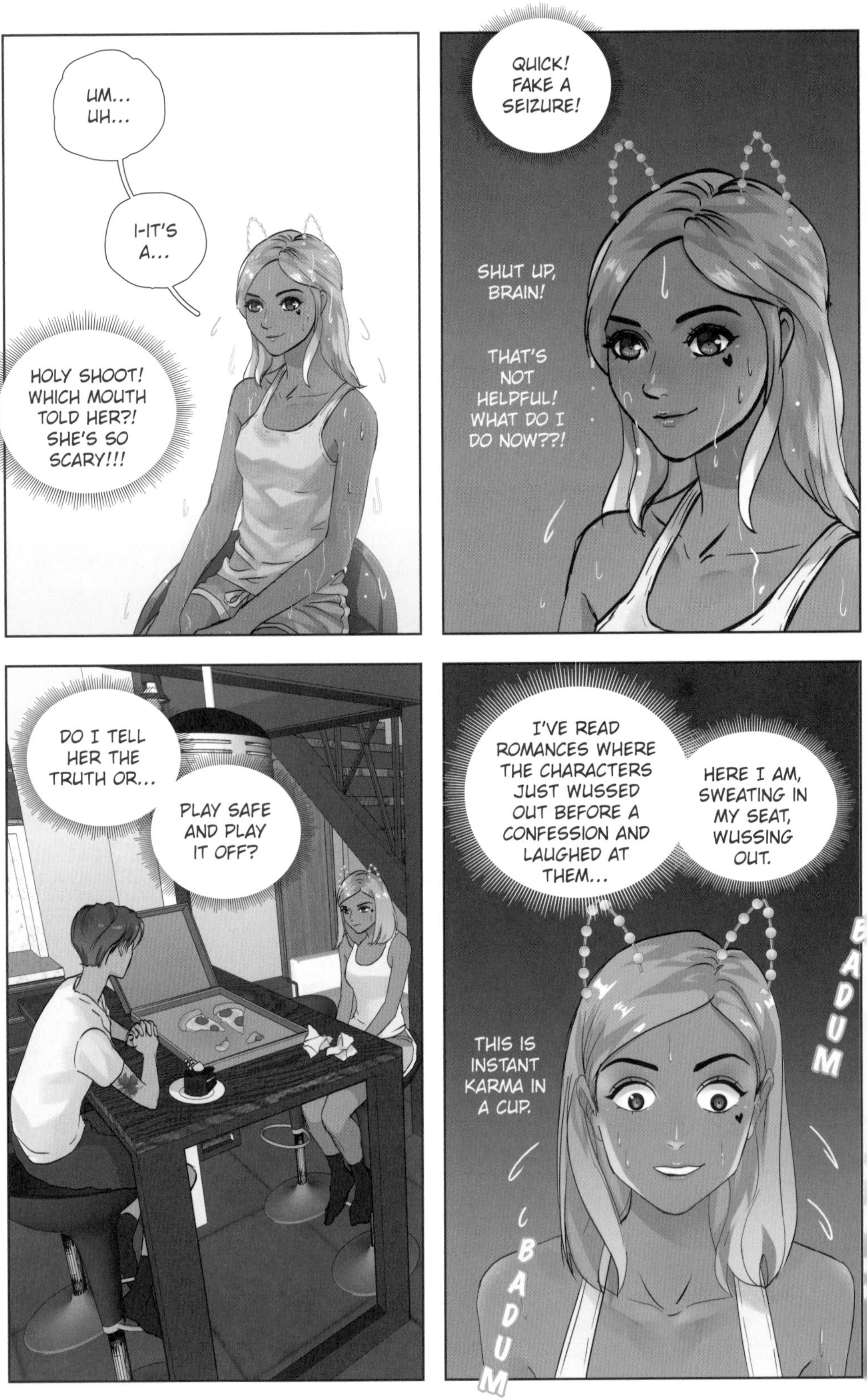
UM... UH...
I-IT'S A...
HOLY SHOOT! WHICH MOUTH TOLD HER?! SHE'S SO SCARY!!!
QUICK! FAKE A SEIZURE!
SHUT UP, BRAIN!
THAT'S NOT HELPFUL! WHAT DO I DO NOW??!
DO I TELL HER THE TRUTH OR...
PLAY SAFE AND PLAY IT OFF?
I'VE READ ROMANCES WHERE THE CHARACTERS JUST WUSSED OUT BEFORE A CONFESSION AND LAUGHED AT THEM...
HERE I AM, SWEATING IN MY SEAT, WUSSING OUT.
BADUM
THIS IS INSTANT KARMA IN A CUP.
BADUM

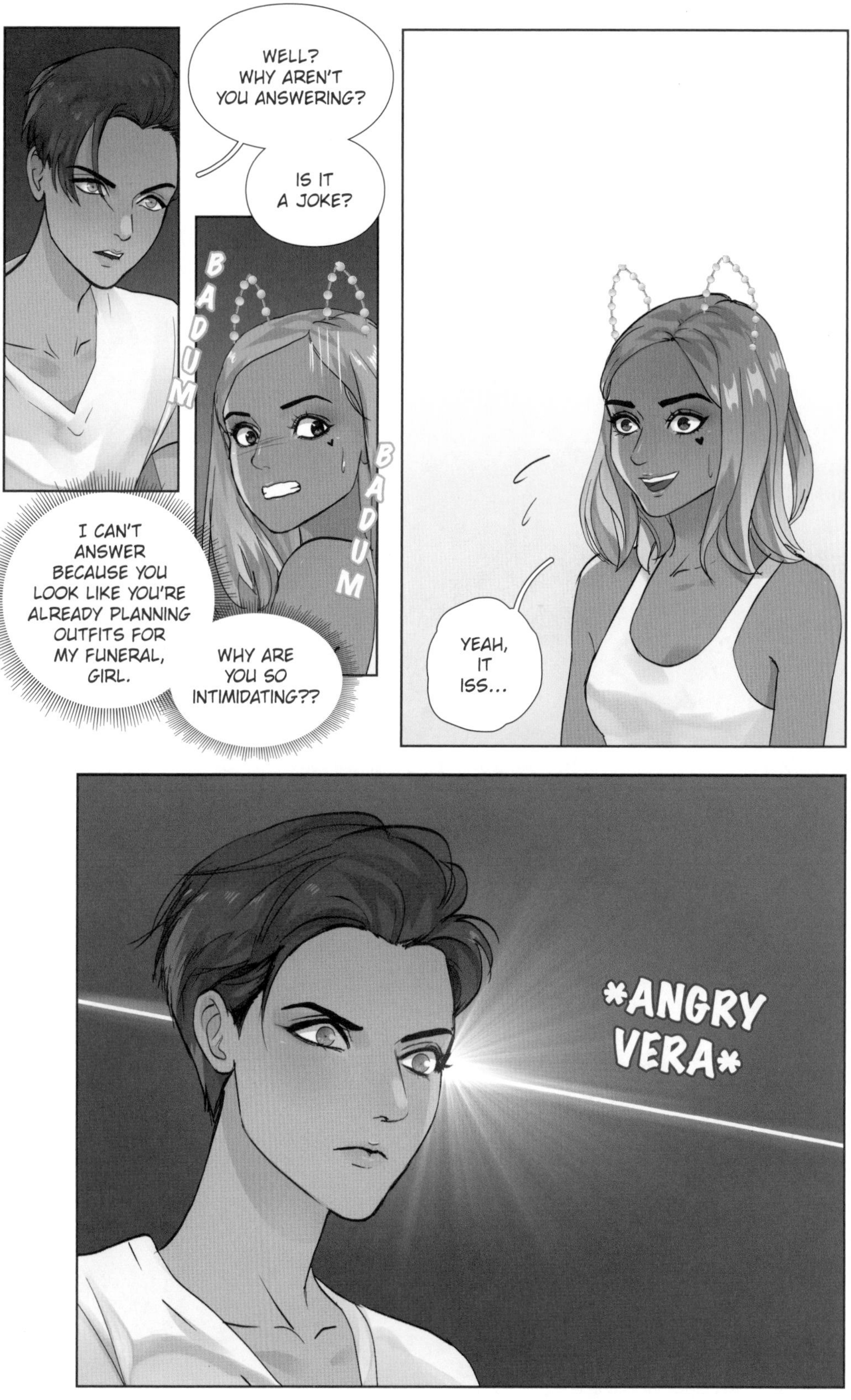
WELL? WHY AREN'T YOU ANSWERING?
IS IT A JOKE?
BADUM
BADUM
I CAN'T ANSWER BECAUSE YOU LOOK LIKE YOU'RE ALREADY PLANNING OUTFITS FOR MY FUNERAL, GIRL.
WHY ARE YOU SO INTIMIDATING??
YEAH, IT ISS...
ANGRY VERA

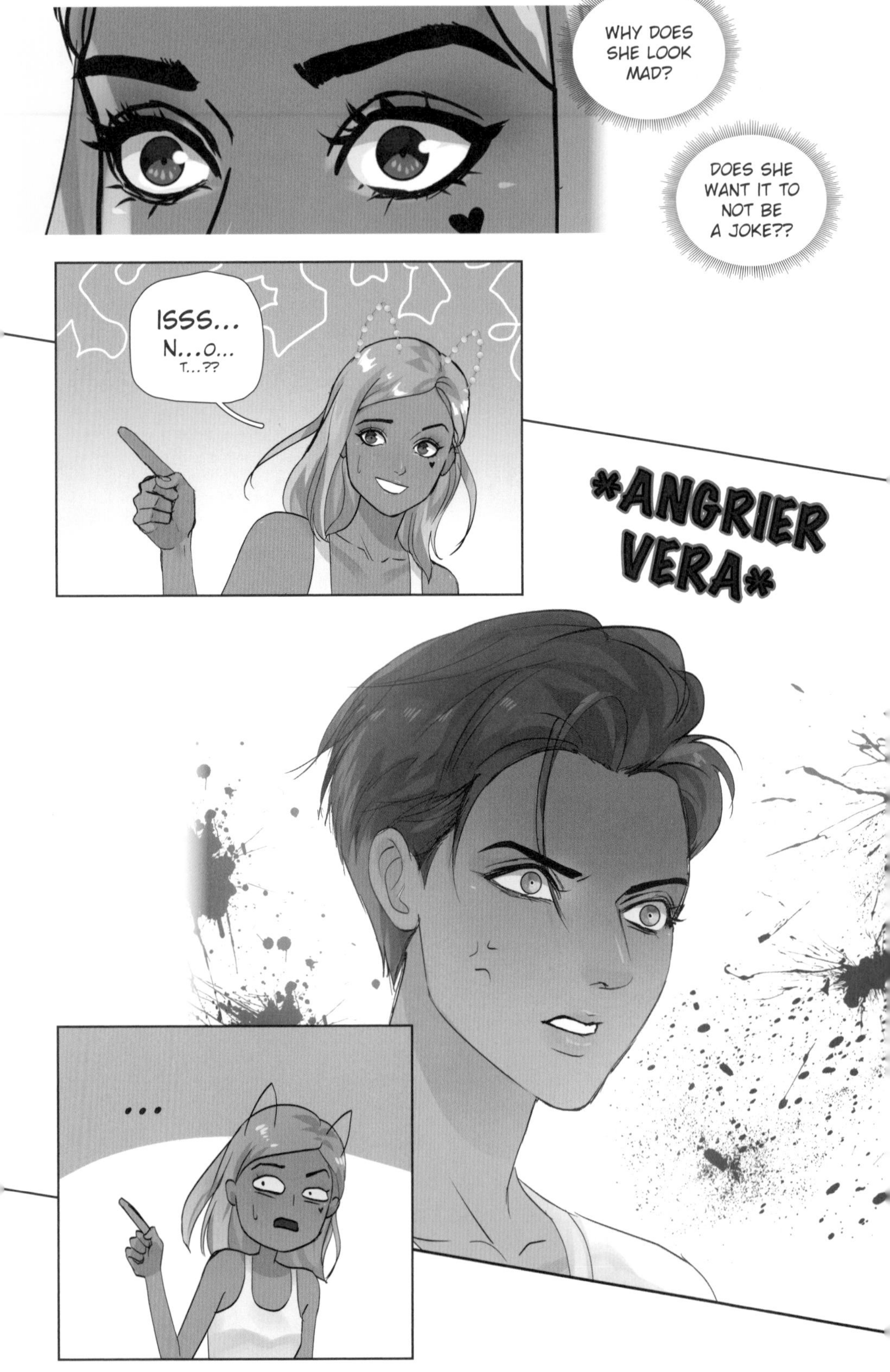
WHY DOES SHE LOOK MAD?
DOES SHE WANT IT TO NOT BE A JOKE??
ISSS... N...O... T...??
ANGRIER VERA
...

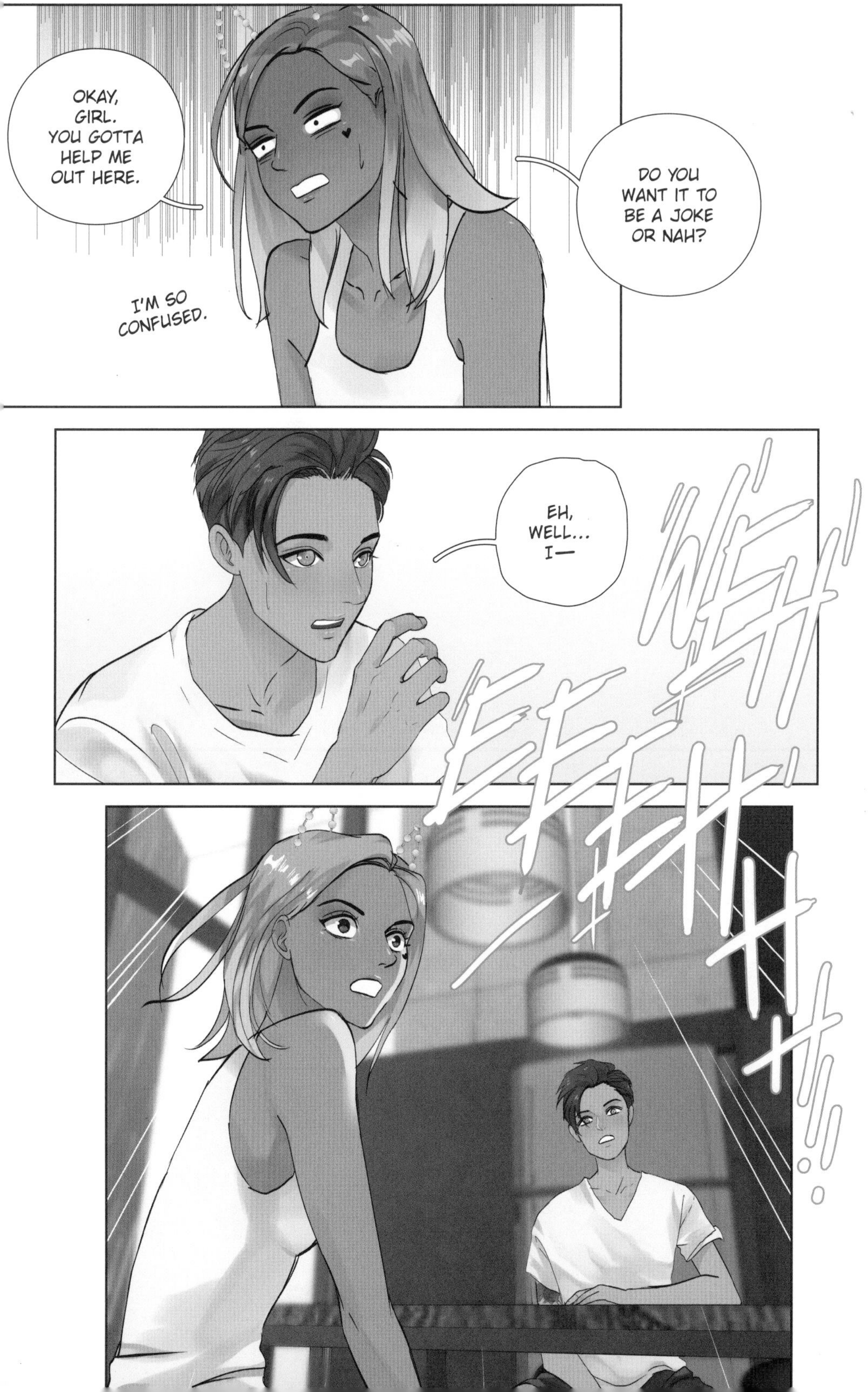
OKAY, GIRL. YOU GOTTA HELP ME OUT HERE.
I'M SO CONFUSED.
DO YOU WANT IT TO BE A JOKE OR NAH?
EH, WELL... I—
WEEEEHHHHH!!!

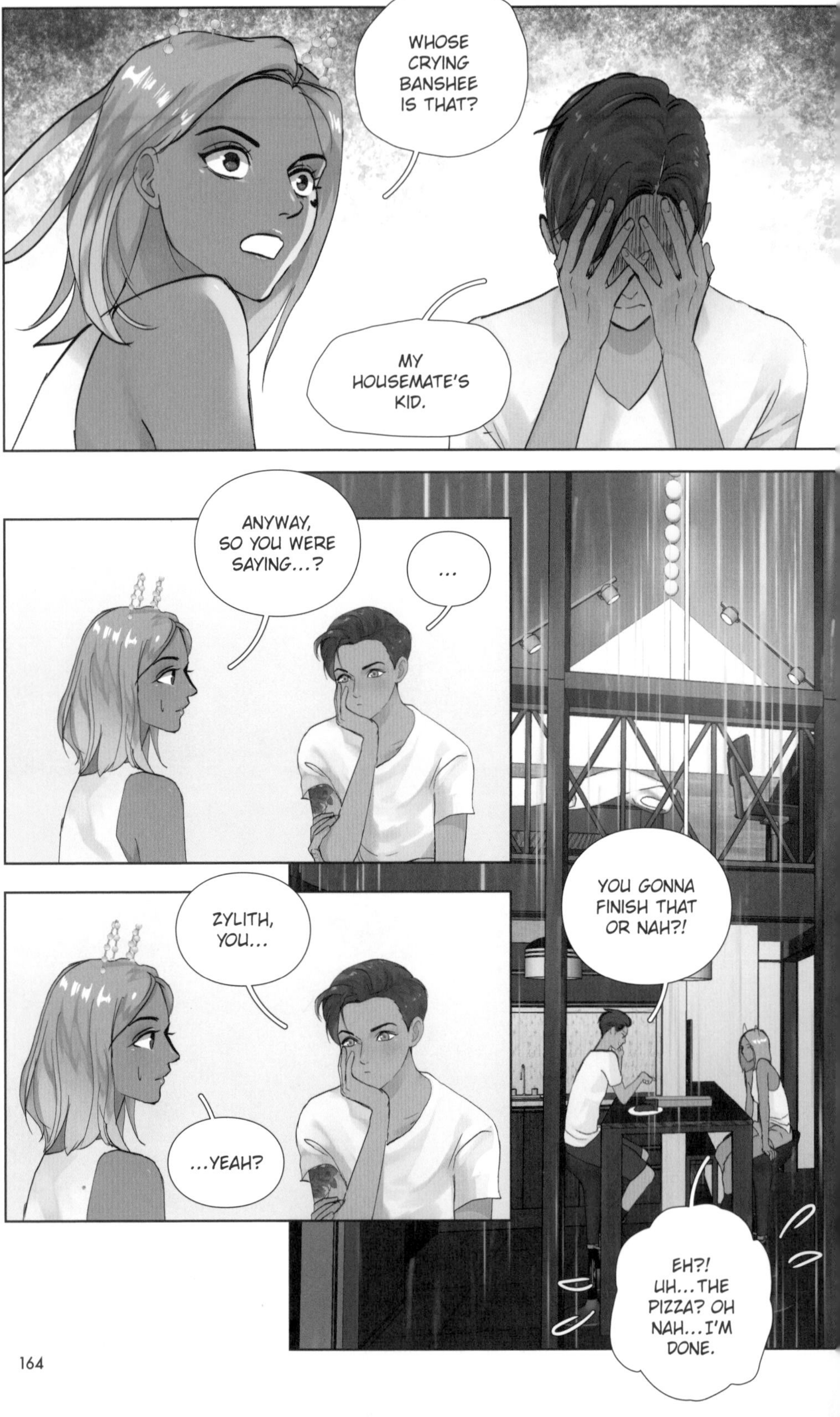
WHOSE CRYING BANSHEE IS THAT?
MY HOUSEMATE'S KID.
ANYWAY, SO YOU WERE SAYING...?
...
ZYLITH, YOU...
...YEAH?
YOU GONNA FINISH THAT OR NAH?!
EH?! UH...THE PIZZA? OH NAH...I'M DONE.

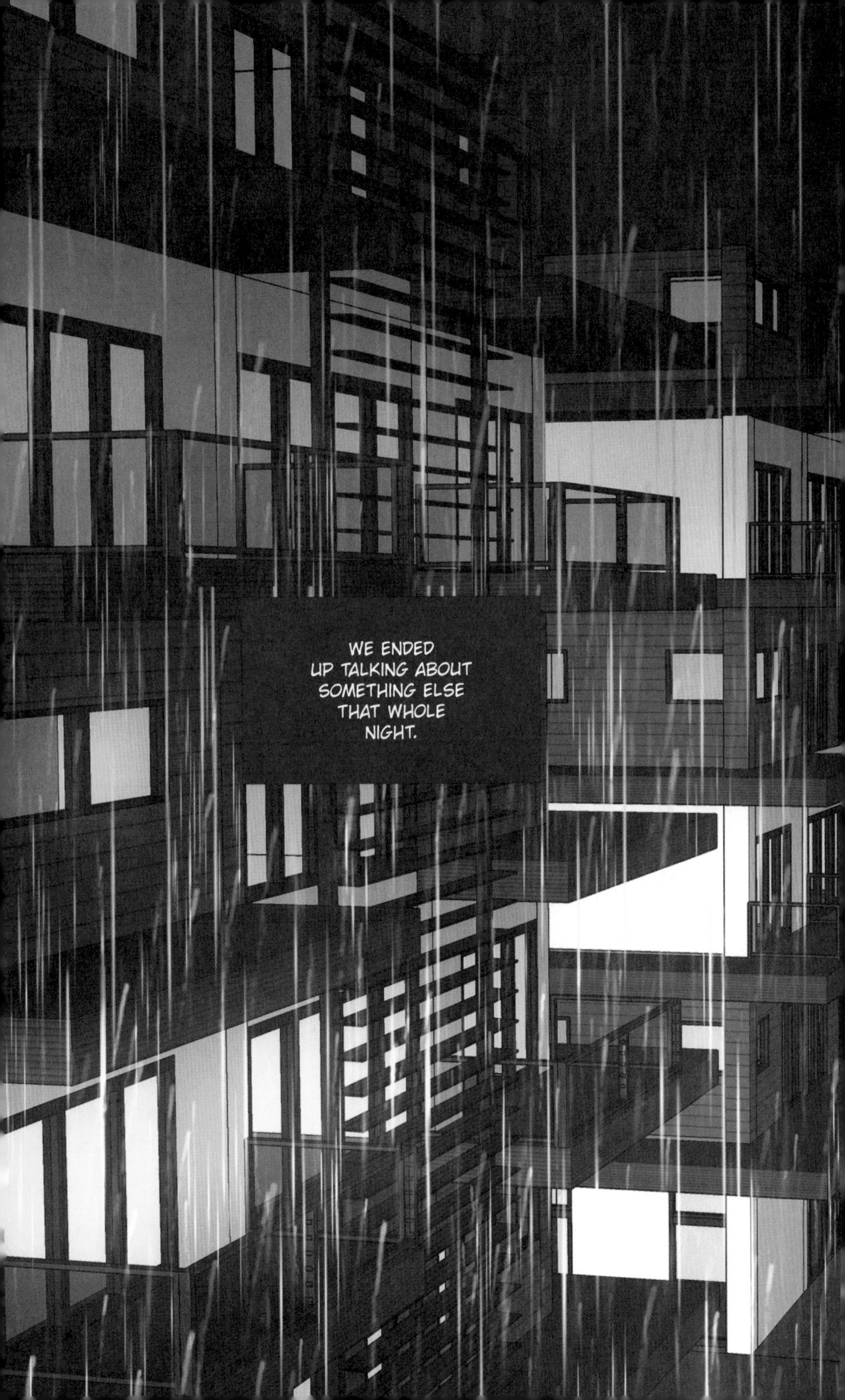
WE ENDED UP TALKING ABOUT SOMETHING ELSE THAT WHOLE NIGHT.

AND I WASN'T BRAVE ENOUGH TO BROACH THE TOPIC AGAIN.

HELLO, HANDSOME.

WHO'S A GOOD PUSSY?!

WHO'S A GOOD PUSSY?!

NOT YOU! ME! I'M THE PUSSY.

UGH! I CAN'T EVEN ASK A GIRL OUT ON A DATE.

ZELAN IS GONNA BE SO DISAPPOINTED IN ME.

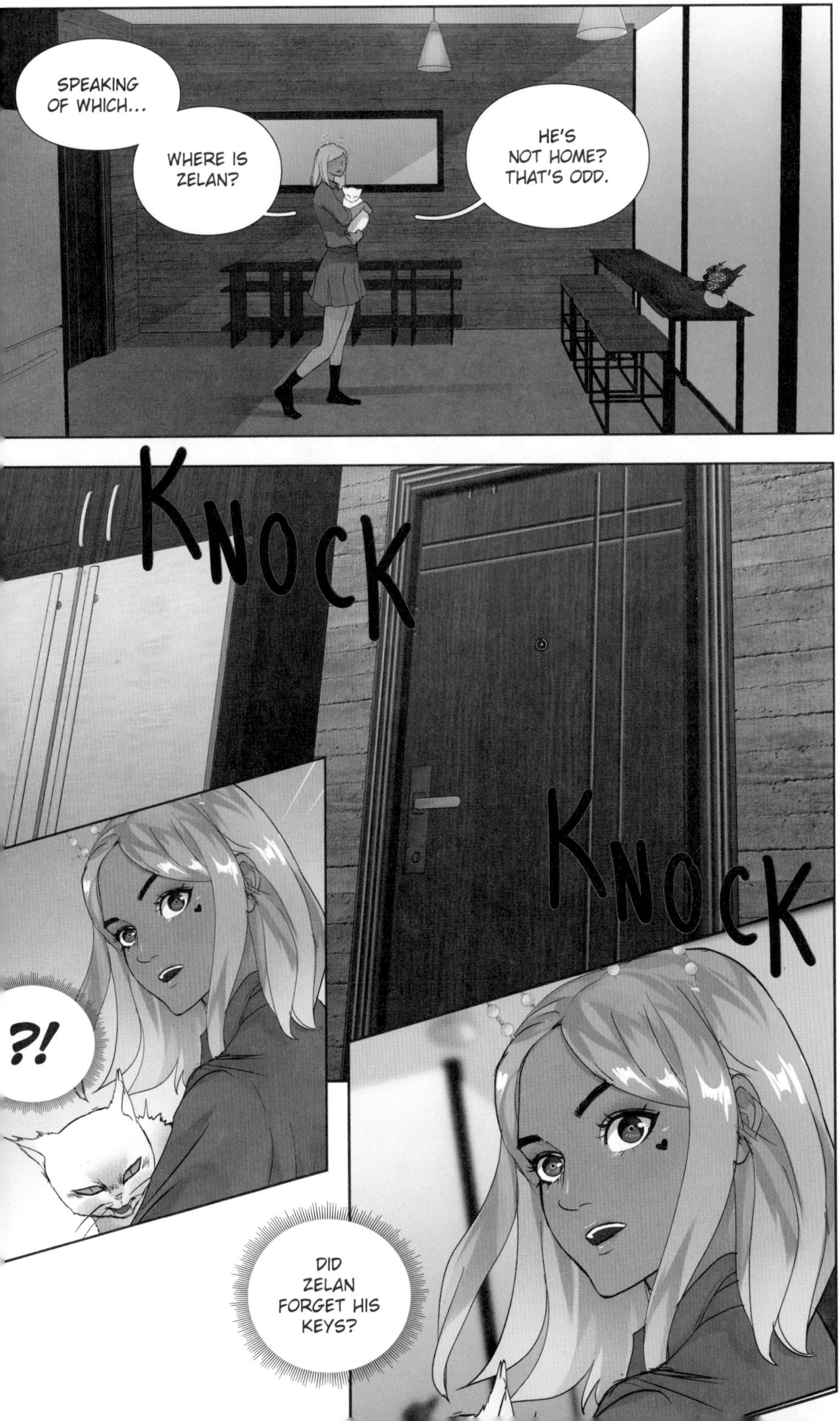
SPEAKING OF WHICH...
WHERE IS ZELAN?
HE'S NOT HOME? THAT'S ODD.
KNOCK
KNOCK
?!
DID ZELAN FORGET HIS KEYS?

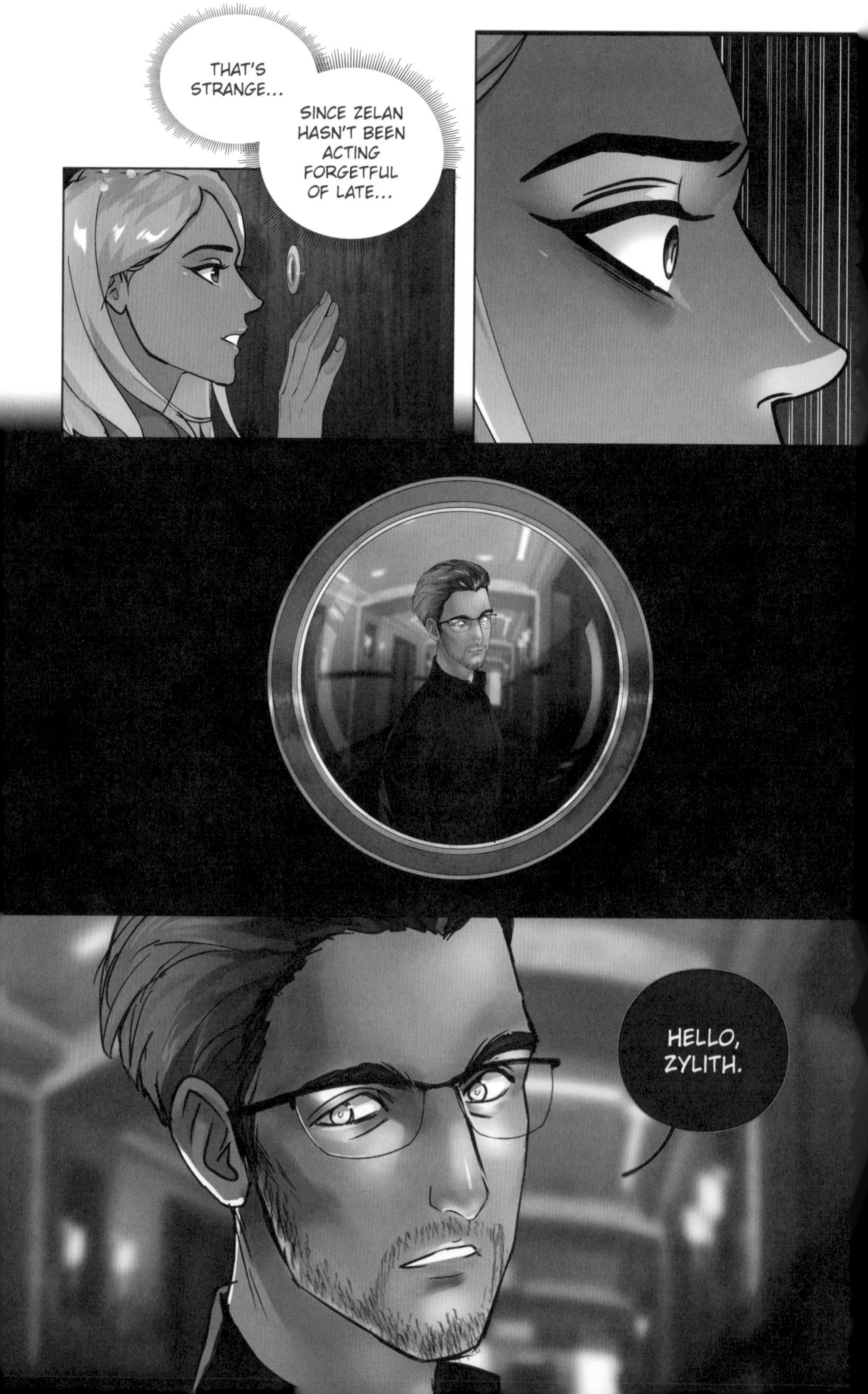
THAT'S STRANGE...
SINCE ZELAN HASN'T BEEN ACTING FORGETFUL OF LATE...
HELLO, ZYLITH.

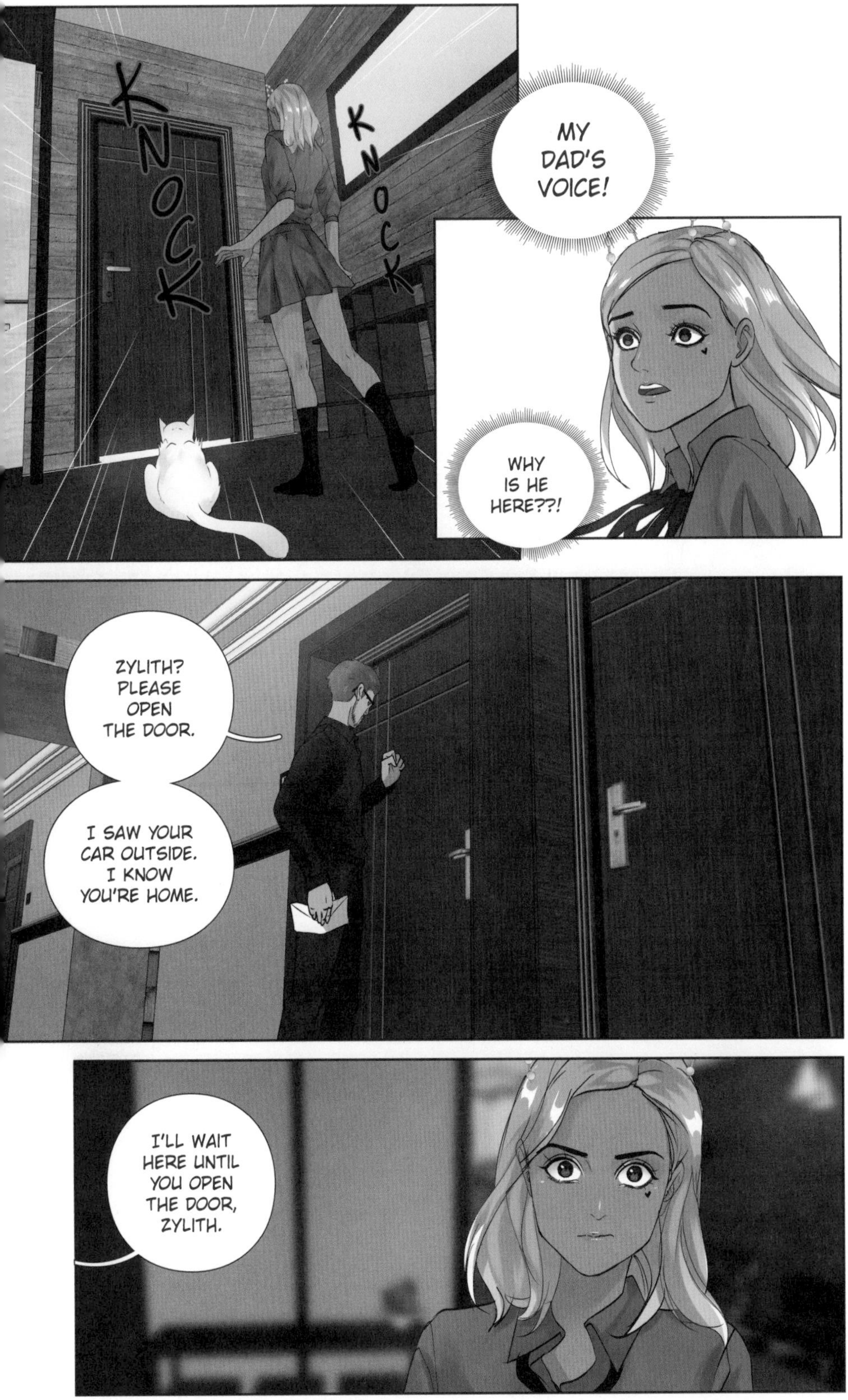
KNOCK
KNOCK
MY DAD'S VOICE!
WHY IS HE HERE??!
ZYLITH? PLEASE OPEN THE DOOR.
I SAW YOUR CAR OUTSIDE. I KNOW YOU'RE HOME.
I'LL WAIT HERE UNTIL YOU OPEN THE DOOR, ZYLITH.

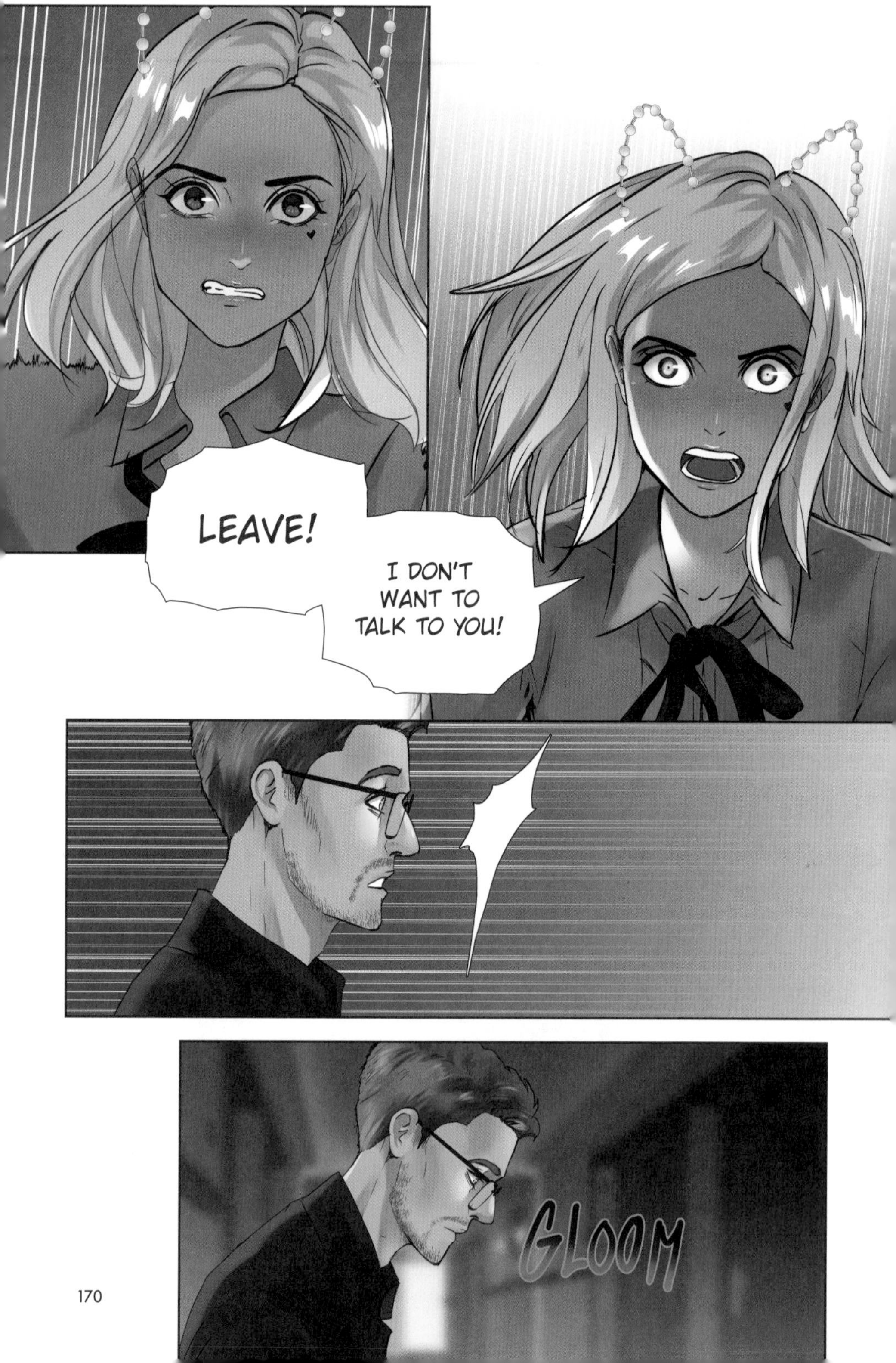
LEAVE!
I DON'T WANT TO TALK TO YOU!
GLOOM

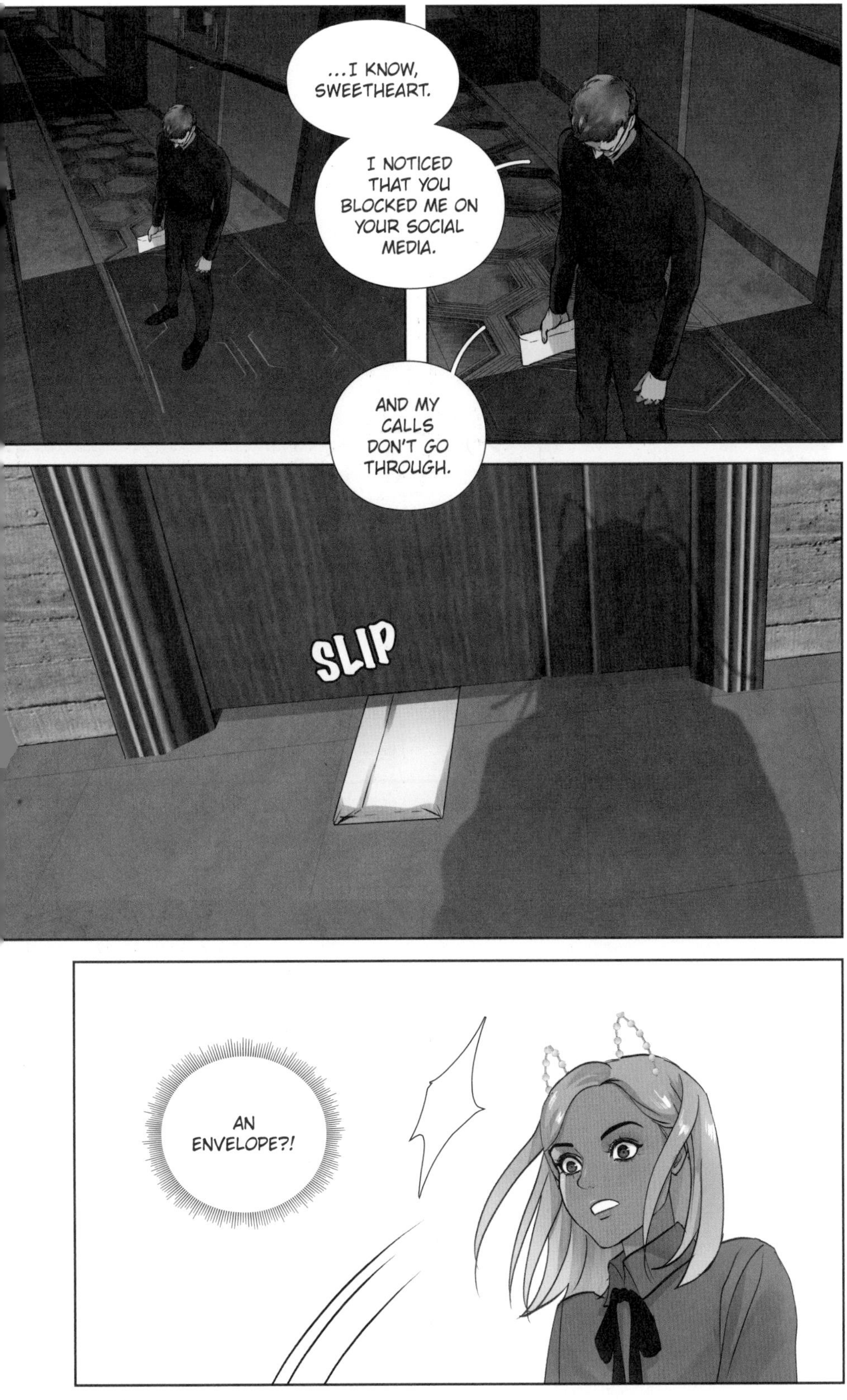
...I KNOW, SWEETHEART.
I NOTICED THAT YOU BLOCKED ME ON YOUR SOCIAL MEDIA.
AND MY CALLS DON'T GO THROUGH.
SLIP
AN ENVELOPE?!

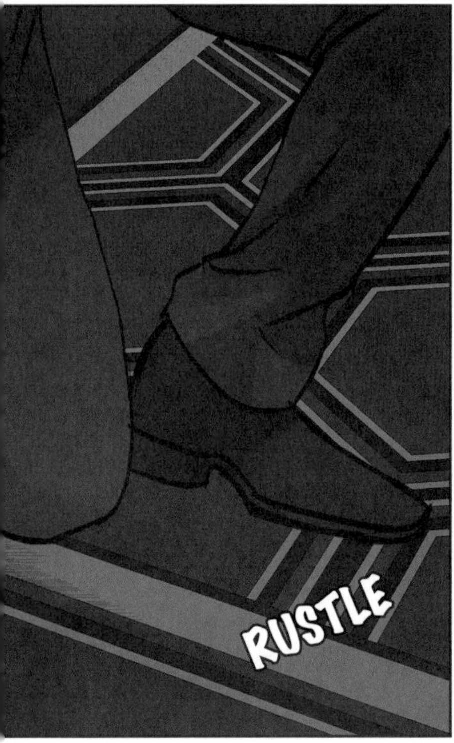
RUSTLE
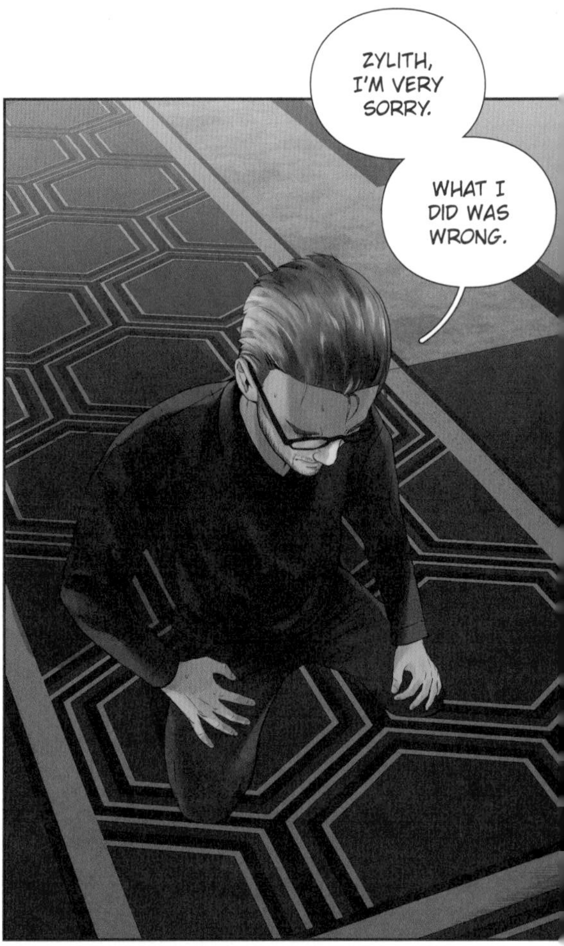
ZYLITH, I'M VERY SORRY.
WHAT I DID WAS WRONG.
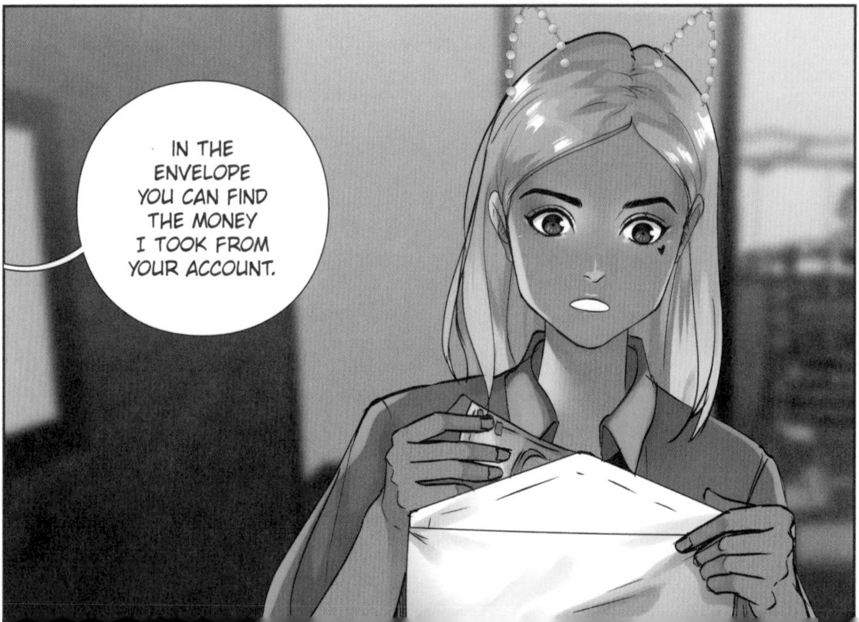
IN THE ENVELOPE YOU CAN FIND THE MONEY I TOOK FROM YOUR ACCOUNT.

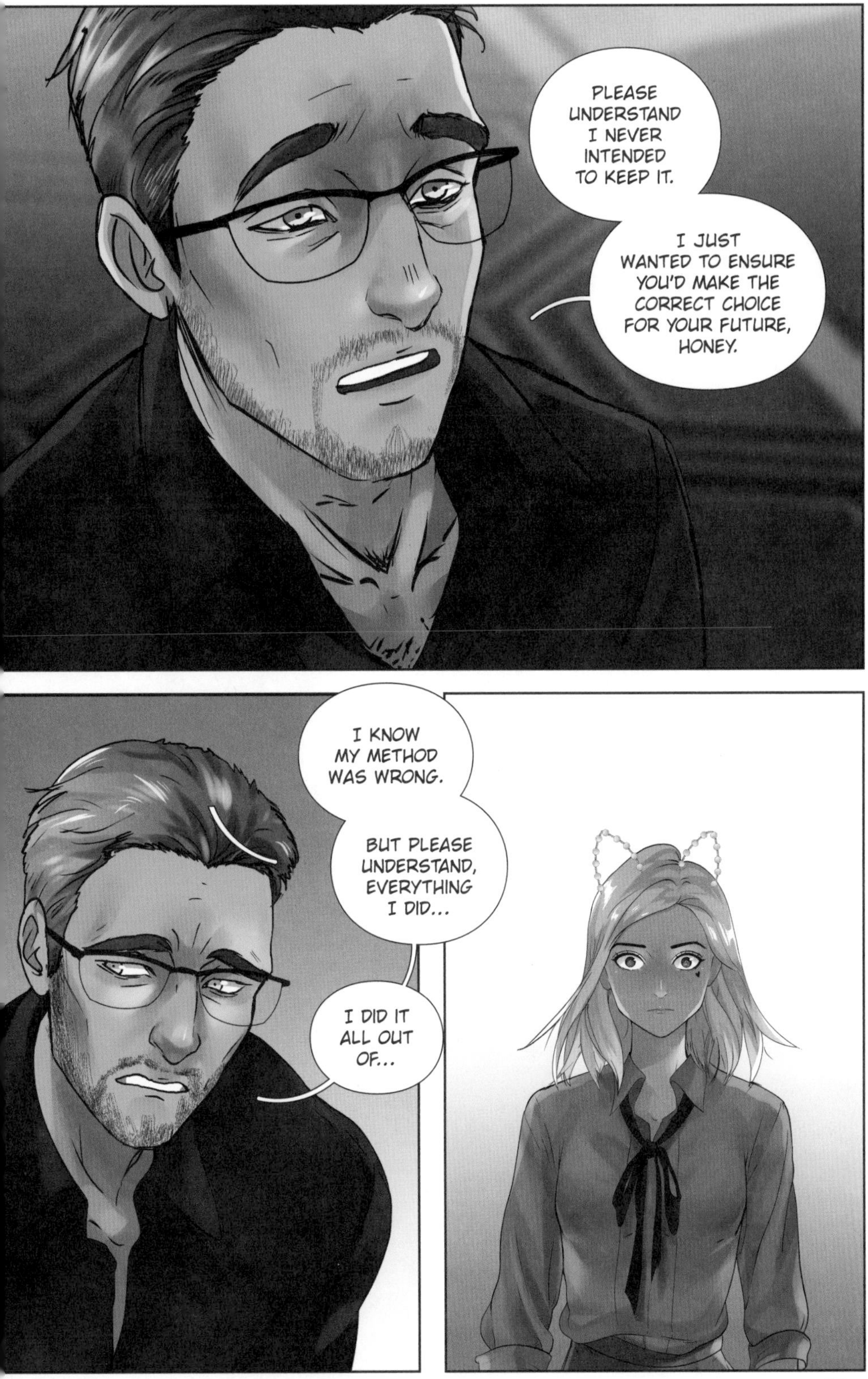

PLEASE UNDERSTAND I NEVER INTENDED TO KEEP IT.
I JUST WANTED TO ENSURE YOU'D MAKE THE CORRECT CHOICE FOR YOUR FUTURE, HONEY.
I KNOW MY METHOD WAS WRONG.
BUT PLEASE UNDERSTAND, EVERYTHING I DID...
I DID IT ALL OUT OF...

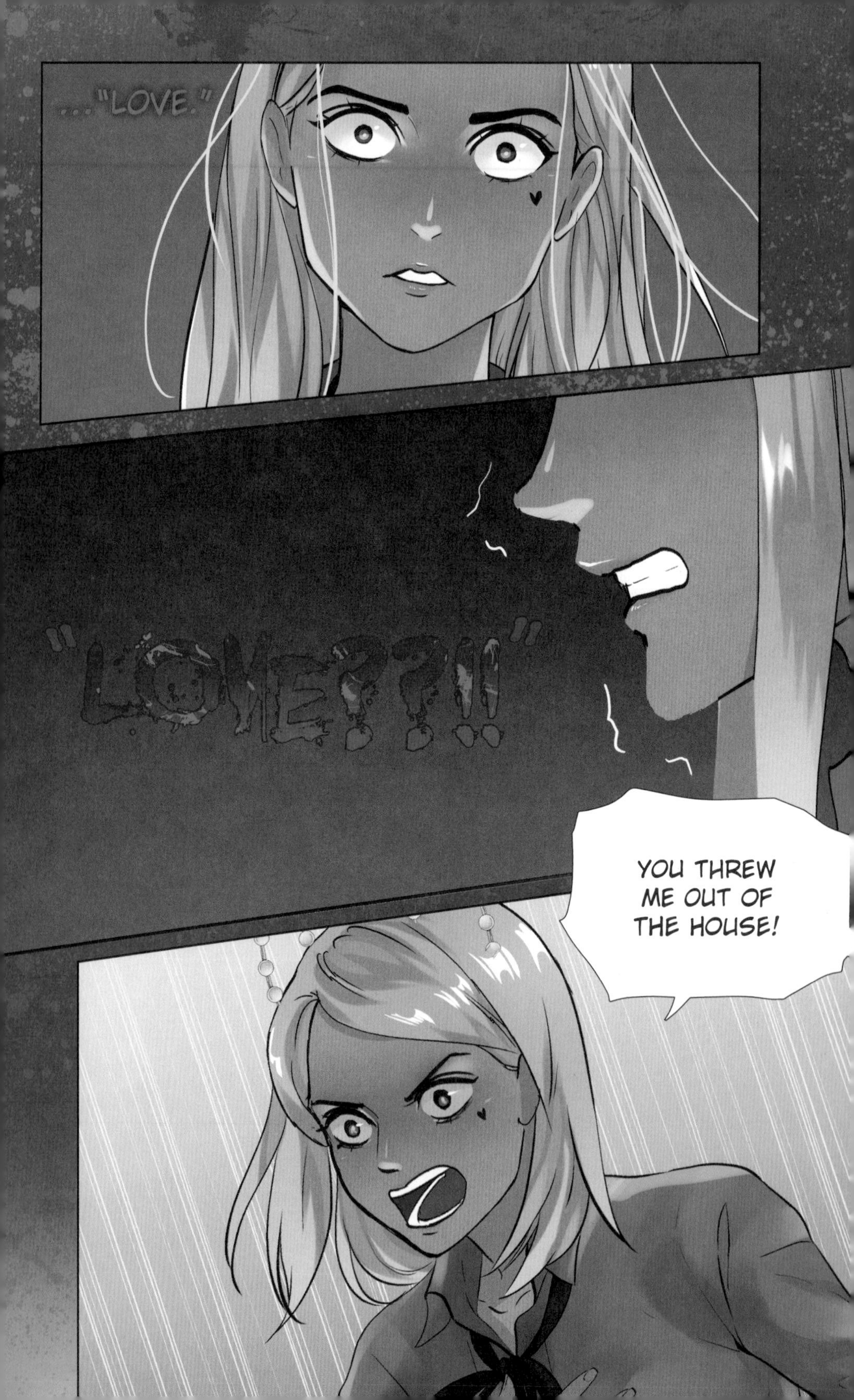
..."LOVE."
"LOVE??!!"
YOU THREW ME OUT OF THE HOUSE!

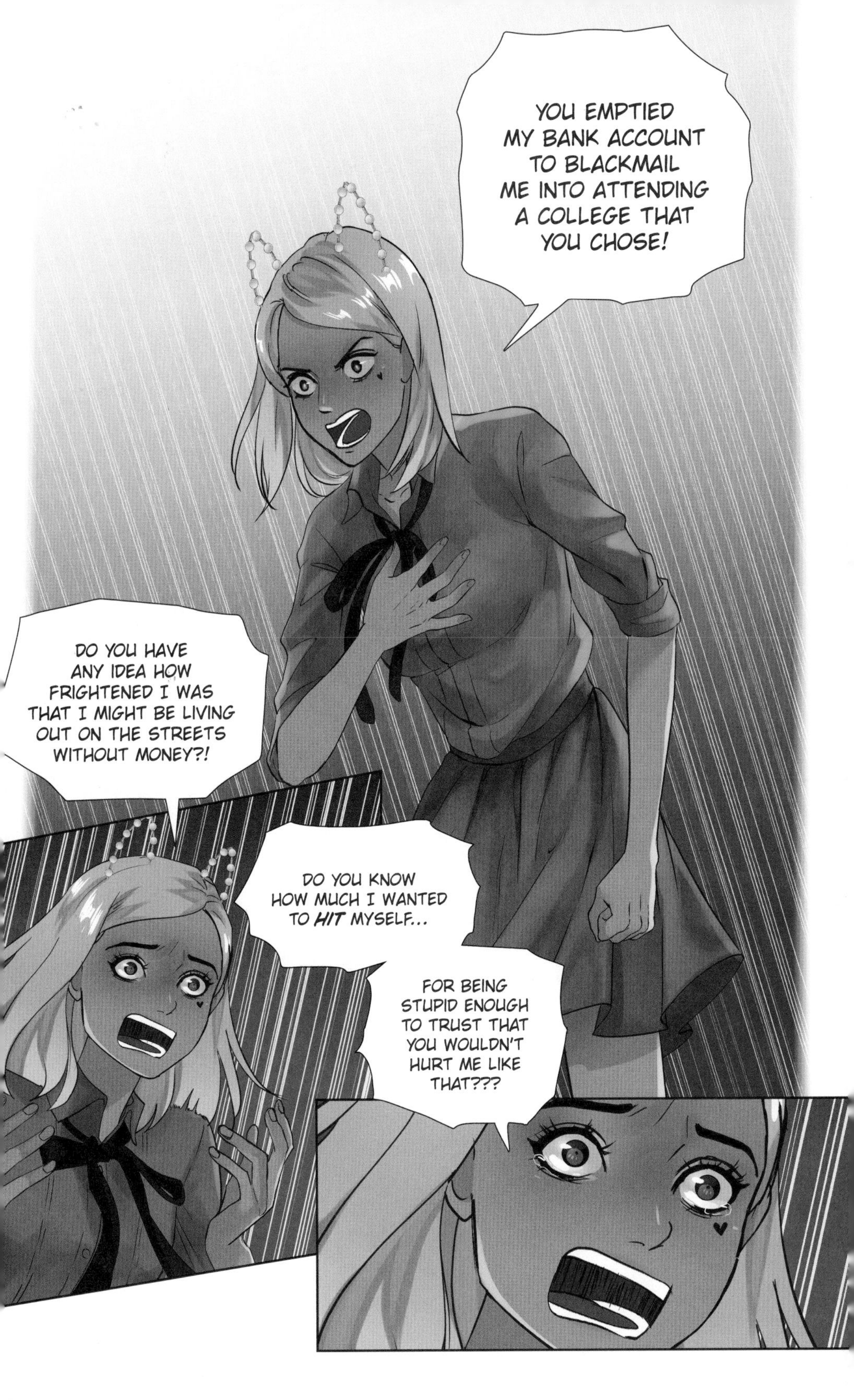
YOU EMPTIED MY BANK ACCOUNT TO BLACKMAIL ME INTO ATTENDING A COLLEGE THAT YOU CHOSE!
DO YOU HAVE ANY IDEA HOW FRIGHTENED I WAS THAT I MIGHT BE LIVING OUT ON THE STREETS WITHOUT MONEY?!
DO YOU KNOW HOW MUCH I WANTED TO *HIT* MYSELF...
FOR BEING STUPID ENOUGH TO TRUST THAT YOU WOULDN'T HURT ME LIKE THAT???

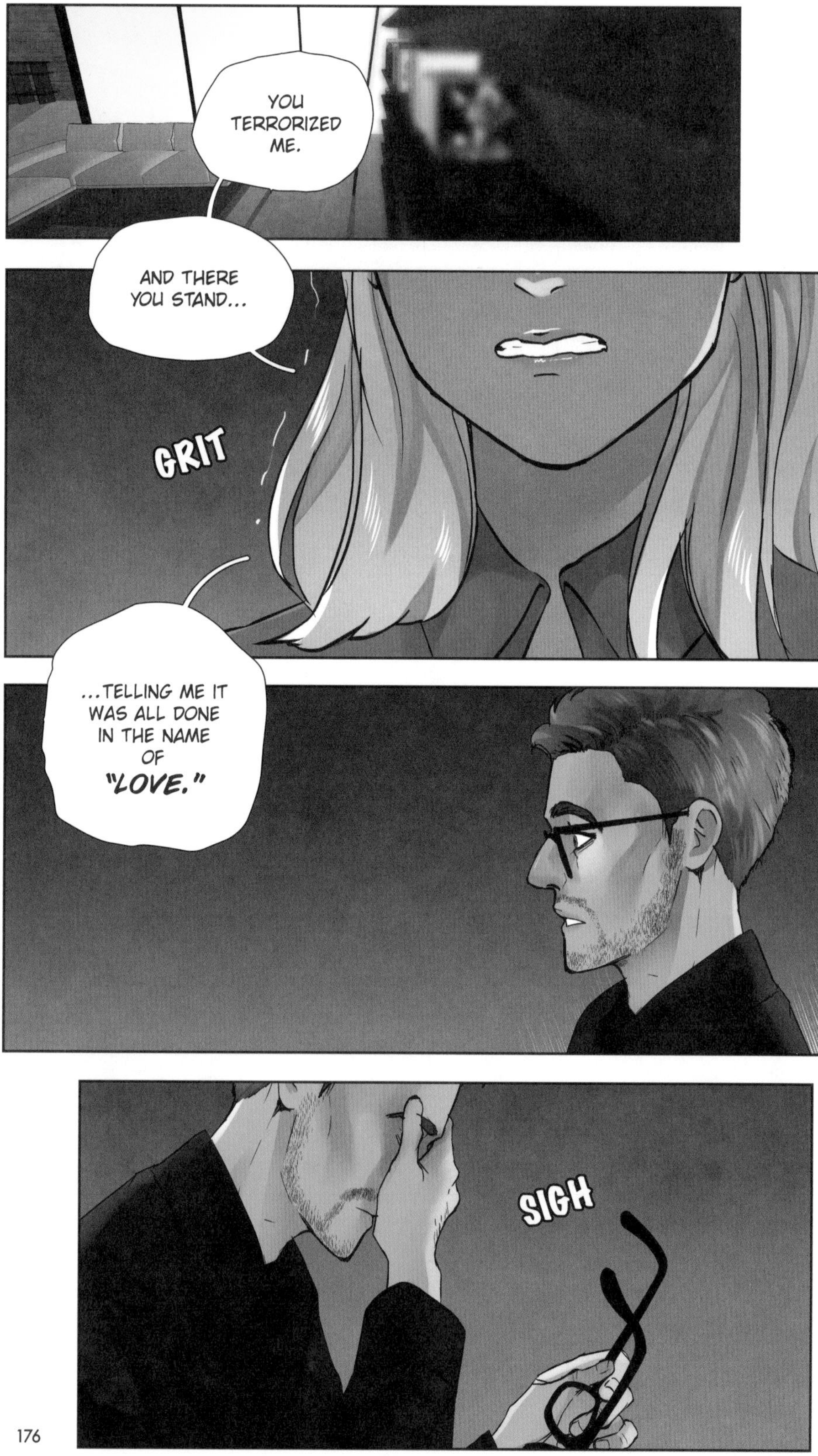
YOU TERRORIZED ME.
AND THERE YOU STAND...
GRIT
...TELLING ME IT WAS ALL DONE IN THE NAME OF "LOVE."
SIGH

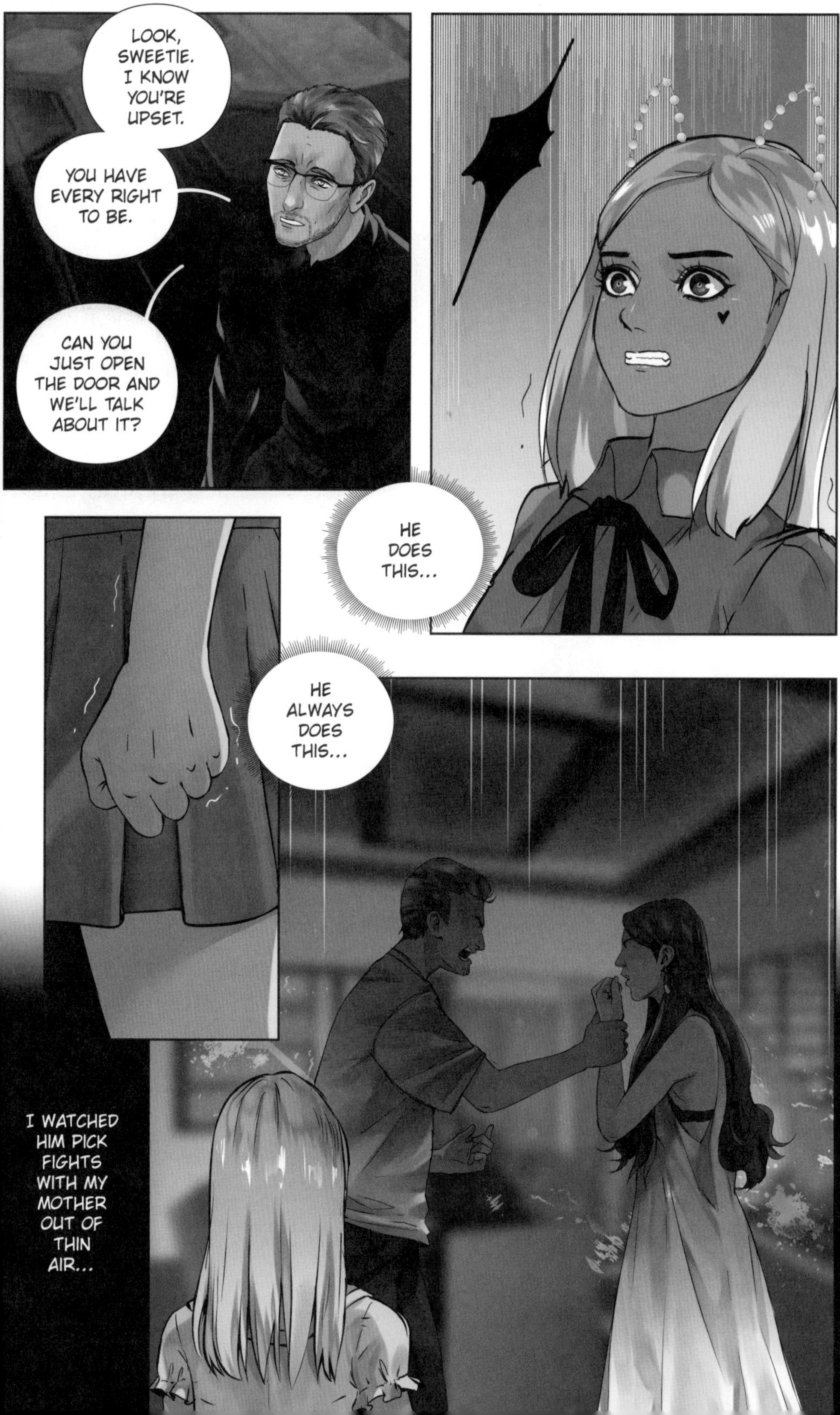
LOOK, SWEETIE. I KNOW YOU'RE UPSET.
YOU HAVE EVERY RIGHT TO BE.
CAN YOU JUST OPEN THE DOOR AND WE'LL TALK ABOUT IT?
HE DOES THIS...
HE ALWAYS DOES THIS...
I WATCHED HIM PICK FIGHTS WITH MY MOTHER OUT OF THIN AIR...

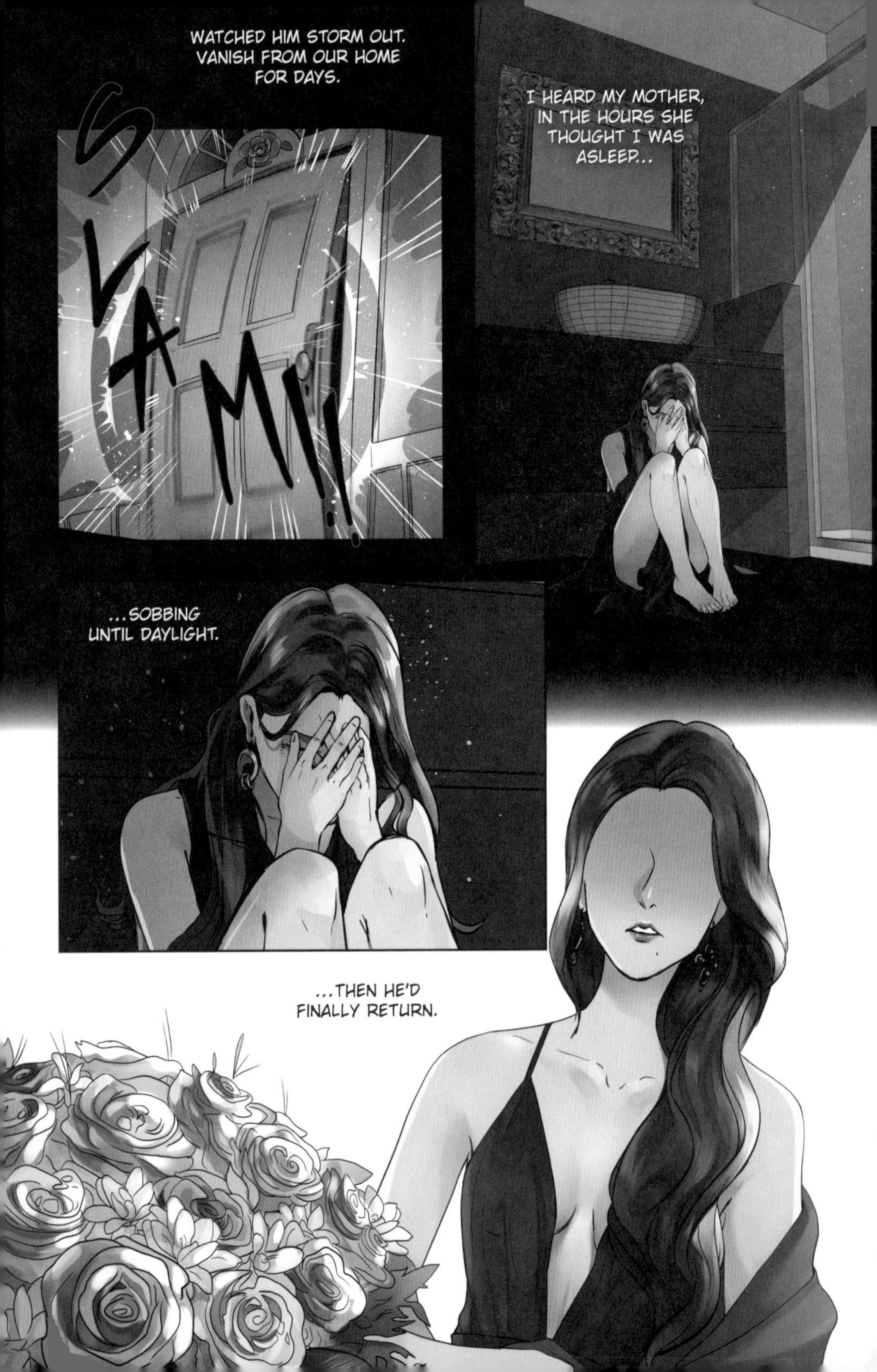
WATCHED HIM STORM OUT. VANISH FROM OUR HOME FOR DAYS.
SLAM!!
I HEARD MY MOTHER, IN THE HOURS SHE THOUGHT I WAS ASLEEP...
...SOBBING UNTIL DAYLIGHT.
...THEN HE'D FINALLY RETURN.

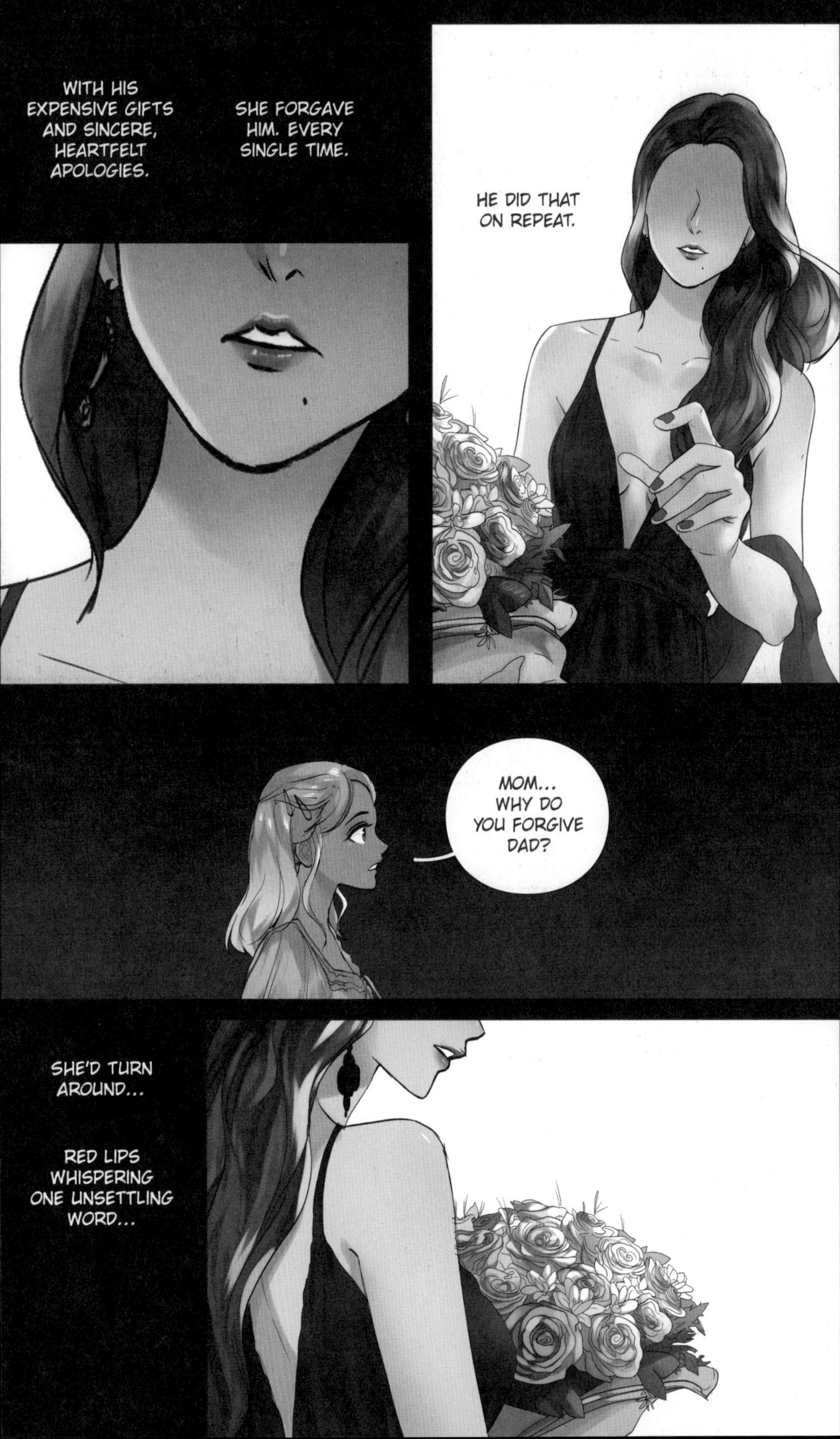
WITH HIS EXPENSIVE GIFTS AND SINCERE, HEARTFELT APOLOGIES.
SHE FORGAVE HIM. EVERY SINGLE TIME.
HE DID THAT ON REPEAT.
MOM... WHY DO YOU FORGIVE DAD?
SHE'D TURN AROUND...
RED LIPS WHISPERING ONE UNSETTLING WORD...

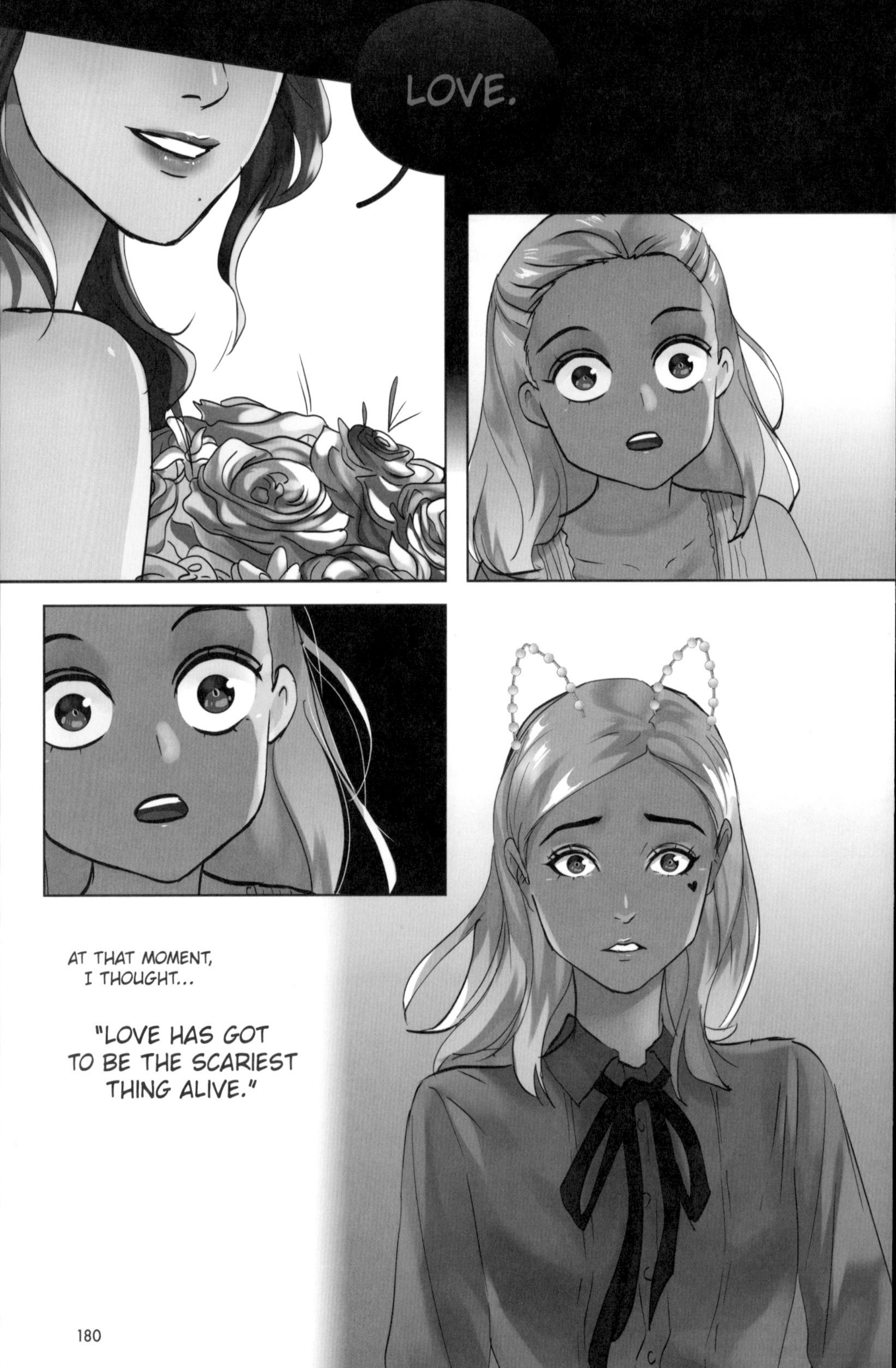
LOVE.
AT THAT MOMENT, I THOUGHT...
"LOVE HAS GOT TO BE THE SCARIEST THING ALIVE."

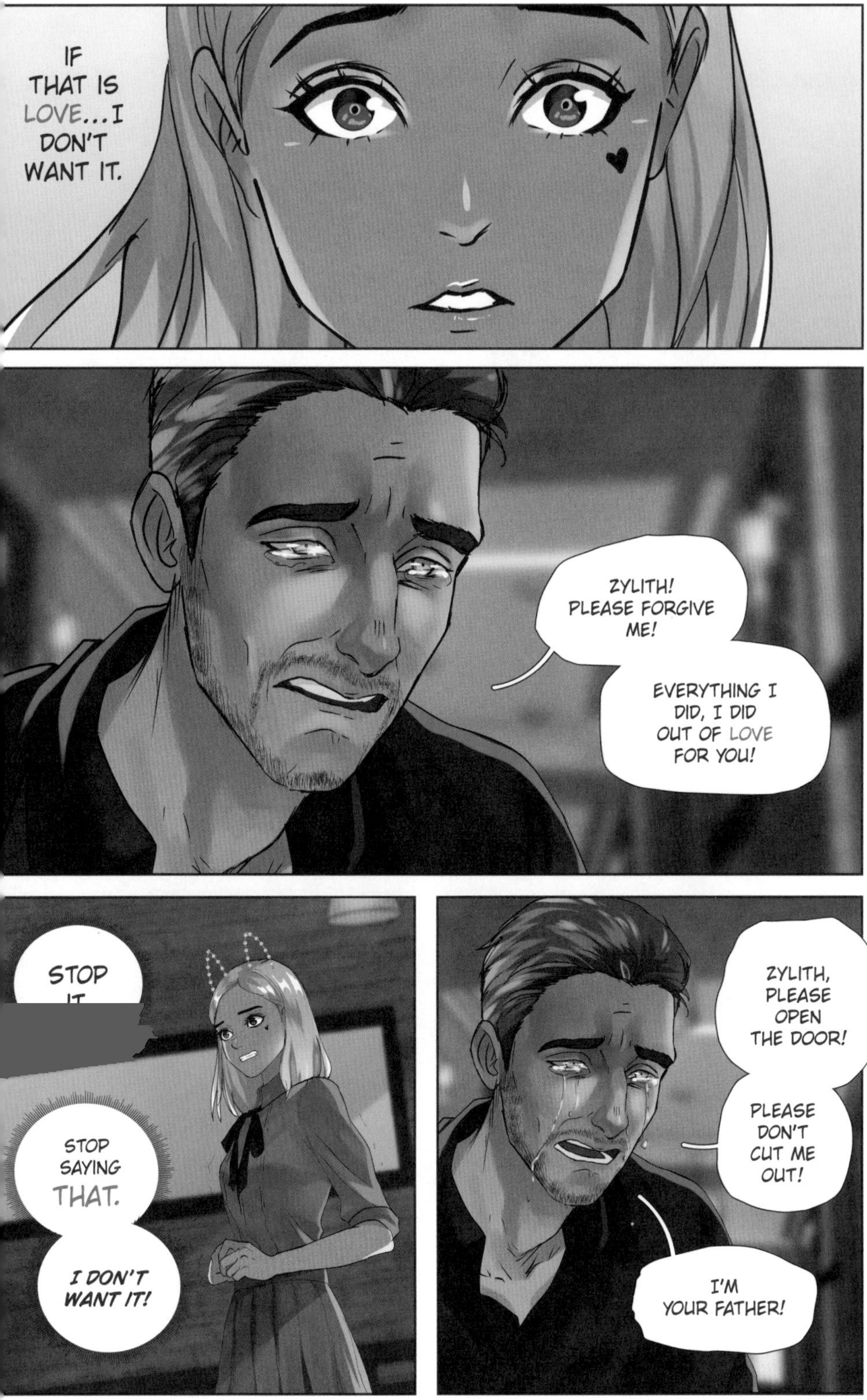
IF THAT IS LOVE...I DON'T WANT IT.
ZYLITH! PLEASE FORGIVE ME!
EVERYTHING I DID, I DID OUT OF LOVE FOR YOU!
STOP [redacted]
STOP SAYING THAT.
I DON'T WANT IT!
ZYLITH, PLEASE OPEN THE DOOR!
PLEASE DON'T CUT ME OUT!
I'M YOUR FATHER!

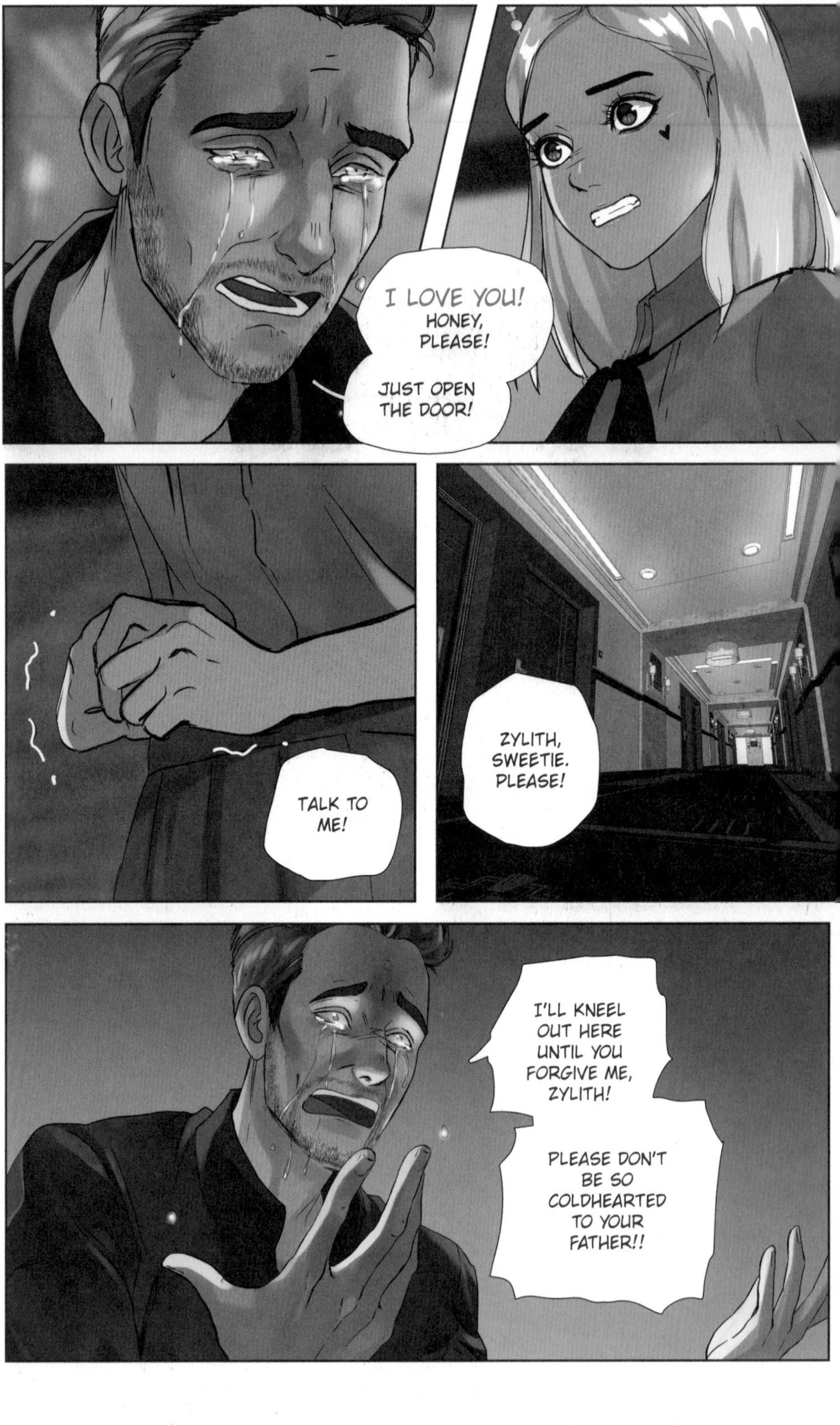
I LOVE YOU! HONEY, PLEASE!
JUST OPEN THE DOOR!
TALK TO ME!
ZYLITH, SWEETIE. PLEASE!
I'LL KNEEL OUT HERE UNTIL YOU FORGIVE ME, ZYLITH!
PLEASE DON'T BE SO COLDHEARTED TO YOUR FATHER!!

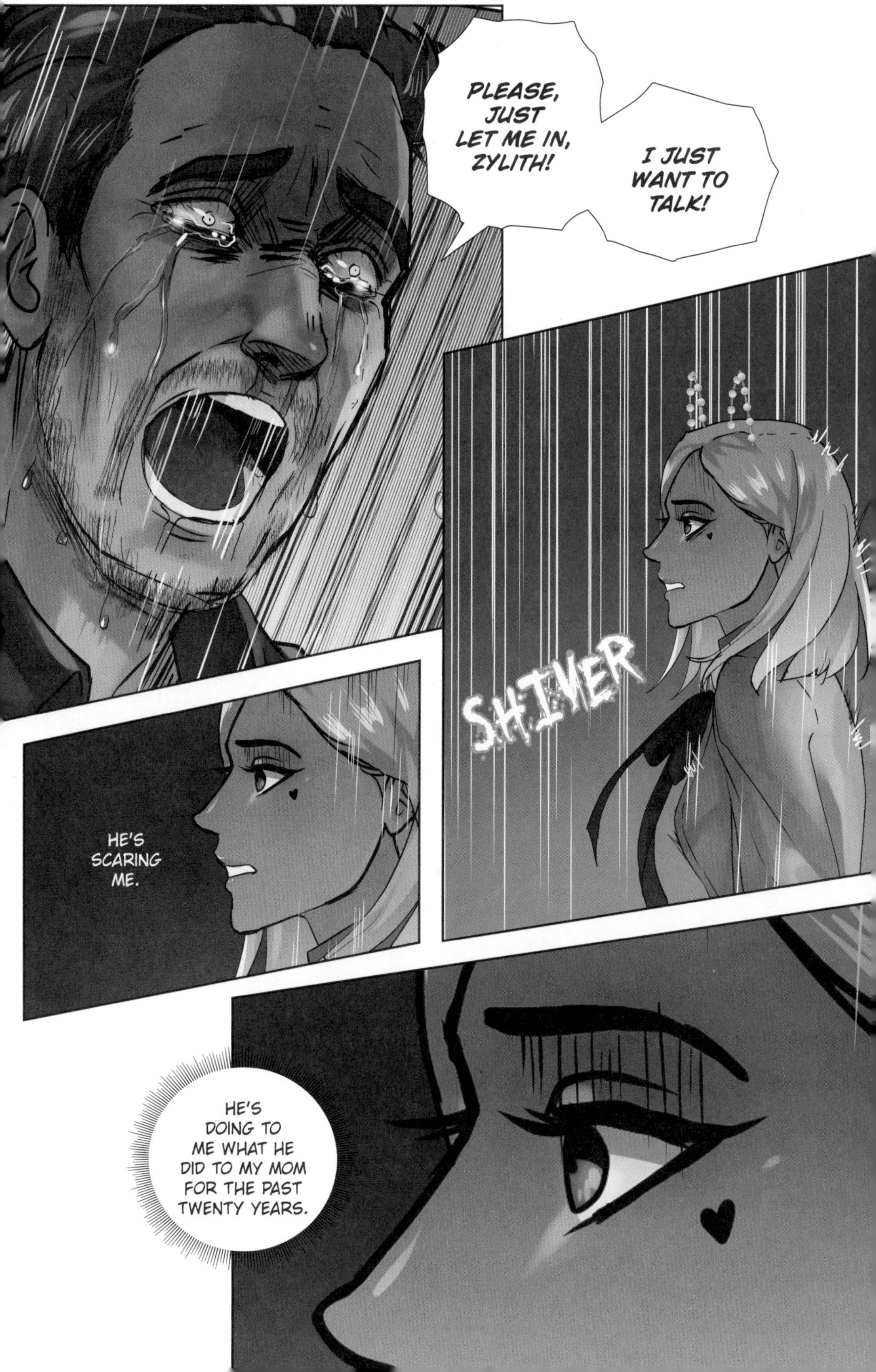

PLEASE, JUST LET ME IN, ZYLITH!
I JUST WANT TO TALK!
SHIVER
HE'S SCARING ME.
HE'S DOING TO ME WHAT HE DID TO MY MOM FOR THE PAST TWENTY YEARS.

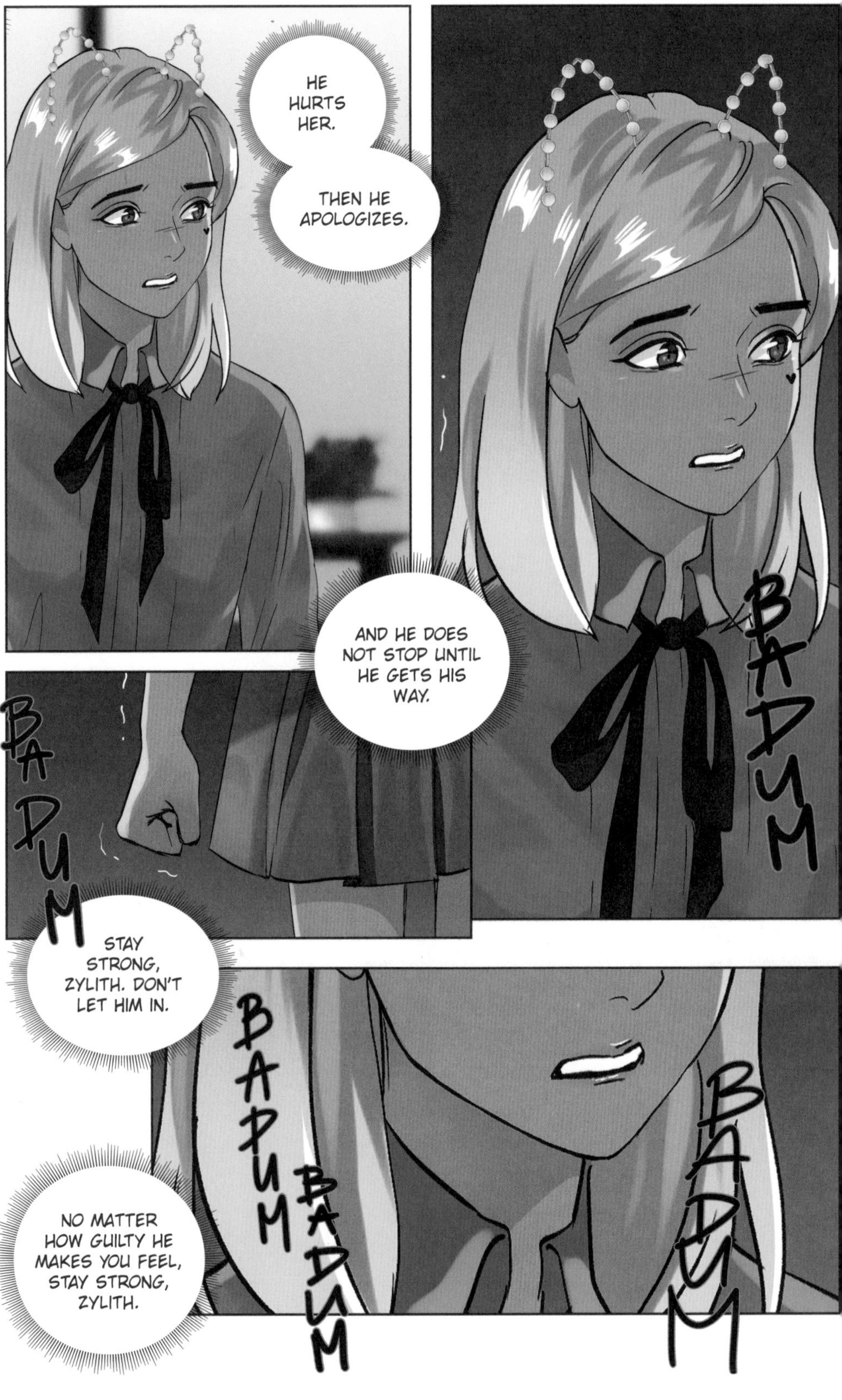

HE HURTS HER.
THEN HE APOLOGIZES.
AND HE DOES NOT STOP UNTIL HE GETS HIS WAY.
BADUM
BADUM
STAY STRONG, ZYLITH. DON'T LET HIM IN.
BADUM
BADUM
BADUM
NO MATTER HOW GUILTY HE MAKES YOU FEEL, STAY STRONG, ZYLITH.

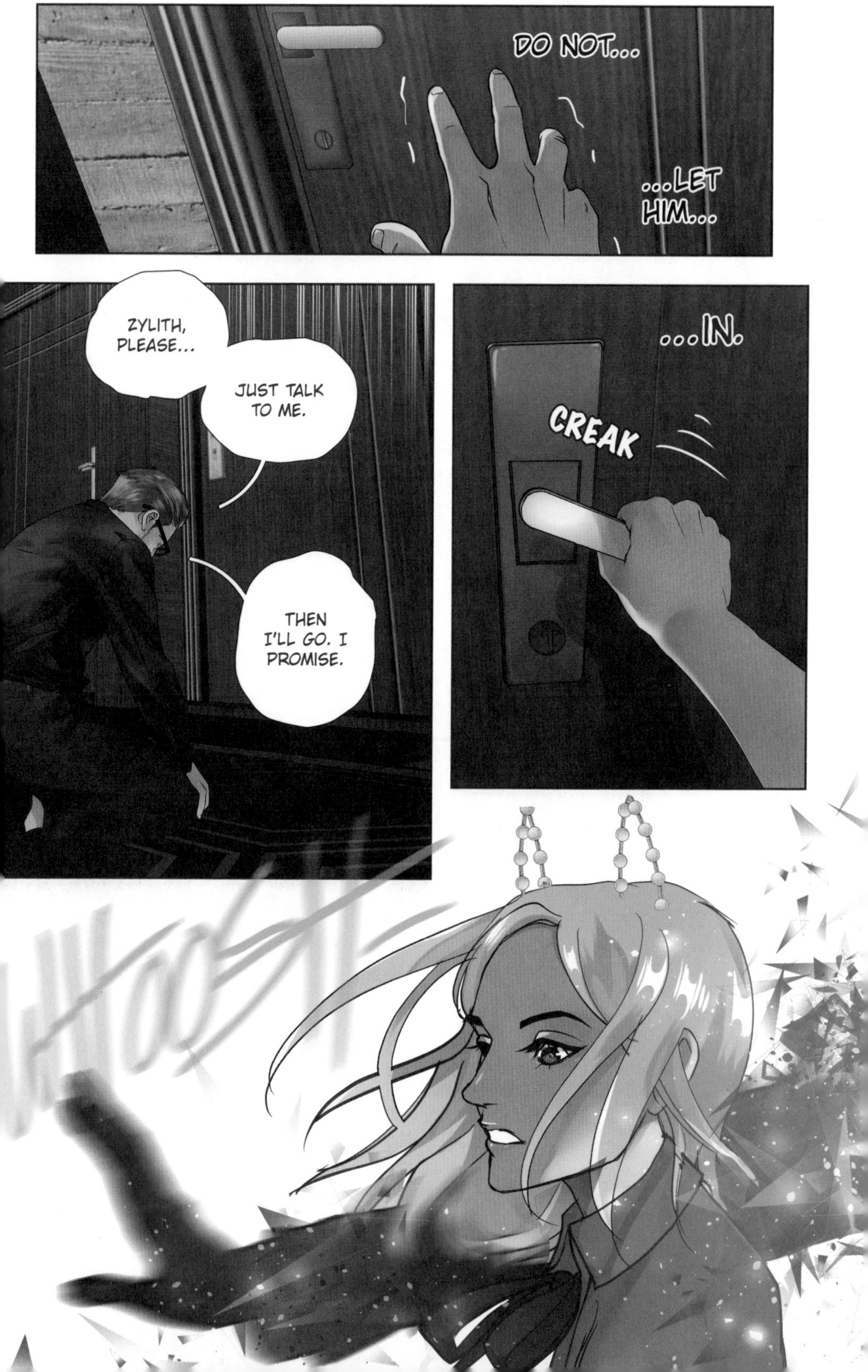
DO NOT...
...LET HIM...
ZYLITH, PLEASE...
JUST TALK TO ME.
THEN I'LL GO. I PROMISE.
...IN.
CREAK

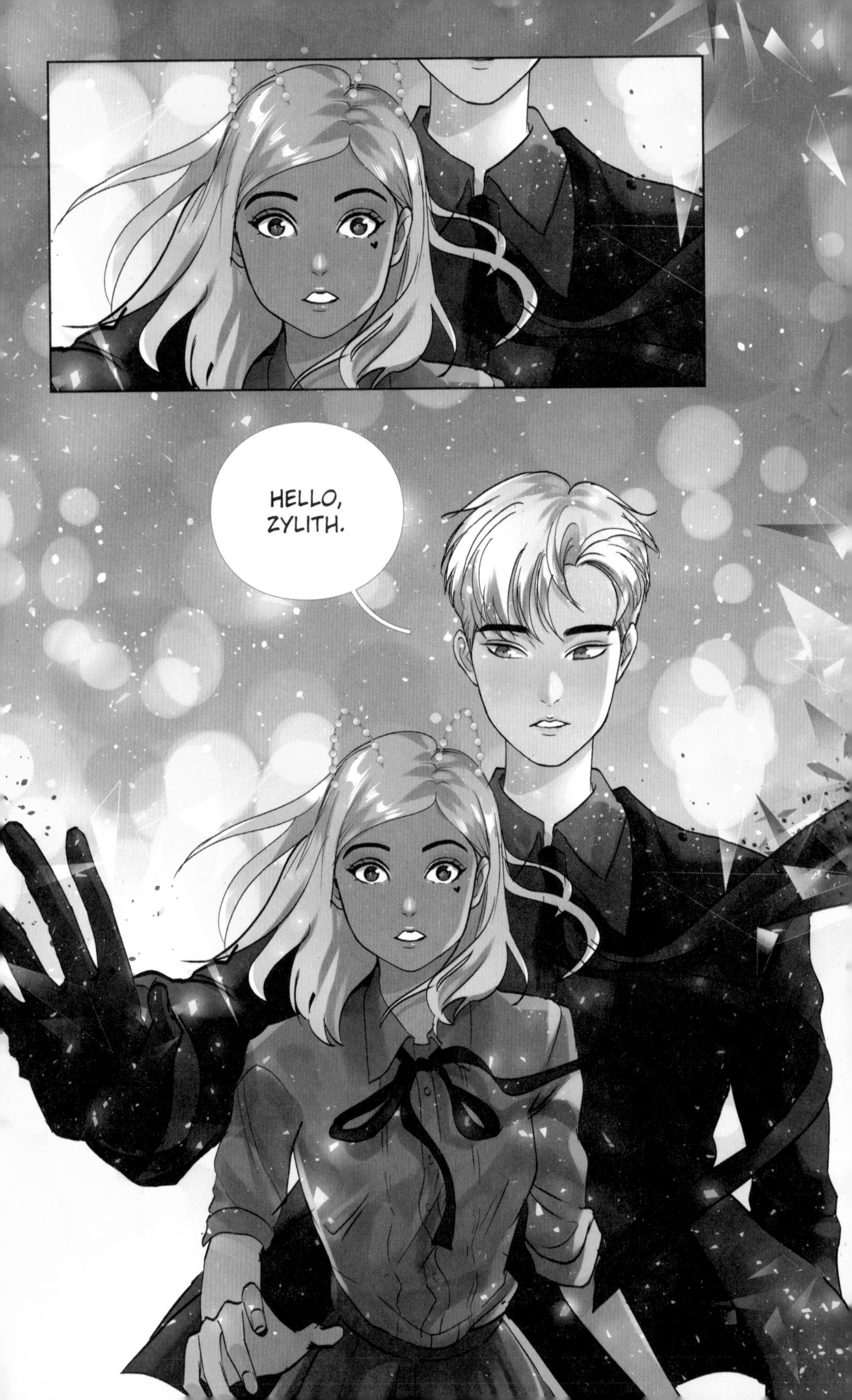
HELLO, ZYLITH.

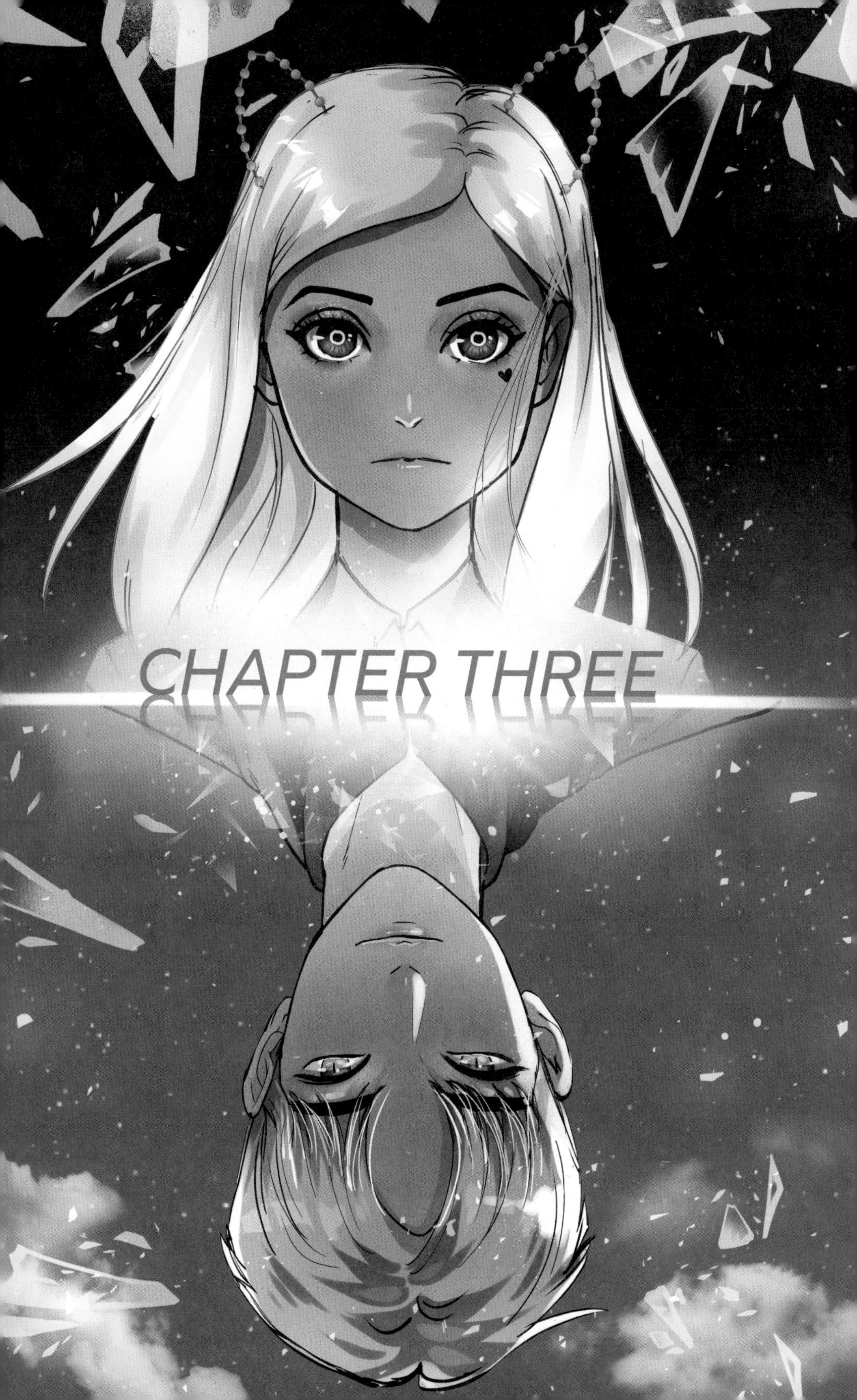
CHAPTER THREE

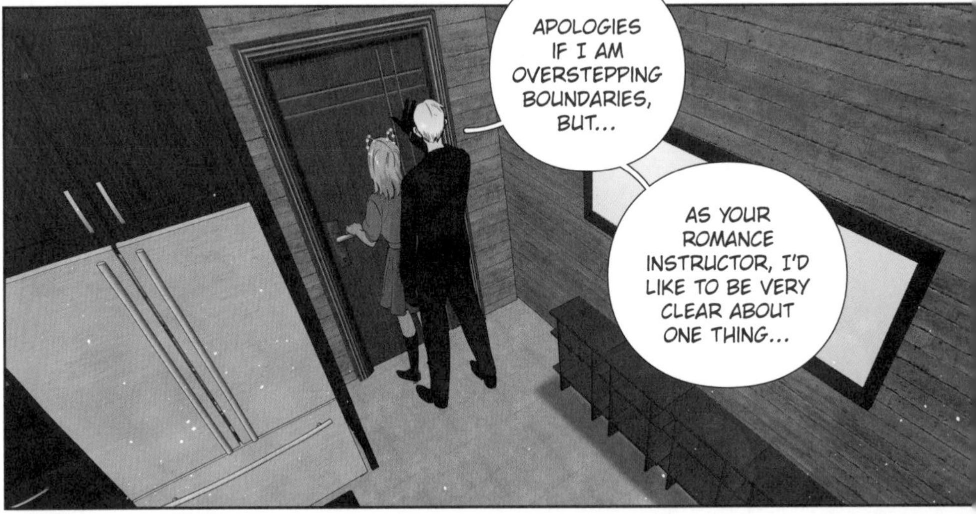
APOLOGIES IF I AM OVERSTEPPING BOUNDARIES, BUT...
AS YOUR ROMANCE INSTRUCTOR, I'D LIKE TO BE VERY CLEAR ABOUT ONE THING...

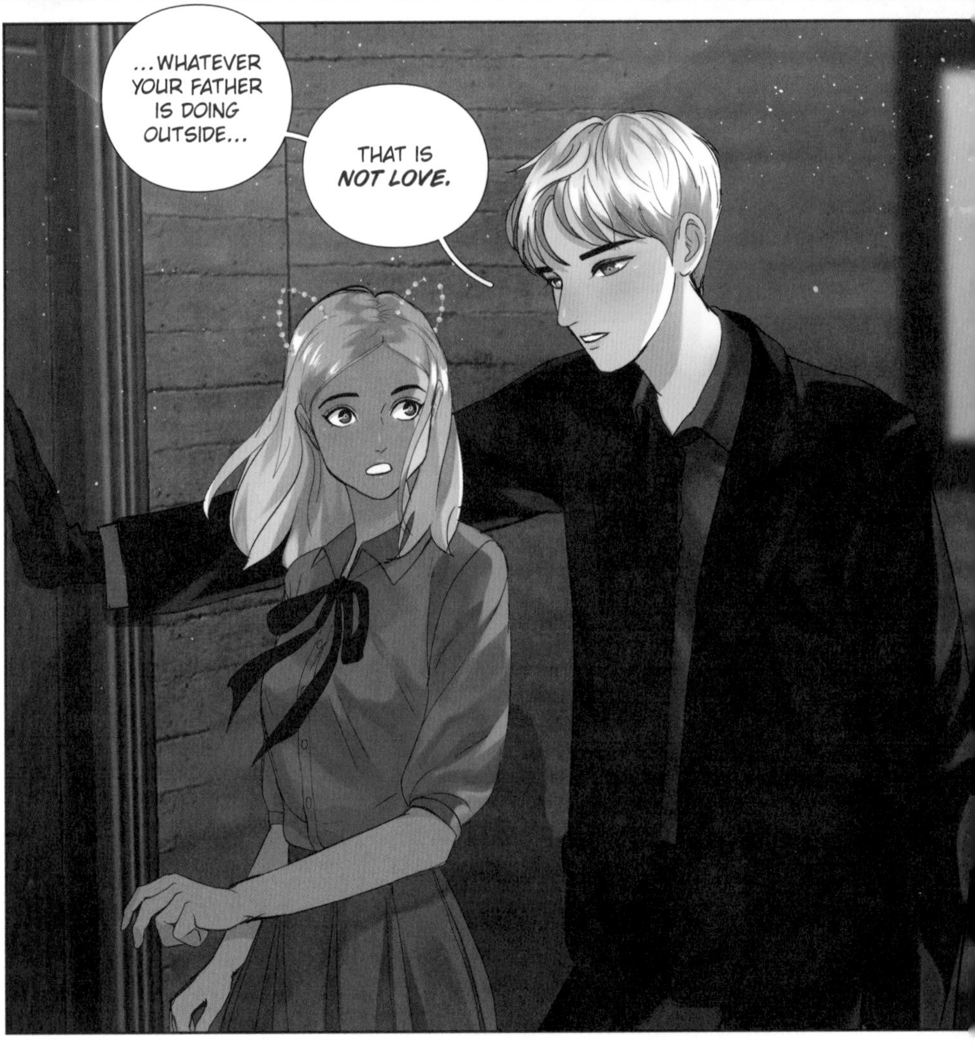
...WHATEVER YOUR FATHER IS DOING OUTSIDE...
THAT IS ***NOT LOVE.***

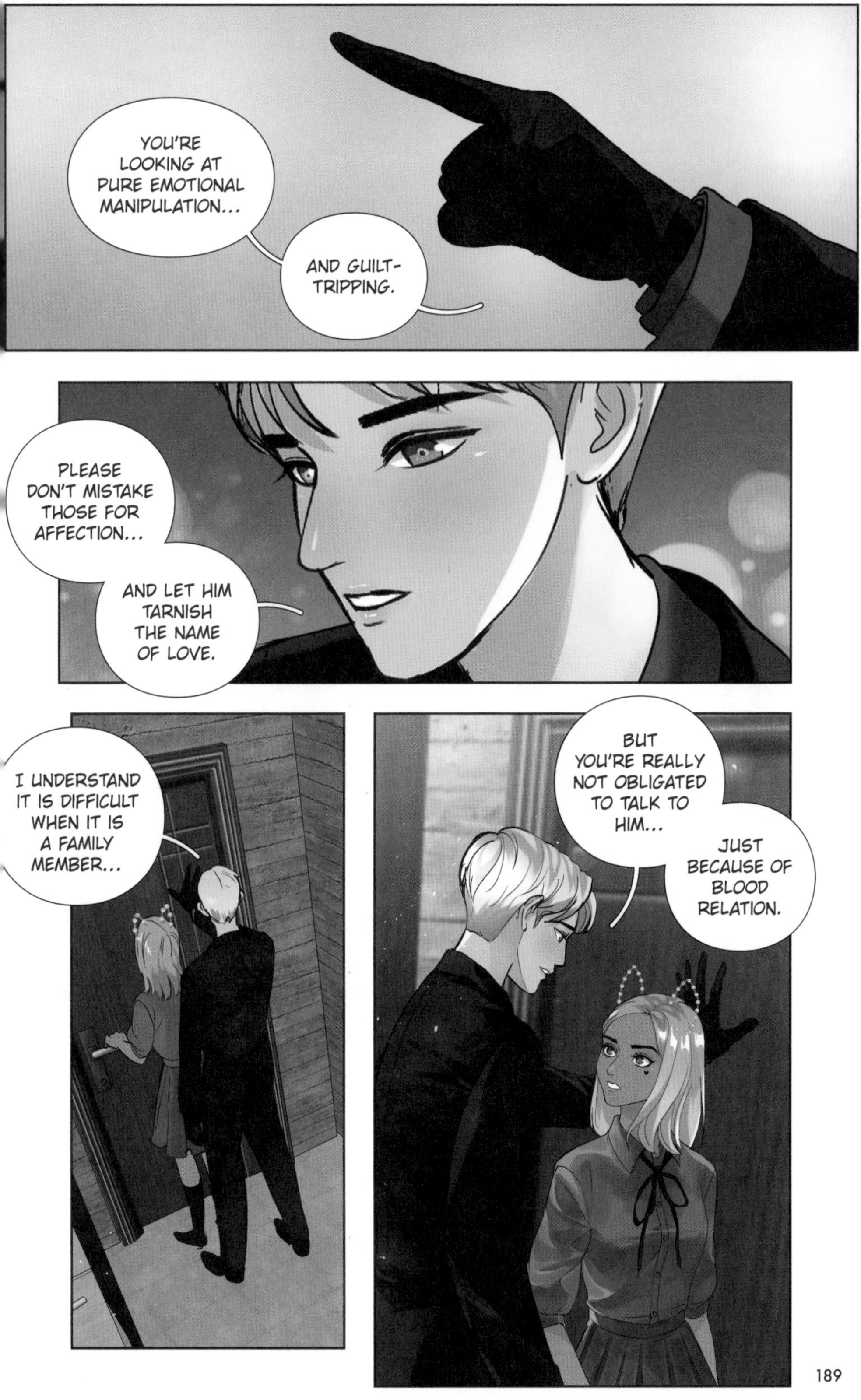
YOU'RE LOOKING AT PURE EMOTIONAL MANIPULATION...
AND GUILT-TRIPPING.
PLEASE DON'T MISTAKE THOSE FOR AFFECTION...
AND LET HIM TARNISH THE NAME OF LOVE.
I UNDERSTAND IT IS DIFFICULT WHEN IT IS A FAMILY MEMBER...
BUT YOU'RE REALLY NOT OBLIGATED TO TALK TO HIM...
JUST BECAUSE OF BLOOD RELATION.

OF COURSE, IF YOU CHOOSE TO OPEN THE DOOR, I WILL NOT STOP YOU.

JUST BE CAREFUL, ALL RIGHT, ZYLITH?

ZELAN...

THERE HE IS AGAIN, WORRYING ABOUT ME. WHY?

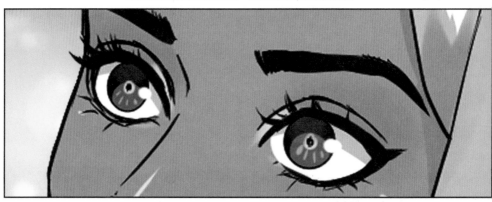

WAIT, SO BLACKMAILING YOUR KID AND THEN CRYING AND BEGGING FOR FORGIVENESS...

THAT ISN'T LOVE?

NO.

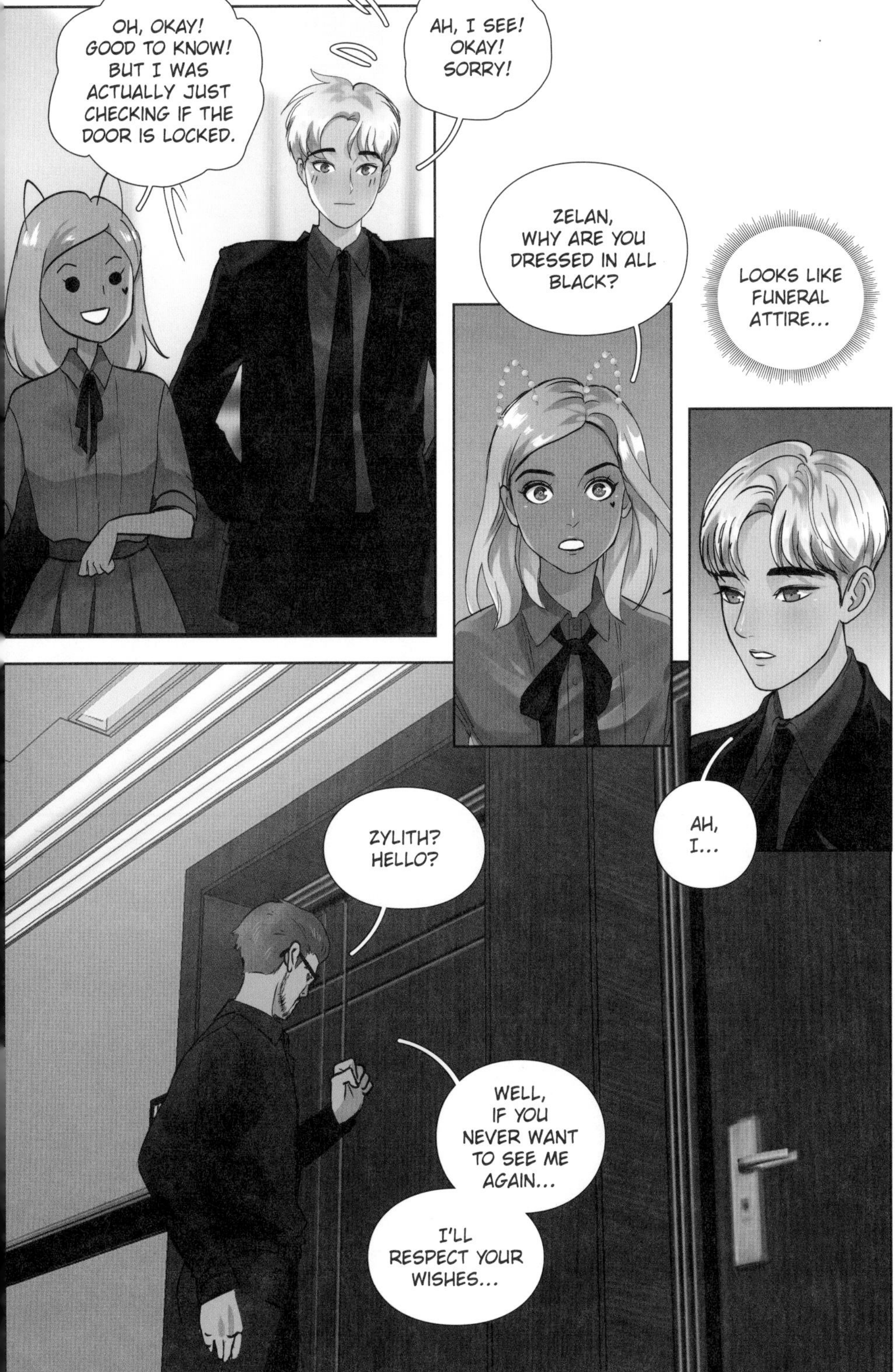
OH, OKAY! GOOD TO KNOW! BUT I WAS ACTUALLY JUST CHECKING IF THE DOOR IS LOCKED.
AH, I SEE! OKAY! SORRY!
ZELAN, WHY ARE YOU DRESSED IN ALL BLACK?
LOOKS LIKE FUNERAL ATTIRE...
AH, I...
ZYLITH? HELLO?
WELL, IF YOU NEVER WANT TO SEE ME AGAIN...
I'LL RESPECT YOUR WISHES...

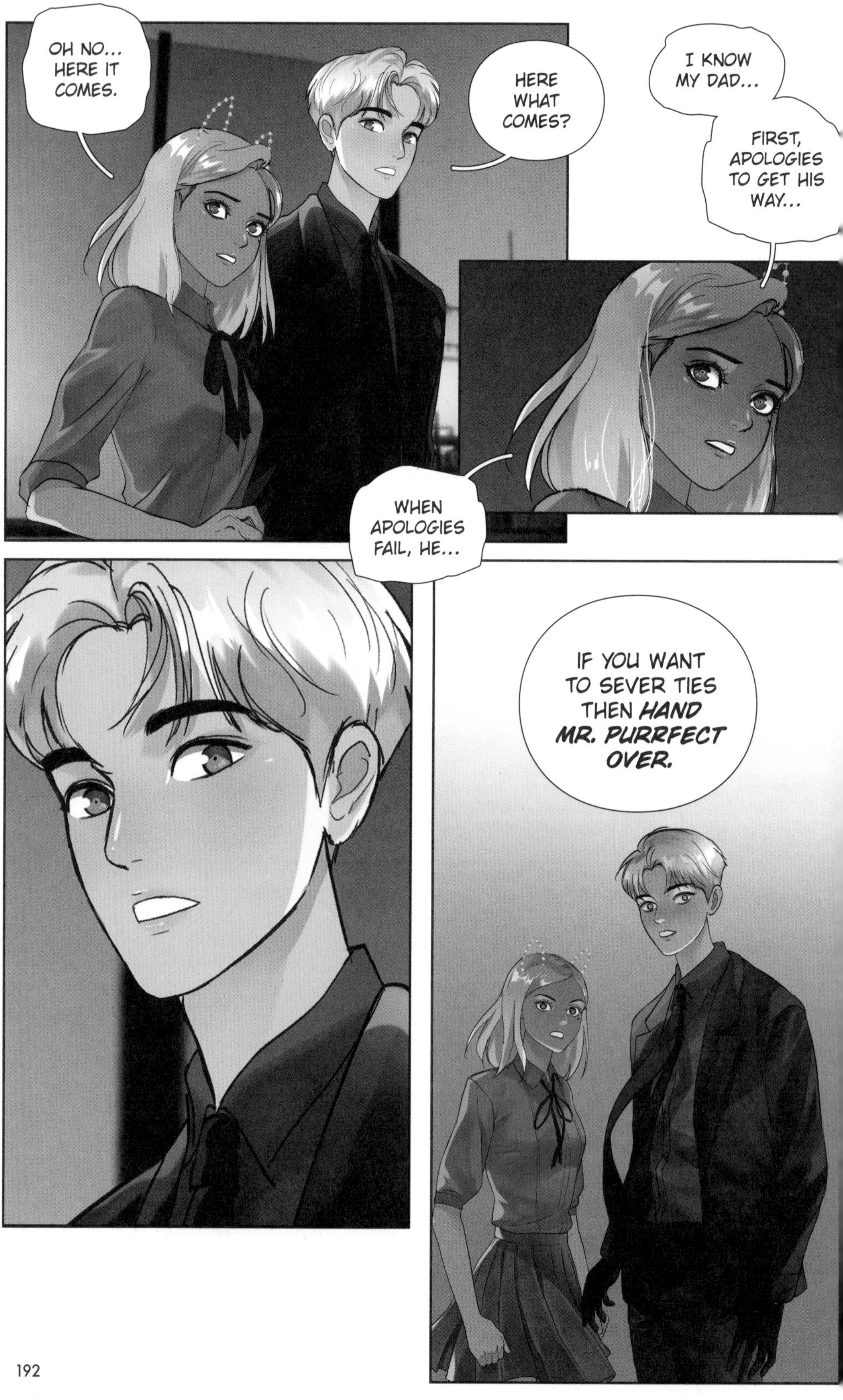
OH NO... HERE IT COMES.
HERE WHAT COMES?
I KNOW MY DAD...
FIRST, APOLOGIES TO GET HIS WAY...
WHEN APOLOGIES FAIL, HE...
IF YOU WANT TO SEVER TIES THEN ***HAND MR. PURRFECT OVER.***

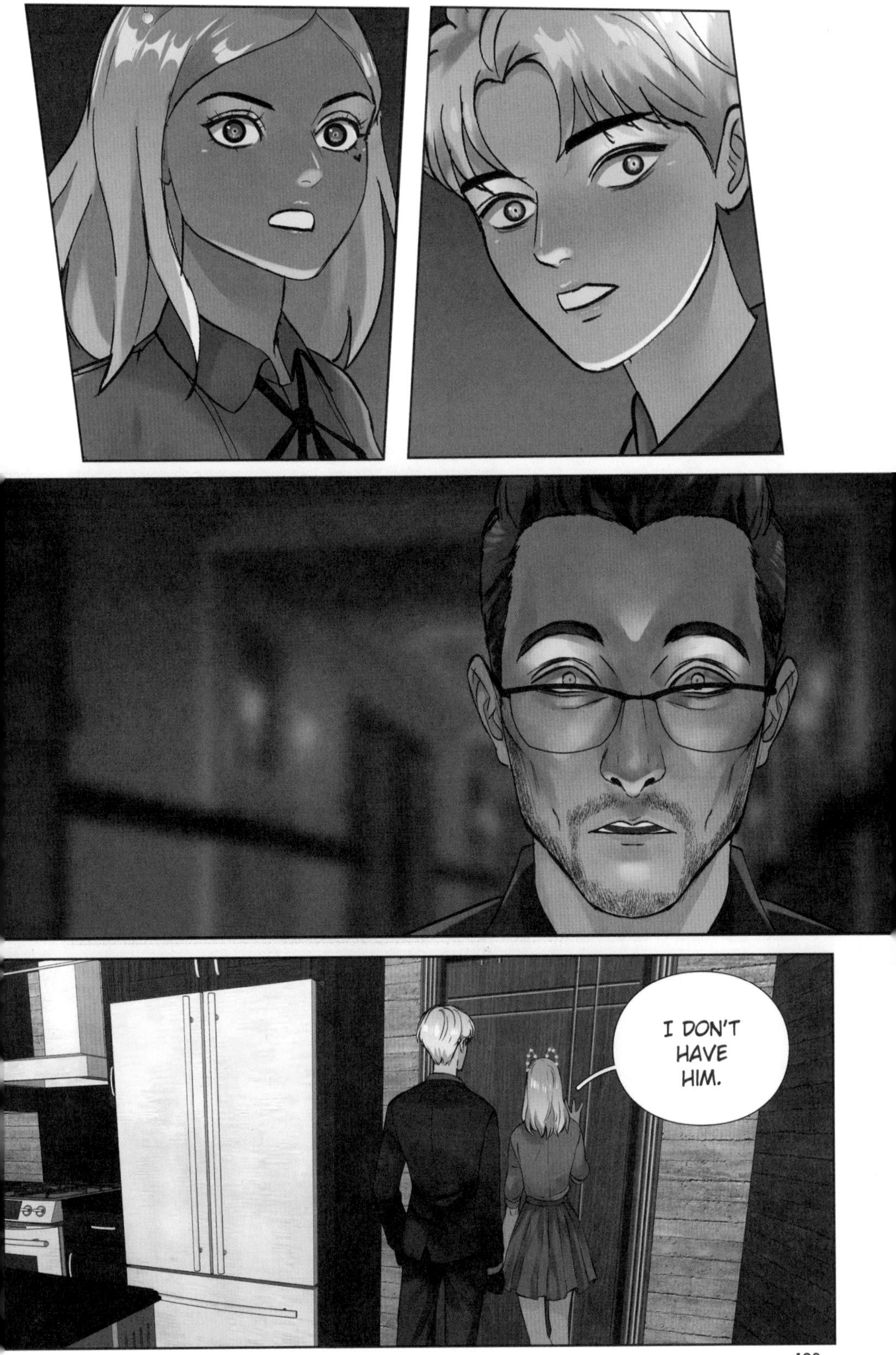
I DON'T HAVE HIM.

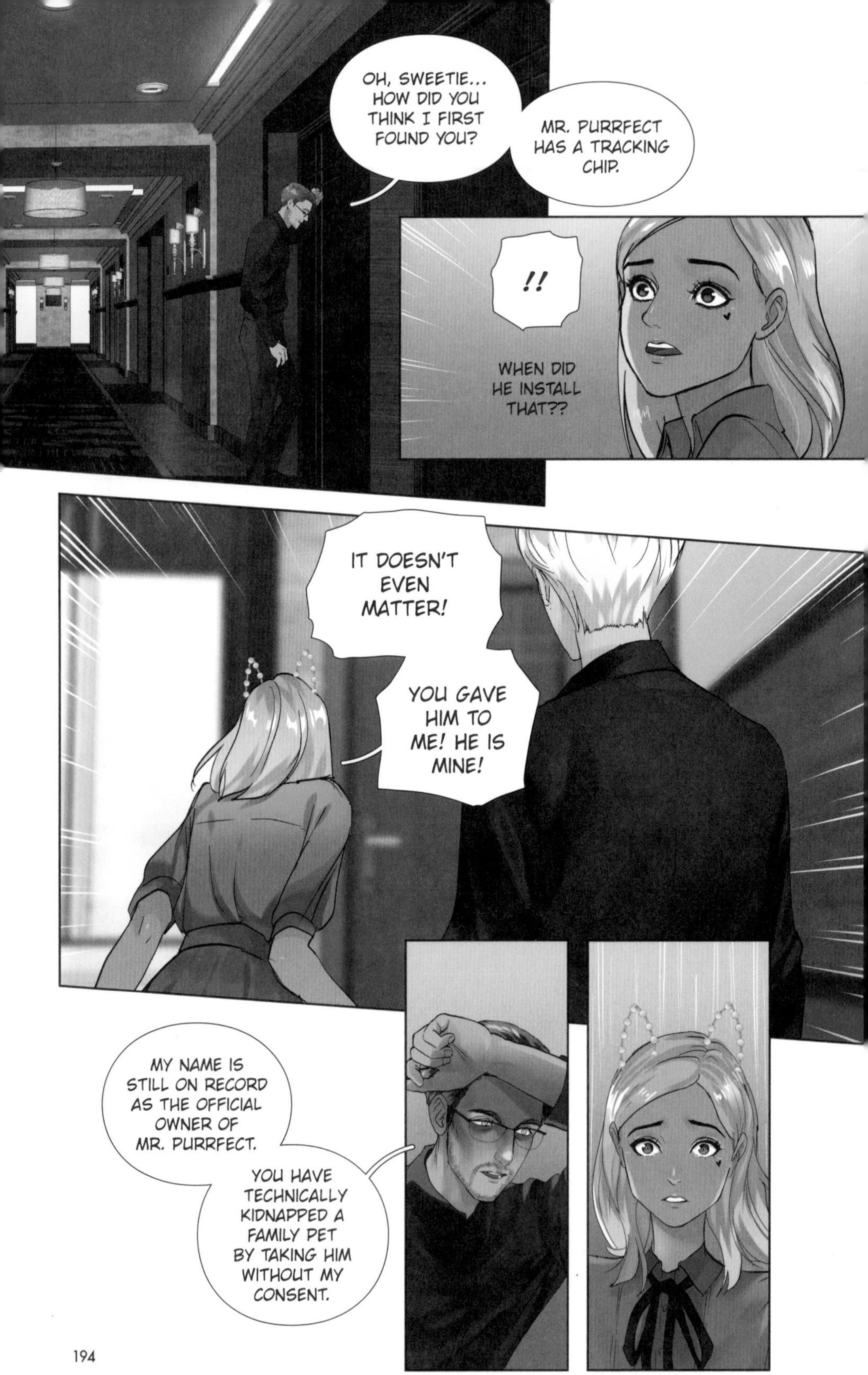
OH, SWEETIE... HOW DID YOU THINK I FIRST FOUND YOU?
MR. PURRFECT HAS A TRACKING CHIP.
!!
WHEN DID HE INSTALL THAT??
IT DOESN'T EVEN MATTER!
YOU GAVE HIM TO ME! HE IS MINE!
MY NAME IS STILL ON RECORD AS THE OFFICIAL OWNER OF MR. PURRFECT.
YOU HAVE TECHNICALLY KIDNAPPED A FAMILY PET BY TAKING HIM WITHOUT MY CONSENT.

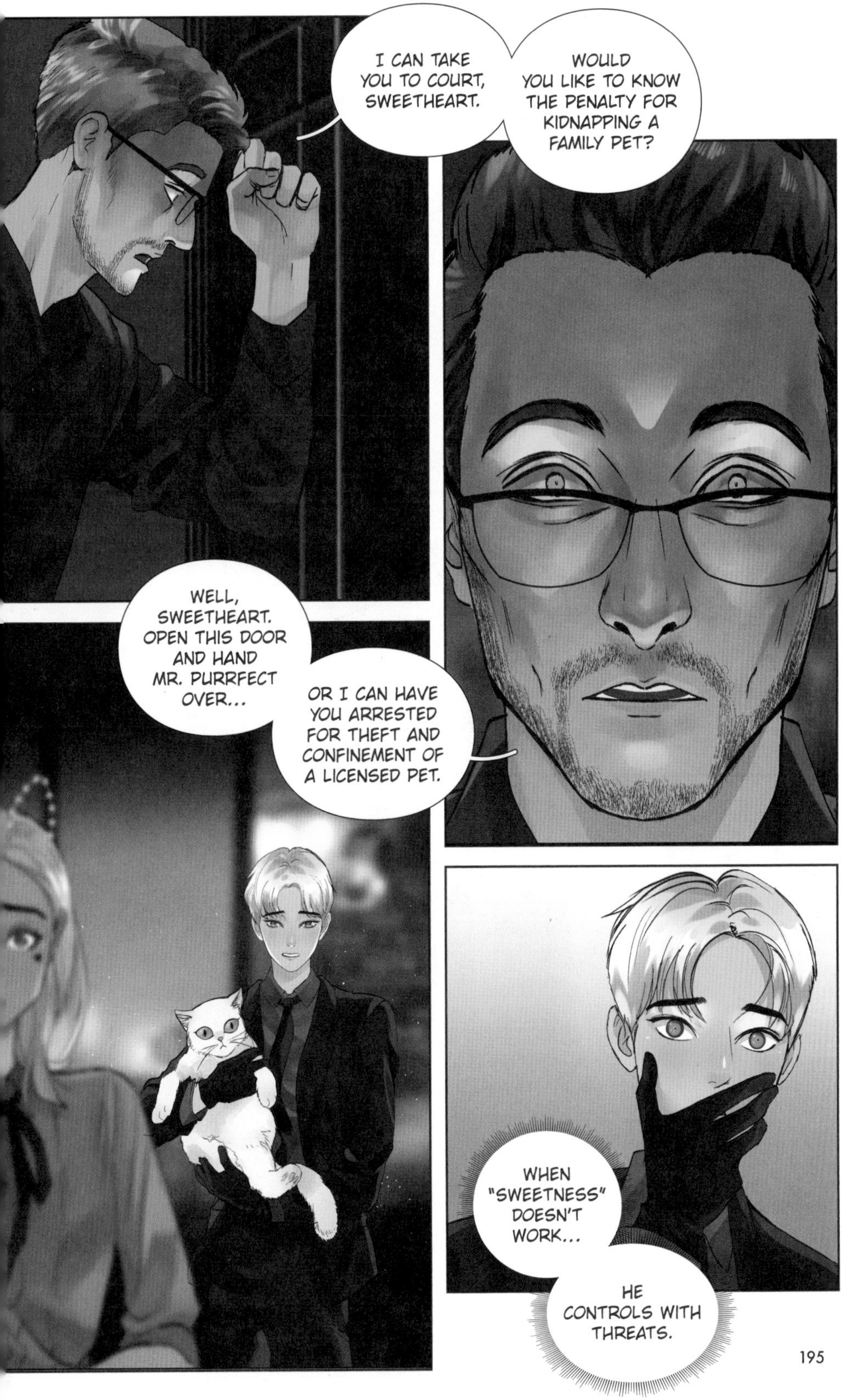
I CAN TAKE YOU TO COURT, SWEETHEART.
WOULD YOU LIKE TO KNOW THE PENALTY FOR KIDNAPPING A FAMILY PET?
WELL, SWEETHEART. OPEN THIS DOOR AND HAND MR. PURRFECT OVER...
OR I CAN HAVE YOU ARRESTED FOR THEFT AND CONFINEMENT OF A LICENSED PET.
WHEN "SWEETNESS" DOESN'T WORK...
HE CONTROLS WITH THREATS.

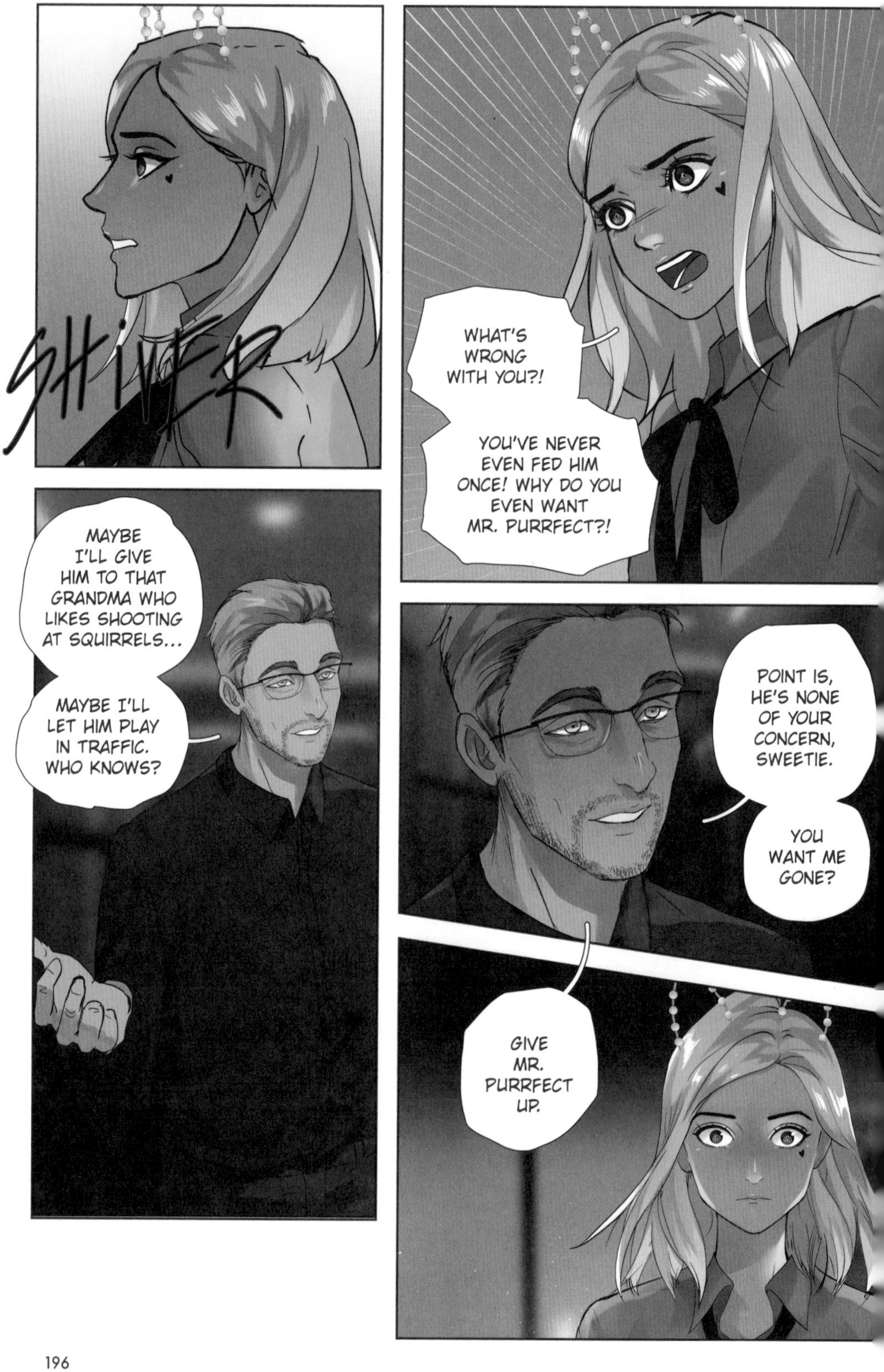
SHIVER
WHAT'S WRONG WITH YOU?!
YOU'VE NEVER EVEN FED HIM ONCE! WHY DO YOU EVEN WANT MR. PURRFECT?!
MAYBE I'LL GIVE HIM TO THAT GRANDMA WHO LIKES SHOOTING AT SQUIRRELS...
MAYBE I'LL LET HIM PLAY IN TRAFFIC. WHO KNOWS?
POINT IS, HE'S NONE OF YOUR CONCERN, SWEETIE.
YOU WANT ME GONE?
GIVE MR. PURRFECT UP.

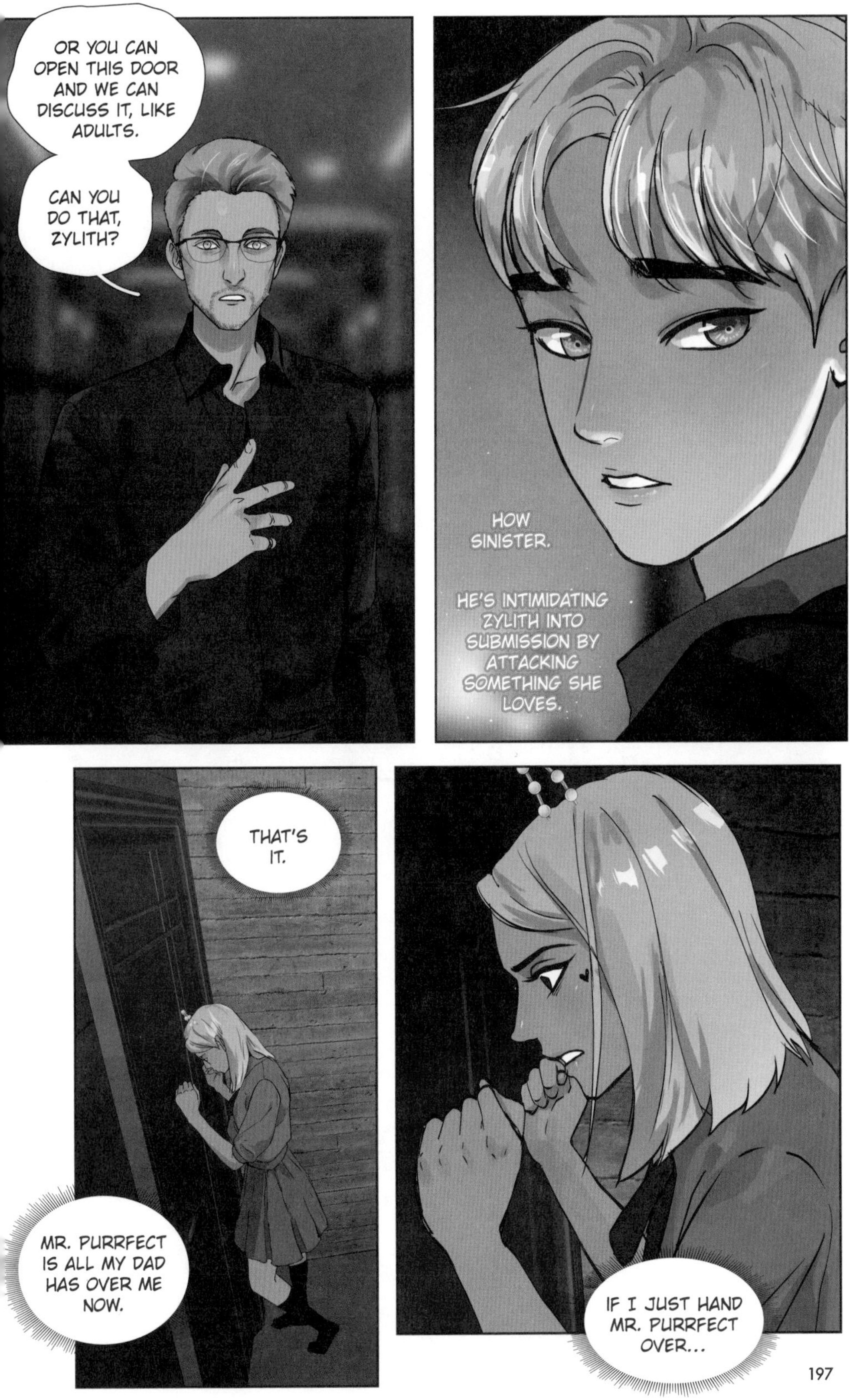
OR YOU CAN OPEN THIS DOOR AND WE CAN DISCUSS IT, LIKE ADULTS.
CAN YOU DO THAT, ZYLITH?
HOW SINISTER.
HE'S INTIMIDATING ZYLITH INTO SUBMISSION BY ATTACKING SOMETHING SHE LOVES.
THAT'S IT.
MR. PURRFECT IS ALL MY DAD HAS OVER ME NOW.
IF I JUST HAND MR. PURRFECT OVER...

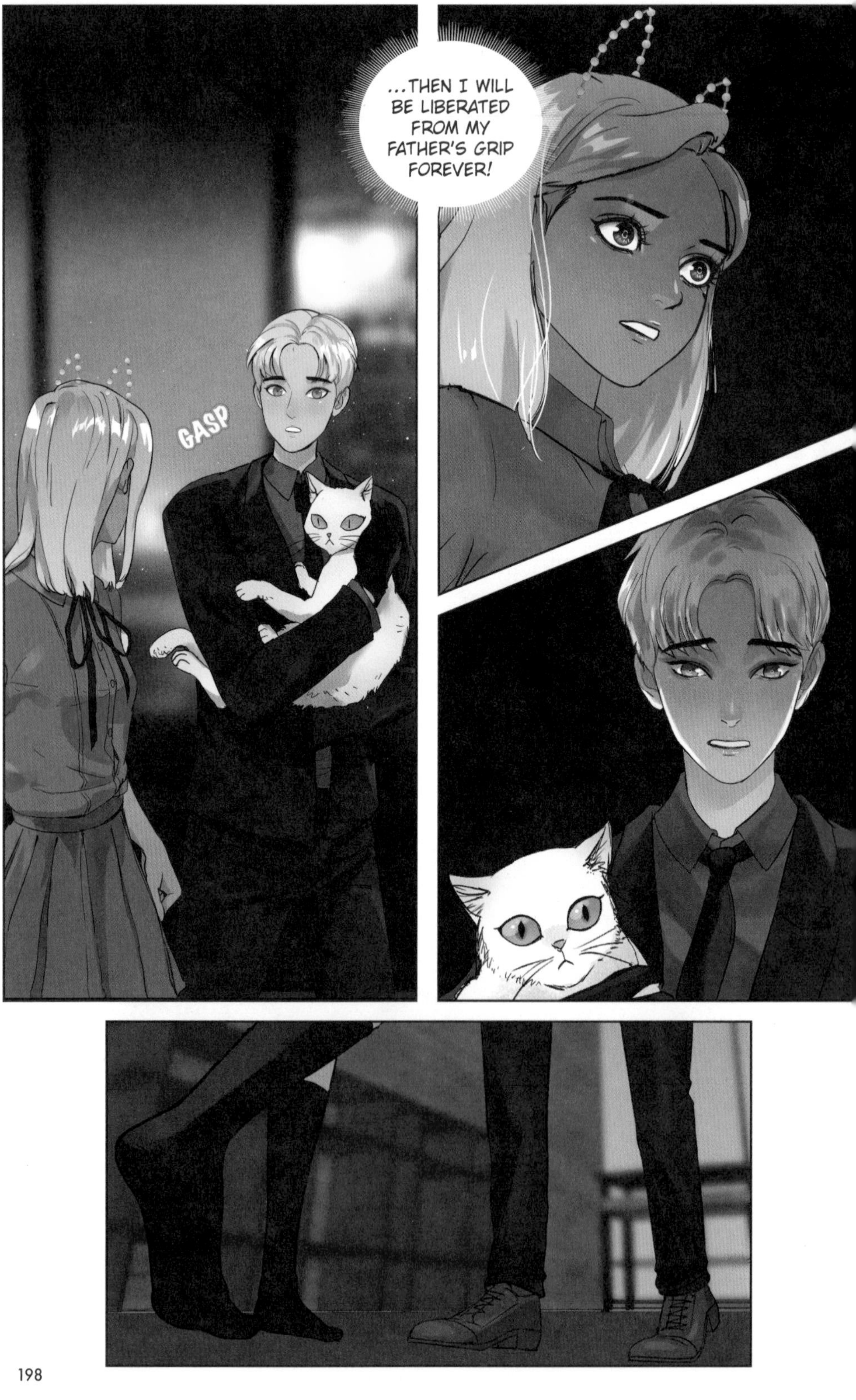
GASP
...THEN I WILL BE LIBERATED FROM MY FATHER'S GRIP FOREVER!

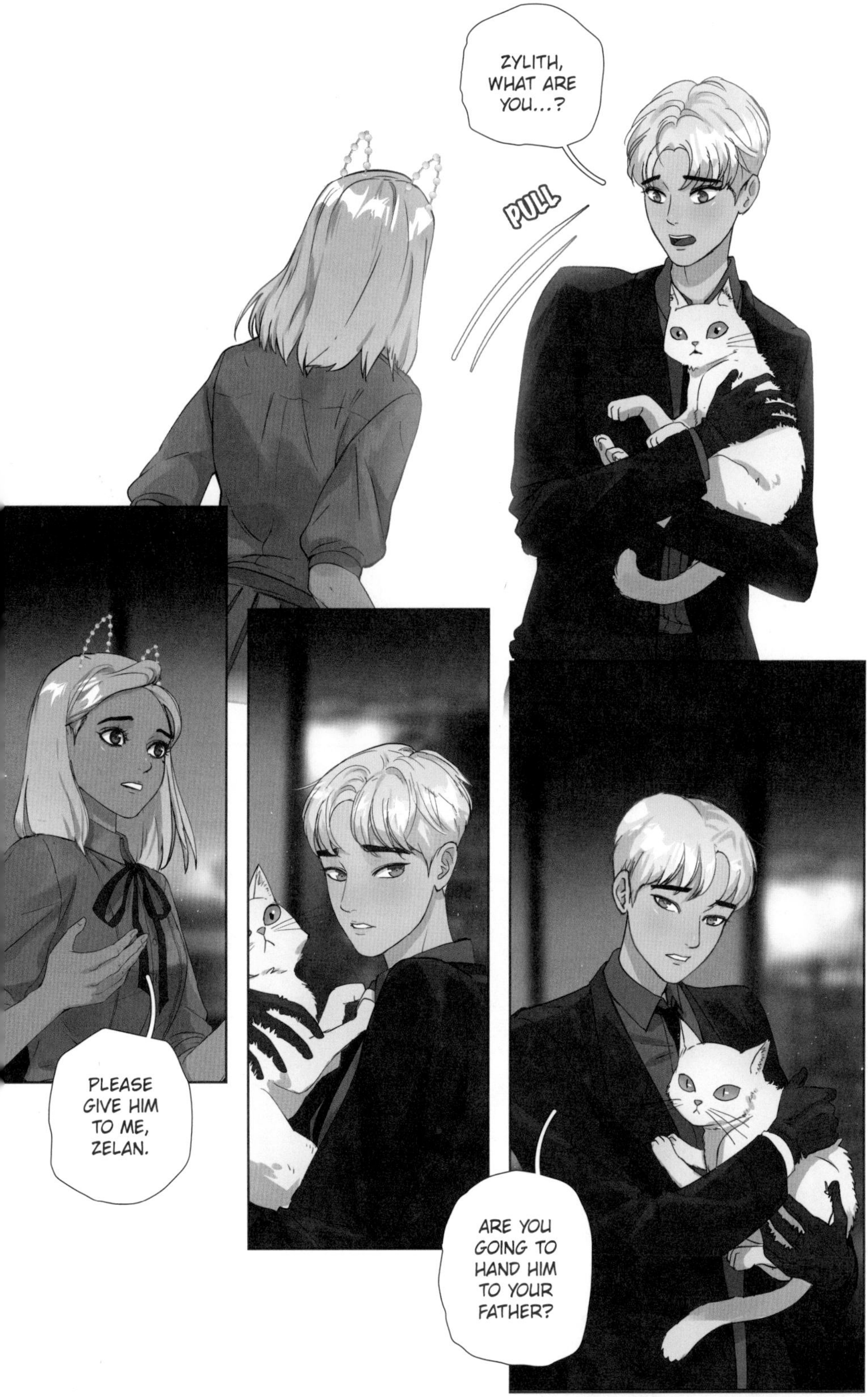
ZYLITH, WHAT ARE YOU...?
PULL
PLEASE GIVE HIM TO ME, ZELAN.
ARE YOU GOING TO HAND HIM TO YOUR FATHER?

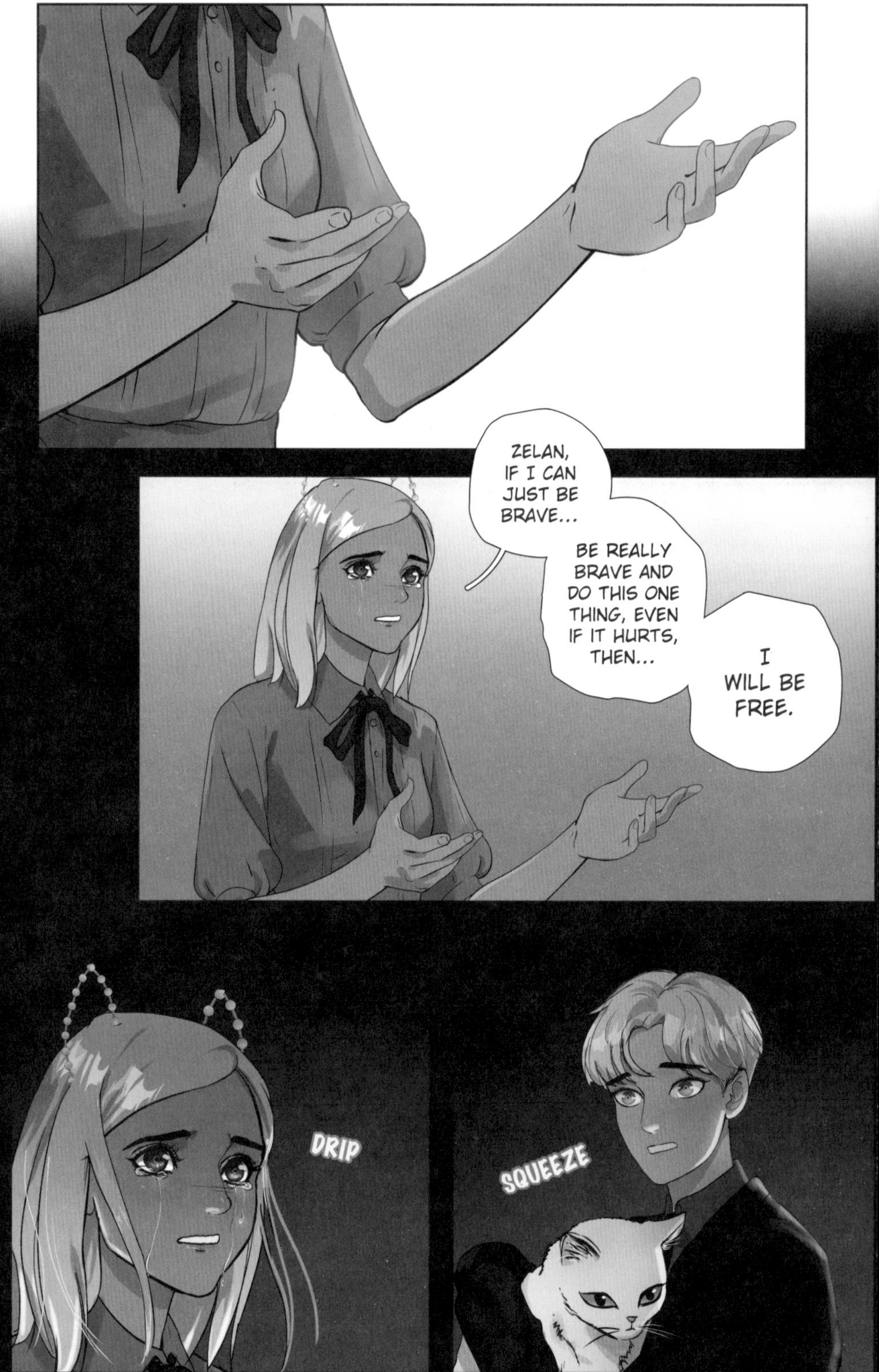
ZELAN, IF I CAN JUST BE BRAVE...
BE REALLY BRAVE AND DO THIS ONE THING, EVEN IF IT HURTS, THEN...
I WILL BE FREE.
DRIP
SQUEEZE

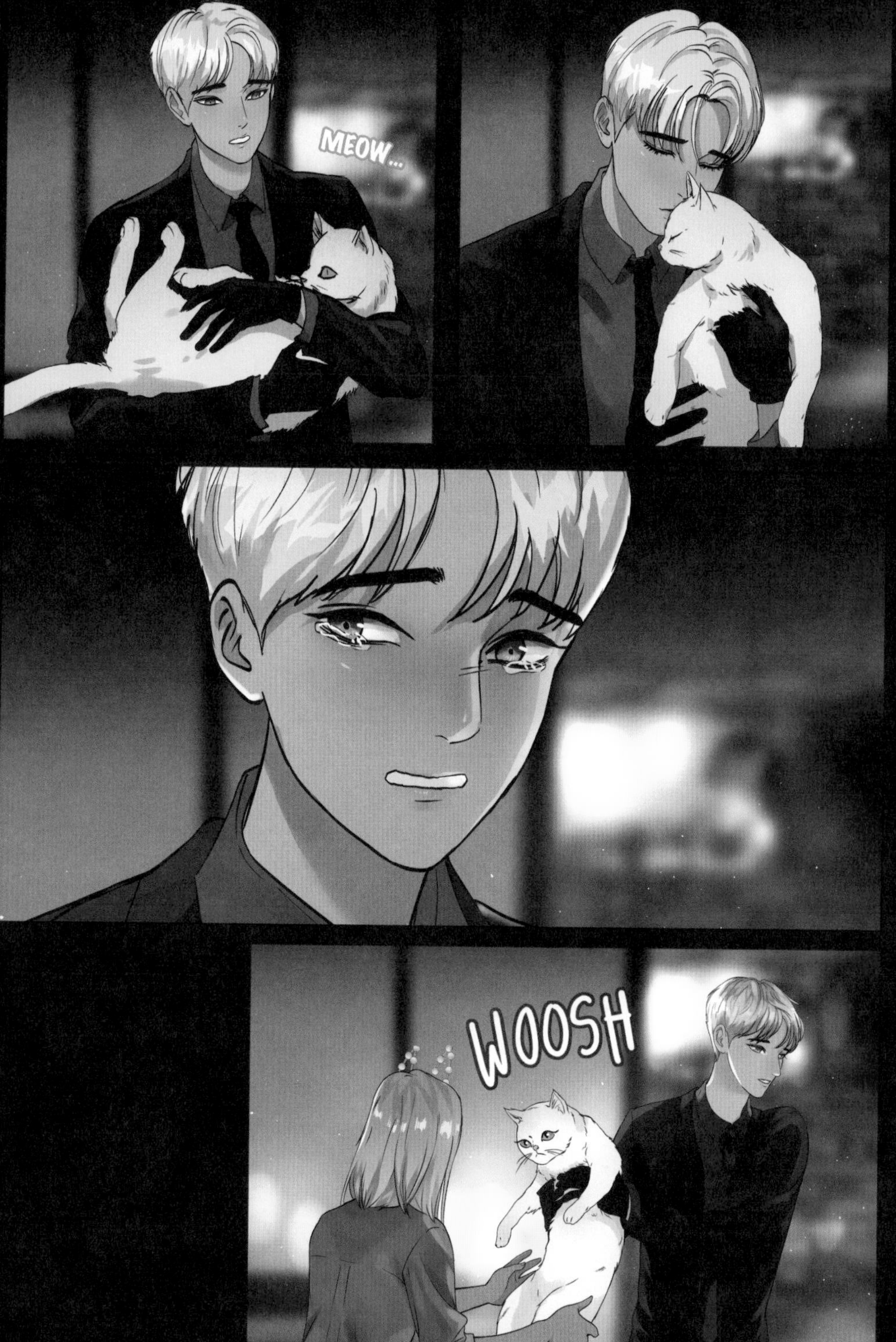
MEOW...
WOOSH

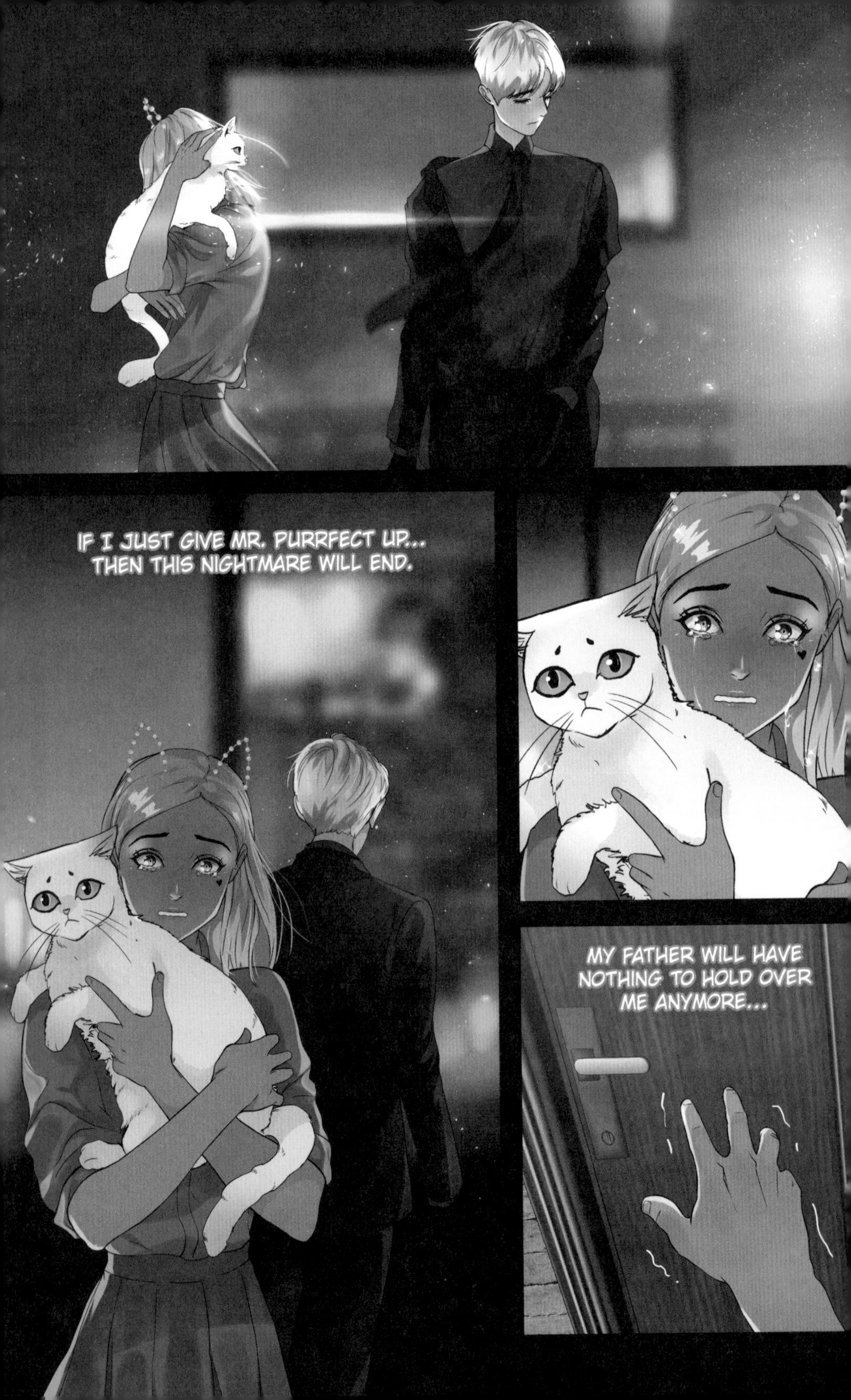
IF I JUST GIVE MR. PURRFECT UP... THEN THIS NIGHTMARE WILL END.
MY FATHER WILL HAVE NOTHING TO HOLD OVER ME ANYMORE...

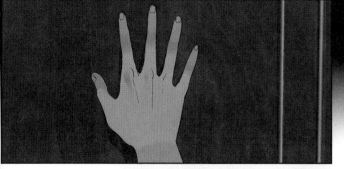

AND I WILL NEVER HAVE TO BE A PUPPET ON HIS STRINGS AGAIN.

I KEPT ON HOPING...

...THAT YOUR INSINCERE APOLOGY WAS SINCERE.

AND I HAD HOPED THAT YOU WOULDN'T INTENTIONALLY HURT ME WITH YOUR ACTIONS.

YOU ALWAYS TOLD ME TO STOP LIVING IN THE CLOUDS.

203

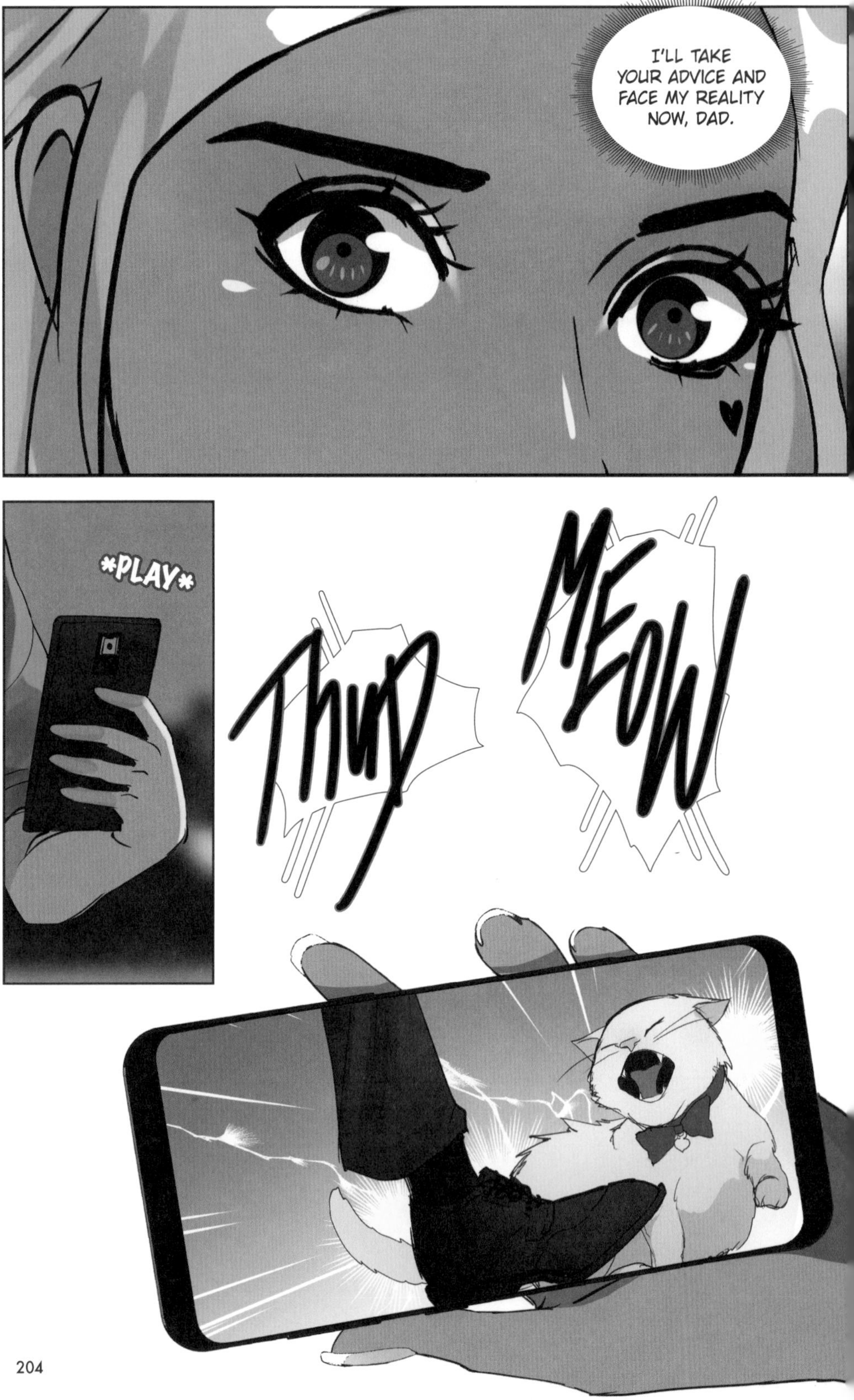
I'LL TAKE YOUR ADVICE AND FACE MY REALITY NOW, DAD.
PLAY
THUD
MEOW

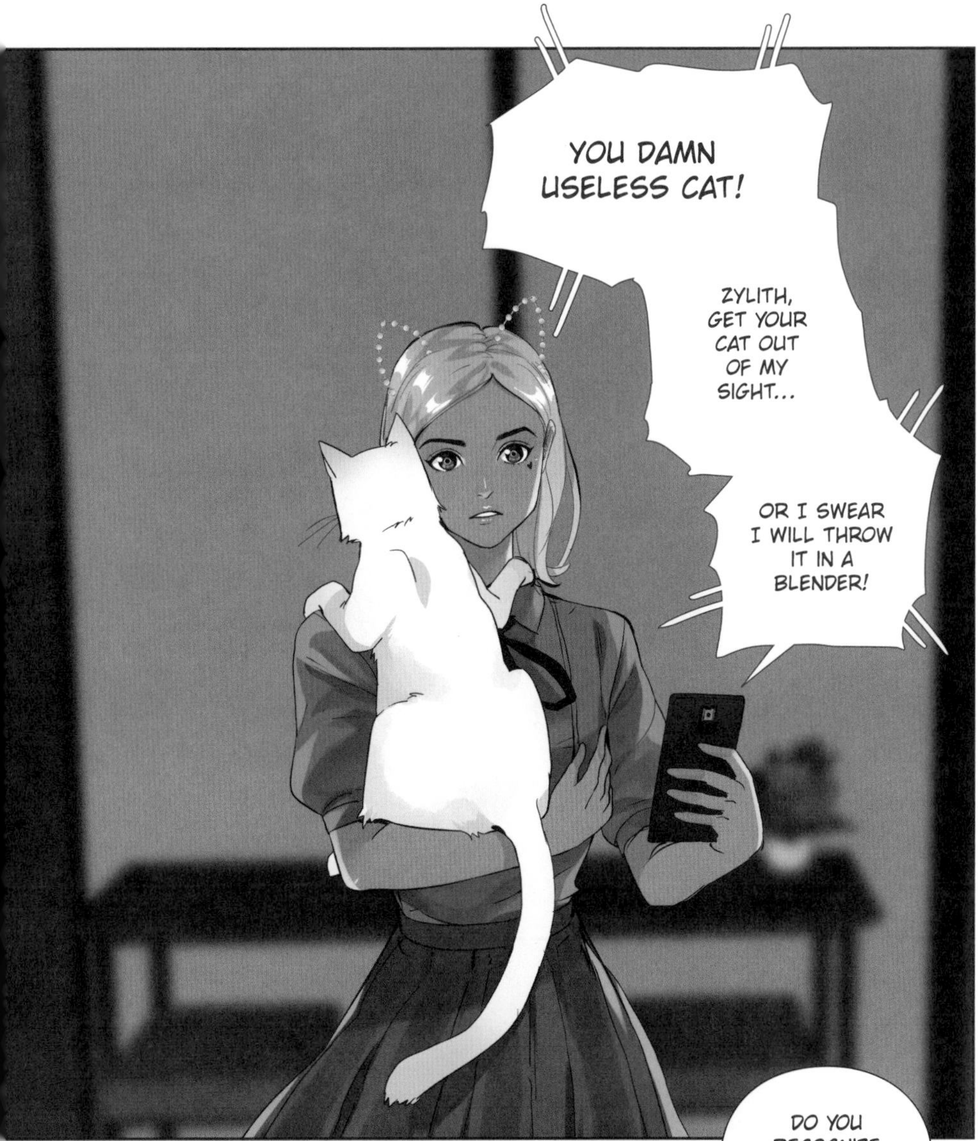
YOU DAMN USELESS CAT!
ZYLITH, GET YOUR CAT OUT OF MY SIGHT...
OR I SWEAR I WILL THROW IT IN A BLENDER!

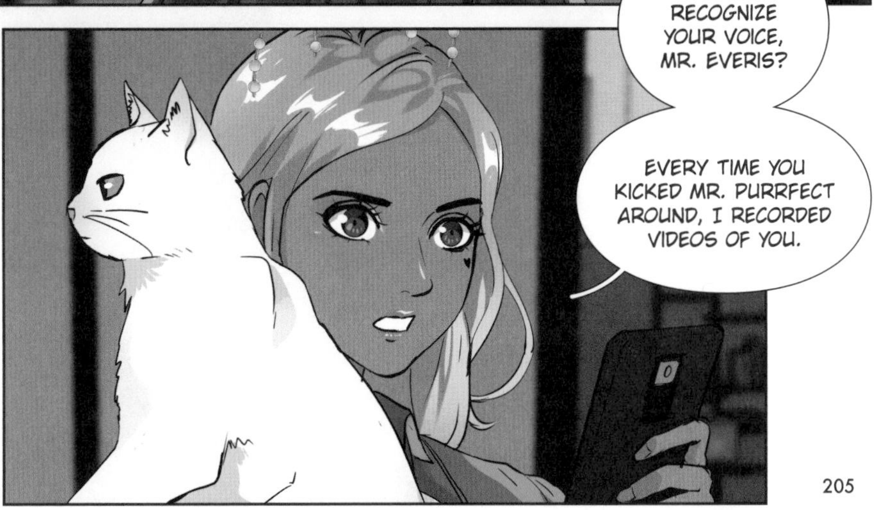
DO YOU RECOGNIZE YOUR VOICE, MR. EVERIS?
EVERY TIME YOU KICKED MR. PURRFECT AROUND, I RECORDED VIDEOS OF YOU.

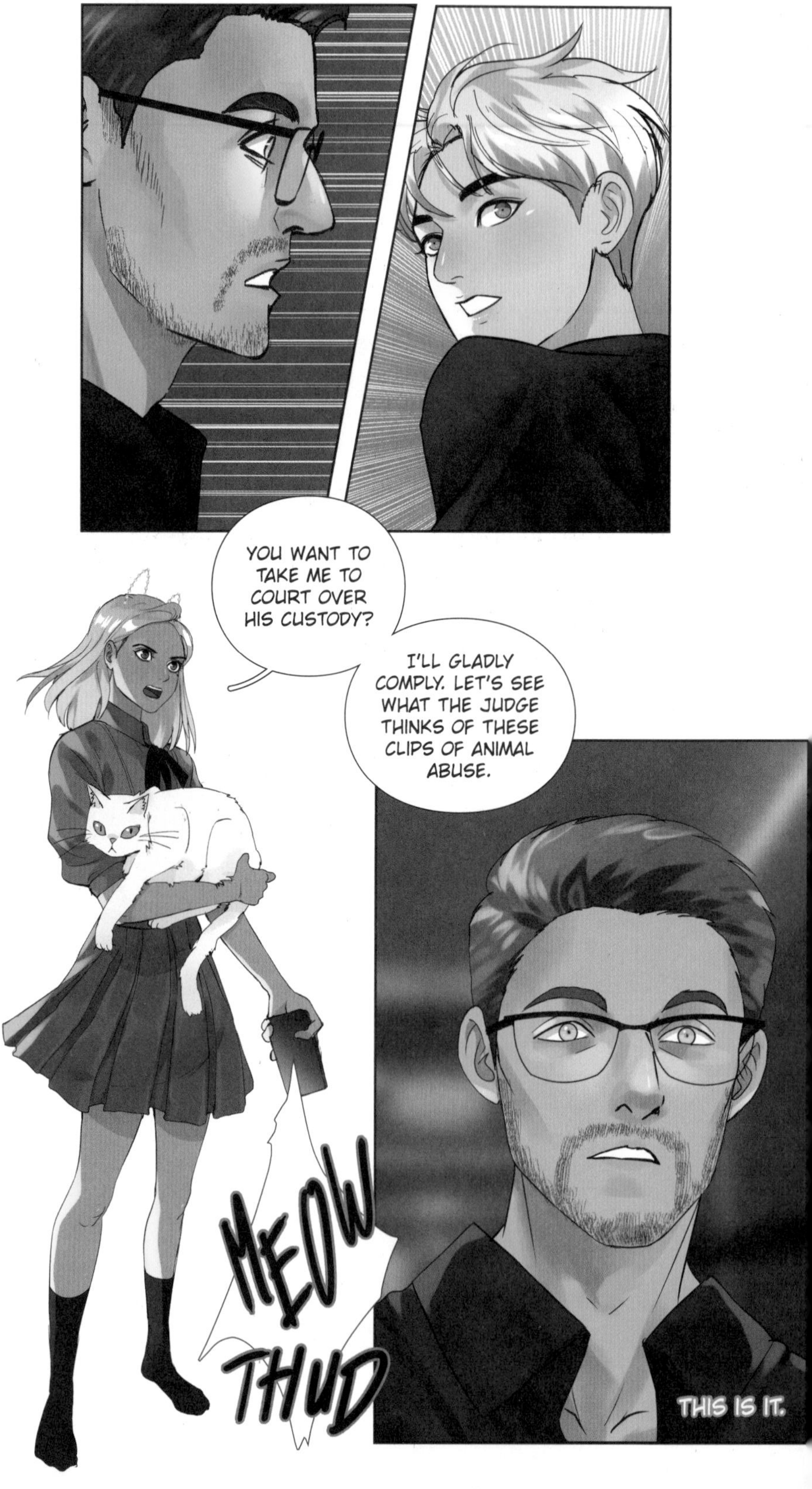
YOU WANT TO TAKE ME TO COURT OVER HIS CUSTODY?
I'LL GLADLY COMPLY. LET'S SEE WHAT THE JUDGE THINKS OF THESE CLIPS OF ANIMAL ABUSE.
MEOW
THUD
THIS IS IT.

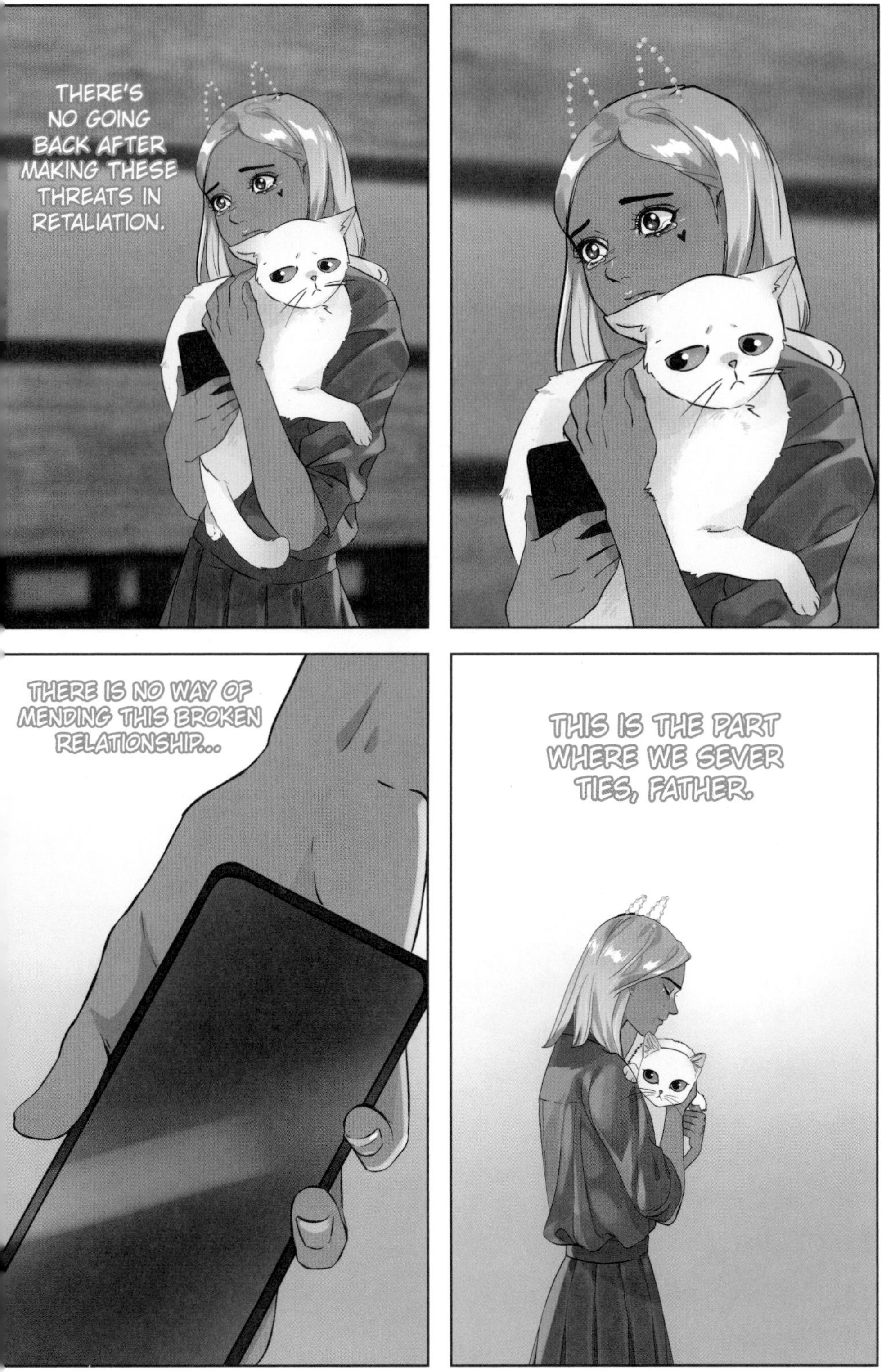
THERE'S NO GOING BACK AFTER MAKING THESE THREATS IN RETALIATION.
THERE IS NO WAY OF MENDING THIS BROKEN RELATIONSHIP...
THIS IS THE PART WHERE WE SEVER TIES, FATHER.

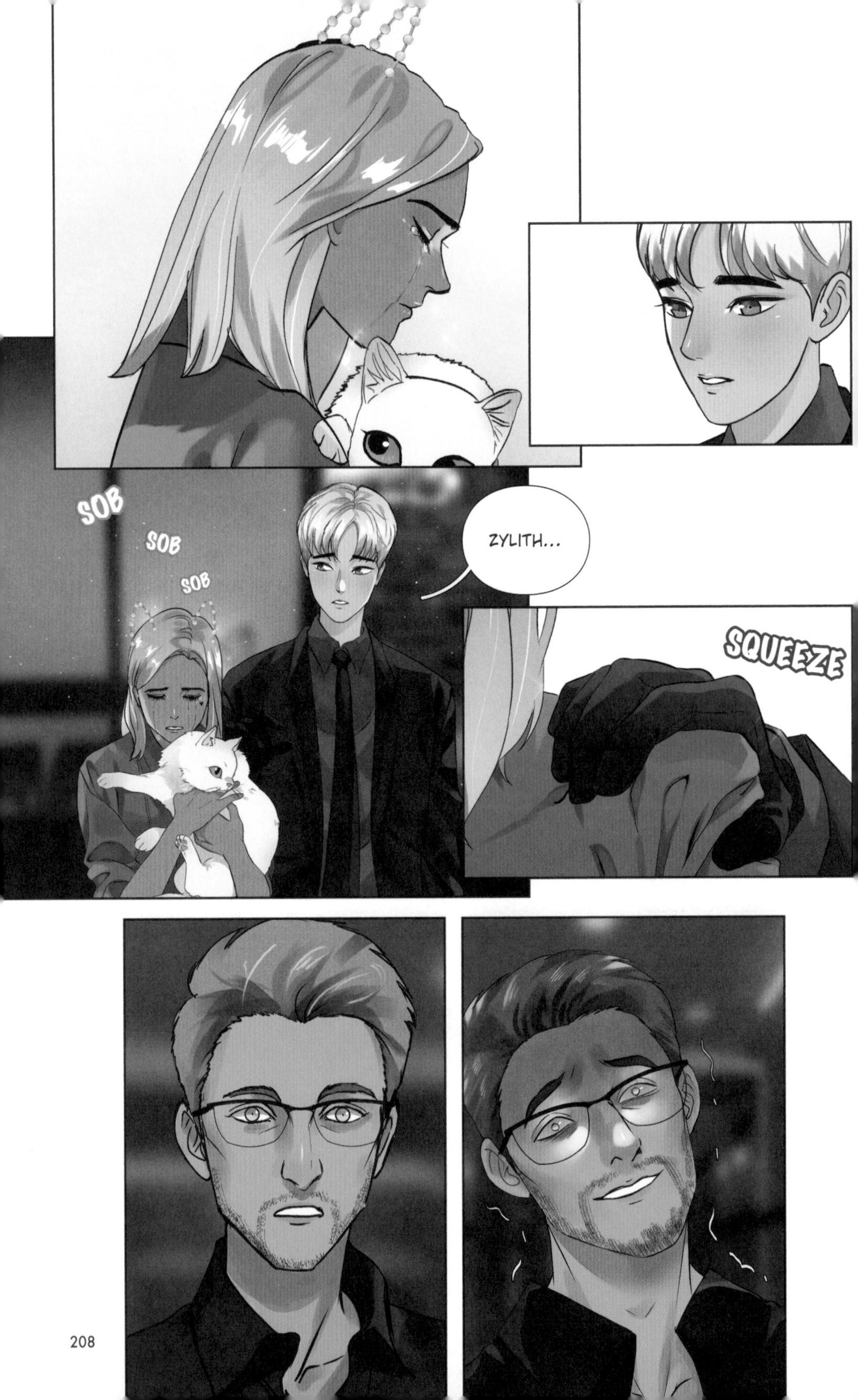
SOB
SOB
SOB
ZYLITH...
SQUEEZE

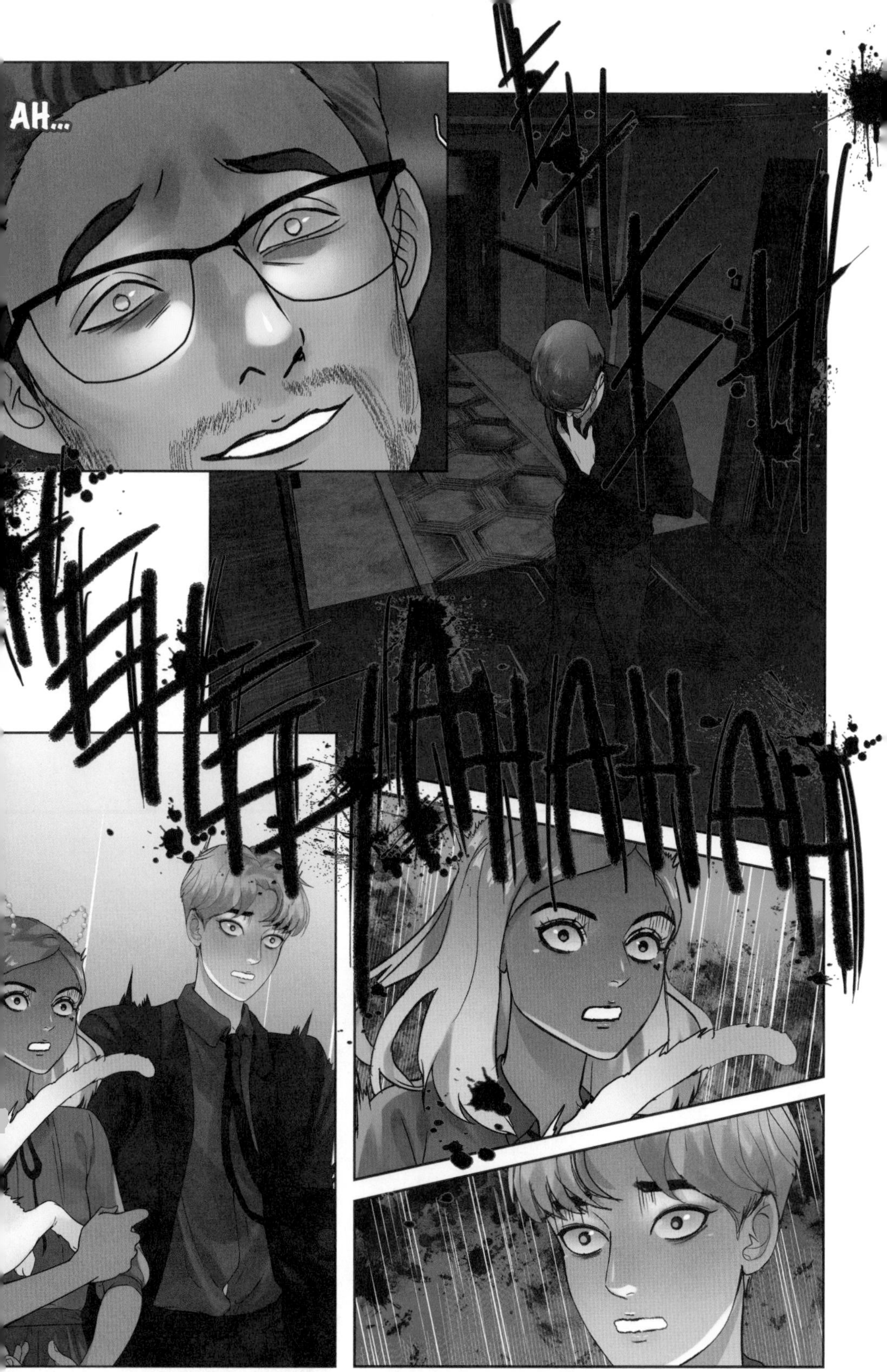
AH...

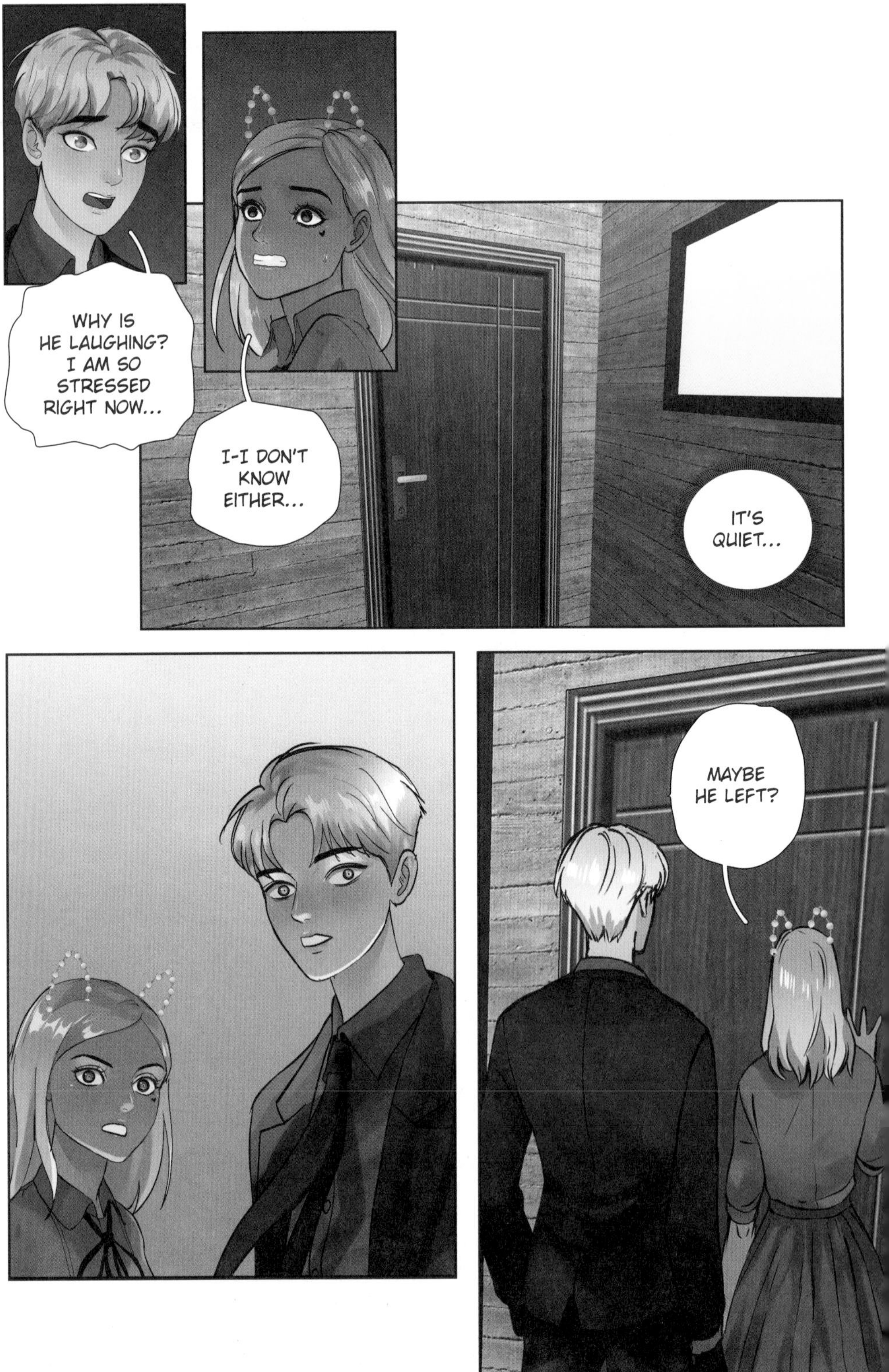
WHY IS HE LAUGHING? I AM SO STRESSED RIGHT NOW...
I-I DON'T KNOW EITHER...
IT'S QUIET...
MAYBE HE LEFT?

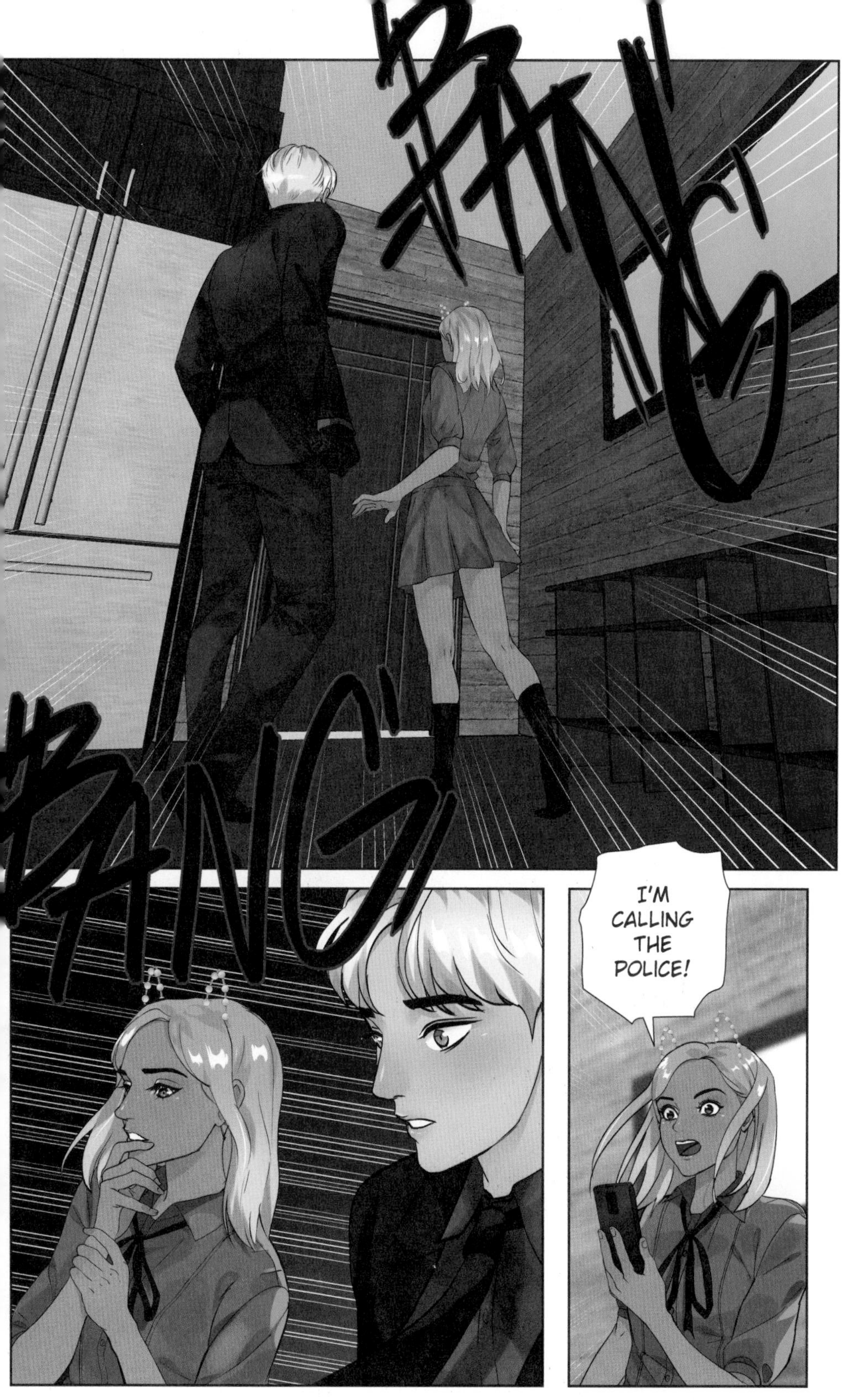
BANG
BANG
I'M CALLING THE POLICE!

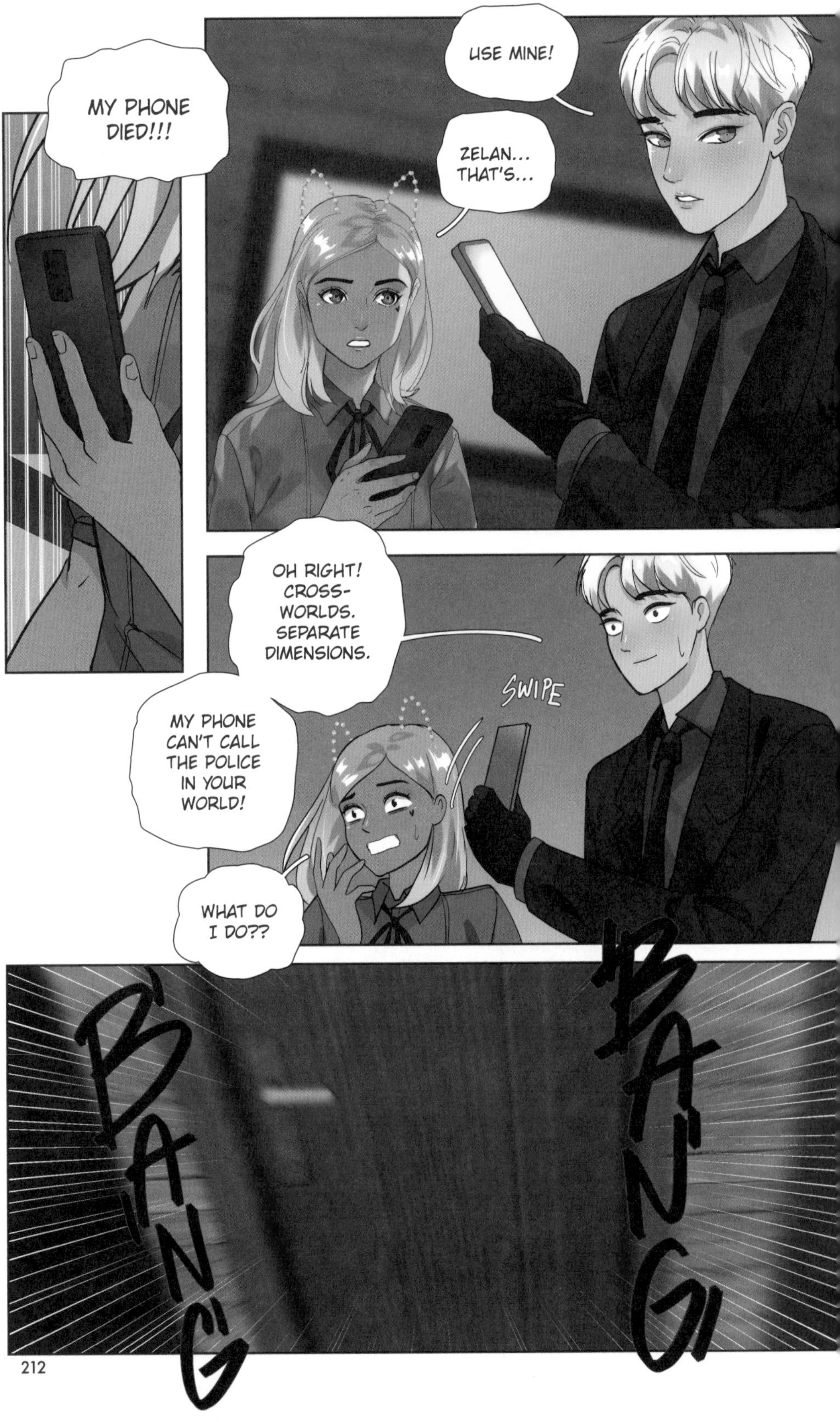

MY PHONE DIED!!!
USE MINE!
ZELAN... THAT'S...
OH RIGHT! CROSS-WORLDS. SEPARATE DIMENSIONS.
SWIPE
MY PHONE CAN'T CALL THE POLICE IN YOUR WORLD!
WHAT DO I DO??
BANG
BANG

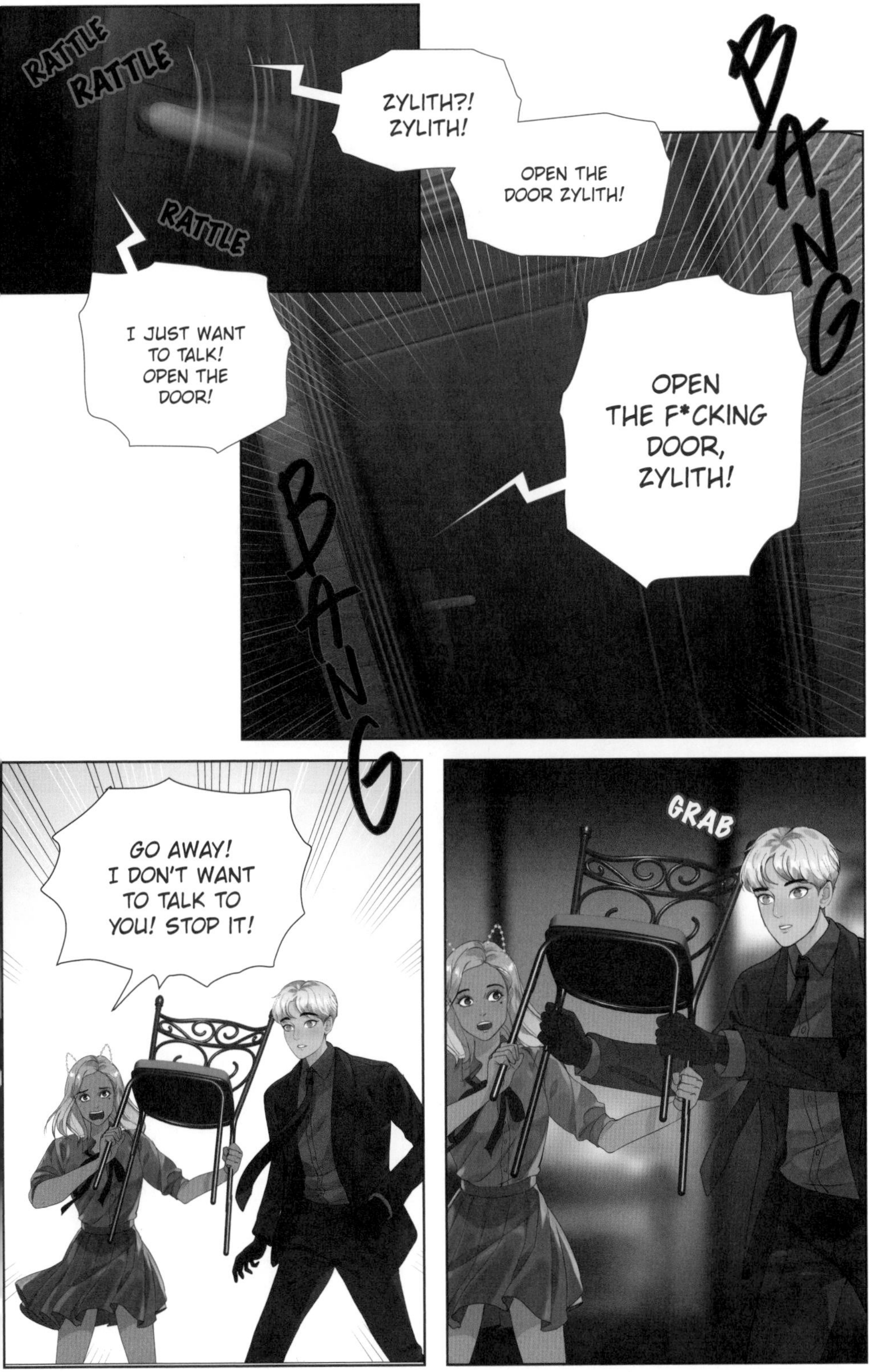
RATTLE RATTLE
ZYLITH?! ZYLITH!
OPEN THE DOOR ZYLITH!
BANG
RATTLE
I JUST WANT TO TALK! OPEN THE DOOR!
OPEN THE F*CKING DOOR, ZYLITH!
BANG
GO AWAY! I DON'T WANT TO TALK TO YOU! STOP IT!
GRAB

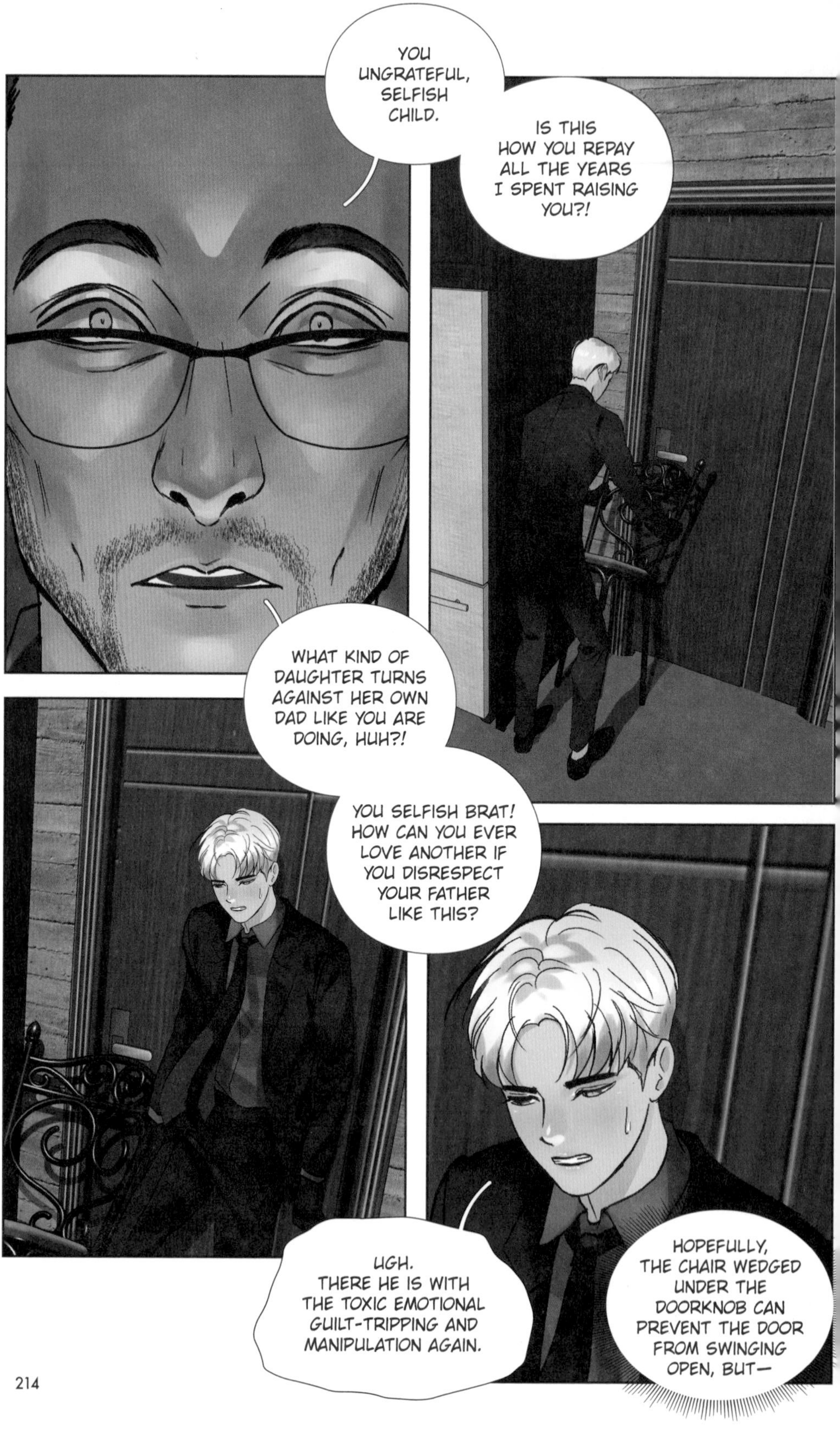
YOU UNGRATEFUL, SELFISH CHILD.
IS THIS HOW YOU REPAY ALL THE YEARS I SPENT RAISING YOU?!
WHAT KIND OF DAUGHTER TURNS AGAINST HER OWN DAD LIKE YOU ARE DOING, HUH?!
YOU SELFISH BRAT! HOW CAN YOU EVER LOVE ANOTHER IF YOU DISRESPECT YOUR FATHER LIKE THIS?
UGH. THERE HE IS WITH THE TOXIC EMOTIONAL GUILT-TRIPPING AND MANIPULATION AGAIN.
HOPEFULLY, THE CHAIR WEDGED UNDER THE DOORKNOB CAN PREVENT THE DOOR FROM SWINGING OPEN, BUT—

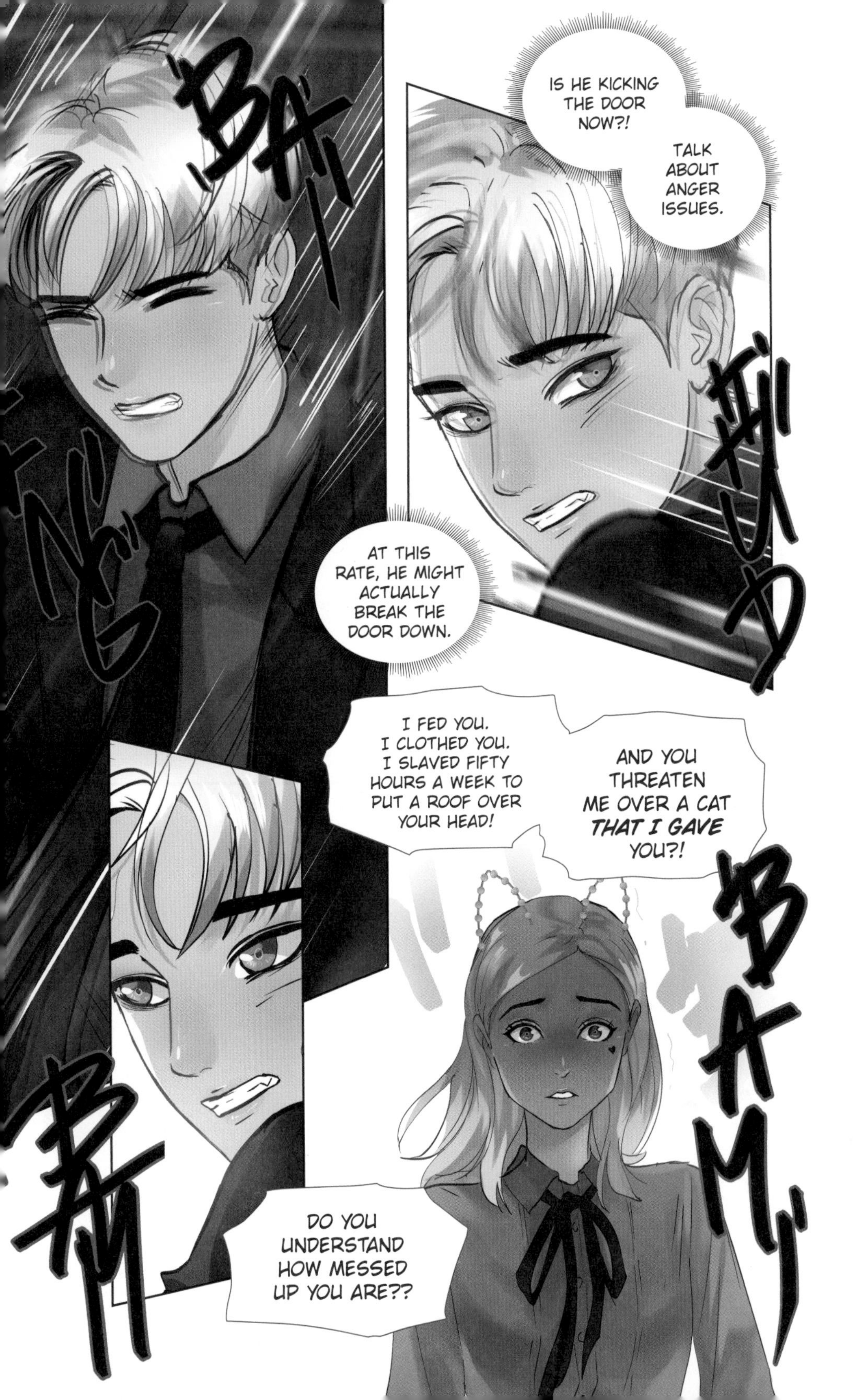
IS HE KICKING THE DOOR NOW?!
TALK ABOUT ANGER ISSUES.
AT THIS RATE, HE MIGHT ACTUALLY BREAK THE DOOR DOWN.
I FED YOU. I CLOTHED YOU. I SLAVED FIFTY HOURS A WEEK TO PUT A ROOF OVER YOUR HEAD!
AND YOU THREATEN ME OVER A CAT *THAT I GAVE* YOU?!
DO YOU UNDERSTAND HOW MESSED UP YOU ARE??

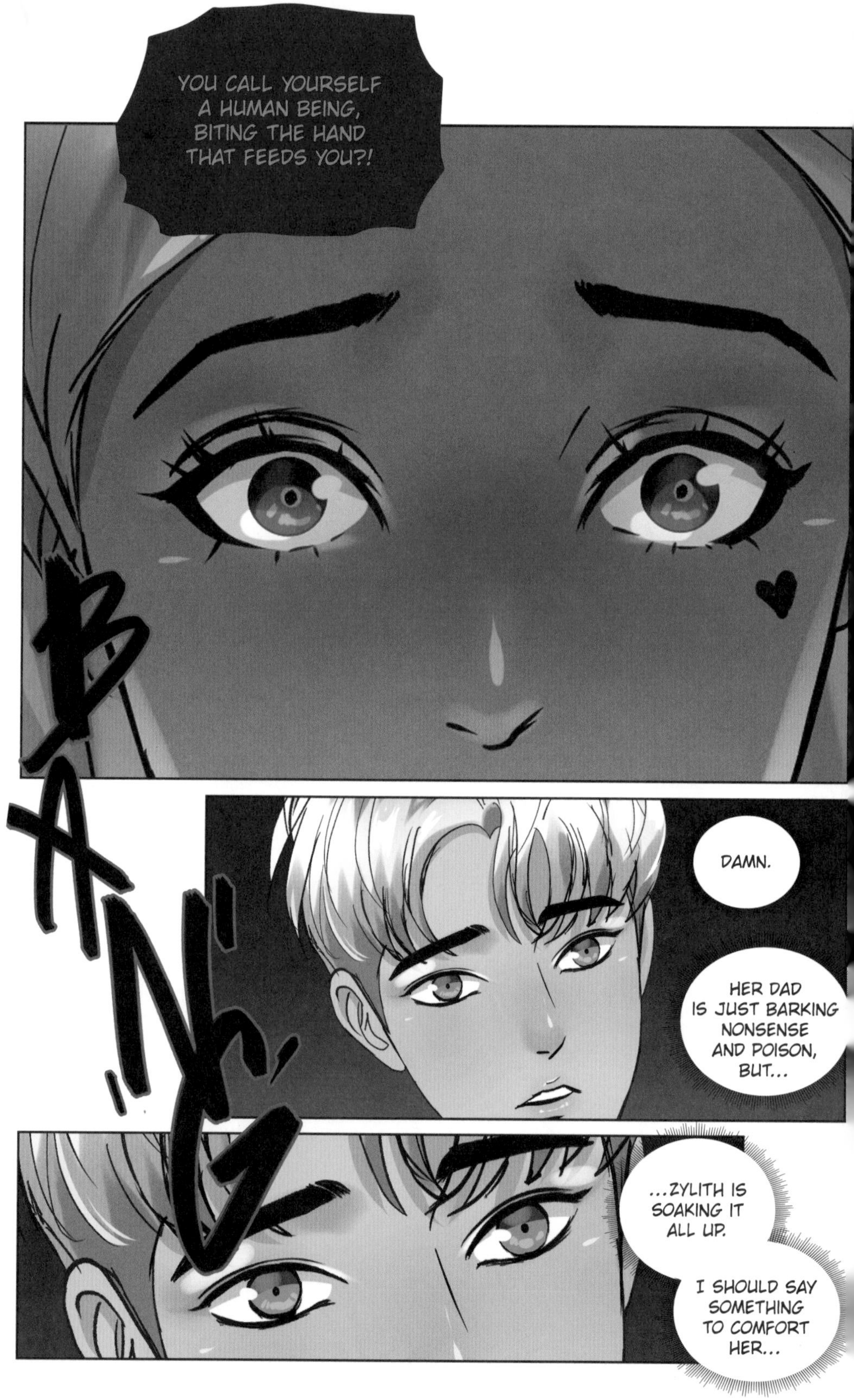
YOU CALL YOURSELF A HUMAN BEING, BITING THE HAND THAT FEEDS YOU?!
BANG
DAMN.
HER DAD IS JUST BARKING NONSENSE AND POISON, BUT...
...ZYLITH IS SOAKING IT ALL UP.
I SHOULD SAY SOMETHING TO COMFORT HER...

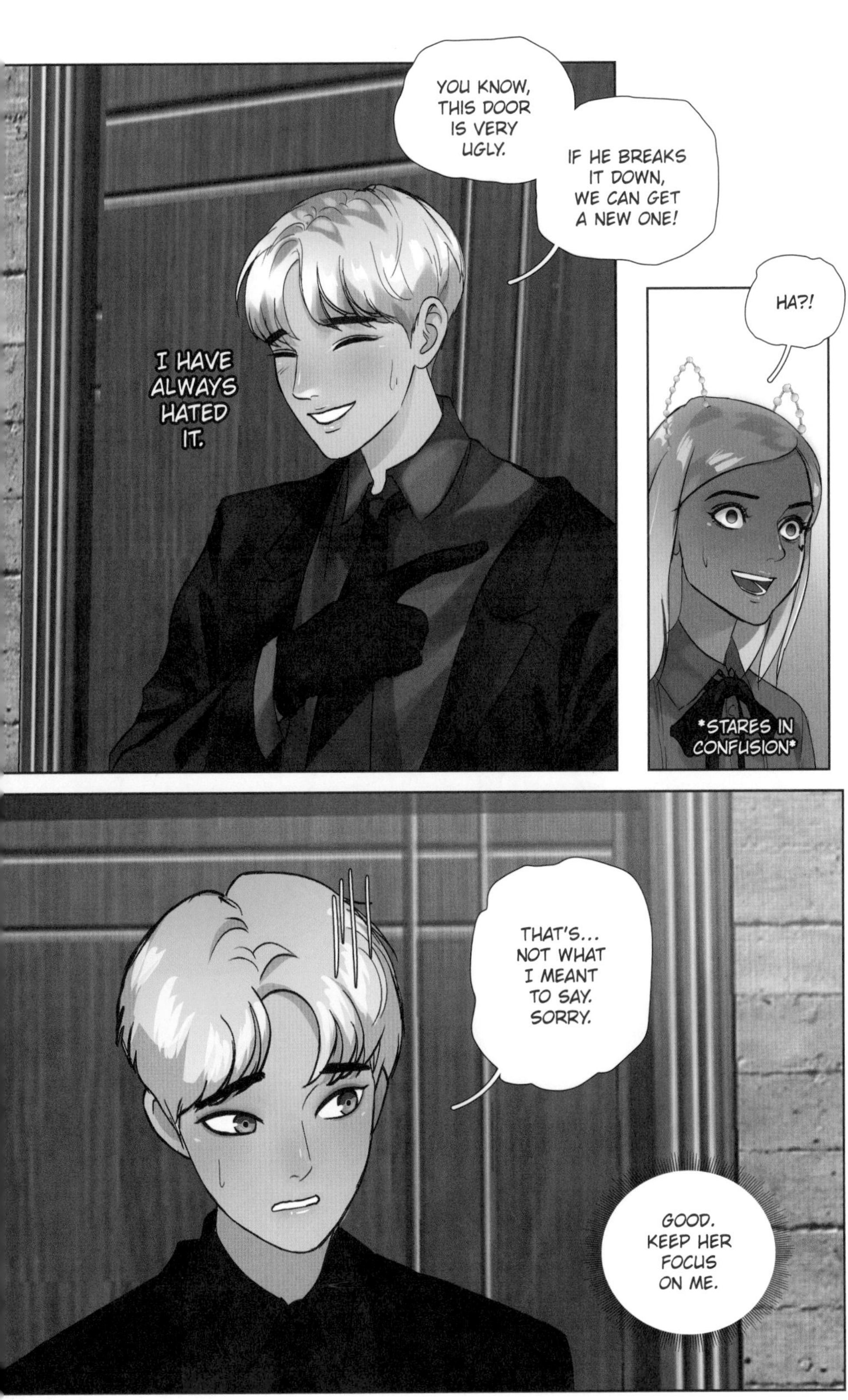
YOU KNOW, THIS DOOR IS VERY UGLY.
IF HE BREAKS IT DOWN, WE CAN GET A NEW ONE!
I HAVE ALWAYS HATED IT.
HA?!
STARES IN CONFUSION
THAT'S... NOT WHAT I MEANT TO SAY. SORRY.
GOOD. KEEP HER FOCUS ON ME.

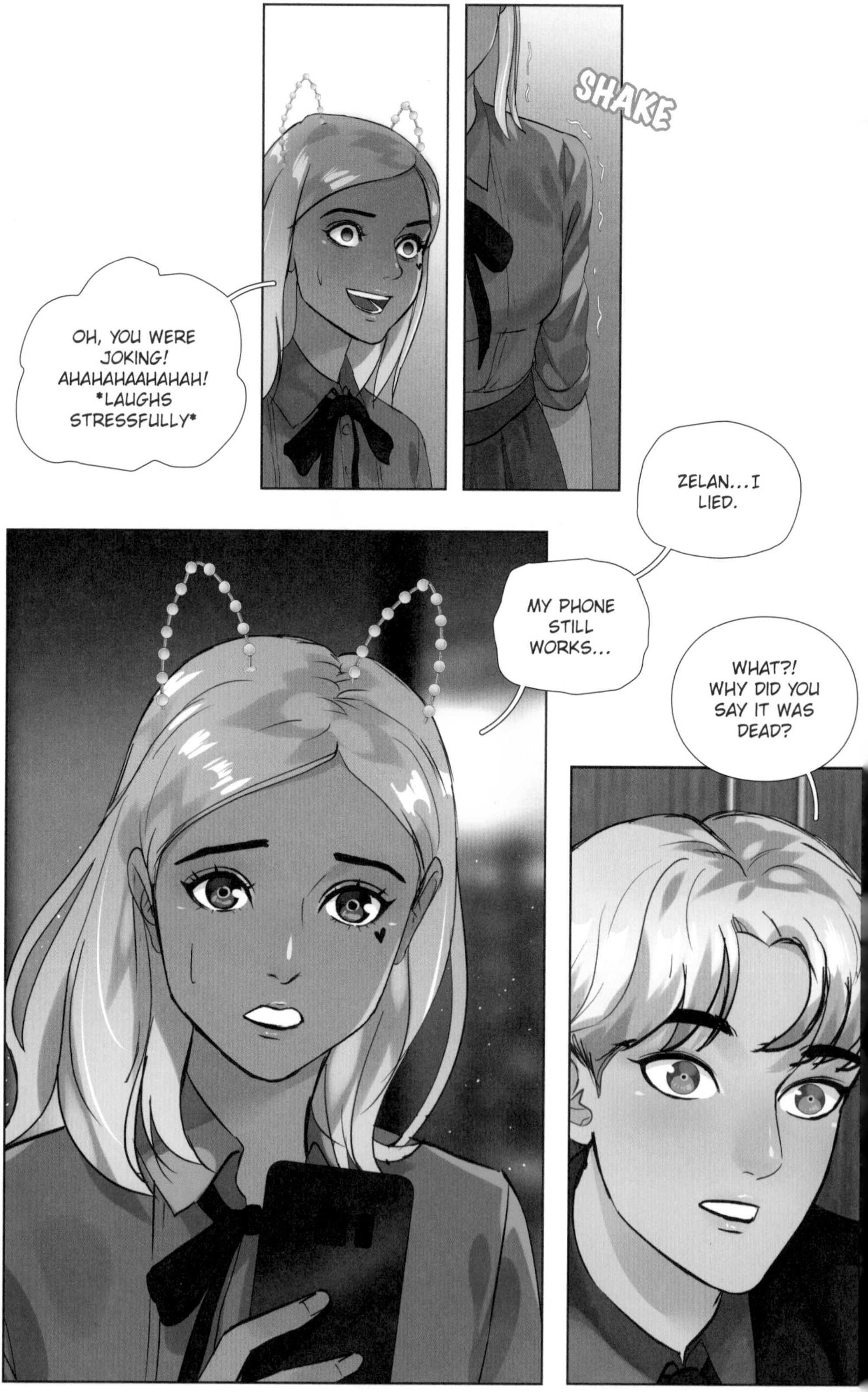
OH, YOU WERE JOKING! AHAHAHAAHAHAH! *LAUGHS STRESSFULLY*
SHAKE
ZELAN...I LIED.
MY PHONE STILL WORKS...
WHAT?! WHY DID YOU SAY IT WAS DEAD?

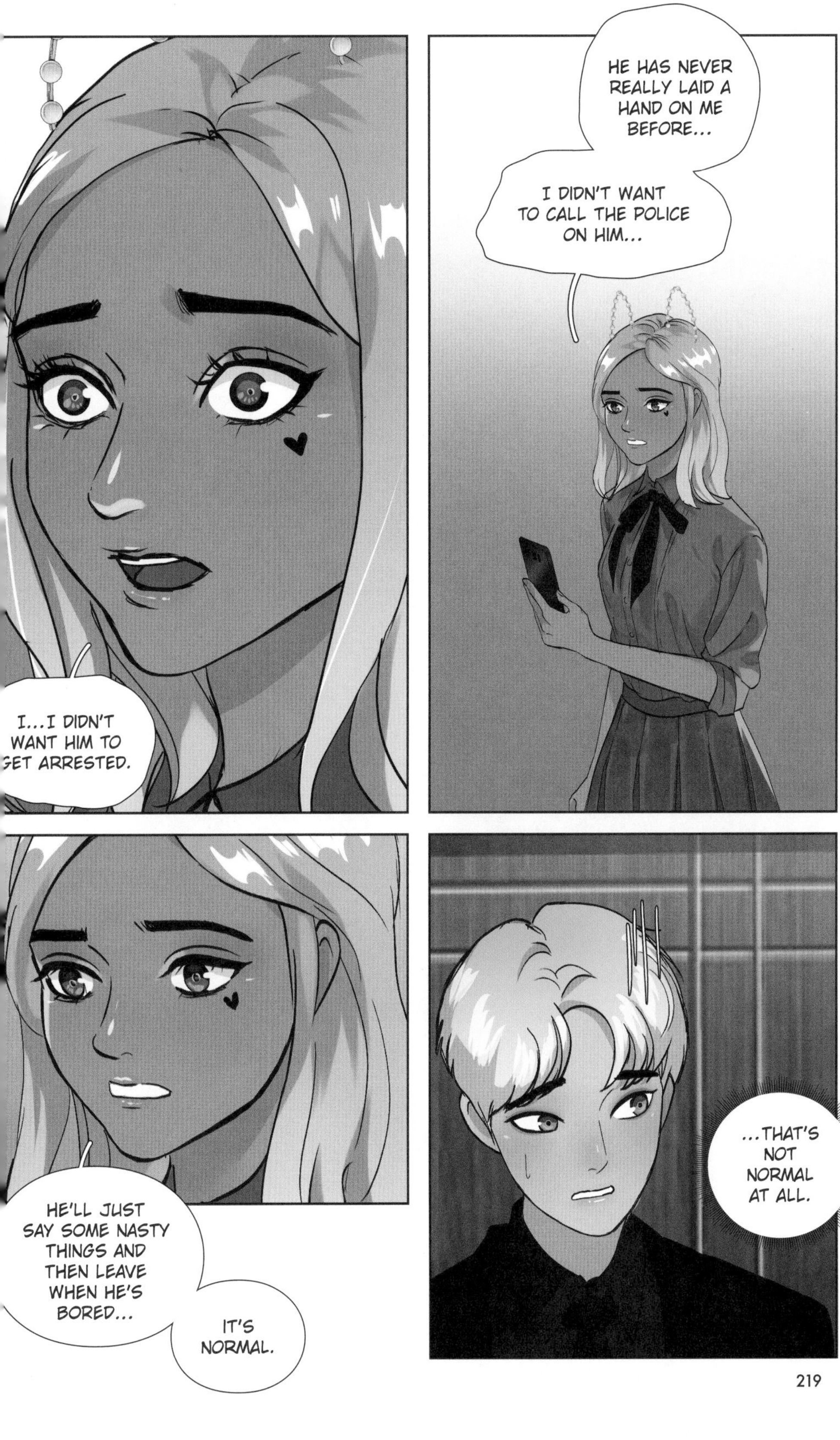
I...I DIDN'T WANT HIM TO GET ARRESTED.
HE HAS NEVER REALLY LAID A HAND ON ME BEFORE...
I DIDN'T WANT TO CALL THE POLICE ON HIM...
HE'LL JUST SAY SOME NASTY THINGS AND THEN LEAVE WHEN HE'S BORED...
IT'S NORMAL.
...THAT'S NOT NORMAL AT ALL.

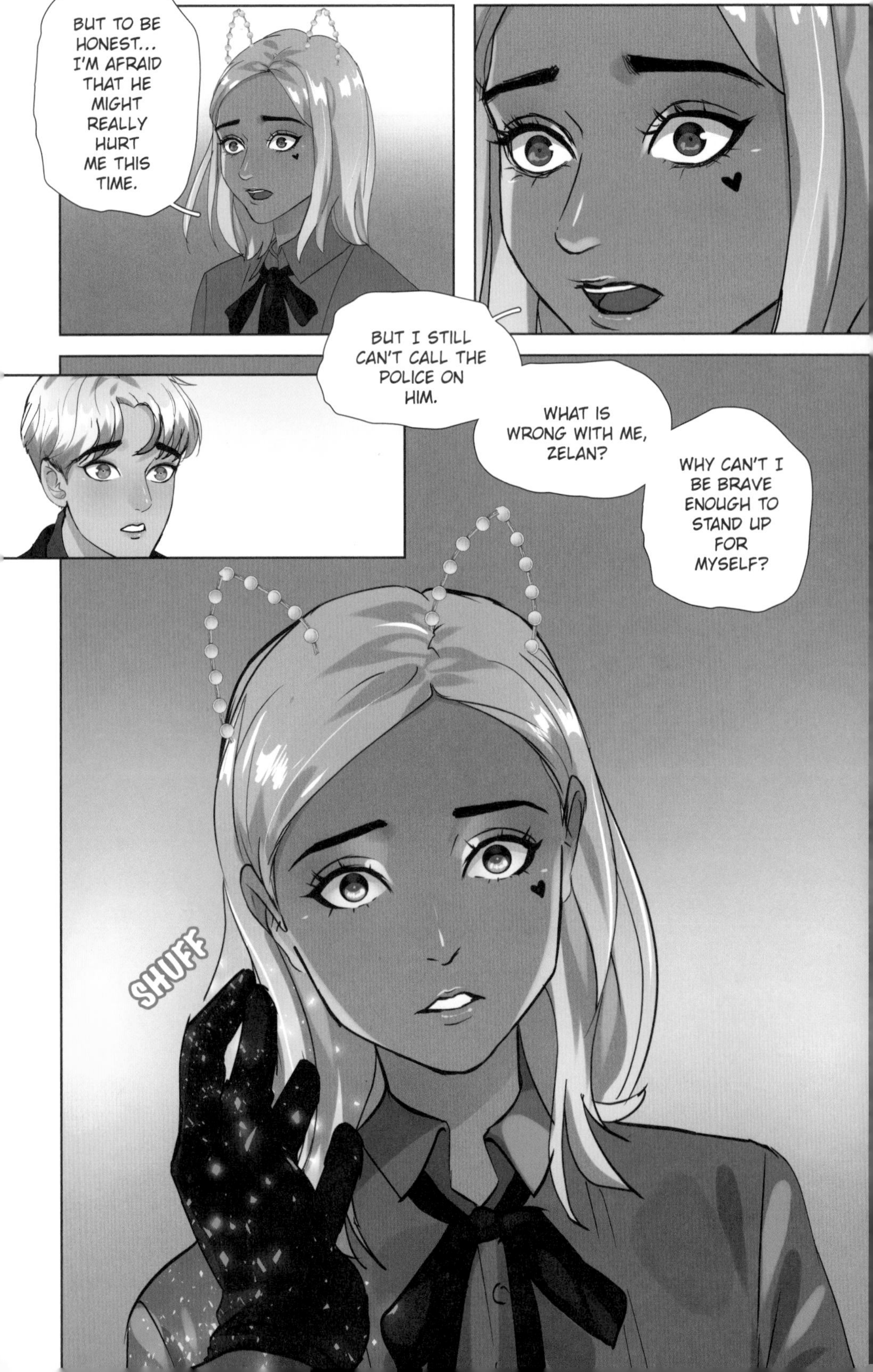
BUT TO BE HONEST... I'M AFRAID THAT HE MIGHT REALLY HURT ME THIS TIME.
BUT I STILL CAN'T CALL THE POLICE ON HIM.
WHAT IS WRONG WITH ME, ZELAN?
WHY CAN'T I BE BRAVE ENOUGH TO STAND UP FOR MYSELF?
SHUFF

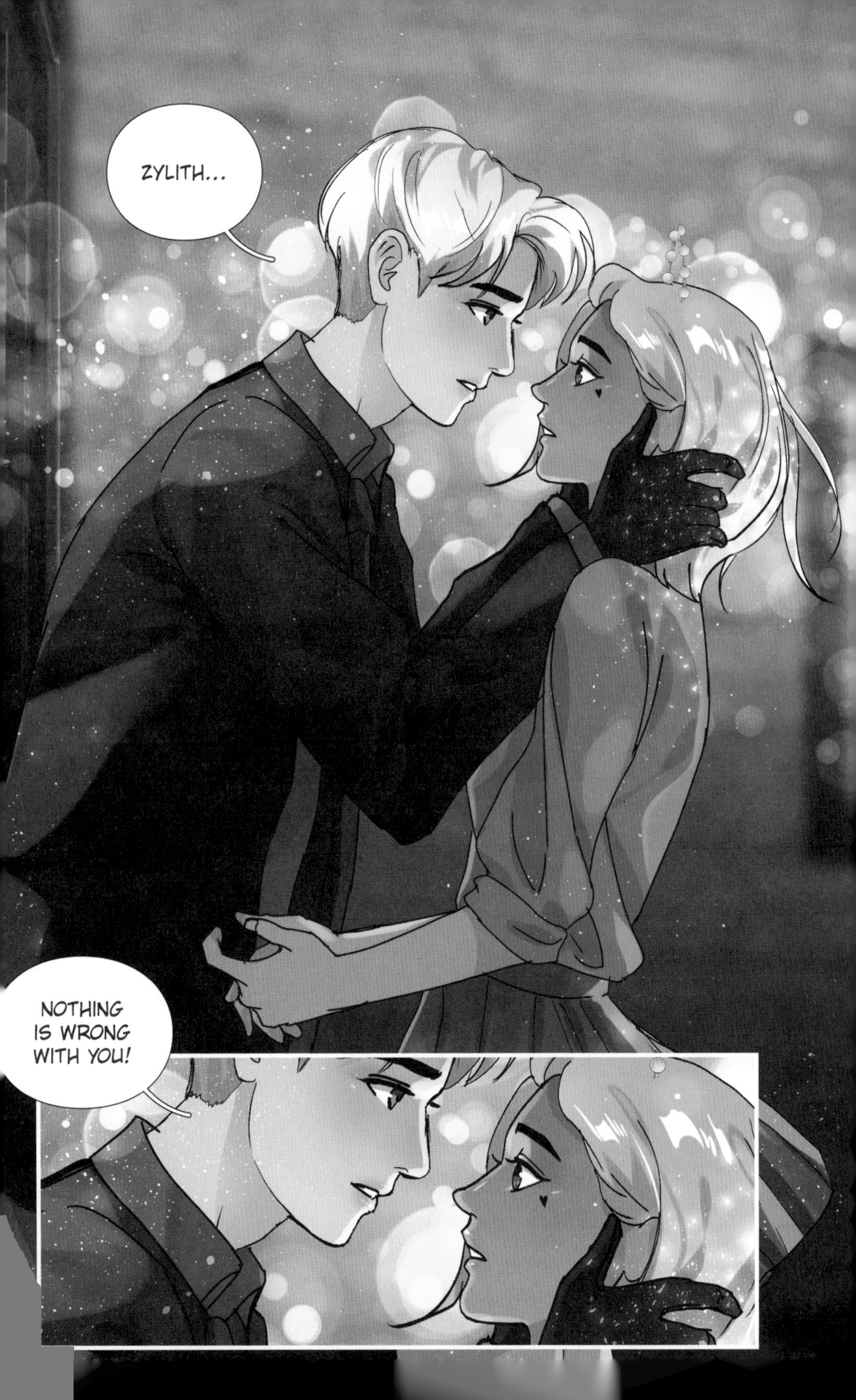
ZYLITH...
NOTHING IS WRONG WITH YOU!

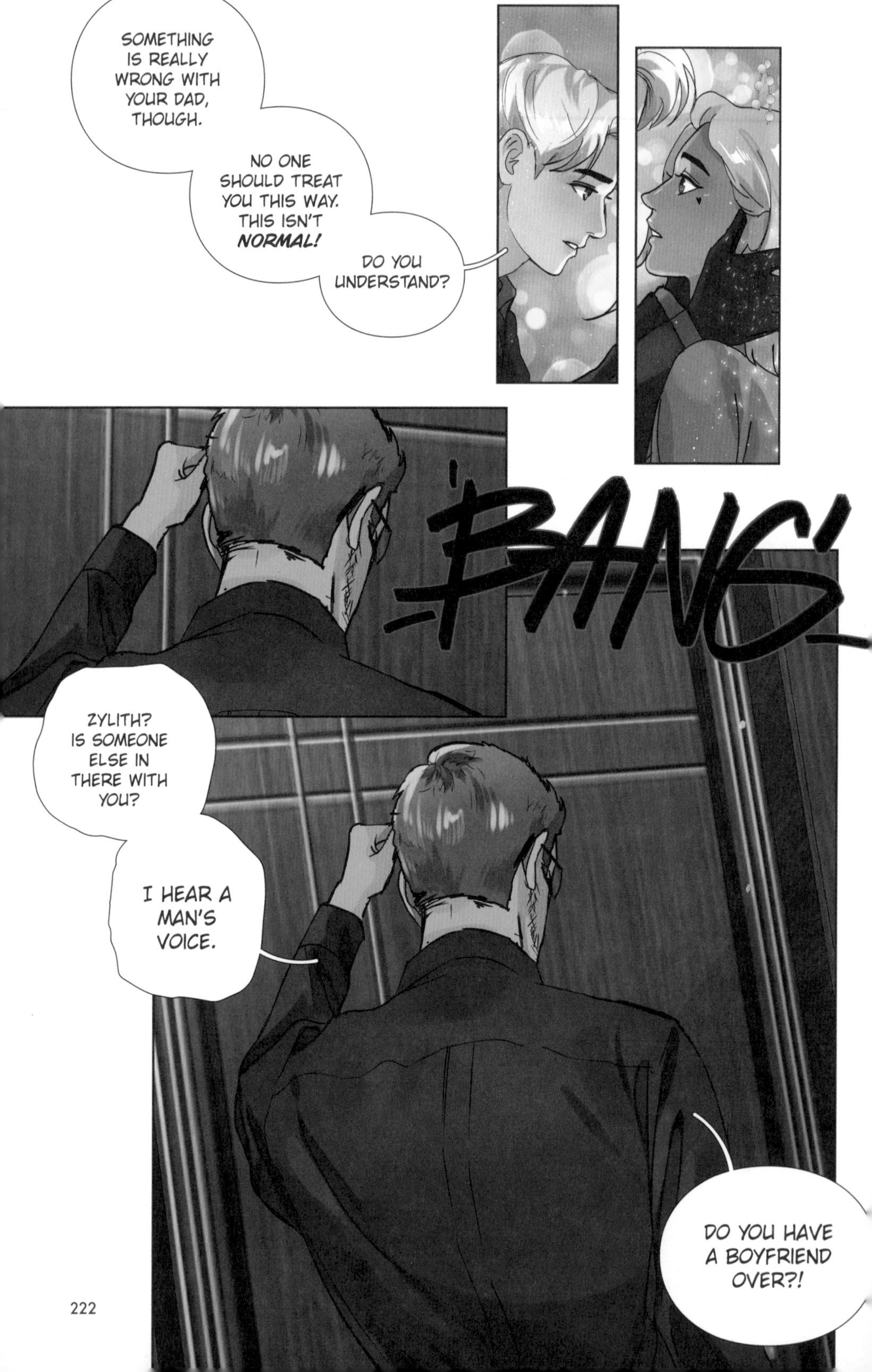
SOMETHING IS REALLY WRONG WITH YOUR DAD, THOUGH.
NO ONE SHOULD TREAT YOU THIS WAY. THIS ISN'T *NORMAL!*
DO YOU UNDERSTAND?
BANG
ZYLITH? IS SOMEONE ELSE IN THERE WITH YOU?
I HEAR A MAN'S VOICE.
DO YOU HAVE A BOYFRIEND OVER?!

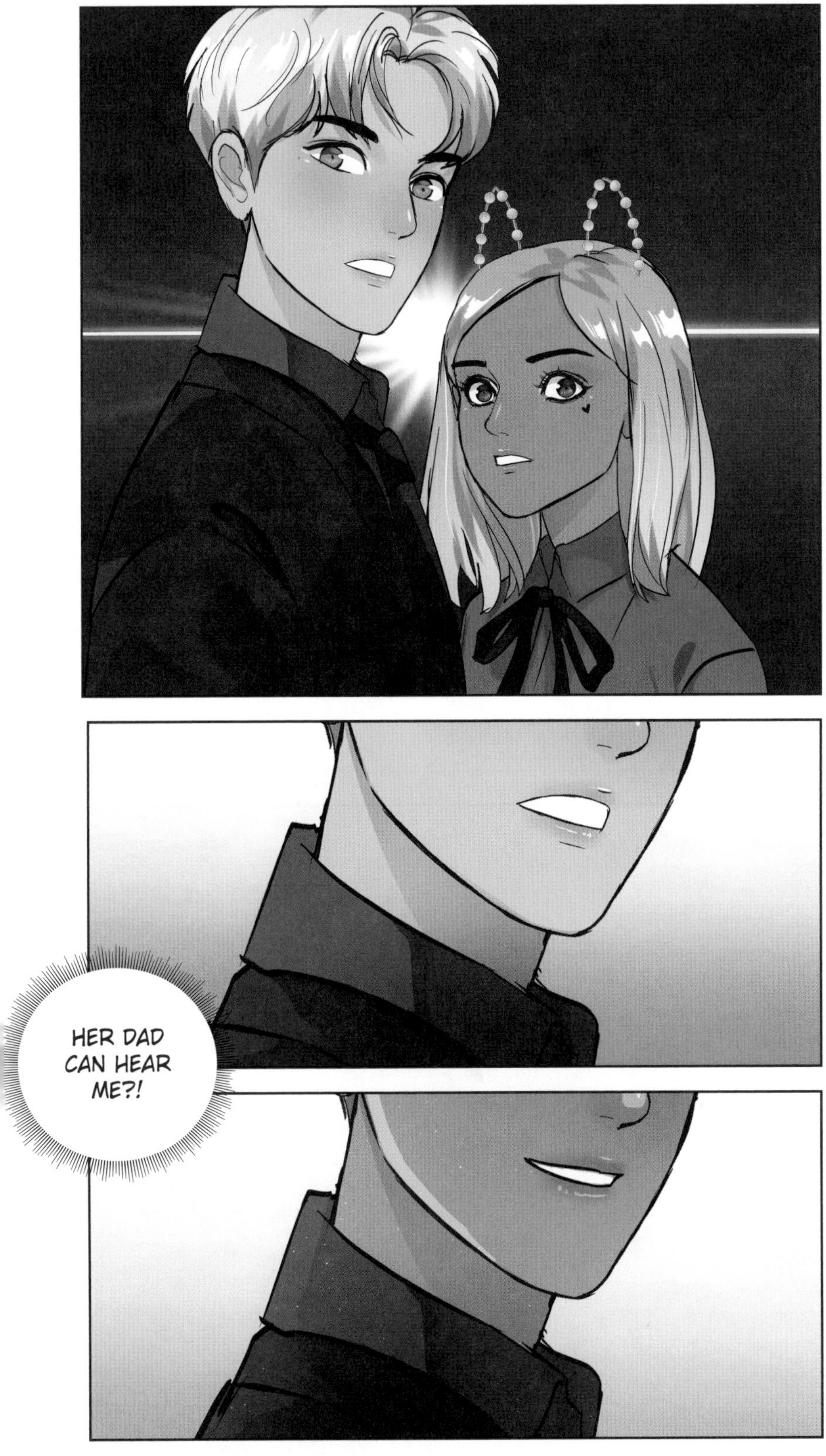
HER DAD CAN HEAR ME?!

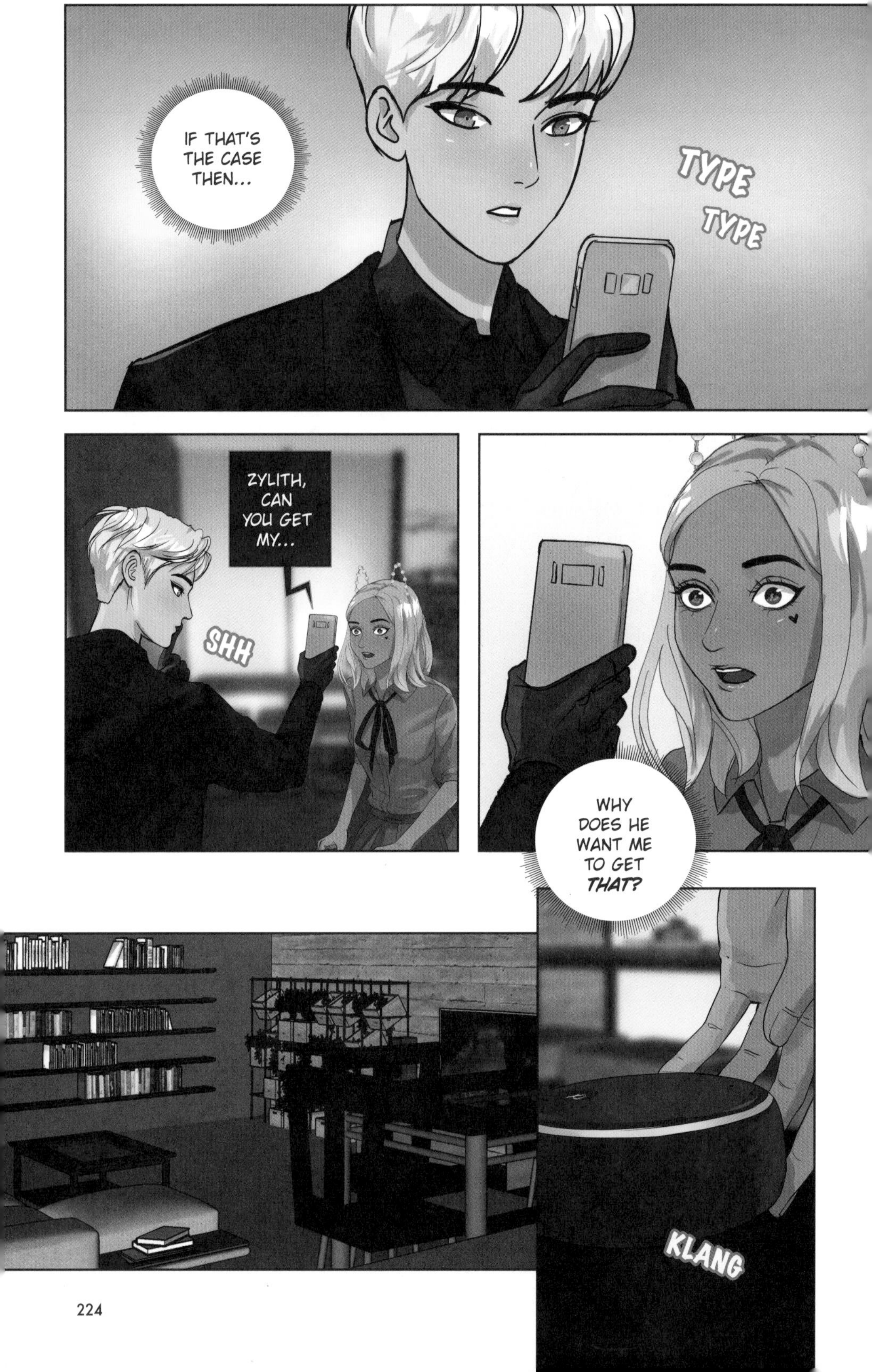
IF THAT'S THE CASE THEN...
TYPE
TYPE
ZYLITH, CAN YOU GET MY...
SHH
WHY DOES HE WANT ME TO GET *THAT?*
KLANG

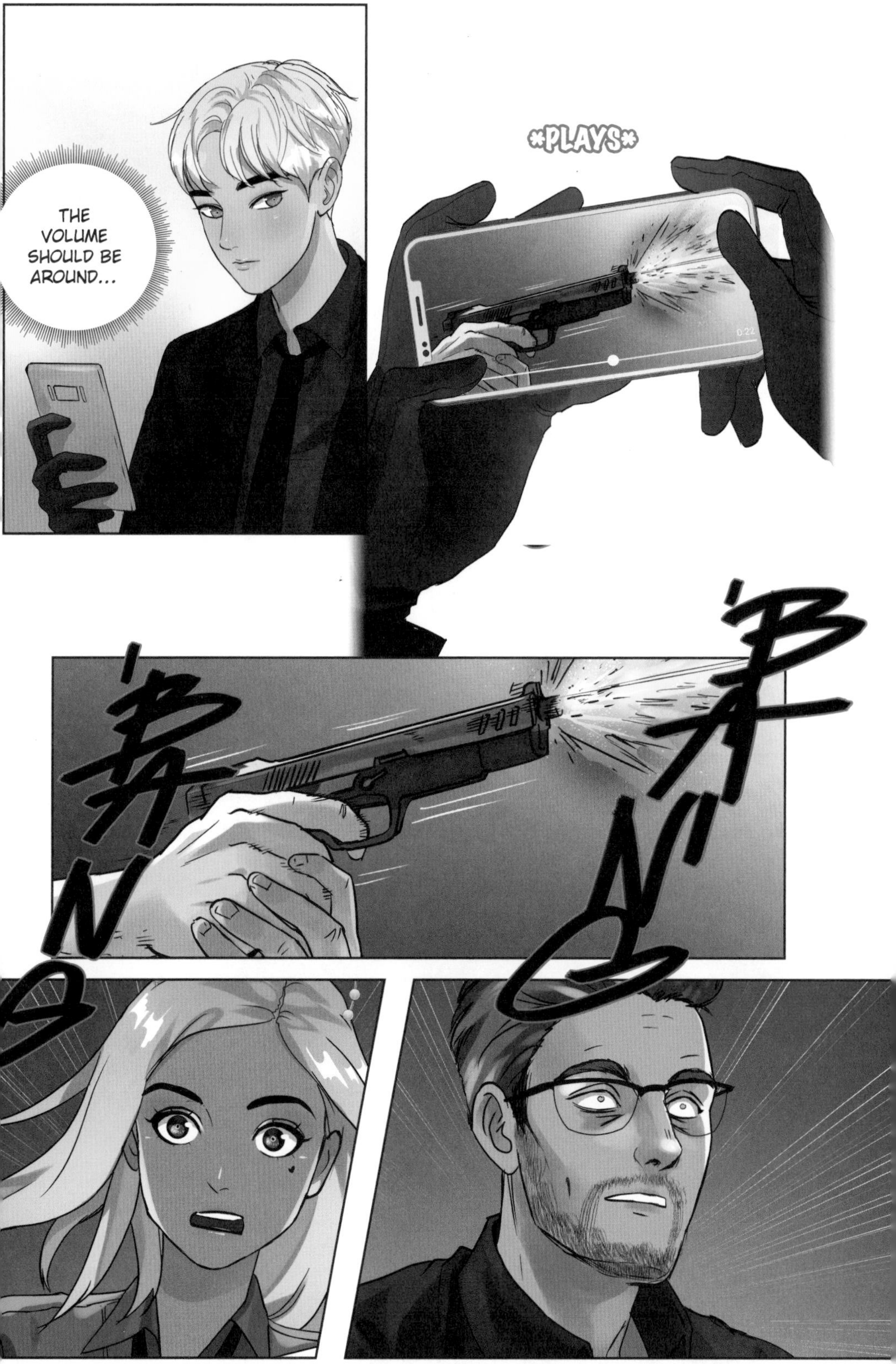
THE VOLUME SHOULD BE AROUND...
PLAYS
'BANG
'BANG

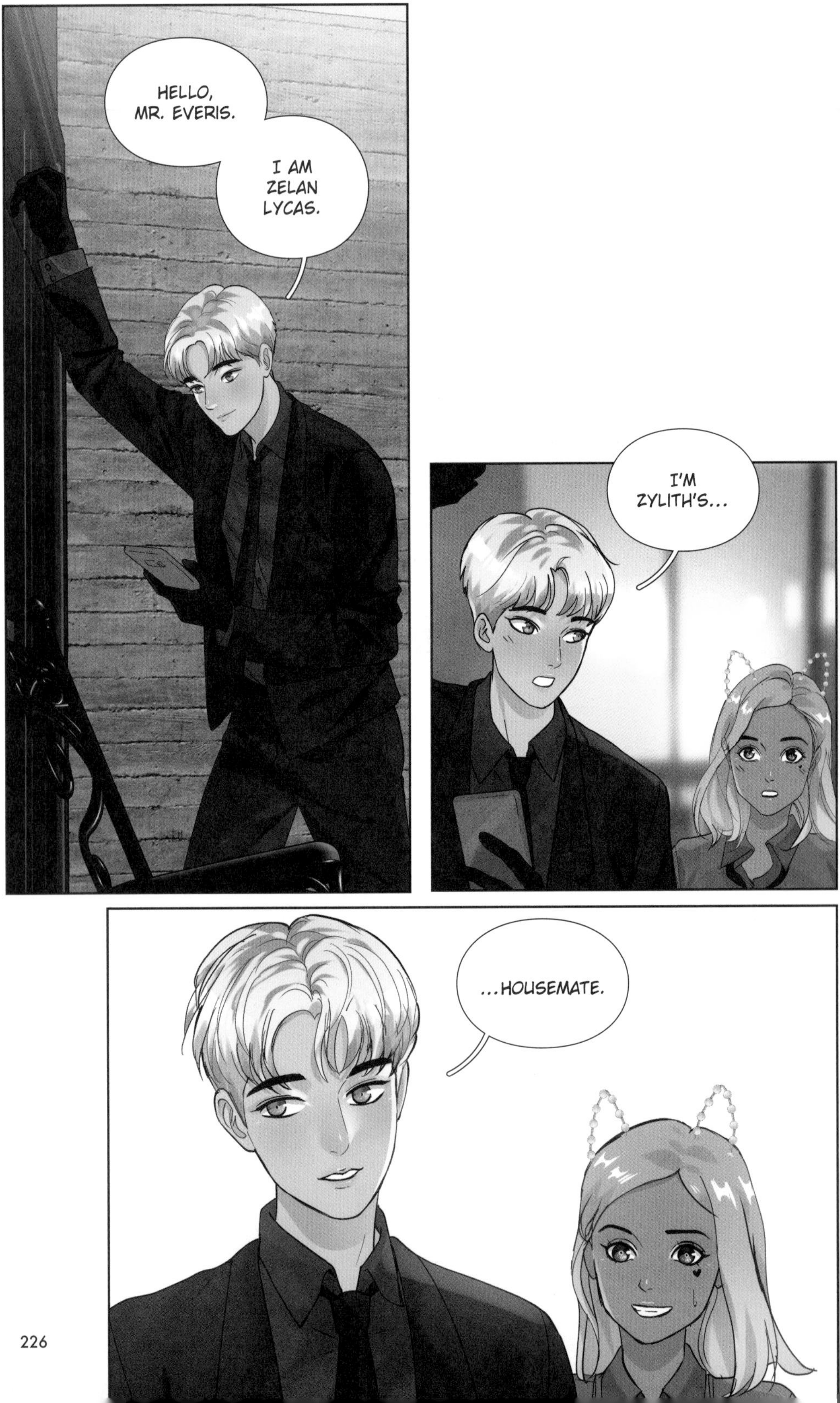
HELLO, MR. EVERIS.
I AM ZELAN LYCAS.
I'M ZYLITH'S...
...HOUSEMATE.

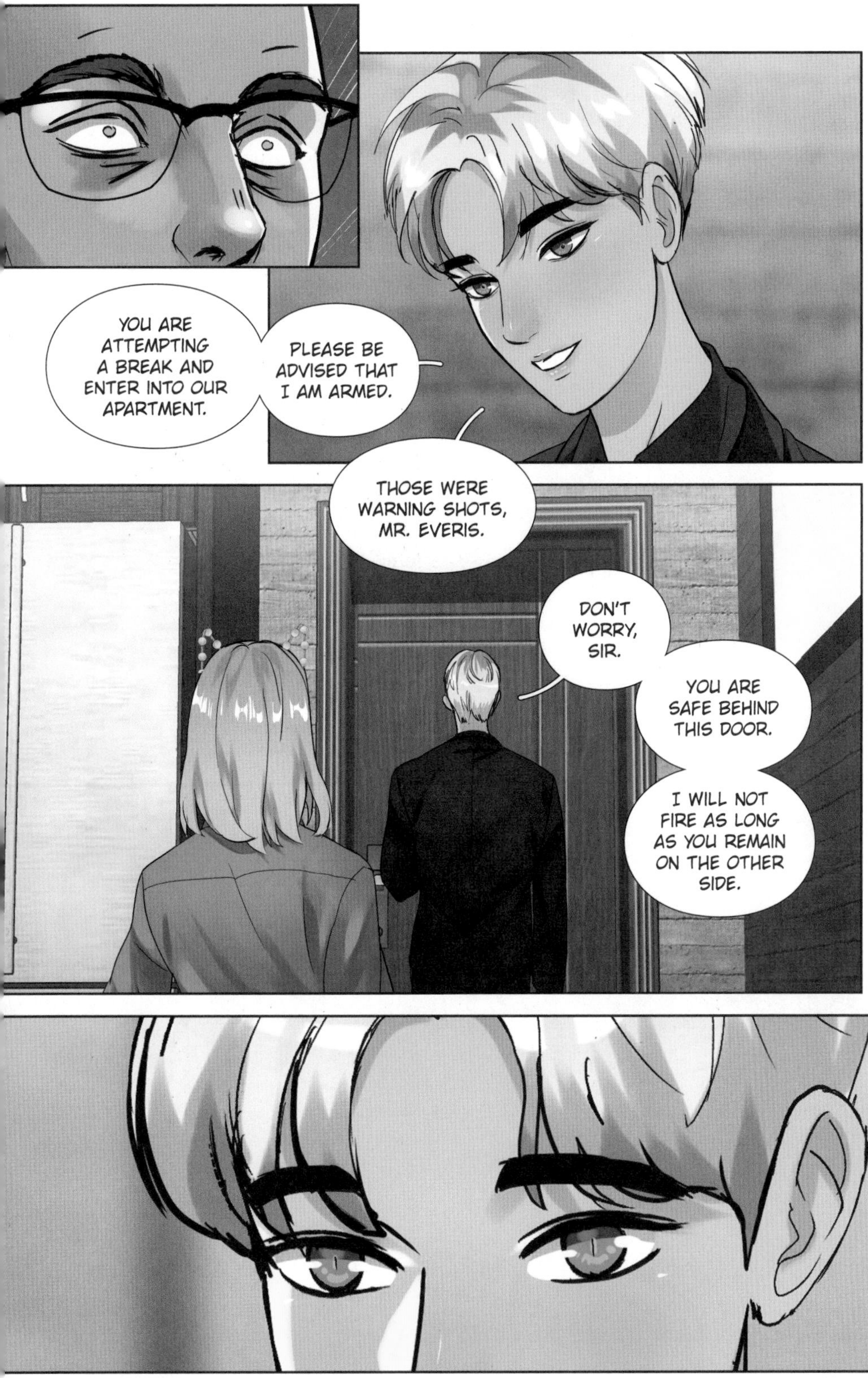
YOU ARE ATTEMPTING A BREAK AND ENTER INTO OUR APARTMENT.
PLEASE BE ADVISED THAT I AM ARMED.
THOSE WERE WARNING SHOTS, MR. EVERIS.
DON'T WORRY, SIR.
YOU ARE SAFE BEHIND THIS DOOR.
I WILL NOT FIRE AS LONG AS YOU REMAIN ON THE OTHER SIDE.

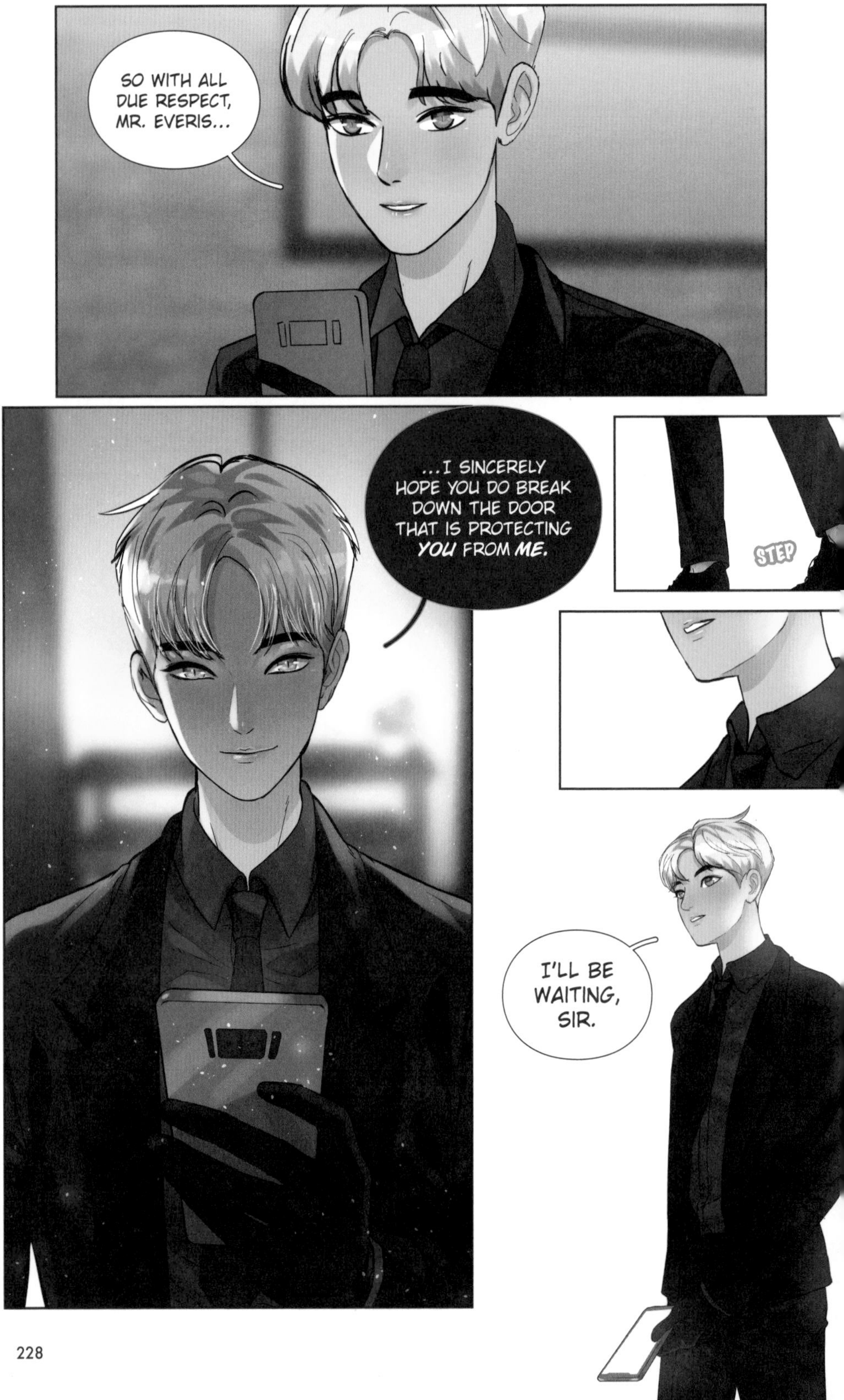
SO WITH ALL DUE RESPECT, MR. EVERIS...
...I SINCERELY HOPE YOU DO BREAK DOWN THE DOOR THAT IS PROTECTING *YOU* FROM *ME.*
STEP
I'LL BE WAITING, SIR.

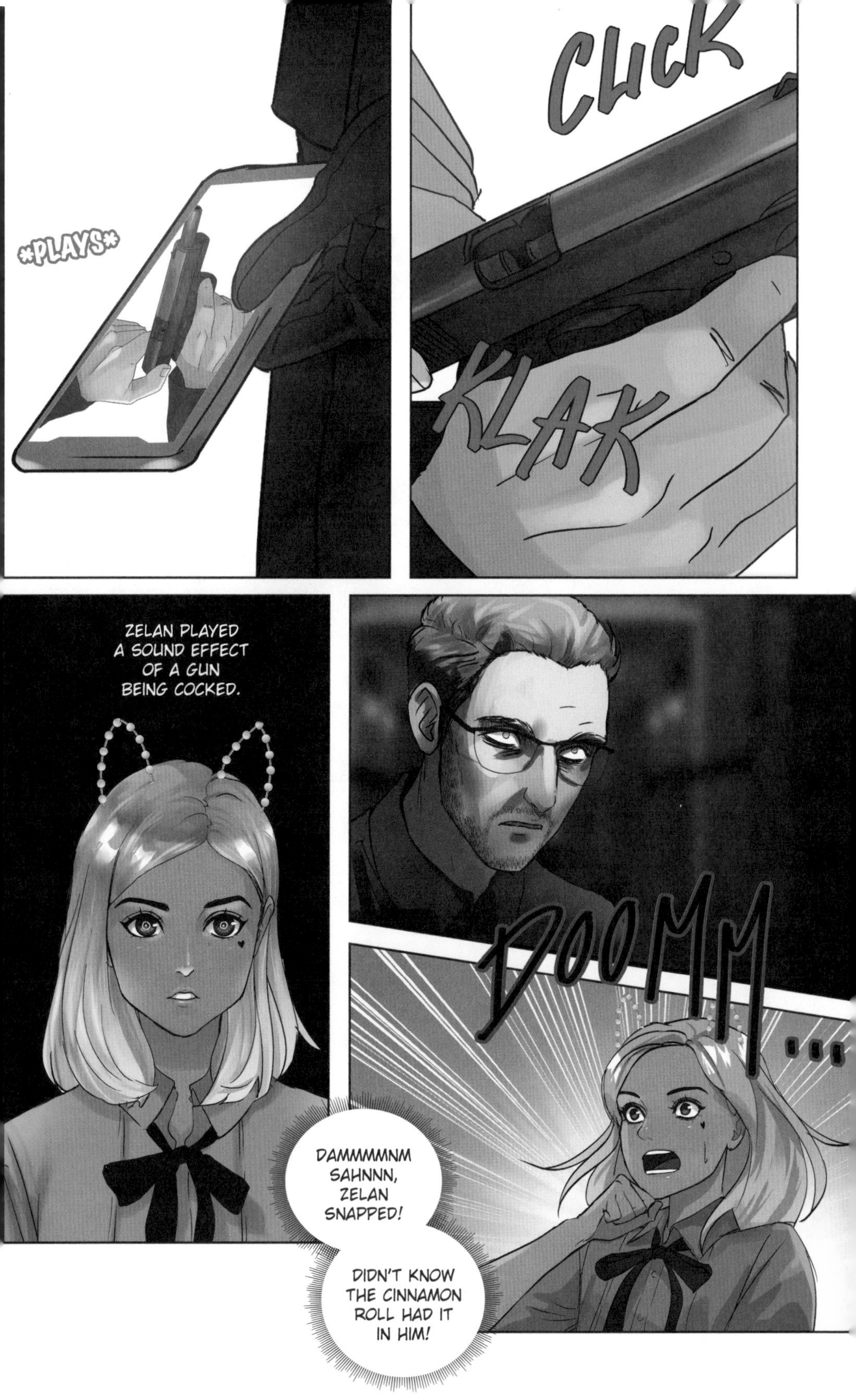
PLAYS
CLICK
KLAK
ZELAN PLAYED A SOUND EFFECT OF A GUN BEING COCKED.
DOOMM
...
DAMMMMNM SAHNNN, ZELAN SNAPPED!
DIDN'T KNOW THE CINNAMON ROLL HAD IT IN HIM!

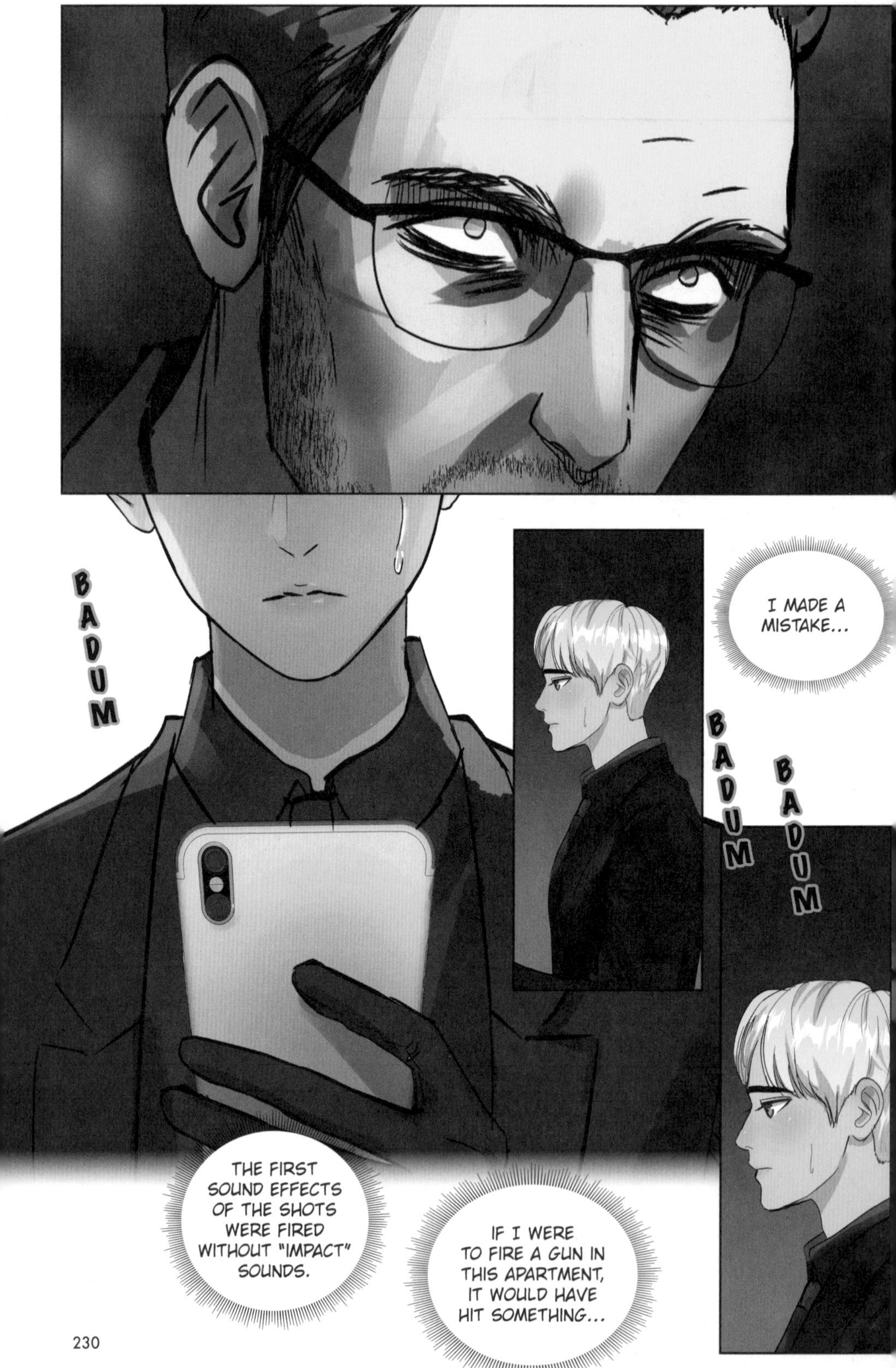
BADUM
I MADE A MISTAKE...
BADUM
BADUM
THE FIRST SOUND EFFECTS OF THE SHOTS WERE FIRED WITHOUT "IMPACT" SOUNDS.
IF I WERE TO FIRE A GUN IN THIS APARTMENT, IT WOULD HAVE HIT SOMETHING...

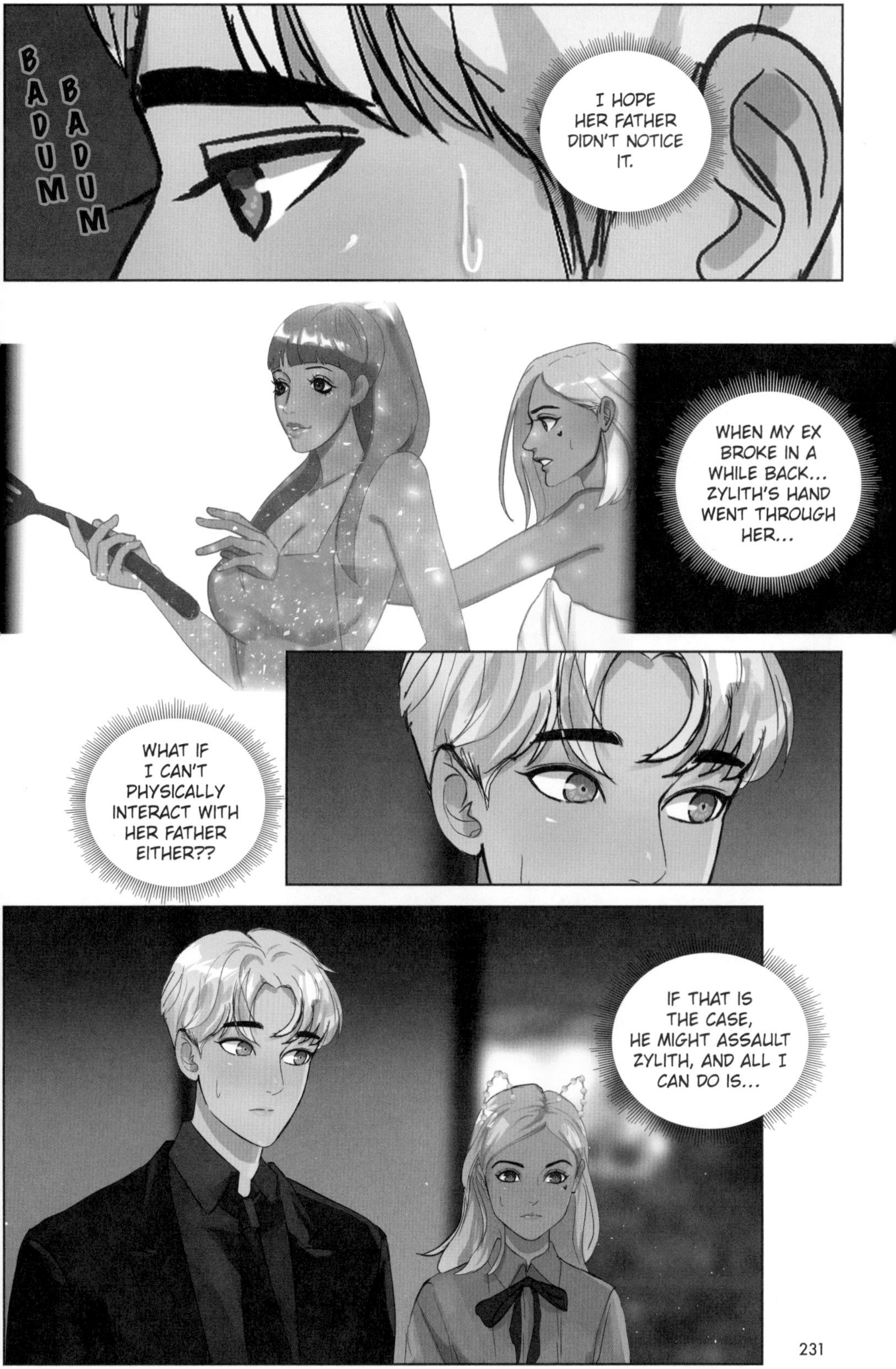
BADUM BADUM
I HOPE HER FATHER DIDN'T NOTICE IT.
WHEN MY EX BROKE IN A WHILE BACK... ZYLITH'S HAND WENT THROUGH HER...
WHAT IF I CAN'T PHYSICALLY INTERACT WITH HER FATHER EITHER??
IF THAT IS THE CASE, HE MIGHT ASSAULT ZYLITH, AND ALL I CAN DO IS...

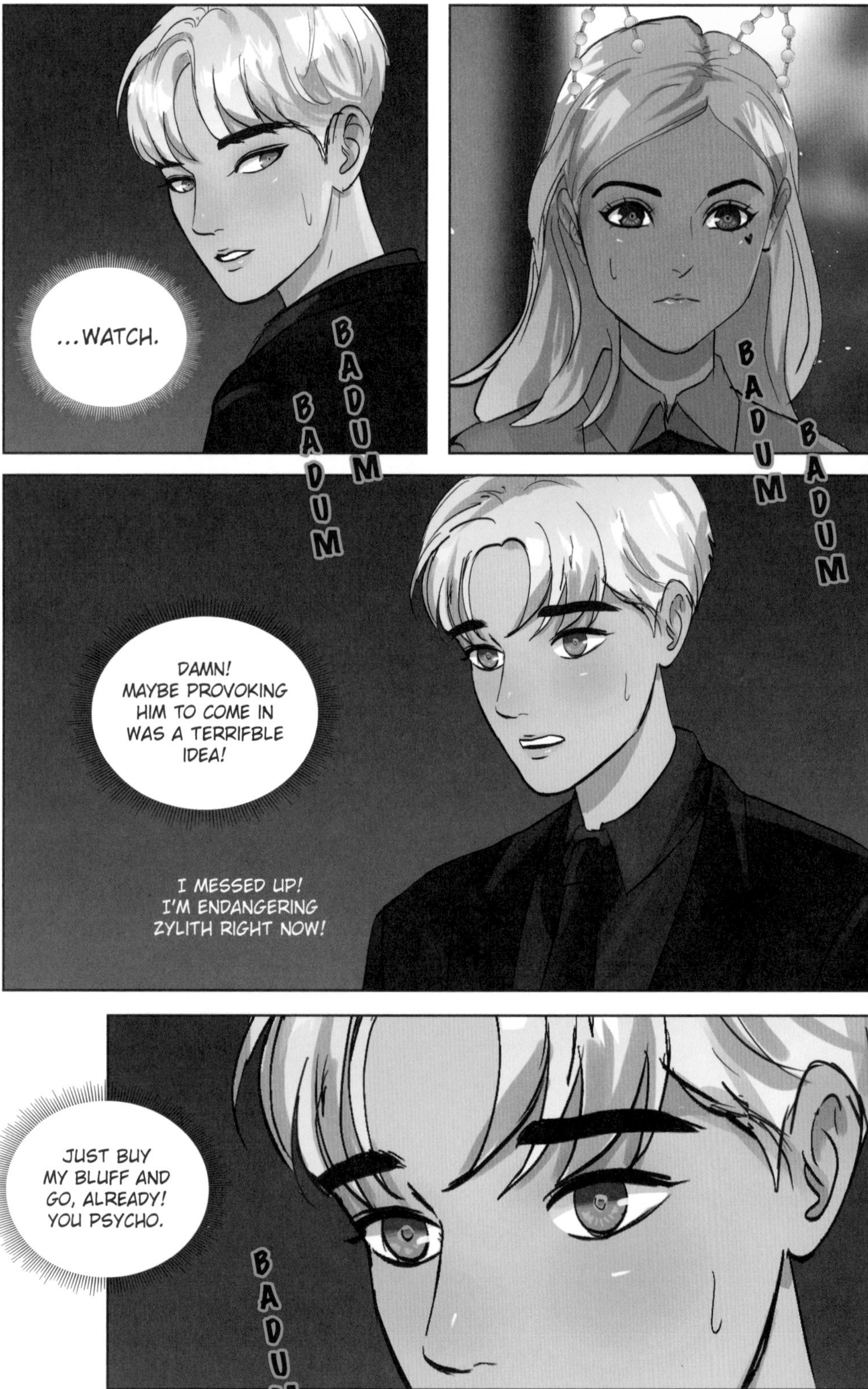
...WATCH.
BADUM
BADUM
BADUM
BADUM
DAMN! MAYBE PROVOKING HIM TO COME IN WAS A TERRIFBLE IDEA!
I MESSED UP! I'M ENDANGERING ZYLITH RIGHT NOW!
JUST BUY MY BLUFF AND GO, ALREADY! YOU PSYCHO.
BADUM

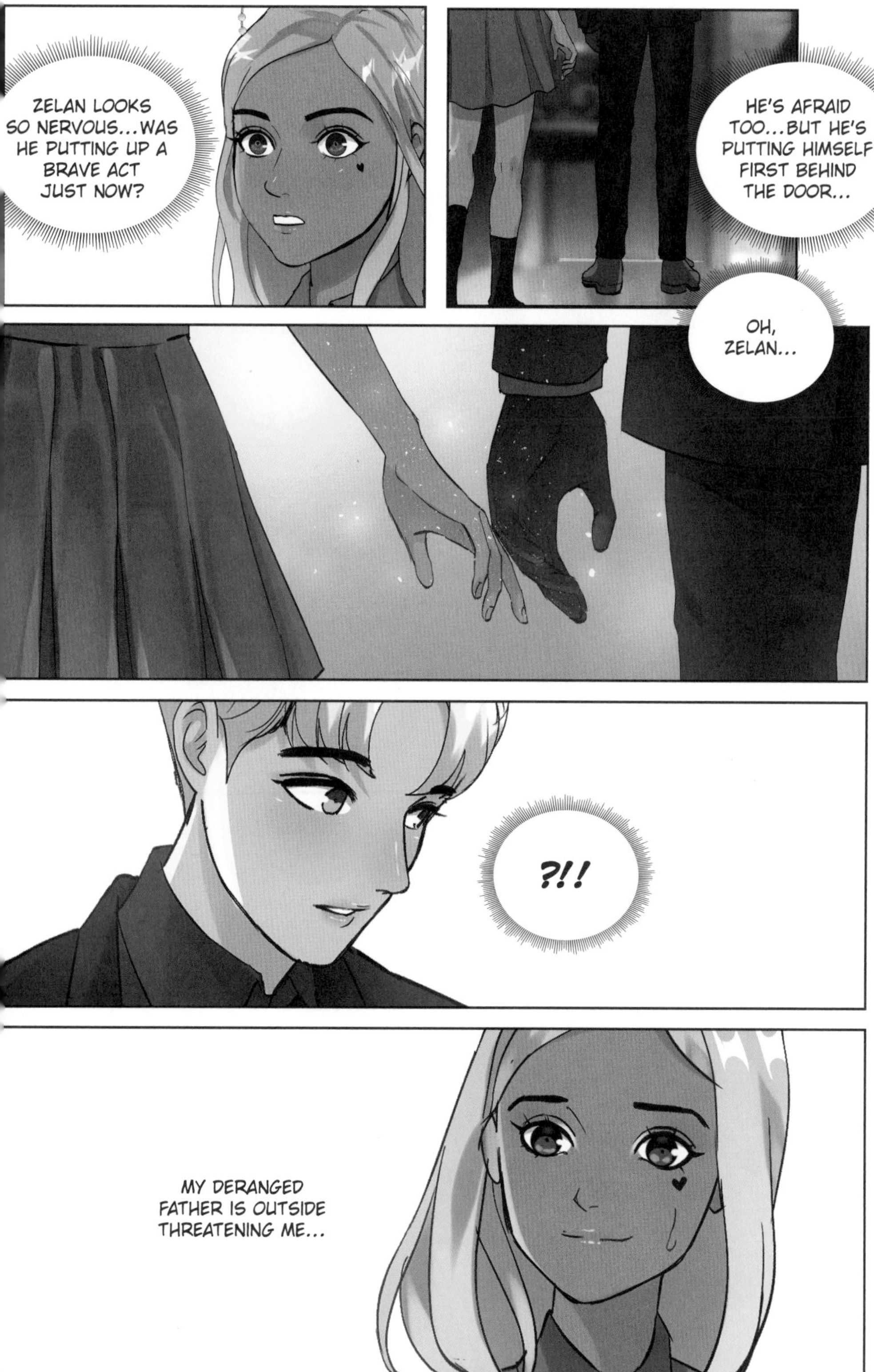
ZELAN LOOKS SO NERVOUS...WAS HE PUTTING UP A BRAVE ACT JUST NOW?
HE'S AFRAID TOO...BUT HE'S PUTTING HIMSELF FIRST BEHIND THE DOOR...
OH, ZELAN...
?!!
MY DERANGED FATHER IS OUTSIDE THREATENING ME...

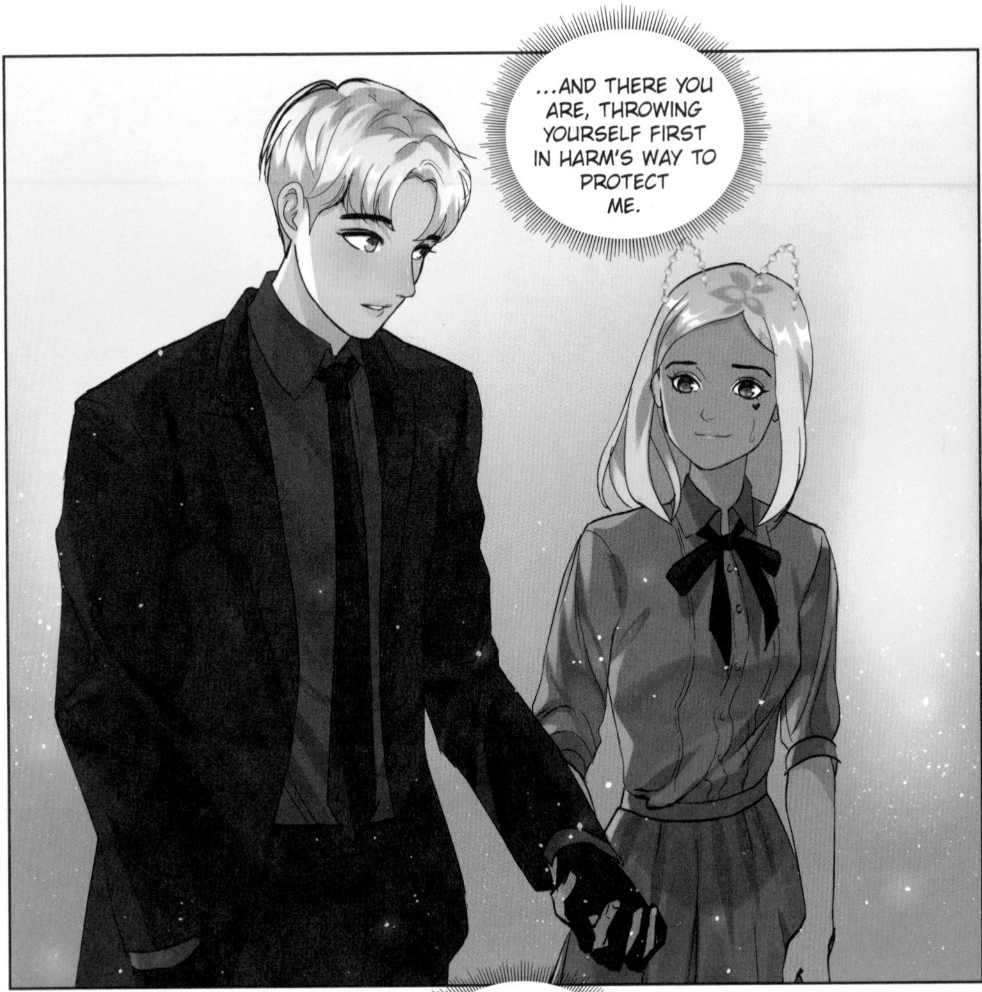
...AND THERE YOU ARE, THROWING YOURSELF FIRST IN HARM'S WAY TO PROTECT ME.

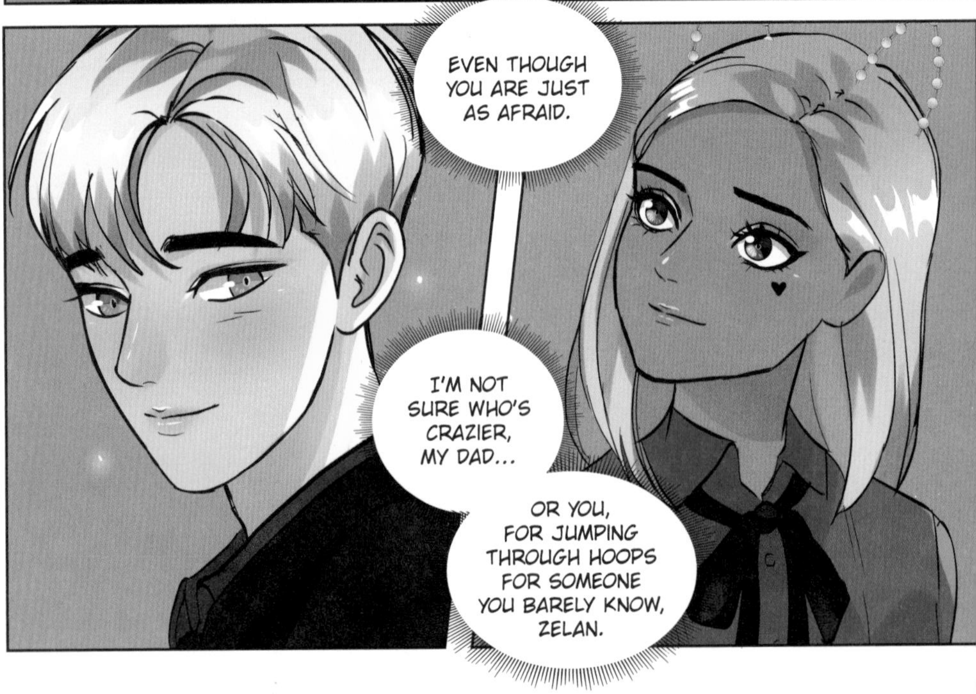
EVEN THOUGH YOU ARE JUST AS AFRAID.
I'M NOT SURE WHO'S CRAZIER, MY DAD...
OR YOU, FOR JUMPING THROUGH HOOPS FOR SOMEONE YOU BARELY KNOW, ZELAN.

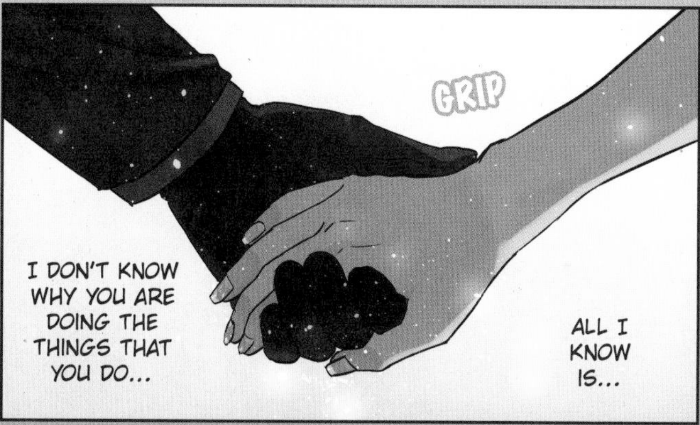
GRIP
I DON'T KNOW WHY YOU ARE DOING THE THINGS THAT YOU DO...
ALL I KNOW IS...

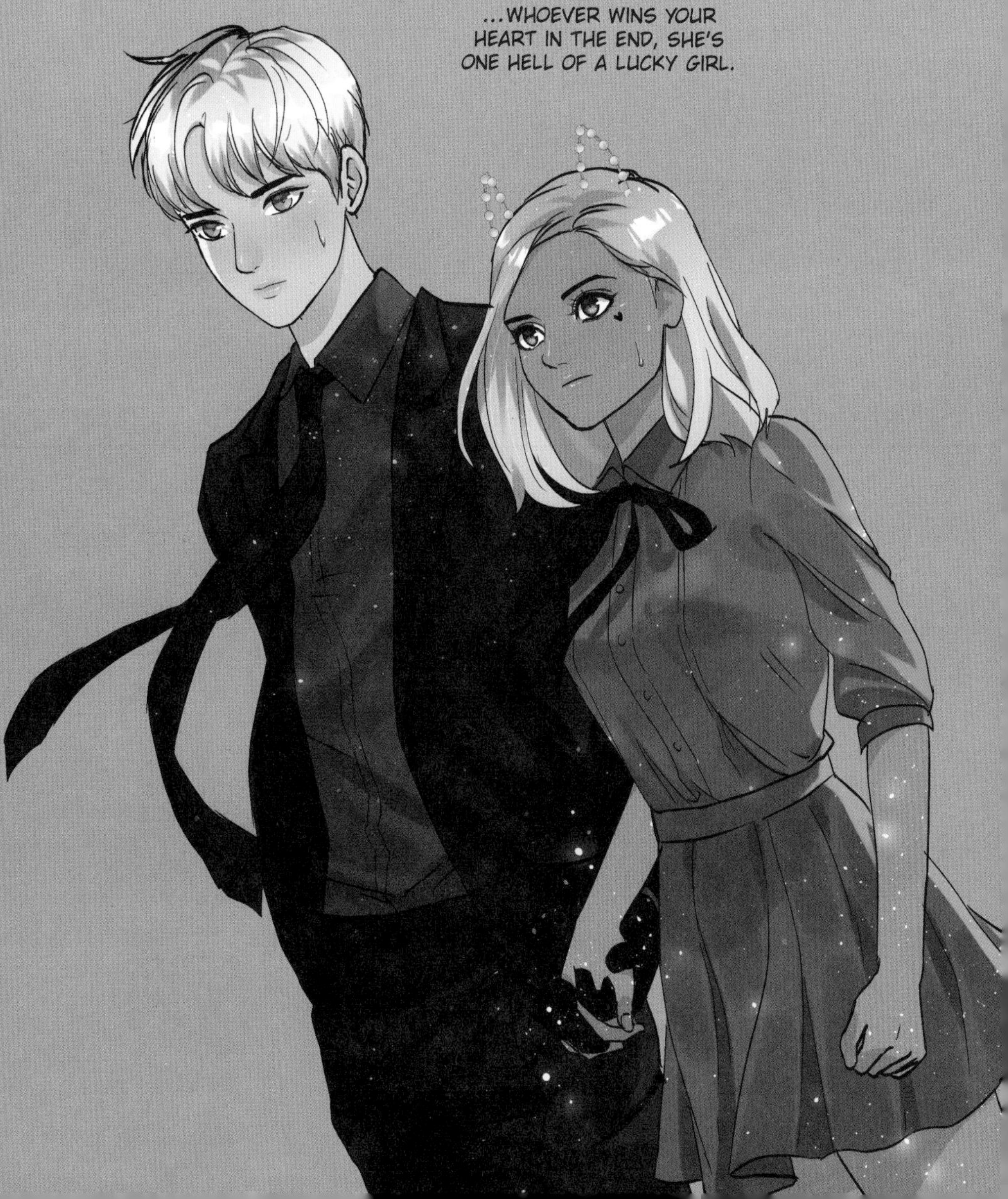
...WHOEVER WINS YOUR HEART IN THE END, SHE'S ONE HELL OF A LUCKY GIRL.

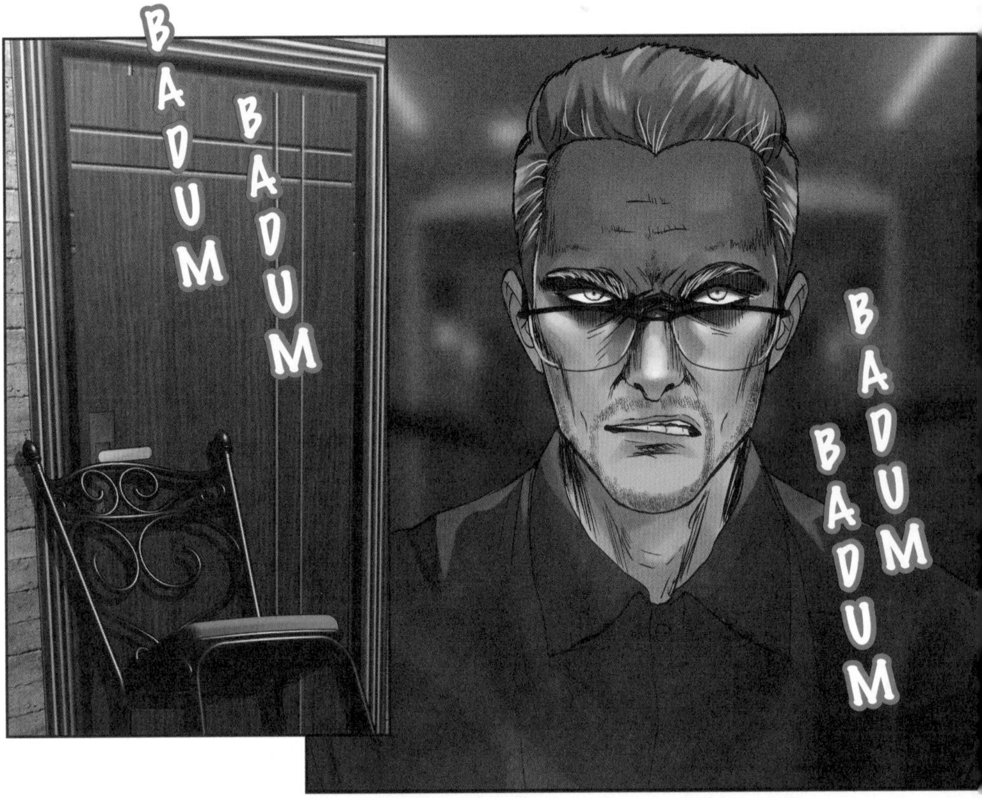
BADUM
BADUM
BADUM
BADUM

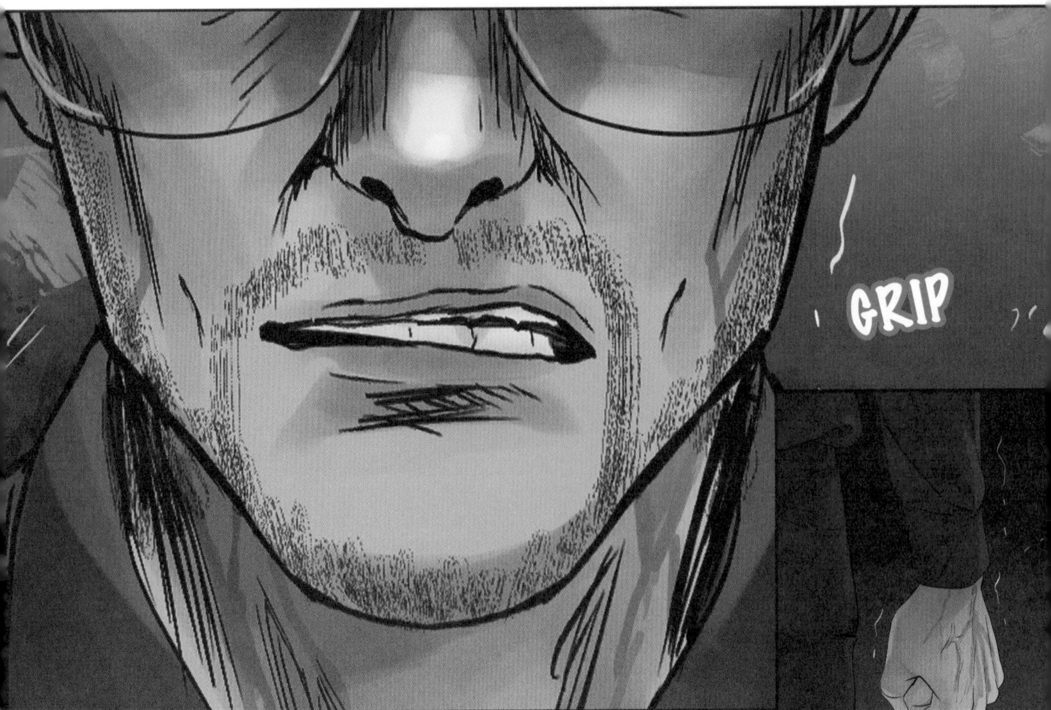
GRIP

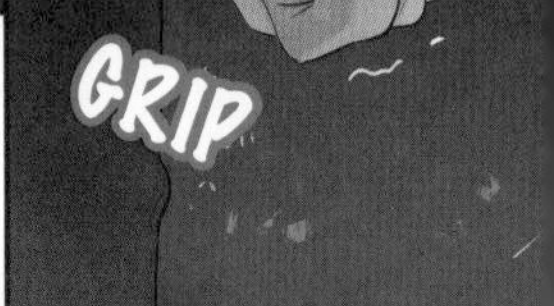
GRIP

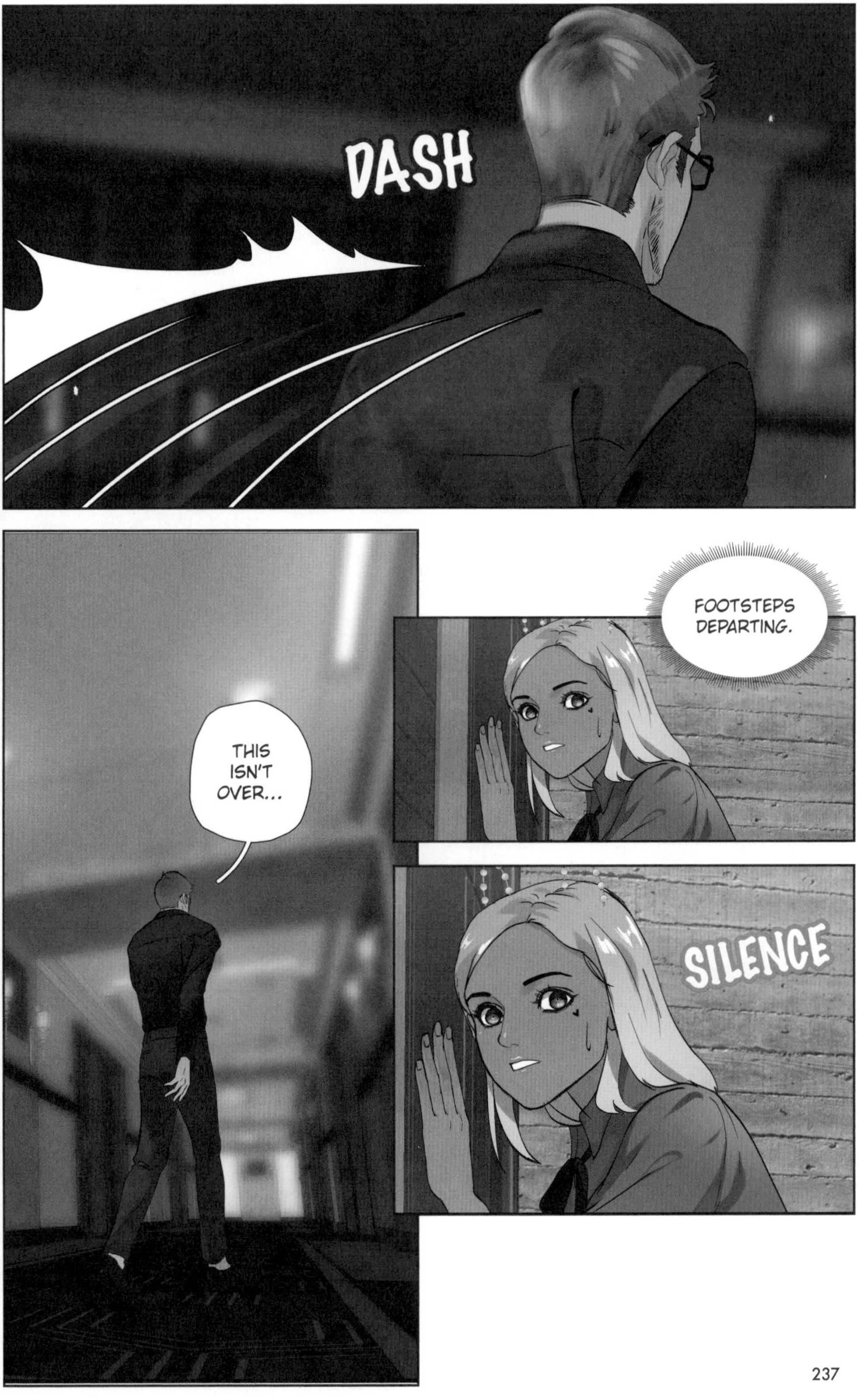
DASH
THIS ISN'T OVER...
FOOTSTEPS DEPARTING.
SILENCE

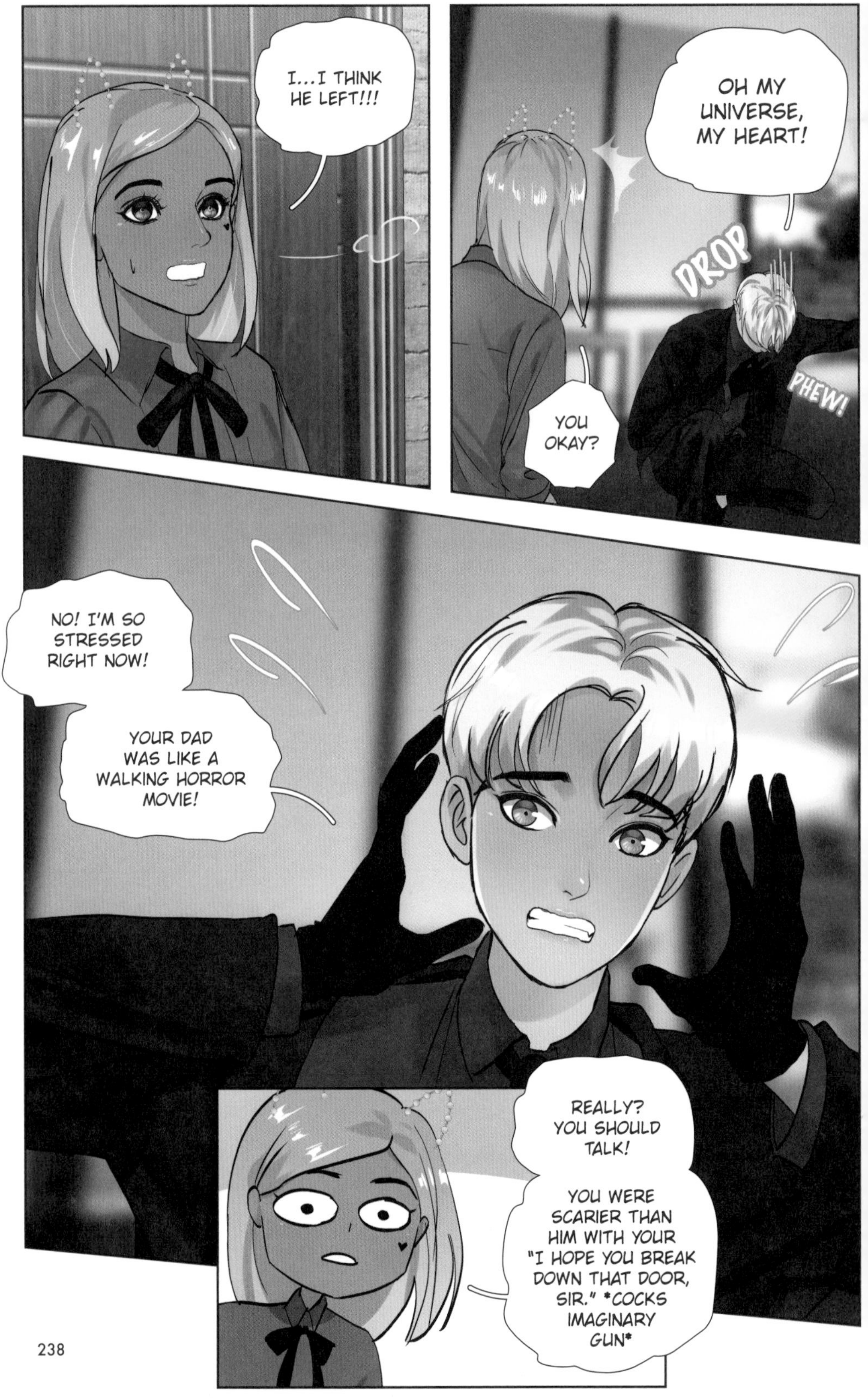
I...I THINK HE LEFT!!!
OH MY UNIVERSE, MY HEART!
DROP
PHEW!
YOU OKAY?
NO! I'M SO STRESSED RIGHT NOW!
YOUR DAD WAS LIKE A WALKING HORROR MOVIE!
REALLY? YOU SHOULD TALK!
YOU WERE SCARIER THAN HIM WITH YOUR "I HOPE YOU BREAK DOWN THAT DOOR, SIR." *COCKS IMAGINARY GUN*

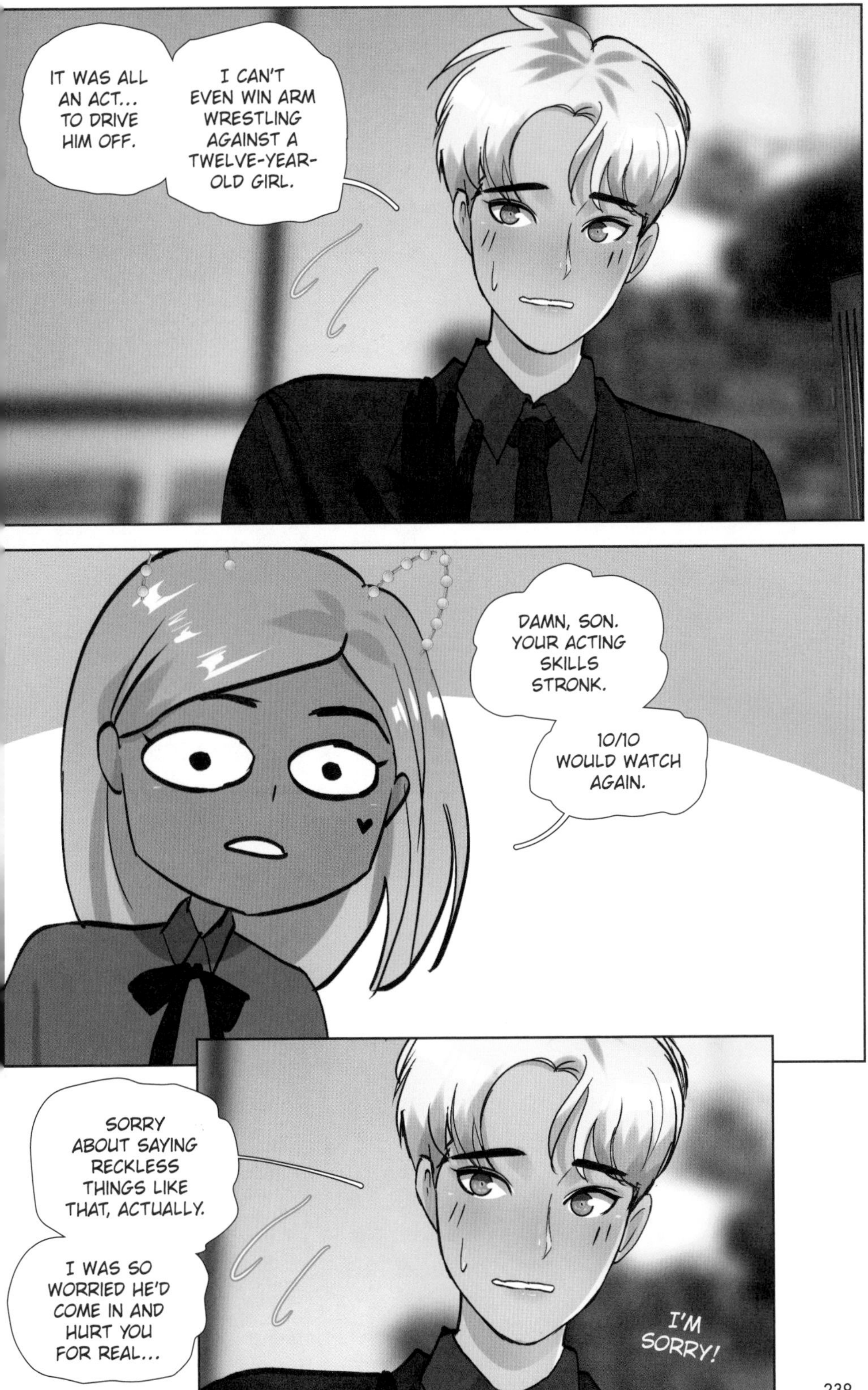
IT WAS ALL AN ACT... TO DRIVE HIM OFF.
I CAN'T EVEN WIN ARM WRESTLING AGAINST A TWELVE-YEAR-OLD GIRL.
DAMN, SON. YOUR ACTING SKILLS STRONK.
10/10 WOULD WATCH AGAIN.
SORRY ABOUT SAYING RECKLESS THINGS LIKE THAT, ACTUALLY.
I WAS SO WORRIED HE'D COME IN AND HURT YOU FOR REAL...
I'M SORRY!

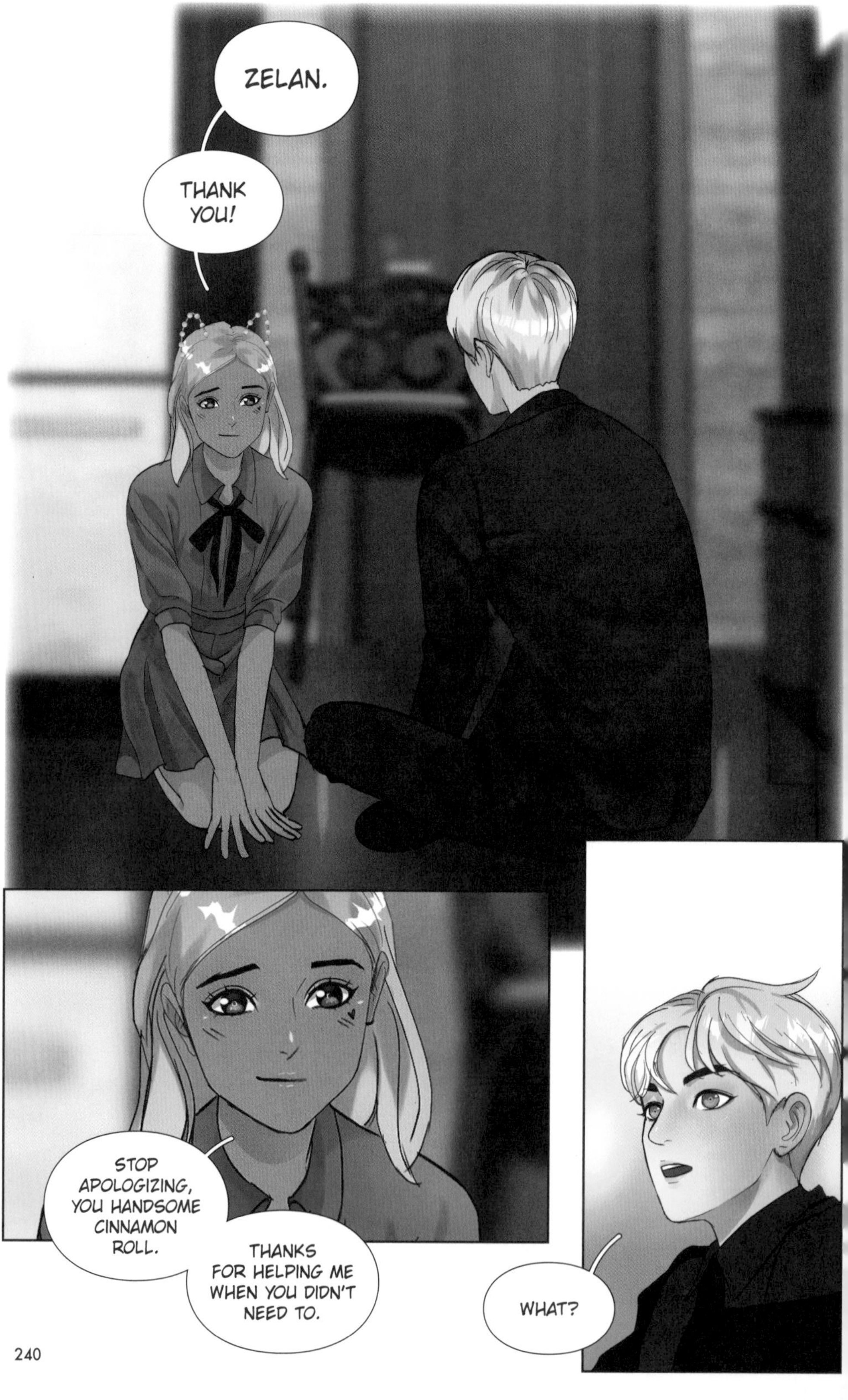
ZELAN.
THANK YOU!
STOP APOLOGIZING, YOU HANDSOME CINNAMON ROLL.
THANKS FOR HELPING ME WHEN YOU DIDN'T NEED TO.
WHAT?

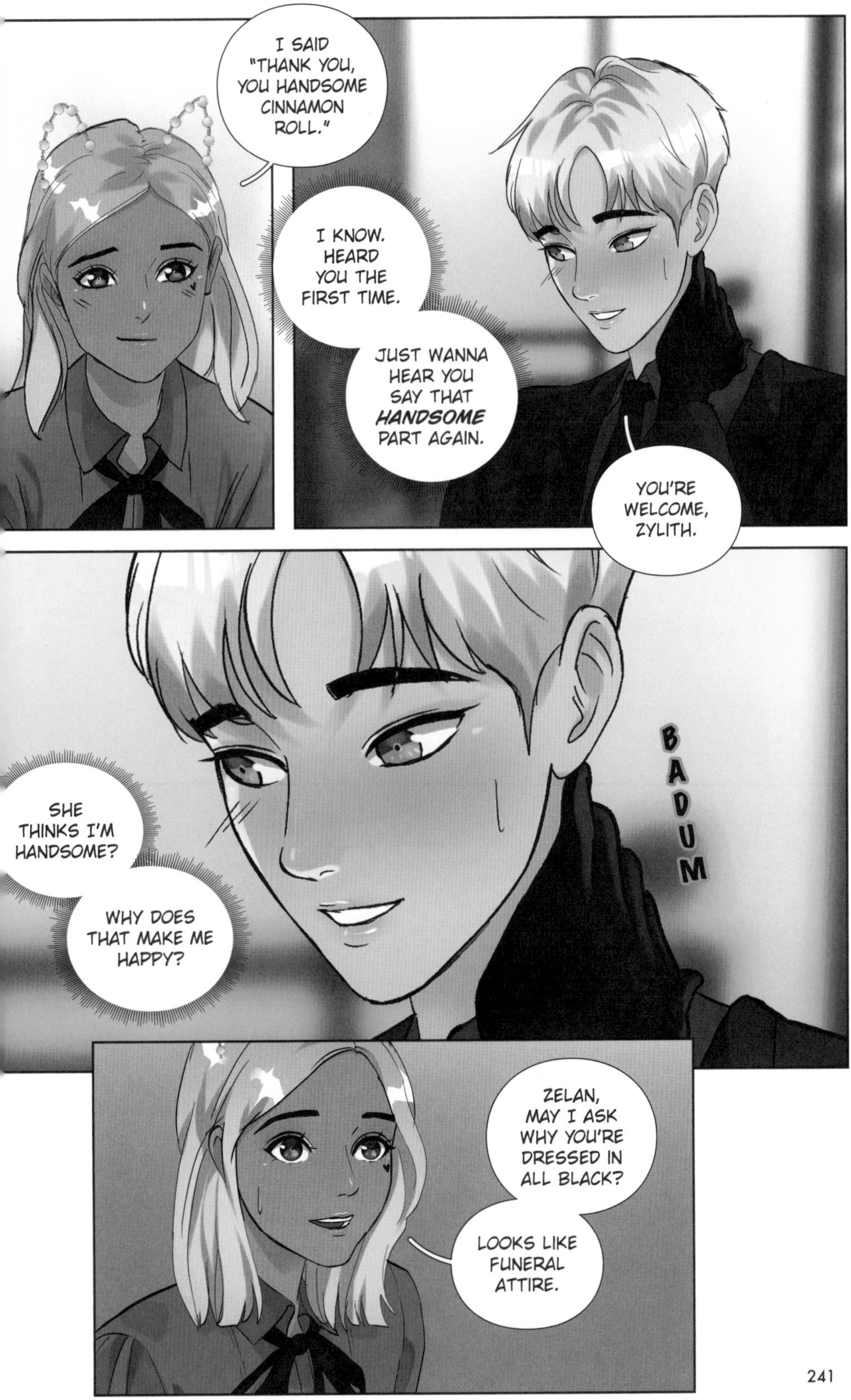
I SAID "THANK YOU, YOU HANDSOME CINNAMON ROLL."
I KNOW. HEARD YOU THE FIRST TIME.
JUST WANNA HEAR YOU SAY THAT **HANDSOME** PART AGAIN.
YOU'RE WELCOME, ZYLITH.
SHE THINKS I'M HANDSOME?
WHY DOES THAT MAKE ME HAPPY?
BADUM
ZELAN, MAY I ASK WHY YOU'RE DRESSED IN ALL BLACK?
LOOKS LIKE FUNERAL ATTIRE.

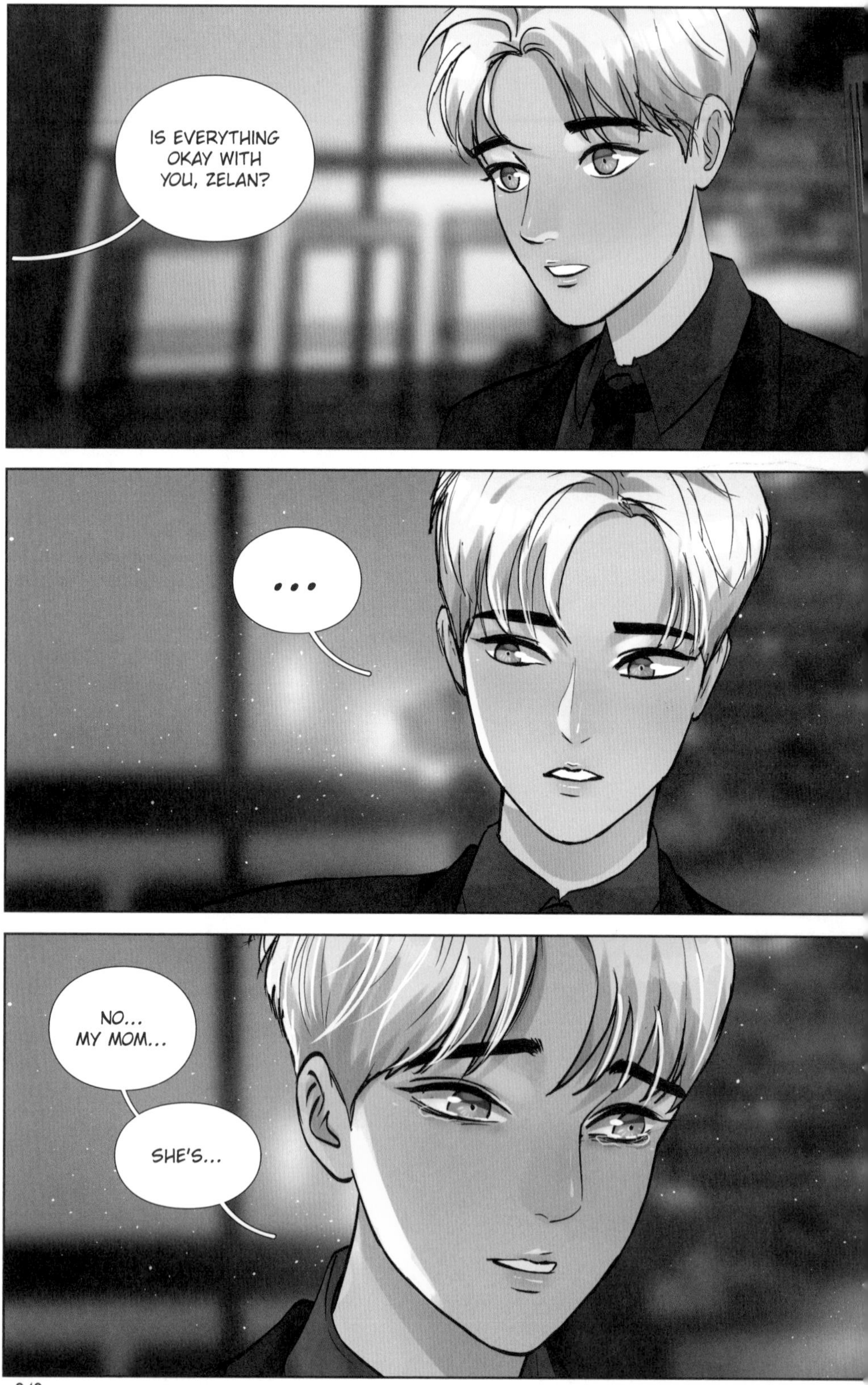
IS EVERYTHING OKAY WITH YOU, ZELAN?
...
NO... MY MOM...
SHE'S...

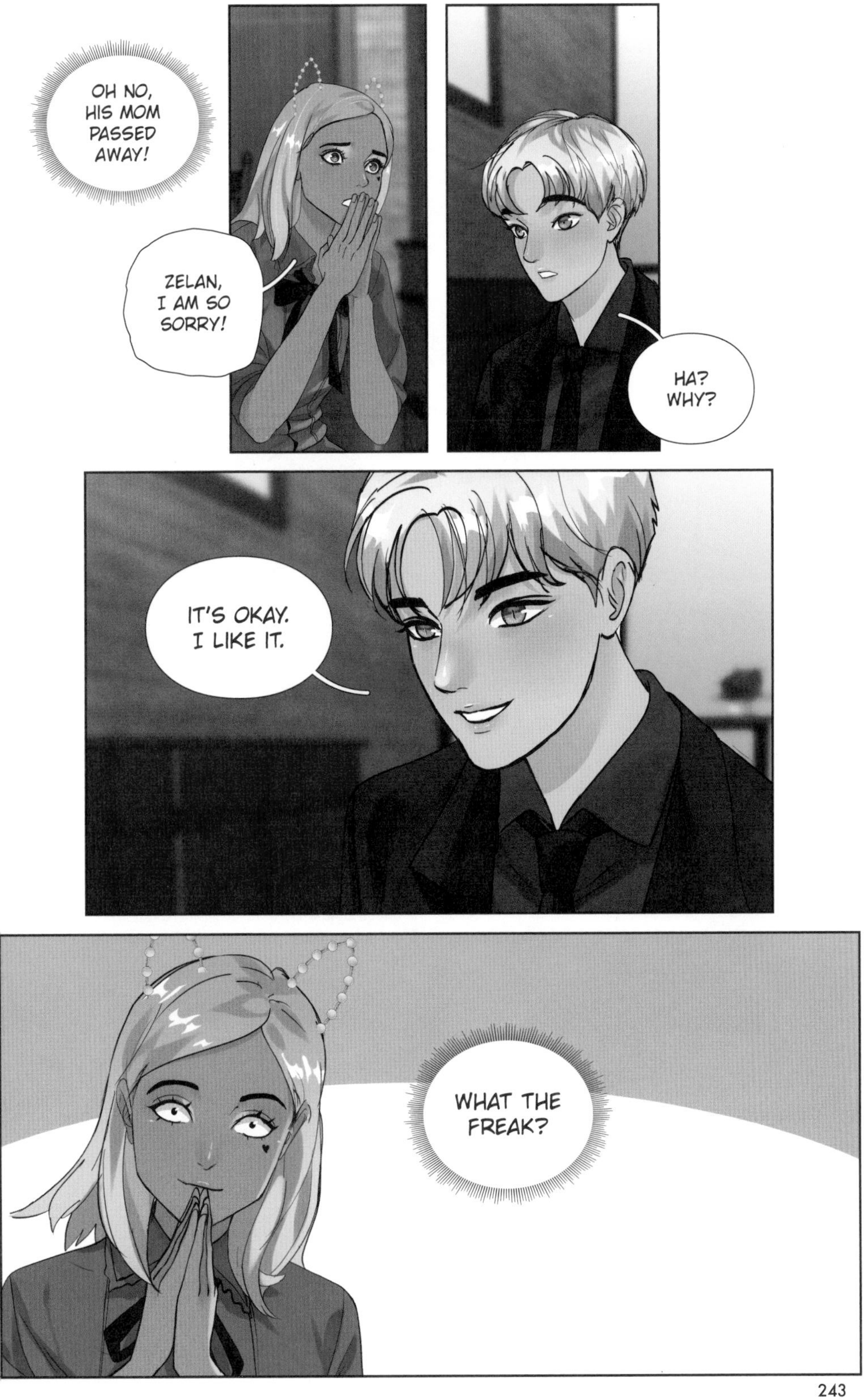
OH NO, HIS MOM PASSED AWAY!
ZELAN, I AM SO SORRY!
HA? WHY?
IT'S OKAY. I LIKE IT.
WHAT THE FREAK?

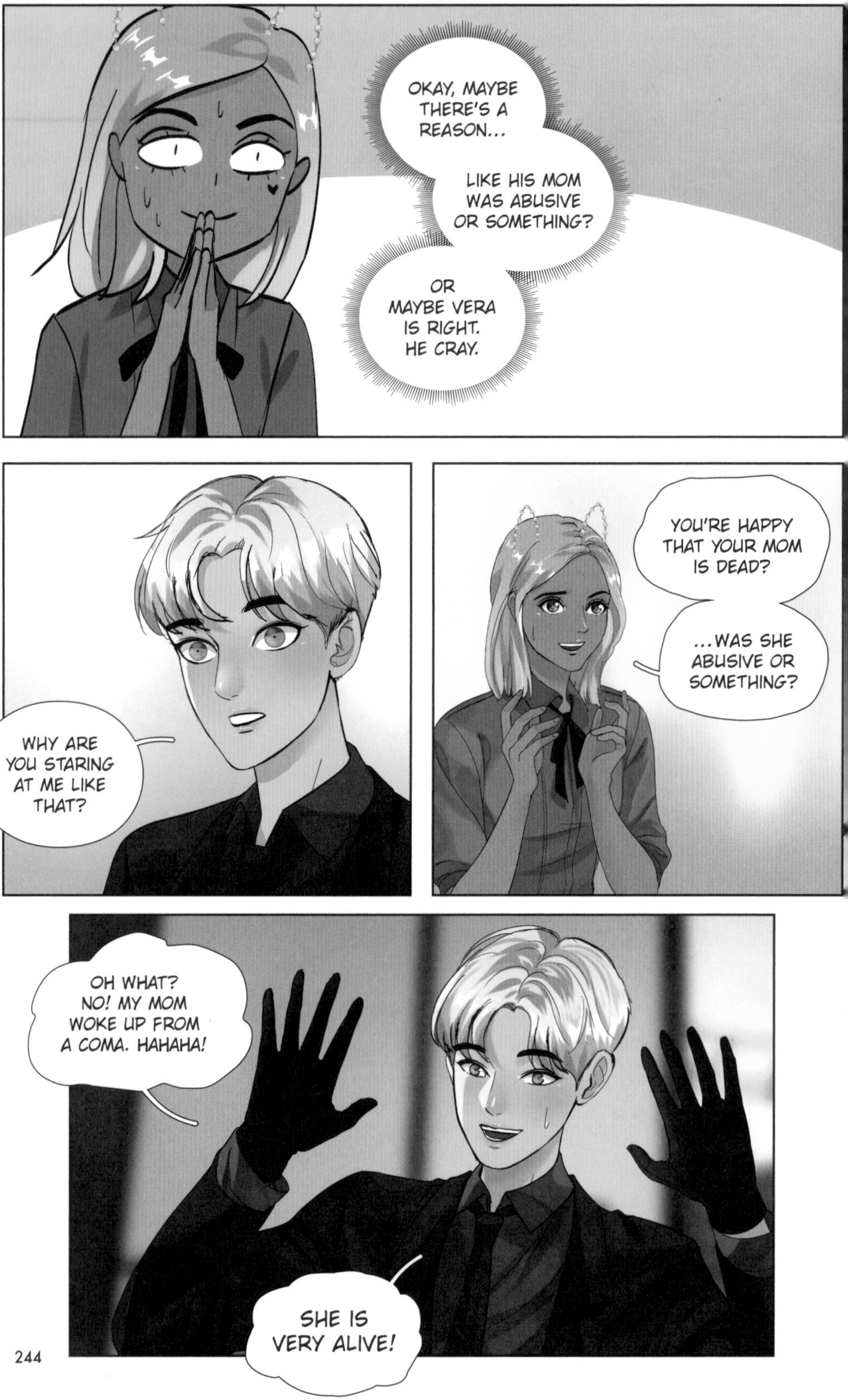
OKAY, MAYBE THERE'S A REASON...
LIKE HIS MOM WAS ABUSIVE OR SOMETHING?
OR MAYBE VERA IS RIGHT. HE CRAY.
WHY ARE YOU STARING AT ME LIKE THAT?
YOU'RE HAPPY THAT YOUR MOM IS DEAD?
...WAS SHE ABUSIVE OR SOMETHING?
OH WHAT? NO! MY MOM WOKE UP FROM A COMA. HAHAHA!
SHE IS VERY ALIVE!

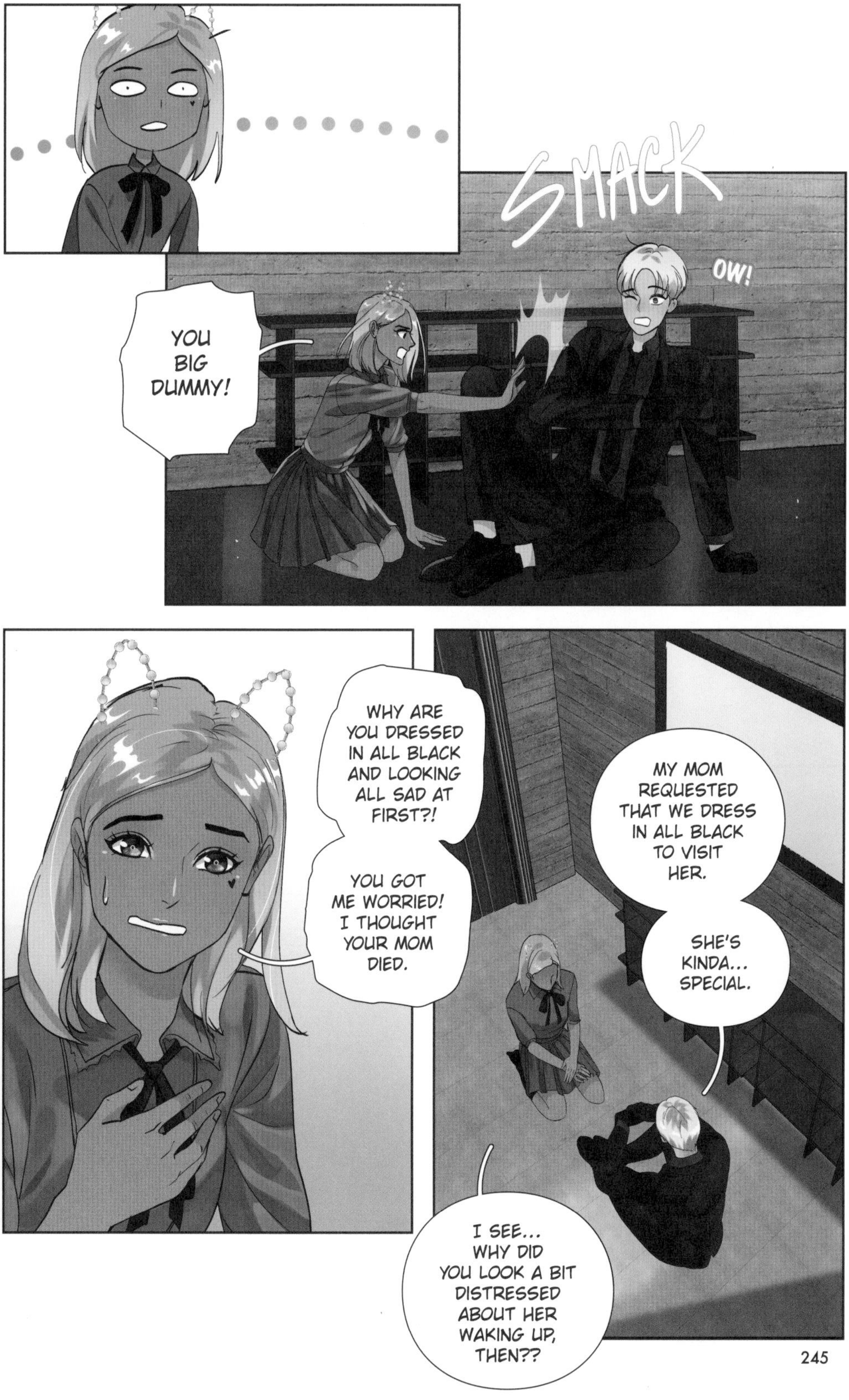
SMACK
OW!
YOU BIG DUMMY!
WHY ARE YOU DRESSED IN ALL BLACK AND LOOKING ALL SAD AT FIRST?!
YOU GOT ME WORRIED! I THOUGHT YOUR MOM DIED.
MY MOM REQUESTED THAT WE DRESS IN ALL BLACK TO VISIT HER.
SHE'S KINDA... SPECIAL.
I SEE... WHY DID YOU LOOK A BIT DISTRESSED ABOUT HER WAKING UP, THEN??

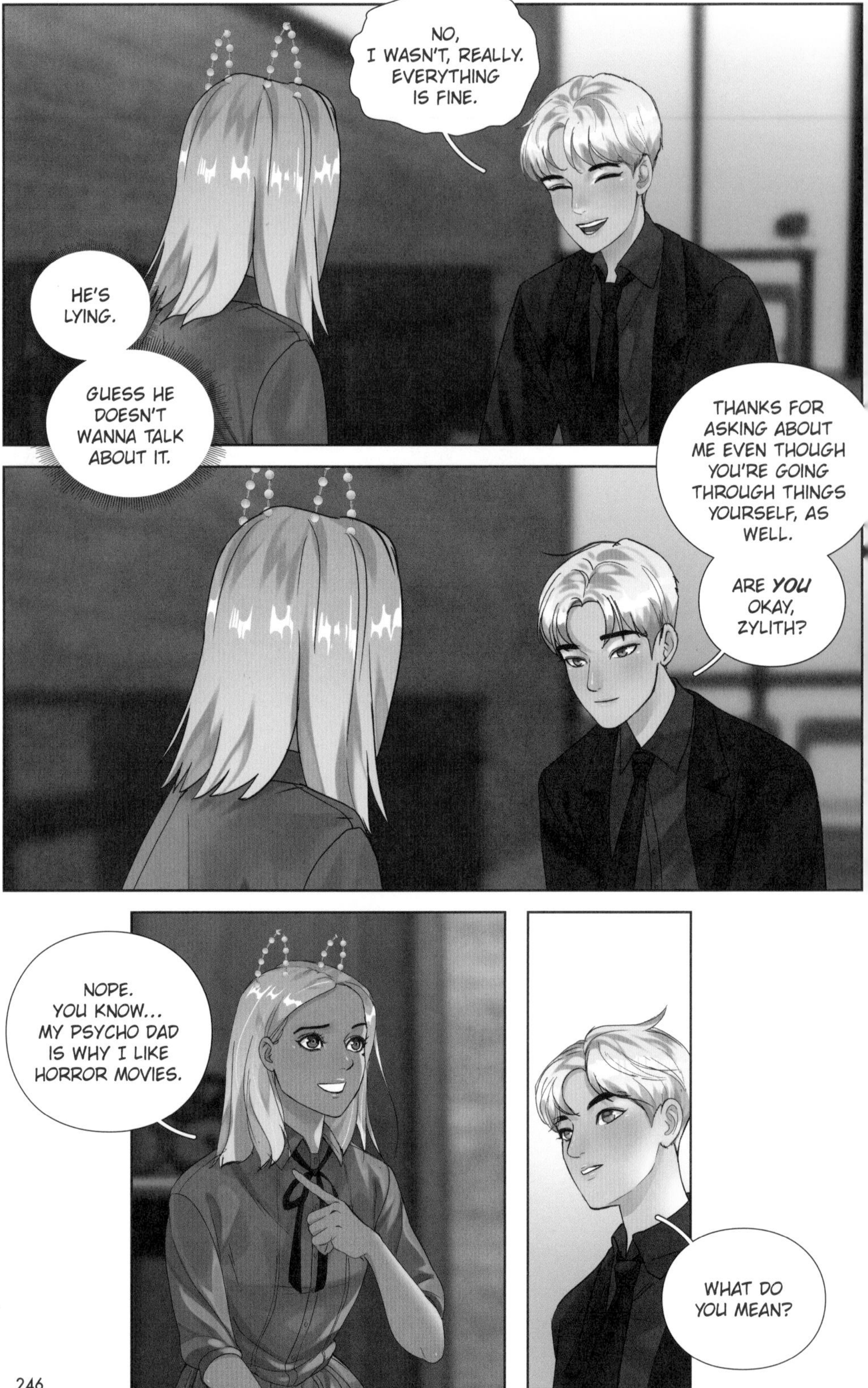
NO, I WASN'T, REALLY. EVERYTHING IS FINE.
HE'S LYING.
GUESS HE DOESN'T WANNA TALK ABOUT IT.
THANKS FOR ASKING ABOUT ME EVEN THOUGH YOU'RE GOING THROUGH THINGS YOURSELF, AS WELL.
ARE ***YOU*** OKAY, ZYLITH?
NOPE. YOU KNOW... MY PSYCHO DAD IS WHY I LIKE HORROR MOVIES.
WHAT DO YOU MEAN?

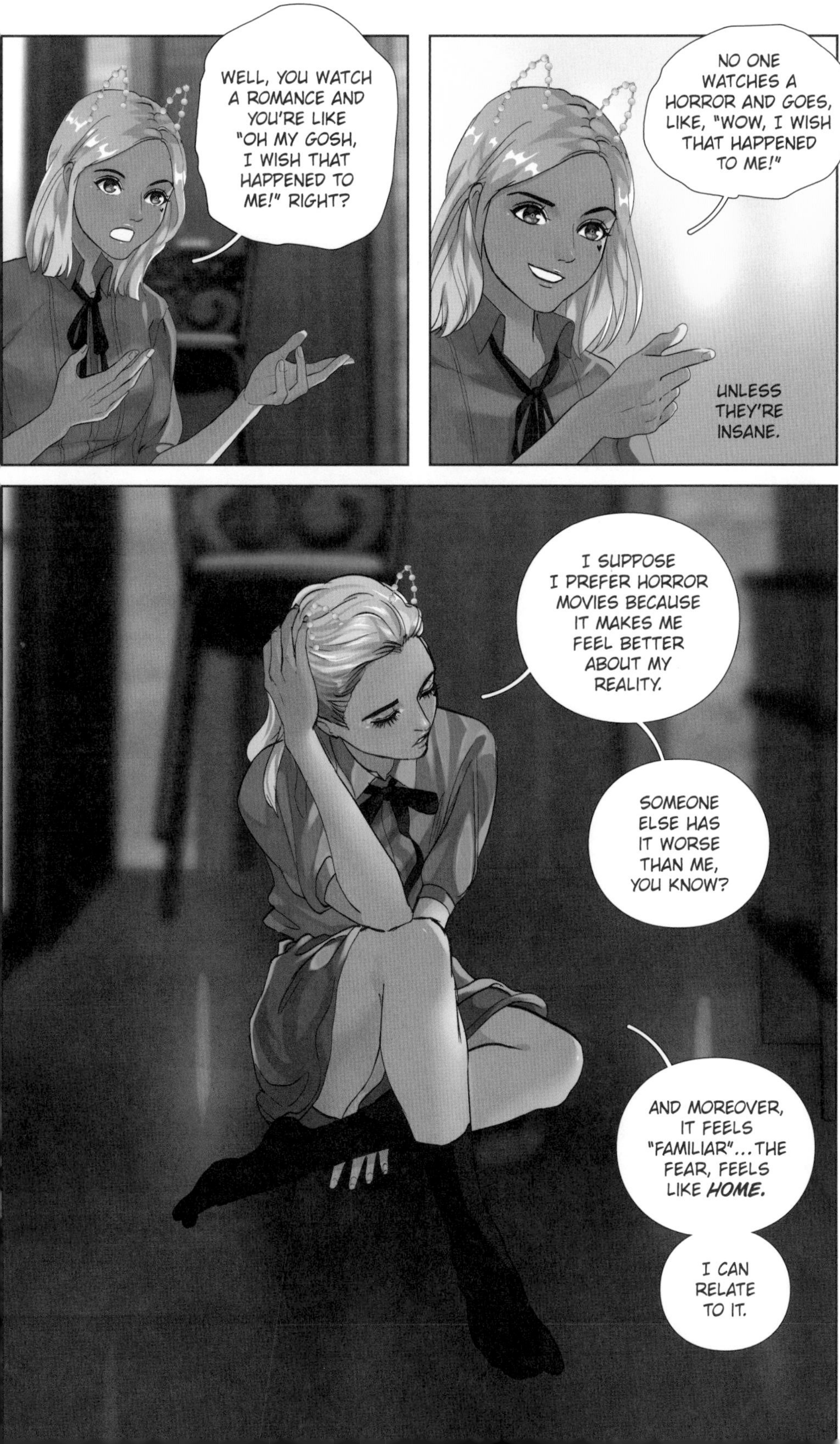
WELL, YOU WATCH A ROMANCE AND YOU'RE LIKE "OH MY GOSH, I WISH THAT HAPPENED TO ME!" RIGHT?
NO ONE WATCHES A HORROR AND GOES, LIKE, "WOW, I WISH THAT HAPPENED TO ME!"
UNLESS THEY'RE INSANE.
I SUPPOSE I PREFER HORROR MOVIES BECAUSE IT MAKES ME FEEL BETTER ABOUT MY REALITY.
SOMEONE ELSE HAS IT WORSE THAN ME, YOU KNOW?
AND MOREOVER, IT FEELS "FAMILIAR"... THE FEAR, FEELS LIKE *HOME.*
I CAN RELATE TO IT.

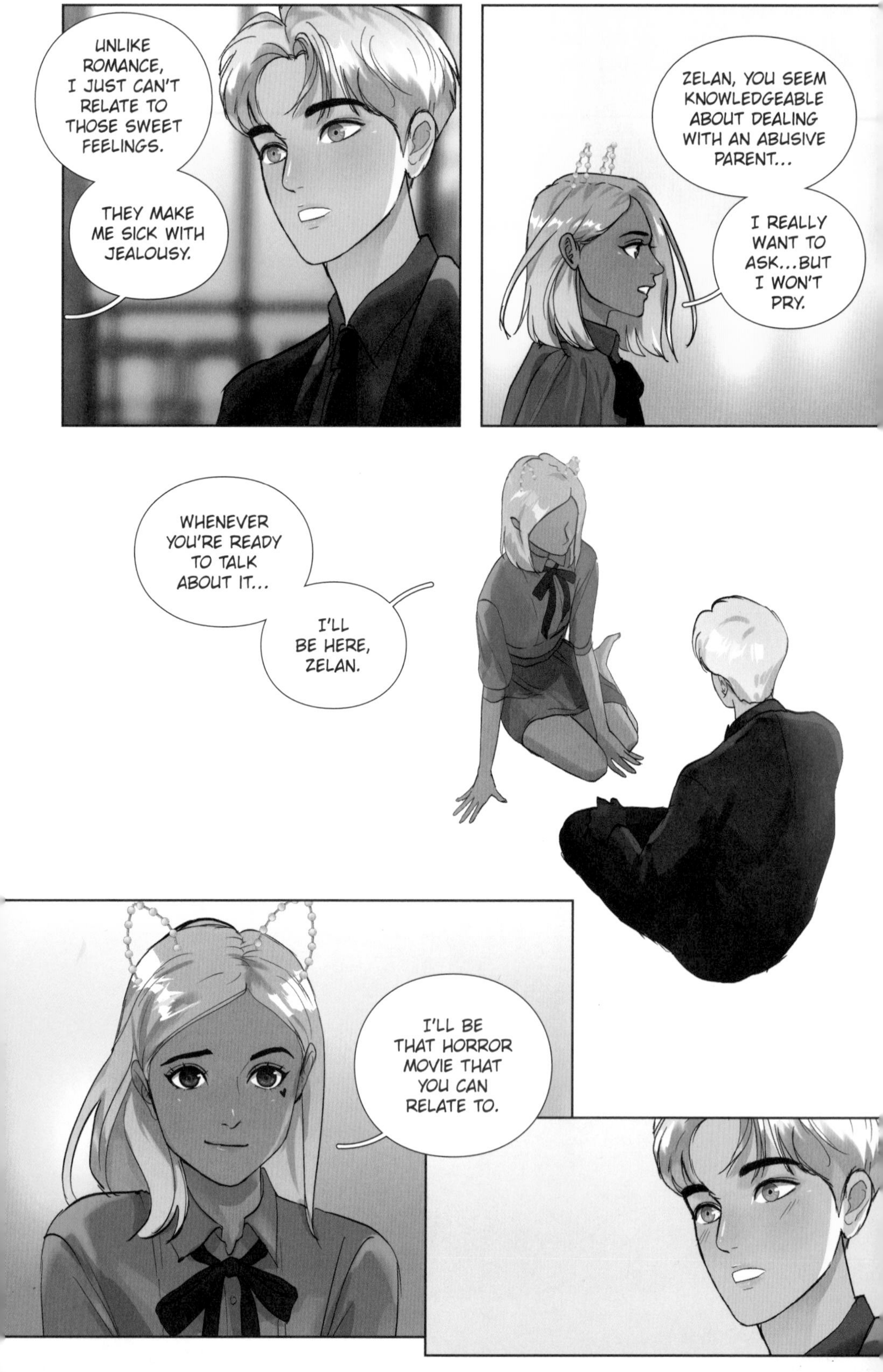
UNLIKE ROMANCE, I JUST CAN'T RELATE TO THOSE SWEET FEELINGS.
THEY MAKE ME SICK WITH JEALOUSY.
ZELAN, YOU SEEM KNOWLEDGEABLE ABOUT DEALING WITH AN ABUSIVE PARENT...
I REALLY WANT TO ASK...BUT I WON'T PRY.
WHENEVER YOU'RE READY TO TALK ABOUT IT...
I'LL BE HERE, ZELAN.
I'LL BE THAT HORROR MOVIE THAT YOU CAN RELATE TO.

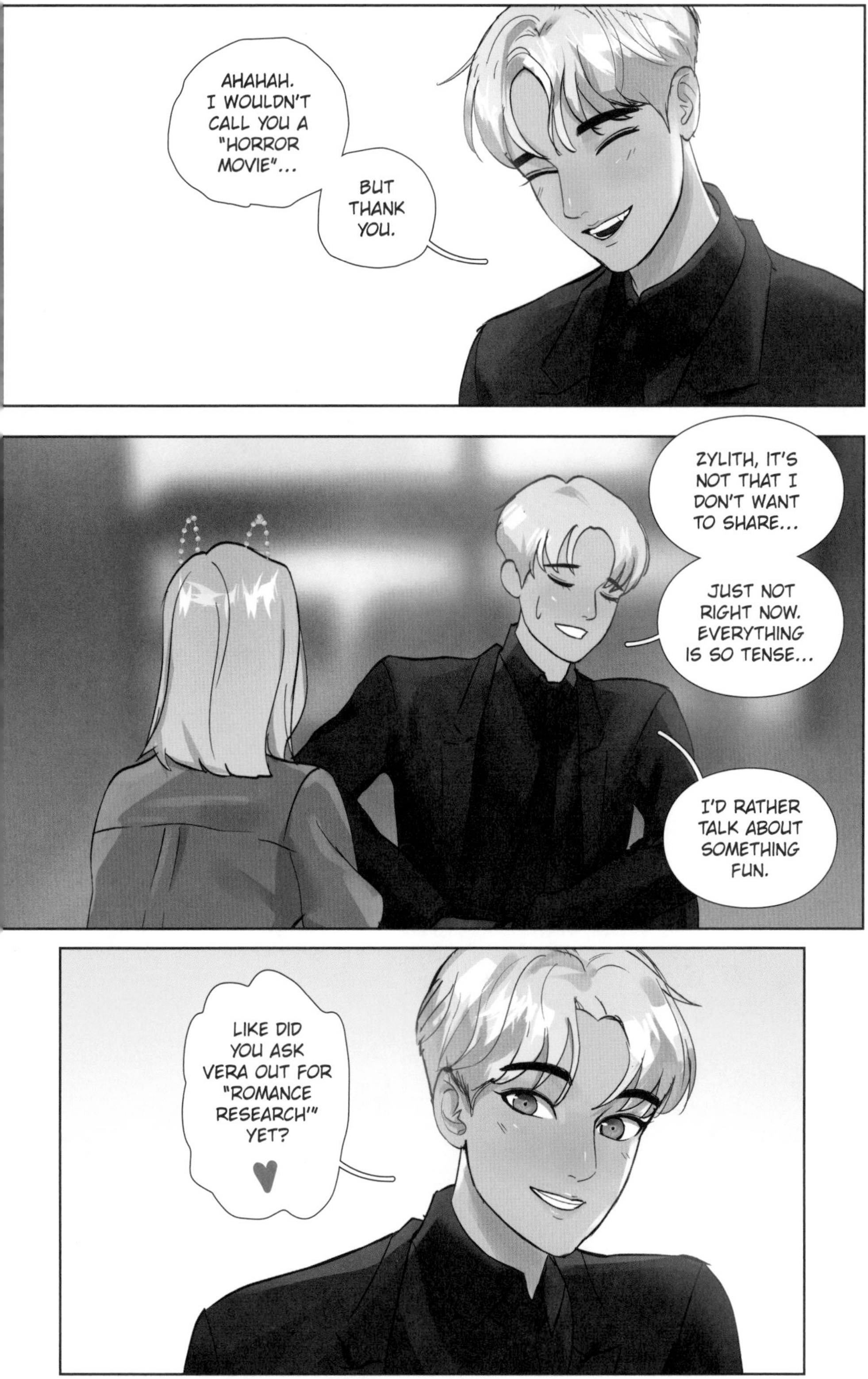
AHAHAH. I WOULDN'T CALL YOU A "HORROR MOVIE"...
BUT THANK YOU.
ZYLITH, IT'S NOT THAT I DON'T WANT TO SHARE...
JUST NOT RIGHT NOW. EVERYTHING IS SO TENSE...
I'D RATHER TALK ABOUT SOMETHING FUN.
LIKE DID YOU ASK VERA OUT FOR "ROMANCE RESEARCH'" YET?

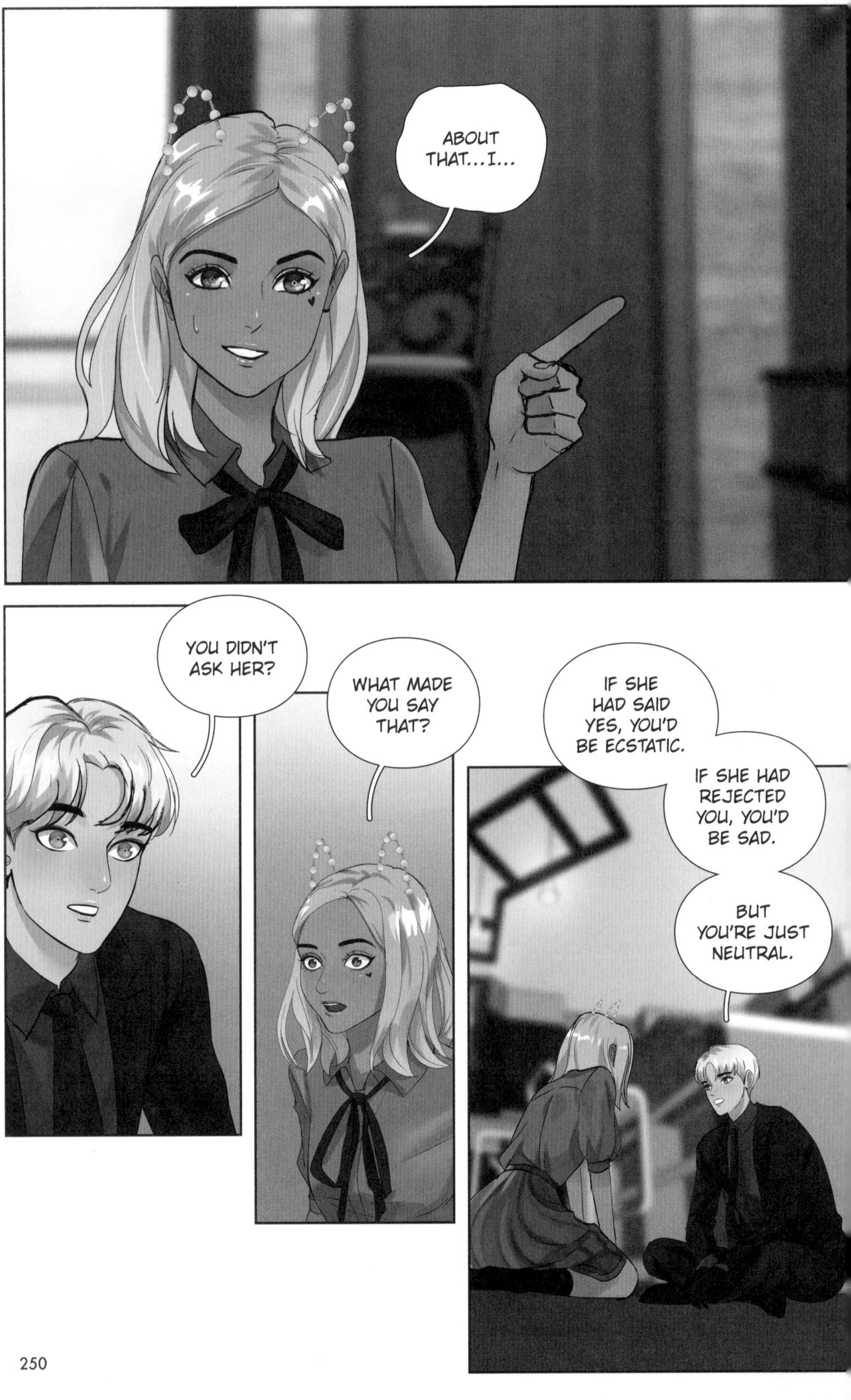
ABOUT THAT...I...
YOU DIDN'T ASK HER?
WHAT MADE YOU SAY THAT?
IF SHE HAD SAID YES, YOU'D BE ECSTATIC.
IF SHE HAD REJECTED YOU, YOU'D BE SAD.
BUT YOU'RE JUST NEUTRAL.

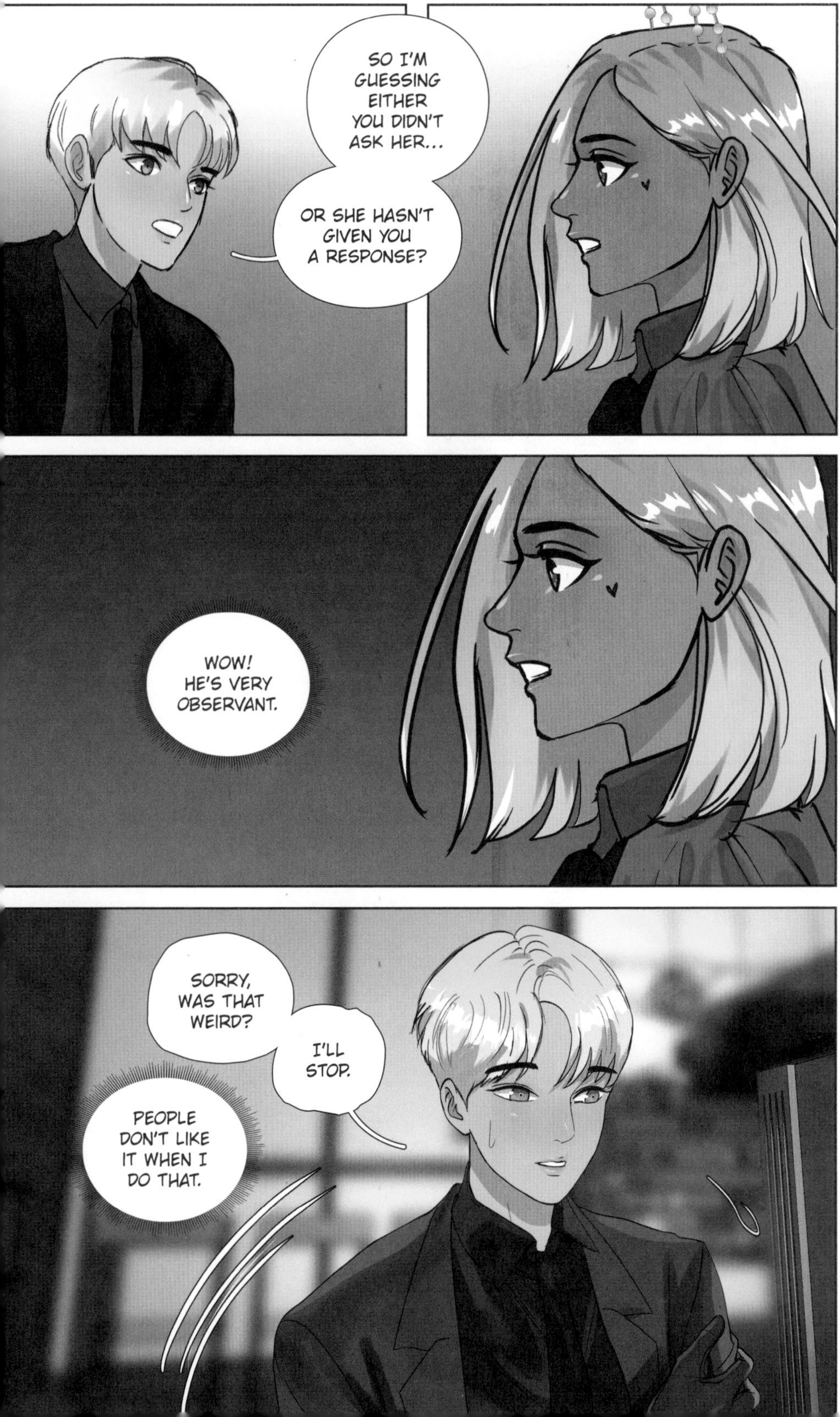
SO I'M GUESSING EITHER YOU DIDN'T ASK HER...
OR SHE HASN'T GIVEN YOU A RESPONSE?
WOW! HE'S VERY OBSERVANT.
SORRY, WAS THAT WEIRD?
I'LL STOP.
PEOPLE DON'T LIKE IT WHEN I DO THAT.

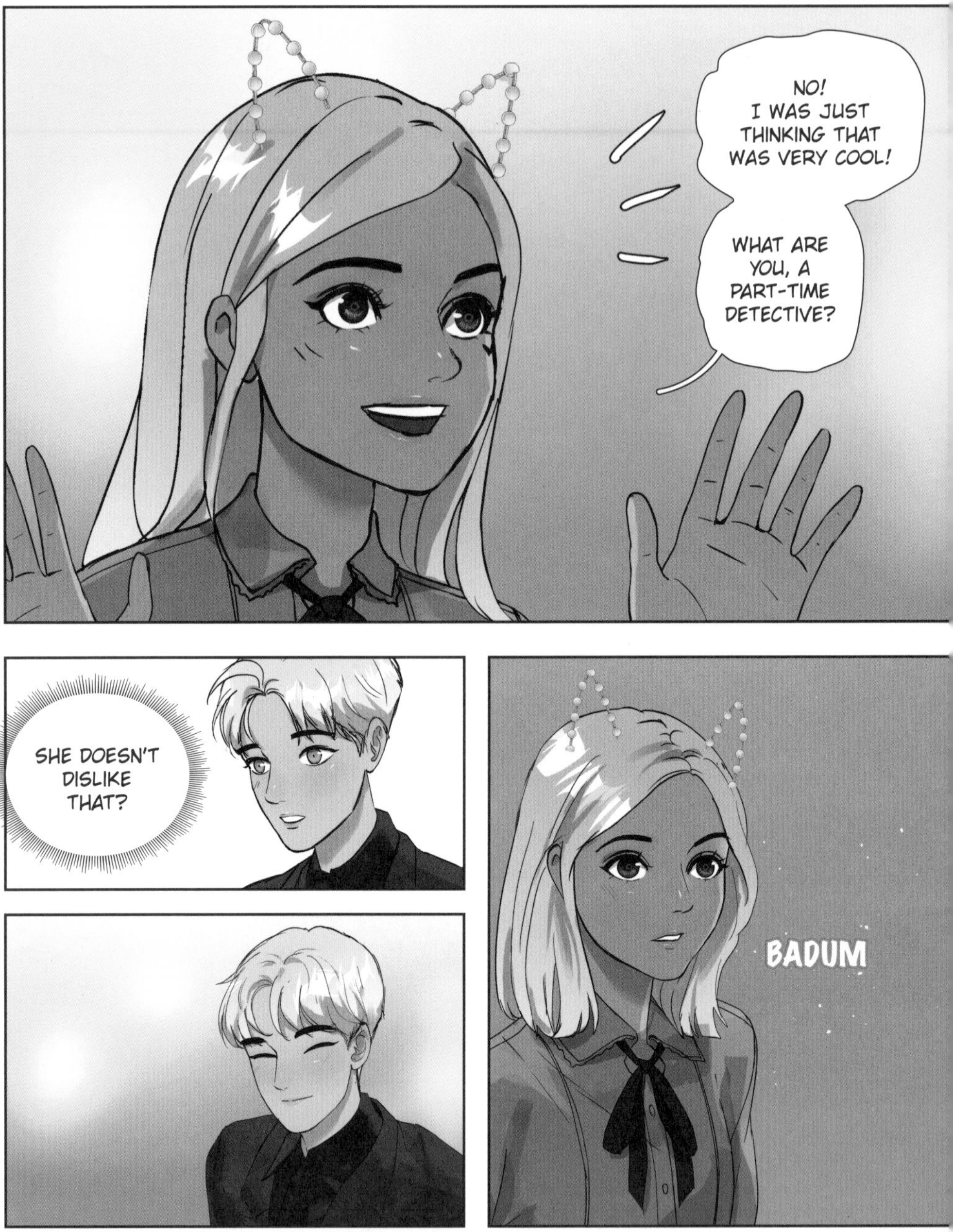
NO! I WAS JUST THINKING THAT WAS VERY COOL!
WHAT ARE YOU, A PART-TIME DETECTIVE?
SHE DOESN'T DISLIKE THAT?
BADUM
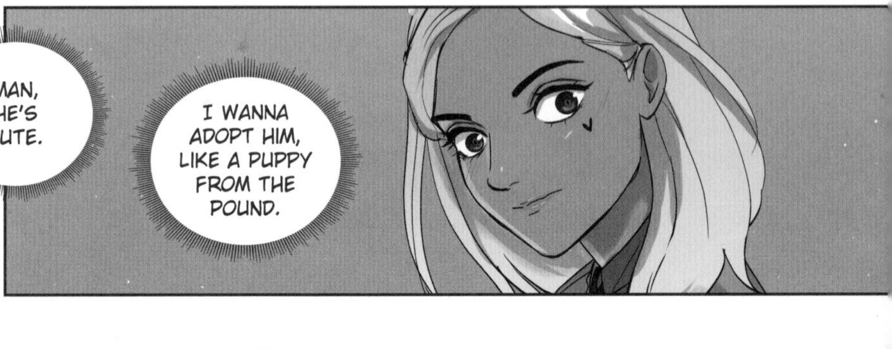
MAN, HE'S CUTE.
I WANNA ADOPT HIM, LIKE A PUPPY FROM THE POUND.

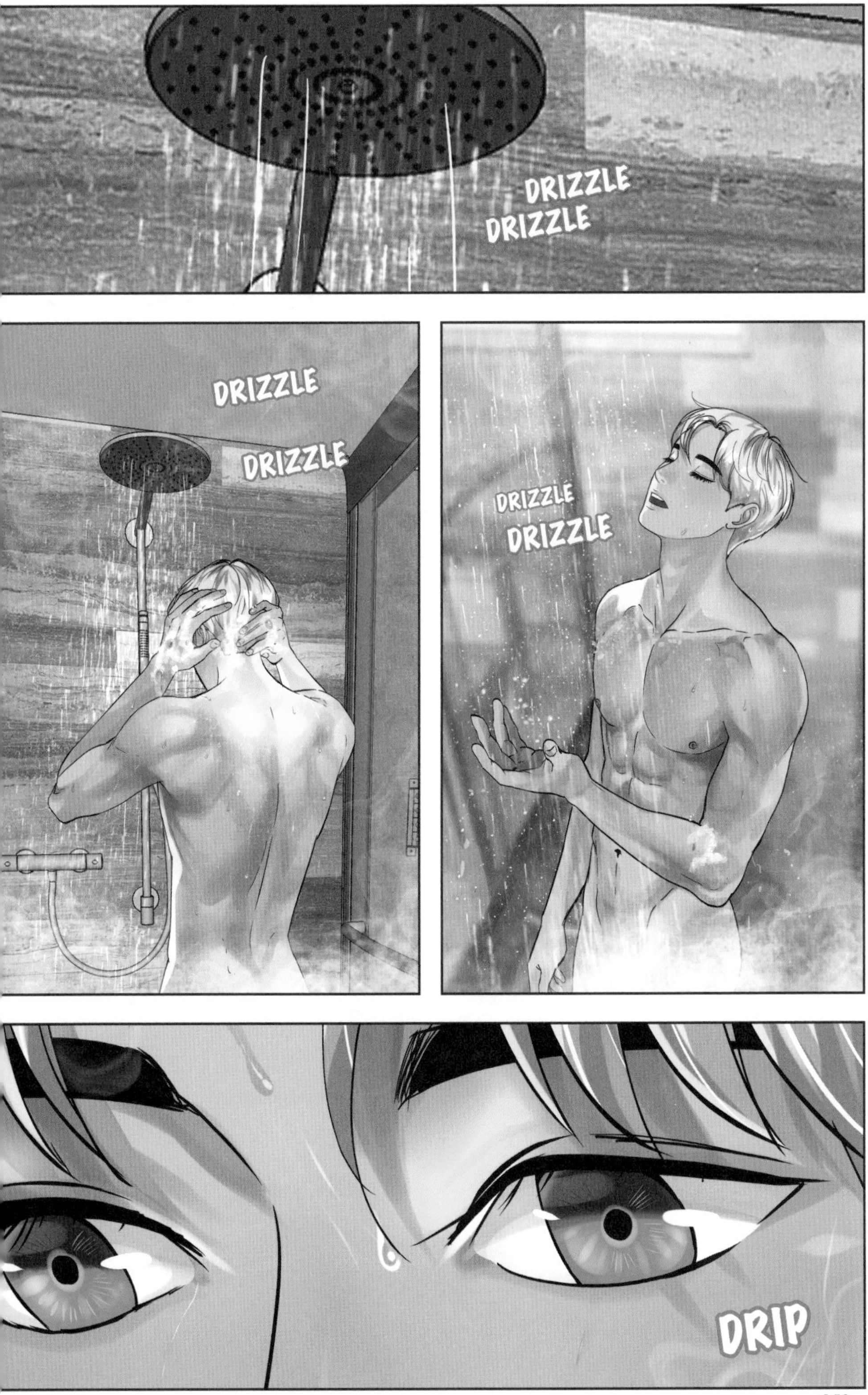
DRIZZLE
DRIZZLE
DRIZZLE
DRIZZLE
DRIZZLE
DRIZZLE
DRIP

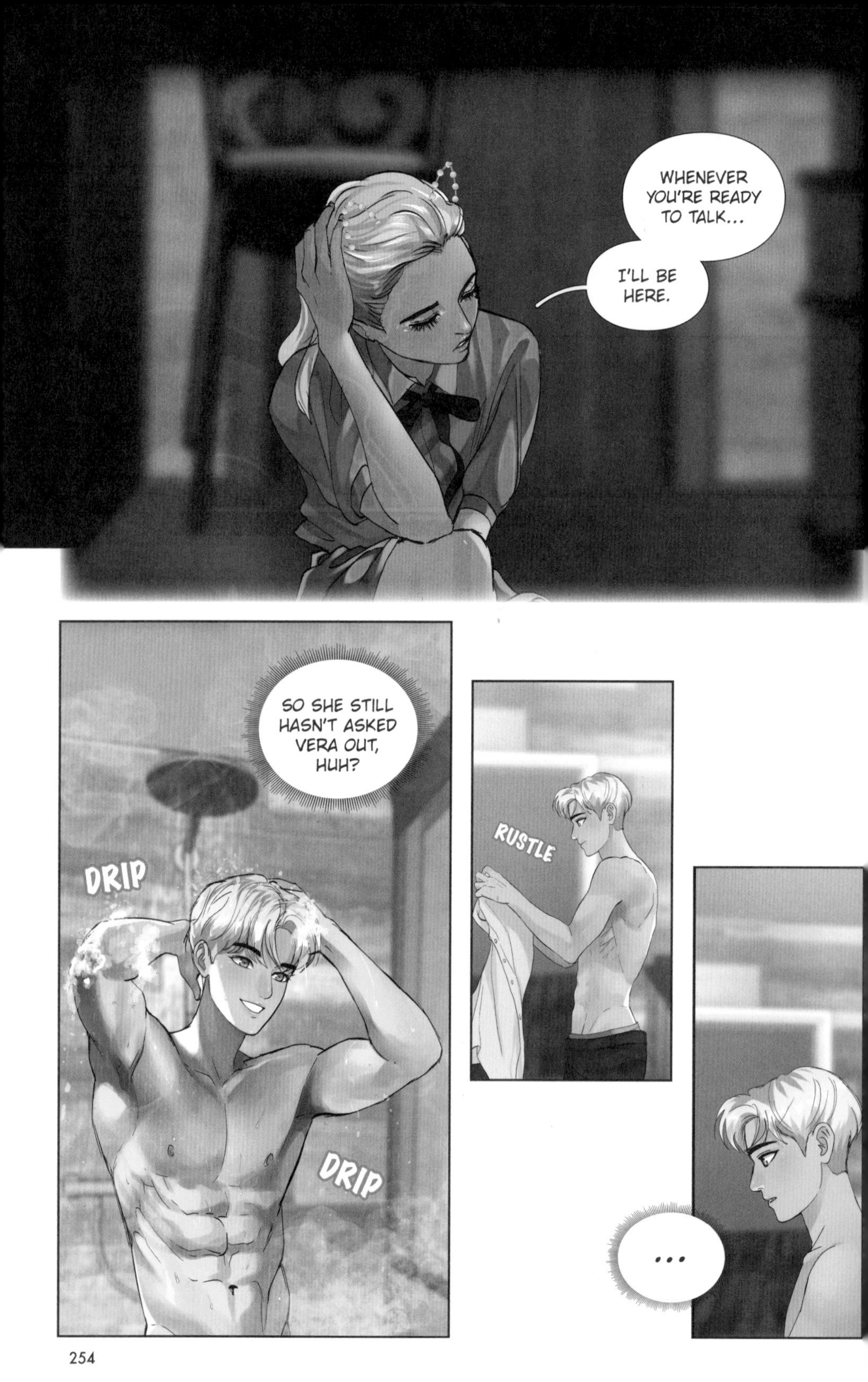
WHENEVER YOU'RE READY TO TALK...
I'LL BE HERE.
SO SHE STILL HASN'T ASKED VERA OUT, HUH?
DRIP
DRIP
RUSTLE
...

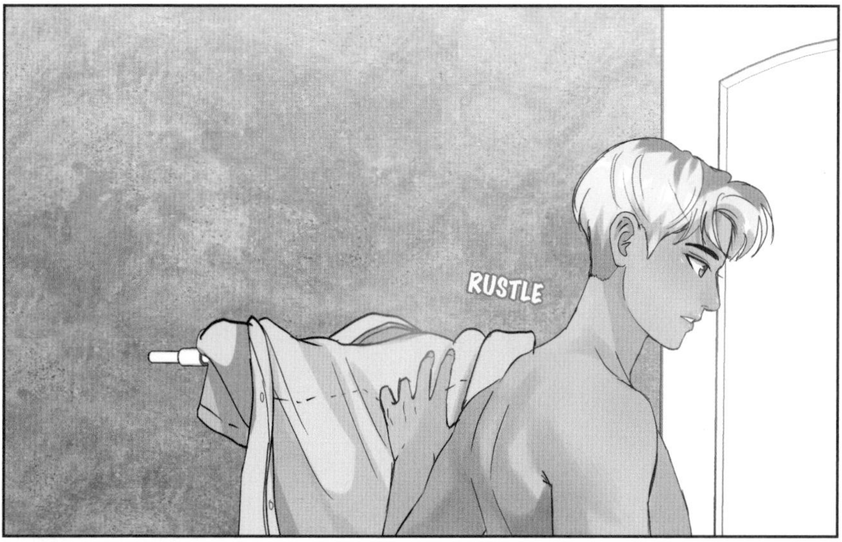
RUSTLE

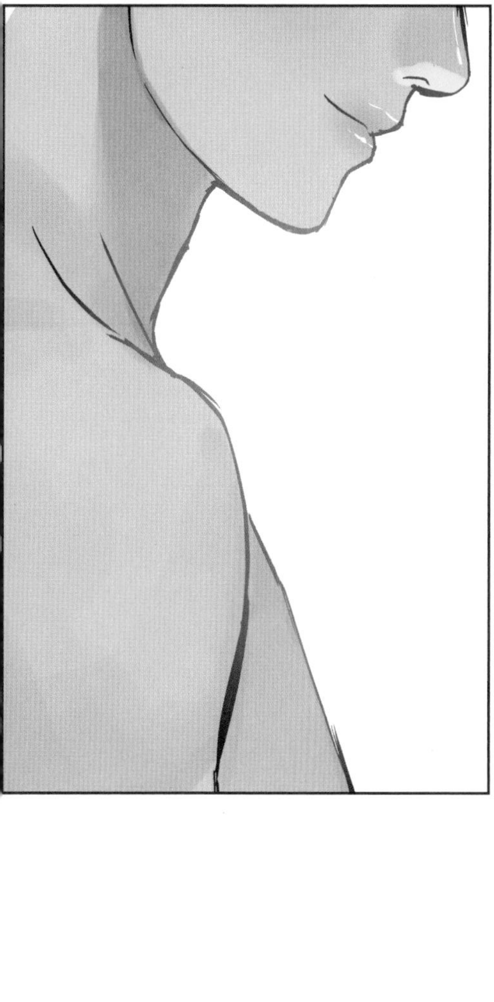

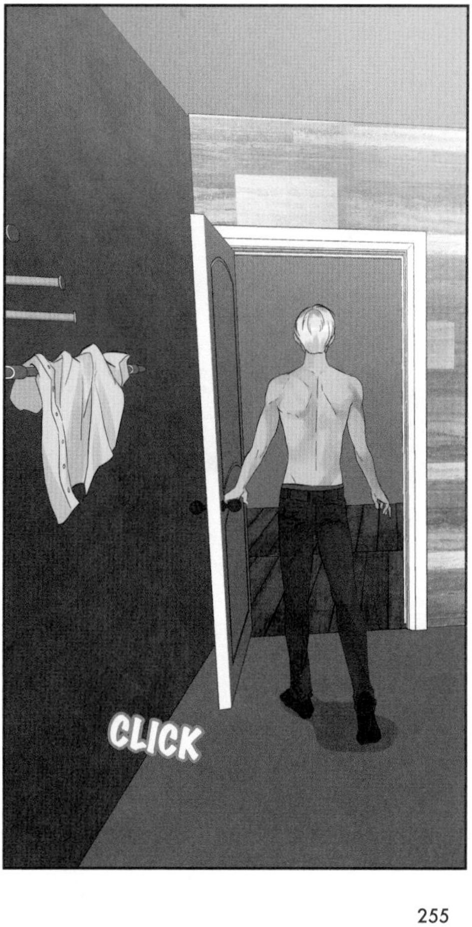
CLICK

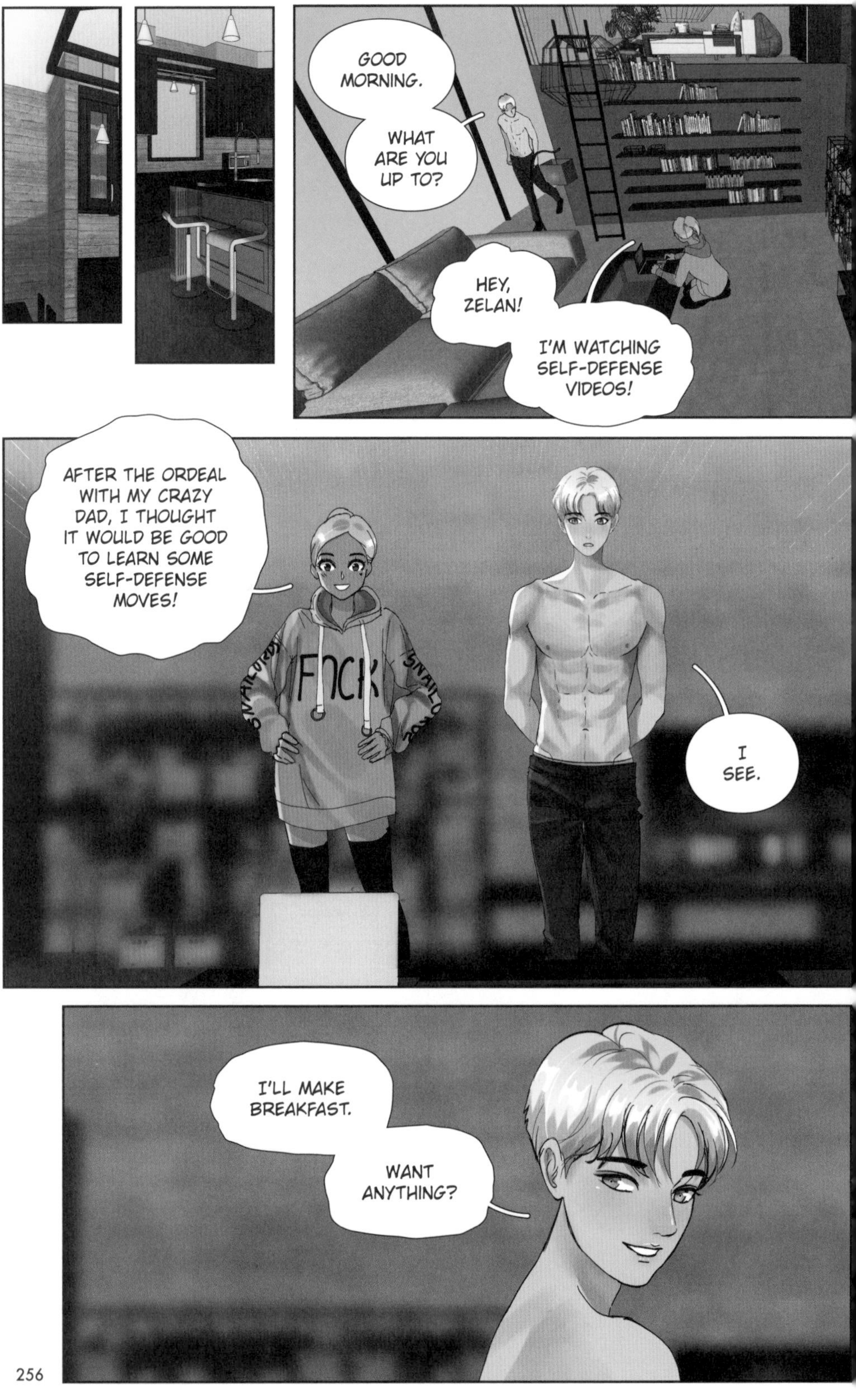
GOOD MORNING.
WHAT ARE YOU UP TO?
HEY, ZELAN!
I'M WATCHING SELF-DEFENSE VIDEOS!
AFTER THE ORDEAL WITH MY CRAZY DAD, I THOUGHT IT WOULD BE GOOD TO LEARN SOME SELF-DEFENSE MOVES!
I SEE.
I'LL MAKE BREAKFAST.
WANT ANYTHING?

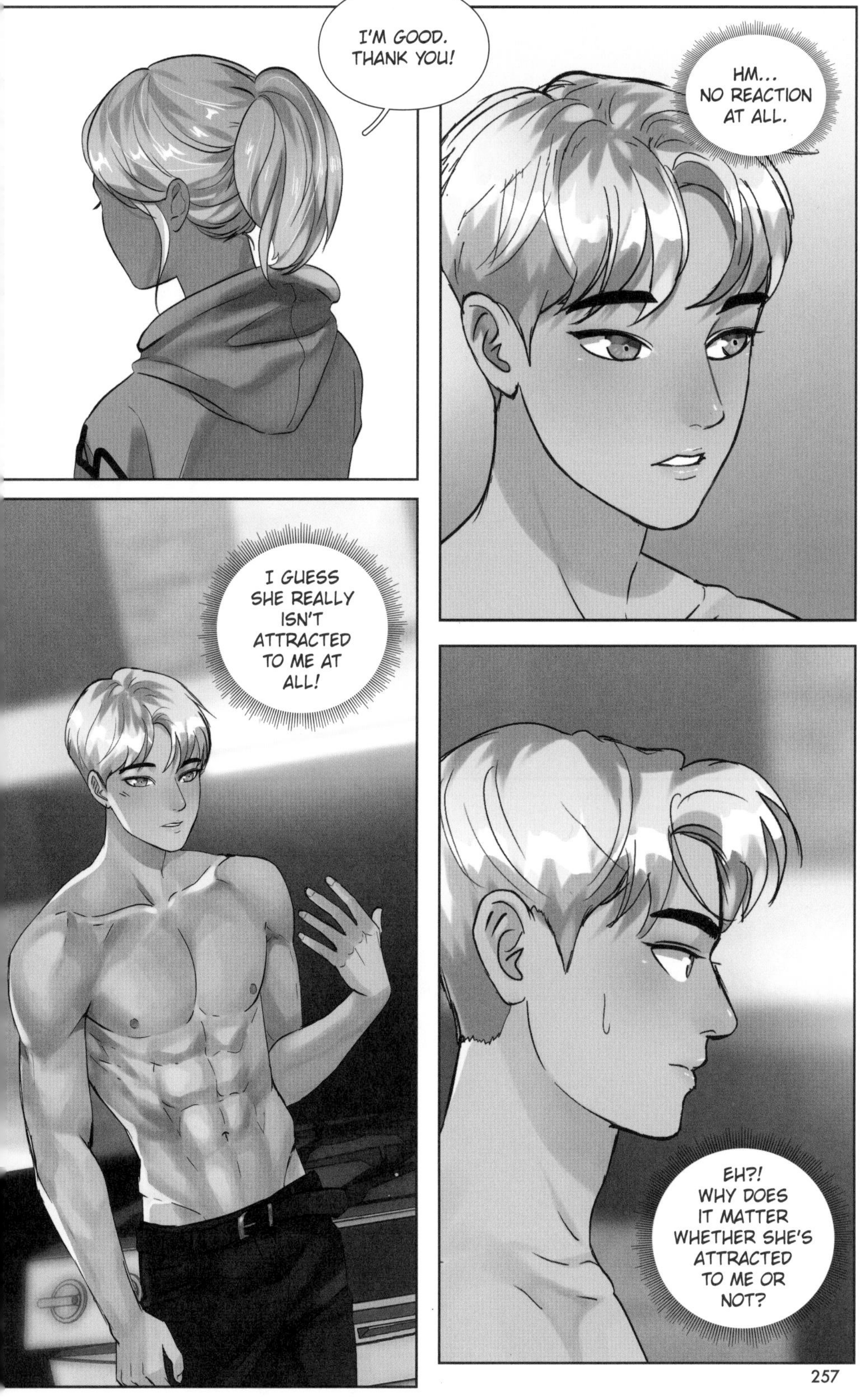
I'M GOOD. THANK YOU!
HM... NO REACTION AT ALL.
I GUESS SHE REALLY ISN'T ATTRACTED TO ME AT ALL!
EH?! WHY DOES IT MATTER WHETHER SHE'S ATTRACTED TO ME OR NOT?

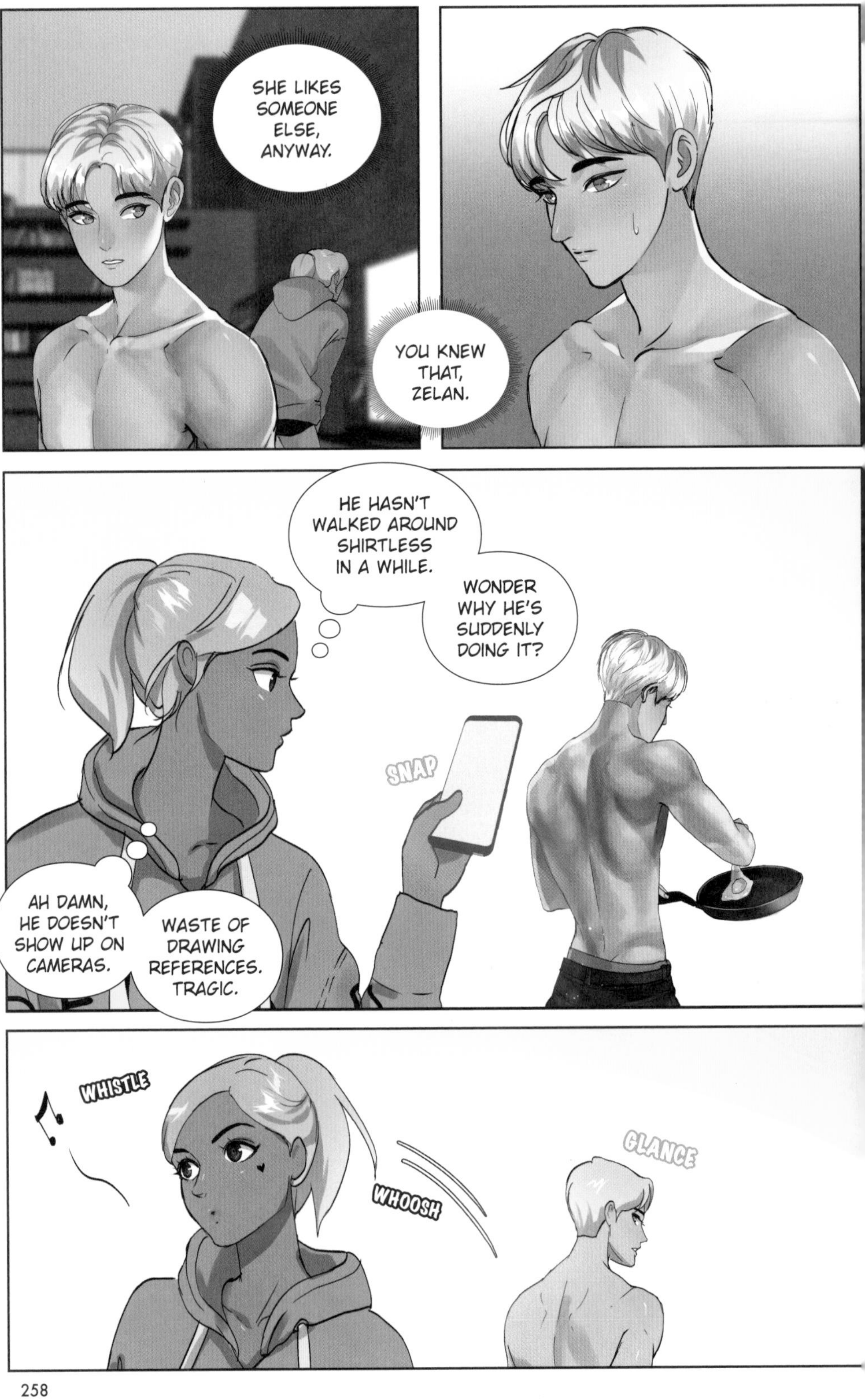
SHE LIKES SOMEONE ELSE, ANYWAY.
YOU KNEW THAT, ZELAN.
HE HASN'T WALKED AROUND SHIRTLESS IN A WHILE.
WONDER WHY HE'S SUDDENLY DOING IT?
SNAP
AH DAMN, HE DOESN'T SHOW UP ON CAMERAS.
WASTE OF DRAWING REFERENCES. TRAGIC.
WHISTLE
WHOOSH
GLANCE

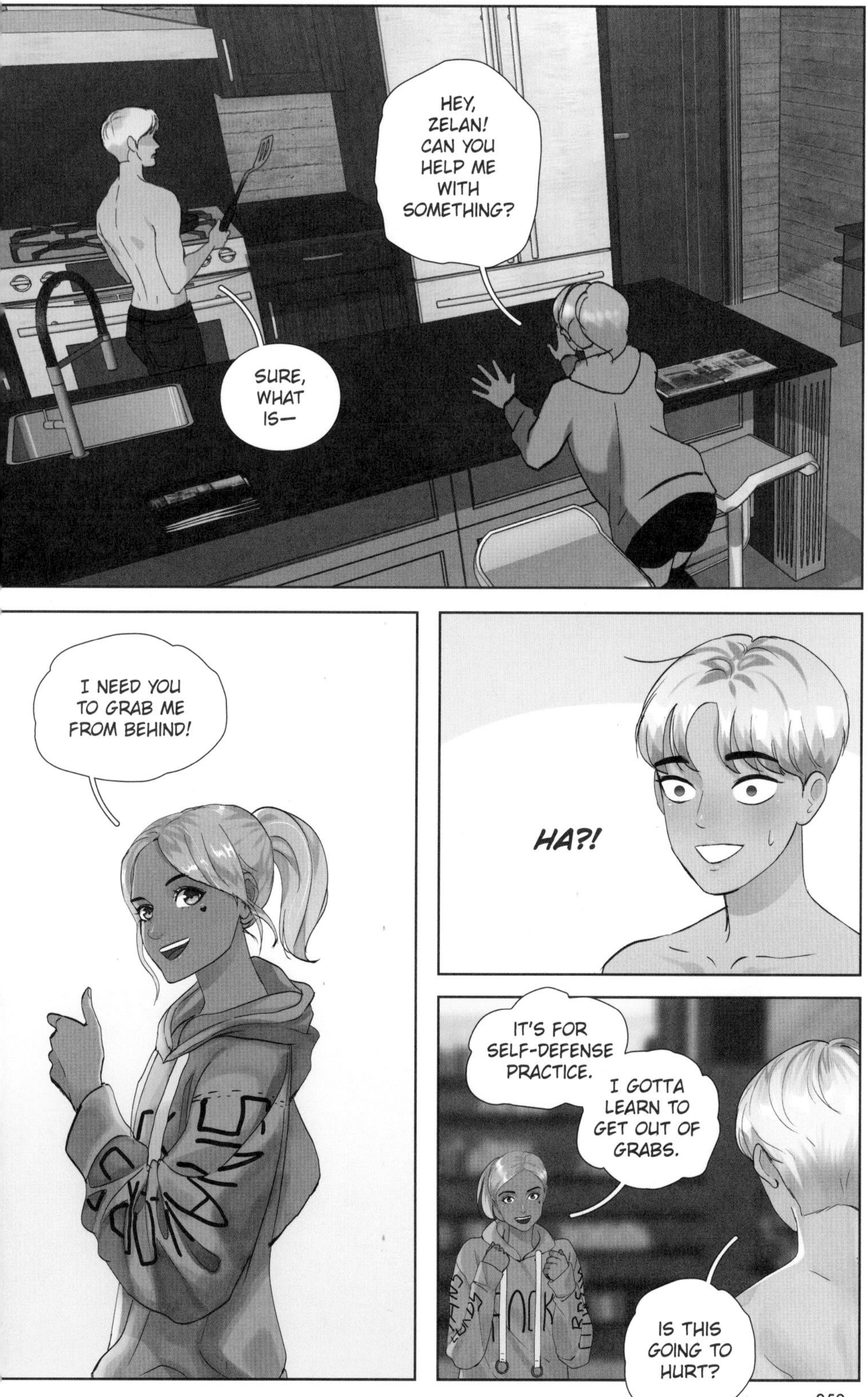
HEY, ZELAN! CAN YOU HELP ME WITH SOMETHING?
SURE, WHAT IS—
I NEED YOU TO GRAB ME FROM BEHIND!
HA?!
IT'S FOR SELF-DEFENSE PRACTICE.
I GOTTA LEARN TO GET OUT OF GRABS.
IS THIS GOING TO HURT?

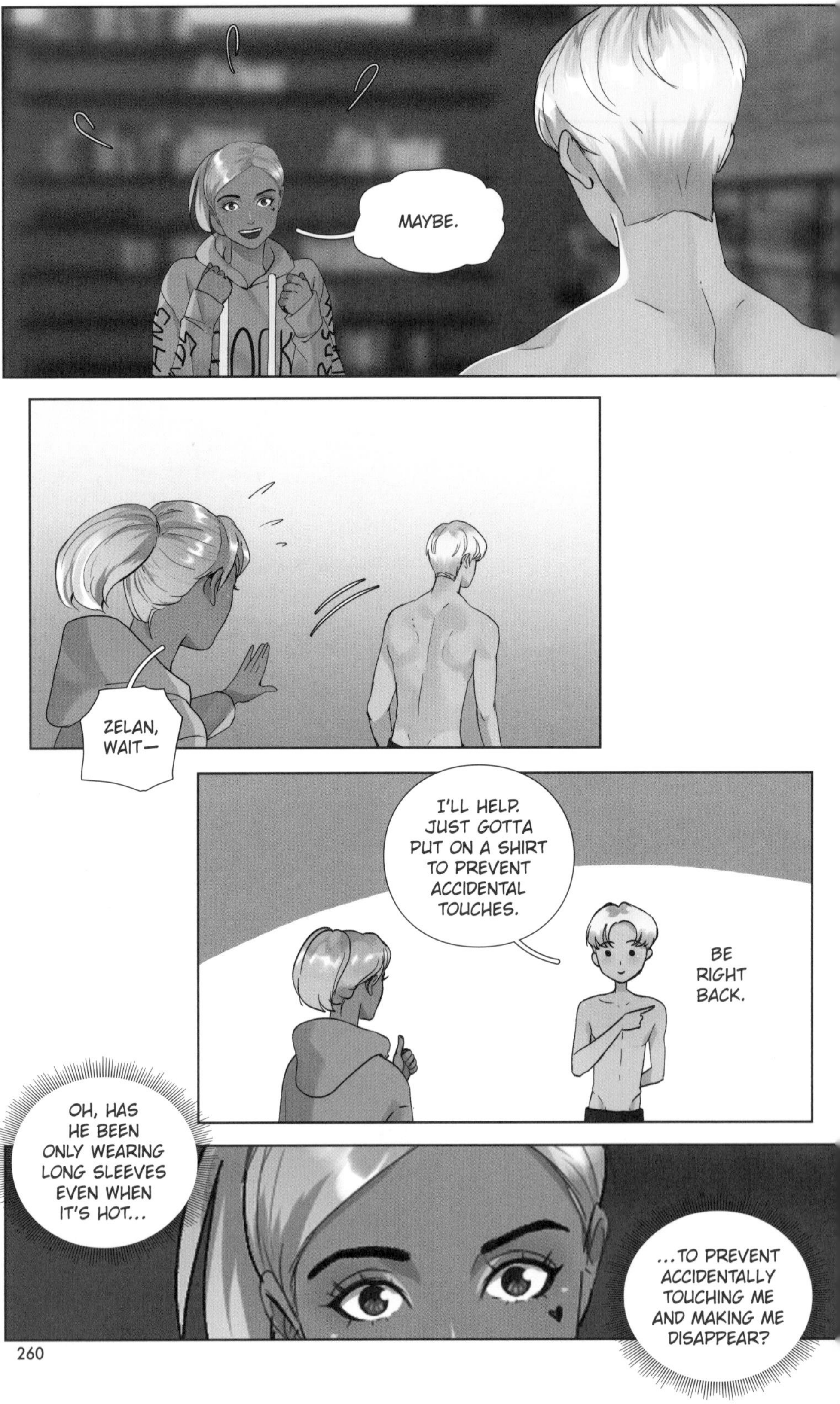
MAYBE.
ZELAN, WAIT—
I'LL HELP. JUST GOTTA PUT ON A SHIRT TO PREVENT ACCIDENTAL TOUCHES.
BE RIGHT BACK.
OH, HAS HE BEEN ONLY WEARING LONG SLEEVES EVEN WHEN IT'S HOT...
...TO PREVENT ACCIDENTALLY TOUCHING ME AND MAKING ME DISAPPEAR?

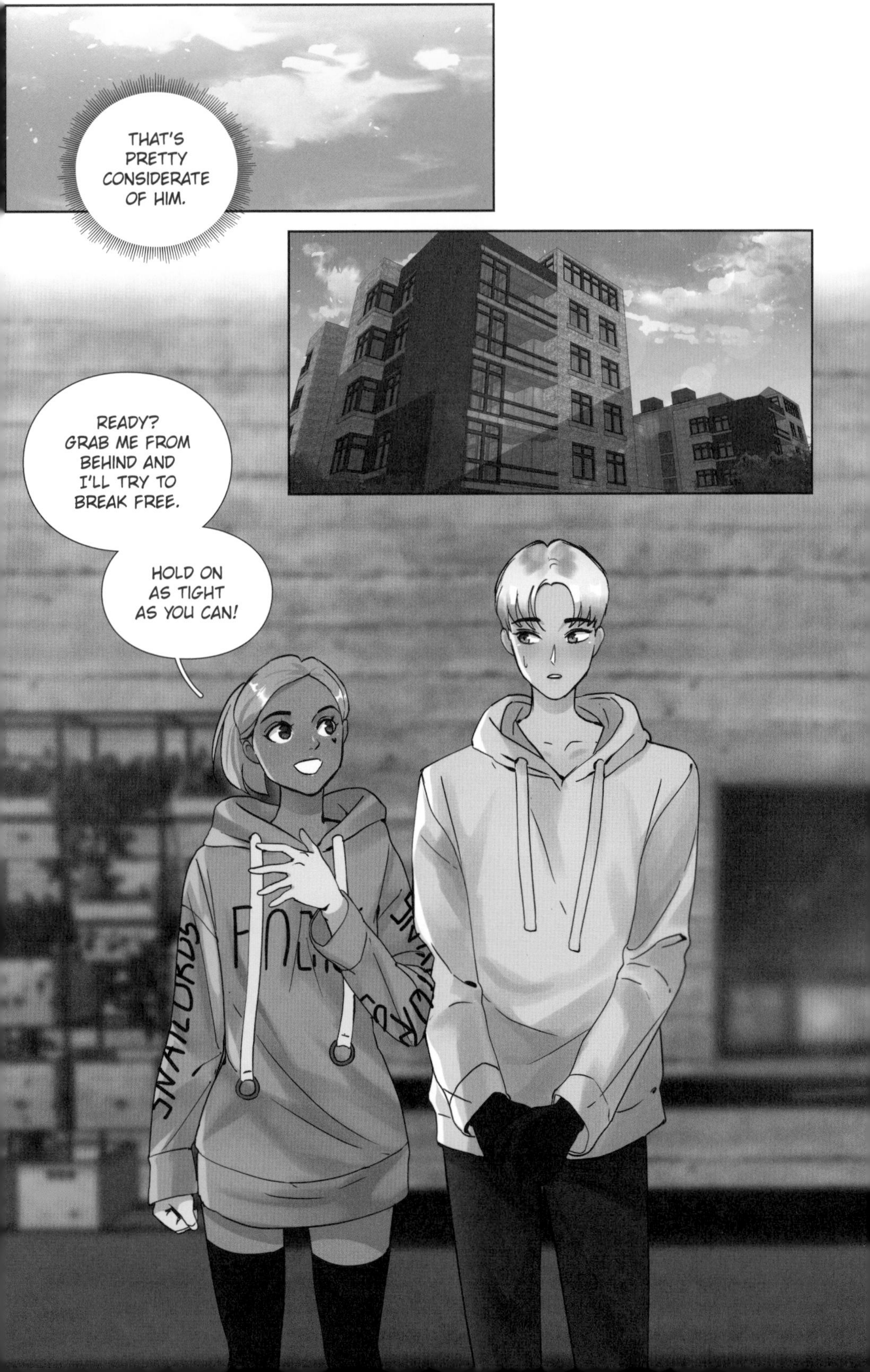
THAT'S PRETTY CONSIDERATE OF HIM.
READY? GRAB ME FROM BEHIND AND I'LL TRY TO BREAK FREE.
HOLD ON AS TIGHT AS YOU CAN!

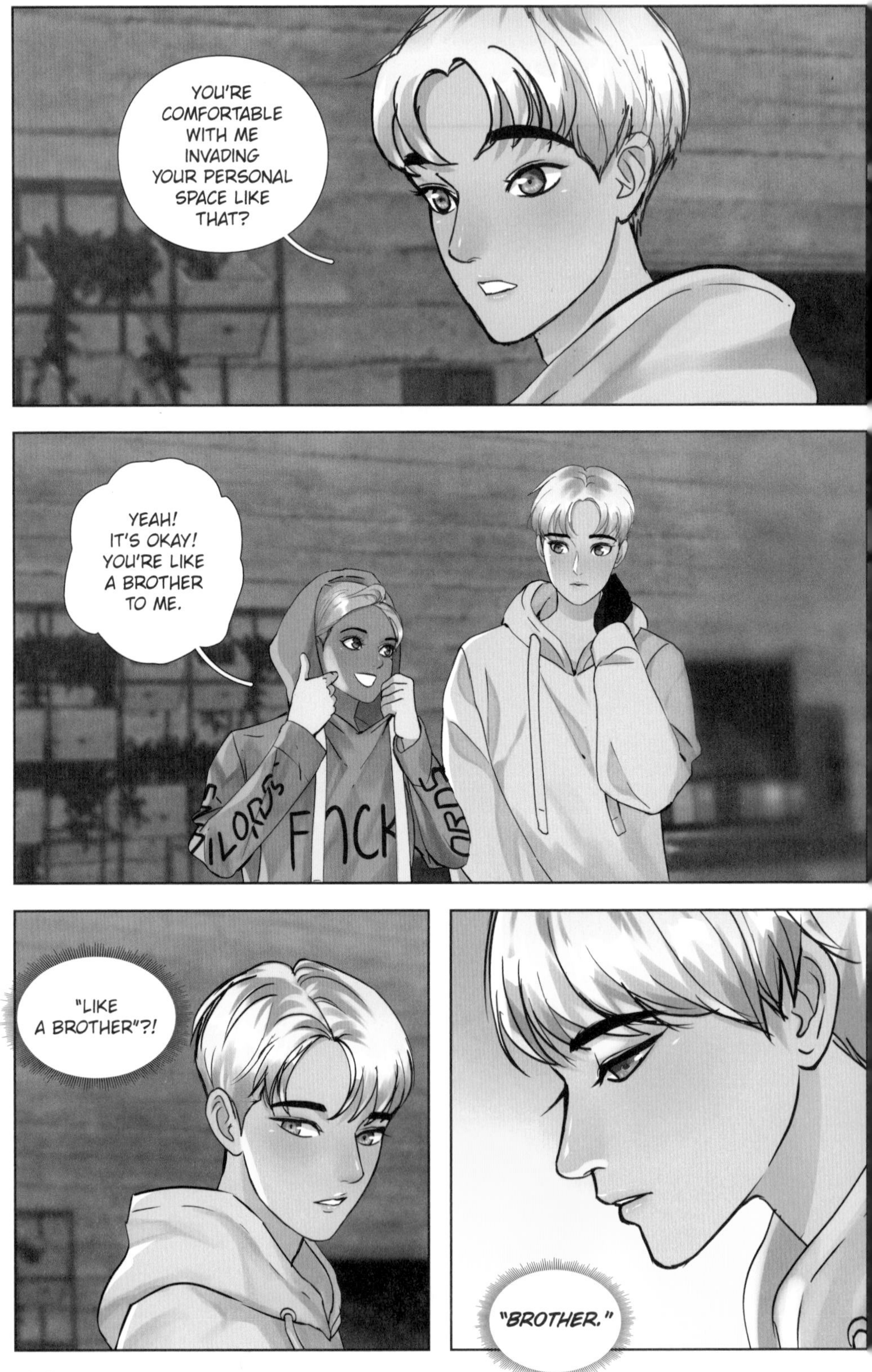
YOU'RE COMFORTABLE WITH ME INVADING YOUR PERSONAL SPACE LIKE THAT?
YEAH! IT'S OKAY! YOU'RE LIKE A BROTHER TO ME.
"LIKE A BROTHER"?!
"BROTHER."

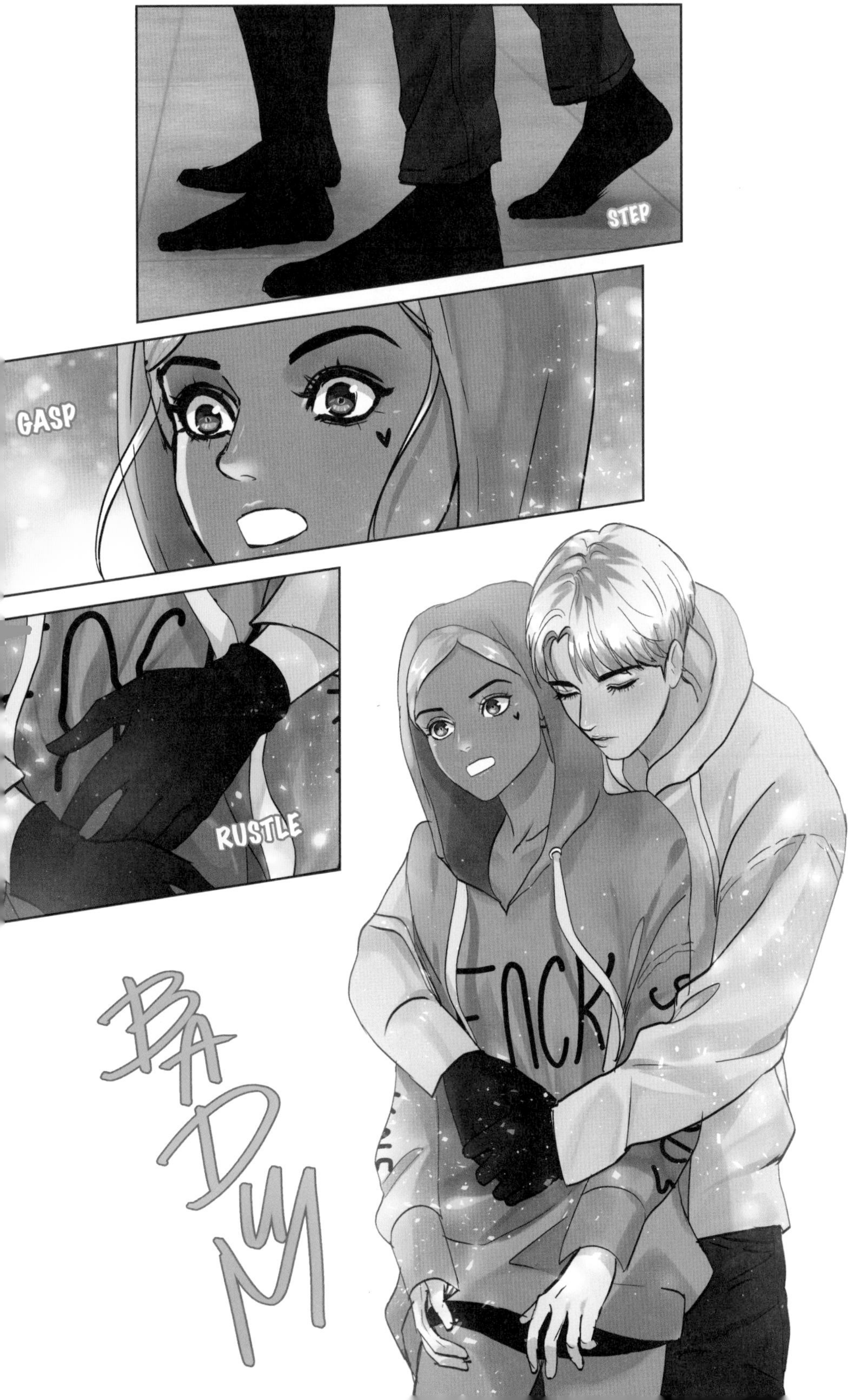
STEP
GASP
RUSTLE
BADUM

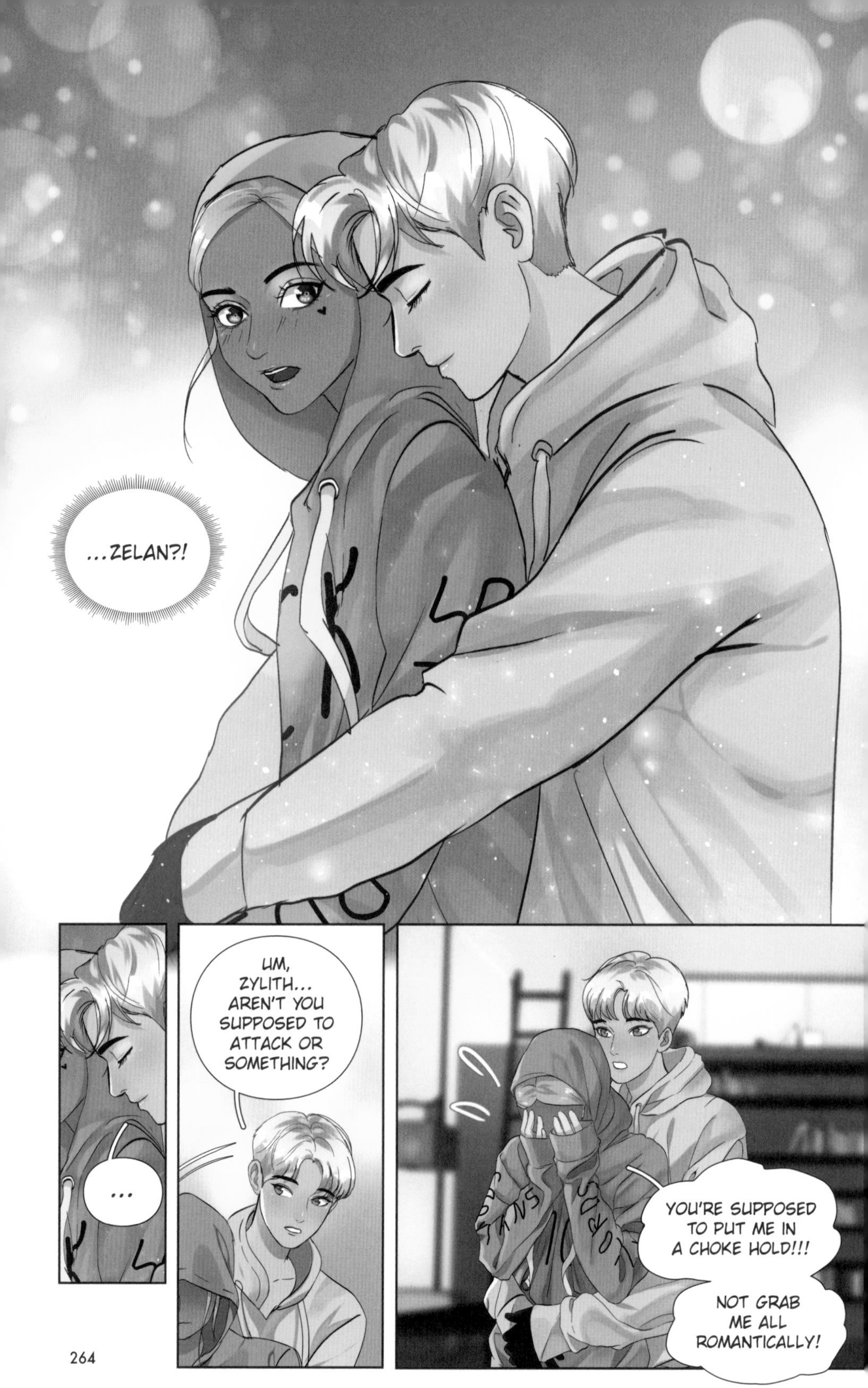
...ZELAN?!
...
UM, ZYLITH... AREN'T YOU SUPPOSED TO ATTACK OR SOMETHING?
YOU'RE SUPPOSED TO PUT ME IN A CHOKE HOLD!!!
NOT GRAB ME ALL ROMANTICALLY!

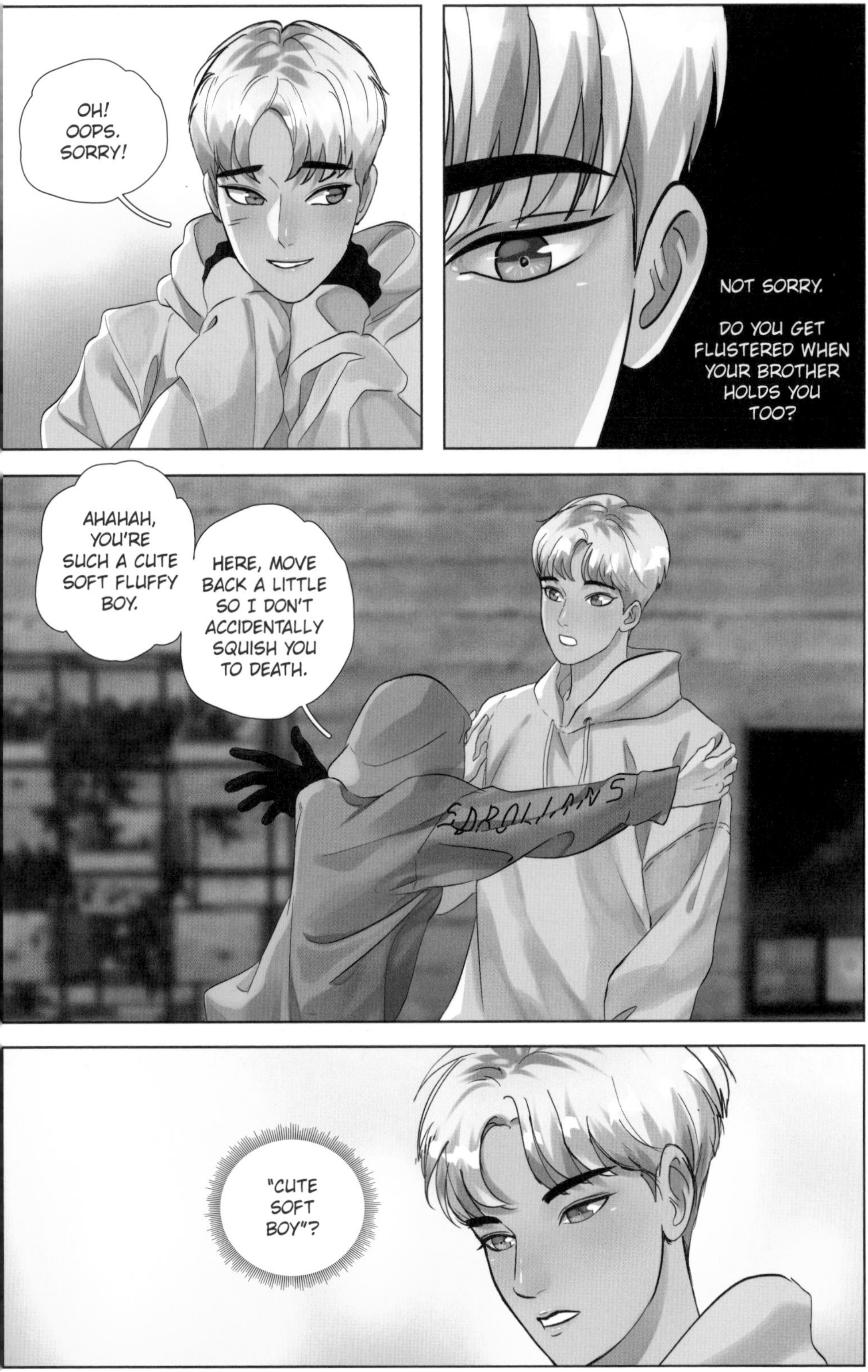

OH! OOPS. SORRY!
NOT SORRY.
DO YOU GET FLUSTERED WHEN YOUR BROTHER HOLDS YOU TOO?
AHAHAH, YOU'RE SUCH A CUTE SOFT FLUFFY BOY.
HERE, MOVE BACK A LITTLE SO I DON'T ACCIDENTALLY SQUISH YOU TO DEATH.
"CUTE SOFT BOY"?

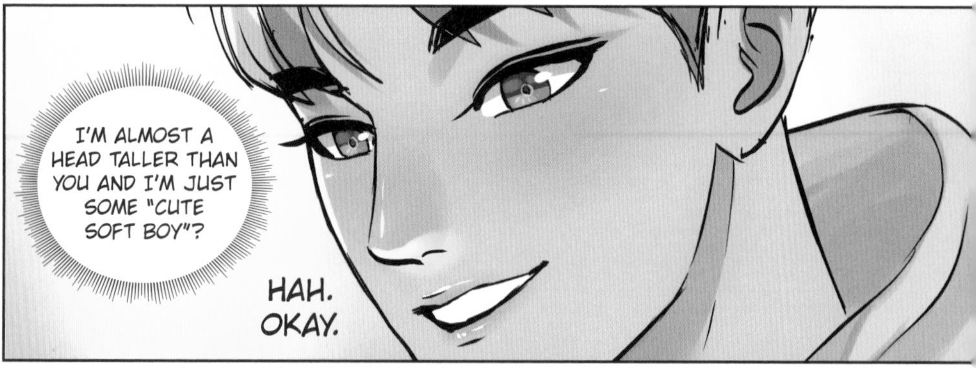
I'M ALMOST A HEAD TALLER THAN YOU AND I'M JUST SOME "CUTE SOFT BOY"?
HAH. OKAY.

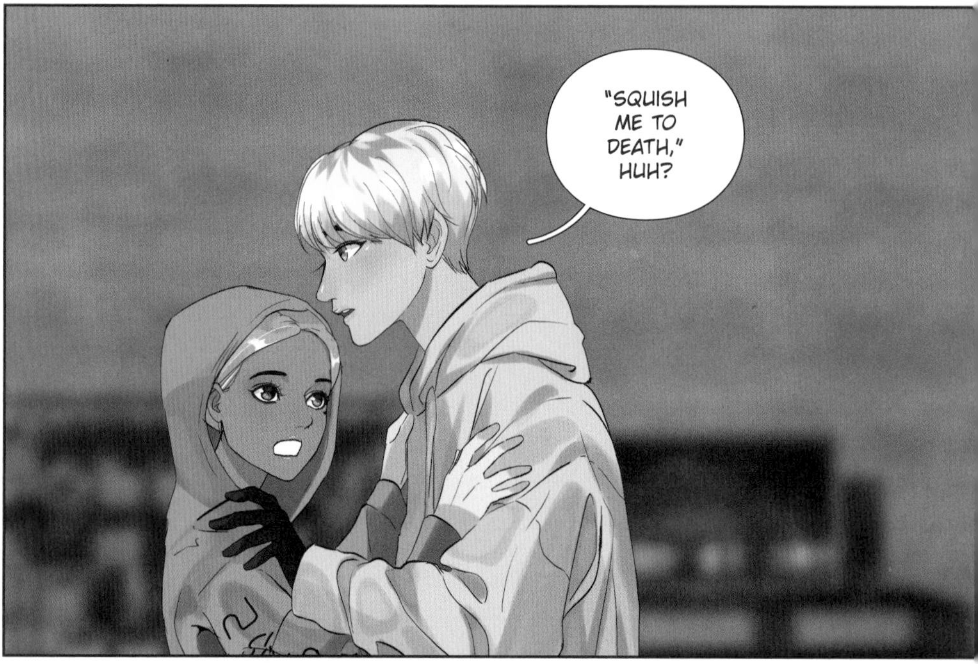
"SQUISH ME TO DEATH," HUH?

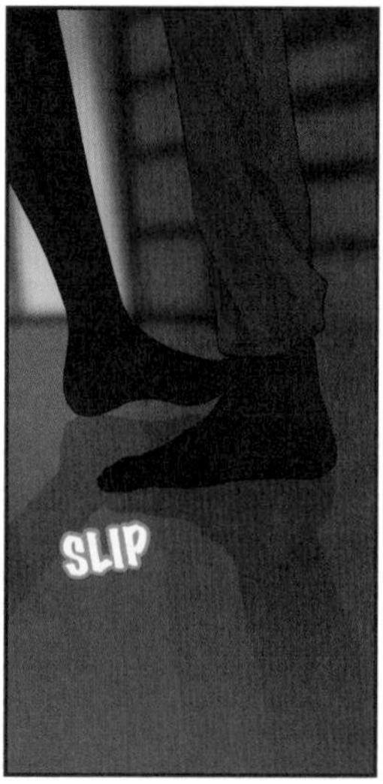
SLIP

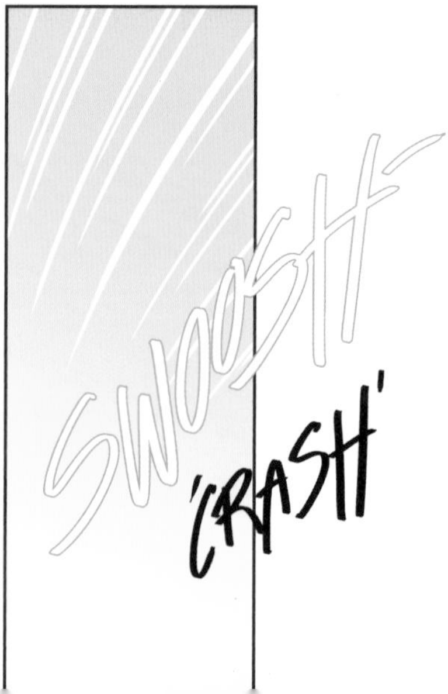
SWOOSH
CRASH

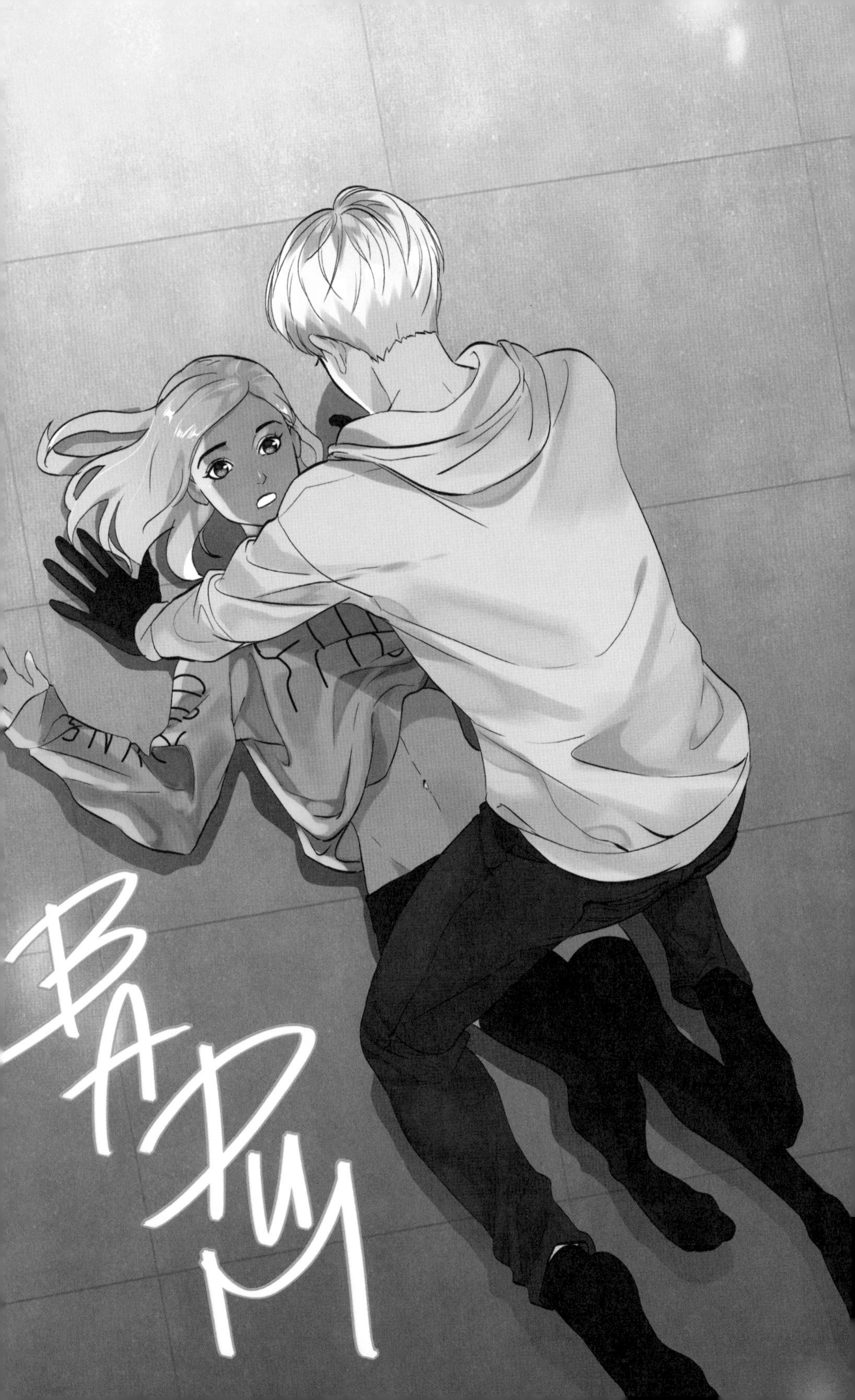
BADUM

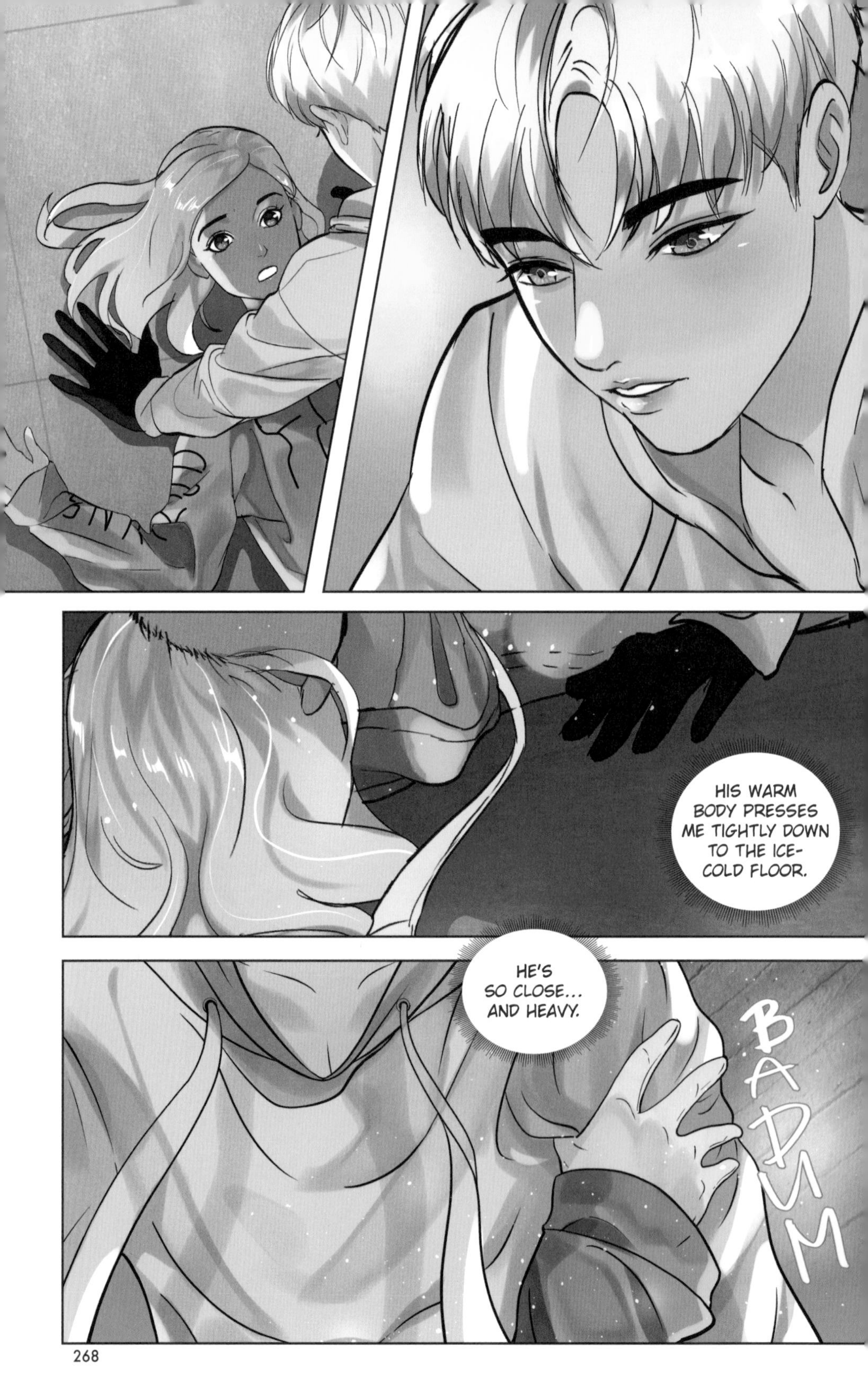
HIS WARM BODY PRESSES ME TIGHTLY DOWN TO THE ICE-COLD FLOOR.
HE'S SO CLOSE... AND HEAVY.
BADUMM

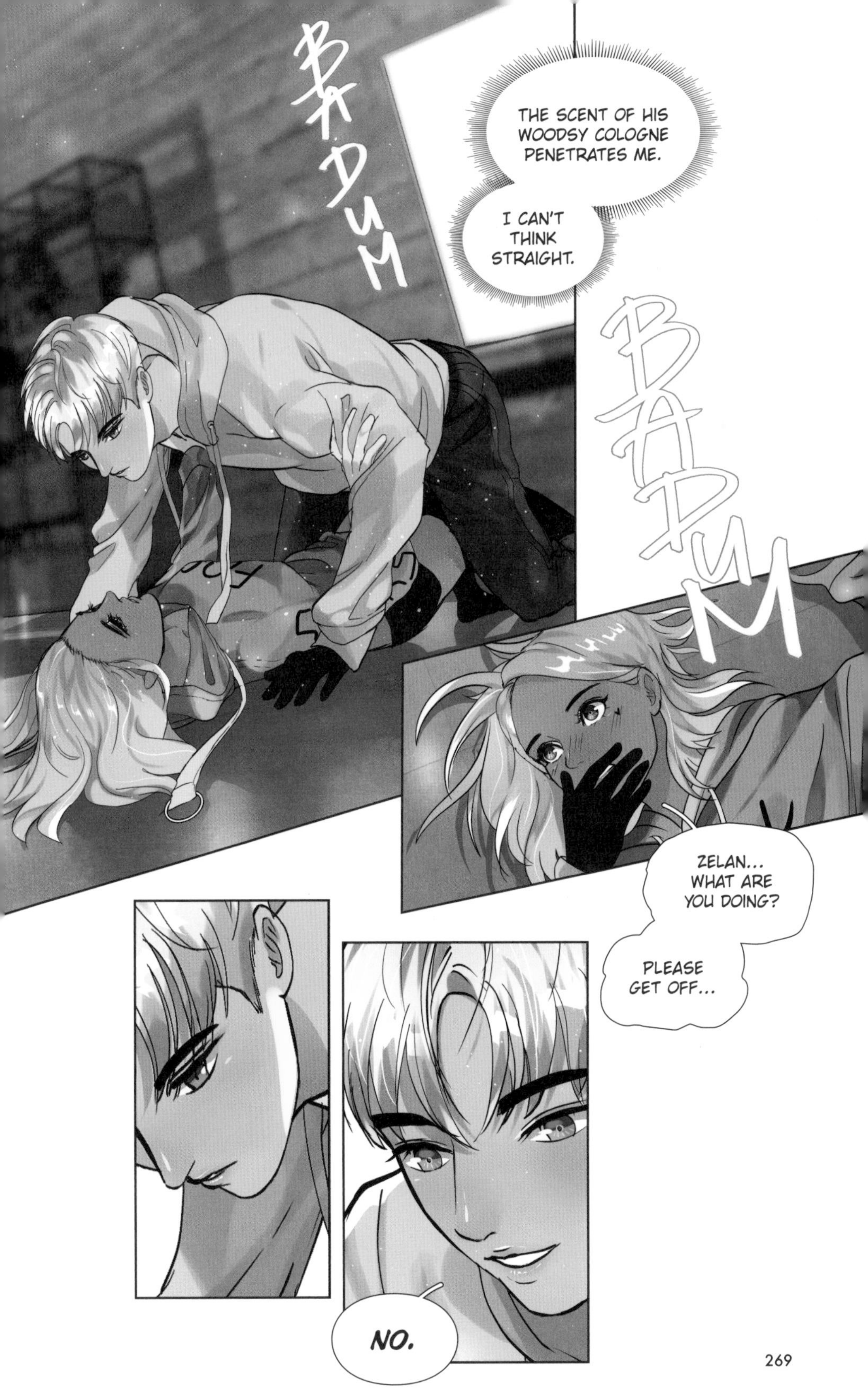
BADUM
THE SCENT OF HIS WOODSY COLOGNE PENETRATES ME.
I CAN'T THINK STRAIGHT.
BADUM
ZELAN... WHAT ARE YOU DOING?
PLEASE GET OFF...
NO.

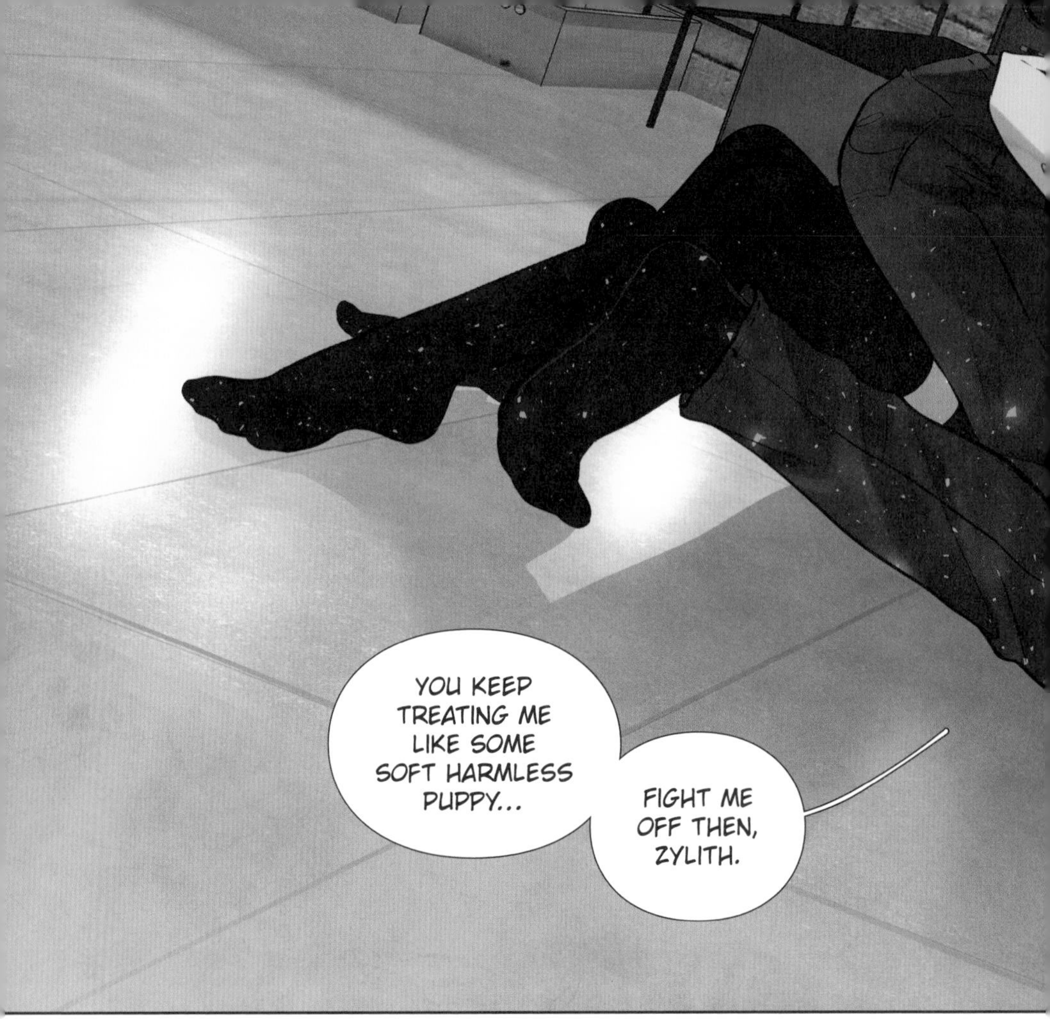
YOU KEEP TREATING ME LIKE SOME SOFT HARMLESS PUPPY...
FIGHT ME OFF THEN, ZYLITH.

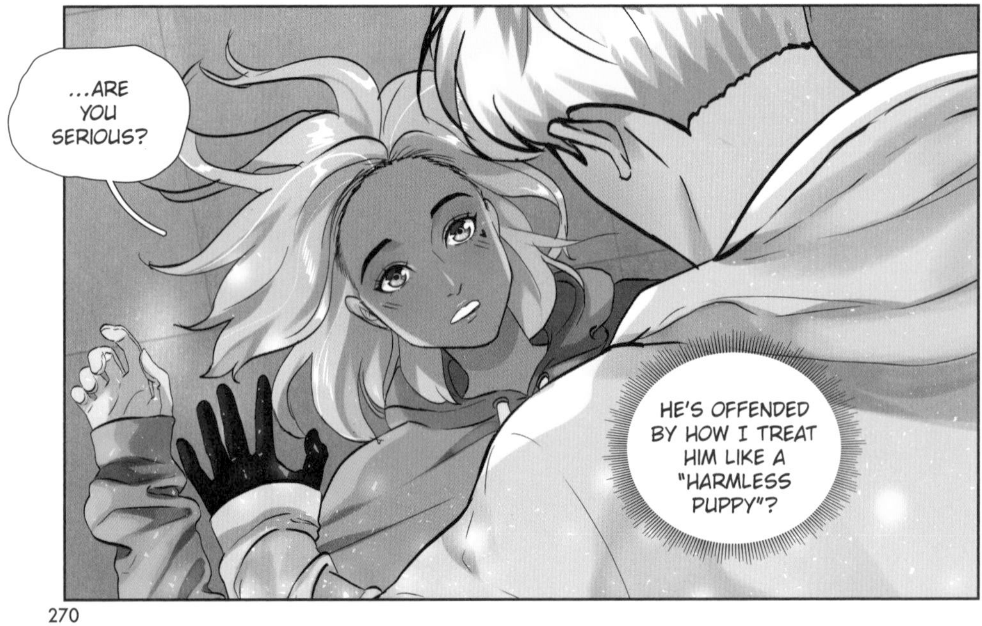
...ARE YOU SERIOUS?
HE'S OFFENDED BY HOW I TREAT HIM LIKE A "HARMLESS PUPPY"?

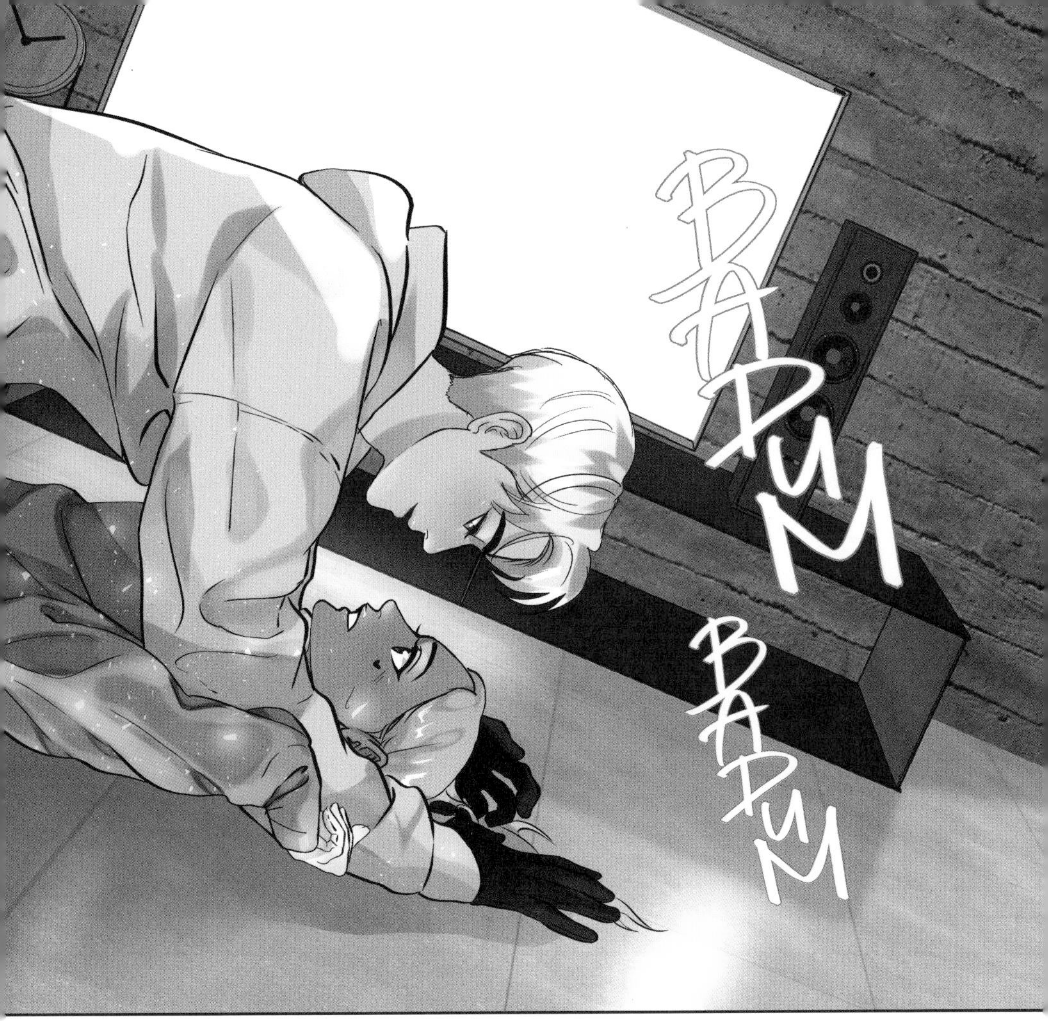
BADUM
BADUM

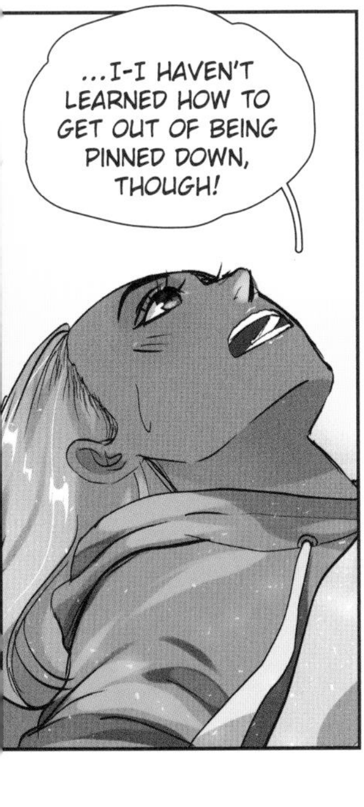
...I-I HAVEN'T LEARNED HOW TO GET OUT OF BEING PINNED DOWN, THOUGH!

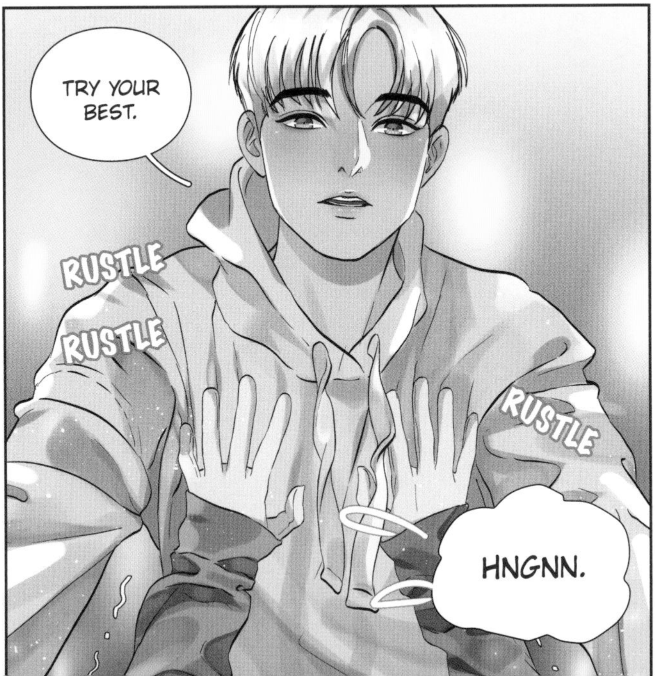
TRY YOUR BEST.
RUSTLE
RUSTLE
RUSTLE
HNGNN.

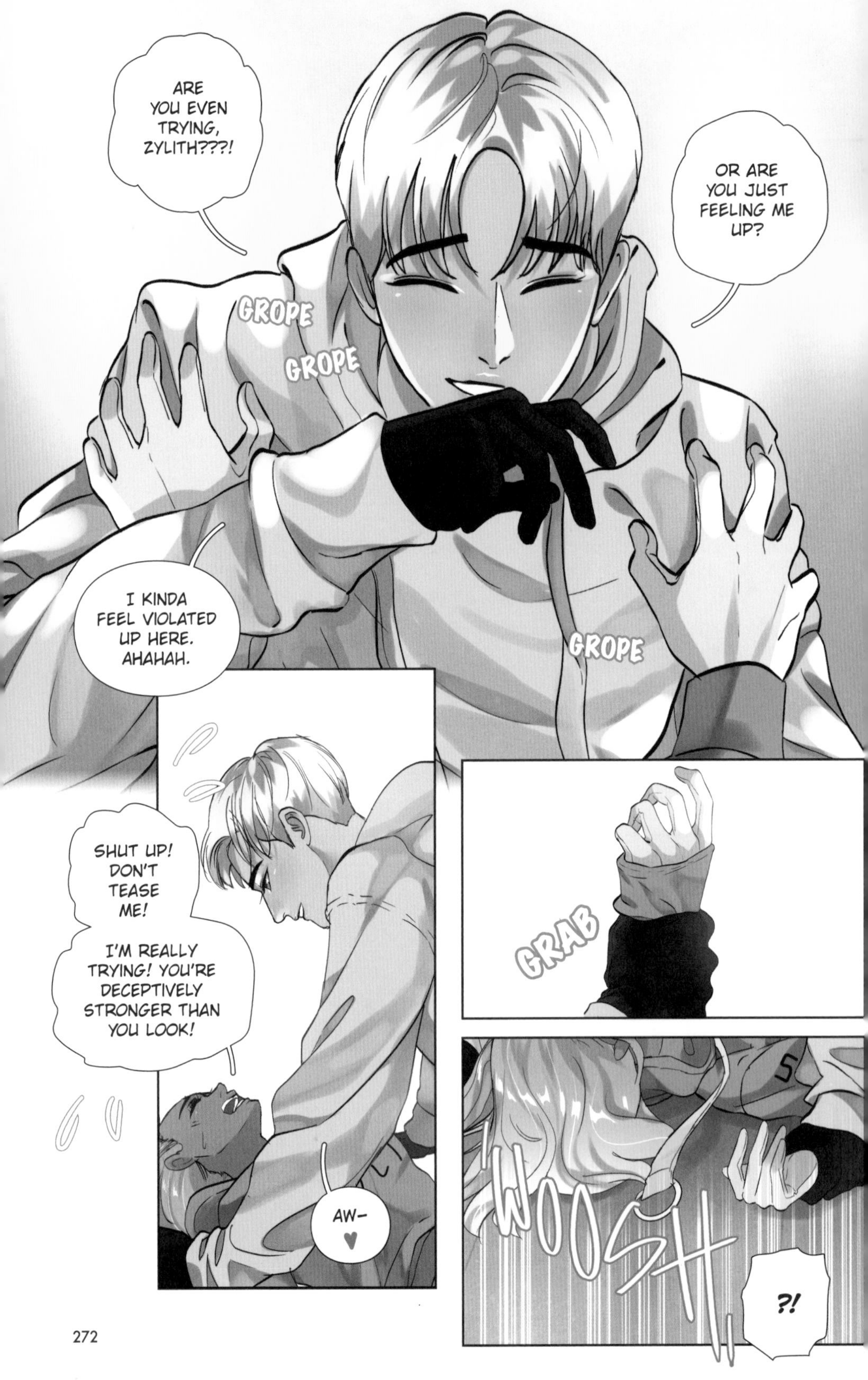
ARE YOU EVEN TRYING, ZYLITH???!
OR ARE YOU JUST FEELING ME UP?
GROPE
GROPE
I KINDA FEEL VIOLATED UP HERE. AHAHAH.
GROPE
SHUT UP! DON'T TEASE ME!
I'M REALLY TRYING! YOU'RE DECEPTIVELY STRONGER THAN YOU LOOK!
AW-♥
GRAB
WOOSH
?!

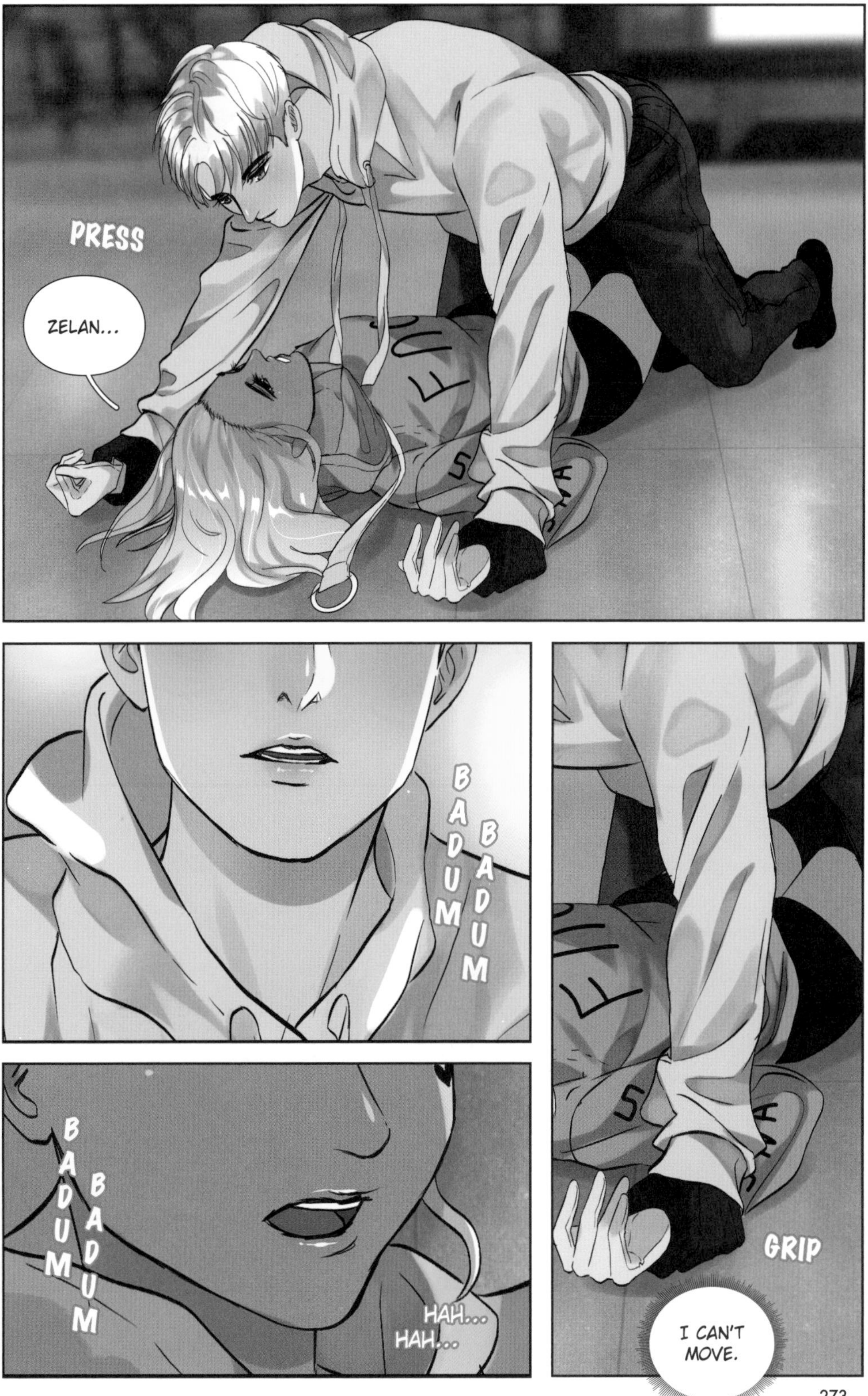
PRESS
ZELAN...
BADUM BADUM
BADUM BADUM
HAH... HAH...
GRIP
I CAN'T MOVE.

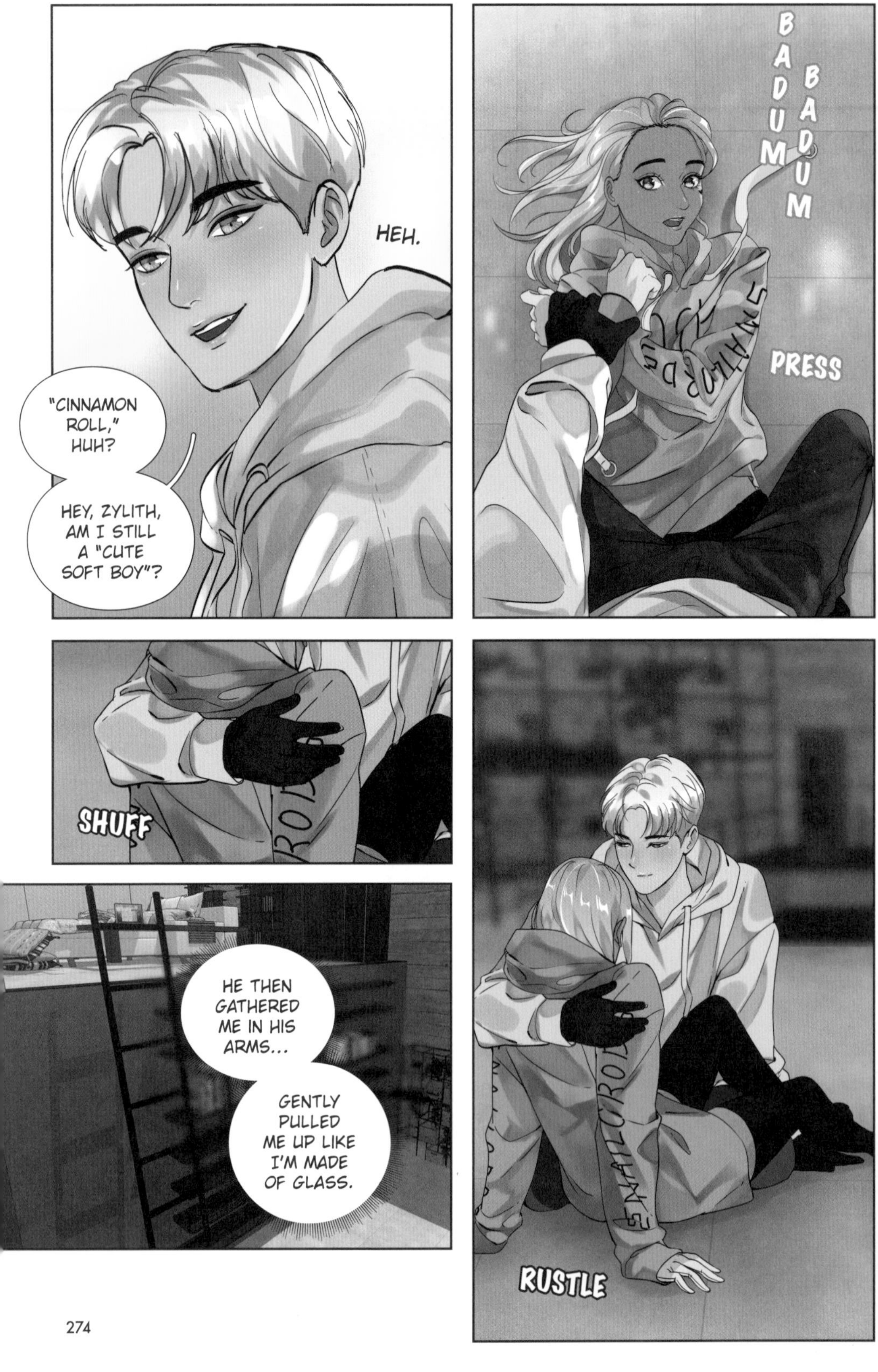
HEH.
"CINNAMON ROLL," HUH?
HEY, ZYLITH, AM I STILL A "CUTE SOFT BOY"?
BADUM
BADUM
PRESS
SHUFF
HE THEN GATHERED ME IN HIS ARMS...
GENTLY PULLED ME UP LIKE I'M MADE OF GLASS.
RUSTLE

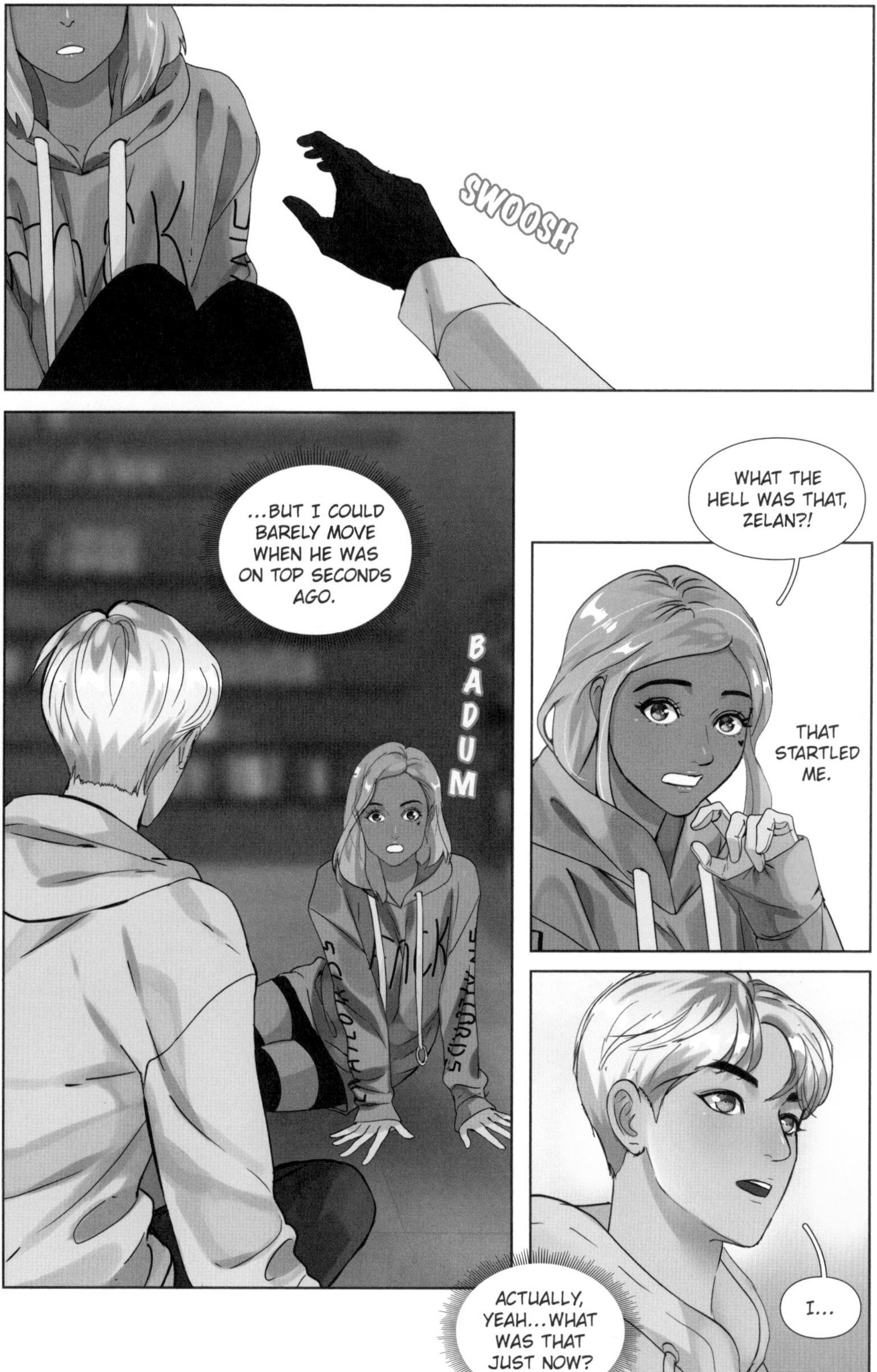
SWOOSH
...BUT I COULD BARELY MOVE WHEN HE WAS ON TOP SECONDS AGO.
BADUM
WHAT THE HELL WAS THAT, ZELAN?!
THAT STARTLED ME.
I...
ACTUALLY, YEAH...WHAT WAS THAT JUST NOW?

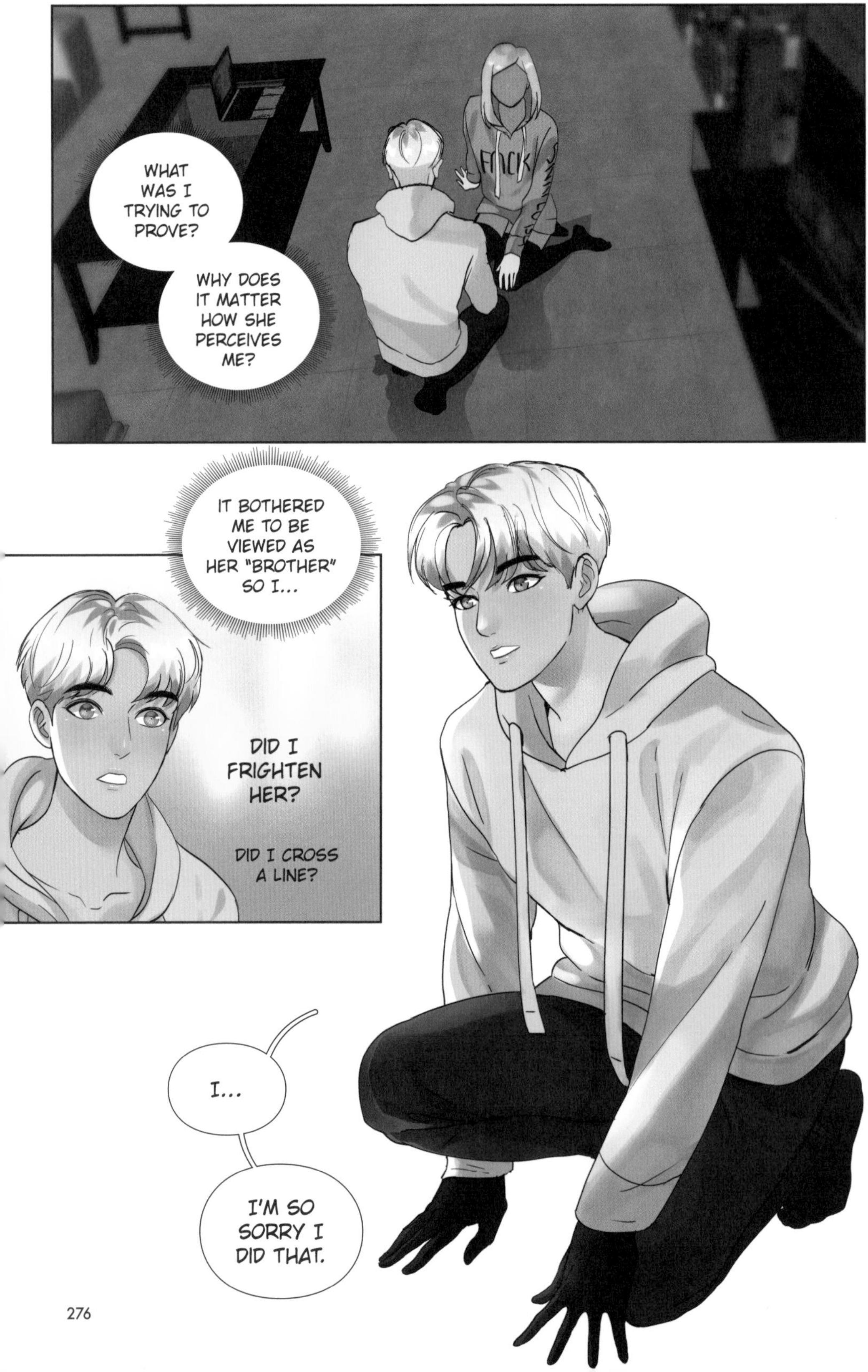
WHAT WAS I TRYING TO PROVE?
WHY DOES IT MATTER HOW SHE PERCEIVES ME?
IT BOTHERED ME TO BE VIEWED AS HER "BROTHER" SO I...
DID I FRIGHTEN HER?
DID I CROSS A LINE?
I...
I'M SO SORRY I DID THAT.

THAT WAS VERA'S TEXT TONE.

ZYLITH DOVE FOR HER PHONE RIGHT AWAY.

OF COURSE. SHE LIKES SOMEONE ELSE.

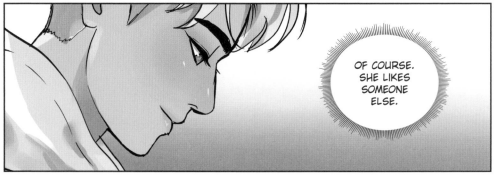

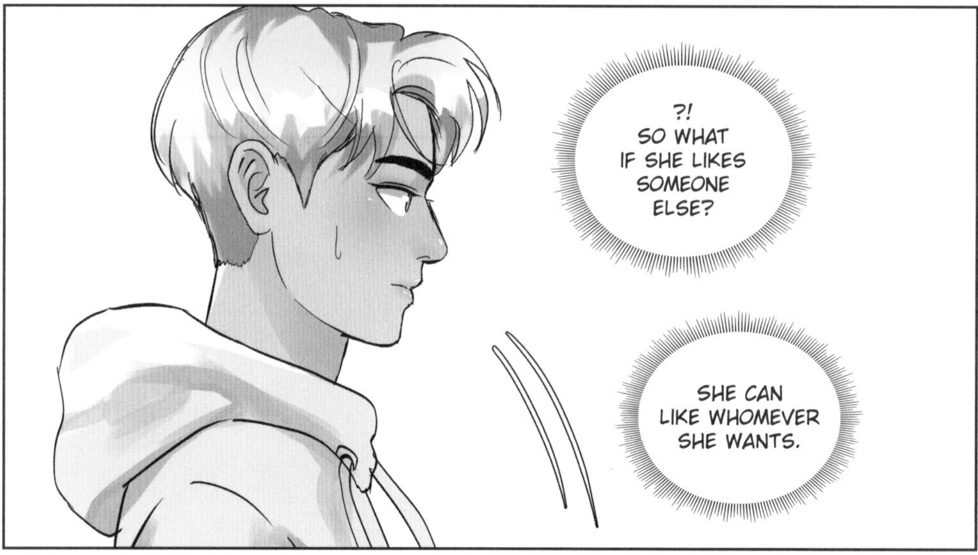
?!
SO WHAT IF SHE LIKES SOMEONE ELSE?
SHE CAN LIKE WHOMEVER SHE WANTS.

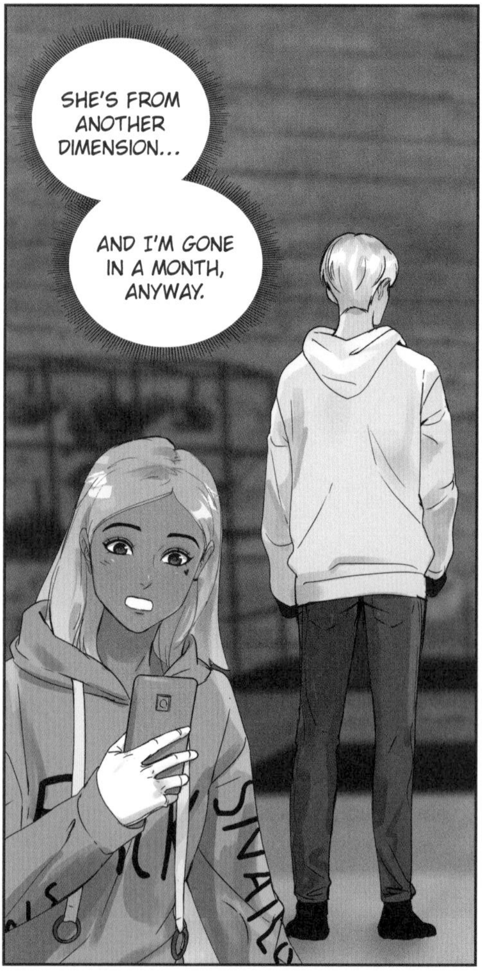
SHE'S FROM ANOTHER DIMENSION...
AND I'M GONE IN A MONTH, ANYWAY.

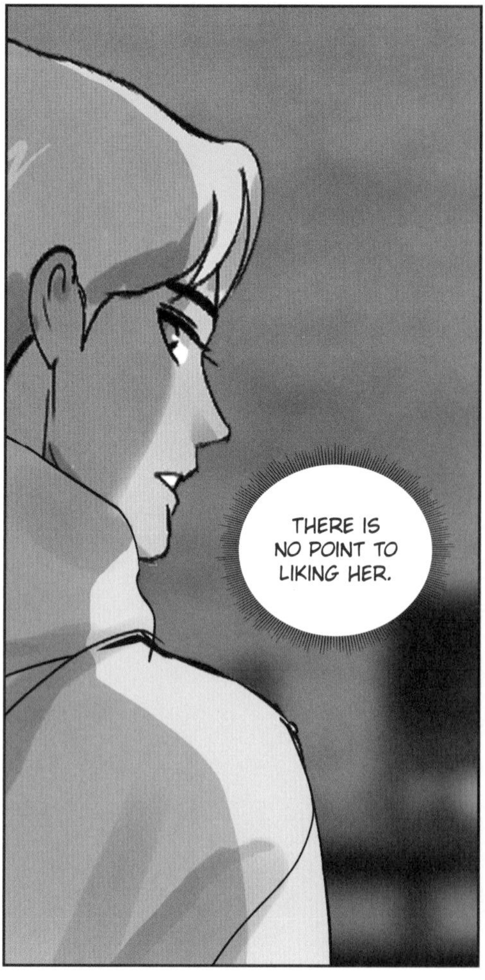
THERE IS NO POINT TO LIKING HER.

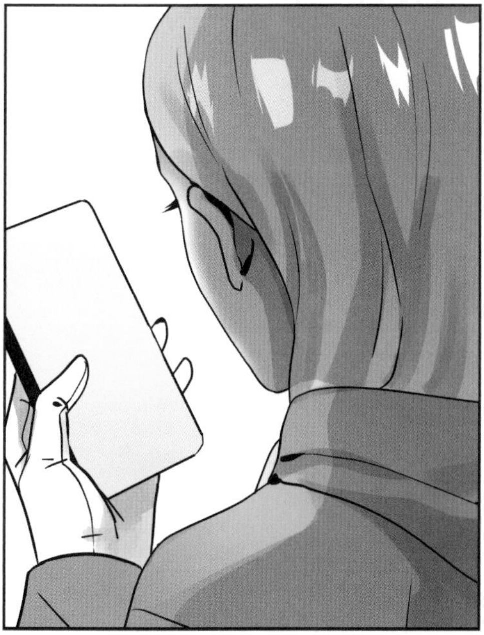

WE CAN'T EVEN HAVE DIRECT SKIN CONTACT WITHOUT HER VANISHING FOR DAYS.

PHYSICAL INTIMACY IS OUT OF THE QUESTION.

MOREOVER, WHAT HAPPENS WHEN THE RIFT BETWEEN OUR DIMENSIONS SEALS ITSELF?

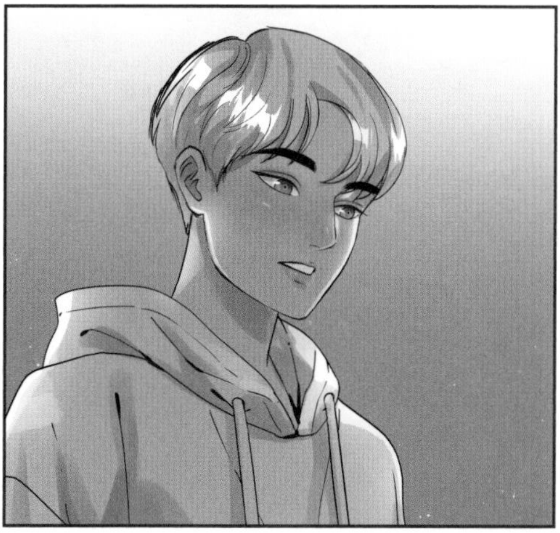

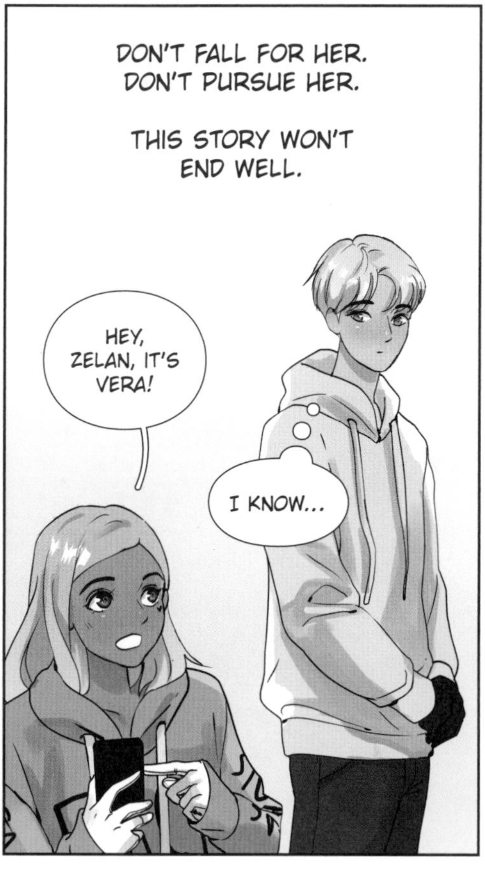
DON'T FALL FOR HER.
DON'T PURSUE HER.
THIS STORY WON'T END WELL.
HEY, ZELAN, IT'S VERA!
I KNOW...

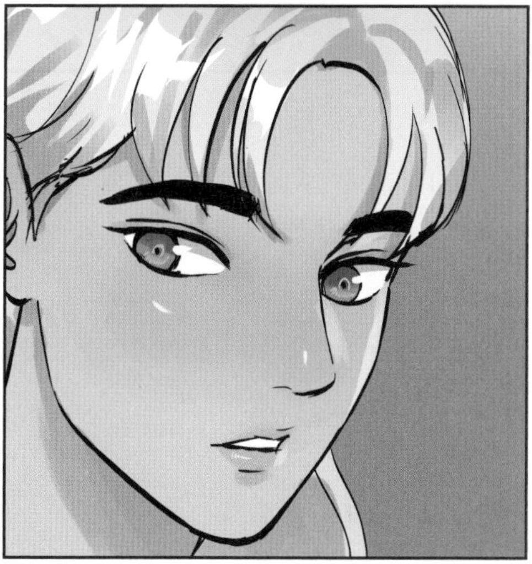

THIS IS DANGEROUS.

I NEED HER TO BE TAKEN BY SOMEONE ELSE...

TO DROWN OUT THESE TEMPTATIONS TO WIN HER ATTENTION.

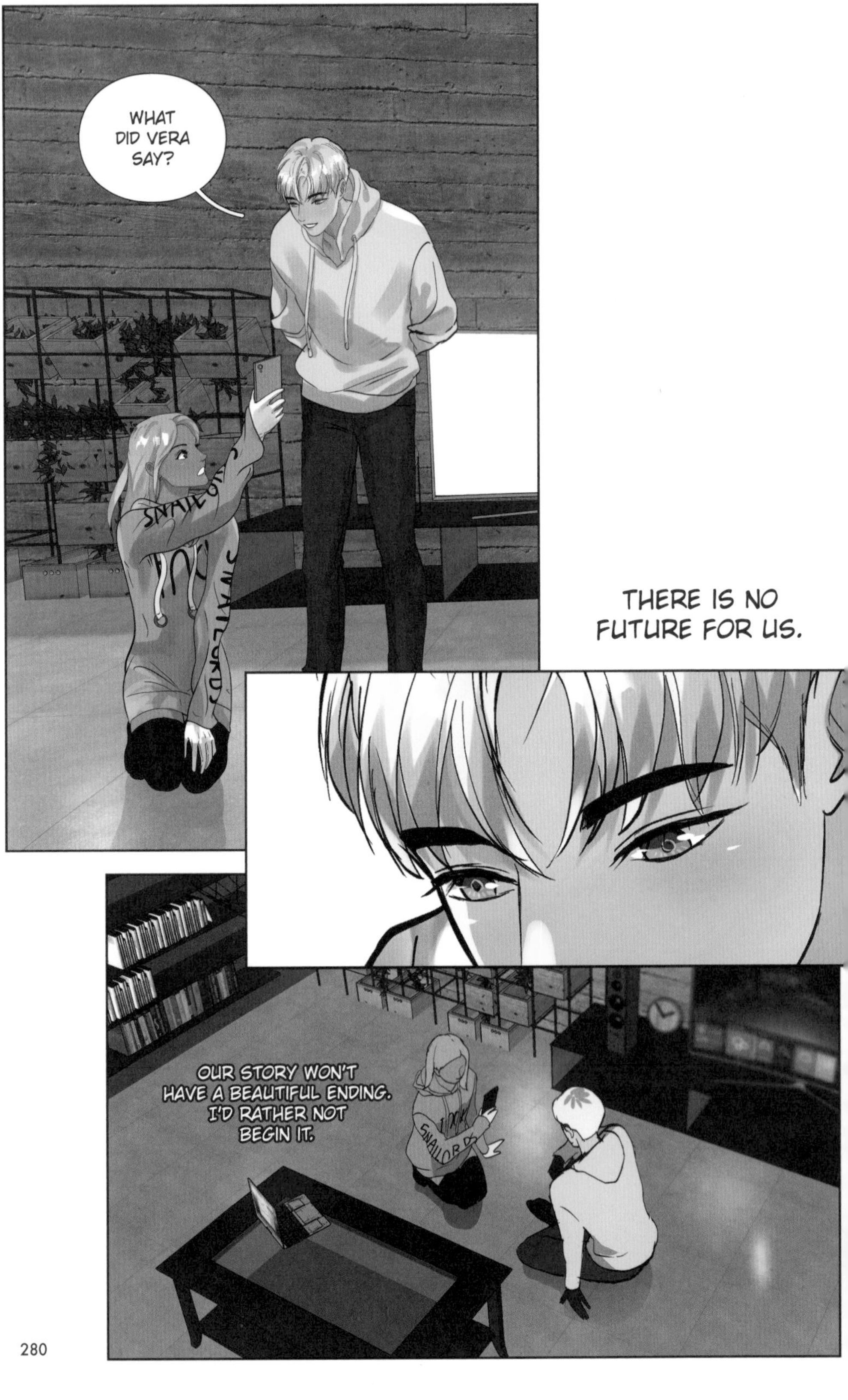
WHAT DID VERA SAY?
THERE IS NO FUTURE FOR US.
OUR STORY WON'T HAVE A BEAUTIFUL ENDING. I'D RATHER NOT BEGIN IT.

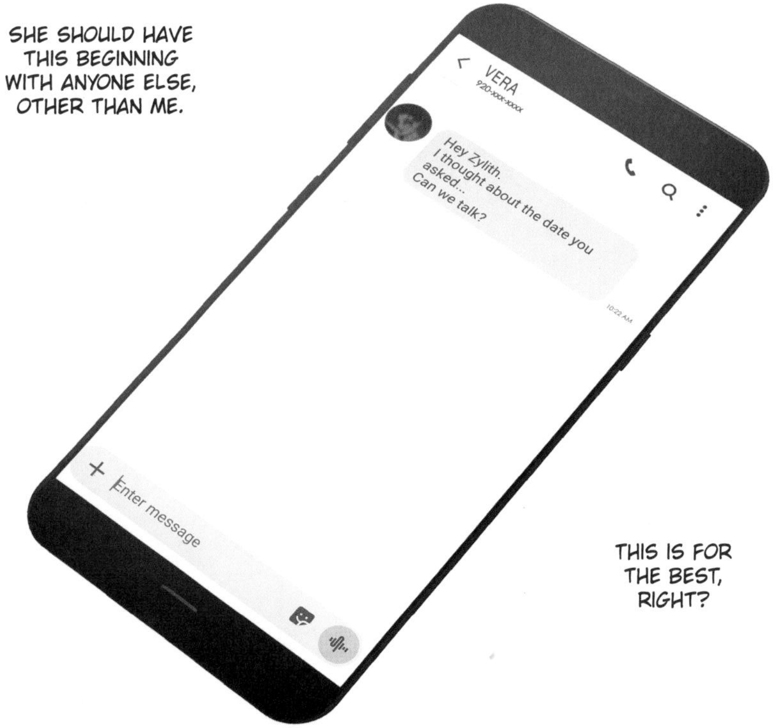
SHE SHOULD HAVE THIS BEGINNING WITH ANYONE ELSE, OTHER THAN ME.
VERA
920-xxx-xxxx
Hey Zylith.
I thought about the date you asked...
Can we talk?
10:22 AM
Enter message
THIS IS FOR THE BEST, RIGHT?

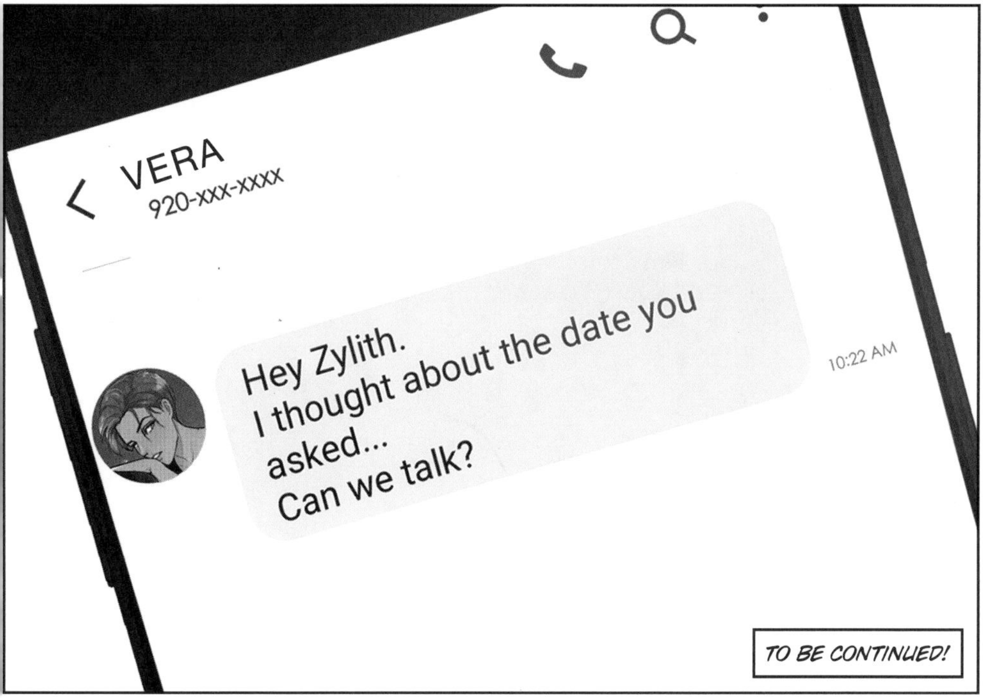
VERA
920-XXX-XXXX
Hey Zylith.
I thought about the date you asked...
Can we talk?
10:22 AM
TO BE CONTINUED!

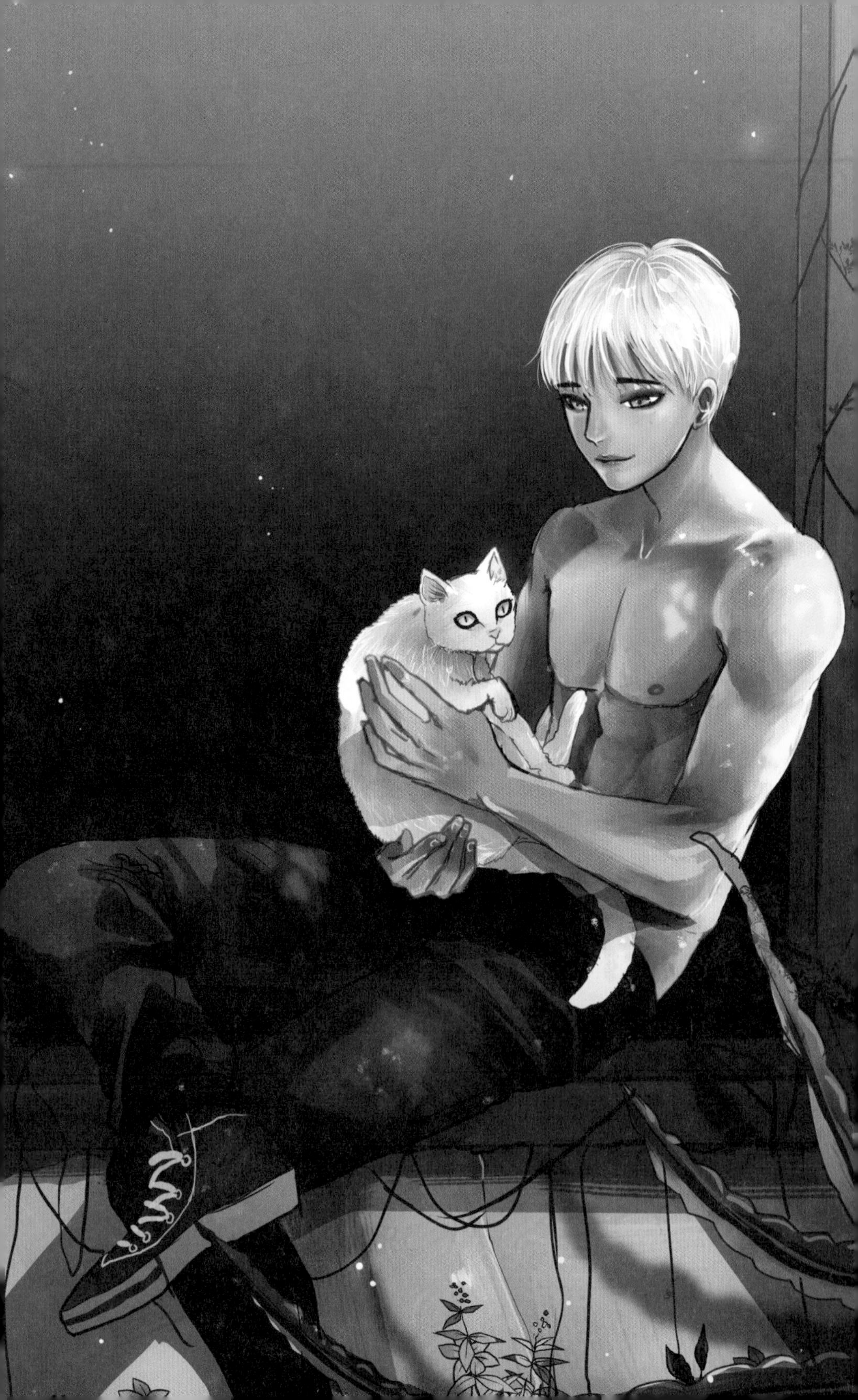

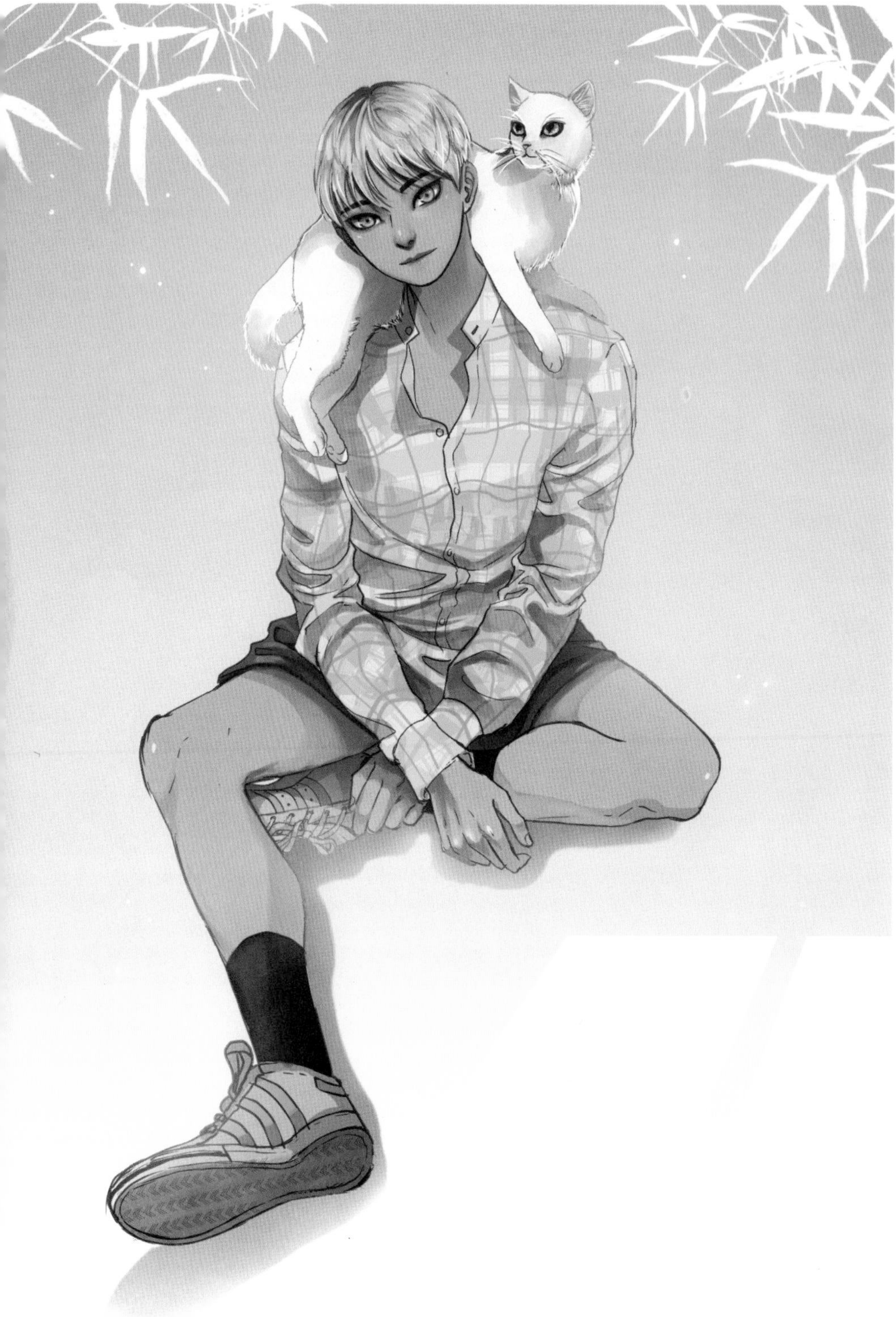

snailords
Aidyn Arroyal

SNAILORDS

Aidyn Arroyal aka Snailords (he/they) is a manga, comic, and WEBTOON artist. He's best known for his romance WEBTOON series *Freaking Romance* (completed) and thriller WEBTOON series *Death: Rescheduled* (ongoing).

He is also the creator of *Snailogy* and *Snailed It*, two slice-of-life comics series.